NC21934

N850YR

Introduction to Aviation Insurance and Risk Management

Third Edition

Introduction to Aviation Insurance and Risk Management

Third Edition

by
Alexander T. Wells, Ed. D.
and
Bruce D. Chadbourne, Ed. D.

KRIEGER PUBLISHING COMPANY
MALABAR, FLORIDA
2007

Original Edition 1992
Second Edition 2000
Third Edition 2007

Printed and Published by
KRIEGER PUBLISHING COMPANY
KRIEGER DRIVE
MALABAR, FLORIDA 32950

Library of Congress Cataloging-In-Publication Data

Introduction to aviation insurance and risk management / edited by Alexander T. Wells and Bruce D. Chadbourne. — 3rd ed.
p. cm.
Includes bibliographical references and index.
Contents: The aviation insurance industry — Principles of insurance and risk management — Aviation insurance — Other lines of insurance.
ISBN 1-57524-274-5 (alk. paper)
1. Insurance, Aviation. 2. Insurance. 3. Risk management. I. Wells, Alexander T. II. Chadbourne, Bruce D.

HG9972.3.I68 2007
368.5'7600973—dc22

2006048707

10 9 8 7 6 5 4 3

Contents

Preface

Publication of the third edition of *Introduction to Aviation Insurance and Risk Management* will extend its life into the 21st Century, which unquestionably will be the most remembered period in the history of aviation. The aviation industry entered a new era as a result of the terrorist attacks of September 11, 2001 and the Iraq war. General aviation, including business aviation, and commercial aviation have been faced with record financial losses, resulting in massive restructuring. Faced with losses, lower interest rates and heated competition, aviation insurers and reinsurers have experienced no less a stress in the marketplace. Consolidations and mergers that began with brokers and agents years before, took place with the insurance carriers at a rapid pace during the 1990s and into the new millenium. No other time in history has proven to be as difficult as the current situation.

The need for a well-trained and educated aviation insurance professional at this time could not be more appropriate. This has been recognized by the industry as evidenced by growth in the AIA-sponsored *Certified Aviation Insurance Professional* (*CAIP*) program. As a result, the AIA Education Institute felt the timing was right to prepare a third edition of the text used in the aviation insurance course that is a part of the CAIP program.

Revision provides the opportunity to improve the book. Old material can be deleted, and newer, more timely material added. Building on a tested framework of subject areas, we have tried to make the most of this recent opportunity to contribute to the metamorphosis of the book. However, unlike previous editions, a number of industry professionals have contributed to this revision. The end product, we trust, is one that is both quite familiar and clearly superior to its predecessor.

Despite these changes, the primary purpose of the book remains the same—to introduce the basic principles of insurance and risk with their special application to the aviation industry. It is designed for several similar, yet distinct audiences: the college student enrolled in an aviation or insurance program who, as a prospective manager, must recognize and appreciate the basic concepts and underwriting techniques peculiar to insuring against aviation risks; the corporate pilot, fixed base operator, or other individual in the aviation industry who is charged with the responsibility of protecting a firm's assets; and an individual in the insurance business such as a trainee with an aviation insurance company or an agent or broker who needs to know more about this specialized field of insurance.

This text should provide a foundation of general knowledge in a subject that plays a significant role in any aviation related business. It is operational in nature in that it was designed to provide the readers with basic information they need to know. The approach is introductory, not exhaustive. The book is not a treatise on aviation insurance; it does not pretend to be the last word on the subject, for that would take a working knowledge of underwriting. It offers a logical approach to building a foundation for future study.

CHACTERISTICS OF THIS BOOK

This book employs a number of features that are designed to facilitate student learning. The main ones are:

1. Chapter Outlines. Each chapter opens with an outline of the major topics to be covered.

2. Chapter Objectives. After the outline, each chapter includes a list of objectives that the student should be able to accomplish upon completing the chapter.
3. Logical Organization and Frequent Headings. Insurance can easily become overwhelming in its multitude of topics, concepts, practices, and examples. The material covered has been put in a systematic framework so that students know where they have been, where they are, and where they are going in the text. Frequent headings and subheadings aid organization and readability.
4. Key Terms. Each chapter concludes with a list of key terms used in the text.
5. Review Questions. Review questions at the end of each chapter cover all of the important points.
6. Policies/Endorsements. Included at the end of chapters 8, 9,10, and 12 are sample applications, policies, and endorsements.
7. Glossary. The glossary includes over 600 key terms appearing at the end of the chapters, as well as many others in the text of significance in the insurance and legal professions.
8. Self-Tests. Close to 1,000 objective questions, including multiple-choice, true-false, fill-in, and matching, are included for students to review the materials covered in each chapter.

ORGANIZATION OF THE TEXT

Introduction to Aviation Insurance and Risk Management is designed to acquaint the student with the basic principles of insurance and risk with their special application to the aviation industry. This book should provide a foundation of general insurance principles and practices, an introduction to the specialized field of aviation insurance, and general lines of insurance that must be considered by the aviation enterprise.

The following is an outline of *Introduction to Aviation Insurance and Risk Management.*

Part One: The Aviation Insurance Industry

Chapter 1. **Aviation Insurance in the United States: A Historical Perspective.** Chapter 1 provides a historical sketch of the aviation insurance industry in the United States from its beginning at the end of the end of World War I through the start of the new millenium.

Chapter 2. **Insureds and Liability of the FAA**. This chapter introduces the student to the market for aviation insurance space manufacturers, the air carriers, various segments of the general aviation industry, airports, and individual pilots. The last section of this chapter deals with liability incurred by the FAA arising out of its operation and management of the airway system.

Chapter 3. **Insurers.** Chapter 3 concludes the first part of the book with a review of the major domestic aviation underwriters, Lloyd's of London, and other international markets. Other topics include selecting an insurer, insurance channels of distribution, and selecting an agent or broker.

Part Two: Principles of Insurance and Risk Management

Chapter 4. **Risk and Insurance**. The beginning chapter of Part Two introduces the concept of risk, listing its classifications and the factors which affect pure risks. Insurance is defined and the role of the law of large numbers is examined along with the prerequisites of an insurable risk. The valuable practice of reinsurance and its importance in aviation risk transfer is explored.

Chapter 5. **Risk Management**. The discussion of risk continues with chapter 5 where the nature and development of the profession of risk management is examined. The five steps in the risk management process are discussed in detail with emphasis on risk handling techniques and their selection. Risk management procedures which are especially useful for small aviation business organizations are identified.

Chapter 6. **The Legal Foundation for Insurance**. Chapter 6 introduces the reader to applicable laws including the principle of indemnity on which insurance is founded. This discussion is followed by a comprehensive review of legal liability including the principle of negligence and liability under contracts. Equitable compensation for aviation damages under the tort system is discussed. State and federal statutes along with international agreements that influence the degree of care required to be shown passengers and establish liability procedures are presented.

Chapter 7. **Insurance Contracts**. This chapter prepares the reader for the in-depth analysis of aviation insurance policies which follows in chapters 8 and 9. Prerequisites of an enforceable contract are discussed along with the importance of the application and binder. Policy format, unique characteristics of an insurance policy, the Law of Agency, and the types of authority possessed by an agent are presented.

Part Three: General Aviation Insurance

Chapter 8. **Aircraft Hull and Liability Insurance.** The opening chapter of Part Three introduces the student to the aircraft hull and liability contract. Coverages, exclusions, limits of liability, and conditions are thoroughly explored. Extensions to the basis coverages are also covered along with additional considerations for business aircraft operators.

Chapter 9. **Airport Premises Liabilty and Other Aviation Coverages**. This chapter rounds out our discussion of the principal lines of aviation insurance by covering airport premises, products, and hangar keepers' liability plus several additional liability coverages written in conjunction with premises liability. Additional specialized lines such as aerial application, individual and corporate non-ownership, manufacturer's product liability, excess liability, loss of use coverage, loss of license insurance, and pilot accident insurance are covered.

Chapter 10. **Underwriting and Pricing General Aviation Risks.** Chapter 10 completes Part Three by analyzing the process of underwriting and pricing general aviation risks. The need for underwriting is reviewed followed by an in-depth discussion of aviation exposures. The major factors in underwriting aircraft, rotorcraft, and airport risks are then explored. The chapter concludes with a discussion on pricing aviation risks including reporting form contracts.

Part Four: Other Lines of Insurance

Chapter 11. **Airline and Space Insurance**. The subject of airline and space insurance is new to the third edition. A brief history of airline insurance in the U.S. is covered followed by topics of underwriting and rating airline accounts. A thorough discussion of space insurance is included followed by types of coverages, how rates are determined and future space underwriting issues.

Chapter 12. **Aviation Business Property Insurance and Transportation Insurance**. This chapter identifies the various commercial property insurance coverages that are available to transfer real and personal property risk exposures. Major risk management decisions areas unique to commercial property risks are compared and contrasted. The transportation insurance portion covers legal liability of common carriers, the Cargo Legal liability Endorsement and the inland transit policy.

Chapter 13. **Workers' Compensation, Automobile, and Bonds.** Aviation business organizations are required to provide employees with workers' compensation benefits. The purchase of commercial insurance or the establishment of a self-insurance program are the methods of dealing with this risk. The Business Auto Policy is used by aviation businesses to transfer property damage and liability risks associated with the ownership and operation of motor vehicles. Fidelity and surety bonds are used for the risk of employee theft and financial losses due to the breach of contracts by independent contractors.

Chapter 14. **Employee Benefits and Business Use of Life Insurance.** This final chapter covers one of the most expensive areas for aviation businesses-employee benefits. Risk managers are often involved in handling those benefit programs which are insurance based. Group life, medical care, and disability income programs, along with an in-depth analysis of retirement plans for both large and small businesses are presented. The business use of life insurance is focused on the problems of business continuation, reimbursement for the loss of a key person, and split-dollar plans that assist in the retention of personnel.

Acknowledgments

Teamwork is a reality in the insurance business. It takes brokers, agents, underwriters, adjusters, loss prevention personnel, and a myriad of other specialists to leverage their special capabilities in attempting to produce a desired result. Both of these ideas played a role in the development of this edition. While we were involved in each stage of the book's revision, the special expertise of many AIA members who updated, revised and in fact provided major portions of new material made the third edition a reality. In this regard, we owe a special debt of gratitude to the following individuals:

Dave Barder	Caledonian Insurance Group, Inc. – Mercer Island, WA
Tom Bradshaw	Menger Underwriting Services, LLC – Fort Worth, TX
Jeff Bruno	Global Aerospace – Short Hills, NJ
Michael Clark	Phoenix Aviation Managers, Inc. – Kennesaw, GA
Ernest DrSpain	W. Brown & Associates Insurance Services – Irvine, CA
Beverly Fant	Acordia – Atlanta, GA
Nancy Gratzer	Marsh USA, Inc. – Atlanta, GA
Perry Gray	Swiss Reinsurance Company – New York, NY
Wayne Gregory	US Specialty Insurance Company – Dallas, TX
Darrell Hyde	CS&A Aviation Insurance – Cumming, GA
Doug Johnson	Insuranceamerica Aviation, Inc. – Stone Mountain, GA
Frank Kimmel	Kimmel Aviation Insurance Agency, Inc. Greenwood, MS
Dave McKay	U.S. Aviation Underwriters – New York, NY
Nicholas Methven	Global Aerospace – Short Hills, NJ
Corky Nason	Nason Associates, Inc. – Overland Park, KS
Beckie Rodriguez	ABC Program – St. Louis, MO
Scott Ross	Global Aerospace – Short Hills, NJ
Kim Stufflet	Preferred Aviation Underwriters – Lawrenceville, GA
Frank Turtola	Global Aerospace – Short Hills, NJ

The committee members of the AIA Education Institute played a significant role in shaping the book by identifying individual contributors and offering many suggestions and insightful comments to enhance the final product. We sincerely appreciate their time and effort in this endeavor.

A special thanks is due Tom Fry, President of AIA during 2003 through 2005, who spearheaded this project from its inception in March, 2003. Unlike the previous editions, this revision was a team effort that required a special leader to shepherd, oversee and encourage the committee and its contributors. Tom was that individual.

We extend our gratitude to the AIA staff and particularly Gary Hicks, Executive Director, and Mandie Bannwarth, Director of Marketing and Membership Services for their invaluable assistance in arranging committee meetings and following up on the progress of contributors.

Finally, we would like to thank Robert Krieger for agreeing to publish the third edition of this book and to the other members of the Krieger team for their individual efforts including Bill Page and Elaine Rudd who guided us through the editing and production processes.

Bruce D. Chadbourne, Ed.D
Professor – College of Business
Embry-Riddle Aeronautical University
Daytona Beach, FL

Alexander T. Wells, Ed.D
Professor – Worldwide Campus
Embry-Riddle Aeronautical University
Daytona Beach, FL

PART ONE
THE AVIATION INSURANCE INDUSTRY

Chapter 1

Aviation Insurance in the United States: A Historical Perspective

OUTLINE

Introduction
The Formative Period
Establishment of the United States Aviation Insurance Market
Aviation Insurance Reaches Maturity
Nearly Five Decades following the Senate Investigation
Aviation Insurance in the New Millenium
Conclusion

OBJECTIVES

At the end of this chapter you should be able to:
Describe some of the early attempts in underwriting aviation risks in the immediate post-World War I period.
Identify several of the early aviation underwriters and discuss their contribution to the field of aviation insurance.
Explain the factors which caused the establishment of the aviation insurance market during the mid-to-late 1920s.
Discuss the advantages of the group approach to underwriting.
Identify the three leading aviation insurance groups up to World War II.
Recognize several of the independent insurers who entered the market in the post-World War II period.
Summarize the reasons for and the findings of the Senate investigation into aviation insurance during August 1958.
Discuss the factors in the aviation industry during the 1960s and 1970s that influenced the aviation insurance market during this period.
Describe the aviation insurance market during the 1980s and 1990s and how these two decades differed from the two preceding decades.
Discuss the effect that the tragedy of September 11, 2001 had on all segments of the aviation insurance industry.

INTRODUCTION

The history of transportation and the development of insurance are curiously interwoven. Whenever a new means of travel was sought, a multitude of hazards to people and property presented themselves, calling for new methods of protection.

The perils of the sea which beset sailors for centuries, were among the earliest of these transportation hazards, and the first known forms of insurance probably were the "bottomry contracts" early Greek merchants placed on the small and primitive vessels which ventured into the Mediterranean.

Civilization progressed. The steam engine was developed to propel individuals over metal rails with the danger of fog-hidden signals, derailment and overturn. The insurance industry expanded to compensate people for personal injuries received in railroad accidents and to safeguard investors when their property was damaged or destroyed.

The automobile came and brought its own peculiar hazards. Automobile insurance was developed in all its forms to protect against fire, theft, collision, comprehensive physical damages, and liability.

Latest of all, a new era of transportation began, when on December 17, 1903 the Wright brothers gave birth to the air age at Kitty Hawk, North Carolina. Since that date aviation has changed from a few test flights to orbiting celestial bodies, from sliding along sand dunes to spanning oceans, from feats of isolated daring to casual acceptance. Speeds have increased a thousandfold, as have altitude and range capabilities. No longer is the sky the limit. Ahead lie risks and rewards as vast as space itself. We have new airplanes that fly with greater fuel efficiency, huge air freighters that move the nation's goods, an expanding general aviation fleet, and the vehicles for space exploration and research. Insurance also keeps abreast of endeavors to conquer space and time.

One hundred years ago, aviation insurance was barely recognized. Today it is part of the space age. Aviation insurance began in 1911 when the first policy was developed by Lloyd's of London. In July 1912 Lloyd's agreed to cover legal liability only on some aircraft participating in an air meet. Unfortunately, the weather was bad, the crashes were numerous, and the losses on the policies were so bad that the underwriters completely gave up insuring airplanes.

Few policies were issued before World War I, and those few were more or less confined to legal liability or personal accident coverages. The risk of insuring against loss from physical damage to the unstable and frail aircraft of those days was more than even the most courageous underwriter would undertake. World War I ended civilian aviation and until 1919 the demand for insurance coverage lapsed. The return of peace set underwriters to thinking again about the possibilities of this form of travel. There was comparatively little flying at the time however, and what flying existed did not produce enough business to feed a competitive market with an adequate premium income.

THE FORMATIVE PERIOD

After World War I civilian air transportation and the aviation insurance market began in the United States. Many returning pilots bought surplus war aircraft Curtiss Jennies, de Havilland DH-4s, and S.E. 5s and went into business. A Curtiss Jenny which had cost the government close to $17,000 sold for as high as $750 including a new OX-5 engine and as low as $50. These happy-go-lucky barnstormers toured the country putting on shows and giving rides to the local townsfolk. Some insurance companies experimented with the risk of insuring them, but the loss experience was poor and withdrawals from the market were frequent.

Nevertheless, in meeting the needs, the Travelers Insurance Company announced on May 1, 1919, a comprehensive insurance program for air risks. Aviation insurance became a reality.

The lines of insurance written by the Travelers applied to the maintenance, operation, and use of aircraft for private and commercial purposes, including the transportation of passengers. The program assumed that airplane use for business as well as pleasure purposes would increase vastly in the next few years.

According to the announcement the lines of aviation business to be written included:

1. **Life Insurance.** The company was prepared to issue aviation risk life insurance upon the one-year nonrenewable term plan, with a $5,000 limit.
2. **Accident insurance for owners and pilots.** The policy provided death, dismemberment, and loss of sight benefits, also indemnity for total and partial disability.
3. **Trip accident ticket insurance.** The company prepared to furnish transportation-by-air companies with an accident ticket to be sold to passengers. These tickets were issued to take effect as of date and hour of issue and to end at 4 A.M. the following day. The ticket provided $5,000 for accidental death benefit and disability benefits.
4. **Workers' Compensation insurance.**
5. **Public liability and property damage insurance.**[1]

The stated purpose was "offering insurance to encourage the manufacture, improvement and use of aircraft."

Public liability policies were designed for injuries occasioned by collision in the air resulting in injuries to occupants of other aircraft. They did not include the passenger hazard of the insured's aircraft. Public liability policies also included injuries caused to others on the ground while landing or taking off or because of articles accidently dropped from the aircraft while in flight. Property damage coverage provided for the liability of the insured for damage to the property of others not carried on the aircraft. This early Travelers' program did not include coverage against damage to the aircraft itself (the aircraft hull insurance).

A few days after the Travelers' announcement, on May 6, at a convention of the Aero Club of America in Atlantic City, New Jersey, the agency of Payne and Richardson issued Aero Tickets to an illustrious group of Americans, including President Woodrow Wilson and the Wright brothers. Aero Ticket Number One was sold to President Wilson at a premium of $5 for $5,000 accidental death benefits. "In issuing aircraft trip tickets,' commented the *Weekly Underwriter* that week, "the Travelers increased the reputation of that company for initiative in the insurance business."[2]

Unfortunately, the early development of air transportation did not measure up to the Travelers' expectations. After struggling to write aviation insurance business independently for 12 years, the Travelers was finally forced to cease in 1931, after several tragic air disasters that year wiped out the company's reserves for aviation business. The Travelers did not reenter the aviation insurance market until 1939, when the company joined the United States Aircraft Insurance Group (USAIG).

In the next three years after 1919 there were, besides the Travelers, five other companies active in aviation insurance:

1. The Home Insurance Company
2. Queen Insurance Company of America
3. Globe and Burgers Insurance Company
4. National Liberty Insurance Company
5. Fireman's Fund Insurance Company

Early Aviation Underwriters

In May 1920 Horatio Barber, an underwriter at Lloyd's, came to the United States and became an aviation underwriter for the Hartford Accident and Indemnity Company. In 1924 the Hartford dropped out of all aviation coverages except public liability and property damage liability and in 1925 it and the Travelers were the only American companies writing any aviation insurance. Finally the Hartford group dropped out entirely in 1926.[3] Hartford joined the USAIG on September 1, 1929.

Following the termination of his contract with the Hartford, Barber and his partner, Baldwin, in 1926 became the aviation underwriting managers for the Independent Fire Insurance Company and its casualty affiliate, the Independent Indemnity Company of Philadelphia. This initial entry of Barber and Baldwin, as an organization, into the field of aviation insurance in America lasted three years. In September 1929 the Independent withdrew from the office of Barber and Baldwin and entered the field as a competitor. Finally in October 1930 the Independent retired from the aviation insurance field. The Barber and Baldwin Agency remained in business until 1948, writing business through Lloyd's and other British companies. Their success was largely attributable to underwriting hull coverages with very high deductibles, using very difficult and complicated policy conditions and charging very high rates.

Since the very early days another individual, and the company he organized, continuously played an important role in the development of the aviation insurance market in the United States. This man was the late J. Brooks B. Parker. The firm he organized, Parker & Co., International, Inc. (later the Parker Aviation Division of Frank B. Hall and Company, now a part of the AON Risk Services) has been recognized as the world's first brokerage house specializing in aviation insurance and a pioneer in aviation since its founding in 1919.

One of the original founders of the Aero Club of the University of Pennsylvania in 1908, Mr. Parker joined Chubb & Son as a marine underwriter upon graduation in 1911. He entered the first class of army flying schools in May 1917, graduated as a pilot, and because of his marine insurance training, he established his own brokerage firm.

In exploring ever-broadening coverages to meet the insuring needs of clients, Parker & Co. originated many of the forms and methods of writing this type of coverage. In addition to his insurance qualifications, Mr. Parker knew aircraft manufacturing and airlines from having assisted in the formation of several carriers. For example, Parker & Co. placed insurance coverages for Pan American World Airways from its formative days and for many years afterwards. Parker & Cc. induced the Continental Casualty Company to enter the aviation insurance field so that flight insurance for international air passengers could be sold by Pan American ticket agents.

Parker & Co. modernized the merchandising method of air travel insurance by selling the policy over the counter in airports. Later, Parker & Co. expanded its operation in the international market, particularly in Latin American countries, and became a significant reinsurance broker.

ESTABLISHMENT OF THE UNITED STATES AVIATION INSURANCE MARKET

Gradually, commercial aviation became stabilized. Several factors were responsible. The Air Mail Act of 1925 provided for the carriage of mail by private carriers. The Air Commerce Act of 1926 established the first airway rules and regulations as well as the licensing of aircraft and airmen. In 1927 the successful transatlantic flight of Charles Lindbergh brought about the release of large amounts of capital for the building up of the aviation industry. Public attention focused on the almost forgotten possibilities of flying as a means of transportation. Between 1926 and 1928 17 domestic airlines commenced air mail services. At the same time, two American airlines started foreign operations. Altogether in 1928 there were 294 airplanes in service, having flown 10,472,024 miles and carried 52,934 passengers.[4] In addition, there were also airplanes conducting aerial service operations (which means all activities that may not be properly classified as scheduled transport or private flying). In 1929 the aviation industry included 6,684 licensed aircraft in the United States, 10,215 licensed pilots, and 948 established airports. During the first six months of 1929, 153 manufacturers produced some 970 commercial aircraft and 22 manufacturers each produced more than 10 aircraft. The average value of the aircraft, including engines, constructed during 1929 was $9,519.[5]

Lindbergh's historic flight had also stimulated popular interest in the aviation insurance business in the Western Hemisphere. Consequently, the competition for this business really began in the period 1927–1929, when three major groups of aviation underwriters established themselves in the market.

USAIG

On July 1, 1928, the first entry, the United States Aircraft Insurance Group with the United States Aviation Underwriters, Inc., serving as managers, commenced the acceptance of aviation risks in New York City. The group had as a nucleus eight members in all, four fire insurance companies and four casualty companies. The original four fire members were National Union Fire Insurance Company, United States Fire Insurance Company, North River Insurance Company, and Pacific Insurance Company. The first four casualty members were Maryland Casualty Company, New Amsterdam Casualty Company, New York Indemnity Company, and United Fidelity and Guarantee Company.

The necessity for including within the same management organization both fire and casualty companies arose because in many states, legislation permitted an insurance company to write only one of the three major lines of business, i.e., fire (and marine), casualty, or life. By joining a number of companies, the underwriting manager could meet all the insurance needs of various aviation interests.

On August 24, 1928, the first policy, No. AF251, was issued to Canadian Colonial Airways, Inc. During the year, the USAIG suffered its first catastrophic loss. A Colonial & Western Airway's Ford Tri-Motor crashed on the edge of the Newark, New Jersey, airport, killing all 14 passengers, the pilot being the sole survivor. The group paid $29,680 on account of the total destruction of the aircraft and ultimately paid a liability loss amounting to $193,000, which included $189,119 for passenger liability, and the balance for workers' compensation and for the liability for property damage to others[6].

AAU

The catastrophe occurred on March 11, 1929. On the very next day, the Associated Aviation Underwriters (AAU) entered the aviation insurance field. The idea was hatched when Owen C. Torrey (then vice president of the Marine Office of America) and J. Russell Parsons (a partner of Chubb & Son) met and decided that insurance for airplanes would be required. For many years, AAU was jointly owned by The Chubb Corporation and CNA Financial Corporation. In 2001 it merged with British Aviation Insurance Group to form Global Aerospace.

Initially AAU included 17 companies in its group. Later that year it reinsured the outstanding liability of the Transportation Companies when these companies retired from the aviation field. Again in 1930 when the Independent Companies retired from the aviation insurance field, the AAU reinsured their outstanding liabilities. Later, when the Aero Insurance Underwriters retired from the writing of scheduled airlines, the burden of providing insurance for the airlines fell on the Associated Aviation Underwriters and the USAIG.

Aero Insurance Underwriters

The Aero Insurance Underwriters came into the aviation business as successors to the original firm of Barber & Baldwin, Inc. After the Independent Companies withdrew from the office of Barber and Baldwin, the Aero Underwriters Corporation was organized as a holding company for the newly created Aero Insurance Company, Aero Indemnity Company, Aero Engineering and Advisory Company, and the old firm of Barber and Baldwin, Inc. In 1932 the Aero Underwriters Corporation and its subsidiaries were placed in liquidation. Barber retired and returned to Europe and in November of that year the Aero Insurance Underwriters came into being under the management of George L. Lloyd. The major companies in the Aero Insurance Underwriters group were the Royal-Globe Insurance Companies and the Great American Insurance Companies. Later when the Aero dissolved in 1948, the Royal-Globe Group entered the aviation market independently and the Great American Companies joined the USAIG.

Many of the companies previously associated with the Barber and Baldwin office joined Aero Insurance Underwriters which then became a group that followed a pattern initially established by the USAIG.

The National Continental Aviation Insurance group was formed in Chicago in the summer of 1929, but it did not make adequate progress and later retired from the business in April 1933. Thereafter until the end of the Second World War, AAU and the USAIG, representing over one hundred insurance companies, handled practically all the insurance transactions in the aviation market.

The Group Approach to Underwriting

The group, as an approach to underwriting aviation risks, has spanned the period between the day when the financial speculator first saw an opportunity in civil aviation for those who were willing to take a risk and the present time when airlines and the aerospace industry have become an accepted part of our complex economic structure. The success of the group approach represents the finest example in American insurance of the pooling of faith, knowledge, and facilities in a common undertaking involving the fortunes of both fire and casualty companies, which have been inseparably intertwined in providing the insurance protection for the American aerospace industry.

It all started from the idea of two comparatively young men who foresaw the need for better insurance for the aviation industry. One was David C. Beebe, who had a background of flying experience and insurance experience in the marine field. In 1927 Beebe resigned from Marsh & McLennan and traveled to England, Germany, and other European countries on his own to study problems of aviation insurance and to learn, if possible, how it could be underwritten successfully in America. At that time aviation insurance, though still experimental, was developed more thoroughly in Europe. His research convinced him that this form of indemnity could be handled safely only by insurance pools or groups of companies.

Upon his return Beebe approached Major Reed M. Chambers and convinced him to enter the insurance field. Together they hoped to build up aviation insurance where it could be of real service to American aviation. Major Chambers was a leading figure in American aviation. Following a brilliant flying career in the Army in France during World War I, he remained in aviation and in 1926, along with Eddie Rickenbacker, organized Florida Airways, the forerunner of Pan American World Airways. Major Chambers knew the technical end of aviation and the industry had complete confidence in his judgment. He gave the new insurance organization immediate prestige among possible buyers of coverage.

In the formation of their group, Beebe and Chambers approached the initial insurance companies on three grounds:

1. To promote American patriotism. American aviation was deserving of support to bring it up to the standard of other countries.
2. The most economical way to write aviation insurance was to pool the resources that might be of service to each member company.
3. The proposed new group would be composed of specialists in aviation.

The group method of operation initially selected by the United States Aviation Underwriters, Inc. (USAU) for the handling of aviation risks has been followed and is still the favored method of operation used by many companies.

The advantages of the group approach to underwriting was summarized by the pioneering Mr. Beebe as follows:[7]

A. For the benefit of assureds of the USAIG, the group plan
    1. Brings to each assured security unequalled in the aviation insurance field.
    2. Brings to each assured the experience and advice of underwriters gained in handling the problems of a larger number of assureds than underwriters acting for any one company individually would have the opportunity to acquire.

B. For the benefit of agents and brokers, the group plan
    1. Brings to agents of each member company facilities for a class of business that no company up to the present time acting individually (either in the United States or elsewhere) has been able to offer for more than

a brief unsatisfactory experimental period.

2. Brings to each agent of a member company the ability to deliver to his assured a policy of the company he represents in an amount, and covering hazards that a conservative company would under other circumstances not provide. It also brings complete facilities for all required forms of aviation protection through one channel.
3. Brings to each broker facilities for all required forms of aviation protection through one channel, and permits the broker or his assured to select that member fire or casualty company in which policies are desired.
4. Does not take away from any agent of any member company any power or authority which he may have had prior to the formation of the USAIG, but brings to each, new facilities and a new source of income that he did not previously have.

C. For the benefit of the participating member companies the group plan
   1. Brings to each member company a small share in the large spread developed through the combined agency and brokerage channels of all members collectively.
   2. Distributed the large catastrophe hazard inherent in air risks in a manner not presently possible through outside reinsurance.
   3. Effects economies in operation through the maintenance of one centralized Aviation Department and the elimination of all possible duplication of effort.
   4. Permits the purchase of necessary outside reinsurance on a wholesale basis for the reason that reinsurers have the same advantage of a small share in the larger spread that is enjoyed by the participating direct writing companies themselves.
   5. Alone can produce a volume of aviation business sufficient to justify the expense of (a) a specialized underwriting staff, (b) the accumulation and analysis of detailed pertinent statistics, (c) comprehensive investigations and surveys, and (d) educational and loss prevention work.
   6. Relieves home office executives of member companies from pressure by agents to accept undesirable business for purely agency reasons, and permits selective underwriting by the managerial staff.
   7. Provides the advantages enumerated above without destroying the identity or individuality of the participating member companies.

With Beebe as president and Chambers as vice president, the United States Aviation Underwriters, Inc., (USAU) began operation to serve as underwriting managers for the United States Aircraft Insurance Group. The group approach initially selected by the USAU for the handling of aviation risks has been followed ever since.

Shortly after the formation of USAIG, AAU, and Aero Insurance Underwriters, the country experienced its great depression. Commencing in 1930, there was a serious decline in the volume of aviation insurance business. This trend continued for three or four years, but in the middle of the decade the business began to come back. In 1935 and 1936, aviation insurance business took a distinctly upward trend and in the late 1930s prior to World War II, it started to climb at a rapid pace. During the war years premium volume receded for a while but then increased slightly. United States entry into World War II cast an ever-increasing influence over American aviation and American aviation insurance.

The war changed the business of aviation insurance underwriting considerably. In the prewar days aviation insurance was written principally for:

1. Scheduled airlines
2. Manufacture of civil aircraft
3. Fixed base operators and flying schools
4. Private owners
5. Aircraft sales distributors
6. A small number of military manufacturers

During the war, the available business for the aviation underwriting market changed to:

1. Scheduled airlines
2. Manufacturers of military aircraft
3. Civilian pilot training program
4. Civil Air Patrol
5. Army training schools

All these businesses were directly or indirectly under government control or influence. Consequently, the three groups pooled resources and placed them all at the service of the government a valuable contribution to the war effort. Still they continued to dominate the American aviation insurance market. In 1942 over 96 percent of the aviation insurance business reported to the New York State Insurance Department was written by the three underwriting groups.

On June 10, 1932, the Superintendent of Insurance of New York State called a meeting of all insurance companies engaged in transacting aviation insurance. The purpose was to establish some coordination and uniformity in rates and rules so that the required regulation could be properly administered. An industry committee was appointed to accomplish this purpose. On September 21, 1932, a plan subscribed to by all existing elements of the aviation insurance market was presented to the department and was accepted on September 30, 1932. The original subscribers to this plan were: Associated Aviation Underwriters, Aero Insurance Underwriters (successors to Barber and Baldwin, Inc.), National Continental Aviation Insurance Association, United States Aircraft Insurance Group, and the Travelers Insurance Companies.

On October 7, 1932, these groups and the companies they represented organized a rather loose advisory rating and statistical organization and adopted articles of association containing rules and regulations. The name agreed upon for this organization was the Board of Aviation Underwriters and it assumed countrywide jurisdiction. Over the years its importance diminished and finally in 1945 the Board of Aviation Underwriters ceased functioning. Thereafter the various companies and groups writing aviation insurance filed their rates directly with the New York State Insurance Department.

AVIATION INSURANCE REACHES MATURITY

The growth of aviation insurance has paralleled the growth of the aviation industry itself. As American aviation achieved world supremacy during and after World War II, American aviation insurance business established a strong position in the world aviation insurance market. As was true of the post-World War I years, the postwar years of 1946 and 1947 brought increased aviation activities and the further expansion of aviation insurance business. A great number of returning pilots and new air carriers expanded the aviation industry. At the same time a considerable number of new underwriting organizations staffed with inexperienced underwriters entered the aviation insurance field.

The overexpansion of the aviation insurance business resulted in poor loss ratios for all underwriters and a reduction of rate levels below those necessary to write the business successfully. As a result, many withdrew from the market in 1947, including one of the major groups, the Aero Insurance Underwriters. During 1947 the remaining underwriting groups increased rates significantly for all types of coverage and cancelled or refused to renew a large number of accounts which had shown poor loss experience. After these years of painful adjustment, the aviation insurance market gradually stabilized by 1948.

Entry of Independent Underwriters

The vast expansion of general aviation in the postwar years prompted several insurance companies to write the aviation business independently. Numerous companies tried but soon withdrew. Among the survivors were the Royal-Globe Insurance Companies, the Insurance Company of North America, the American Mercury Insurance Company, and several mutual insurance companies associated in the Mutual Aviation Casualty Underwriters group. Following its withdrawal from the Aero Insurance Underwriters at the end of 1947, the Royal-Globe Insurance Companies entered the aviation insurance field on January 1, 1948, by establishing their own aviation department. Specializing in the business and pleasure risks including corporate aircraft operators, this market continued to underwrite aviation business until the early 1970s when the combination of recession in the general aviation industry and severe competition in the aviation insurance field forced them to withdraw as an independent and subsequently join the USAIG.

As early as 1927 the Insurance Company of North America (INA) expressed its interest in aviation insurance and conducted an investigation to determine whether it would be advisable to write the various forms of aviation insurance. Seven years later, in 1934, the Insurance Company of North America and affiliated fire companies joined the Hull section of the USAIG. The Indemnity Company of North America, however, stayed outside the group and commenced writing aviation liability business on its own during World War II as an accommodation to its agents.

Immediately after the war, the North American Companies decided that they could best serve the industry and their agents by divorcing themselves from any underwriting syndicate and by writing this form of insurance directly through their agents. On January 1, 1946, INA announced its entry into the aviation field, and established a new aviation department.

INA started with those lines of aviation insurance which were most valuable to the local agency system and endeavored to confine writings largely to owners of private airplanes, including corporate operators, aircraft dealers, and fixed base operators. In 1982 INA merged with Connecticut General Corporation to form CIGNA Property and Casualty Corporation. In 1999 ACE Ltd., one of the largest underwriters of aerospace insurance in the world acquired CIGNA and formed ACE USA Aerospace.

An entirely new firm, the American Mercury Insurance Company, with its headquarters in Washington, D.C., entered the aviation insurance market in 1949. Unlike North America and the Royal-Globe Companies, the American Mercury was organized to write aviation business exclusively, although its charter powers authorized it to write all lines of business except surety, life, and annuity. The company obtained its business, to a considerable extent, from members of the Aircraft Owners and Pilots Association and the National Aviation Trades Association. The company terminated its agreement with the Aircraft Owners and Pilots Association on January 1, 1963. On the same date, the Aircraft Owners and Pilots Association entered a new agreement with the newly organized Aviation Employees Insurance Company (AVEMCO) to solicit members' business through direct mail. This agreement would continue until 1986 when AOPA terminated AVEMCO as its designated insurer.

At the close of World War II, several mutual insurance companies also saw the prospect of the expansion of general aviation activities and thus began the growth of the general aviation insurance market. In order to strengthen their entry into the field and to obtain a meaningful share of the business, these mutual companies decided, in 1945, after a careful study, to associate themselves in a new group called Mutual Aviation Casualty Underwriters. With the group facilities available, the agency-writing companies among the group were also enabled to accommodate their agents in writing aviation risks.

Challenge of the Jet Era

The real test of strength of the American aviation insurance market came in 1954 when the industry entered the jet age. In July 1954 a Boeing 707 took off from Renton, Washington, to Baltimore, Maryland, on a test flight. This prototype was the first of a long line of jet aircraft to follow in the next five decades.

This development presented an unprecedented challenge to the USAIG when the group was called upon to provide insurance coverage of over $5 million on a single plane in test flight. To meet the huge requirements, the USAIG not only utilized the full capacities of its member companies but mobilized the world insurance market through Lloyd's. The test flight was successful, and the Americans aviation insurance market has since built up a substantial capacity to meet the ever-increasing needs for far larger amounts.

The enlarged underwriting capacities of the two groups did not meet the entire insurance requirements of the aviation industry, particularly in the area of products liability for aircraft manufacturers. Since the early 1950s, the liability of an aircraft manufacturer to a third party for allegedly defective products has become a serious problem. An aircraft crashing into a heavily populated area with resulting fire and explosion could prove to be disastrous to the manufacturer of the aircraft or of the component part which may have caused the accident. Furthermore, grounding liability coverages were not available on the market then.

Consequently, in 1952 certain members of the Aerospace Industries Association became concerned and initiated a study of the aviation insurance market. To explore the possibilities of providing adequate insurance protection against products liability, the Aircraft Builders Council, Inc., was organized. The council developed a plan of aircraft products liability insurance and the so-called ABC Plan became operative in 1955.

The Plan provided manufacturers with the third-party liability insurance for damages arising out of the products hazard, with a limitation of $5 million for personal injury or property damage for any one occurrence and, in addition, third-party liability insurance for damages arising out of the products hazard for loss of use of completed aircraft caused by grounding, up to a limit of $5 million. The insurance was available for a qualified manufacturer of aircraft, aircraft engines, propellers, missiles, and component parts. Coverage applied to both the sales of military and commercial aircraft, aircraft parts, and missiles. Military and commercial coverages could not be purchased separately. The Plan was underwritten by two domestic mutual companies and Lloyd's of London and British companies. The two domestic companies are Liberty Mutual Insurance Company and Employers Mutual of Wausau.

Senate Investigation of the Industry

Aero Insurance Underwriters, as previously mentioned, went out of existence on January 1, 1948. Subsequently another group called Aero Associates was formed in 1949 by an insurance broker, George Stewart, president of Stewart, Smith & Co. The group originally consisted of the American Fidelity and Casualty Company and the American Fidelity Fire Insurance Company. In 1950 the Eagle Star Insurance Company joined the group, and in 1954 Zurich Insurance Company was substituted for American Fidelity and Casualty Company. As originally formed, 50 percent of

Aero was owned by Stewart, Smith & Co. and the other 50 percent by the American Fidelity Companies. When Stewart entered the market in 1949 through the formation of Aero Associates, he conducted a market survey which indicated there was room for another group to provide more capacity.

In the early days Aero Associates was quoting prices approximately 20 percent less than the other two groups. Stewart was satisfied that additional business could be obtained at rates lower than those charged by the two existing groups. From 1954 to 1958 Aero Associates showed underwriting losses for each year. Zurich offered to buy out Stewart, Smith's 50 percent ownership in Aero Associates, but was not able to interest any other underwriters in entering the group after it took control of Aero Associates. As a result, Aero Associates ceased operations and Zurich joined the USAIG on January 1, 1958.

Despite the enormous growth of the aviation industry and the vast increase in insurance that such growth entails, where formerly there were three available American groups, now there were only two. It was against this background that the Subcommittee on Antitrust and Monopoly of the Committee of the Judiciary of the United States Senate, headed by the late Senator O'Mahoney, started its investigation of the situation and commenced public hearings which lasted from August 6, 1958, through August 15, 1958. Throughout the hearings, the Subcommittee indicated that its overriding concern was with the extent and effectiveness of competition.

In summarizing its findings, the Subcommittee made its conclusions and recommendations in a report published in August 1960. The major items among its conclusions were:

1. In 1943, a report of the Civil Aeronautics Board criticized the concentration of the aviation insurance business in the hands of three competing groups or markets. Despite the phenomenal growth of the commercial aircraft industry in the intervening years, only two groups or syndicates were available to furnish the insurance for the operation and continued growth of the industry.
2. Adequate reinsurance facilities had not developed in the United States.
3. Reverse competition had occurred in the air trip insurance business where the three insurers were engaged in a struggle for market position, not through lower rates or wider coverages to buyers, but through the payment of enormous rentals to airports.
4. State regulation of aviation insurance was not completely effective in eliminating the restrictive market practices discovered by the Subcommittee.

No specific actions aimed at correcting the above situations were undertaken by the federal government or by the New York State Insurance Department. The Justice Department, however, and a Federal Grand Jury later conducted lengthy investigations and hearings on the allegations of the Subcommittee. The conclusion of both was that no action was warranted.

FIVE DECADES FOLLOWING THE SENATE INVESTIGATION

Expansion, modernization, and increasing complexity characterized all segments of the aviation industry during the turbulent 1960s. A decade that began with radial-engine transports and ended with the Concorde, it was also the decade which saw the first manned space launch in April, 1961 when Yuri Gagarin logged 1.8 hours in *Vostok I* and Neil Armstrong and Buzz Aldrin landed on the moon in July, 1969. Airline traffic soared, fed by a strong economy and the Vietnam War. By the mid-sixties the major carriers were placing orders for wide-body jets to carry the ever-increasing number of passengers.

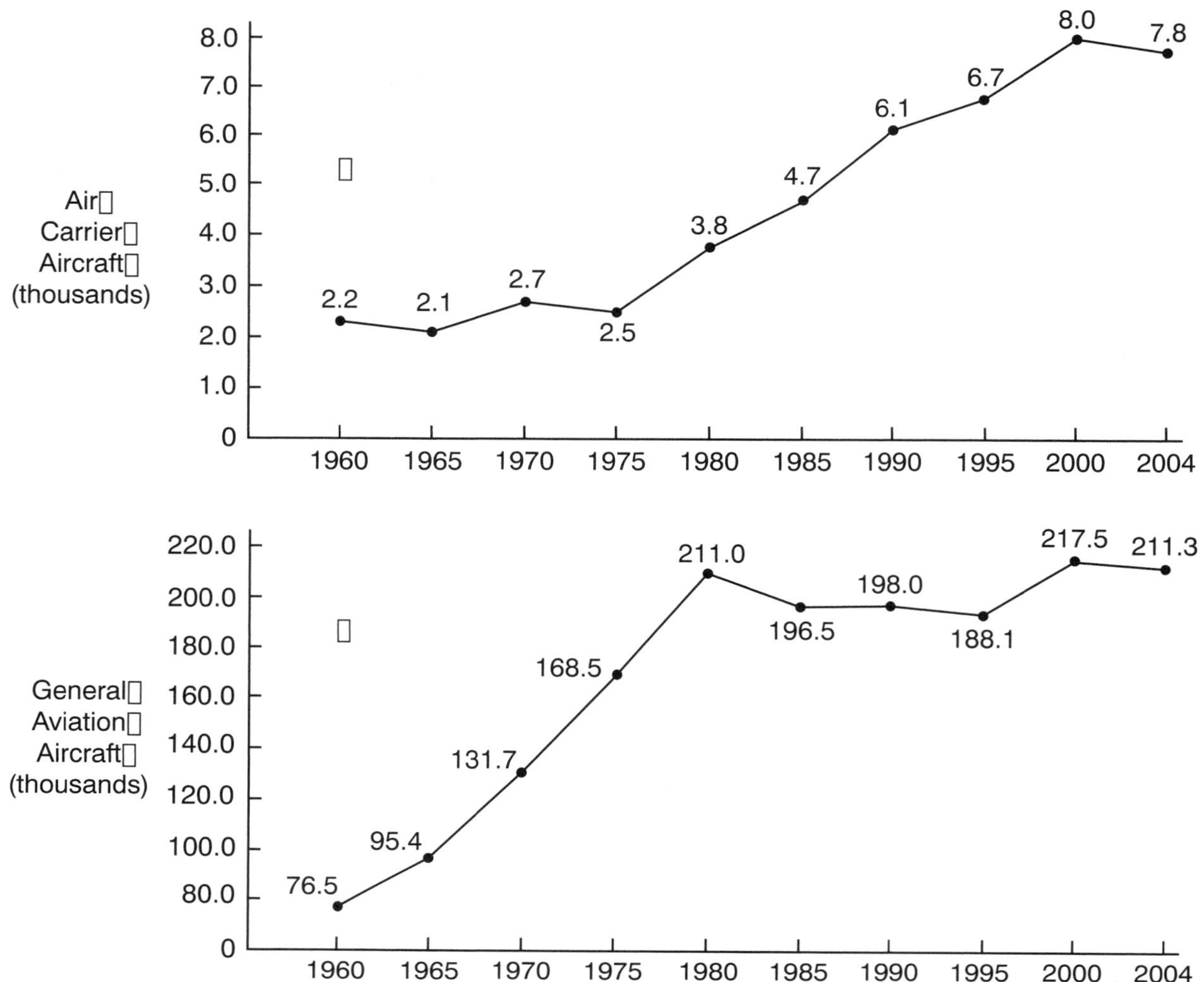

Figure 1.1 Active U.S. Civil Aircraft for Selected Years as of December 31. Source: FAA Statisitcal Handbook of Aviation (current edition)

As for general aviation, the 1960s were boom times, with more pilots using more airplanes than ever before. General aviation manufacturers were having a heyday, introducing new models and producing an average of more than 9,000 airplanes per year. Four airplanes in particular that were introduced in the 1960s the Cessna 172, the Piper Cherokee, the Beech King Air 90, and the Lear 23 proved to be bellwether designs for years to come. The general aviation fleet almost doubled during the 1960s and new aircraft shipments hit a high of 15,768 units in 1966 (see figures 1-1, 1-2 and 1-3).

Significant changes also took place in the aviation insurance market. New underwriting groups were formed and the market expanded and became more competitive. General Aviation Underwriting Corporation was organized in Dallas, Texas, in 1962 and was composed of 10 insurance companies specializing in general aviation risks. A pool by the name of Aviation Insurance Managers (AIM) was formed in 1962 by Southern Marine & Aviation Underwriters, surplus lines brokers, and served as aviation insurance managers for eight companies. AIM was headquartered in New Orleans with offices in Los Angeles and San Francisco. Another company, American

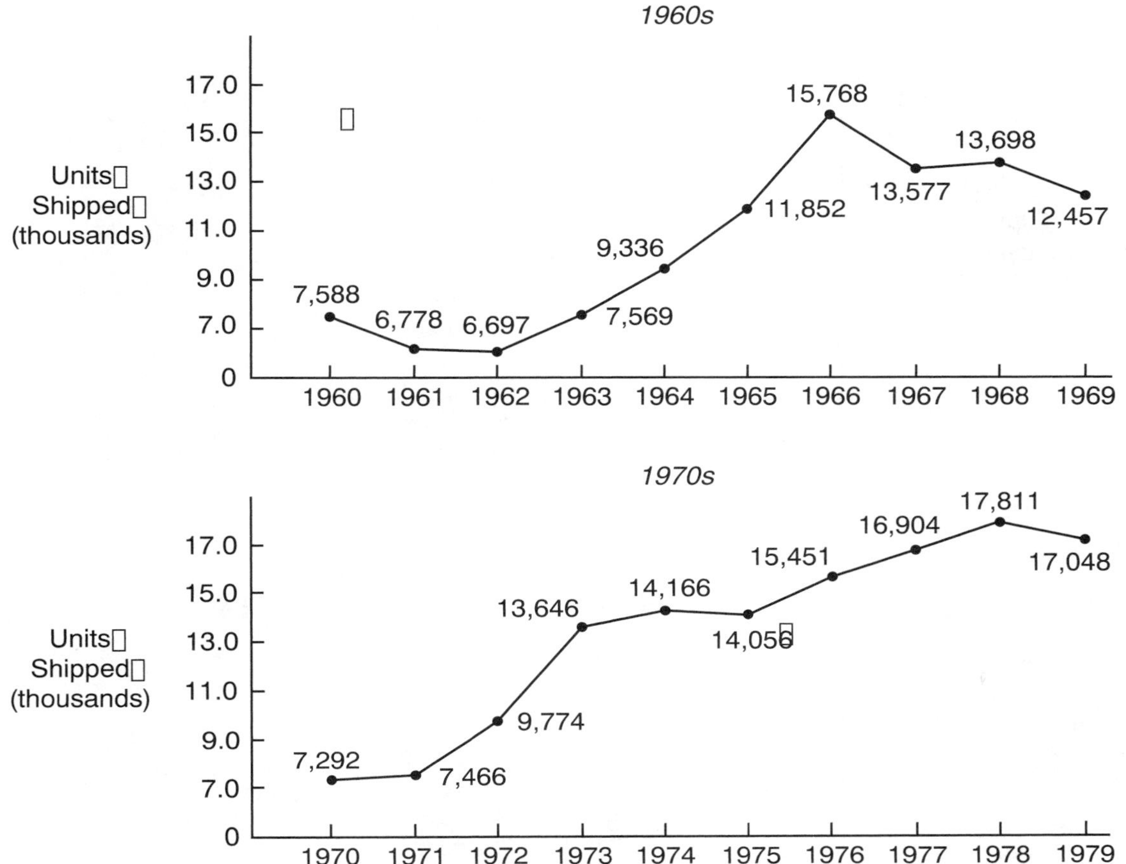

Figure 1.2 Annual Shipments of New U.S. General Aviation Aircraft by Units Shipped Durring the 1960s and 1970s.
Source: GAMA Statisitcal Databook (current edition)

Aviation Underwriters, based in Houston, Texas, included two companies and was managed by Cravens, Dargan & Co.

Six other groups were formed during the 1960s, all primarily seeking business in the growing general aviation market. These were Airway Underwriters, Ann Arbor, Michigan; Aviation Office of America (AOA), Dallas, Texas; International Aviation Underwriters, Dallas, Texas; Northwestern Underwriters, Portland, Oregon; Southeastern Aviation Underwriters, Atlanta, Georgia; and Transport Indemnity Company, Los Angeles, California.

In addition, there were a number of independent companies entering the market or expanding their operations. In 1963 the direct writer, Aviation Employees Insurance Company (AVEMCO) became the designated insurer for the Aircraft Owners and Pilots Association (AOPA) replacing American Mercury Insurance Company whose relationship with AOPA covered 25 years. The Ohio Casualty Company, Royal-Globe Insurance Companies and the Insurance Company of North America expanded their writing and opened regional offices staffed with aviation underwriters.

At the same time, the mutual insurance companies became more active in the aviation market. The most prominent were Liberty Mutual of Boston, the Lumbermens Mutual Casualty of Chicago, and the Employers Mutual of Wausau.

The entry of these numerous groups and companies into the market during the

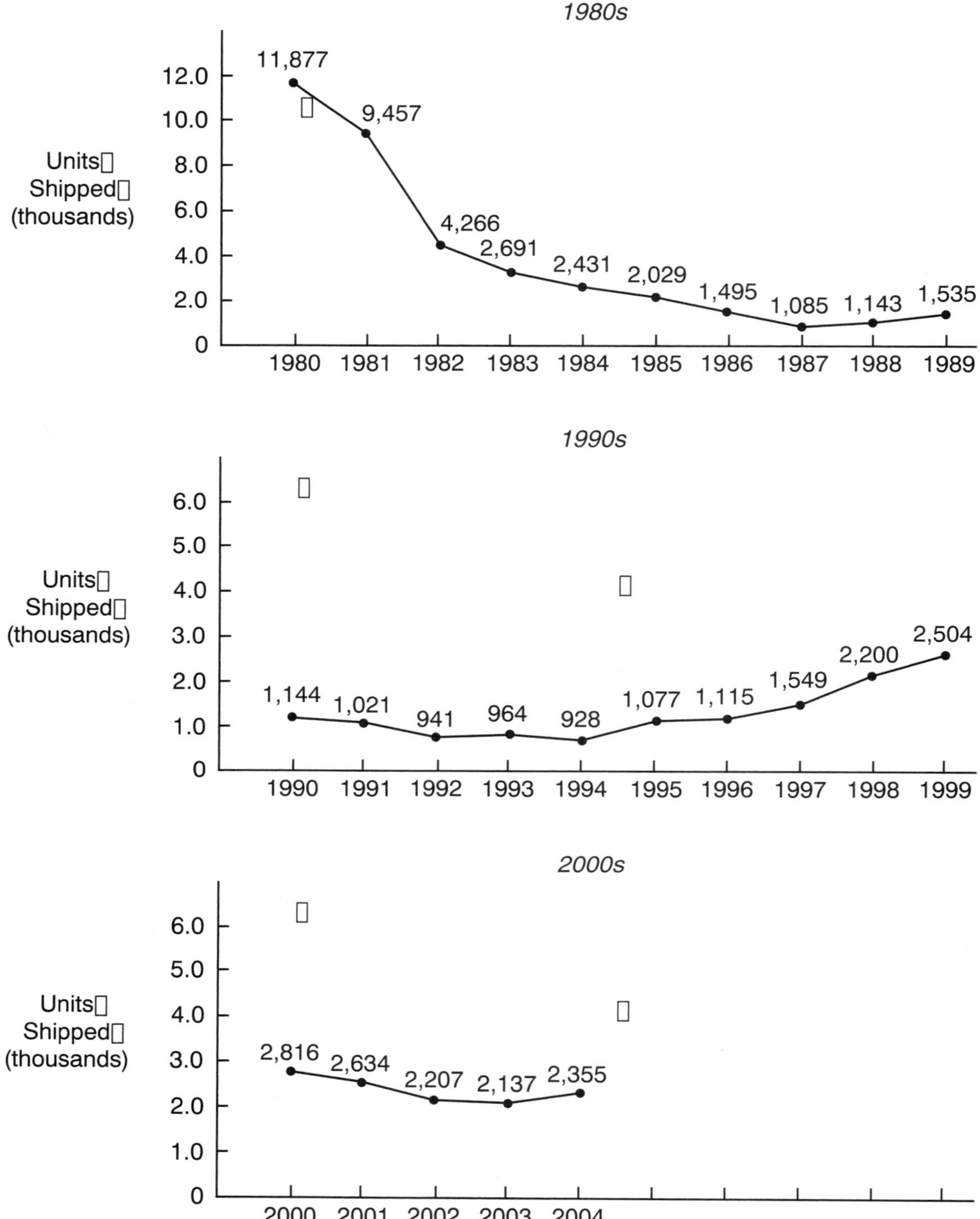

Figure 1.3 Annual Shipments of New U.S. General Aviation Aircraft by Units Shipped Durring the 1980s,1990s and 2000s.
Source: GAMA Statisitcal Databook (current edition)

1960s, particularly in the general aviation field, fostered a high degree of competition for business and as a result, caused a reduction in the level of premium rates for all classes of business. Reinsurance facilities also expanded. Up to the 1960s at least 50 percent of the American aviation insurance business was reinsured with a foreign market, primarily British companies and Lloyd's.

In 1961 the American Mutual Reinsurance Company organized a "Scheduled Airlines Pool" to write excess liability coverage. Insurance Company of North America also expanded its reinsurance capabilities to participate in the insurance of major air carriers. Other reinsurance organizations, such as the Excess and Casualty Reinsurance Association, General Reinsurance Corporation, also provided additional reinsurance capacity for all lines of aviation insurance business.

Parker & Company, the vigorous motivating force in the aviation market in its earlier days, again paved the way for the formation of a new aviation reinsurance pool in 1963 called the Interocean Reinsurance Pool. Participants in the pool included 11 strong independent insurers, both stock and mutual, such as the Continental Casualty Company, Allstate Insurance Company, and Nationwide Mutual Insurance Company.

The expansion of all segments of aviation continued into the 1970s. More airplanes were sold during this decade than before or since. The general aviation aircraft fleet increased from 132,000 to 211,000 aircraft and production hit a high of 17,800 aircraft in 1978 (see figures 1-1 and 1-2). New aircraft were introduced in record numbers, particularly trainers such as Piper's Cherokee and Tomahawk models, Cessna's 150 and 152 and Beech's Sierra and Sundowner, to name a few.

However, there were some clouds on the horizon. Fuel prices soared during the 1970s and manufacturers looked to more fuel-efficient aircraft for the future. Airspace congestion was another problem that the industry had been studying since the mid-sixties. As a result, the Airport and Airways Development Act was passed in 1970 to provide the revenue needed to expand and improve the airport/airway system over a 10-year period. Finally, the industry was faced with ever-increasing federal regulations during the 1970s. Terminal Control Areas (TCAs) were introduced around the country's busiest airports which required two-way communications with Air Traffic Control (ATC), VOR navigation capability and altitude-reporting transponders. Increasing regulations particularly impacted the personal pleasure pilot.

It was also during the 1970s that attention of the general aviation industry started focusing on product liability. The number of suits increased as well as the size of awards. Insurance premiums increased from $51 per new airplane in 1962 to $2,111 in 1972. It would be a sign of things to come for the aircraft manufacturers and no doubt, one of the major causes for the precipitous decline in the production of general aviation aircraft during the 1980s (see figure 1-3). Product liability insurance costs for the general aviation airframe builders totaled about $135 million in 1985 and based on unit shipments of 2,000 aircraft that year, the price exceeded $70,000 per airplane. This was more than the selling price of many basic two- and four-place aircraft.

These phenomenal cost increases during the first five years of the 1980s came at a time when the industry's safety record continued to improve (see figure 1-4). Improved safety notwithstanding, the number of product liability suits continued to increase. Even more significant was the exponential growth in settlements, judgments, and legal costs.

By 1986 Cessna Aircraft Company decided to drop its piston aircraft production and self-insure up to $100 million. Piper decided to operate without the benefit of product liability coverage and Beech insured the first $50 million annual aggregate exposure with their own captive insurance company.

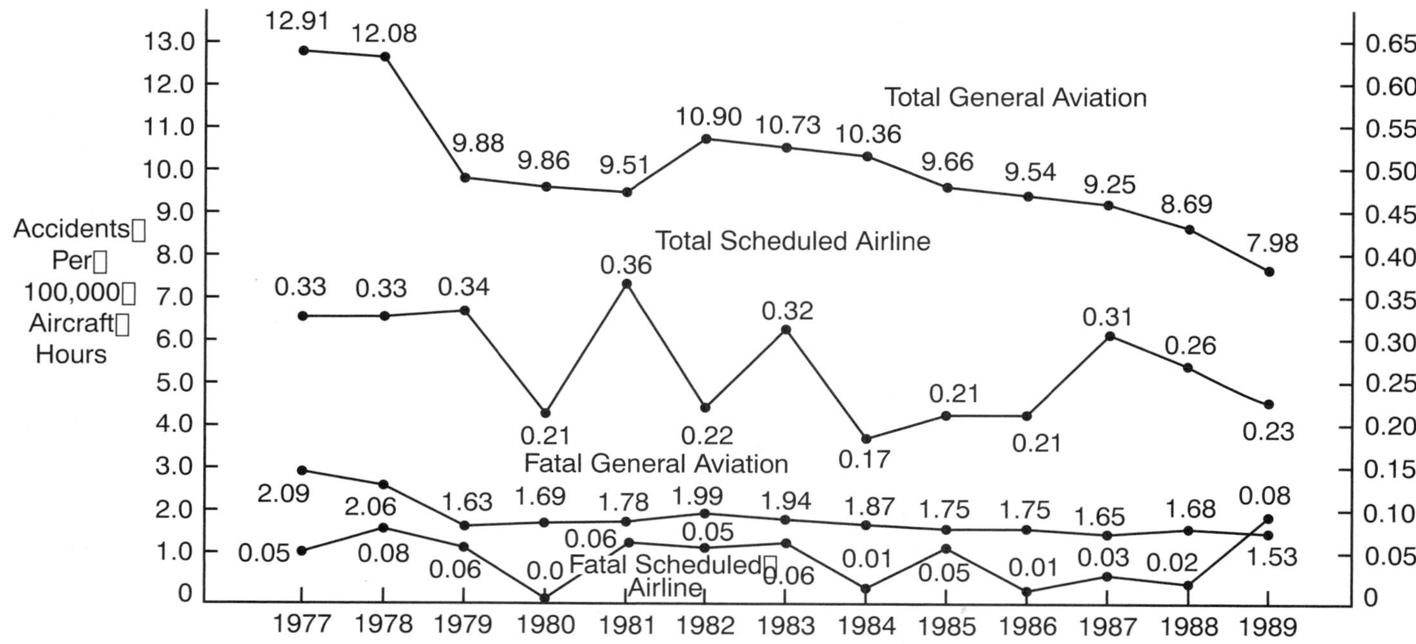

Figure 1.4 Annual Rates for U.S. Civil Aircraft per 100,000 Aircraft Hours Flown from 1977 to 1989.
Source: National Transportation Safety Board Current Annuaal Report

Other factors were also working against the private business and pleasure flyer. Airline deregulation in 1978 at first caused a decrease in the use of business aircraft, as the air carriers, including many new ones, served new markets and competed for customers with lower fares. Business aircraft were harder to justify. But as the airlines concentrated their flights at hub cities and merger mania struck the industry in the early 1980s, service to many smaller communities was dropped or severely cut back as competition decreased. The use of corporate aircraft started to rebound. The major manufacturers focused more attention on turboprops and jets. By this time they had been purchased by larger conglomerates.

In 1980 Beech Aircraft was acquired by Raytheon Corporation which eventually dropped the Beech name in 1997. Beech survived the 1980s by concentrating on its traditional role as a supplier of business airplanes. With over 90 percent of the executive turbo-prop market firmly in the hands of various King Airs. Beech still offered its four-place Bonanza F-33A, a six-seat Bonanza A-36 or turbo-charged B-36, and a twin-engine Baron 58.

Beech acquired the rights to Mitsubishi's Diamond Business jet in 1986. This was actually Beech's third attempt at jets. The company had entered into marketing agreements for the French-made Moraine-Saulnier MS-760 in 1955 and the British-made Hawker BH-125 in the 1970s, but neither venture had been overly profitable. This time, however, Beech was in a position to take over the production of its jets, which it redesigned and built as the Beech Jet-400A.

Cessna was acquired by General Dynamics in 1985 but apparently found the field of general aviation to be too far removed from its core military business, which was in decline during the post-Cold War period, so Cessna was sold to Textron in 1992. After dropping its piston aircraft production in 1986 Cessna was satisfied building Caravan single-engine turbo-props, operated primarily under contract to Federal

Express over small-parcel freight routes. Cessna also produced its line of six Citation business jets.

Piper's owner, Banger Punta Corporation, was bought by Lear Siegler, which was bought by Forstmann Little & Company. In 1987 M. Stuart Millar, an entrepreneurial businessman purchased the company and unlike the other light aircraft manufacturers redirected the company's attention to single-engine aircraft. Piper dropped its product liability insurance in an attempt to discourage lawsuits, prices were cut, and enthusiasm ran high for a while. Unfortunately, the company slipped into Chapter 11 bankruptcy in 1991, unable to build airplanes cheaply enough to fill the large backlog of orders taken at bargain prices. It was purchased in 1992 by another entrepreneur, A. Stone Douglas. A trickle of airplanes continued to flow from the production lines under the protection of the court. Finally, in 1995, The New Piper Aircraft Corporation was formed from the assets sale of Piper Aircraft Corporation.

The rest of the U.S. general aviation industry held on through the 1990s by staying small, merging, or diversifying. Mooney had been owned by the French firm Euralair since 1984 and was still building single-engine aircraft in the Kerrville, Texas, plant it occupied in 1953. Learjet was sold to the Canadian firm Bombardier, but it remained based in Wichita, Kansas. The stretched Model 55 grew into the Model 60, certified in late 1992.

Specialty aircraft builders hung on by exploiting their particular niche, such as manufacturers of fabric-covered tail-wheel airplanes (Husky, Maule, Taylorcraft, American Champion), amphibian flying boats (Lake) custom-made and steel-tube classic aircraft (Bellanca, Waco Classic), and other personal airplanes (Commander 114-B and the American General Tiger, a rebirth of the Grumman AA-58).

Historically, the general aviation industry has paralleled the economic cycle of the national economy. The 1980s proved to be an exception to that analysis. In the early 1980s, general aviation followed the rest of the economy into a recession. Interest rates were at an all time high when the new administration took office in 1980. Everything from housing starts to durable goods sales including autos and general aviation aircraft sales plummeted. The economy began to recover in 1983 but general aviation did not. In fact, the number of general aviation aircraft delivered fell from a high of 17,811 in 1978 to 928 in 1994. (see figures 1-2 and 1-3).

No doubt high interest rates, the ever-increasing cost of new aircraft with relatively few design changes since the 1970s, higher fuel and other operating expenses including maintenance and hangaring charges, and the availability of used aircraft all had an effect on new aircraft sales. Other analysts cite changing tastes and preferences among the traditional business and pleasure aircraft users as contributing to the decline during the 1980's. Interest in sports cars and boats which require less training and recurrency seemed to have peaked during the 1980's. Another financial pressure working against aircraft ownership took place in 1986 with the passage of the Tax Reform Act which eliminated the 10 percent investment tax credit (ITC). Finally, the foreign aircraft manufacturers entered the traditionally American-dominated market in a much bigger way during the 1980s.

The number of fixed base operators (FBO's) followed the general aviation industry during its downward cycle. In the post-world War II era and continuing through the 1950s, 1960s, and 1970s, the number of FBO's accelerated dramatically. Much of the expansion of the industry after World War II can be directly related to the G.I. Bill, which provided funding for the majority of flight training that occurred throughout this period. Flight training was clearly a catalyst for growth in the industry, as newly licensed pilots created additional demand for aircraft, which increased manufacturing-and-sales-related activities and ultimately, increased demand for aircraft fueling, maintenance, and other services. By 1980, it was estimated that more than 10,000 FBO's were operating throughout the United States. Over the ensuing years the number of FBO's declined by more than two-thirds resulting in an approximate figure of 3,000 by the mid 1990's.

Airplane shipments had declined 95 percent from the previous decade, and the industry had lost over 100,000 jobs. Cessna Aircraft Company, the largest general aviation manufacturer in the world, had stopped making single-engine piston airplanes. Piper Aircraft had shut down most of its piston production lines.

A review of all the lawsuits defended by one company over a 10-year period found that the NTSB had not attributed the cause of these accidents to design defects. Yet, that company had paid nearly $535,000 per accident in litigation costs. Finally, Congress, airplane manufacturers, owners, and pilot groups all agreed that legislation was the only solution to solving the frivolous lawsuit problem.

Signs of optimism appeared in 1994 with the passage of the General Aviation Revitalization Act limiting products liability suits and with Cessna's announcement that it would resume production of single-engine aircraft in 1996. The New Piper Aircraft Corporation was formed, and in 1995, general aviation aircraft shipments began an upward climb reaching 2,200 in 1998. This was the first year since 1985 that the industry shipped more than 2,000 aircraft (see figure 1-3). In the four years since passage of the General Aviation Revitalization Act more new aircraft models were delivered than in the entire decade that preceded it. General Aviation experienced its best safety record in 1998 since record keeping began in 1938. A new wave of optimism fell over the industry as it approached the new millenium.

Aviation Insurance in the 1980s

In the late 1970s, the aviation insurance industry rode a crest of profitability. Insureds were pleased with the competitive rates and coverage available from a number of insurers who had entered the market during the 1960s and 1970s. Several factors contributed to this favorable situation. All segments of aviation, including the airlines and general aviation, grew at a record-breaking pace. There was enough business for all insurers. Of course, some withdrew from the market and others merged as a result of competitive pressures, but for the most it was a period of steady growth and favorable loss experience. Insurance company investments paid off handsomely due to very high interest rates. Consequently, insurance companies offered lower rates to insureds, knowing that losses would be covered by investment income. The keen competition fueled further premium reductions. Premium quotations to insureds were not necessarily based on losses but on beating the competition and maintaining the cash flow. The result was more competition and artificially depressed rates.

In the early 1980s, the bubble finally burst. Interest rates dropped and the insurers found themselves in a crisis. Income from investments fell by half or more and payments for losses increased. From 1980 to 1985, general aviation aircraft shipments plummeted from 11,877 aircraft in 1980 to 2,029 units in 1985 (see figure 1-3). This also happened to fixed base operations during the same period. Many FBOs went out of business, merged, or drastically scaled back their operations. The result was no growth in insurable units, further intensifying competition and helping to depress rates even further. Southeastern Aviation Underwriters (SEAU), based in Atlanta and specializing in general aviation business, was acquired by the American International Group (AIG) in 1983. National Aviation Underwriters, formed in Saint Louis in 1945 and specializing in FBO's, was merged into AVEMCO in 1985. Phoenix Aviation Managers with headquarters in Atlanta was founded in 1983 to write general aviation business.

A major social change impacted the insurance industry during this period: the growing frequency and tendency to sue. In 1985, an estimated 16.6 million private suits were tried in state courts, with one private civil suit for every 15 Americans.

With the high media visibility of general aviation accidents, plus a more pervasive legal system, a trend had begun where general aviation cases were not settled so much on individual value as they were on the available limits of the insurance policy.

Another factor added to the crisis in the mid-1980s. Fueled by both the availability of inexpensive insurance and reinsurance capacity and real growth in individual net worth, the popularity of large limits grew substantially. This factor impacted all segments of aviation heavily due to case settlements being equated to the policy limits. Higher liability limits also increased settlement expenses, dollars that do not compensate any victims but are spent on legal fees, accident investigation, and so forth. These factors contributed to a treadmill of increasing competition, decreasing rates, and increasing expenses. That had to stop, and it did, in 1985. International and American airlines sustained a record number of passenger fatalities in 1985. It was estimated that the world airlines had hull and liability losses of $ 1. 8 billion in 1985 on premium income of approximately $750 million. This ended a period of more than two years during which American airlines had no fatalities in passenger jet operations.

Rapid rate increases followed in order to bring premium levels back into proportion with losses, combined with restructuring in coverages and limits. Airline hull and liability rates rose dramatically in 1985 and 1986 as insurers attempted to recoup their losses. Some air carriers saw premiums rise by as much as 50 percent during this period. In 1986 the International Air Transport Association (IATA) formed its own Bermuda-based captive insurance company. Known as the Airline Mutual Insurance, Ltd., this facility was designed to provide an alternative market for the air carriers.

The general aviation aircraft manufacturers saw their insurance rise 500 percent from 1980 to 1986. Concomitantly, a number of aviation underwriters, including some of the Lloyd's of London syndicates, withdrew from the market. This left aviation with a capacity shortage. What capacity was available was almost entirely assigned to the airlines, leaving little for general aviation. Insurance, even for the blue-chip corporate aviation segment, was difficult to get at non-inflated rates. In some cases, premiums increased 150 percent over previous years and with restrictions in coverage and limits.

The airlines had an exceptionally fine safety record in 1986. It is estimated that the world's aviation underwriters generated in excess of $1 billion in airline premiums that year while suffering a relatively low $300 million in losses. The picture changed dramatically. More money poured into the aviation insurance market as those underwriters and syndicates who had withdrawn from the market came back with vigor. More money also became available from reinsurers on the European continent and in Tokyo who sensed profit-making opportunities. At the same time, airlines went through a frenzy of mergers and acquisitions as deregulation took hold, reducing the number of individual companies (accounts); and the general aviation fleet had stopped growing (see figure 1-1). The result was a softening of the market as supply (capacity) exceeded demand (insureds seeking coverage). In such a market, an insurance company has two ways to maintain or increase business: lure customers from the competitors by reducing rates or by insuring risks that it formerly chose not to insure. Both of these factors benefited all segments of aviation during the last three years of the 1980s.

The weakening of the U.S. dollar was added to the competitive environment, since many risks underwritten in this country are reinsured abroad, particularly with Lloyd's of London and other British companies. The favorable exchange rate allowed foreign underwriters to cover U.S. aircraft at an effective discount.

The rate war which broke out during the late 1980s also spawned a number of creative features including profit sharing under which an insured received a return premium for no losses and 18-month policies instead of the traditional 12-month term.

By late 1989, aircraft hull and liability insurance rates reached the lowest point in the 80- year history of aviation insurance. Aircraft operators of virtually all categories of aircraft, airline, corporate, general aviation, and even helicopters, which traditionally found their rates high and coverage difficult to obtain were looking at a fiercely competitive aviation insurance market.

A professionally flown corporate jet with a value from $10 to $15 million took a $.90 per $100 hull rate in 1986. By 1987, this rate had fallen to $.65 and a typical rate for this type aircraft in 1988 was $.40 per $100 of value. In 1989, business aircraft operators were experiencing rates as low as $.20. The premium for liability coverages typically carried by a corporate operator including a $100 million limit fell from about $50,000 in 1987 to $10,000 in 1989. Higher limits of liability were readily available and formerly additional coverages such as voluntary settlement (admitted liability) and medical payments were included in the premium.

Airline premiums also took a steep downward slide during the late 1980s. At the end of 1987, airline hull rates were half of what they were at the beginning of that year, while liability rates were 30 percent lower for, in many cases, double the liability coverage. Premium reductions continued during 1988 and 1989 despite poor underwriting experience in 1988. There were 24 total losses of western built jets costing $413 million compared to the average per year between 1980 and 1987 of 19 costing $194 million and 879 passenger fatalities against an average of 650.

It has been estimated that the worldwide airline premium fell from approximately $1.2 billion at the start of 1987 to less than $600 million by the end of 1989.

Even fixed base operators (FBOs) and other segments of the general aviation community experienced rate reductions though less dramatic than the corporate and airline operators. Product liability plagued aircraft manufacturers also benefited from the soft underwriting market of the late 1980s, experiencing reductions in the neighborhood of 30 percent between 1987 and 1989.

Aviation Insurance in the 1990s

The fierce competition which started in 1986 showed no sign of abating in the early 1990s. In 1993 at the International Airline Insurance Conference in London it was estimated that during the five-year period from 1988 to 1992 industry premium value totaled $3 billion while claims amounted to $6.42 billion, resulting in a total loss for the period of approximately $3.42 billion. The prevailing soft market conditions, characterized by abundant capacity and severe competition, were caused by a number of factors: (1) Consolidation in the airline industry. Regional carriers, whose history traced back to the 1940s such as Frontier, Ozark, Piedmont and Republic (formerly North Central, Southern and Hughes Air West) were all absorbed by the major carriers. Carriers formed after deregulation such as People Express, Air Florida and Midway merged with larger carriers or went bankrupt. Finally, in 1991 Eastern and Pan Am folded their wings after limping along for several years under bankruptcy. Consolidation also affected the commuter/regional markets as well with the number of carriers dropping from 179 in 1986 to 144 in 1991. Fewer carriers meant fewer accounts for the aviation insurance industry. (2) The recessionary economy of the early 1990s resulted in losses exceeding $12.7 billion for the scheduled airline industry between 1990 and 1993. There was tremendous pressure to cut costs including their insurance premiums. The carriers renewed their interest in establishing their own captive insurance company in Bermuda. Backed by IATA, this alternative insurance facility with its potential to attract major accounts put more pressure on the insurance market to keep rates low. (3) While the accident rate for the air-

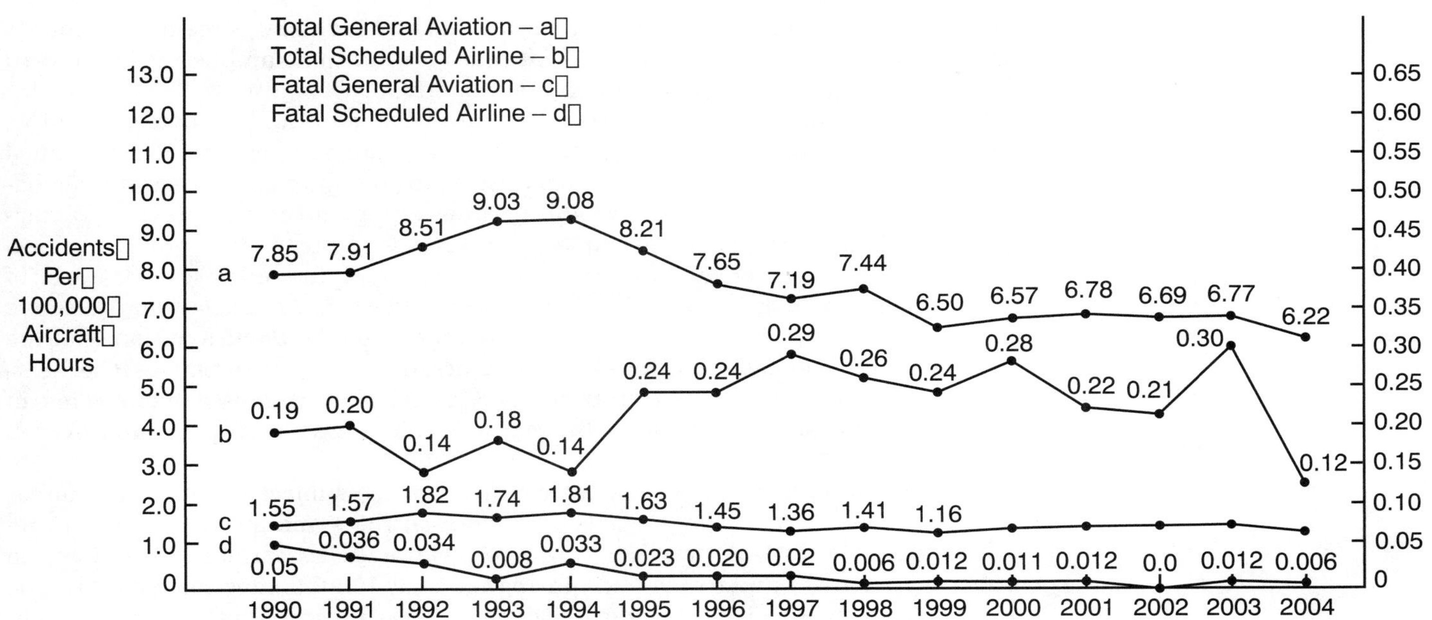

Figure 1.5 Accident Rates for U.S. Aircraft per 100,000 Aircraft Hours Flown from 1990 to 2004.
Source: National Transportation Safety Board.

lines and general aviation remained fairly steady during this period (see figures 1-4 and 1-5) the size of the awards continued to rise as courts became more liberal in awarding damages for fatalities and injuries. (4) The number of new general aviation aircraft shipments continued its 17-year downward slide from 17,811 in 1978 to a historical low of 928 in 1994. The total active general aviation aircraft fleet which was over 211,000 aircraft in 1980 dropped to 188,000 by 1995, an 11percent decline. Fewer exposure units exacerbated an already intensely competitive insurance market attempting to maintain market share. (5) Many smaller aviation insurance companies founded during the late 1970s and early 1980s during the zenith of general aviation growth reduced rates to maintain cash flow and stay in business. Even the established insurance companies held off raising rates for fear of losing market share and inviting new insurance companies.

It was inevitable that market forces had to eventually push rates higher across the board. Another factor causing underwriters to reassess overcapacity in the market was the reinsurers. Carriers that were heavily reinsured began to feel the squeeze as reinsurers tightened their policies and demanded adequate pricing.

Airline rates began to increase as early as 1991 with some carriers experiencing 100 to 150 percent increases in their premiums. Rate increases averaging 50 to 80 percent continued into 1993 when underwriters began to break even on their airline book of business. Other classes of aviation business such as general aviation, aircraft, engine and component manufacturers, and service organizations rates are largely influenced by airline underwriting results. It is generally accepted that if the airline portfolio is losing money there will be pressure on underwriters to increase rates on all classes of aviation business in order for them to have any chance of making money on the overall portfolio of aviation business.

Aircraft and component manufacturers fared much better than the air carriers during the recovery period between 1991 and 1993. Increases were on the order of

10 to 20 percent per year for clean renewals and upward to 20 percent for accounts with a loss history. Considering the soft market conditions and better loss record than the airlines, these increases were more tolerable.

Rates for business aircraft operators rose between 5 and 10 percent, and as much as 20 to 25 percent for individual owners who had no safety record established with an insurer. Corporate accounts operating turbine equipment experienced modest increases particularly in their liability rates for higher limits. This class of business has consistently had an exemplary loss record.

Helicopter operators and FBO's experienced annual rate increases in the area of 15 to 30 percent during this period. In addition, underwriters became very selective in accepting new business or in renewing current accounts. Some aviation insurers ordered an independent analysis of maintenance and in-flight procedures before setting rates or imposing policy restrictions. Greater concern was demonstrated in reviewing an insured's operating history, loss experience, reputation and overall dedication to safe operations.

The aviation insurance business continued to be subject to conflicting forces during the mid-1990s. The pressure for increased rates and for more diligent and restricted underwriting practices continued. However, the dramatic increases in rates experienced by many insureds during the early 1990s abated considerably. The edge still remained with the underwriting side of the business rather than the selling side. Yet competition among insurers for the more attractive accounts tempered the impetus to charge more. Liability coverage remained the most underfunded side of the pricing equation even though hull rates were still not considered adequate. Emphasizing the industry consensus that liability rates were too low, a judgment in 1994 established an $8.1 million award to the heirs of one passenger killed in a USAir crash at New York's LaGuardia Airport in 1992. Underwriters were more selective in offering higher liability limits at rock bottom prices. There was still a lot of resistance in achieving adequate prices because of the intense competition for better classes of business. While total underwriting capacity was less than what it was a few years before there was enough for the better accounts. Marginal accounts found underwriters uncompromising in their pricing and policy restrictions. Poorer risks still faced large increases in rates or were denied coverage.

Passage of the General Aviation Revitalization Act (GARA) of 1994, ushered in a new wave of optimism to the general aviation industry. With some exceptions, GARA imposed an 18-year statute of repose limiting products liability suits for aircraft having fewer than 20 passenger seats not engaged in scheduled passenger-carrying operations. Cessna immediately announced that it would resume production of single-engine aircraft in 1996. The New Piper Aircraft Corporation was formed, and in 1995, general aviation aircraft shipments finally increased after an 18-year decline. The aviation industry's growth was positive in all segments by just about all measures. The nation's scheduled airlines reported record profits in 1995 and 1996. Business flight activity was on the rise. New and used aircraft sales activity also was on the increase. More efficient, new airframe and engine designs began emerging from the flight-test hangars and moving to production facilities.

Insurance rates continued their upward climb during 1994 and 1995. Underwriters attributed the increases to high profile, high-cost accidents and the cost of reinsurance. A typical eight-passenger business jet operator, as an example, saw its liability premium for $100 million coverage rise from $9,000 to $14,500 during this period. Once again, the market seemed to have peaked around this time, and a softening in the market beginning in 1996 continued throughout the remaining years of the decade. The example business jet operator saw its liability premium drop to $12,500 in 1996. The air carriers and manufacturers also experienced substantial decreases in premiums during the late 1990s.

Losses worldwide and the cost of reinsurance will always remain major factors in rate increases or declines. Reinsurance giant, Lloyd's of London, began to make a comeback in 1996 after some devastating losses during the late 1980s and 1990s. However, instead of Lloyd's being mentioned as the exclusive source of treaty reinsurance, a small group of domestic reinsurers such as Prudential has entered the arena.

The aviation insurance market has experienced soft and hard business cycles for the past several decades. The cycle of rate softening started in 1999 and precipitated a consolidation in the industry, similar to what the brokerage and agency business experienced for years. Instead of competing for market share on an individual basis, larger aviation insurers acquired smaller companies and as such, an entire book of business.

Phoenix Aviation Managers, founded in 1983 and specializing in general aviation business acquired Southern Marine and Aviation Underwriters in 1995. Avemco, founded in 1960 and the only direct writer in the aviation insurance market, that in 1985 acquired National Aviation Underwriters, was itself acquired by Houston Casualty Company in 1997. Now operating as HCC Aviation Insurance Group, this insurer also acquired U.S. Specialty Insurance Company, Signal Aviation Underwriters, Southern Aviation Insurance Underwriters and Continental Insurance underwriters. The Great American Insurance Companies' Aviation Division was created in 1997 following the acquisition of a book of aviation business from the former Aviation Office of America. AIG Aviation, Inc., a subsidiary of the American International Group (AIG), formed in 1983 after acquiring Southeastern Aviation Underwriters, acquired Commercial Aviation Underwriters (COMAV) in 1997. In 1999 CIGNA Aerospace, formed in 1982 with the merger of INA Corporation and Connecticut General was acquired by ACE Ltd., to become ACE USA Aerospace. Finally, in 2001 Associated Aviation Underwriters merged with British Aviation Insurance Group to form Global Aerospace.

While the impact of this consolidation on the market is too early to tell, the financial strength of many carriers has been substantially improved according to ratings given by A. M. Best and Company. Underwriting philosophy is also changing. Some carriers have stopped competing against one another for certain classes of business. Some are not offering renewal on existing accounts or providing new business quotations to accounts they may have been interested in previously. The natural fear in a market experiencing consolidation is that rates may increase and some insureds may have difficulty finding coverage. There is no question that the late 1990s brought new challenges to the aviation insurance industry; but this is nothing new if we reflect on the history of aviation insurance.

AVIATION INSURANCE IN THE NEW MILLENIUM

The aviation insurance market went through one of its many cycles starting in 2000. Underwriters in the United States had to address a loss experience of close to 200 percent over the previous 10 years. Major pressure by the reinsurance markets caused a reexamination of rates. Significant rate increases were applied to all segments of the industry in the fall of 2000. Particularly hard hit were the rates for excess liability and higher primary limits. Rates continued to trend upward during the spring and summer of 2001. On September 11, 2001, four commercial airliners, two American Airlines and two United Airlines, were hijacked by nineteen terrorists resulting in crashes into the north and south towers of the World Trade Center in New York City and the Pentagon in Washington, DC. The fourth airliner crashed in a field in Pennsylvania. These events rocked the insurance markets throughout the world, resulting in the largest single reserve for any aircraft claim. The reserves for claims in the aviation market were somewhere between $7and $9 billion with the other insurance coverages suffering tremendous losses. The total estimate for this loss is estimated to be between $50 billion and $75 billion dollars and the final number will be calculated many years from now after all of the losses are known and the subrogation actions between the various carriers are completed.

Rate increases followed the September 11, 2001 loss as well as the worldwide cancellation of all terrorism coverage by underwriters. Underwriters who had never written terrorism coverage and those in London who had underwritten terrorism coverage were in a state of shock which led to either lack of total terrorism coverage or substantially increased rates. Not since the introduction of the 747s in the late 1960s and early 1970s had so many governments been called upon to provide coverage for a particular type of insurance. Rates continued on an upward spiral into 2002. All of these increases were not uniform and it is estimated that the rates during this period of time doubled or some cases, went even higher. The rates for some classes drastically increased, certainly more than 100 to 200 percent, particularly for fixed based operators, propeller repair facilities, aerial applicators, and small fixed based operators without aircraft.

Crisis in the market with large rate increases usually lead to decrease in capacity, reduced limits available and quite often, to a loss of an insurance market. The crisis of 2001 led one of the markets, ACE USA, to cease underwriting on a direct basis. ACE USA continues to underwrite governmental business and airport liability through its office in New Orleans but all other aviation insurance is written through its participation in USAIG.

Unlike other increases the higher rates have continued to hold relatively steady with the exception of the airline business which started a downward spiral in January of 2003. Another unusual factor involving changes in the new century has to do with products liability. Rates remained at historically high levels and trended slightly upward throughout 2003 and 2004. The big unknown factor in the aviation insurance industry today, as in most cycles, is the profitability of reinsurance and its effect on rates and policy conditions.

Since 2000, U.S. aviation has been jolted by a number of unanticipated events that have significantly impacted the demand for air travel and the sale of airliner, corporate and general aviation aircraft. These include the September 11th terrorist attacks, conflict in the Middle East, the SARS epidemic, and a rapid run-up in world oil prices. The impact of these events on airlines, general aviation, aerospace manufacturers, aviation insurance and economic growth have been immediate and significant.

Although the effects from these events have also been global in scope, the greatest impact by far has been on U.S. legacy airlines. By the end of 2005, six U.S. mainline carriers were currently operating under Chapter 11 Bankruptcy protection (Aloha Airlines, American Trans Air, Delta, Hawaiian, United Airlines, and U.S. Airways), and several others appeared to be on the brink. Although demand recovered well in 2005, competition remained strong and profits remained elusive for the fifth consecutive year. Following a three-year run of declining shipments and weak billings, the market for general aviation products and services also staged a relatively strong recovery in 2004. General aviation aircraft shipments and billing were stimulated by growth in U.S. economic activity as well as by accelerated depreciation allowances for the operators of new aircraft.

CONCLUSION

In conclusion, it is worth repeating that few chapters in the annals of human history have been as romantic as the conquest of the sky. Although the air age began only a little over 100 years ago at Kitty Hawk, it has now soared into outer space and is evidence of the tremendous resourcefulness of imagination, skill, fortitude, and capital that have been dedicated to the accelerated expansion of the aviation industry. Many factors have contributed to this expansion. Of no less significance is the strong backing it has received from the American insurance industry. Willingness to underwrite and accept the risks of flight, particularly in the formative and uncertain years of aviation, has been a mighty factor in persuading people to invest their money in aircraft manufacturing and air transportation and in fostering the confidence of the air travelers. The recognition of aviation's needs did not come easily to the insurance underwriters and they should be highly complemented for their pioneering study of the industry and for their coverage in venturing into an extremely hazardous new field without the stabilizing protection of past experience. It is this coverage that has made the aviation insurance business what it is today, and as Lloyd's of London aided in awarding in England "supremacy of the seas," so does our aviation insurance business give to America supremacy of the air. Today the American aviation underwriters prepare to meet the gigantic challenge of the space era, supersonic aircraft, and passenger capacities of 600 seats or more.

REVIEW QUESTIONS

1. What was the first company to write aviation insurance in the post-World War I period? What lines did it underwrite? Why did it withdraw from the market?
2. Describe the contributions to the field of aviation insurance made by the following pioneer underwriters: Horatio Barber, J. Brooks, B. Parker, and David C. Beebe.
3. What factors caused the aviation industry to become stabilized during the mid-to-late 1920s and thus permitted the growth of aviation insurance? Who were the three major aviation insurance groups to become established in the late 1920s?
4. Why has the group approach to underwriting aviation insurance been so successful over the years? How did the nature of insuring aviation risks change during the war years? Why do you think that the Board of Aviation Underwriters was not successful?
5. Who were the leading independent aviation insurers during the fifties and sixties? Which one is the only survivor today?
6. Why did the introduction of jet equipment into the airline fleets during the late 1950s present such a problem to the underwriters? Why was the Aircraft Builders Counsel formed? Why did the select Senate committee investigate the aviation insurance industry in August 1958? What were its findings?
7. Describe the various segments of the aviation industry during the 1960s and 1970s in terms of growth and other trends which affected the aviation insurance market.
8. Historically, the general aviation industry paralleled the economic cycle of the national economy. Why were the 1980s an exception to that relationship?
9. What factors caused the tremendous increase in premiums for all segments of the industry during the mid-1980s? Why did rates decline so precipitously from 1986 through the remainder of the decade?
10. How did the events of September 11, 2001 affect the aviation insurance industry?

REFERENCES

[1] The Travelers Insurance Companies, *The Travelers 100 years,* published by the Travelers in commemorating the Companies' 100th anniversary on April 1, 1964, pp. 90-93.
[2] The Travelers Insurance Companies, ibid.
[3] Beebe, David C., Comments of the United States Aviation Underwriters, Inc., on *A Study of Aviation Insurance by the Civil Aeronautics Board.* New York, May 8, 1944.
[4] Aeronautical Chamber of Commerce, *Aircraft Year Book,* 1929.
[5] Beebe, ibid., p. 98
[6] Beebe, ibid., p. 93

Axe, J. H., *Aviation Insurance.* Insurance Institute of America, New York, 1931. Civil Aeronautics Board, *A Study of Aviation Insurance.*

Rhyne, Charles S., *Aviation Accident Law.* Columbia Law Book Company, Washington, D.C., 1941. Sweeney, S. B., *Nature and Development of Aviation Insurance.* University of Pennsylvania Press, Philadelphia, 1927.

[7] Beebe, ibid., p.2

Chapter 2

Insureds and Liability of the FAA

OUTLINE

The Challenges of Space
The Aviation/Aerospace Manufacturers
Air Carrier and Air Taxi Operators
Business and Pleasure Aircraft Operators
Fixed Base Operators
Special Use Aircraft
Airport Owners and Operators
Individual Pilots
Liability of the FAA

OBJECTIVES

At the end of this chapter you should be able to:
Recognize the potential for aviation insurance with the growth of space exploration.
Identify some of the members of the AIA and GAMA and describe the primary aviation insurance coverage purchased by them.
Explain the circumstances in which a manufacturer might be liable for defective products.
Understand why common carriers must exercise the highest degree of care and how this factor affects their negligence.
Distinguish between the following classes of general aviation aircraft business: industrial aid, business and pleasure, fixed base operators, and special use aircraft.
Describe several situations in which FBOs are subject to liability.
Describe the airport and individual pilot as a market for aviation insurance.
Identify the major areas in which the Federal Aviation Administration (FAA) may incur liability and how the Federal TORT Claims Act affects the liability exposure of the FAA.

THE CHALLENGES OF SPACE

Many years ago, science fiction writer Ray Bradbury wrote about a spacecraft capable of transporting hundreds of Earthlings and diverse agricultural and scientific equipment to the developing Martian colonies, and then shuttling back to Earth for another load.

Considering the success and routine nature of the recent space shuttle flights, the fictional writings of Ray Bradbury and his *Martian Chronicles* have turned into real possibilities. During the next decade, the insurance industry will come face to face with these possibilities.

Insurance protection for the space and space-related industries has been available in the commercial market since the mid-1960s when Early Bird became the world's first commercial communications satellite. Complete details of the intricacies of this unique niche in the aviation insurance marketplace are contained in a later chapter.

THE AVIATION/ AEROSPACE MANUFACTURERS

The *aviation / aerospace manufacturers* include those companies engaged in research, development, and manufacture of aerospace systems, including manned and unmanned aircraft; space-launch vehicles and spacecraft; propulsion, guidance, and control units for all of the foregoing; and a variety of airborne and ground-based equipment essential to the testing, operation, and maintenance of flight vehicles. Virtually all of the major aerospace manufacturers are members of the *Aerospace*

Industries Association (AIA) or the *General Aviation Manufacturers Association* (GAMA).

The aerospace manufacturers include several hundred firms backed by thousands of subcontractors, vendors, and suppliers. The principal product line-aircraft, missiles, space systems, and related engines, and parts—and equipment is characterized by high performance and high reliability—hence high technology and high unit value.

The AIA had 96 regular and 182 associate member companies at the beginning of 2005, including such firms as:

AAI Corporation
Aerojet
The Boeing Company
Curtiss-Wright Corporation
Dassault Falcon Jet Corporation
DuPont Company
Eclipse Aviation
General Dynamnics Corporation
General Electric Company
Goodrich Corporation
Harris Corporation
Honeywell, Inc.
IBM Corporation
ITT Industries, Defense and Electronics
Kaman Aerospace Corporation
Laser Technology, Inc.
Lockheed Martin Corporation
Northrop Grumman Corporation
Parker Aerospace
Raytheon Company
Rockwell Collins, Inc.
Rolls-Royce North America, Inc.
Silicon Graphics, Inc.
Textron, Inc.
3M Company
United Defense
United Technologies Corporation

The GAMA represents 15 airframe manufacturers and numerous engine, avionics and components manufacturers. Association members include the following firms:

Airplane Manufacturers

Boeing Business Jets
Bombardier Aerospace
Cessna Aircraft Company
Cirrus Design Corporation
Dassault Falcon Jet Corporation
Diamond Aircraft Industries
EADS Socata
Embraer Aircraft Holding, Inc.
Gulfstream Aerospace Corporation
Mooney Aerospace Group, Ltd.
Piaggio Aero Industries S.P.A.
Pilatus Aircraft, Ltd.
The New Piper Aircraft, Inc.
Raytheon Aircraft Company
Sabreliner Corporation

Engine Manufacturers

Honeywell Engines
Lycoming Engines
Pratt & Whitney Canada
Rolls-Royce North America
Teledyne Continental Motors
Williams International

Avionics Manufacturers

Avidyne Corporation
Century Flight Systems, Inc.
Garmin International, Inc.
Honeywell Aerospace Electronic Systems
L-3 Communications Avionics Systems
Meggitt/S-TEC
Rockwell Collins, Inc.
Safe Flight Instrument Corporation
Universal Avionics Systems Corp.

Component Manufacturers

Aircraft Technical Publishers
Airtechnics, Inc.
Argo-Tech Corporation
B/E Aerospace, Inc.
CAE SimuFlite
Crane Aerospace & Electronics
DeCrane Aircraft Holdings, Inc.
Dukes Inc.
Flight Safety International, Inc.
Goodrich Corporation
Hamilton Sundstrand Corporation
Hartzell Propeller, Inc.
Jeppesen
Kelly Aerospace, Inc.
The NORDAM Group
Parker Hannifin Corporation
Perkin Elmer Fluid Sciences
PPG Aerospace
Precision Aerospace Group, LLC
Smith's Aerospace Mechanical Systems-Yakima
Unison Industries
Woodward Governor Company

While these manufacturers and subcontractors require many forms of insurance coverage, the principal aviation industry insurance coverage is products liability. The products liability policy provides coverage for damages arising out of the use of goods or products manufactured, sold, handled, or distributed by the company. Grounding coverage is also provided which protects the company if its product causes an aircraft to be withdrawn from service by order of the FAA or other regulatory body, because of the existence or alleged existence of a like fault, defect, or condition in two or more such aircraft which presents a serious safety hazard if not corrected immediately.

Beyond the more obvious aviation/aerospace manufacturers whose prime product is destined to be part of an aircraft, a great deal of the aviation product business is generated by manufacturers of small parts, off-the-shelf items, and raw materials which may find their way into aircraft production without the knowledge of the company. Most general liability policies exclude aviation liability and consequently many of these subcontractors and suppliers must purchase aviation products liability to obtain protection in the event that their products become part of an aircraft.

Manufacturing Defects

Aviation manufacturers are responsible for defects in the component parts they incorporate to the same extent as the manufacturer and supplier of such component parts. Where a defect can be traced to the component part manufacturer, that manufacturer may also be subject to liability.

Aircraft are inherently sophisticated machines. They require much more than simply a functionally aerodynamic design. Modern aircraft must be safe to operate and maintain and must minimize the chance of injury from unintended but foreseeable misuse.

An allegation of negligent or defective design is often defended on the theory of contributory negligence or unforeseeable misuse. In many instances, such a defense suggests the further question: Did the design itself cause the human error? For example, when instruments or gauges are inconspicuously located or insufficiently illuminated, it can be reasonably expected that many persons may not see them at a crucial moment, thereby causing an accident. An investigator might conclude that the pilot failed to heed instructions. However, designs which do not take the human response factor into consideration may be found defective. Aircraft design is very likely to have an effect on pilot behavior. The control system may be too sensitive and may react violently to the exercise of very little pressure, or it may be stiff and require excessive force in emergency maneuvers, and other instruments may be ambiguously labeled, mislabeled, or unlabeled.

Design-induced error may also play a role in the performance of maintenance, repair, or inspection services. Examples of design deficiencies causing a maintenance error include an oil gauge that is inadequate to warn of a dangerously low oil level: the design and use of replacement parts which are imperceptibly different yet interchangeable; or a part which is not reasonably accessible for required lubrication.

A manufacturer may also be held liable unless it provides adequate instructions for proper use of the product and warnings about potential dangers. The concept of a marketing defect has been applied many times to aviation accidents. The duty to provide adequate warnings or instructions continues after the product is sold. Aircraft manufacturers ordinarily satisfy their postsale duty to warn through the issuance of service bulletins or service letters. Much of the information contained in these service bulletins is obtained from the aircraft operators themselves and through the manufacturers' field service personnel. They can be routine or urgent, depending upon the severity of the risk. Additionally, Federal Aviation Regulations require the manufacturer to report serious failures, malfunctions, and defects to the Federal Aviation Administration (FAA) regional office within 24 hours.

If the FAA decides that an unsafe condition exists which warrants immediate corrective action, it may issue an Airworthiness Directive (AD). Once an AD is issued, it has the force of law and, therefore, provides constructive notice to all aircraft owners, operators, and overhaul facilities. If the AD calls for immediate corrective action, failure to take such action may subject violators to criminal and civil prosecution, including the grounding or seizure of aircraft or the revocation of the airworthiness certificate.

Prior to 1994, aircraft manufacturers had been subject to liability for their product with no time limitation. During the period from 1958 to 1994 it was not uncommon to see a successful lawsuit against a manufacturer for an alleged design defect in a 25-30-year-old airplane. The problem was so bad that by 1986 most U.S. manufacturers had ceased production of piston-engine aircraft entirely. In response to this issue, after much lobbying by various aviation groups, Congress passed the General Aviation Revitalization Act of 1994. The purpose of the act was to limit manufacturers' liability by placing a time limit of 18 years on civil actions against a manufacturer. This Act amended the Federal Aviation Act of 1958.

There are some exceptions to the act, most notably if a plaintiff can prove with specificity that the manufacturer misled the FAA as to the compliance of the aircraft with regulations for its airworthiness or type certificate, then action is allowed beyond the time limit.

The Act accomplished what it was originally intended to do, which was limit the liability of new aircraft manufacturers and, as promised, some of the manufacturers restarted their piston-engine production lines.

The unintended consequence of the act was to increase the liability exposure of FAA repair stations, replacement part providers and other repair facilities that worked on or provided parts for the aircraft after the time limit ran out. The act did not address this issue and the cost and availability of liability insurance for many repair facilities has become a new crisis.

AIR CARRIER AND AIR TAXI OPERATORS

The air carrier industry consists of a vast network of routes connecting cities throughout the country, and indeed the world. Over this network, a large number of air carriers transport passengers and cargo on scheduled and charter service. In 1978 Congress mandated the deregulation of the airlines and since that time it has been difficult to keep up with the failures, mergers, and acquisitions that have occurred causing a shake-up felt throughout the entire industry.

The scheduled airline system today consists of the so called "legacy carriers," the major airlines that have survived since the inception of deregulation, numerous "low fare" carriers and various regional and localized carriers that either compete with the "legacy carriers" or provide supplementary routes to act as feeders for the larger operators

The air carrier service provided by the scheduled airlines is complemented by the air taxi and charter operators who supply on-demand service for passengers and cargo shippers. These carriers operate a wide variety of aircraft ranging from large jets to small single-engine equipment.

Like any business, the air carriers need a wide range of insurance coverages including fire insurance on buildings, automobile coverage, workers' compensation, premises liability protection, and life and health insurance for their employees. Principal among their aviation coverages is aircraft hull and liability protection. Hull coverage provides protection against loss of or damage to their owned or leased aircraft. Liability coverage is designed to pay on behalf of the insured air carriers all sums which they become legally obligated to pay as damages for bodily injury or property damage arising out of an accident or occurrence as defined in the policy.

Liability of the Air Carriers

Air carriers, air taxi operators, and most charter services are considered common carriers. As such, they have a duty to exercise the highest degree of care for the safety of their passengers. A plaintiff must prove negligence to recover; however, a common carrier will be liable for the slightest negligence. The theory underlying the expanded liability of common carriers is that the law imposes a special relationship between carriers and persons who have committed themselves into the hands of the carrier for transport. Therefore, the higher degree of care generally applies only to paying passengers.

Wreckage or debris from midair collisions or other accidents may cause death, personal injury, emotional distress, and property damage on the ground. Similar harm may be caused by dumping fuel or wastes. Persons suffering such damages have no contractual relationship with the air carrier; however, the carrier still has a duty to exercise ordinary care. Persons on the ground can recover against the carrier only with proof of negligence. Similarly, air carriers, like other aircraft operators, owe a duty of ordinary care to other aircraft. This duty includes a requirement to comply with all Federal Aviation Regulations, to adhere to filed flight plans, to operate at proper altitude and speed, and to look out for other aircraft.

The scheduled and nonscheduled air carriers as a class of business represent a tremendous volume of premium for a relatively few insurance markets which can provide the substantial limits of liability required. There are approximately 7,000 air carrier aircraft operated by the majors, nationals, and regionals. These are supplemented by another 4,000 or so aircraft operated by air taxi operators.

NONCOMMERCIAL AIRCRAFT OPERATORS

Corporate operated aircraft flown by professional pilots employed exclusively for the purpose of operating and managing the aircraft are referred to as the *industrial aid* class of business. Industrial aid is considered the preferred type of business in aviation insurance. A unique branch of aviation, it embraces a select group of highly skilled, professional pilots flying on behalf of corporations. Close to 10,500 aircraft fall into this class and their loss experience compares very favorably with that of the scheduled air carriers.

Aircraft, which range from large jets to single-engine and twin-engine piston aircraft, may be owned or leased by corporations for transporting guests and employees primarily for business. Many corporations operating aircraft have their own flight department with an operations manual detailing such procedures as pilot training, maintenance, and flight procedures. Others contract with a flying service to schedule, maintain, and crew the aircraft. Corporate aircraft supplement regularly scheduled airlines.

Aircraft hull and liability coverage is a prime consideration of corporate aircraft operators. Other major aviation insurance coverages carried by corporate operators include:

- Medical Payments—Provide voluntary payments to passengers and crew for medical expenses incurred due to an injury involving the aircraft. Payments are made without regard to liability or negligence.
- Guest Voluntary Settlement (Admitted Liability)—A form of liability protection under which voluntary settlement can be made at the request of the insured, whether or not the aircraft owner is liable, with respect to the death or dismemberment of a passenger. Coverage closely follows a traditional AD&D policy. If the coverage is written "including crew" GVS will pay a death benefit to a crew member in addition to workers' compensation.
- Non-Owned Aircraft Hull and Liability—Covers the insured's liability arising out of the use of non-owned aircraft.

Single-engine or multiengine aircraft owned by an individual, corporation, or less than three individuals, and operated by the owner for personal recreation or in connection with the insured's business, is considered as a *business and pleasure class*. If owned by three or more individuals it is often termed a *flying club*. Flying clubs refer to nonprofit organizations formed for the purpose of owning and operating aircraft at a reasonable per capita cost.

The majority of aircraft fall into the business and pleasure or flying club class. An estimated 144,000 active general aviation aircraft fall under this category. As with the industrial aid class, usage does not contemplate operating the aircraft for a charge as defined in each individual policy. Business and pleasure is often considered a desirable class. Underwriting and rating in this category can vary considerably, however, depending upon the capability and ability of pilots to operate the aircraft to be insured. Factors that are considered include the pilot's total time as well as the time in the particular make and model aircraft, and the year of the manufacture of the aircraft. Owners of aircraft used for business and pleasure normally carry hull and liability coverage as well as medical payments coverage.

FIXED BASE OPERATORS

The fixed base operators (FBOs) class refers to the airport-based, commercial operations which provide some or all of the following activities: line services, aircraft and engine maintenance, sale of parts and accessories, aircraft sales, charter and rental of aircraft, corporate flight services, and flight training.

Line services are the primary business of the fixed base operator, which include selling fuel and oil, providing storage and general services for aircraft regularly based at the airport, and also providing these for transient airplanes. In recent years, with the growth of the regional carriers, many FBOs have established contractual arrangements with the air carriers, including fueling, exterior cleaning, interior cleaning, deicing, turbine starting, and minor maintenance services.

Maintenance and repair service is another basic part of the fixed base operator's business. The large, well-equipped repair stations include facilities for complete maintenance, overhaul, and rebuilding airframes and power plants, and a full complement of equipment for repairing, testing, calibrating, installing, and replacing avionics components. The sale of parts and accessories is also an important segment of business for most FBOs.

Larger FBOs often sell new and used aircraft. The design and installation of interiors on larger new airplanes are an important segment of business for some FBOs. A full line of this work includes layout of the cockpit, placement of the avionic components and other systems, and design and installation of accommodations for the passenger cabins, as well as exterior custom painting.

Most fixed base operators, even the relatively small ones, own at least a few planes that can be rented for short periods of time. Many have only small single-engine planes, intended for use by private pilots flying for pleasure. Others have a more complete line of aircraft available for chartering, including turboprop and jet aircraft for business purposes.

Some of the larger fixed base operators offer a complete corporate flight service for business customers. Under such an arrangement, the owner or FBO supplies the aircraft and the FBO provides the personnel, and is responsible for conducting flight operations, performing maintenance, and handling administrative matters.

Another service provided by many FBOs is training new pilots and retraining experienced pilots. Some facilities are fully accredited and FAA-certified, and they handle all phases of flight and ground school training. In addition to offering single-engine pilot rating, some are equipped to offer the full range of training for multiengine, instrument, and air transport ratings.

Some FBOs have arrangements with private and public organizations to offer various specialized commercial flight services. These include aerial advertising, aerial photography, fire fighting, fish spotting, mosquito control, pipeline and powerline surveillance, and wildlife conservation.

The best educated guess is that there are 2,400 fixed base operations of different sizes at public-use airports in the United States. These FBOs operate about 20,000 aircraft for air taxi, instructional, and rental purposes. Some extremely specialized aviation operations found on public airports do not qualify as true fixed base operations but are nevertheless necessary to aviation. These include engine manufacturers and remanufactures, avionics specialists, propeller specialists, and certain flight training specialists who do nothing but recurrent flight training for professional and semiprofessional pilots of high-performance aircraft.

Fixed base operators vary widely in size, scope of services offered, type of facility, size of investment, and management expertise. Consequently, as a class, underwriting and rating individual risks can vary considerably.

The primary coverages considered by commercial operators include aircraft hull and liability, airport premises liability, hangarkeepers legal liability, and products and completed operations liability. Two additional coverages are quite frequently purchased by FBOs. They are non-owned aircraft liability and non-owned physical damage, coverage. Non-owned physical damage is often referred to as in-flight hangarkeepers liability, an older term. The terms had slightly different meanings at one time but have developed into the common term of non-owned physical damage liability in most policies today. Non-owned coverage is designed to protect the commercial operator when operating an aircraft he does not own or lease. The operation can be for the benefit of the aircraft owner or the FBO.

FBO Liability

When a fixed base operator is engaged in the sale or lease of aircraft, it may be held liable for injuries resulting from defective aircraft which it has sold or used as a demonstration model. Prior to GARA, most defective aircraft cases were brought against the manufacturer, but today the FBO may be on the front line.. Aircraft sales organizations are also liable for breach of any express warranties or breach of the implied warranty of merchantability. Plaintiffs seeking to recover for economic loss, such as damage to the aircraft itself, must usually bring a warranty action rather than one in liability.

The duty of an aircraft dealer to test and inspect an aircraft prior to sale will vary with the facts of each case. Under a negligence theory, the seller of a product manufactured by another is under no duty to determine whether that product is defective. The courts have identified a number of exceptions to this rule.

The dealer may have a duty of inspection and a subsequent duty to warn where one or more of the following factors are present: the seller is put on notice of the hazard; the aircraft is used; the dealer makes representations or express warranties; or the dealer undertakes to inspect, prepare, or repair the aircraft prior to sale. If such a duty is imposed, a breach of that duty would enable the plaintiff to recover under the rules of negligence.

An FBO, as an owner and lessor of aircraft, may also be held vicariously liable for the negligence of a student or renter pilot. This will usually depend on a state's interpretation of the Federal Aviation Act which defines the operation of aircraft to include those persons who authorize operation by others. The states are divided on this issue. However, even where there is no vicarious liability, an FBO lessor or renter may still be liable for negligent entrustment by leasing or renting an aircraft to a person the FBO should have known to be incompetent.

One of the most common functions of an FBO is fueling aircraft. Misfueling (using the wrong type of fuel) or contaminating fuel may constitute FBO negligence. Numerous cases have held FBOs and others liable for negligence in the repair, maintenance, or modification of aircraft. Maintenance facilities also frequently assume the responsibility to inspect aircraft. When this is the case, failure to discover defects may constitute negligence. Even where a thorough inspection is not required, a maintenance company may be negligent if it fails to warn the owner of a dangerous condition which it does observe.

FBO liability for aircraft storage often depends on the principles of bailment, which require proof of the FBO's care, custody, and control of the aircraft of others. When the FBO assumes the position of bailee, it owes the owner a duty of ordinary care and can be held liable for negligence when the aircraft is damaged either on the ground or resulting from a flight test.

SPECIAL USE AIRCRAFT

It is estimated that an additional 15,000 aircraft are used for special use. These include aircraft used for aerial applications, aerial advertising, aerial photography, fire fighting, fish spotting, mosquito control, police traffic control, pipeline/powerline surveillance, weather modifications, and wildlife conservation. Other uses include sight-seeing, experimentation, research and development, testing, touring gliders, parachuting, helicopter hoisting, external load operations, log hauling, and offshore oil operations.

While the risks presented by special use aircraft represent some of the most perilous activities in aviation, some parts of the class are considered favorably by underwriters. Insurance coverages include the basic aircraft hull and liability and airport premises liability protection.

Other owners and operators use aircraft exclusively for pleasure, including gliders, ultralights, and experimental aircraft, homebuilts, antique aircraft, and warbirds. Special aircraft hull and liability contracts have been designed to meet the needs of these individuals.

AIRPORT OWNERS AND OPERATORS

There are over 18,000 airports in the United States ranging in size from Chicago O'Hare and Atlanta Hartsfield-Jackson to private grass strips. Included in this number are heliports, stolports, and seaplane bases. Airports generally fall into one of the following three categories: private use, public-use publicly owned, and public-use privately owned.

Private-use airports are those that are not open to the general public, but are restricted to the use of their owners and invited guests of the owners on an exclusive basis. *Public-use publicly owned airports* range in size from the major airports serving a metropolitan area to a small single grass strip owned by a local community. *Public-use privately owned* airports generally are located on the outskirts of a metropolitan area and serve as the general aviation airport for the community.

From an insurance standpoint, the primary coverage is airport premises liability. Other coverages frequently purchased are contractual liability and independent contractors liability. Another coverage unique to airports is air meet liability. Air meet liability covers the insured's liability arising out of the sponsorship of an air meet or air show.

Airport Liability

Persons using a commercial airport are public invitees and the owner or operator of the airport owes them the duty of ordinary care in maintaining and operating the premises in a reasonably safe condition. When an airport is strictly private and noncommercial, owners and operators are required only to refrain from willful, wanton, or reckless conduct. Even this lesser standard of care, however, has been construed to require a warning of known hazards to invitees.

The primary obligation of a commercial airport is to maintain its runways in a safe condition and keep them free from obstructions. When it is necessary to close a runway or to leave obstructions on it, an airport must notify the Federal Aviation Administration, which in turn will issue a Notice to Airmen (NOTAM) warning pilots of the situation. Runway obstructions have been held to include persons and vehicles, and the airport may be liable to the owner and occupants of the aircraft and the persons on the runway.

The duty of an airport to maintain its premises in a safe condition extends beyond the runways to include the airspace used for takeoffs and landing approaches. Thus an airport could be held liable for its failure to warn of nearby powerlines or bird-nesting areas. However, where the pilot should have been aware of a hazard, such as the presence of birds, the pilot's negligence or contributory negligence may defeat or reduce liability.

An airport may also provide storage and parking service much the same as an FBO. The liability of the airport in this role, like that of the FBO, depends upon the extent of control over the aircraft. Where the airport takes full possession and control of the aircraft, a bailment is created which imposes upon the airport a duty to use ordinary care in safeguarding the plane.

The airport authority is also responsible for ensuring a safe environment for passengers using the terminal area and parking garage. Moveable sidewalks, escalators, and elevators as well as recently washed or waxed floors can result in minor premises accidents.

INDIVIDUAL PILOTS

There are over 600,000 active pilots in the United States, including approximately 250,000 private pilots, many of whom do not own, but instead rent, borrow, or lease small aircraft for business and pleasure purposes. The personal non-owned aircraft policy is designed for such individuals. It provides liability and medical payments coverage. Optional non-owned aircraft physical damage liability coverage may be purchased. This coverage provides protection for damage to a rented or borrowed aircraft if the insured is held legally liable.

Pilot Liability

The majority of aircraft accidents are attributed to pilot error. Pilot liability is generally governed by the rules of negligence, except as modified by state statutes. When a pilot is an agent or employee acting within the scope of authority or employment at the time of an accident, the pilot's liability can be imputed to the pilot's principal or employer.

The pilot-in-command (PIC) of an aircraft is directly responsible for and is the final authority for the operation of the aircraft. The PIC must, before each flight, become familiar with all the available information concerning that flight, including weather conditions, airport conditions, alternative airfields, aircraft condition, nature of the terrain over which the plane will be flying, and any pertinent information contained in the latest Airman's Information manual, Advisory Circulars, and NOTAMs. The PIC must be designated in the flight plan.

Before a pilot can be held legally responsible, it must be shown that he or she knew all facts material to the safe operation of the aircraft. The pilot can expect the air traffic controller or Flight Service Station to supply all pertinent facts which he or she is not in a position to know.

The pilot owes a duty of reasonable care both to passengers and to other air traffic. This duty is an objective one, and does not vary with the pilot's experience. The standard of care in many situations is governed by Federal Aviation Regulations (FARs), which deal extensively with who may operate an aircraft, as well as where, when, and how the aircraft is to be operated. Violation of an FAR may constitute negligence per se depending on state law.

The pilot assumes several specific responsibilities. Primary among these is the duty to operate the aircraft in a safe manner. Negligence can arise as a result of improperly operating the controls in the cockpit. For example, pilots have been held liable for turning a fuel valve off, for improperly adjusting the wing flaps and causing a stall, for improperly setting a propeller in a cruising rather than climbing position, and for improper throttle adjustment. Improper operation may also include the performance of dangerous acrobatic maneuvers, flying below minimum safe altitudes, and flying through controlled airspace without reporting the aircraft's position.

Pilots flying under Visual Flight Rules (VFR) are required under the FARs to "see and avoid" and to separate themselves from other air traffic. This includes a duty to maneuver the aircraft in order to avoid blind spots, and a duty to keep a lookout for other aircraft which may be operating negligently.

In addition to the duty to see and avoid other traffic, the pilot must exercise equal caution in avoiding other obstructions. The most common of these are wires and power lines, which are often extremely difficult to detect.

A pilot will sometimes be found negligent for proceeding in the face of a known hazard. Such hazards include adverse weather, wake turbulence, or unsafe aircraft conditions such as wing or engine icing, being out of balance or over the weight capacity, or proceeding while low on fuel. This is distinct from the liability imposed for a negligent failure to appreciate the hazard.

Pilot liability can sometimes be established on a theory other than negligence. A pilot who flies with an expired medical certificate or in violation of the terms of a certificate such as a student pilot carrying passengers or a private pilot flying for hire, may be liable for willful misconduct entitling the plaintiff to punitive damages (payments above compensatory damages to punish the defendant). The same result can be reached when a pilot flies while under the influence of alcohol or drugs.

Activities, such as aerial application, have been held in some jurisdictions to constitute an ultra hazardous activity which may make the operator strictly liable (liability without fault) for any resulting accident.

LIABILITY OF THE FAA

Before 1996, the Federal Aviation Administration (FAA) was charged by Congress with the promotion and regulation of civil aviation to ensure safe and orderly growth of the airway system. In the 1996 FAA Reauthorization Bill, the charge of the FAA was changed to one of regulation only. It carries out its responsibilities in aviation safety by issuing and enforcing safety rules and regulations; certificating airmen, aircraft, aircraft components, air agencies, and airports; conducting aviation safety-related research and development; and operating and managing the air traffic control system.

As an agency of the federal government the FAA generally enjoys immunity from liability under the Doctrine of Sovereign Immunity.

Around 1947 Congress passed the Federal Tort Claim Act (FTCA). The FTCA provides a limited waiver of the federal government's sovereign immunity when its employees are negligent within the scope of their employment. Under the FTCA, the government can only be sued under circumstances where a private person acting on behalf of the United States government is liable to the claimant in accordance with the law of the place where the act or omission occurred. Thus, the FTCA does not apply to conduct that is uniquely governmental, that is, incapable of performance by a private individual.

As a result of the FTCA, the FAA may incur liability in the following areas:

Certification of Aircraft

The FAA is responsible for prescribing minimum safety standards for the design, construction, and performance of most aircraft, aircraft engines, and propellers. The first certification step requires manufacturers to obtain approval of each proposed design. Approval results in the issuance of a type of certificate. Once a type of certificate is issued, the manufacturing and quality control process is set up. If a prototype is produced in accordance with the design specifications approved in the type of certificate, then a production certificate is issued authorizing mass production of the aircraft or component. Each aircraft manufactured is then inspected as to its general condition for safety and to determine whether it conforms to the type certificate. Each aircraft passing the inspection is issued an airworthiness certificate, which represents final FAA approval for use of the aircraft. In the event that major modifications are later made to an aircraft so that the design no longer complies with the original type certificate, a supplemental type certificate is required prior to a recertification of the modified aircraft's air worthiness.

Because of the extensive inspection and certification process, the negligent failure of the FAA to discover an accident-causing defect may give rise to a suit. However, recent court decisions have severely restricted the criteria under which the FAA may be sued for liability due to the certification process.

Certification of Airmen

The FAA also has responsibility for certifying pilots and maintenance technicians. In so doing, the FAA may be held liable for negligence in the certification process.

Air Traffic Control

Early cases alleging ATC negligence usually held that the pilot in command of an aircraft was directly and primarily responsible for the safe operation of that aircraft and that consequently an air traffic controller had no duty to the aircraft except to adhere to the requirements of the Air Traffic Control Manual. Since the mid-1950s it has become well established that air traffic controllers have a duty of due care to pilots and that the government is not immune from liability for ATC negligence. While the pilot in command remains the primary and final authority for the safe operation of the aircraft, both the pilot and the air traffic controller are concurrently responsible.

Federal Aviation Regulations, mandate aircraft separation in numerous situations. All aircraft flying under Instrument Flight Rules must maintain separation and many times must rely entirely on ATC for separation information and instructions since they cannot keep a visual lookout for traffic.

All aircraft operating in "controlled airspace" must maintain varying degrees of separation as outlined in the FAR's. Even though the pilot in command is charged with the obligation to "see and avoid" ATC has a primary responsibility for traffic separation and procedures in and around busy airports and traffic corridors.

The degree of separation required and the obligation of ATC in each instance are clearly outlined in the FAR's. After an accident occurs, it is often not as clear how well the parties fulfilled their obligations and a court interpretation of the FAR's may ultimately decide the liability of the FAA in a particular situation. In any event, it is clear there are many opportunities for the FAA to incur liability in the performance of their ATC function.

Weather Information

Weather conditions are important in the safe operation of aircraft. Weather does not directly cause the accident, but instead induces pilot error or creates conditions which the pilot is unable to handle. In some cases, however, weather conditions such as hail, ice, and severe turbulence can directly cause aircraft failure or cause a loss of control over the aircraft. The FAA Flight Service Station (FSS) is the main distributor of weather information for aviation use. The FSS has primary responsibility for providing pilots with both preflight and in-flight weather briefings. Air traffic controllers advise pilots of current weather conditions as necessary, although their most important function is traffic control.

Negligence on the part of the FAA can occur when an air traffic controller gives the pilot-in-command inaccurate or misleading information. Failure of an air traffic controller to report wind shear could result in negligence rendering the FAA liable. (A wind shear is a rapidly changing wind which moves in a sharp vertical drop before diverging into a horizontal flow near the earth's surface.)

Aeronautical Charts

The FAA is authorized to arrange for the publication of aeronautical charts and maps in order to promote the safe and efficient flow of air traffic. Under certain situations, the FAA can be held liable for an erroneous or misleading chart.

Airport Hazards

The FAA has been held liable for negligence in the failure to warn of known ground hazards at airports and near flight paths on much the same basis as for weather hazards. Where an obstruction or dangerous condition exists at an airport, the FAA must include a warning in its weekly Notice to Airmen (NOTAM). Pilots are responsible for reviewing the current NOTAMS.

KEY TERMS

Aviation/aerospace manufacturers
Aerospace Industries Association (AIA)
General Aviation Manufactures Association (GAMA)
Legacy air carriers
Air taxi and charter operators
Industrial aid
Business and pleasure
Flying club
Fixed base operators
Special use
Private-use airports
Public-use

REVIEW QUESTIONS

1. Discuss some of the challenges of space exploration that will face aviation underwriters into the twenty-first century.
2. Name some of the leading aerospace manufacturers who are members of AIA and GAMA. What is the purpose of products liability? Why do subcontractors and suppliers need this form of coverage? What is meant by a manufacturing defect?
3. Name several of the legacy air carriers. What are the principal lines of aviation insurance carried by the air carriers and air taxi operators? Why must air carriers and air taxi operators exercise the highest degree of care? How does this affect their negligent acts?
4. Why is the industrial aid class of business considered one of the best by aviation underwriters? Describe one unique coverage provided industrial aid accounts. Most aircraft risks fall into which class of business?
5. Describe some of the services provided by FBOs. Give some examples of how

liability may arise out of these operations. List the principal aviation insurance coverages purchased by FBOs. What are special use aircraft?

6. Discuss the variety of airport risks. What are the major liability exposures faced by airport authorities? What type of aviation insurance is sold to active pilots who do not own an aircraft? Why is the pilot in command such an important element in determining negligence following an accident?
7. How might the FAA incur liability in carrying out its responsibilities?

Chapter 3

Insurers

OUTLINE

Overview of the Industry
Major Aviation Insurers
Other Aviation Insurance Markets
Lloyd's of London
Selecting and Insurer
Insurance Agents and Brokers
Insurance Channels of Distribution
Selecting an Agent or Broker

OBJECTIVES

At the end of this chapter you should be able to:
Identify the major aviation insurance companies and the classes of aviation business written by them.
Distinguish between a direct-writing company and one that sells its security and services through the agency system.
Understand how Lloyd's of London differs from other contemporary insurance markets.
Describe how aviation insurance is placed through Lloyd's of London.
Summarize the important considerations an insured must take in selecting an insurer.
Distinguish between an agent and a broker.
Identify several of the largest aviation insurance brokerage firms in the United States.
Discuss some of the factors an insured must consider in selecting an agent or broker.

OVERVIEW OF THE INDUSTRY

Today there are over 5,000 insurers in the United States organized under a variety of ownership forms and writing a variety of coverages. It is estimated that probably no more than 300 of these write aviation insurance and the majority belong to some pool or association.

The divisions of the insurance business according to underwriting lines are somewhat arbitrary, as a result of the gradual development of different branches of insurance and of the laws which controlled them. The original charters were so broad that the early U.S. insurance companies wrote all lines of insurance. Over the years, state insurance laws were tightened restricting companies to one or another of the following lines:

1. Life and Health coverages
2. Fire, marines, and allied forms of property insurance
3. Casualty and surety business

Companies were prohibited from engaging in more than one of the three categories. Up until the 1940s it was quite common for an insurer to write separate hull (physical damage to the aircraft) and liability (protection against the insured's negligent acts) policies. The method of evading the restrictions imposed by state laws was to organize subsidiary companies, owned in part or wholly by the parent company.

During the 1940s there was great pressure to abandon the strict categories and gradually the state laws were amended. One state after another passed multiple-line laws. At present, such laws exist in all states. This makes it possible for any company except a life insurance company to engage in all forms or property and liability insurance.

The first combined aircraft hull and liability policies appeared during the 1950s and soon became a significant marketing factor. This multiple-line underwriting approach continues today with the result that many life insurance companies are buying property and liability insurance companies, and the latter are buying life insurance companies. Although combinations of life and property companies have existed for years, recently the tempo of acquisition has been speeded up. Some industry analysts foresee only two policies in the future, one covering life and health insurance and the other covering all property and liability losses.

Aviation insurance has remained as one of the few specialty lines and although there has been a trend to combine policies within the field, it has not been caught up in the tide of combining the major property and casualty lines of insurance. The reason for this relates to the basic nature of the aviation risk. Aircraft and the perils of flight present many unique problems for the aviation insurer. One factor is the constant exposure to a catastrophe loss. Another is the wide diversity of risks resulting in a relatively limited number of insureds (spread of risk) in any one category. Finally, the rapidity of change in aircraft and aviation risks compared to other lines of insurance has required the need for a specialist to underwrite such risks.

MAJOR AVIATION INSURERS

There are several different kinds of aviation insurers. By far the largest share of the domestic aviation market is handled by the two largest of the multicompany aviation pools, the *United States Aircraft Insurance Group* (*USAIG*) and *Global Aerospace*. These two markets handle all aviation insurance exposures and write the biggest share of the domestic air carriers, aircraft manufacturers, and large airports.

Three other markets have grown considerably during the past two decades and now participate in virtually all classes of aviation insurance. They are *AIG Aviation, Inc.* a subsidiary of the American International Group of Companies; *ACE USA Aerospace*, a subsidiary of ACE Ltd.; and the *HCC Aviation Insurance Group.*

Each of these five markets specializes in aviation insurance and all underwriters, field representatives, claims adjusters, and loss prevention engineers are thoroughly trained in handling problems associated with the aviation field. Regional officers are located throughout the country, where quotations are made and policies issued. Their facilities are available to any independent agent of each member or associate company. Neither a special agency appointment nor a special license is required. Generally, no binding authority is given to most agents; however, some agents and brokers who produce large quantities of business may have authority for some selected risks. Agents and brokers not representing any of the member companies of these pools may be appointed provided certain requirements are met.

United States Aircraft Insurance Group
One Seaport Plaza
199 Water Street
New York, NY 10038

Second largest of the domestic aviation underwriters, United States Aircraft Insurance Group (USAIG) was formed in 1928 and today includes 34 of the world's major insurance companies. Member companies include ACE American Insurance Company, General Reinsurance Corporation, Hartford Fire Insurance Company, Liberty Mutual Insurance Company, National Liability & Fire Insurance Company, Zurich American Insurance Company. The individual insurance companies collectively function as an insurance market for all types of aviation and aerospace accounts. The actual underwriting of these accounts is done by United States Aviation Underwriters, Inc., which manages the USAIG and is responsible for selecting business, specifying rates, binding coverages, issuing policies, arranging reinsurance, collecting premiums, and settling claims on USAIG's behalf. USAIG was acquired in the early 1980s by General Re which in turn was acquired by Berkshire Hathaway in 1998.

Aviation insurance for individuals and companies domiciled in Canada is provided by the Canadian Aircraft Insurance Group (CAIG). The CAIG is managed by Canadian Aviation Insurance Managers, Inc. CAIM maintains underwriting and claims officers in Toronto and Vancouver to serve policyholders and insurance agents and brokers throughout the provinces. USAIG provides a broad spectrum of insurance for the aviation community. Coverages include insurance for physical damage to airline, private and corporate aircraft as well as liability insurance for owners, operators, and aircraft service facilities.

Additional aviation coverages include medical coverage, liability insurance for owners or operators of airports and helicopters (and their tenants), products liability coverage for manufacturers of aircraft and aircraft components, and workers' compensation insurance for aviation-related accounts. USAIG's aerospace coverages include launch and initial operations insurance for satellites and in-orbit satellite insurance. Insurance is provided for owners, operators, manufacturers, and users of satellites, plus launch vehicle operators. Coverages can include asset value, loss of revenue, and extra expenses.

Staffed by aviation insurance underwriters, claims, and loss prevention specialists, USAU maintains 17 domestic branch offices in Atlanta, Chicago, Dallas, Denver, Houston, Los Angeles, Memphis, Minneapolis, New York, Orlando, Phoenix, Pittsburgh, San Francisco, Seattle, St. Louis, Toledo, and Wichita. See Chapter 1 for the early history of USAIG.

Global Aerospace
(US Headquarters)
51 John F. Kennedy
Parkway Short Hills
New Jersey 07078

Largest of the multicompany pools, *Global Aerospace* underwrites on behalf of some of the world's largest and most secure insurers and reinsurers. By combining the strengths of Associated Aviation Underwriters (AAU) and the British Aviation Insurance Group—who's roots date back to 1924—Global Aerospace was formed in 2001 to insure the risks of ownership, operation, and maintenance of aircraft. Global Aerospace is on the of largest aerospace insurance groups in North America, underwriting all types of aerospace insurance including, airlines, airports, aviation products manufacturers, satellites, aviation businesses, and corporate, business, and private aircraft throughout the Western Hemisphere. Global Aerospace also offers safety and engineering surveys for policyholders, and claims management services.

Global Aerospace functions as the aerospace insurance department for four member companies: National Indemnity, Munich Re, Tokio Marine Nichido and Mitsui Sumitomo. Business is written through licensed insurance brokers and agents of member companies, and appointment and licensing of agents is handled exclusively by Global's member companies. All business is transacted directly with Global Aerospace.

Underwriting and claims specialists staff its eight North American branch offices located in Atlanta; Short Hills, New Jersey; Chicago; Dallas; Kansas City; Los Angeles; Seattle; (claims only) and Toronto, Canada. Global Aerospace's corporate headquarters is located in London. See chapter 1 for early history of AAU.

AIG Aviation, Inc.
100 Colony Square
Atlanta, Georgia 30361

AIG Aviation is a subsidiary of the American International Group, Inc. one of the leading U.S.-based international insurance organizations and among the nation's largest underwriters of commercial and industrial coverages. AIG Aviation was created from the former Southeastern Aviation Underwriters (SEAU) when the latter was acquired by AIG in 1983.

Over the years AIG has grown into one of the largest aviation underwriters worldwide. In 1997 AIG acquired Commercial Aviation Insurance (COMAV). COMAV specialized in underwriting general aviation and agricultural business. This has given AIG Aviation access to the agricultural markets and has expanded its own general aviation book of business. AIG's current product line also includes corporate aircraft, major and regional airlines, fixed base operators, airport and products liability, helicopters, and satellites. Policies are issued through the following companies: American Home Assurance Company, National Union Fire Insurance Company of Pittsburgh, The Insurance Company of the State of Pennsylvania, and the New Hampshire Insurance Company. AIG Aviation has a staff of dedicated safety and loss control engineers who perform detailed safety surveys of customers' flight operations and provide methods for mitigating liability exposures. The company maintains its home office in Atlanta, with regional offices located in Chicago; Dallas; Princeton, New Jersey; Scottsdale, Arizona; Los Angeles; New York; and London.

ACE USA International & Specialty Aerospace
1601 Chestnut Street
Philadelphia, Pennsylvania 19101

ACE USA Aerospace is the operating Unit of *ACE USA International & Specialty Division*. ACE USA is wholly owned by ACE Limited and together with ACE Global Markets, London is a major provider of Aerospace insurance.

ACE USA International and Specialty Aerospace focuses on two specific product segments: (1) Airport & Special Risks, and (2) Satellites. In addition, ACE USA is a Member of the USAIG Pool where it participates in a broad range of aviation products. Claims are serviced by a dedicated Aerospace claims unit in Chicago.

HCC Aviation Insurance Group
16415 Addison Road
Dallas, Texas 75248

HCC Aviation Insurance Group, formed in 1997, is a wholly owned subsidiary of HCC Insurance Holdings, Inc., an international specialty insurance group based in Houston, Texas. Prior to January 1999, HCC Aviation was underwriting aviation business under the name of Aviation & Marine Insurance Group (AMIG). AMIG was formed from the former U.S. Specialty Insurance Company, Southern Aviation Underwriters, Continental Insurance Underwriters, and Signal Aviation Underwriters.

HCC Aviation underwrites all classes of general aviation business primarily focusing on pleasure and business aircraft, industrial aid, and commercial accounts, both fixed wing and rotorcraft. HCC Aviation also offers a wide range of coverages including physical damage, aircraft liability, and chemical liability for the agricultural aviation industry. The company also provides workers' compensation for the aviation industry in conjunction with corporate clients.

The HCC Aviation Insurance Group operates out of the home office in Dallas and the western regional office in Glendale, California.

XL Aerospace

XL Aerospace entered aviation lines in 1997 first in London and then in the U.S. under the name Brockbank Insurance Services, Inc. While Brockbank was a wholly owned subsidiary of XL Capital, it was before the XL branding began. XL Aerospace is the aviation and space arm of the XL Capital Group, a Bermuda-based insurance group. XL underwrites aviation business through its London office and its Santa Barbara, California office. In addition to these company offices XL has entered into a long-term agreement with W. Brown & Associates, a Managing General Underwriter, to produce a majority of its general aviation portfolio. Risks domiciled in the United States are typically written using XL Specialty Insurance Company, and those that are domiciled elsewhere are written using our Lloyd's of London platform.

XL underwrites most lines of aviation insurance. They have a major book of worldwide airlines, manufacturers, suppliers, and significant volume of general aviation business. In addition XL has a keen view of niche segments within the aviation market and utilizes technology to help underwrite these segments successfully.

U.S. Specialty Insurance Company
16415 Addison Road
Addison, Texas 75001

U.S. Specialty Insurance Company, formed in 1987, is a wholly owned subsidiary of HCC Insurance Holdings, Inc., an international specialty insurance group based in Houston, Texas.

U.S. Specialty concentrates on all classes of general aviation business primarily focusing on pleasure and business aircraft, industrial aid, and commercial accounts, both fixed wing and rotorcraft. General Aviation is augmented by the Special Risk Department, which specializes in the more challenging aircraft, warbirds, antique, float, experimental and homebuilt aircraft. U.S. Specialty also offers the full spectrum of coverages including physical damage, aircraft liability, and airport liability. All business is handled through the Addison, Texas, office.

OTHER AVIATION INSURANCE MARKETS

The are a number of smaller aviation insurance markets which tend to specialize either in a particular class of business such as agricultural aircraft, helicopters, or antique and experimental aircraft or to restrict their writings to single-engine and light-twin business and pleasure risks. These markets include: Avemco Insurance Company and Phoenix Aviation Managers, Inc.

Avemco Insurance Company
411 Aviation Way
Frederick, Maryland 21701

The only direct writing company, *Avemco Insurance Company* was formed in 1960 and served for many years as the designated insurer for the Aircraft Owners and Pilots Association (AOPA). Direct writing companies market their policies directly to the public through company representative rather than by using independent agents. In 1974 Avemco acquired Airway Underwriters, a small general aviation insurer, based in San Antonio, Texas. National Aviation Underwriters (NAU) became a wholly owned subsidiary of Avemco in 1985. NAU had a long and illustrious history in the general aviation insurance business particularly as an underwriter of FBOs. Originally formed as a reciprocal exchange in 1945 by several St. Louis area FBOs the company expanded its operation over the years, writing a cross-section of general aviation risks, airports, helicopters, agricultural operators, and FBOs of all sizes.

In the summer of 1997 Avemco was acquired by HCC Insurance Holdings, Inc. and now operates as one of its subsidiaries under its own name as a direct writer. Avemco's traditional market niche has been the private owner of general aviation aircraft, airports, and FBOs. It also provides insurance for financial institutions and "stop-loss" health insurance. All business is handled through the Frederick, Maryland office.

Phoenix Aviation Managers, Inc.
1255 Roberts Blvd.
Kennesaw, Georgia 30144

Phoenix Aviation Managers, Inc. is a wholly owned subsidiary of Old Republic International Corporation, and writes its policies primarily through Old Republic Insurance Company. Founded in 1983, the company's major focus is to write general aviation business. Although most classes of business are entertained, its strengths are pleasure and business aircraft owners, FBOs, and flight schools.

In 1995 Phoenix started an airport and special risk division after acquiring the book of business from Southern Marine & Aviation Underwriters (SMAU) when the latter retired from the business. This division concentrates on aircraft and other government business, including government-operated helicopters. Airports range from small country airports to major international airports. The company also writes workers' compensation, primarily to support other lines of business.

An agricultural division was established in 1998 to handle this specialized class of business. Located in Memphis, Tennessee, this division is the result of the merger of the former Crump Aviation Underwriters and SMAU. Crump Aviation Underwriters was a successful specialty market for many years concentrating on helicopters and agricultural operators.

Phoenix Aviation maintains its home office at Kennesaw, Georgia, with regional offices in Dallas, New Orleans, and Pasadena, California.

LLOYD'S OF LONDON

In a colorful history spanning three centuries, *Lloyds's of London* has created tremendous impact of the world's insurance business. Lloyd's was originally a market exclusively for marine insurance, writing the first policies in the 1680s. Today, however, nearly 75 percent of its annual premium writings come from nonmarine sources. Risks of every conceivable description are accepted by Lloyd's underwriters from all continents and most countries either directly or by means of reinsurance. Since 1911 when Lloyd's underwriters issued the first standard aircraft insurance the Lloyd's aviation market has been a world leader insuring approximately 20 percent of the world's aviation business and war risks. More than half of the aviation market's premiums are from North American Risks, including hull and liability coverage for airlines, aircraft manufacturers' products liability, airport liability, commuter airlines and corporate fleets, air cargo liability, helicopters, and satellite coverages. Personal coverages such as loss of license for aircrews and personal accident coverages for passengers and crew members are also underwritten.

Lloyd's is not a company as such but an association of individual and corporate underwriting members formed into *syndicates* whose underwriters actually accept the risks.

Lloyd's membership is drawn from many sources, both foreign and domestic. All members of Lloyd's must provide capital equivalent to their risk-assessed capital requirement. In the case of corporate members they must deposit at least 50 percent of the premiums permitted to write or more if their risk-based capital assessment requires. For individual members this means assets equal in value to a minimum of 40 percent of the premiums they are permitted to write. In addition, there are minimum capital requirements for both corporate and individual members.

Corporate and individual members must also make annual contributions to Lloyd's Central Fund which was established to meet policyholders' claims in the event of members being unable to meet their underwriting liabilities.

All premiums are automatically paid into a trust find, which is held by the syndicate's managing agent. The use of these funds is restricted, ensuring that the money is available to meet policyholder claims and other underwriting expenses.

New underwriting members are introduced by firms of underwriting agents who see to most of the formalities connected with joining, advise the new members as to which syndicate they should join, and deal with their accounts. Each syndicate specializes in some class of insurance—marine, nonmarine, or aviation. In addition to the specialist aviation syndicates, Lloyd's also allows marine syndicate to write aviation business. A team of underwriting managers runs each of the syndicates. Some of the underwriting managers are members of Lloyd's; the rest are professional underwriters hired by the syndicates. Modernization and market forces have reduced syndicate numbers in recent years and encouraged the growth or larger, better-financed syndicates.

In a syndicate, members participate according to the amount of premium that the proportion of their applicable deposit entitles them to write. For example, Suppose an air carrier needs hull coverage with an insured value of $5,000,000 at a premium of 1 percent, that is $50,000, and an underwriting member has a 1 percent share in a syndicate, which includes 125 members with carrying shares. If the lead underwriter in the syndicate accepts a 10 percent line on the insurance on behalf of the syndicate, it will receive a premium of $5,000 of which the underwriting member will be liable for 1 percent of 10 percent of $5,000,000 or $5,000. The underwriting member is not liable for the sums due from any other member of the syndicate.

LLOYD'S BROKERS

The only persons who may present business to underwriters at Lloyd's are the several hundred insurance brokers who are approved by the Committee of Lloyd's and are known as *Lloyd's brokers*. American agents and brokers doing business, with Lloyd's must work through an approved Lloyd's broker.

The Lloyd's broker's primary duty is to negotiate the best available terms for his clients. To this end he is free to place risks wherever he thinks fit whether at Lloyd's, with another British companies, or both. On receiving a request for insurance coverage, a Lloyd's broker first makes out the "slip"—a sheet of folded paper with details of the risk. The next step is to negotiate a rate of premium with the underwriters' expert in that particular type of business. Lloyd's thrives on competition and the broker may obtain several quotes before deciding on the best one—bearing in mind what his client will be prepared to pay and what level of premium is required to get the risk adequately covered in the market. The lead underwriter, having set the rate, takes a proportion of the risk on behalf on his syndicate.

Armed with this lead, the broker approaches as many other syndicates as are needed to get the slip fully subscribed. Large aircraft liability risks are usually spread over the whole London market, coverage being shared by Lloyd's underwriters and the insurance companies. Spreading a risk as widely as possible is one of the principles of insurance, which enables Lloyd's, and the London market to withstand the pressure of heavy claims, which might otherwise be ruinous.

In addition to the underwriters at Lloyd's, there are several thousand other staff members employed as lawyers, claims adjusters, actuaries, data processing personnel, and clerical staff. Lloyd's maintains a policy-signing office through which all policies issued at Lloyd's pass, and a central accounting system of Lloyd's transactions, thus relieving underwriters of all this detailed work.

When paying claims the Lloyd's broker informs the leading underwriter at Lloyd's (who originally set the terms and conditions of the risk) and Lloyd's claims office, who act on behalf of other following Lloyd's underwriters who have also underwritten the risk. Once the claim has been approved by both the leader and the Lloyd's claims office, the claims office initiates settlement, transferring claims funds from the underwriters to the broker.

Lloyd's central accounting system ensures that the claim is paid directly to the brokers account and the accounts of the underwriting syndicates are then debited. In the unlikely event that funds prove inadequate to meet the claim, the payment to the policyholder is not affected: the managing agent obtains more funds from the syndicate members. Claims arising on syndicates no longer trading continue to be paid in the same way through a run-off company.

All Lloyd's policies are backed by the market's unique four levels of security: the premiums trust funds; individual and corporate member's funds at Lloyd's the personal resources of individual members; and the Central Fund.

International Market

The international aviation market is truly cosmopolitan and to some extent reflects the global nature of the aviation industry. Apart from the United States, which has its own domestic marketplace, the most important center for aviation insurance is in Europe, primarily in London, but also in Paris, Munich, and other cities where the aviation reinsurance companies reside.

Lloyd's of London was the driving force in aviation insurance through the 1960s and, in conjunction with the London and European aviation insurance companies, provided the majority of the aviation premium capacity.

This is still true today, but to a slightly lesser extent. Today, it is not unusual to find United States. domestic insurers like United States Aviation Insurance Group (USAIG) and Houston Casualty Company (HCC) writing business outside the U.S.A. in places such as Central and South America, Africa, and Pacific Rim countries.

With the advent of the A380, configured to carry up to 550 passengers, airlines will be approaching the aviation insurance marketplace for limits of $2.5 billion to $3 billion when the aircraft makes its commercial debut in 2006. This will stretch the existing capacity but some new capacity is expected to enter the marketplace because of the three exceptionally profitable years following the tragedy of September 11, 2001.

It is hard not to emphasize the importance of the Lloyd's market when discussing international aviation insurance. For nearly a century, Lloyd's has been the center for international aviation business. Lloyd's underwriters and brokers alike derive most of their business from abroad and have developed a worldwide network of correspondents. It is also true that Lloyd's London insurance companies and their European counterparts still write the majority of U.S. aviation business either as direct writers or as reinsurers. Their ability to write the needed liability limits particularly the large liability limits required by the airlines, major airframe and engine manufacturers means that they have to be involved in some capacity. In other parts of the world it is Lloyd's London and the European insurance companies expertise in evaluating the risks and rating them that provides the much needed insurance product for the aviation industry.

This ability to underwrite risks which are far away has improved greatly because of ease of communications due to the fax machine and more recently e-mail and the internet. In the sixties most London brokers relied on telexes which tended to give only brief details of the risk to be placed. Since those days, underwriters have demanded much more information and frequently travel abroad to visit their clients, whether they are the insured, local broker, or local insurance company. This gives them the opportunity to put into perspective the culture, philosophy, and operating conditions of the insured or prospective insured. This has been a feature of U.S. underwriting for decades and has provided with a sound underwriting capability.

The major non-U.S. airlines are all underwritten and placed in Lloyd's London and European marketplace. However, it is not unusual to find a U.S. market like United States Aviation Insurance Group (USAIG) also participating. Global Aerospace which resulted from the merger of British Aviation Insurance Group and Associated Aviation Underwriters (AAU) is headquartered in London and now is considered a London insurance company.

The country of domicile of the airline will dictate whether it will be a reinsurance of a local insurance company or will go into the market as a direct placement. This is dependent on the local insurance laws of the country in question. With the current (2005) airline premium income close to $3 billion (including U.S. airlines) this is the largest source of premium income to the worldwide aviation insurance market.

The results of the worldwide airline premium income and losses can impact the world's general aviation rates/premiums since the same underwriters and reinsurers who write the airlines also write the general aviation book of business. Therefore, airline results can and do affect underwriters' and reinsurers' attitude to other classes of business worldwide. This can also to a lesser extent be said of the space/satellite market, which although slightly different in composition still can have significant losses which affect other sectors of the aviation marketplace worldwide.

Canada

Canada, like the United States has its own domestic market. The main insurers are Canadian Aviation Insurance Group (CAIG) which is the Canadian branch of USAIG, Global Aerospace, AIM Underwriting, and Gerling Canada part of the Gerling Global Group. The remainder of the capacity is written in Lloyd's London and European insurance companies.

From the perspective of a U.S. broker, placing Canadian business in a U.S. or London market is not particularly attractive, as half of the commission/brokerage must be earned and/or given to a Canadian broker. However, the reverse is not true.

Central and South America

Central and South American countries are probably the most interesting to a U.S. market and brokers or agents largely because of the proximity and ease of access.

Houston Casualty Company (HCC) and USAIG both write business in this part of the world. HCC writes a tremendous amount of rotor wing business as well as general aviation business. USAIG prefers to write the corporate aviation accounts. American International Group wrote a great deal of its Central and South American business out of their Atlanta office. However, this is now written in its London underwriting office.

It was not too long ago that most business in this part of the world was not considered up to U.S. standards. However, today that is not true and many of the operations are comparable to U.S. firms.

As with any operation, an on-site survey is essential to ascertain the culture, philosophy, equipment, training methods, and operational integrity of the operator. In addition, the U.S. broker will need to meet the local reinsurance or direct broker and the local fronting company.

In many, if not all Central and South American countries, the U.S. broker will be looked upon as a reinsurance broker and may be required to be licensed by the local Ministry or Superintendent of Banks and Insurance. Licensing often takes place after the account has been "won" but still needs to be complied with to retain the account(s). Normally, this can be facilitated by working with a local broker. Also, foreign insurance companies might have to be on a "white list" (approved by governmental authorities) before being acceptable.

Most, if not all, Central or South American countries' insurance laws require that a minimal portion of the liabilities and in some cases the hull physical damage coverage, be placed with a local insurance company that will then reinsure 100 percent of it through the reinsurance broker to the market in the United States. or London/Europe. This is referred to as "fronting" and from the point of view of the local company serves the purpose of:

a. Supporting the local insurance market.
b. Providing income to the local insurance market with fronting fees to the local insurance company and commissions to local direct and reinsurance brokers.
c. Providing a vehicle, the local insurance policy, to charge the governmental taxes.
d. In some cases the local insurance company will retain a portion of the risk, normally no more than 10 percent.

In some cases the local insurers may have an underwriting facility, normally a line slip, which will either need to have the rates agreed to by the reinsurers prior to binding or will have a schedule of rates/premiums that reinsurers' have determined as adequate and that the local insurer must adhere to.

In some rate cases, the local insurance company may have an aviation reinsurance treaty that will allow it to write aviation risks generally limited to certain classes of business.

One important aspect of working in Central and South America is client loyalty. Like the rest of the world, the cost of insurance is often the overriding factor in determining whether the account is retained or lost. However, just as in the United States, service is also a very important factor. Therefore, it is vital to visit clients and prospects on a regular basis so as to build up client loyalty. The reverse is also true and taking out the underwriters to visit these clients can be very beneficial.

Australia and New Zealand

Australia and New Zealand have their own sophisticated domestic aviation insurance market, although on occasion business other than airline accounts have been written in the U.S. However, in general all aviation business is either written domestically or by the Lloyd's, London and European markets.

In Australia there is the Australian Aviation Pool which primarily writes general aviation accounts.

In marked contrast to the United States tort liability environment, the award levels in these two countries are much lower. In New Zealand there is the "Accident Compensation Act" which limits awards to low levels by American standards. Australia does not have a similar act, but its legal system helps to keep award levels in check, albeit somewhat higher than in New Zealand.

Africa and the Middle East

Africa is somewhat like South America in that the insurance process is similar. The only country where it really differs is in South Africa which has a level of sophistication not seen in the rest of the continent. They have a small but effective market which uses Lloyd's brokers when necessary to access Lloyd's and London/European markets.

The Middle East has developed its aviation infrastructure in the last 30 years and it now boasts very modern jet fleets in many of the countries or emirates. These are generally insured in the Lloyd's and London and European marketplace sometimes as a reinsurance of a local domestic insurance company that might accept a small retention.

Europe

The level of aviation insurance sophistication in Europe rivals or surpasses that in the United States. This is in part due to the fact that Lloyd's, having been a market for aviation insurance for nearly a century, has led the way in providing the insurance products required by the industry. Lloyd's has always been regarded as an entrepreneurial marketplace with many innovators among its ranks. This spirit coupled with a depth of aviation insurance knowledge not available anywhere else has helped to provide generations of professional aviation insurance personnel to fill the positions in brokering, underwriting, and claims throughout Europe and elsewhere.

Another important factor influencing Europe is that it is the home of most of the major aviation reinsurance companies including Swiss Re, Munich Re, and Hanover Re. The interaction among the reinsurance companies and the direct writers with their brokers acting as intermediaries generally occurs for the January 1st and July 1st treaty renewals but regular dialogue is ongoing.

Rest of the World

The rest of the world comprises some huge land masses including China, Russia, India, Pakistan and the remainder of the Far East. From a U.S. aviation insurance professional's viewpoint, there is little likelihood of involvement in this part of the world. The majority of the aviation business is handled by local brokers/intermediaries and is placed either as a reinsurance of local insurance companies or directly into the Lloyd's London and European markets. It is certainly possible that markets like USAIG might be asked to participate in airline and corporate business, but this is likely to come through to them from the various Lloyd's brokers they deal with.

One of the largest worldwide insurance groups is American International Group otherwise known as AIG. It writes its worldwide book of aviation business through its London office and therefore can only be accessed through Lloyd's brokers for business outside the United States. However, its capabilities are formidable and its reach is truly worldwide.

SELECTING AN INSURER

In many respects the most important consideration an insured faces in selecting insurance is the integrity of the insurer. The company's financial condition, underwriting philosophy, claims policy, service, and premium rates are more important considerations than whether it is a direct writer or sells its policies through independent agents and brokers. Alfred M. Best, Inc. publishes an annual book entitled *Best's Insurance Reports: Property-Liability* which is a comprehensive analysis of insurers that considers the following four factors: (1) underwriting results, (2) management efficiency, (3) adequacy of reserves, and (4) soundness of investments. From the analysis of these four factors, *Best's* assigns a rating to each insurer: A+, A, B+, C+, and C. Risk managers generally establish a criterion like B+ or better for the past four years, before placing their risk with a particular company.

Theoretically, direct writing companies should offer insurance coverages at lower rates because of the absence of the agent's or broker's commission (often between 5 and 25 percent); however, this is not necessarily true. It pays the insured to shop around and get various quotations before selecting an insurer. Another complicating factor is that aviation insurance policies vary tremendously, particularly in rates and policy wording, neither of which is established by state insurance departments or rating bureaus. Each policy differs in some aspect—even policies from the same company. A company which is very competitive in writing policies for corporate aircraft flown by professional pilots may be uncompetitive in both policy wording and rating when it comes to low time pilots in high performance single-engine aircraft.

Companies writing aviation insurance can range from a small department within a large general insurer, to a company which only writes aviation business. While most insurers retain some of the risk before reinsuring the balance, some retain none of the risk and pass it all off through various reinsurance treaties to other insurers. These so-called *front companies* generally last as long as they protect their reinsurance companies. Once underwriting results deteriorate, the reinsurers pull out and the front companies are forced out of business.

Most aviation insurers fall within the top four categories of *Best's* ratings. Unfortunately, as in any industry, marginal firms appear during growth periods in the aviation industry and then retire during recessionary periods. As noted, there are fewer markets now than during the past four decades. An insured should find out how long the insurer has been in business. What is its reputation for paying claims? Having an experienced independent agent or broker review a specimen policy from the company is also a wise procedure before selecting an insurer.

INSURANCE AGENTS AND BROKERS

In marketing insurance, agents and brokers are the intermediary primarily used by insurers to sell their policies and services. Legally, an insurance *agent* in the property and casualty field is a representative of an insurer, and is delegated authority through an agency contract to act on behalf of the insurer. An insurance *broker* is a person who, for a consideration, solicits and negotiates the placing of risks for an insured and is considered as the agent of the insured and not of the insurer. The agent and the broker are both compensated by commission paid by the insurance company. In practice, the distinction between agents and brokers is complicated by the fact that many agents may be licensed both as agents and brokers.

Although there are relatively few aviation insurance companies, there are many agents and brokers who place aviation insurance. The insurance section of the *World Aviation Directory* lists the major agents and brokers in the United States. Another excellent listing can be found in the membership directory of the *Aviation Insurance Association* (*AIA*). AIA, located in Kansas City, Missouri, can be reached by calling 1-800-354-7918.

Insurance agencies and brokerage firms come in all sizes from one or two person operations specializing in aviation to a large corporation placing all classes of business with separate departments staffed with specialists. Some brokerage firms with offices throughout the country place millions of premium dollars and are as large as some insurance companies.

INSURANCE CHANNELS OF DISTRUBUTION

Insurance policies are distributed through two channels: American Agency system and the direct writing system. The American Agency system is the traditional approach and independent agents are appointed and authorized by insurance companies to represent them in a given territory. The agent is compensated solely by commission, and has the right to solicit renewal business and to sell this right to others. Independent agents will establish agency agreements with multiple companies so that they can satisfy their clients' many different insurance coverage needs.

The direct writing system, traditionally used by life insurance companies, has become increasingly popular in the property and casualty field. Insurance companies select this form of distribution when they desire more control over marketing their product. Direct writers operate through exclusive or captive agents, or write insurance directly and eliminate agents from the transaction. Captive agents represent only one insurer, are paid either by commission or salary, and unlike independent agents, do not have ownership rights to the renewals on the insurance they write, or use and control of policy records.

Which system is better? Proponents of the American Agency system claim that the insurance buyer enjoys certain advantages, such as greater convenience, personalized service, local assistance in settling claims, greater selectivity among insurers, and a more knowledgeable agency force. Direct writer advocates state that the insurance buyer enjoys much lower costs and greater specialization in certain coverage areas.

SELECTING AN AGENT OR BROKER

Agents and brokers representing various companies can get quotations from the non-direct-writing underwriters but not the direct-writing companies. While it may be faster and more convenient to deal with the direct-writing companies, an independent agent or broker enables the insured to have a local contact who will shop around among the underwriters for the best policy and coverages for the insured's operation. Perhaps the most important factor is that in the event of a claim, the local agent or broker as the intermediary will represent the insured in any dealings with the company. This is not to say that the direct-writing companies are incompetent. They are very competent, and in many cases they are less expensive. Avemco, a direct-writer and now part of HCC Insurance Holdings, Inc., has an exceptionally fine reputation in the industry in handling fixed base operator accounts including fair claim treatment and loss prevention and engineering services. An insured must select an agent or broker carefully. The agent or broker must have an in-depth knowledge of the insurance business. Other than by reputation or experience, it is difficult for the insurance buyer to predetermine the level of competence. If the agent or broker has acquired professional designations, like *Chartered Property and Casualty Underwriter* (*CPCU*) *or Chartered Life Underwriter* (*CLU*), then a commitment has been made to acquire insurance knowledge because these designations are awarded only after passing 10 examinations requiring about four years of study. In 1998 the Aviation Insurance Association established their international *Certified Aviation Insurance Professional* (*CAIP*) program in which individuals can take a certification exam upon completing a series of courses. It is anticipated that the CAIP designation will become the standard of professionalism in the aviation insurance industry.

The agent or broker must also have time and facilities for providing necessary services; good contacts with the insurance market so that prompt and favorable action for clients can be obtained; knowledge of insurers to use for special situations; an effective claim follow-up service; and finally, the respect and cooperation of the clients, competitors, insurers, and claims adjusters. An agent's competitors are valuable source of information.

It has been said that "if you have the right agent or broker, the price is right. If you have the wrong agent or broker, no price is right. " Many agents and brokers have considerable experience in placing the more familiar lines of property and casualty insurance. Most of the risks the general agent or broker handles are far more standardized than aviation lines. For example, the average FBO presents a number of risks which the average agent or broker, being unaware of how an FBO operates, would have no idea how to handle. How can agents recognize loss exposures if they are unable to recognize the differences in methods of operations?

We might use a general practitioner for our more common medical ailments, but not for open heart surgery. The analogy holds for the insurance industry. While an agent may be extremely competent in the general areas of property and casualty insurance, the individual may have very little aviation insurance experience or it might be limited to a few business and pleasure risks.

An insured must consider an agent's or broker's years of experience in the insurance business and the breadth of exposure to the various lines. Does the agent primarily handle personal lines, small or large accounts, or across-the-board business? Does the agent specialize in aviation insurance? What types of risks are handled? Which markets are represented? Is there any experience in dealing with aviation claims? How long has the agent been placing aviation risks? Has the agent attended seminars or courses, or received other specific instruction on aviation insurance such as a company correspondence course? Is anyone in the office an active pilot? Answers to these questions help the insured make an informed decision.

INDEPENDENT ADJUSTING SERVICES

Normally an insured will notify the agent or broker first in the event of a loss. While all of the aviation insurers have claims personnel, the company will generally assign the loss to one of the number of independent adjusters located throughout the country. Agents and brokers work very closely with these adjusters as well as company claims personnel in handling the claim. An organization which represents many of these independent adjusters is called the *Organized Flying Adjusters*.

KEY TERMS

- United States Aircraft Group (USAIG)
- Associated Aviation Underwriters (AAU)
- AIG Aviation, Inc.
- ACE USA Aerospace
- British Aviation Insurance Group (BAIG)
- Global Aerospace
- HCC Aviation Insurance Group
- Avemco Insurance Company
- Phoenix Aviation Managers, Inc.
- Lloyd's of London
- Syndicates
- Lloyd's brokers
- *Best's Insurance Reports: Property-Liability*
- Front companies
- Agent
- Broker
- *World Aviation Directory*
- Aviation Insurance Association (AIA)
- Chartered Property and Casualty Underwriter (CPCU)
- Chartered Life Underwriter (CLU)
- Certified Aviation Insurance Professional (CAIP)
- Organized Flying Adjusters

REVIEW QUESTIONS

1. When did the first combined aircraft hull and liability policies appear in the market? Why did it take until this time?
2. Who are the two major domestic aviation insurance groups? Describe the classes of business they write. Which major insurance company underwrites aviation risks for its own account and is not a member of a group? Name four other aviation insurance markets. Who is the largest direct writer?
3. What is a Lloyd's syndicate? Can any agent or broker place business directly with Lloyd's of London? What is the role of the lead underwriter? The Lloyd's brokers?
4. What is *Best's Insurance Reports*? What are the advantages and disadvantages of selecting a direct-writing company? What are so-called front companies?
5. Discuss some of the things that an insured must consider in selecting an insurer. Why might it not be a good practice to buy aviation insurance on price alone?
6. What is the difference between agents and brokers?
7. Why is it important for an agent or broker placing aviation business to have an understanding of the aviation industry? What characteristics should an insured consider in selecting an agent or broker?

PART TWO
PRINCIPLES OF INSURANCE AND RISK MANAGEMENT

Chapter 4

Risk and Insurance

OUTLINE

Concept of Risk
Classifications of Risk
Factors Affecting Risk
Fundamental Characteristics of Insurance
Insurance as a Method for Handling Risks
Probability Theory and the Law of Large Numbers
Requirements of an Insurable Risk
Social Values of Insurance
Reinsurance

OBJECTIVES

At the end of this chapter you should be able to:
Define risk and explain how it relates to insurance.
Define and differentiate degree of risk and chance of loss.
Explain the classifications of risk.
Explain the following types of loss exposures: personal, property, liability, and failure of others.
Discuss the burden of risk and its transferability.
Define insurance and explain its fundamental characteristics.
Define the law of large numbers and state its significance in insurance.
Identify the requirements for an insurable risk.
Explain the social values of insurance.
Define reinsurance.
Differentiate between facultative and treaty reinsurance and illustrate quota share, surplus share, and excess of loss reinsurance.

CONCEPT OF RISK

Individuals and businesses are surrounded by innumerable risks every day. Risks are pervasive. Even the water we drink and the air we breathe involve risk. Pollution can cause an unlimited amount of financial loss from lost wages, extensive medical expenses, condemned real estate, and changes in production processes necessitated by social pressures and governmental regulations. Risks exist regardless of awareness. Through the years, research has shown that exposure to certain elements in the environment will eventually cause severe health problems. Examples include lead and mercury poisoning, carcinogens like asbestos, red dye # 2, agent orange, and cigarettes.

What is the meaning of the term risk? Risk is a concept with multiple meanings depending upon the context, and discipline in which it is used. A statistician, economist, decision theorist, and an insurance theorist would all define risk differently. The following are examples of various definitions of risks:

- Chance of loss; possibility of loss; or uncertainty.
- The dispersion of actual from expected results.
- Variation in outcomes.
- The probability of an outcome different from the one expected.

Even though different, these definitions do have two common threads: uncertainty as to outcome, and a loss of some kind. The definition that facilitates communication and understanding of risk as it applies to insurance is concise: *risk* is the uncertainty concerning financial loss. Examples of risk are everywhere, ranging from the unavoidable to those assumed by choice, i.e., the risk of losing one's pilots license because of poor health or the risk of starting an air taxi service. Indeed, anyone who owns property automatically assumes the risk of financial loss by such perils as fire, windstorm, theft, or liability for negligence by their use. The inability to predict with accuracy when these perils may cause losses is a risk that property owners acquire with ownership. Insurance is purchased to transfer these risks resulting from perils which an individual or business may face each day. Therefore, the major function of insurance is to substitute certainty for uncertainty in one's personal or business activities. Insurance does not remove the risk of misfortune, because the mere fact that an aircraft is insured does not guarantee that it will not be stolen or destroyed. What insurance does accomplish is to provide full or partial compensation in the event an insured property is lost or damaged.

Underwriters often use the word risk in a different manner to describe the object of potential loss, or the object insured. Thus, an aircraft may be referred to as "the risk" in a hull and liability policy. Underwriters will also refer to the different uses of aircraft such as business and pleasure, industrial aid, airline, commercial, and so forth as different "classes of risk."

Loss

As was mentioned above, risk involves the possibility of a financial loss. Insurance is widely purchased because people are anxious to avoid loss. *Loss* may be defined as the unintentional parting with something of value. The adjective unintentional is an essential component of this definition. If an FBO owner gives his chief pilot an expensive watch for meritorious service, he has certainly parted with something of value. He would probably not admit that he had suffered a loss. The theft of a radio is an obvious loss because the owner has unintentionally parted with the value of the property. Loss does not necessarily imply the loss of a tangible article. For example, a person who is responsible for another pilot while flying an airplane and becomes liable for damages resulting from his negligence, has lost property surely as much as a person who loses possession of a tangible object.

Chance of loss is the long-run relative frequency of a loss. If we place all risks on a continuum with the two ends represented by 0 and 1, the 0 position says that there is no chance of a loss occurring. At the other end, 1, the chance of loss is 100 percent because the event is certain to happen. In both of these extremes, there is no risk because there is no uncertainty. The closer the chance of loss moves on the continuum toward the 1 position, the more likely a risk manager will seek insurance to transfer the burden of loss. Chance of loss may conveniently be expressed as a fraction, and it indicates the probable number of losses out of a given number of exposures and expresses it as a percentage. Expressed as a fraction, the numerator represents the probable number of losses, and the denominator represents the number of times that the event could possibly occur. For example, if 1,000 aircraft are exposed to the peril of theft and 10 of them can be expected to be stolen each year, we can say that the chance of loss is 10/1000 or 1 percent.

Degree of risk is related to the likelihood of an occurrence and can be defined as the accuracy with which losses can be predicted. Situations with a high probability of loss are riskier than those with a low probability, and have a greater degree of risk. The distinction between chance of loss and degree of risk can be clarified by using the data in Table 4. 1. The chance of loss in each company for year six is 6 percent (average loss of 3/50). Since the fleet size is 50, the expected loss would be 3 aircraft. Charter Co. A's annual losses varied from 2 to 4, whereas Charter Co. B's varied from 0 to 7. The actual loss experience is more stable for Charter Co. A. Therefore,

Table 4.1 Aircraft Losses in Two Similar Charter Companies Fleet Size =50 Aircraft Each

	Year					
	1	2	3	4	5	6
Charter Co. A Loses	2	4	2	3	4	(3)
Charter Co. B Loses	7	1	2	0	5	(3)

actual losses are more predictable because of the low degree of variability. The more predictable the loss, the smaller the degree of risk. Even though the chance of loss is the same (6 percent) for each company, the degree of risk is smaller for Charter Co. A.

Insurance companies generally find it imprudent to insure exposures which are likely to occur in a large number of cases, say 25 to 50 percent of the total number of risks outstanding. Chance of loss and degree of risk are important in insurance because they are the basis upon which rates are established. A reasonable degree of accuracy in measuring loss probabilities is necessary if adequate and equitable insurance premiums are to be developed. In addition, the chance of loss and degree of risk affect the decision how risks should be handled by the risk manager. If the chance of loss is high, risk avoidance or risk retention coupled with a major loss-prevention program might be the best method of dealing with an identified risk. On the other hand, if the chance of loss is quite small, the best approach may be to simply ignore the risk.

CLASSIFICATIONS OF RISK

The classification of risk is important in risk management because it identifies those risks that are the primary responsibility of the risk manager, and must be dealt with in an organized and systematic manner. By using the definition of risk as uncertainty concerning financial loss, all risks that do not have financial consequences have been eliminated from consideration by the risk manager.

Risks can be divided into static risks and dynamic risks. This classification was made by Alan H. Willett, in his book *The Economic Theory of Risk and Insurance*, 1951. *Static risks* are caused by the normal perils of nature and the dishonesty of other individuals, and involve either the damage or destruction of the asset or a change in its possession as a result of dishonesty or human failure. Static losses occur over time with regularity, and as a result, are generally predictable. *Dynamic risks* are associated with changes, especially changes in human wants and improvements due to technology. Market depreciation resulting from consumer needs and wants changing, and losses due to product obsolescence are examples of dynamic losses. Although dynamic losses affect a large number of individuals and businesses, they are less predictable than static losses because they do not occur with any predictable regularity. Dynamic risks are not the responsibility of the risk manager. Since static losses are predictable and are eligible for transfer to an insurance company, they are the responsibility of the risk manager.

Risks may also be divided into fundamental and particular risks. This distinction is based on C. A. Gulp's discussion of risk in his text *Casualty Insurance*, 1956. *Fundamental risks* are group risks that are impersonal in origin and effect. They are primarily caused by social, political, or natural occurrences. Because they are group risks, they affect large portions of the population simultaneously. Examples of fundamental risks include war, unemployment, drought, and natural disasters like floods. The losses from these types of exposures are so great that the federal government through social insurance programs and subsidization has accepted the burden of loss. *Particular risks* are personal in origin and effect and tend to arise out of individual occurrences. Examples of particular risks are the loss of income due to death or disability, and the loss of property by such perils as fire, windstorm, theft and vandalism. The payments to others for injury and property damage caused by negligence are additional examples. Since particular risks are individual, they are inappropriate for social insurance or governmental subsidy, thus are the responsibility of the risk manager.

The most useful classification of risks from the risk management perspective divides risks into pure risks and speculative risks. Albert H. Mowbray, *Insurance, Its Theory and Practice in the United States*, 5th edition, 1961, is responsible for this distinction. A *pure risk* exists when there is a chance of loss, but not a chance of gain. When a pilot takes title to an airplane, there is a possibility that something may happen to damage or destroy the airplane. If a loss should occur, there is no chance for a gain in value. In contrast, a *speculative risk* is one that involves the possibility of a loss or a gain. Gambling is a good example of a speculative risk. Similarly, when an FBO embarks on a new charter service or establishes a flight school, it assumes speculative risk. The investment required to start up these businesses may be lost if the target market does not accept the service. Certainly the FBO fully anticipates a profit from the introduction of this new service.

The distinction between pure risks and speculative risks is important because speculative risks are not transferable to an insurance company. Insurance only deals with pure risks. Insurance is not designed to enable the insured to realize a profit from a covered loss, but only to protect the asset already owned. The insurance contract, therefore, does not bring into existence any new risks but offers protection against a risk that is already present. By purchasing insurance, property owners are not seeking to enrich themselves at the expense of anyone else, but merely to protect what they already possess. Figure 4.1 summarizes the classifications of risk and shows that those on the left side—pure, static, and particular—are considered the responsibility of the risk manager. Because these risks are individual risks and their occurrences are predictable they can, if desired, be transferred to an insurance company. The right side includes risks that are quite real and do impact the operating efficiencies of a business. Other responsible persons and committees within the organization manage these risks, particularly speculative and dynamic ones.

Classifications of Pure Risks

Because risk managers have the responsibility of managing pure risks, it is useful to describe the various pure risks faced by individuals and business firms. Even though the word “risk” is used to denote the property or person exposed to losses, it is more prevalent to use the term *loss exposure* to identify the possibility that a particular property or person may suffer loss from a specific peril. Pure risks that exist for individuals or organizations may cause personal, property, or liability exposures.

Personal risk exposures involve those situations in which there is a possibility of loss of income or property as a result of the person’s inability to earn an income. Earning power is exposed to the following three perils: premature death, long-term disability from accident or illness, and advanced age. Life, accidental death and dismemberment, long-term disability income and loss of license insurance are examples of insurance designed to protect against personal loss exposures.

Aircraft owners and operators face the possibility of not only direct loss to their airplane, but also indirect losses that are called *consequential losses*. If an airplane is damaged by a windstorm, the *direct loss* is the actual cost of repairs. The *indirect losses* are the time and effort required to arrange for the repairs, the loss of use of the aircraft while repairs are being made, and the additional cost of renting a substitute airplane. Property risks, then, involve the following three types of losses: 1) direct loss to the property, 2) loss of use of the property or its ability to generate

RISK

PURE	SPECULATIVE
STATIC	DYNAMIC
PARTICULAR	FUNDAMENTAL

Figure 4.1 Classifications of Risk

revenue, and 3) additional costs incurred due to the direct loss. Aviation hull coverage with a Loss of Use Endorsement is an example of insurance designed to protect against these property exposures.

Under our system of law, a person can be held responsible for causing injury or damage to the person or property of others through negligence or carelessness. In certain circumstances, liability may be imputed to the owner of an airplane, or the owner of an airport, even though others caused the incident. Liability may also result from intentional interference with other persons or their property. Examples include assault, false imprisonment, libel and slander, and trespassing over or on others' property. Thus individuals or business firms are exposed to the possibility of liability loss by having to pay the cost to defend themselves against lawsuits. In addition, there is the potential loss of accumulated assets or future income that is needed to pay damages awarded to third parties by juries. An airport owner purchasing a Commercial General Liability policy with a Personal Injury Protection Endorsement is an example of insurance that is available to protect against liability exposures.

FACTORS AFFECTING RISK

There are two factors that work together to cause losses. They are perils and hazards. A *peril* is the actual cause of a loss such as a fire, windstorm, theft, collision, negligence, crime, premature death, or any number of other causes. The cause of a loss is often casually called a risk. From a risk management standpoint, it is more correct to define risk as uncertainty about financial loss, and peril as the cause of the loss. Perils may be grouped according to their origin as either natural, human, or economic. Natural perils include floods, mud slides, windstorm, and hail among many others. These types of perils are largely beyond risk management control. Human perils include dishonesty, vandalism, and acting negligently. The frequency and severity of these perils can be controlled to some extent through proper selection techniques, and loss control measures. Economic perils are classified as speculative risks and are not the responsibility of risk management. These perils stem from the actions of large number of persons or governments or loss caused by changes in the business cycle that result in unemployment and loss of purchasing power. Whether or not a peril is covered by an insurance policy can be determined only by examining the insuring agreements and the exclusion section of the policy.

Hazards are the various factors that contribute to uncertainty in any given situation. It is common to speak of a hazard as anything that may conceivably bring about a loss, whereas a peril is used to denote the factor that actually causes the loss. Another way of looking at hazards is to consider them as factors that contribute to the possibility of loss.

There are physical, moral, and morale hazards. Location, construction (in the case of a building) and their use can represent *physical hazards* which are objective characteristics increasing the chance of a loss. An aircraft tied down at an airport located near a high crime area like south Florida would certainly be more susceptible to loss by theft than one tied down in Asheville, North Carolina. Construction affects the probability and severity of loss. While no building is fireproof, some types of construction are less susceptible to loss from fires and windstorms than others. Use of the property may also create physical hazards. A light single-engine aircraft used exclusively for flight instruction by a fixed base operator will have a greater probability of loss than the same aircraft operated by an individual for personal use who has 500 logged hours in the airplane.

Moral hazard is an individual characteristic of the insured that increases the probability of loss. Dishonesty or lack of integrity in an individual can increase the chance of loss to 100 percent. For example, dishonest insureds increase arson losses. Insureds have been known to try to over insure or inflate the value of an aircraft and then destroy it by some means to collect the insurance. Insurance companies make every effort to avoid the moral hazard because in theory it is uninsurable. Underwriters attempt to determine if there is a moral hazard by obtaining credit and inspection reports and character references.

Morale hazards, unlike moral hazards, do not involve dishonesty. Instead, morale hazards represent an attitude of carelessness and lack of concern that increases the chance of a loss occurring. This indifference to loss is due to the realization of the insured that losses will be reimbursed by the insurance company. Poor housekeeping on the part of an FBO by allowing spare parts, oily rags, and trash to accumulate in a hangar are examples of morale hazards. Morale hazard is also exemplified when aircraft owners lend their planes to others without checking licenses, total hours, and hours in the particular aircraft.

Because some hazards exist in all lines of insurance, companies are vitally interested in the individuals and business firms they insure. *Adverse selection* may be defined as insuring a group of risks which represents an above- average expectation of loss. Adverse selection may also be defined as the tendency of poor risks to seek insurance. Individuals with a family history of coronary artery disease are more likely to seek adequate health insurance than individuals without this history. When workers' compensation insurance companies require hangar inspections and life insurance companies require physical examinations, it is not their intent to insure only the very best of risks. Rather, their purpose is to make sure that they obtain an average spread of risks. It is a motto in insurance circles that companies must select or they will be selected against.

FUNDAMENTAL CHARACTERISTICS OF INSURANCE

There are two fundamental characteristics of insurance:

- transferring or shifting risk from one person or business firm to a group
- sharing in the losses when they occur.

If insurance did not exist, the burden of losses due to individual carelessness or acts of God would remain with the owner of the property. If another caused the loss, common law allows the injured party to shift the burden of the loss to the other party. To be successful in this shift, the injured party must prove negligence in a court of law and the negligent party must have sufficient resources to pay for the damages awarded by the court. Since many risks subject persons and businesses to unacceptable levels of potential loss, insurance is purchased to automatically transfer the burden of loss and to provide the resources when required to pay others for negligent actions.

INSURANCE AS A METHOD FOR HANDLING RISK

The major purpose of insurance is to provide security for individuals and companies by means of a group operation of combining risks. Insurance enables the individual or company to obtain greater protection by combining with others who are also exposed to this risk than they could obtain by meeting it themselves. The major social advantage of insurance is that it permits spreading risks so that a loss, which would be unbearable for one person or company, may be borne with relative ease by a large number of insureds.

Corporations are licensed to sell insurance policies in one or more states. In order to meet losses and to pay for their operating expenses, insurance companies establish rates, which are the prices for a given amount of insurance. The insurance contract is often referred to as a *policy* to distinguish it from other legal documents.

Insurance is often referred to as an "intangible" since the policyholder receives in essence a piece of paper rather than a physical product. In exchange for a premium, the company promises to pay in the event of loss. Because the benefits of insurance often lie in the future and individuals and companies are not aware of all the risk to which they are exposed, insurance companies have generally found it necessary to employ agents to sell their products to the public. The purpose of the agent is to explain policies to the public and to convince potential clients of the benefits of insurance.

Definition of Insurance

Insurance may be defined in many ways, depending upon the standpoint from which it is viewed.

1. From a legal standpoint, insurance is a contract whereby the insurance company agrees to make payments to a party, generally called the *insured*, should the event insured against in the contract occur. Thus, we may look upon all insurance as a series of contracts whereby the insurance company agrees to indemnify the insured against certain losses. The principle of indemnity applies to all lines of insurance except life, accident, and sickness. *Indemnify* simply means to make the insured whole, to return his property to the state that it was in prior to the loss no better and no worse.
2. From a social standpoint, we may look upon insurance as a method of combining a large enough group of units to make the loss predictable. This method enables individuals or companies to obtain insurance at a reasonable rate and thus to protect themselves against the possibility of unforeseen losses.
3. From an accounting standpoint, insurance may be defined as a method of substituting a small certain loss for a large uncertain loss. In other words, in purchasing insurance the insured suffers a monetary loss by paying a small premium that he would otherwise not have to pay; in return, however, he obtains protection against the possibility of a large loss that may or may not occur.

PROBABILITY THEORY AND THE LAW OF LARGE NUMBERS

USAIG agrees to insure an aircraft hull valued at $800,000 against physical damage for $0.75 cents per $100 of value or $6,000 per year. How can it afford to pay $800,000 to the owner of this airplane in the event of a total loss when it only collected $6,000? How can it be reasonably confident that all of the premiums collected will be sufficient to pay its claims? A brief discussion on the law of large numbers and probability theory will assist in understanding the answers to these two questions.

The law of large numbers can be illustrated by flipping a coin. It is obvious that flipping a quarter one time will result in a 50/50 chance that the coin will land on heads. Since the coin has no memory, the next flip of the quarter will have the same 50/50 odds that heads will appear again. How many heads would you expect if the quarter was flipped 10 times, 25 times, and 1,000 times? Only with the 1,000 flips will the outcome be reasonably predictable. (500 heads and 500 tails) What appears to be an out and out guess, becomes instead a predictable experience if the event is

Table 4.2 Sample 1,000 Airplanes- Average Value $60,000

Year	Aircraft Destroyed	Difference	Difference Squared
1	10	0	0
2	7	3	9
3	13	3	9
4	9	1	1
5	11	1	1

repeated a sufficient number of times. The *law of large numbers* can be defined as a device for reducing risk by combining a sufficient number of homogeneous exposure units (airplanes, automobiles, houses, etc.) to make their individual losses collectively predictable. In other words, a large number of coin flips is required for the underlying probability of 50 percent heads and 50 percent tails to become a reality. It is obvious that the coin flip is useful for illustrating the law of large numbers but is not practical for insurance companies to assist them in determining the chance of loss on insured aircraft. They must use the empirical method that is the statistical manipulation of past history to predict future losses with confidence. Statistical inference is the tool used. Table 4.2 is a five-year historical sample of aircraft losses and will be used to explain how predictions about future losses of the total population of similar airplanes could be made. Chance of loss is .01 of 1 percent. (average loss 10/tota1 exposure 1,000) If the statistical analysis stopped here, then the insurance company would predict that out of each 1,000 airplanes, 10 would suffer a loss in any one year. Because the range of loss in the sample is between 10 and 13 losses, preparing to pay for only 10 losses may prove to be inadequate.

One of the most popular measures of dispersion in a group of historical losses is called *standard deviation*. Standard deviation is a statistical calculation that measures the concentration of the losses about their mean or average, and aids in improving the accuracy for predicting future losses. In the above sample, the mean is 10 and the standard deviation is 2. The smaller the standard deviation in relation to the mean, the less the dispersion or variation and the more consistent are the losses.

In a normal population of airplanes, automobiles, homes, etc., 68.27 percent of the losses will fall within the range of the mean minus or plus 1 standard deviation (8 to 12 losses), 95.45 percent of the losses will lie within the range of the mean minus or plus 2 standard deviations (6 to 14 losses), and the range of 3 standard deviations (4 to 16 losses) will include 99.73 percent of all losses. With the use of standard deviation, the insurance industry has a tool to predict future losses with confidence, which allows it to charge appropriate premiums, and assures financial stability.

Using the sample data with a mean of 10 and a standard deviation of 2, there is 95.45 percent probability that losses for year 6 will lie between 6 and 14 losses. If 99.73 percent certainty is desired, then the actual losses will fall between 4 and 16 losses. This use of statistical inference can be applied to all homogeneous units in the total population and helps explain how an insurance company can determine premium rates at the beginning of the policy year which establishes adequate reserves to pay the expected losses.

Requirements for an Insurable Risk

It is not possible to insure every personal and business risk. Certain criteria or requirements must be met.

1. *A large number of homogeneous risks must be present.* Since insurance de-

pends upon the law of large numbers, it is essential that the insurance company be able to insure a large number of homogeneous risks so that losses will be predictable and an adequate premium may be determined before policies are sold. Where the insurance is such that few persons would be interested in its purchase, its issuance is usually not practical. Insurance in these cases is not impossible, however, and policies to cover unusual hazards are written by a few markets.

Unlike automobile insurance, aircraft risks represent a considerably smaller number of exposure units. In addition, aircraft risks can vary a great deal depending upon the use and the qualifications of the pilot. Aircraft types and values include a wide range, from low valued older single-engine aircraft to multimillion dollar jets. All these factors compound the underwriter's problem of developing a homogeneous grouping of risks for rating purposes and still have a sufficient number of aircraft to obtain credibility in the rating structure.

2. *The number of losses must be predictable to a reasonable degree.* The price that an insurance company charges is directly related to the number and extent of the losses it expects. In order to establish a rate, the underwriter must have some basis upon which to determine the probable losses. Because of the catastrophic nature of aviation risks, this also is a difficult factor. A company may enjoy reasonably good experience for a period of years and then several catastrophes could wipe out all accumulated reserves. The ultimate nightmare of any aviation underwriter is to have two jumbo jets colliding over New York City at rush hour.

   In the case of new risks, such as the insurance on the first wide-body jet or a new satellite, there is no adequate basis for determining the rate. The insurance must be either refused or else must be written at a premium that is only a guess.
3. *The object to be insured must be of sufficient value to warrant the purchase of insurance.* Insurance is only practical when the loss of the insured article will cause some financial hardship to the individual. People generally do not insure objects of very small value such as fountain pens and pencils. Insurance is not practical since the cost of transferring such risks would be disproportionate to the value of the item. Where the article may easily be re placed from current income, insurance is seldom feasible. It should also be noted that insurance is not designed to cover ordinary repair and maintenance costs. When the article is one that will gradually wear out, insurance cannot be written to cover the "wear and tear hazard."
4. *The loss must be accidental.* Insurance is not designed to cover losses that are certain to occur. Preferably the loss should be both accidental and outside the control of the insured. An accident normally means an event which is unexpected, unforeseen, and outside the control of the insured.

   Underwriters exclude damage, under the physical damage portion of an aircraft hull and liability policy, which is "*due and confined to the wear and tear deterioration*" and so forth. Consequently, an engine that breaks down because it is improperly maintained would not be covered. However, if the engine stopped while in flight, causing a crash with resulting damage, the aircraft would be covered including the engine.
5. *The event insured against must be unlikely to occur to all insured risks simultaneously.* Insurance companies are interested primarily in situations where the loss may be expected to occur to only a very small percentage of the exposed units at any given time. Underwriters normally exclude losses arising out of war, rebellion, insurrection, and so forth because any of these

events could affect all insureds at the same time. In addition, it is quite common for underwriters to maintain mapping books in which they keep track of all aircraft risks at a particular airport. Too many risks at one location could result in a catastrophic loss, for instance, if a tornado hit that particular airport.

6. *The loss must be definite*. It must be difficult or impossible for the insured to pretend that he has suffered a loss when he has not done so. Life insurance is ideal from this standpoint, since it is rather difficult to feign death.

SOCIAL VALUES OF INSURANCE

Insurance plays an important role in our economy in a number of ways.

1. *Insurance introduces security into personal and business situations*. The purpose of all forms of insurance is to provide payment in the event of unexpected losses. Insurance acts as a stabilizing factor in protecting both businesses and individuals against unexpected losses. The unique value of insurance lies in its ability to grant a large amount of protection in return for a small premium. It is only through the purchase of insurance that many of the personal and business risks, which confront every individual, can be successfully met.
2. *Insurance serves as a basis of credit, especially in business situations*. Without adequate insurance protection no financial institution would lend money for the purchase of capital goods.
3. *Insurance provides a means of capitalizing earning power*. Every person, in a materialistic sense, possesses a monetary value based upon his future earnings. The greater the future earnings, the greater is the present "life value" of the person. The death of a working individual is no less disastrous from a monetary standpoint than is the destruction of an income-producing machine. Payments in the event of death or disability are largely based upon an estimate of the deceased individual's future earnings. Future earnings will depend upon such factors as the individual's annual income, present age, and state of health.
4. *Insurance aids in the development of the economy*. Large reserves are set up to meet future policy obligations, and these reserves are invested throughout the economy. Life insurance companies, such as Metropolitan and Prudential, were a major source of funding for major air carriers when they accepted their first jumbo jets in the early 1970s.
5. *Insurance performs a social function by analyzing risks and making protection available at a reasonable cost*. Since risk is their business, insurance companies have become experts at analyzing the risks to which businesses and individuals are all exposed. Insurance companies maintain large loss prevention and engineering staffs that assist businesses in reducing hazards. Safety inspectors from the insurance company are often located at a major insured's facility and work closely with company personnel in developing and managing safety programs.
6. *Insurance distributes the cost of accidents among a large group of persons*. We have seen that insurance may be defined as a method of substituting a small certain loss for a large uncertain loss. By distributing the cost of accidents among a very large group of persons, the cost of such misfortunes can be more easily borne.
7. *Loss-prevention methods are encouraged*. By allowing discounts for certain loss prevention methods, insurance companies provide a financial incentive for business firms to improve their safety measures. For example, the intro duction of sprinkler systems is often financially advantageous to an insured

because of the consequent reduction in fire insurance rates. Companies will offer the most attractive rates to corporate fleet operators that have provided for recurrent flight training for their crews.

8. *Insurance agents provide a professional service.* The tendency today is not to sell policies on a hit-or-miss basis; rather the goal of the better agencies and brokers is to develop a clientele of satisfied policyholders who will look to them for their insurance needs and who will recommend their services to others. Agents survey the needs of their clients in a systematic manner and tailor coverages to fit these needs.
9. *Insurance reduces cost.* Insurance may actually enable a company to sell its products or services at a lower cost, because through insurance the insured is able to cover many business risks for a small premium. If the company were unable to do so through insurance, it would be necessary to charge a higher price for products or services to compensate for these risks.

REINSURANCE

Most risk managers have little direct connection with reinsurance or the reinsurance market. Due to the reinsurance mechanism, the tasks of selecting and working with insurance companies and trying to maintain a balance between coverages, costs, and services provided are much more efficient. Reinsurance makes it easier to have all of the insurance on a large or complex risk written with one policy, with a single expiration date, rather than multiple policies with different and, possibly, conflicting terms and conditions.

Reinsurance (insurance of insurance) is an agreement between an insurance company which issues a policy, referred to as the *ceding company* or primary insurer, and another type of insurance company, called the *reinsurer*. Under the terms of the agreement, the reinsurer agrees to accept that portion of the risk that is beyond the ceding company's desired retention. The reinsurer in turn may obtain reinsurance from another reinsurer, referred to as *retrocessional reinsurance (reinsurance of reinsurance)*.

The basic purpose of all reinsurance is to spread losses—to protect an insurance company from the consequences of one or more catastrophic losses, or from the accumulation of a number of losses from a single occurrence. In addition, reinsurance does increase the insurance company's underwriting capacity to write new and large risks. When an insurance company receives a large volume of insurance on a particular aircraft or airport in excess of the amount it wishes to retain, it can reinsure the portion that exceeds its risk appetite. This procedure increases the underwriters' flexibility as to the size and type of risk and the volume of business they can accept. In addition, if the volume of business received by a company from all its agents is in excess of the amount that can be supported by the insurer's financial position, it can reinsure a portion of the business. It's a very simple process for relieving strain on the surplus and reserves of an insurance company.

The great bulk of aircraft hull and liability premiums is derived from risks which have a loss potential in excess of the retention limits of a single insurance company. In aviation, as in any other form of insurance where catastrophic risks and capacity problems exist, reinsurance plays an important role. The use of reinsurance may allow an independent insurer to rival the gross capacity of group underwriting associations on large risks. It is also used by group underwriters to spread the loss potential they have assumed. It would be difficult to imagine any sizable aviation risk where reinsurance would not be involved.

The insurance coverage for the ValuJet DC-9 that crashed into the Florida Everglades on May II, 1996, killing all 110 of its crew and passengers, illustrates how the reinsurance mechanism allows the industry to manage catastrophic losses. The airplane was insured with $4 million hull coverage and $750 million in liability insurance. According to ValuJet's certificate of insurance, obtained by the *National Underwriter* from the U.S. Department of Transportation, the insurers of the risk were Lloyd's and various London companies, 25.5 percent; U.S. Aircraft Insurance Group, New York, 20 percent; La Reunion Adrienne, Paris, 20 percent; Assurance Aviation France, Paris, 10 percent; Associated Aviation Underwriters, New York, 19 percent; American Home through AIG Aviation, New York, 7.5 percent; CIGNA (now ACE USA Aerospace), Philadelphia, 5 percent; and Somerset Aviation, New York, 2 percent. This loss was also covered by the reinsurance protections purchased by each of the mentioned insurers, illustrating the spread of risk concept of insurance and one of the major principles of reinsurance (Catastrophe Protection).

Placing Reinsurance

There are two general methods for arranging or placing reinsurance: facultative and treaty. *Facultative reinsurance* is an agreement between the ceding company and the reinsurer, in which the reinsurer becomes involved in the underwriting of the risk, and has the right to accept or reject the entire risk before coverage is granted. Facultative reinsurers evaluate each transaction and decide on terms and premiums acceptable for the risk to be covered. This reinsurance is generally purchased on extremely hazardous or unusual risks and on risks or coverage that require unusually high limits. Aircraft liability is a coverage that is usually reinsured with facultative agreements because of extremely high limits required by owners and operators of aircraft.

Treaty reinsurance, on the other hand, is an agreement where the reinsurer automatically assumes a portion of the ceding company's liability on every risk written. This type of reinsurance agreement has several advantages to the ceding company. It is automatic, so there is no delay in placing the insurance. It is also economical since there is no necessity to shop around for reinsurance. A reinsurance treaty agreement can be written to provide a broad spectrum of coverages or it can be very narrow, applying only to a particular line of business, like hull coverage. The terms of the treaty are negotiated prior to writing the coverage, and once in place, the reinsurer has no involvement in or influence over the underwriting of the coverages which will be received from the ceding company.

Types of Reinsurance

Regardless of whether the agreement is facultative or treaty, there are essentially two ways in which risk is shared under reinsurance agreements in the field of property and liability insurance. The first arrangement is called *proportional reinsurance* or pro rata reinsurance and includes quota share and surplus share reinsurance. Under *quota share reinsurance*, the ceding insurer and reinsurer agree to share premiums and losses on some predetermined proportional basis. Their limits of liability are expressed as percentages, rather than dollar amounts. For example, Insurance Company "A" and "XYZ Re" enter into a quota share agreement whereby premiums and losses are shared 60 percent and 40 percent. Thus if a $100,000 loss occurs, Company "A" would pay $60,000 and "XYZ Re" would pay $40,000 of the loss. Premiums are also shared on the same percentage basis. However, "XYZ Re" would usually be required to pay a ceding commission to "A" to help pay for the acquisition expenses incurred in writing the insurance.

The second type of proportional reinsurance is called *surplus share reinsurance*. Under this format, the reinsurer agrees to accept insurance in excess of the ceding company's retention limit or line, expressed in dollars. When a policy is written with coverage over the retention limit, the excess amount of risk is ceded to the reinsurer up to a maximum limit. Like quota share, the ceding company and the reinsurer share premiums and losses based on the fraction of total insurance retained by each company. For example, assume that "A" Insurance Company has a $300,000 retention limit (called a line) for aircraft hull insurance, and "XYZ Re's" capacity is four lines or $1,200,000 (4 X $300,000). With this arrangement, "A" can accept from its agents and brokers hull coverage up to $1,500,000 on anyone airplane. If a hull policy is written for $500,000, "A" will take $300,000 or 3/5 of the insurance and "XYZ Re" will take $200,000 or 2/5 of the insurance. These fractions determine the amount each will pay for a loss and how each will participate in the premium.

The second type of reinsurance arrangement is called *nonproportional reinsurance*. The most common form of nonproportional reinsurance is *excess of loss reinsurance* where the reinsurer becomes liable to pay only when the losses incurred by the ceding company exceed some predetermined dollar figure. For example, "A" Insurance Company is comfortable with paying $100,000 on any one hull loss. "XYZ Re" agrees to pay all losses that exceed the $100,000 limit up to $1,000,000. Since the majority of losses would be expected to take place within the $100,000 retention of the ceding company, a relatively small share of the premium would be paid to "XYZ Re". Thus, the distribution of premium and losses are *not* proportional to one another. The reinsurer, "XYZ Re" would not be involved in any loss until the size of the loss exceeds the limit of $100,000. One advantage of excess of loss reinsurance is that it allows the ceding insurer to retain the bulk of the premium while at the same time affording protection against large losses. This form of reinsurance is most appropriate for insurers writing business where both the frequency and severity of losses are reasonably predictable, and the expected smaller losses can normally be quantified as less than the total premium collected by the ceding insurer. Premiums for excess of loss reinsurance are generally calculated on a net rate basis, meaning that there is no commission paid to the ceding insurer, and the price of reinsurance reflects only the reinsurer's costs to provide the excess limits plus its required profit margin.

Reinsurance Markets

The reinsurance market, as it currently exists, began in London in 1688, with the sharing of risk conducted at John Lloyd's coffeehouse and the growth of the institution that became Lloyd's of London. The event that triggered the formation of one of the largest reinsurers today, Swiss Re, was a fire in Glarus, Switzerland, in 1861. This devastating fire threatened to bankrupt a number of the local insurers, demonstrating that the ability of local insurers to withstand unusually large claims was limited. The need for a strong local reinsurer was clear.

The domestic reinsurance market dates from around 1917, and has enjoyed major growth in premium income and capacity since World War II. All of the American aviation insurance markets employ the use of reinsurance to a greater or lesser degree depending on their retention limits.

The international reinsurance market consists of European and Asian companies that also have branch offices in the United States. The London market and the professional reinsurance companies such as Munich Re and Swiss Re (those reinsurers that conduct reinsurance business only as opposed to being a "reinsurance division of a composite insurer) play an important role in the aviation market by supporting the major airline, airport, and space risks that require large capacity in this global economy today. Another major market of reinsurance consists of the offshore companies domiciled in Bermuda, the Cayman Islands, Barbados, and the Turks and Caicos Islands. Many of these companies started as captives of large insurance companies for the purpose of providing a share of the company's insurance or reinsurance needs, while taking advantage of the very favorable tax treatment.

The global reinsurance market is undergoing dramatic structural changes and has undergone many mergers since the 1990s. With the changes in the global reinsurance landscape we now have fewer American reinsurers and larger (by size) international reinsurers. Currently, the world's five largest reinsurance groups by brand name, Munich Re, Swiss Re, Hannover Re, Berkshire Hathaway Group/Gen Re (formerly General Re), and Lloyd's of London accounted for only 17 percent of the market in 1980. In 2005 they accounted for 46 percent of the market, in terms of gross premium written.

KEY TERMS

Risk
Loss
Chance of loss
Degree of risk
Static risks
Dynamic risks
Fundamental risks
Particular risks
Pure risk
Speculative risks
Loss exposure
Consequential loss
Direct loss
Indirect loss
Peril
Hazard
Physical hazards
Moral hazards
Morale hazards
Adverse selection
Insurance
Insured
Indemnify
Law of Large Numbers
Standard deviation
Reinsurance
Ceding company
Reinsurer
Retrocessional reinsurance
Facultative reinsurance
Treaty reinsurance
Proportional reinsurance
Quota share reinsurance
Surplus share reinsurance
Nonproportional reinsurance
Excess of loss reinsurance

REVIEW QUESTIONS

1. Identify and explain the two key words found in the definition of risk.
2. Define degree of risk and chance of loss.
3. Differentiate between and give an example of pure and speculative risk.
4. What is a peril? Distinguish between physical, moral, and morale hazards.
5. Define the law of large numbers and explain its role in insurance.
6. Identify three important social values of insurance.
7. Identify the requirements for an insurable risk.
8. Differentiate between facultative and treaty reinsurance agreements.
9. Explain quota share, surplus share, and excess of loss basis of reinsurers' acceptance of risk from ceding companies.

REFERENCES

Dobbyn, John F., *Insurance Law* (2nd ed.). West Publishing Co., St. Paul, Minnesota, 1989.

Rejda, George E. *Principles of Risk Management and Insurance* (7th ed.). Addison Wesley Longman, Inc. New York, 2001.

Vaughn, Emmett J. and Therese M. Vaughn. *Fundamentals of Risk and Insurance* (9th ed.). John Wiley & Sons Inc. New York, 2003.

Chapter 5

Risk Management

OUTLINE

Development of Risk Management
The Process of Risk Management
Risk Management Techniques for Small Businesses

OBJECTIVES

At the end of this chapter you should be able to:
Discuss the evolution of risk management as a profession.
State the objective of the risk management process.
Discuss the following two steps in the risk management process: identification and measurement of risk.
Explain the importance of understanding supplemental or expansion coverages.
Explain the two major techniques for handling risk: risk control and risk finance.
Discuss the criteria used in selecting a specific technique for dealing with risks.
Discuss opportunities and risks involved in self- insurance programs.
Explain the major risk management techniques that are especially useful for small businesses

DEVELOPMENT OF RISK MANAGEMENT

On December 20, 1995, American Airlines Flight 965 from Miami crashed into a mountain on its approach to the Cali, Columbia, airport. This tragic loss of property and lives illustrates the magnitude of the problem of managing aviation risk. The experienced pilots flying the relatively new Boeing 757 were quite familiar with the terrain. Cause of the accident was initially thought perhaps to be the result of a terrorist attack or bombing. This was dismissed when it was determined that at the time of the accident, the plane was 13 miles off its intended course. The crash investigation revealed that the radar at the airport had been blown up by guerrillas in 1991 and not replaced. There were language barriers between controllers at the airport and the flight crew. Since some unusual elements of risk with this specific airport were known prior to the crash, should American Airlines have been serving the airport? This is the type of decision that the risk management process is designed to evaluate and help answer. *Risk management* deals with the systematic identification of a company's exposures to the risk of loss, and with decisions on the best methods for handling these exposures in relation to corporate profitability. Risk managers are responsible for identifying all exposures that create pure risks and establishing programs to handle them.

A company faces the challenge to assess an almost unlimited number of possible events that have financial implications. Risk management calls for familiarity with all facets of the business as well as a seasoned, balanced judgment. A professional risk manager directs the management of risk in larger corporations, such as the major air carriers, aircraft manufacturers, or large corporate fleet operators. In smaller firms, such as fixed base operators, it may be the part-time responsibility of the treasurer or controller, or the president. It is essential to assign responsibility for this vital activity so that it receives the attention it warrants and is not perceived as simply purchasing insurance policies. Whether the function is performed by a professional risk manager or another competent employee, their objective or goal is to manage pure risks to assure the financial solvency of the firm against the consequences of financial loss, at the lowest possible cost.

Prior to 1930, little thought was given to the management of pure risk. Insurance was often purchased in a haphazard manner in an attempt to deal with observed risks facing a business by an employee who was often called the *insurance manager*. Insurance management predominately dealt with selecting the agent/broker and administration of the insurance program. Risk management has evolved from insurance management by widening the scope of responsibility to both insurable and uninsurable pure risks and then selecting the appropriate technique for dealing with them.

The history of modern risk management traces its origin to 1931 when the American Management Association established its Insurance Division for exchanging information among members. In 1932, the Insurance Buyers of New York was organized. Membership included insurance managers of businesses located in the New York metropolitan area. This organization was succeeded by the American Society of Insurance Management, Inc. (A.S.I.M.) in 1955. The purpose of this organization was to serve its member entities by proactively providing the highest quality products, services, and information to manage all forms of business risk. In 1975, to reflect the evolution of risk management as a profession, the name was changed from A.S.I.M. to its current name, the *Risk and Insurance Management Society* (RIMS). RIMS serves nearly 3,800 businesses and organizations represented by over 9,200 individuals with risk management responsibilities throughout the United States and Canada. Many factors contributed to the evolution of risk management from the days of the insurance buyer to the professional risk manager of today. Some of the more important factors include:

1. Growth in size, complexity, and diversification of businesses have required centralization and delegated responsibility for the management of risk to a specialist;
2. Advancements in technology have changed the nature and structure of physical hazards as businesses strive for increases in productivity; and
3. Statutes have been passed placing greater responsibility on business to provide a safer product or service while preserving the environment. The courts have become more liberal to injured parties, and the public has become more aggressive in asserting its rights.

THE PROCESS OF RISK MANAGEMENT

The risk management task can be viewed as either a decision-making process or a management process. As a decision-making process, it is an adaptation of the scientific problem-solving technique that begins with defining the problem, searching alternatives, evaluating alternatives and selecting, implementing, and monitoring the elected alternative. In risk management, the problem is exposure to accidental financial loss. The logical sequence to deal with this problem consists of identifying and analyzing loss exposures, examining alternative techniques for dealing with those exposures, selecting the most promising techniques, implementing the chosen technique and monitoring the results to see, in fact, if the loss exposure has been dealt with efficiently. The decision-making process is both repetitive and self-reinforcing. It is repetitive because past implemented choices of handling loss exposures must be continually re-evaluated in light of the following:

- Changes in a firm's operation;
- Changes in the relative costs of alternative risk management techniques;
- Changes in legal requirements; and
- Changes in a firm's basic objectives.

It is also self-perpetuating because the final step of monitoring will often reveal the need to revise decisions when a significant change in conditions causes the risk management program to fall short of its goals. This reassessment typically requires the decision-making process to start at the beginning again.

When viewed as a management process, risk management entails the traditional four functions of management: planning, organizing, implementing, and controlling. This second view of risk management is interrelated with the overall organizational objectives to conserve assets, both material and human, and to protect the firm's ability to generate earnings. Both approaches are appropriate since the concepts of risk management are useful for both large national firms and small family-owned businesses.[1]

A formal goal statement of risk management reads: *"It is the objective of Ace Aviation, Inc. to manage, control, minimize or eliminate risk, to the end that its personnel be protected from hazards, the financial condition of the organization not be seriously jeopardized, and its material resources be conserved to the maximum extent possible and practical."*[2] The components of this overall goal can be broken down between pre-loss and post-loss objectives. Pre-loss objectives include:

- Efficiency of operations;
- Tolerable uncertainty—helping management carry out operational decisions effectively without being paralyzed by worry;
- Legality—ensure compliance with laws and regulation; and
- Humanitarian conduct—social responsibility.

Post-loss objectives include: (listed by degree of necessity—essential to desirable)

- Survival
- Continuity of operations—no interruptions;
- Profitability;
- Stability of earnings; and
- Growth.

It is the responsibility of the risk manager to direct and administer the program and to formulate and make recommendations as required. To accomplish these objectives, the risk management process involves the following steps.

Risk Identification

Risk identification is the process of systematically and continuously identifying all of the resources for which a corporation is responsible, and all of the accidental loss exposures that could materially affect these resources. This may be the most important step in the process because the risk manager cannot deal with risks that remain unidentified. It is not easy to recognize the hundreds of risks that can lead to an unexpected loss. Unless you have experienced a fire loss for example, it is difficult to realize how extensive fire losses can be. Damage to the building and its contents are obvious, but the following will illustrate the many other potential losses:

- Damage or destruction that smoke or water from dozens of fire hoses can create;
- Damage to employees' property (clothing, tools, and personal belongs) and to leased property or property left for repair;
- Cost of business lost during weeks or months required to rebuild and repair; and
- Loss of business to competitors from customers who may not return when business reopens.

The process begins with an extensive physical inspection of company facilities

Aircraft Liability and Hull

Named Insured ______________________________

Insurer ______________________ Policy # ______________ Term__________

Agency ______________________ Form ______________ Premium__________

Limits:

Bodily Injury	$__________	Each Person	$__________	Each Occ.	Incl. Pass. __________
Property Damage	$__________	Each Occ.			
B.I. & P.D.-C.S.L.	$__________	Each Occ.			Incl. Pass. __________
Vol. Settlement	$__________	Each Person	$__________	Each Acc.	Incl. Crew__________
Medical Payments	$__________	Each Person	$__________	Each Occ.	Incl. Crew__________
Physical Damage	$__________	Max.	$__________	Deductible	

On Ground __________ Taxiing & On Grouind __________ In Flight, Taxiing & On Ground __________

Loss of Use	$__________	Each Day		
Baggage Liability	$__________	Each Pass.	$__________	Each Occ.
Hanger Damage	$__________	Each Occ.		

Use Limitations:

Purpose ______________________________

Territory ______________________________

Number of Passengers ________ Pilot Warranty______________________

Insured Aircraft ______________________________

Must report non-owned aircraft used for more than ______ consecutive days.

	Have	***Need***	***Comments***
1. Broad Named Insured	______	______	______________
2. Notice: Canc. ___ Non-Ren. ___ Reduc. ___	______	______	______________
3. Notice of Loss Modification	______	______	______________
4. Cov. for Unintentional E&O in App./Dec.	______	______	______________
5. Satisfactory Other Insurance Clause	______	______	______________
6. Waiver of Subrogation	______	______	______________
7. In Accord with Umbrella	______	______	______________
8. Non-Owned Aircraft Liability	______	______	______________
9. Employees Included as Insureds	______	______	______________
10. Fellow Employee Exclusion Eliminated	______	______	______________
11. Contractual Exclusion Eliminated	______	______	______________
12. Rotor Aircraft Exclusion Eliminated	______	______	______________
13. Assault & Battery to Prevent Injury or Damage	______	______	______________
14. Permission for Use by Others & Reimbursement	______	______	______________
15. Modification of FAA Certification Requirement	______	______	______________
16. War Risks	______	______	______________
17. Automatic Increase in Value	______	______	______________
18. Foaming of Runway Costs	______	______	______________
19. Search & Rescue Costs	______	______	______________
20. Engine Mechanical Breakdown	______	______	______________
21. ______________	______	______	______________
22. ______________	______	______	______________
23. ______________	______	______	______________
24. ______________	______	______	______________
25. ______________	______	______	______________
26. ______________	______	______	______________
27. ______________	______	______	______________
28. ______________	______	______	______________

Figure 5.1 Risk Analysis Questionnaire

and operations. This survey can be reinforced by the use of a *risk analysis questionnaire* that is available from a property and casualty insurance company or its representative. Checklists of potential losses are included in the questionnaire to uncover hidden exposures common to many firms. Figure 5.1 illustrates a questionnaire to be used for aircraft liability and hull coverage. Flow charts, detailing the firm's entire operating processes, may suggest further hazards. Reports on past losses experienced by the firm can be invaluable, as can analysis of financial statements and reports.

The risk identification process is further enhanced as the risk manager becomes more aware of the types coverages that may be available from underwriting companies. For example, Host Liquor Liability exposures resulting from serving alcoholic beverages aboard the aircraft or on covered premises, might not be considered an exposure area until the risk manager becomes aware that insurance coverage for such exposures might be available. Figure 5.2 offers a list of some additional coverage features that might be available to certain risks.

As the aviation insurance industry has evolved over the years, many *"supplemental"* or *"expansion" coverages* have become available due primarily to competition among markets. Many such coverages were added to policies by special endorsement. Many have now found their way into revised and broadened policy forms (e.g., Global Aerospace's "Broad Horizon" policy form and AIG Aviation's "Gold Medallion" policy form).

Many of these broadened features were originally reserved for corporate owned, noncommercial, professionally flown and maintained turbine powered aircraft ("Industrial Aid" uses). Over time some of them have become available to smaller single-engine "Pleasure and Business" risks.

All of the features listed in Figure 5.2 may not be available from every underwriting company and may vary in content and wording. Following the list in Figure 5.2 is a brief explanation of each. Each policy or endorsement must be reviewed for specific details. (See Chapter 8 - Aircraft Hull and Liability Insurance for more discussion about typical coverages as well as some of the features listed in Figure 5.1)

Feature Comments

Below are brief descriptions of the "expansion" coverages. The descriptions are general in nature and for reference and discussion only. Actual policy and endorsement wordings should be consulted.

Aircraft Retrieval (off airport landing)

Suppose an aircraft experiences an in-flight emergency requiring an immediate landing. The pilot does a perfect landing on an available interstate highway (or open field), and there is no damage to the aircraft. Usually the DOT won't allow the aircraft to take off from the interstate or other conditions make flying the aircraft back to an airport impossible, requiring that the aircraft be dismantled, loaded on a truck, and hauled to the nearest airport for reassembly. There has been no loss since the aircraft is not damaged, therefore a standard policy does nothing. This "expansion" coverage states that, in such an event, the company will pay for the related costs to disassemble, move, and reassemble the aircraft even though there has been no physical damage to the aircraft.

Automatic Increase in Hull Value for Modification

The insured value stated in the policy automatically increases as modifications are made or equipment is added by the amount spent as evidenced by the insured's records. The insured must report the improvements to the company within 60 days and pay any resulting additional premium. Prior notification is not required.

Baggage and Personal Effects

Damage to these items is not covered in a standard policy because of the "care, custody, or control" exclusion. This feature makes an exception to the exclusion

Features	Comments
Aircraft Retrieval (off airport landing)	
Automatic Increase in Hull Value for Modification	
Baggage/Personal Effects – Property Damage	
Broad Form Definition of Aircraft	
Broad Form Definition of Named Insured	
Cancellation Notice – # of Days	
Cargo Legal Liability	
Contractual Liability	
Cost Reimbursement	
Cross Liability	
Damage to Hangar & Contents	
Delete Pilot Requirements for Maintenance Flights	
Emergency Costs (Foam Runway, etc)	
Engine Breakdown	
Excess Auto – Airport Premises	
Excess Work Comp Employer Liability	
Extra Expense – Spare Parts Rental	
Extra Expense – Substitute Aircraft	
Fellow Employee Exclusion – Deletion of	
Guest Voluntary Settlement (GVS) – Broad Form	
Hangarkeepers' Liability	
Host Liquor Liability	
Incidental Medical Malpractice	
Lay-Up Credit for Scheduled Aircraft	
Mechanics' Tools	
Mexican Liability Policy	
Mobile Equipment Liability	
Non-Owned Aircraft Liability	
Non-Owned Aircraft Medical Payments	
Non-Owned Guest Voluntary Settlement	
Non-Owned Physical Damaage to Aircraft	
Personal Injury Liability	
Premise Liability, Airport	
Premise Medical Payments	
Premium Insurance – Hull	
Products Liability, Sale of Aircraft, Parts, Maintenance	
Profit Commission on Renewal	
Search & Rescue	
Spare Parts and Engines	
Territorial Limits	
TRIA – Terrorist Risk Insurance Act	
Trip Interruption	
War Risk – Hull	
War Risk – Liability	
Approved Pilots	
Approved Uses	

Figure 5.2 Additional Coverage Features

with respect to damage to personal effects of passengers (currency and certain other property are not covered).

Broad Form Definition of "Aircraft"

Expands the definition of "aircraft" to include equipment, such as avionics, removed from aircraft even if it has been temporarily replaced. The temporary replacement equipment is also covered since it would now be a part of aircraft.

Broad Form Definition of "Named Insured"

Expands the definition of "Named Insured" to include subsidiary and parent companies as additional named insureds if financially controlled by the named insured.

Cancellation Notice - # of Days

Can extend the number of days required for prior written notice to named insured if the policy is cancelled at the request of the company. Normal notice period is 30 days.

Cargo Legal Liability

Seen more as a contingency coverage for noncommercial risks in case the named insured should carry cargo for a third party.

Contractual Liability

Covers liabilities of others that the named insured assumes under contracts. Contracts needs to be submitted to the company and additional premium, if any, paid. Does not require prior approval.

Cost Reimbursement

Permits uses where direct costs of operation of the aircraft are reimbursed to the named insured.

Cross Liability

Liability will cover claims by one insured against another.

Damage to Hangar and Contents

Covers damage to temporary use of non-owned hangars and contents that are in the care, custody, or control of the insured (otherwise excluded under the "care, custody, or control exclusion).

Delete Pilot Requirements for Maintenance Flights

Pilots employed by an FAA approved repair station are automatically approved pilots with respect to test flights after repairs.

Emergency Costs (Foam Runways, etc.)

Provides reimbursement to the named insured for incurred costs of runway or aircraft foaming, and fire, crash control, or rescue expenses.

Engine Breakdown

Writes mechanical and electrical breakdown back into policy from the "wear and tear" exclusion. Typical wear and tear and hot starts still excluded.

Excess Auto Liability - Airport Premises

Provides excess liability over insured's automobile liability for auto claims while on airport premises. Usually requires underlying auto liability limit of $1,000,000.

Excess Work Comp Employers Liability

Provides excess employers liability over insured's workers' compensation employers' liability insurance for employees injured as a passenger in insured aircraft. Usually requires underlying employer's liability limit of $1,000,000.

Extra Expense for Spare Parts Rental

Reimburses for costs of the rental of temporary replacement components that replace those damaged in a covered physical damage loss, for the period of repair. Requires a waiting period of 10 days.

Extra Expense for Substitute Aircraft

Provides reimbursement to the named insured for costs of rental or lease of a temporary replacement aircraft when the insured aircraft is being repaired following a covered physical damage loss. It does not provide coverage if another aircraft is available to insured at no cost. It only pays that portion of such costs that exceed the costs to operate the insured aircraft if it had not been damaged. A waiting period of 7 days is required.

Fellow Employee Exclusion, Deletion of

Most standard policies exclude liability coverage for a claim from an injured employee against another employee of the same employer. The workers' compensation exclusion and most state laws preclude an injured employee from making a claim against his employer if he is injured on the job. However, the pilot, if a fellow employee, could be vulnerable in such an event. Since the pilot is often a likely candidate for a liability claim, the deletion of this standard exclusion can provide liability protection for him that would not otherwise exist.

Guest Voluntary Settlement (GVS)– Broad Form

GVS coverage is broadened to include weekly indemnity and permanent and total disability. The basic GVS coverage is only for death or dismemberment as defined.

Hangarkeepers' Liability

As an "expansion coverage," this is a contingency coverage for a noncommercial operation. It provides protection if an aircraft belonging to someone else is in the care, custody, or control of the insured and is damaged as a result of the insured's negligence. Such coverage is otherwise excluded under the "care, custody, or control" exclusion.

Host Liquor Liability

Provides liability coverage for claims arising from the serving of alcoholic beverages on the insured aircraft or covered airport premises.

Incidental Medical Malpractice

This is contingency coverage for losses arising out of the furnishing of medical or emergency assistance for noncommercial operators.

Lay-up Credit for Scheduled Aircraft

This feature returns a portion of the hull premium on renewal if an aircraft is withdrawn from service for other than repair of covered damages. Normally requires a minimum lay-up period of 30-60 days and prior notice to the company.

Mechanics' Tools

Provides physical damage coverage for direct and accidental damage to or loss of mechanics tools. Does not cover "loss of use".

Mexican Liability Policy

Liability policy issued by a Mexican insurance company to meet the requirements of the Mexican government.

Mobile Equipment Liability

This is liability coverage regarding the use of equipment such as tugs, Auxiliary Power Units (APUs), etc., not subject to motor vehicle registration and designed for use principally off public roads.

Non-Owned Aircraft Liability

Extends basic liability coverage to apply to the use of a non-owned aircraft.

Non-Owned Aircraft Medical Payments

Extends basic Medical Payments coverage to apply to the use of a non-owned aircraft.

Non-Owned Guest Voluntary Settlement

Extends GVS to apply to the use of a non-owned aircraft. (See Guest Voluntary Settlement above.)

Non-Owned Physical Damage to Aircraft

Provides property damage liability if insured's negligence results in physical damage to a non-owned aircraft being operated by or in the interest of the insured.

Personal Injury Liability

Liability coverage for "personal injury" offenses including false arrest, detention or imprisonment, malicious prosecution, libel, slander, etc., arising out of aircraft operations.

Premise Liability, Airport

Extends liability coverage to include claims arising out of the use of airport areas by the insured in connection with the ownership, operation, maintenance, or use of aircraft.

Premise Medical Payments

Extends Medical Payments coverage to include losses occurring on airport areas used by the insured in connection with the ownership, operation, maintenance, or use of aircraft.

Premium Insurance – Hull

Some policies require that the entire hull premium is fully earned with respect to an aircraft on which a total loss has been paid. This feature stipulates that the earned hull premium, just as the liability premium, be calculated on a pro-rata basis.

Products Liability, Sale of Aircraft, Parts, Maintenance

Protection for claims arising out of the sale of a listed aircraft, parts, or maintenance for losses that occur during the policy period. Can cover claims from the sale of an aircraft during a prior period provided the loss occurs during the current period.

Profit Commission on Renewal

A portion of the hull premium is reimbursed on renewal depending on the amount of any hull loss paid, if any.

Search & Rescue

This provides reimbursement to the insured of expenses incurred for search and rescue operations performed by or at the request of the named insured.

Spare Parts and Engines

Physical damage coverage for spare parts and engines held in inventory for the insured aircraft.

Territorial Limits

The policy territorial limits can be extended beyond the standard the United States, Canada, Mexico, and Bahamas. The broadest extension would be "Worldwide."

TRIA – Terrorism Risk Insurance Act

Optional coverage, beyond the typical "war risk" coverages, which is mandated by the Terrorism Risk Insurance Act enacted November 26, 2002 in response to the effect on insurers of the terrorist attack on 9/11/01.

Trip Interruption

Reimbursement to the insured for reasonable expenses for food, travel, and lodging of passengers incurred from the place where the insured aircraft suffers a covered physical damage loss to the intended final destination or back to the point of origin if the trip is cancelled.

War Risk – Hull

Writes back many of the physical damage exclusions under the "war risk" exclusion such as strikes, riots, civil commotion, labor disturbances, malicious acts or acts of sabotage, and hi-jacking.

War Risk – Liability

Writes back many of the liability exclusions in the "war risk" exclusion (see War Risk – Hull above).

Other exposures might exist where there are generally no coverages offered by the usual aviation insurance underwriters. Liability arising out of environmental damages from fuel or deicing chemical spills is excluded in most aviation insurance policies ("Pollution Exclusion"). Environmental Pollution Liability insurance would be sought from specialty underwriters specializing in that type insurance.

Coverage for engine breakdown due to wear and tear is excluded under aviation insurance policies. On some larger jets with engines worth around $250,000 and above, engine breakdown insurance might be available, usually from a Surplus Lines market (e.g., Lloyd's of London, etc.)

Figure 5.2 and explanations from article by Darrell Hyde on CS&A Aviation Insurance's web site under "HELPFUL ARTICLES"; www.aviationinsurance.com

The risk manager, often working closely with an agent or broker, looks for five major types of risk. They are:

1. *Property losses*. Property that is owned or under the care, custody, or control of the business is examined. This involves an extensive physical inspection of the company facilities and operations. Property can be divided into two broad classes, *real property,* and *personal property*. Real property includes unimproved land, buildings, and other structures attached to land. Insurable value of property is rather easily obtained either internally or by outside appraisal. Value of unimproved land is more difficult to establish and is influenced by location, mineral resources, and vegetation. Losses due to earth movement, fire, and rising waters can have major future value implications. Personal property includes all property other than real property and is classified as either tangible or intangible. Examples of tangible personal property include money and securities, accounts receivables, inventory, furniture, equipment, machinery, data processing hardware, software and media. Mobile personal property is an important subclass due to their large dollar cost and liability exposures associated with its use. Airplanes, autos, trucks, and earth-moving equipment are examples. Property may be damaged by many common perils: fire, theft, windstorm, hail, carelessness, and vandalism. Intangible property would include goodwill, copyrights, licenses, and leases. This type of property is most difficult to value.

   In assessing the value of property, a risk manager must select a valuation standard. No one standard is appropriate for all classes of property. The following represent the choices of arriving at an insurable value:

   - Historical cost. The original cost of the property paid by the company. Generally, this is a poor indicator of the cost to replace property at today's prices.
   - Book value. The accounting term is determined by subtracting accumulated depreciation expense from historical cost. No help at all in establishing property value. A corporate jet that has been depreciated for six years has a book value of zero.
   - Replacement cost. One of the most useful standards for buildings and some personal property. If buildings are not new, then appraisals are required to determine replacement values. This is especially true for older buildings where code changes influence the cost of repairing the damage.

- Functional replacement cost. The cost of acquiring a replacement that, while not identical to the property being replaced, will perform the same function with equal efficiency. This standard is most useful for property subject to rapid changes in technology. Computer hardware offers an excellent example. A five-year-old computer is not replaceable since the particular model and technology are no longer in production. For this type of property, the standard should not be replacement cost, but functional replacement cost that would generally be at a lower valuation.
- Agreed value. Some real and personal property loss exposures lend themselves to this method. Parties to the insurance contract agree at the inception of the policy the maximum amount that will be paid in the event of a total loss. This method was used to insure ocean-going vessels and their cargo. Impossible to evaluate the extent of loss with the ship on the ocean floor. Most aircraft hull coverage is now written on this method for similar reasons.
- Market value. Established by a willing seller and a willing buyer transacting business under no compulsion to do so. As a valuation standard, this method is call actual cash value (ACV), and represents the replacement cost of an item minus its market depreciation. Very common in valuing loss potential of personal property like office contents, machinery, and autos, trucks and aircraft. Used price guides are available to assist in this process. Some personal property can be insured on a replacement basis by requesting an endorsement.

2. *Loss of use of property*. In addition to the direct loss of the property, a business may lose the use of the property while it is being repaired or replaced. For example, a charter company not only suffers the cost of repair to its airplane caused by an accident, but also the loss of revenue due to the cancellation of charter flights. Damage to buildings often triggers extra ex penses. For example an FBO may authorize overtime to shorten the interruption period, or it may reopen in temporary quarters (additional rent) using leased furniture and equipment. These losses are called indirect or consequential losses.
3. *Liability losses*. A business faces the possibility that it will be held liable for property damage or bodily injury suffered by a member of the general public or personal injury, medical expenses, and lost wages to an employee hurt on the job. For example:

    - A customer in the firm's building trips on a broken step;
    - A defect in a product causes injury to the user;
    - An employee is negligent in repairing an airplane;
    - The firm's automobile is involved in a negligent accident; and
    - An employee is seriously injured while on the job.

4. *Criminal and fraud losses*. Robbery and burglary from the outside are obvious perils. Exposure to employee theft, embezzlement, or forgery are areas of great concern in organizations with large dollar exposures or expensive inventory and they are often over looked.
5. *Key person losses*. Loss of the services of key persons through death, disabling injury or disease will often cause major reductions in revenue because their talents are difficult to replace. This is especially true in small organizations. Death of major stockholders in family-owned businesses or a general partner in a partnership present especially difficult problems of not

only loss of revenue but also the orderly transfer of their equity in the business.

Risk Measurement

Once the risks of loss have been identified, the next step is to measure both the maximum possible loss and the maximum probable loss that can occur. This data will determine the relative importance of potential losses and serve as a guide to the best techniques for risk handling and limits of coverage to be carried. For a risk manager of a large corporation, this may be a complex mathematical process using computer models involving statistical analysis and probability. For the small firm, it must, by necessity, be a process involving considerable intuition and intelligent guesswork.

Probability of loss is measured by analyzing the following four factors. *Frequency* is a measure of how often a particular type of loss will occur. Risk managers' research past loss experience of their firms to estimate future losses that may be expected. Generally, smaller losses are apt to occur more frequently than larger losses. *Severity* has to do with the amount of loss that is apt to be sustained. Again, past losses are reviewed to determine the range in cost of those losses. *Variations* in future losses, as to both frequency and severity, must be predicted. This information is essential to assist the risk manager in deciding what to do about various loss exposures. The fourth factor concerns the *impact* of a loss. Most small businesses would be able to pay out of current income a $1,000 windstorm loss, but a $10,000 fire loss would severely stress their cash reserves. A $75,000 hangar loss would probably force some to go out of business. Larger businesses could easily handle the $10,000 loss and some might be in position to absorb the loss of a $ 100,000 airplane. The impact of a particular loss, or a series of losses, will vary depending upon the size of the organization, its current financial condition, and the indirect loss potential of the damage to their property. Therefore, all losses from a single event must be considered, as should the ultimate financial impact on current and future operations. For example, on an average day an FBO may have anywhere from three to five transient aircraft stored in the tie-down area. On the weekend this number may double including several multiengine aircraft. Several times during the year around holidays or special events this number may quadruple. What limits of liability should be carried under the FBO's hangarkeepers' coverage? This is just one of a number of questions which must be answered in the risk measurement process.

Risk Handling Techniques

After the risk manager has identified and measured the risks facing the firm, a decision must be made as to how to best handle them. There are two basic approaches available to the risk manager, risk control and risk finance.

Risk control techniques are used to alter the exposure to either reduce the firm's expected property, liability, and personal losses or to make the annual loss experience more predictable. Risk control can be achieved by risk avoidance, loss prevention, loss reduction, segregation, and contractual transfer. When *risk avoidance* is employed, the risk is avoided in the first place, or the activity is discontinued once the hazards are known. A company may decide not to use private aircraft or allow employees to fly aircraft for business to avoid the potential loss exposure that comes from owning and operating an aircraft. An FBO may discontinue selling a product or providing a service when recent court decisions demonstrate a high product liability exposure. An air taxi would remove aging aircraft from its fleet to eliminate the higher crash risk that those aircraft impose. Risk control can also be achieved by using loss prevention techniques. *Loss prevention* is an attempt by companies to prevent losses from occurring by reducing hazards. This method may not eliminate all chance of loss. It reduces loss frequency without necessarily affecting all chance of loss. FBOs may establish certain procedures in parking aircraft to assure that when they bring them in and out of the hangar they avoid "hangar rash" claims. Establishing visitor areas, posting no smoking signs in the maintenance area, improving housekeeping procedures, venting paint room fumes, and giving proficiency check rides to all renter pilots are examples of loss preventive techniques that can be initiated at a moderate cost but can significantly decrease the chance of loss. If losses cannot be prevented, the use of *loss reduction* techniques is appropriate. The objective of this method is to reduce the severity of losses once they have occurred. Pre-loss methods would include erecting a firewall between two parts of a warehouse, and post-loss measures include fire alarms and automatic sprinkler systems. Examples of loss reduction methods that will dramatically reduce the extent of bodily injury and the cost of medical care and lost wages include:

- Safety programs which include first aid training;
- Frequent inspections of the premises; and
- Instructions on proper ways to lift heavy objects, handle dangerous equipment, and procedures to follow when the task requires two employees.

The *segregation* method focuses on reducing an organization's dependence on a single asset by making individual losses smaller and perhaps more predictable. This can be accomplished by either separating the property or duplicating the property. When a business uses two warehouses in different areas to store critical inventory and operates passenger and cargo aircraft at less than capacity are examples of the separating property. When the duplication strategy is used, the duplicate system is not used unless the primary system is damaged or destroyed. Examples include duplicate accounting records, spare parts, and redundancy in aircraft systems. Neither separation nor duplication will reduce the severity of loss to a single unit. Each unit might still be subject to total loss, but by following this technique, each unit is less significant to the organization.

The *contractual transfer* method uses contractual agreements to shift the loss exposure associated with an asset or activity from one firm to another. Tailoring a lease or rental agreement covering real or personal property is an example. The lessor and the lessee can apportion and transfer property and liability loss exposures. Another example involves subcontracting specific activities where people can transfer responsibility and consequently the liability for these activities.[2]

Risk finance, the second broad option, can be divided between active risk retention and risk transfer. *Active risk retention* means that the risk has been identified and measured and a decision made to absorb any losses by one of the following internal financing methods:

- Current financing;
- Establishing a designated reserve;
- Borrowing from a line of credit; and
- Establishment of a self-insurance program.

There are a great number of pure risk exposures that may be retained as a matter of policy. The extent of this risk retention will depend upon the size of the firm, its ability to pay for losses, the loss frequency, and the loss severity. For example, an FBO may decide not to insure against theft of shop tools or the loss caused by collision of older cars and trucks. In some cases, firms may decide to retain a portion of a risk by accepting insurance coverage with a deductible that represents a portion of all property losses that the insured agrees to pay. A $5,000 in motion and a $1,000 not in motion deductible in aircraft hull policies is an example.

When considering the size of the deductible the firm will accept, it is important to be aware of the possibility of deductible *pyramiding*. The probability of this happening increases when a loss involves more than one type of insurance, with each having its own deductible clause. Coverages where separate deductible clauses might apply include the following:

- Commercial building and contents;
- Boiler and machinery;
- Business interruption;
- Money and securities; and
- Accounts receivable

Deductibles of $500 dollars that are perceived as reasonable could become $2000 or more if an occurrence involved multiple policies simultaneously. This pyramiding possibility is important as risk managers evaluate the size of the deductible in insurance policies. Care must also be taken to be sure that as decisions are made between risk retention and risk transfer that consideration is given to the problem of *loss accumulation*. It is not uncommon for businesses to retain the physical damage risk to older aircraft, automobiles and other tangible personal property, because the maximum loss of any one property can be safely absorbed. However, if a number of properties are damaged or destroyed during the same year, the assumed risk is far in excess of what was expected.

Some firms use the impact of active risk retention on earnings per share as a valuable guideline to determine the upper limits of a corporate risk retention program. For example, a drop of one cent per share caused by an uninsured loss may be acceptable, but a drop of five cents per share would be unacceptable. The risk manager can calculate what dollar amount of loss is reflected by a one cent per share dip in earnings and then retain risks up to that dollar amount and transfer excess potential loss to insurance companies.

One of the most dangerous forms of risk retention is called *passive risk retention*. This occurs when risks are inadvertently retained due to an improperly done risk analysis and/or failure to keep it updated. Recent legislation that holds firms liable for pollution caused by underground storage of fuel is an example.

Self -insurance is really not insurance at all because there is no transfer of risk to others. Reserves are established within the company to pay losses. It is important to distinguish between a risk retention program and a self-insurance program. Active risk retention is referred to as noninsurance because the firm can predict fairly accurately the frequency and severity of some losses during a stated period so that losses can be paid out of current resources. There can be self-insurance only if the number of exposure units is sufficiently large for the law of large numbers to work and the amount of risk in each location is such that the magnitude of the loss will not jeopardize the companies financial future. Workers' compensation insurance is a popular candidate in large firms for a self- insurance program because it commonly develops more premium costs than other property lines of coverage and it has a higher claim frequency with low severity and a greater degree of predictability. The major benefits of a workers' compensation self-insurance program are:

1. The firm's cash flow is improved through the elimination of required advance premiums;
2. Improved loss experience due to closer involvement by key personnel which results in more effective loss control; and
3. Meaningful savings through reduced administrative costs.

The major disadvantages of a workers' compensation self-insurance program are:

1. Number of employees may be insufficient to spread the cost of the claims, especially if several deaths occur or if a large number of employees are injured in a common accident.
2. Work force levels are unstable or characterized by high turnover. Administrative costs increase and untrained employees have a higher incidence of accidents.
3. Contributions made to the reserve are not tax deductible, where as premiums paid to insurance companies enjoy this favorable tax treatment.
4. Loss of insurance company services like plant inspections, safety and first aid training for employees, and extensive record keeping.
5. No control over increases in employee benefit levels because a state commission establishes them.

The other method of risk finance is *risk transfer*. The transfer is usually to an insurance company. There are several benefits of purchasing insurance to transfer the burden of financial loss. The firm is guaranteed protection against large and uncertain losses in exchange for a small certain premium cost. Thus, insurance does provide an element of stability and peace of mind to a business. It also enhances the probability that the firm can borrow money at competitive rates. Risk transfer can also be accomplished by making another person or firm responsible for losses. One common transfer that does not involve insurance is shifting an unacceptably hazardous risk to another firm. For example, to cut down on personal property damage exposure to inventory, an FBO may cut parts inventory to the minimum and reorder from suppliers more frequently. This approach will reduce the chances of a large loss to inventory and transfers to the suppliers much of the FBO's exposure to loss of inventory. Similarly, an FBO may choose to engage the services of an aircraft paint facility rather than start its own, thus transferring the loss exposure associated with operating a paint booth. Another common form of noninsurance risk transfer is through hold harmless agreements. Companies that buy and operate business aircraft often find it necessary to enter into these agreements with the aircraft manufacturer, the firm that adapts the plane to their use, or an airport, hangar, or maintenance service. To protect their interests, owners may add a contractual or assumed liability clause to their aviation coverage that recognizes the agreement. The clauses protect them in the event of loss or damage to the aircraft at a time when it is the responsibility of a party with whom they have a contract. In most cases, this coverage is not automatic, and insurance companies require advance approval prior to accepting the additional liability.

Selection of Specific Techniques

After reviewing the basic techniques for dealing with loss exposures, the risk manager must determine the best technique for handling each specific exposure. Many risk managers believe that as a general rule, at least one risk control technique and one risk finance technique should be considered for each risk. For instance, the risk of aircraft theft can be reduced by installing passive alarm systems, hangaring at night, removal of a key engine part, and so forth. These measures constitute risk control. At the same time, the risk can be transferred through the purchase of aviation hull coverage. Because the risk control measures have effectively reduced the risk, savings in hull premiums will occur. The following 2 x 2 decision matrix is useful to derive some general conclusions using frequency and severity characteristics of losses.

	High Frequency	Low Frequency
High Severity		
Low Severity		

Losses that have been evaluated and judged to have high severity and high frequency characteristics should be avoided. They are probably not transferable due to their high frequency, so unless it is possible to reduce both of these dimensions, avoidance is the appropriate choice. Those risks characterized as high frequency and low severity should be retained and prevention/reduction techniques applied by the firm. Transfer would be inappropriate because of the administrative costs associated with the large number of small claims. Transfer is the only choice for risks with high severity and low frequency. The magnitude of the loss dictates that the firm should not attempt to pay these losses out of company resources or borrowed funds. The use of prevention/reduction techniques here would also be suitable. Aircraft liability exposure is a good example of this risk. The last box in the matrix holds risks that have low severity and low frequency characteristics. These risks can basically be ignored because they have minor impact on company resources or profitability when they occur.

Federal income tax considerations do enter into the proper choice for dealing with risks. A business decision to purchase insurance or actively retain the risk and to determine the size of the deductible, is influenced by the fact that all premiums for property and liability insurance as well as the cost of all uninsured losses are deductible business expenses. For a business in the 34 percent tax bracket, each dollar spent for premiums or unreimbursed losses will actually cost only 66 cents. For example, a business which purchases a hull and liability aircraft policy for its corporate aircraft and pays $10,000 annual premium, is actually only paying $6,600, because the premium expense is deductible. At the end of the tax year, this business's annual revenue was reduced by the $10,000 premium expense that lowered its taxes by 34 percent or $3,400. As a result, the net cash outflow for the policy was $6,600. In self-insurance programs, the cost of contributions to the reserve fund are not considered an expense, thus no deductibility. Obviously, when claims are paid from the fund, these costs do receive favorable tax treatment.

Periodic Evaluation

To be effective, any risk management program must be regularly reviewed. The procedure that is becoming popular is the *risk management audit*. This audit is not intended to be a fidelity watchdog like a financial audit by a CPA, but is concerned with identifying, controlling, and protecting all pure risks faced by the firm. It is an objective analysis of the entire risk management program and is usually conducted by someone outside the organization. Among the areas which should be audited are:

1. Possible alternatives such as deductibles, retrospective rating or other loss sensitive plans, self-insurance, and other methods which will have positive impact on the firm's cash flow.
2. Analyzing exposures to loss and determining which risks should be eliminated, reduced, insured, self-insured, or just retained.

3. Loss records should be analyzed to determine changes in frequency and severity of risk exposures.
4. The effectiveness of the current safety activities and loss prevention programs and measuring management's attitudes toward loss control.
5. Evaluation of the current insurance program in terms of level of protection, services provided by insurers, and premium costs.

When the audit is completed, a written report is submitted indicating the findings and specific recommendations concerning areas of deficiency. The scope of the audit will certainly vary depending upon the size of the firm and the frequency of audits. Oftentimes, limited projects are undertaken to assist risk management in solving current specific problems. Examples include:

- Deciding the most economical way to handle product claims
- Analyzing the effect of increased deductibles on cash flow
- Improving the communication between risk management and other key personnel
- Studying the feasibility of consolidating all company units under one insurance program
- Establishing a procedure for assessing the qualifications of agents/brokers and insurance carriers being used

In the final analysis, the risk manager wants to be assured that the company's overall risk management policy is being carried out and that the company as a whole is cooperating in this vitally important area.

RISK MANAGEMENT TECHNIQUES FOR SMALL BUSINESSES

Large firms have used the principles and concepts of risk management for many years to provide optimum loss protection at the lowest possible cost. The savings realized through loss prevention and loss reduction techniques easily outweigh the expense involved in staffing a formal risk management department. Smaller companies generally find the implementation of these programs unfeasible, since the savings potential would not support the additional costs incurred.

The growth of small businesses due to inflation and successful marketing has changed their perspective on the management of risk. These firms now view insurance as part of their overall financial management, and use risk management tools that were once only used by large firms. Initially, most small firms start to accept larger deductibles or retain the entire risk themselves. They also actively consider self-insurance on selected risks. Because these various techniques have specific tax and insurance consequences, a smaller firm generally works on its program with its accountant, legal counsel, and a full-service insurance company, that can help assess the insurance problems involved and structure a plan that responds to the firm's specific needs.

Small firms within an industry group can often take advantage of the newer policies that insurance companies have developed to help small businesses reduce or stabilize their insurance costs while maintaining adequate protection. One of the most efficient and economical products is the *package policy*. Package policies bundle multiple coverages into a single policy to specifically meet the needs of various industries and business operations. These policies eliminate the necessity of purchasing many individual policies that often are more expensive and may provide overlapping or superfluous coverages. The possibility of passive risk retention is also greatly reduced. The Commercial General Liability Policy that is purchased by airport owners and fixed base operators is an example of a package policy.

The purchase of insurance through membership in national trade associations is often an efficient and effective way of transferring risk. This pooling of risk by small businesses, like FBOs, allows them to benefit from the economies associated from the law of large numbers. For example, member firms of the National Air Transportation Association (NATA) have an opportunity to become part of the most successful workers' compensation group program in the general aviation industry. The NATA plan was created in April 1975 with the following three objectives:

1. Provide NATA members with a dependable long-term market for workers' compensation insurance;
2. Structure the plan in such a way that if the overall loss experience of the participating members was favorable, all participants would share a cash dividend at the end of the policy year.
3. Make joining the plan as easy as possible.

Today after 32 years of continuous operation, the plan has exceeded every goal established by its founders:

- Since inception, the total dividends distributed to participants have exceeded $22,000,000 and the average annual dividend has exceeded 20 percent.
- The number of participants has continued to grow—from 76 original members in 1975 to over 545 members today.
- USAIG (United States Aircraft Insurance Group), one of the largest aviation insurance organizations, has provided the coverage since the plan's inception.

A major advantage of small firms joining together, called risk pooling, is the loss reduction programs that insurance companies are willing to offer such groups as a result of the savings generated. The insurance companies loss control specialists will develop a loss reduction program responsive to the needs of the specific group, which is either communicated directly to the insured firms or to the trade association's insurance or loss control committee. Emphasis in loss control programs concentrates on reducing frequency, rather than accident severity. There are two principal reasons for this focus: firms can easily measure the effectiveness of the loss control program at frequent intervals; and studies show that the severity of losses from accidents is unpredictable. Greater savings in loss expenses can be achieved by significantly reducing the total number of accidents. An additional benefit of risk pooling for smaller firms is that pooling helps level out the cost of insurance by combining it with others in their trade group and reviewing the group's loss experience as a whole, thus averaging highs and lows over the long run.

KEY TERMS

Risk Management
Insurance Manager
Risk and Insurance Management Society (RIMS)
Risk Analysis Questionnaire
Supplemental or expansion coverages
Real property
Personal property
Frequency
Severity
Risk control
Loss Prevention
Loss Reduction
Segregation
Contractual transfer
Risk finance
Active risk retention
Pyramiding
Loss accumulation
Passive risk retention
Self-insurance
Risk transfer

Risk avoidance

Risk management audit

Package policy

REVIEW QUESTIONS

1. Differentiate the principal job responsibilities between an insurance manager and a risk manager.
2. What role did the American Management Association play in the evolution of risk management?
3. State the major objectives of risk management.
4. Identify and explain the first two steps in the risk management process.
5. Name and explain four dimensions of a risk that must be measured by the risk manager.
6. Explain the difference between risk control and risk finance.
7. Explain the techniques of loss prevention and loss reduction and give an example of each.
8. Differentiate between active risk retention, passive risk retention, and self-insurance.
9. Explain how small firms can take advantage of risk management concepts.

REFERENCES

[1] Head, George L., and Stephen Horn II. *Essentials of Risk Management* (2nd ed.). Volume 1. Insurance Institute of America. Malvern, Pennsylvania, 1991, p2.

[2] Levick, Dwight E., CPCU *Risk Management and Insurance Audit Techniques*. Shelby Publishing Corporation, Boston, Massachusetts, 1988. p. 299.

Vaughn, Emmett J., and Therese Vaughn. *Fundamentals of Risk and Insurance* (9th ed.). John Wiley & Sons., New York, 2003.

Williams, C. Arthur., and Richard M. Heins *Risk Management and Insurance* (6th ed.). McGraw-Hill, Inc. New York, 1989.

Chapter 6

The Legal Foundation for Insurance

OUTLINE

Nature and Types of Law
Concept of Indemnity
Legal Liability
Aviation Damages
State Statutes
Federal Statutes and International Agreements

OBJECTIVES

At the end of this chapter you should be able to:
Distinguish between the traditional divisions of law.
Discuss the legal principles of indemnity, insurable interest, and subrogation as they pertain to insurance contracts.
Describe the legal basis for liability and explain why this is important to insurance consumers.
Define torts and explain how they occur.
Describe the four requirements that must be met before a person can be held legally responsible for a negligent act.
Explain what is meant by "degree of care required."
Compare and contrast negligence per se, vicarious liability and gross negligence.
Summarize three common defenses for a negligent act.
Describe the concept of strict liability for defective products.
Identify and define five intentional torts.
Describe how liability may be incurred under contract.
Distinguish between special and general losses.
List the variables in determining recoverable special damages.
Explain the reason for punitive damages and wrongful death statutes.
Distinguish between survival statutes and guest statutes.
Explain the rationale and benefits of the General Aviation Revitalization Act (GARA).
Explain the purpose of the Foreign Sovereign Immunities Act and the Warsaw Convention.
Identify the two major parts of the Aviation Disaster Family Assistance Act of 1996.

NATURE AND TYPES OF LAW

What is law and how is it defined? Early philosophers spent considerable time attempting to formalize their views on the nature of law. Plato is credited with saying that law is a form of social control, an instrument of the good life, the way to the discovery of reality, the true reality of the social structure. Aristotle said that law is a rule of conduct, a contract, an ideal of reason, a form of order. Cicero said that law is the agreement of reason and nature, the distinction between the just and the unjust. Today there is no one universally acceptable definition of law. The traditional view states that *law is the body of principles, standards, and rules which the courts apply in the decision of controversies brought before them*. Since the insurance policy is a legal contract, knowledge of certain fundamental legal principles is useful to the risk manager for understanding its nature and the manner in which it is interpreted. The general purposes of our legal system are to keep order, to settle disputes, and to prescribe a code of conduct for its members.

Law is traditionally divided into two general types—statutory and common. *Statutory law* consists of laws that have been passed by duly authorized bodies, such as the federal and state governments. *Common law* is often referred to as "unwritten law" and as "judge-made law," because it consists of the great body of past court decisions. Under our English system of common law, courts are bound by the traditions of the legal profession to follow precedents that have been well established by prior decisions. It is somewhat misleading to speak of the common law as "unwritten," since past court decisions are published and available to all members of the legal profession and to the public.

A third type of law—*administrative law*—is becoming increasingly more important. Rulings by a state insurance commissioner are theoretically only interpretations of the state insurance laws but often have the practical effect of new legislation. Administrative bodies, such as the Federal Aviation Administration, are often given power to "interpret" legislation which they enforce, and thus have in effect limited legislative powers. The FAA has brought enforcement actions against pilots who are not in control of the aircraft and who merely loaned their aircraft to a friend who then committed the flight violation. In a 1996 administrative law decision, the Administrator of the FAA affirmed a civil penalty ($4,000 fine) against the innocent owner of an aircraft, who was not in control or piloting the aircraft at the time of the flight violation. (*In re: Matter of Fenner*, FAA Order No. 96-17, Docket CP93So414, May 3, 1996)

Statutory law on insurance consists of applicable legislation passed by the federal and state governments. Since 1944, insurance has been held to be subject to regulation by the federal government. *Public Law 15*, however, provided that it was the intention of Congress that states should continue to regulate insurance to the extent that they did so effectively and for the most part, statutory regulation of insurance remains on the state level. The objectives of state regulation is to establish policies and procedures that will (1) assure that all insurance companies licensed in each state remain financially sound; (2) see that all policyholders are treated fairly, and (3) control premium rates to see that they are not inadequate, excessive, or discriminatory.

CONCEPT OF INDEMNITY

The basic legal principle that affects the operation of insurance is the concept of indemnity. Webster defines *indemnity* as "compensation or remuneration for loss or injury sustained." Simply stated, it means that the insurer agrees to pay for no more than the actual loss suffered by the insured (to make him whole: no better, no worse off). Obviously, if insureds could gain by having an insured loss, some would deliberately cause losses.

Insurance is not designed to enable the insureds to realize a profit (such as gambling), but to protect assets that they already have. The insurance contract, therefore, does not bring into existence any new risk but offers protection against a risk that is already present. By taking out insurance, the insureds are not seeking to enrich themselves at the expense of anyone else, but merely to protect what they already have. Therefore, gambling and insurance are opposites: one creates risk, the other reduces it. The concept of indemnity is supported by two legal principles: insurable interest and subrogation.

Insurable Interest

An *insurable interest* is a prerequisite to a valid contract. It is defined as an interest when its possessor would be financially injured by the occurrence of the event insured against. From a legal standpoint, the absence of an insurable interest at the required time means that the contract is a wagering contract and therefore is unenforceable. If, for example, a life insurance company discovers that the applicant on a policy has no insurable interest in the person whom they insured, the company could refuse to make payment.

The amount of the insurable interest in most lines of property and liability insurance is determined by the value of the property involved or the value of the legal obligation in question. In life insurance the amount of the insurable interest is immaterial. If an insurable interest exists in life insurance, it is legally sufficient to support any amount of life insurance that the person is able to secure.

An insurable interest in property contracts is normally based upon the ownership of the property. This is not essential, however, as a person who has an equitable title in the property or who has a relationship so that he is financially dependent upon the existence of the property may also have an insurable interest. A mortgagee has an insurable interest in the property pledged as security for a debt. For example, a bank holding a loan on an aircraft certainly has an insurable interest in the aircraft. Lessors and leasees of aircraft also have an insurable interest.

Possession may give the holder of property an insurable interest. Thus a bailee (one holding property of another) has an insurable interest in property left in his care and custody. A fixed base operator who provides hangarage, maintenance, repair, or even tie-down space is a bailee.

Generally speaking, an insurable interest in the property or liability field must exist only at the time of loss, and need not exist when the policy was originally issued. The amount of the insurable interest is determined by the interest of the policyholder in the property that is insured.

In the case of life insurance, every person has an insurable interest in his own life. He also has an insurable interest in those persons to whom he is related by blood, marriage, or business in a way that he may reasonably expect to benefit financially by the continuation of their lives. In the case of life insurance, an insurable interest need exist only at the time the policy was originally issued.

Subrogation

The right of subrogation also supports the principle of indemnity. *Subrogation* is the right of the insurance company, after paying the insured for a covered loss, to take over all the insured's legal rights against negligent third parties. This occurs in hull coverage when someone else caused damage. It is not the purpose of insurance to enable policyholders to realize a profit. If it were not for the right of subrogation, the policyholder might recover twice, once from the insurance company and once from the third party who caused the accident, or the negligent party (tort-feasor) could escape liability although responsible for the loss. The right of subrogation exists in most lines of property and liability insurance and is applicable independently of any policy provision. To bring it to the attention of the policyholder, most property and liability policies contain a specific provision that the insurance company will take over all legal rights against third parties upon payment of a loss. A subrogation clause is also included in many proof-of-loss forms that are required in the claim process.

A second type of subrogation can arise when loss occurs to a rented airplane. If the lessor, the owner of the airplane, does not have a policy where the insurance company has waived rights of subrogation, then the renter pilot is not covered as an additional insured. Any damage to the airplane caused by the renter pilot will be paid by the owner's policy, and the insurance company will then have subrogation rights to sue the renter pilot. Obviously, it is prudent for renter pilots to inquire if they are covered under the owner's policy as an additional insured. Otherwise, a non-owned aircraft policy should be purchased.

The right of subrogation does not accrue to the insurance company until the insured has been fully indemnified for his loss. This is to prevent any third party who may have caused the loss from being subjected to two lawsuits—one from the policyholder and one from the insurance company. The policyholder must be careful not to take any actions which would defeat the company's right of subrogation, such as signing statements admitting liability for an accident.

The majority of courts direct that when funds are recovered from the negligent third party the insured must be compensated first to the extent that the loss exceeded the policy limit. This frequently is how the insured recoups the deductible expense. The insurer is then compensated up to the amount of proceeds paid to the insured, and the balance of the fund, if any, goes to the insured.

LEGAL LIABILITY

Airline liability exposures often result in large losses. In *Air Evac Inc. v. Aeronautical Accessories Inc.*, 124F.3d 207 (8th Cir. Sept. 5, 1997), the United States Court of Appeals for the Eighth Circuit awarded $1.07 million in a case involving a helicopter accident. The pilot and several passengers were injured when the pilot lost control of the helicopter because of his loss of visual contact with the ground. The visual problem developed, because of the malfunction of the "nightscanner" light that is a searchlight mounted on the helicopter. The pilot was unable to turn it off. The following two cases illustrate the magnitude of the product liability exposure for aircraft manufacturers and repair stations. In *Smith / Dempsey v. Beech Aircraft Corp.*, CV-93-160-TUCRMB (D. Ariz. May 9, 1997), plaintiffs were awarded approximately $60 million in a wrongful death suit against Beech Aircraft Corporation for the wrongful deaths of a pilot and his passenger when the Baron they were flying entered into an unrecoverable flat spin. Plaintiffs successfully argued that the Beech Baron had an undue spinning tendency when the aircraft's attitude was less than 45 degrees. The court found that Beech had negligently designed the vertical tail of the Baron. The defect caused an unreasonable risk of harm and Beech failed to warn of the defect, and it failed to provide adequate instructions concerning the Baron's tendency to flat spin. The second product liability case involved a twin-engine aircraft that had an engine failure while in route to its home base in Virginia; the pilot survived the ensuing crash but suffered severe injuries. The repair shop that had recently worked on his engine paid its full insurance limits of $1million.

Nature of Legal Liability

In order to understand liability risk, it is helpful to make a division of the various types of legal wrongs. Any action that results in harm to another person may be either a criminal act or a civil act. A *criminal act*, such as arson or theft, is a crime against society and is punished by the state. A *civil wrong* is a wrong against a specific person and constitutes an invasion of the rights of another party. The usual remedy that an injured party is seeking in a civil suit is damages—a sum of money that will reimburse the victim for the financial losses incurred as a result of the defendant's wrong. Some wrongful acts are of a dual nature, subjecting the wrongdoer to both criminal and civil penalties. For example, if John steals Roger's airplane, the state could bring a criminal action against John, and Roger could also bring a civil action to recover damages arising from the theft. Civil wrongs are divided into two types: torts and breaches of contracts.

A *tort* is defined as a wrongful act committed by one person against another (other than a breach of contract) for which the law provides a civil remedy in the form of damages. Contracts may involve legal wrong when implied warranties are violated, bailee responsibilities are not fulfilled, or contract obligations are breached.

Torts

Torts arise out of (1) negligence, (2) strict liability, and (3) intentional acts. Most tort claims are based on negligence.

1. Negligence

Negligence may be defined as "a failure to exercise due care" or "failure to do what a reasonable person would have done under the circumstances, or doing something, which a reasonable man would not have done under the circumstances." No one is expected to be perfect, and the law does not require perfection. There are numerous unavoidable accidents for which it would be unfair to hold anyone legally responsible.

The right of recovery for damages due to negligence exists because society expects every person to conduct himself in such a way as not to injure other members of society. As a matter of self-protection, society requires that every person take into account the result of his actions on other persons. If a person fails to exercise such due care and bodily injury or property damage results, the injured party may have a right to reimbursement.

Before a person can be held legally responsible for bodily injury or property damage, four requirements must be met: (1) a legal duty, (2) a wrong, (3) a proximate relationship between the wrong and an injury or damage, and (4) an injury or damage.

A *legal duty* to act, or not to act, depends on the circumstances and persons involved. A bystander has no legal duty to try to prevent a robbery, but a security officer does. The courts decide whether or not a legal duty is owed to someone else, and many factors may determine the degree of care required (to be discussed shortly). The judge decides questions of law and the jury, questions of fact.

A *wrong* is a breach of legal duty, based upon a standard of conduct that is determined by what a prudent person would have done or not done in similar circumstances. Criminal wrongs and other kinds of civil wrongs (breach of contract or warranty) are not so pertinent as negligence is in this description of liability. To do a wrong, the act or omission must be voluntary. Thus, if a person in the course of avoiding great danger injures another person without intent, there is held to be no voluntary act and hence no liability. Negligence usually involves injury that is unintentional. On the other hand, it is no defense if the act, which injures a party, was done without intent to do an injury or if the motive behind the act was good and praiseworthy.

A third requisite for fixing liability is found in the rule that the voluntary act of the wrongdoer must have been the proximate cause of the injury. A person is responsible only for damages that are the direct result of negligence on his part. *Proximate cause* is a legal term that refers to the major cause of injury or damage. The test of proximate cause that is generally applied is whether or not the injury or damage would have occurred in the absence of negligence on the part of the defendant. This means that a person cannot be held responsible for injuries or damages which are an unexpected, or unnatural, result of negligence on his part. For example, suppose a pilot crashed on takeoff when his engine malfunctions, and a spectator became so excited watching the accident that he had a heart attack. By no stretch of the imagination could the pilot be held responsible for the spectator's heart attack.

The fourth requirement for negligence liability is that there must be *injury or damage*. The guilty person must pay an amount that reasonably compensates the injured party for: (1) bodily and other personal injuries, (2) loss of income due to disability, (3) pain and suffering, (4) disfigurement, and (5) any other losses for which the negligence is the proximate cause.

Loss of income due to inability to work often comprises a large proportion of *bodily injury* liability cases. As an example of other losses, a husband or wife may collect for the value of the spouse's services as well as for *consortium*, the term that the law applies to the companionship of the mate.

A parent may also collect for the loss of the services of an injured child and for the expenses associated with the injury. In the case of death, the heirs or next of kin may collect damages for the loss of the life. Some states fix a statutory limit for an instantaneous "wrongful" death, but if the party retains or regains consciousness after the injury and ultimately dies, the damage for conscious suffering is added to the damage for the death. Sometimes bodily injury is extended to include cases where no actual physical injury is suffered, but mental anxiety results from near accidents.

Compensation for *property damage* is measured by the difference in the value of the property before and after injury. Although the cost of repair and replacement may serve as a measure of damage, this does not always reflect the actual amount of the damage. If the cost to repair the damaged property is in excess of its value, then the measure of damage would be the value of the property immediately before the accident, less its salvage value immediately following the accident. Indirect losses, such as loss of income, resulting from the inability to use the property may also be a part of property damage liability.

a. Degree of care required. The owner of real estate owes a duty to the public for its care and upkeep and may be held responsible to persons injured on his property if he allows a nuisance to be present. The word nuisance is a legal term meaning a dangerous or defective condition. Thus, an FBO may be held responsible for accidents on the apron area in front his hangar if he fails to keep it free of oil spills or harmful objects. Persons who own or lease property are responsible to members of the public who are injured on their premises under certain circumstances. The degree of care owed to the public depends upon whether such third parties are legally trespassers, licensees, or invitees.

A *trespasser* is one who ventures upon the property of others without the latter' s knowledge or consent. The property owner owes no duty to a trespasser except not to willfully set traps for him. It would not be legal for an airport owner to set up an electric fence around his property without proper warning, even though those who are injured are trespassers. By the same token, a person may not set a trained attack dog upon trespassers without warning.

A *licensee* is one who enters upon the premises of another, with the owner's express or implied consent, principally for his own benefit. An example of a licensee is a salesman or solicitors for charitable organizations. It is often said that a licensee "takes the premises as he finds them." The duty of care owed to a licensee is greater than that owed to a trespasser. The property owner has a duty to warn the licensee of any unsafe condition or activity on the premises.

An *invitee* is a person who is invited, either expressly or by implication, to enter the premises. Examples of invitees are customers entering an FBO's office. The fact that an FBO is open for business is an implied invitation for the public to visit. The duty owed to an invitee requires that in addition to warning of any dangerous conditions, the owner has the obligation to inspect the premises and to eliminate any dangerous condition revealed by the inspection. An FBO, for example, is required to maintain his hangar area in such a manner that members of the public are not injured. His failure to do so constitutes negligence and members of the public who are injured as a direct result may sue and recover.

An FBO owner owes a greater degree of care to someone whom he has invited on his premises (an invitee or guest) than he does to a licensee or trespasser. Some states distinguish between the degree of care owed to business guests or invitees and that owed to social guests to whom a lesser degree is required. If his premises are accessible to children, he may be required to exercise greater care than otherwise. The degree of care required will also depend on the nature of the activities conducted by the individual or firm and on the type of product being handled. A company that manufactures or sells an inherently dangerous item is expected to take more precautions to prevent it causing injury than a firm that handles less dangerous items. The degree of care expected in each instance is commensurate with the risk involved.

An individual pilot operating his own aircraft for business and pleasure purposes owes invited guests (no charge is made) ordinary or reasonable care in the operation of his aircraft. An injured guest may have a cause of action if he can prove that the pilot did not exercise ordinary or reasonable care in the operation of the aircraft. An FBO renting (short-term) or leasing (long-term) aircraft to the public must exercise a higher degree of care than the business and pleasure risk. Similarly, air taxi operators and airlines that charge for their services must exercise the highest degree of care to passengers.

Under unusual circumstances, liability may be imposed because sometimes accidents happen, and it is imposed regardless of the degree of care taken. This is called *absolute liability* and the injured party will be awarded damages even though nothing legally was wrong. Common examples of absolute liability imposed under tort principles include the following:

- Employment connected injuries
- Abnormally dangerous instrumentalities
- Ultrahazardous activities

All states now have enacted worker compensation laws that impose absolute liability on employers for injuries to workers occurring in the course of employment. This represents an exception to the rule that there can be no liability without fault. The worker does not have to prove the employer was negligent to be compensated for lost wages and medical expenses.

Persons injured by an “abnormally dangerous instrumentality” can recover damages without having to prove negligence. Examples of instrumentalities the court might conclude as dangerous would be dynamite, gasoline, noxious chemicals, wild animals kept in captivity, and domestic animals known to be abnormally dangerous.

Activities that are unreasonably dangerous and do bodily injury and property damage are called ultrahazardous activities. Courts have held that the following would generally fall into this category: spraying chemicals on crops from an airplane, using explosives to level old buildings, production of dangerous chemicals, and the handling of propane gas.

b. Negligence Per Se. A statute or administrative regulation, if adopted for the protection of a certain class of persons, may provide the standard of care to such persons in negligence actions. The doctrine of *negligence per se* holds that the violation of such a statute or regulation, when resulting in harm to a plaintiff who is within the class of persons intended to be protected by the statute or regulation, will be considered negligence as a matter of law.

Negligence per se has a wide application in aviation accidents because the Federal Aviation Administration extensively regulates nearly all aspects of civil aviation. These regulations have as their primary purpose the protection of both the flying public and the general public. They govern not only the design and manufacture of aircraft, but also maintenance, crewmembers, air traffic, flight and maintenance schools, instructors, and airports.

c. Nuisance. A *nuisance* includes almost any act or thing that endangers life or health, offends the senses, or damages or interferes with the use of property. Creation or maintenance of a nuisance is a tort entitling the plaintiff to recovery of damages or to equitable relief. It is unnecessary to prove either negligence or intentional malfeasance to maintain an action for nuisance; the essence of the tort is the danger created. Airports and overhead aircraft have often been declared nuisances for the noise vibrations and air pollution created.

d. Res ipsa loquitur. Although the general rule is that the plaintiff (claimant) must prove the negligence of the defendant, the occurrence of an accident under certain conditions is deemed to be prima facie evidence of negligence. This is known as the doctrine of *res ipsa loquitur* the thing speaks for itself. Generally, this rule will apply when the thing that caused the accident is clearly of a kind that does not occur when proper care is exercised.

The doctrine of res ipsa loquitur is not invoked except when necessary evidence is absent or not readily available. Thus, after a plane crash, it may not be possible to determine the cause of the accident. The injured parties are not burdened with proving the negligence of the airline. The doctrine has the effect of justifying an inference of negligence or in some jurisdictions, of establishing a presumption of this nature. For the plaintiff to apply the doctrine, the following requirements must be met:

- The event is one that normally does not occur in the absence of negligence.
- The defendant has superior knowledge of the cause of the accident, and the injured party cannot prove negligence.
- The defendant has exclusive control over the airplane causing the accident.
- The injured party has not contributed to the accident in any way.

e. Vicarious liability. *Vicarious liability*, sometimes referred to as imputed negligence, makes one person responsible for negligent acts of others. All employers are obligated to protect the public from the wrongful acts of their employees. The courts hold an employer liable for the torts committed by his employees in the course of their employment. When an employee commits a tort in the course of employment, both the employee and his employer may be sued. The plaintiff may satisfy his judgment against one or both.

In addition to the liability of employers for the torts of their employees, a number of states have enacted specific aircraft owner statutes for the protection of their citizens that have not been repealed. These laws purport to hold an innocent owner vicariously liable, when the owner grants permission to another to use the aircraft and the aircraft is involved in a negligent incident. Among the states that have permissive user statutes, some impose liability on the owner without limitation. In other states, owners will have only limited liability exposure.

f. Gross Negligence. Occasionally, negligent conduct will be so glaring as to merit an allegation of gross negligence. *Gross negligence* usually involves a positive act rather than an omission to act, and connotes a conscious indifference to the safety of others. It is usually applied in cases where the negligent conduct appears intentional or is so gross as to indicate willful misconduct, wantonness, recklessness, or malice. A finding of gross negligence will in most instances entitle a plaintiff to recover punitive damages.

g. Defenses against negligence suits. An important defense against a suit based upon negligence is that no negligence was actually present. This involves proving that the actions of the defendant were those of a reasonable prudent man.

An *assumption of risk* on the part of the injured party is sometimes used as a defense. Assumption of risk argues that the plaintiff by consenting either expressly or by implication to relieve the defendant of the duty to protect had accepted the risk of injury. The risk may be assumed by written agreement (such as a lease for hangar space) or implied (by taking a ride in an open cockpit stunt plane).

Another possible defense is that the injured party was also negligent and was therefore not entitled to collect. Contributory negligence on the part of the injured party is an important reason for many negligence suits being decided in favor of the defendant. *Contributory negligence* is any degree of negligence on the part of the injured party in connection with an accident. In its strict application, the doctrine of contributory negligence seldom produced equitable results. A very slight degree of negligence on the part of an injured person would prohibit any recovery. Some 48 states have enacted statutes that provide that contributory negligence shall not prohibit recovery for damages. Such statutes apply the concept of *comparative negligence* and provide that damages shall be diminished in proportion to the amount of negligence attributable to the person injured or to the owner or person in control of the property damaged. As an example, in the case of a midair collision, we might find negligence apportioned among the two aircraft owners and even the Federal Aviation Administration and the manufacturers.

The *last-clear-chance* doctrine is an exception to the doctrine of contributory negligence. It states that even though the injured party was negligent, the defendant may be held responsible if he did not take any last clear chance he had of avoiding an accident. A transient pilot who parked his aircraft on an active taxiway is clearly negligent but another pilot using the same taxiway must use a reasonable amount of care to avoid the other aircraft.

2. Strict Liability for Defective Products

Many of the recently reported aviation accident cases involve strict liability claims against the aircraft manufacturer. To a lesser extent, strict liability actions are also maintained against the manufacturer or supplier of aircraft component parts, and in some instances, against the manufacturer or supplier of accessory items not incorporated in the aircraft. Under the concept of *strict liability*, manufacturers and merchandisers of products are held liable for injuries caused by defective products sold by them, regardless of the manufacturers' fault or negligence. Strict liability is distinguished from absolute liability in that the plaintiff must prove the following:

- The product was defective when it left the defendant's control;
- The defect made the product unreasonably dangerous;
- The product was used in the intended manner or a reasonably foreseeable manner; and
- The product was the proximate cause of the plaintiff's injury.

The notion of what constitutes an actionable defect has been expanded over the years. In addition to manufacturing defects, a product can be defective in its design, through deficient instructions on how to use the product, or through a failure to give adequate warnings of foreseeable hazards. The courts recognize three categories of defects: manufacturing defects, design defects, and failure-to-warn defects. The most obvious defect is an error in the construction, fabrication, or assembly of a product or component part. Such flaws will give rise to a cause of action in negligence, although strict liability will avoid the greater burden of proving negligence in the manufacturing process. Manufacturers have long been held liable for negligence in the design of their products. Design defects have posed the most challenges to strict liability theory and have been the area for most of the recent expansion in the application of strict liability. Questions are asked such as does the design incorporate adequate safety devices? Is the design adequate, not only for its intended use, but also for other foreseeable uses and misuses? The technical design factors frequently reviewed include airframe and cabin integrity, restraint systems, cabin and cockpit environment, energy absorption, and the postcrash environment. Warnings or instructions are required when a product is inherently dangerous, dangerous if used incorrectly, or in some way deficient in its capacity for safe use. When a warning or instruction is absent or inadequate, a marketing defect is said to exist.

The defenses to strict liability include contributory negligence, assumption of the risk, the plaintiff's misuse of the product and comparative causation. In addition, *government contractor defense* may shield military contractors from liability for design defects where the design is in compliance with the specifications required under a government contract.

Historically, contractors who complied with government design specifications relied on two principal defenses. The first was based on the negligence rule that a contractor would not be liable for specifications provided by another unless the danger was obvious or unless the contractor had special knowledge or expertise. The other defense required a finding that the contractor was the agent of the government and was, therefore, entitled to share in the government's sovereign immunity. The problem with this defense, at least in the view of most military contractors, was that they were more accurately categorized as independent contractors rather than as agents. However, the government contractor defense will, under certain circumstances, protect the manufacturer from liability for design defects when that design complies with government specifications. Most often it occurs in the case of suits by military personnel arising from design defects in an instrumentality of war.

Broader than the government contractor defense is the *specification defense* that applies to private contracts as well as government contracts. Like the government contractor defense, it applies only to design defects. It is a negligence concept and does not easily apply to causes of action in strict liability. Furthermore, it applies only where the designer provides the specifications and does not merely approve them, and then only when the manufacturer has no reason to know that the design specifications pose a hazard.

Finally, the *state of the art defense* refers to the limits of technological expertise and scientific knowledge relevant to the industry at a particular time. In negligence actions, compliance with industry customs has been recognized as relevant to the issue of whether reasonable care has been exercised.

3. Intentional Acts

Lawsuits may be brought because of injuries or damage caused by intentional torts. *Intentional torts* may arise out of intentional interference with a person or with property. Examples include battery, assault, mental distress, defamation, false arrest or detention, trespass, and conversion.

Battery is the offensive or harmful contact of another without his or her express or implied consent. This action includes contact with anything connected or associated with others, such as the clothes they are wearing, the airplane they are flying, or the cargo they are carrying. *Assault* involves threatened battery. It is an attempt at or a physical threat of violence to another, whereas battery requires actual physical contact.

Liability may originate with intentional acts that cause someone *mental distresses,* which is proven to be both severe and extreme. A creditor, for example, who repeatedly threatens and causes a debtor to suffer a nervous breakdown, can be held liable for infliction of mental distress.

Those who damage our reputation by spreading falsehoods commit the tort of *defamation.* Defamatory acts may be either libel (written) or slander (oral). To be actionable, defamatory statements must be intentionally or negligently communicated to someone other than the defamed party and the defamatory meaning must be reasonably understood by others.

False arrest or detention involves the unprivileged restriction of another's freedom of movement. While the restraint may be brief, it must be total for liability to occur. The restraint must be intended but does not have to be malicious.

Trespass includes an invasion of another's property, whether directly or through some instrumentality. It is generally an intentional tort, and proof of intentional or voluntary trespass will entitle the plaintiff to recover damages even where there is no actual injury. Where actual damages have been sustained, however, the defendant would be liable for such damages without regard to the defendant's intent or negligence. Because negligence is not an element of trespass, the defendant would be liable for the harm done even though it was not a foreseeable consequence of the trespass. Trespass can be an extremely useful theory for the persons on the ground whose property is struck by an aircraft crash. The burden of proof is easily met; the plaintiff need only prove title to the property and a lack of consent. Trespass is also available for property damage caused by aircraft flying below the minimum flight altitudes established by federal regulations.

Conversion is the intentional and unlawful exercise of control over personal property to the detriment of the owner. This tort only applies to tangible personal property that is moveable. An example is when an FBO employee uses an airplane, without the owner's permission, to fly on a weekend vacation. This is called conversion because the owner was deprived of using the airplane and there was some reduction in value to the airplane due to the increased hours on the engines.

Liability Under Contracts

Liability according to contract law is based on the invasion of another's right under contract. It occurs only as a result of a contract between one party and another. Liability under tort law is based on the breach of one's duty to respect the rights of the general public. It may result from either common law or statute law.

A *breach of contract* takes place when one party to a contract refuses to fulfill his part of the bargain. Liability for breach of contract primarily arises out of the sale of products or services. Under certain circumstances a manufacturer, distributor, or dealer may be held liable for breach of an implied or express warranty.

Warranties may be either expressed or implied in connection with the sale of a product. Although there is no statutory definition of *warranty*, it may be said that a warranty is a representation made by a seller of goods as to the character, quality, or title of the goods, which representation becomes a part of the contract for the sale of such goods. When the product fails to live up to the seller's representations, there is a breach of warranty rendering the seller liable to the same extent as for a breach of the contract of sale itself.

The Uniform Commercial Code describes two methods by which a seller creates an *express warranty*: (1) any affirmation of fact or promise made by the seller to the buyer which relates to the goods and becomes part of the basis of the bargain creates an express warranty that the goods shall conform to the affirmation or promise, and (2) any description of the goods which is made part of the basis of the bargain creates an express warranty that the goods shall conform to the description.

Express warranties may be either written or oral. Attempts are often made to prove that statements in advertising, brochures, or other literature create express warranties. In order for such statements to become "part of the bargain," however, the plaintiff must prove justifiable reliance on the statement. Another issue is whether a statement constitutes an affirmation of fact or is merely the expression of an opinion by the seller. An opinion does not create a warranty.

An *implied warranty* exists through operation of law rather than by the agreement of the parties. There are generally two types of implied warranties applicable to aircraft accidents: (1) an implied warranty of merchantability, and (2) an implied warranty of fitness for a particular purpose.

The implied warranty of merchantability requires that the product sold be reasonably fit for the general purpose for which it is manufactured and sold. The warranty does not require any particular agreement by or knowledge of the seller, so long as the seller is in the business of selling such goods. The implied warranty of fitness for a particular purpose applies only where: (1) the seller has reason to know of the use to which the product will be put, and (2) the buyer relies on the seller's judgment or skill in selecting the product. This warranty may be breached, although the product is not otherwise defective. In order to recover, however, the plaintiff must assume the burden of proving these two additional elements, which are not required for other warranties.

Bailee liability

When property is given over to the care of another party, a legal relation of *bailment* is created. Although the ownership of the property is unchanged, it enters the control of the party to whom it is entrusted, known as the *bailee*. This can be in the form of a contract such as a maintenance agreement between two air carriers or simply a handshake as in the case of a private pilot leaving his aircraft with an FBO to be overhauled. These are bailments for hire and usually, the bailee is charged with ordinary and reasonable care of the property entrusted to him, and his liability for the safety of the aircraft does not go beyond such degree of care. Negligence on the part of the bailee, or his employees, would be required to establish his liability in case the property were damaged, lost, or destroyed.

Figure 6.1 illustrates the legal foundation for liability discussed in this chapter. Although liabilities include criminal wrongs, for liability insurance the emphasis is on civil wrongs (common law) and particularly on the many legal wrongs based upon torts. Of greatest importance are torts resulting from negligence (unintentional acts or omissions), which encompass most of the claims for personal injury or property damage to others.

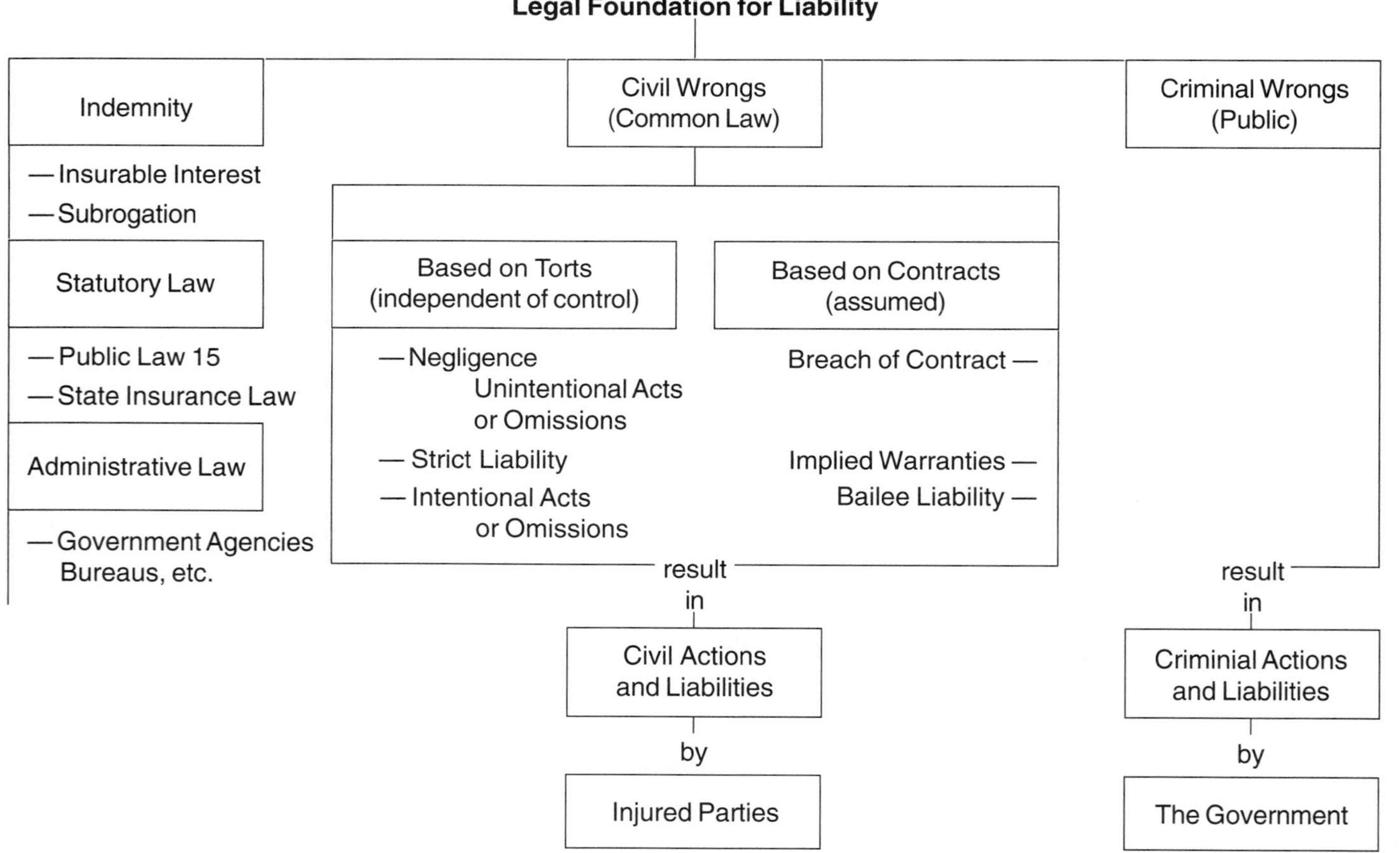

Figure 6.1 Legal Foundation for Liability

Mediation of Aviation Lawsuits

One of the positive changes that has occurred in the administration of our legal system is the greater use of alternative dispute resolution measures to settle lawsuits without going to trial. *Mediation* involves the use of a professional facilitator who allows both parties to present their case in an informal setting. This method does not result in a judgment or an award by a judge or jury, but does culminate with a mutual agreeable settlement. This time and expense saving method of settling disputes should be considered when many of the following factors are present:

- Plaintiffs are willing to accept a realistic percentage of the damages suffered and the defendant is willing to pay this compromised settlement.
- Plaintiff's case is not totally clear especially as it applies to contributory negligence.
- Defendant is plagued with particularly damaging evidence.
- Plaintiff has personal issues that make it undesirable to have a protracted litigation and a public trial.
- Defendant desires to limit exposure to a possible reputation-damaging public trial.
- Defendant's insurance company is a willing partner and aggressively requires its attorney to prepare a mediation plan of action.

AVIATION DAMAGES

The primary aim of the tort system is to provide adequate and equitable compensation and deterrence. The system intends to ensure that plaintiffs are compensated adequately and fairly for their injuries and losses. Adequate means that survivors recover the full amount of their loss. Fairly means that the compensation is proportional to loss, and that people who suffer the same loss receive a similar amount.

The system also intends to deter harmful behavior (such as the manufacture of unsafe products) while not deterring socially desirable behavior (such as advances in technology). To fully satisfy this objective, the tort system requires that tortfeasors pay in some form the full cost of the harm done, and thus have an economic incentive to prevent potential harm to others. The damages stemming from aviation accidents span the entire spectrum of tort law. Recovery will be sought for wrongful death damages, personal injuries, property damage, and economic loss. State law, including various wrongful death and survival statutes will in most cases govern the measure of recovery for each of these losses.

All of the federal acts and a majority of the state statutes provide for recovery of *compensatory damages* by certain designated beneficiaries. These damages represent the combined total of monetary losses that can be inferred from the facts and circumstances of the case. Compensatory damages are normally divided into two categories: special damages and general damages. Exactly what elements constitute compensatory damages under the statutes vary from state to state. Strictly speaking, *special damages* are the financial contributions in terms of support and services that the beneficiary could reasonably have expected to receive had the decedent lived. *General damages* include many intangible losses in addition to the loss of financial support such as loss of society, companionship, consortium, love, care, affection, attention, comfort, and protection.

Special Damages

Virtually all jurisdictions permit recovery for strictly financial losses. However, states differ somewhat in determining the extent of financial loss recoverable and the method used in calculating an award. The important variables in determining the amount of recoverable special damages are the source and amount of the decedent's future income, the decedent's health, and life expectancy, and the relationship between the decedent and the beneficiary. However, these variables can often produce inexplicably different results even within the same jurisdiction.

Financial Support

The estimated amount of future financial support, which the survivors would have received from the decedent, is generally measured by subtracting the decedent's anticipated personal expenses from gross income over the decedent's life expectancy. Promotions and merit pay increases can normally be included if their likelihood is established. Courts have also shown a willingness to consider income estimates based upon a change of careers, if its feasibility and the decedent's intent to do so is proven.

In addition to the decedent's future salary, the courts can consider fringe benefits such as sick leave, insurance, pensions, and room and board received as compensation. This can be particularly significant in cases involving deceased government or military personnel.

Future income is generally calculated over the duration of the decedent's normal worklife expectancy, although retirement benefits can be included over the remainder of the decedent's life expectancy. These include the decedent's age and health at the time of death, race, sex, economic status, environment, occupation, and personality traits. Hereditary factors such as the longevity of the decedent' s parents and grandparents and the presence or absence of hereditary diseases or traits can also be extremely important.

Loss of Inheritance

In many jurisdictions survivor beneficiaries under a wrongful death statute may recover for the loss of the estate they would have inherited from the decedent. This element of damages requires proof of both the probable size of the decedent's accumulated estate and the probability that the beneficiary would have inherited all or part of it. It would also depend on whether the beneficiary would have outlived the decedent based upon their respective life expectancies.

Family Services

Most family members typically provide the household with a number of services that have an ascertainable market value. These may include such things as auto repair, yard work, cooking, cleaning, childcare, home maintenance, driving, shopping, nursing, and so forth. Statutory beneficiaries who have been deprived of these services may recover their value. Minor children have also recovered for the loss of their parents' guidance, education, and nurture as a pecuniary loss, and parents have recovered for the value of their children's services up to the age of majority.

Funeral Expenses

The majority of jurisdictions permit recovery of funeral expenses in wrongful death actions if the beneficiary has paid them or is legally responsible for paying them. It is interesting to note that a minority of jurisdictions denies recovery for funeral expenses altogether, reasoning that death is inevitable and so the expense would be incurred eventually even had death occurred naturally.

General Damages

The death of a family member brings about many intangible losses in addition to the loss of financial support and household services. Recovery for such losses as companionship, consortium, love and protection has been said to derive from a societal belief that a tort-feasor should not escape liability simply because the victim was unproductive. In practice, recovery for intangible losses can provide critical support for families of low-income decedents. General damages fall into two basic categories: (1) loss of society and companionship and (2) grief and mental anguish.

Loss of Society and Companionship

The terms society and companionship have been defined to include love, affection, care, attention, comfort, and protection provided by the decedent. A loss of consortium denotes the marital and sexual relationship between a husband and wife, although it is sometimes used in a broader sense. It is also included in the concept of society and companionship in most jurisdictions. Damages for loss of society and companionship represent an assessment of the qualitative aspects of the personal relationship between the plaintiff and the decedent. It is almost always limited to family members.

Grief and Mental Anguish

An increasing number of jurisdictions are recognizing grief, mental anguish, or mental pain and suffering as compensatory injuries which are separate and distinct from the intangible benefits of society provided by the decedent. However, the majority of jurisdictions continue not to recognize a cause of action for the survivors' grief in a wrongful death case or will permit the claim only in certain narrowly defined circumstances. Some states permit recovery for mental anguish only where the survivor witnessed the accident or observed the scene of the accident soon afterwards.

Survival Claims

Aviation accidents, even when fatal, may result in injuries or damages to the decedent in addition to those suffered by the survivors. Recovery of these losses will depend on the provisions of a state survival statute or a combination survival and wrongful death statute. A survival statute permits recovery of damages to the decedent's estate rather than damages incurred by the survivors. These will typically include the decedent's pain and suffering between the time of injury and the time of death, loss of earnings between the time of injury and the time of death, medical expenses, and lost future earnings less the probable cost of personal consumption and support of dependents.

The fact that the period between injury and death is brief will not by itself preclude recovery for the decedent's pain and suffering. However, the evidence must establish that the decedent experienced conscious pain or was sensitive to and aware of the pain prior to death.

Nonfatal aviation accidents produce similar damages for wrongful death. These include past and future medical expenses, mental and physical therapy, lost earnings and earning capacity, pain and suffering, mental anguish, and loss of society and companionship.

Preimpact Fear and Mental Anguish

The anxiety common to many people while flying can quickly turn to panic or severe anguish when trouble develops, and passengers realize that they are helpless. Historically, the courts have been reluctant to award damages for mental anguish in the absence of some physical impact or other visible manifestation, unless the defendant had committed an intentional tort or was grossly negligent. This doctrine has gradually begun to give way, usually in favor of narrow exceptions to accommodate particular circumstances in which the existence of mental anguish is fairly obvious. For example, in one case, an award for preimpact mental anguish was affirmed because the decedent had been seated over the left wing, and the crash had been caused by the separation of an engine from that wing. From this evidence the jury reasoned that the decedent saw the engine detach at least 30 seconds before the crash.

Postimpact Pain and Suffering

The pain and suffering experienced by the decedent shortly after impact provide the basis for another element of aviation damages. Although the sight of an aircraft wreckage may lead most observers to conclude that death was instantaneous, forensic experts point out that in many cases it is a much more protracted process. The principal issue in recovery of this element of damages is whether the decedent died instantly in the crash.

Postimpact Traumatic Stress

Long-term emotional trauma is another kind of passenger injury for some persons surviving aircraft accidents. This even applies to passengers who have survived an accident or near accident without any physical injuries. The cost of psychiatric treatment and counseling in such cases is a necessary medical expense.

Unfortunately, the common law of many jurisdictions has limited recovery for severe emotional distress. Some states continue to apply the *impact rule*, which permits a cause of action for the negligent cause of emotional distress only where it is accompanied by some physical injury.

Other states have adopted a *zone of danger* rule under which a plaintiff may recover for emotional distress if the plaintiff was in personal danger of impact due to the defendant's negligence.

Bystander Shock and Mental Anguish

The ability of a bystander to recover from the psychological harm caused by an aircraft crash is affected by many of the same rules governing recovery by survivors who have no physical injuries. Consequently, the impact rule can completely bar a claim for emotional distress based on injury to another person. The zone of danger rule is also of little benefit to the bystander unless the bystander feared for personal safety because, for example, of a narrow escape from being struck by the falling aircraft. Where a bystander is related to one of the victims in an aviation accident many states have demonstrated a willingness to employ a forseeability standard of liability. Factors that are considered under the test include the closeness of the relationship between bystander and victim, the location of the bystander at the time of the accident, whether the emotional distress resulted from a direct observation of the accident, and the severity of the resulting distress. Some jurisdictions also require that the emotional distress manifest itself in physical symptoms or injuries.

Damages to Persons and Property on the Ground

Aircraft accidents in populated areas can cause extensive property damage and may cause death or injury to persons on the ground. The full range of damages is available under such circumstances. The limitations in wrongful death and survival actions remain the same as for other victims. Most claims by persons on the ground or their survivors are settled or tried on damage issues only.

Punitive Damages

Punitive damages are assessed in addition to compensatory damages. They are awarded to punish or make an example of a defendant whose conduct has been deemed wanton, reckless, or malicious. The practice of seeking punitive damages in civil cases has increased significantly during the past three decades. It is currently common for the punitive damage award in a particular case to exceed by many times the compensatory damage award in the same case.

Many states that still do not permit recovery of punitive damages in wrongful death cases allow them in a survival action. Punitive damages have also been permitted in cases involving property damage and the loss of the aircraft. In aviation products cases, punitive damages are usually sought when one or more of the following claims are present: (1) knowing violation of an established safety standard, (2) inadequate testing or manufacturing procedures, and (3) failure to warn customers of known dangers.

Very few courts require that the defendant have a specific intent to cause harm before allowing punitive damages. As long as it is established that the defendant had knowledge of a particular defect sufficient to place it at fault in some sense, the majority of jurisdictions permit recovery of punitive damages under a strict liability theory without any finding of negligence.

Aircraft manufacturers have successfully reduced or avoided punitive damage awards by showing evidence of warnings issued to consumers after design defects are discovered. Compliance with government regulations can also be a key factor in establishing good faith.

STATE STATUTES

Wrongful Death

The legal concept of loss to survivors can be traced back at least as far as the passage of Lord Campbell's Act in England in 1846. The passage of this act was a reaction to Lord Ellenborough's 1808 dictum in *Baker vs. Bolfan* promulgating the common law rule denying right of recovery in wrongful death. The denial of recovery in common law meant that recovery for damages had to be statutorily based. Lord Campbell's Act provided decedents' relatives the right to compensation for their financial loss. It became the model for many of the statutory wrongful death acts in the United States. Although the state *wrongful death statutes* modeled after Lord Campbell's Act vary a great deal, particularly in how they have been construed, they all share a common philosophical intent: compensating the decedent's beneficiaries for the financial loss incurred by the wrongful death.

The typical wrongful death statute specified those persons qualified to bring an action. Frequently, such person must be a legal spouse or other dependent, though some states allow recovery by nondependent relatives. In order to prevent duplicative suits, many states require that the next of kin qualify as the estate's personal representative before bringing an action.

Damages recovered under wrongful death statues ordinarily pass directly to the beneficiaries and are not treated as part of the decedent's estate for purposes of allocation or taxation, unless the state statute provides otherwise. Currently, there are no longer any states that place a ceiling on the amount recoverable for wrongful death. However, some states limit damages where the decedent had no dependent survivors or places a ceiling on general as distinguished from special loss.

The primary debate concerning recovery centers on special and general damages. Because the majority of state wrongful death statutes are intended to compensate survivors for their loss, there has been a significant movement in recent years toward inclusion of damages beyond loss of income. In some cases, courts may state that they are limited to financial loss, yet define such loss to include noneconomic elements such as loss of advice, comfort, assistance, care, and protection. Other states have amended their statutes to include such loss explicitly.

The majority of states now recognize recovery for loss of consortium for the death of a spouse. In addition, some states recognize compensation for survivors' grief and mental anguish, and occasionally for the decedent's suffering prior to death. Punitive damages may also be available. The sufficiency of proof concerning these elements varies among the jurisdictions that allow them.

In arguing for noneconomic damages, such as loss of services, guidance, and training, the quality of the decedent's relationship with his or her family members is relevant to the amount which may be awarded for the loss of affection and grief suffered by the survivors, and may serve to alter the amount awarded to the beneficiaries.

Awards for special damages in wrongful death cases are generally calculated based on the decedent's level of economic contribution at the time of death and estimated prospective accumulations throughout the work-life expectancy. Special damages have also been held to include the survivor's or decedent's loss of expected inheritance. The decedent's age, health, habits, qualities, and life expectancy, as well as the number of and situation of dependents, are typical considerations.

Problems may arise in evidence that may be admitted on future earnings potential, such as intention to change occupation, acquire new trade skills, or changed circumstances that make the calculation more difficult. Recoveries limited to pecuniary loss pose particular difficulty where the victim is a child, a homemaker, or an elderly person, since a strict approach may severely limit recovery. The death of such persons frequently has been under compensated in the past. Some states have additional statutes to address the wrongful death of a child. In other states, these cases have contributed to the trend toward the judicial recognition of nonpecuniary losses. The treatment of taxes, interest, and inflation may limit recovery in wrongful death cases and is a subject of dispute among the states. Other elements of wrongful death recovery that are usually paid include medical costs prior to death and funeral expenses.

Extraneous circumstances regarding the lives of the beneficiaries now are more frequently admitted in calculating damages. For example, evidence of a marital affair, lifestyle, or surviving spouse's remarriage since the date of death is becoming admissible in a majority of jurisdictions when offered to prove mitigation of damages.

Survival Statutes

In addition to wrongful death statutes that govern the recovery for survivors, some states also authorize a separate cause of action arising from the continuation of the claim, which the decedent would have had if death had not occurred. Recognition of such claims is contained in state *survival statutes*. A typical survival statute merely states that a cause of action for personal or other injury shall not abate because of the death of a party.

The measure of recovery in a survival action is customarily in keeping with the principle that the cause of action belongs exclusively to the decedent, though the personal representative carries it on. Some states limit survival recovery to pecuniary loss, and may place a ceiling on the amount of recovery.

It is often not clear from the survival statute whether it is to be included as part of the state's wrongful death act, considered as an entirely separate cause of action, or deemed mutually exclusive. Some states specifically indicate that the two provide separate rights of recovery, though they may be consolidated. In some states, consolidation is mandatory. A few cases have held that survival actions are available only if death was not instantaneous and the decedent experienced suffering prior to death.

In jurisdictions that provide a limited recovery of damages under their wrongful death statutes, survival actions may provide alternative means of compensation. In some jurisdictions, elements such as unique and personal damages, prospective accumulations in the decedent's estate, punitive damages, pre-crash mental anguish, and pain and suffering between the time of the crash and the actual time of death may be appropriate in a survival action, even when they are excluded from wrongful death damages.

In some instances, survival actions may be the only available remedy when, for example, the surviving relatives are nondependents or are otherwise ineligible under the state's wrongful death statute.

The effects of a recovery under survival statutes may also be distinct from those of recovery for wrongful death. For example, damages usually pass directly to the decedent's estate and are subject to taxation. Because survival damages generally pass directly to the estates, the ultimate beneficiaries under a will may differ from those beneficiaries eligible under the wrongful death act.

Guest Statutes

Originally, a great many states enacted laws that severely restricted persons who ride as guests in automobiles or other conveyances like boats and airplanes in their right to sue for injuries sustained by them. Today, only a few states have not repealed their guest statutes. The exact terminology of the *guest statutes* differs considerably from state to state, but the impact is similar. In general, the guest passenger is not allowed to recover for damage incurred while riding as a passenger, unless the host operator is found to have been guilty of "gross" or "willful and wanton" negligence. For example, South Carolina's guest statute states that no person transported by the owner or operator of an aircraft as his guest without payment for such transportation shall have a cause of action for damages against such aircraft, its owner or operator for injury, death, or loss in case of accident unless such accident shall have been intentional on the part of such owner or operator or caused by his heedlessness or his reckless disregard of the rights of others. A *guest* is usually defined as one who has not paid for his transportation, although the courts have on occasion interpreted the word more literally in favor of the injured person. The guest statute of Indiana narrows the definition of guest by stating that the owner, operator, or person responsible for the operation of an aircraft is not liable for loss or damage arising from injuries to or the death of his parent, spouse, child or stepchild, brother, or sister resulting from the operation of the aircraft while being transported without payment, unless the injuries or death are caused by the wanton or willful misconduct of the operator, owner, or person responsible for the operation of the aircraft. Some court decisions have held that where the pilot or owner of an aircraft stood to benefit from the presence of his passenger, (such as a business relationship or other motivation) the passenger was not a guest, and therefore could recover for damages if ordinary negligence was the proximate cause of the accident. The courts have also been somewhat liberal in their interpretation of what pilot conduct is sufficient to render the statute inapplicable. Instances range from intoxication and flying into unsafe weather conditions to failure of regular duties such as to inspect or maintain the aircraft.

Difficulty of proof will often complicate guest statute cases. Essential evidence of the parties' mental state in negotiating the ride may be uncertain. Also, the pilot's role in causing the crash may be unknown. Sufficient evidence of facts, which might overcome the statute's operation, must be presented to justify jury consideration. Plaintiffs frequently rely upon a theory of res ipsa loquitur in connection with guest statute cases in order to place the burden upon the defendant to disprove pilot misconduct.

Statutes of Limitations and Repose

Statutes of limitations provide a time limit within which a plaintiff can file suit. The period of time permitted varies with the jurisdiction and the nature of the cause of action. The purpose of these statutes is to relieve the courts of the burden of trying old claims and to give defendants the ability to preserve evidence and prepare a defense. The latter purpose is particularly relevant in aviation cases because technical data and physical evidence that might be lost over time often play a major role in determining the cause of a crash. Negligence claims have limitation periods ranging from one to six years, with a two-year period being most common. Florida's statute of limitation for wrongful death is two years, personal injury four years, and professional malpractice two years. Most warranty actions are governed by the four-year limit imposed by the Uniform Commercial Code, although some jurisdictions hold that implied warranty actions are governed by tort limitations. Tort statutes of limitations generally govern strict liability claims. The likelihood that an aviation accident will result in different losses and will be pleaded under various theories of liability means that several limitations periods may apply simultaneously to the same cause of action.

Like a statute of limitation, a *statute of repose* prescribes a time limit within which a plaintiff can file suit. Manufacturers of durable goods are exposed to possible liability for injuries occurring decades after the manufacture and sale of the product. A statute of repose usually provides a longer period of time than a statute of limitation. However, unlike the statute of limitation period, which commences with the cause of action, a statute of repose commences to run with the manufacture or sale of the product. Thus, it tends to function as an outer limit for filing the suit, without regard to the date of injury. Such statutes are highly controversial because they may act to bar a cause of action before it ever arises.

Statutes of repose are designed primarily to resolve the growing crisis in providing manufacturers with insurance against product liability claims. The so -called "long tail problem" of theoretical perpetual liability has been accused of causing a rapid escalation of insurance premiums and the curtailing or eliminating the manufacture of certain products. The statute of repose will assist insurers to determine an actuarial limit to the risk exposure, thereby stabilizing and reducing insurance premiums.

Proponents of statutes of repose also contend that defending old products is exceptionally burdensome, because evidence concerning their manufacture may no longer be available, and the intervening misuse or alteration is higher but equally difficult to prove after many years. It has further been suggested that the safe use of a product for many years is evidence that the product was not defective at manufacture.

Currently, about half of the states have statutes of repose. The restrictions established by these statutes vary considerably. Many apply only to specific products such as asbestos or nuclear materials. Some apply to all products equally. Most apply to all legal theories, although a few have specifically exempted some causes of action. Statutes of repose establish different periods ranging from five to twelve years. Those, which apply equally to all products, fail to recognize that many products have widely different useful lives.

The *General Aviation Revitalization Act of 1994*, commonly known as *GARA*, is an 18-year statute of repose that was passed by the United States Congress and signed into law by President Clinton on August 17, 1994. The intent of this legislation was to revitalize the general aviation manufacturing industry which found it self almost at the point of extinction. The depth of the problem can be illustrated by looking at the decline in aircraft deliveries from the peak in 1978 of just under 18,000 units to the low point in 1992 when deliveries were below 1,000. The proliferation of product liability suits against the deep pockets of the general aviation manufactures and the increasing product liability insurance costs were the major factors for this crisis. The status of product liability law had degenerated to such a point that is was commonplace for general aviation manufacturers to be faced with lawsuit after lawsuit, claiming that their aircraft were defective even though they had been in successful service for 20, 30, 40 years or more before the accident occurred.

In general, GARA provides that no civil action for damages for death or injury to persons or damage to property arising out of an accident involving a general aviation aircraft may be brought against the manufacturer of the aircraft or the manufacturer of any component, system, subassembly, or other part of the aircraft, in its capacity as a manufacturer if the accident occurred after 18 years beginning on the date of delivery of the aircraft to its first purchaser or lessee, if delivered directly from the manufacturer, or the date of first delivery of the aircraft to a person engaged in the business of selling or leasing such aircraft.

The term general aviation aircraft means any aircraft for which a type certificate or an airworthiness certificate has been issued by the FAA, which at the time the certificate was issued, had a maximum seating capacity of fewer than 20 passengers, and at the time of the accident, was not engaged in scheduled passenger-carrying operations. The act covers small airplanes, helicopters, and seaplanes not engaged in scheduled passenger service. GARA has been held to cover accidents in the United States and accidents abroad. In spite of its broad language, GARA does have the following four exceptions:

1. If the claimant can successfully prove that the manufacturer knowingly misrepresented the airworthiness of an airplane, or concealed or withheld from the FAA required information that is material and relevant to the performance, or the maintenance or operation of such aircraft, or the component, system, subassembly or other part, that is causally related to the harm which the claimant allegedly suffered;
2. If the person injured is a passenger for purposes of receiving treatment for a medical or other emergency;
3. If the person for whose injury or death the claim is being made was not aboard the aircraft at the time of the accident (a bystander perhaps); and
4. To an action brought under a written warranty enforceable under the law but for the operation of this Act.

GARA applies not only to the completely assembled airplane, but also to any new component, subassembly, or other new part, which are added to the aircraft subsequent to its sale. The GARA statute of repose for new parts starts to run from the date of "completion" of the replacement or addition of the new part.

FEDERAL STATUTES AND INTERNATIONAL AGREEMENTS

Foreign Sovereign Immunities Act

Foreign governments may own and/or operate airlines, airports, aircraft manufacturers, and component parts suppliers. Traditionally, claims against such entities were defended on the theory of sovereign immunity. The doctrine of sovereign immunity dates to the common law era of monarchies, when the king's act was equivalent to an act of state and thus immune from judicial action.

To resolve the problems inherent in deciding whether to subject a foreign nation to liability in the courts of this country, Congress in 1976 passed the *Foreign Sovereign Immunities Act.* The act had four main objectives:

1. to codify the restrictive principle of sovereign immunity;
2. to transfer the decision making from the executive to judicial branch;
3. to provide a statutory procedure for suing a foreign state; and
4. to assist in executing a judgment against a foreign state.

The act establishes the basic presumption of immunity from jurisdiction granted to foreign states by Congress and enumerates the exceptions. In general, these immunity exceptions apply (1) when the foreign state has waived its immunity, (2) when the suit arises out of certain types of commercial activity, (3) when rights in certain types of property are at issue, (4) when the claim involves tortuous acts of foreign state officials, and (5) when the claim against the sovereign involves a suit in admiralty to enforce a maritime lien.

The act defines a foreign state to include its political subdivisions and its agencies or instrumentalities, such as an entity whose shares are owned by its government. This definition is broad enough to encompass a variety of government-owned entities involved in aviation, including air carriers and manufacturers. All of these entities possess the right to assert the defense of foreign sovereign immunity.

Most major international air carriers that are government owned or operated have waived the right to assert the defense of sovereign immunity by virtue of the Department of Transportation permit required as a condition of doing business in the United States.

Warsaw Convention

The *Warsaw Convention* is a multilateral treaty intended to regulate international airline transportation uniformly. Its original purpose was to protect the fledgling airline industry from financial ruin. The treaty was negotiated at two international conferences, the first in Paris in 1925 and the second in Warsaw in 1929. The United States was not a participant, but it adopted the treaty in 1934. Discussions concerning the limitation on liability began in 1935 and culminated in 1955 with the negotiation of the Hague Protocol. This document doubled the recovery limit to approximately $16,600. However, the United States remained unsatisfied with the outcome and refused to ratify the Hague Protocol. In 1965, after decades of discontent, the United States denounced the Warsaw Convention unless the limitation on liability was raised to at least $75,000. The result of the threatened withdrawal by the world's largest air carriers was the Montreal Agreement.

In May 1999 the *Montreal Convention*, a special amendment to the Warsaw Convention, was established and applies to any international flight in which the United States is the point of origin, point of destination, or an agreed stopping place. The limit was increased to $75,000. In addition, the air carriers were required to waive the defense based on taking all possible safety measures. The result has been the virtual absolute liability of international air carriers operating in the United States. The Montreal Convention requires notice of the limits on liability to appear on passenger tickets. It requires, in addition, that this notice be printed in 10-point modem type and in ink that contrasts with the ticket stock. Both passengers and airlines, therefore, are conclusively presumed to have assented to its terms.
The limitation on liability does not apply if it is established that the damages resulted from the *willful misconduct* of the air carrier. The standard that has developed for willful misconduct is that the defendant intentionally performed an act with the knowledge that it was likely to result in injury or with reckless disregard of the consequences. Findings range from acts and omissions jeopardizing passengers' safety to misinformation concerning flights or mishandling of baggage or cargo. The treaty also provides that if an air carrier can prove the damages were caused in whole or in part by the negligence of the injured person, the court hearing the case may determine whether contributory or comparative negligence principles ought to reduce or bar liability.

A second provision subject to frequent interpretation involves the requirement that an airline carrier furnish passengers with tickets with adequate notice of the liability rules established by the Convention. Unless the airline can establish that it has met all of the requirements in affording adequate notice, the ceiling on liability provided by the convention will not apply. The crucial question in an adequate notice case is whether the plaintiff can be said to have had reasonable opportunity of protection by obtaining additional insurance.

The treaty provisions apply only to commercial international flights between the 71 signatory nations. This would include scheduled and nonscheduled charter flights. It also applies to commercial travel on successive carriers, even where a connecting flight is entirely within one country, if the parties regard it as a single operation. Each successive air carrier in such an operation is subject to the requirements of the Warsaw Convention.

On September 8, 2003, the United States ratified the Montreal Convention and the following are some of the new significant new benefits:

- Eliminates the meager and arbitrary limits of liability applicable under the Warsaw Convention when passengers are killed or injured in international air carrier accidents. The former limits of liability applied in all cases, except where the harm was due to the carrier's willful misconduct.
- In most cases, American survivors of international aircraft accidents and the

families of American accident victims will have access to U.S. courts in seeking damages for the losses they suffered.

- Requires air carriers to make payments of up to approximately $141,000 of proven damages on behalf of accident victims, without regard to whether the airline was negligent.
- An escalation clause provides that monetary limits and thresholds that survive in the Convention will be adjusted for inflation.
- Provisions on code sharing and similar arrangements clarify that when the airline operating a flight is not the airline from which the transportation was purchased, a passenger may recover from either the airline operating the aircraft at the time of the accident or the airline whose code is carried on the passenger's ticket.
- Furthers U.S. efforts to ensure that U.S. air cargo carriers and shippers can take advantage of technological innovations now available to facilitate and expedite the processing of international air cargo.

The Aviation Disaster Family Assistance Act of 1996

As the result of aircraft disasters like Pan Am Flight 103, ValuJet Flight 592, and TWA Flight 800, Congress passed the *Aviation Disaster Family Assistance Act* on October 9, 1996. The act has two parts—it delineates the responsibilities of the National Transportation Safety Board (NTSB), other governmental agencies, and the airlines in the event of an aircraft accident resulting in major loss of life; and it requires air carriers to submit plans for dealing with this type of disaster. Foreign carriers were included under this requirement by the subsequent passage of the Foreign Air Carrier Family Support Act in December 1997.

The Family Assistance Act expands the duties of the NTSB from just investigating aviation accidents to actively assisting families of victims of aircraft accidents. It is required to coordinate the activities of the American Red Cross, the Department of State, the Department of Health and Human Services, the FBI, the Federal Emergency Management Agency, the Department of Defense and the Department of Justice. The airlines have the responsibilities for notification of families and for the logistical support for victims and family members of the victims. The type of assistance specifically identified in the Act includes aide in identification of victims, recovery efforts, dealing with return of personal effects, and advising the families of the progress of the investigation.

In addition to the expanded role of the NTSB and the requirement of a disaster plan by the air carriers, the act changes the role of insurers for the airlines and their agents and plaintiff's attorneys. The Act provides a 30-day waiting period before any attorney, insurance company or airline litigation representative can contact victims or their families. A violation of the provision carries a fine of up to $1,000. Beyond the 30-day prohibition of solicitation, the families and victims will be able to obtain information directly from the NTSB as opposed to relying on lawyers.

KEY TERMS

Statutory law
Common law
Administrative law
Public Law 15
Indemnity
Insurable interest
Subrogation
Criminal act
Civil wrong
Tort
Negligence
Government contractor defense
Specification defense
State of the art defense
Intentional torts
Battery
Assault
Mental distress
Defamation
False arrest (detention)
Trespass
Conversion

Legal duty
Wrong
Proximate cause
Injury or damage
Bodily injury
Consortium
Property damage
Trespasser
Licensee
Invitee
Absolute liability
Negligence per se
Nuisance
Res ipsa loquitur
Vicarious liability
Gross negligence
Assumption of risk
Contributory negligence
Comparative negligence
Last-clear-chance
Strict liability
Breach of contract
Warranty
Express warranty
Implied warranty
Bailment
Bailee
Mediation
Compensatory damages
Special damages
General damages
Impact rule
Zone of danger
Punitive damages
Wrongful death statutes
Survival statutes
Guest statutes
Guest
Statutes of limitations
Statute of repose
General Aviation Revitalization Act of 1994 (GARA)
Foreign Sovereign Immunities Act
Warsaw Convention
Montreal Convention
Willful misconduct
Aviation Disaster Family Assistance Act of 1996

REVIEW QUESTIONS

1. Distinguish between statutory law, common law, and administrative law.
2. Why is insurance based on the concept of indemnity? Insurance is a form of gambling. Do you agree? How does an insurable interest in life insurance differ from property insurance? What are some relationships other than ownership that can create an insurable interest? How does subrogation support the concept of indemnity?
3. What is the relationship among civil wrongs, torts, negligence, and liability insurance? What is the difference between liability under contracts and under torts?
4. Describe the four parts of a negligence act. Distinguish between the degree of care owed trespassers, licensees, and invitees. What is the justification for different degrees of care? Explain the types of liability hazards to which an FBO is exposed?
5. Distinguish between negligence per se and gross negligence. What is vicarious liability?
6. Discuss assumption of risk and contributory negligence as defenses against negligence suits. What is the purpose of comparative negligence?
7. How does strict liability differ from absolute liability? Discuss several defenses used by manufacturers.
8. What are intentional torts? Why might an airline risk manager be concerned with them?
9. Give some examples of liability arising out of contracts. What is a bailment?
10. Describe the major variables used in determining the amount of recoverable special damages. What are general damages? What is the purpose of punitive damages, wrongful death statutes, survival statutes, and guest statutes?

11. Explain the difference between a statute of limitation and a statute of repose and give an example of each.
12. Why was the General Aviation Revitalization Act passed?
13. Describe the main objectives of the Foreign Sovereign Immunities Act. What is the current situation concerning limits of air carrier liability based on the Montreal convention?
14. Explain the two major parts of the Aviation Disaster Family Assistance Act of 1996.

REFERENCES

Dobbyn, John F. *Insurance Law.* (2nd ed.). West Publishing Co., St. Paul, Minnesota, 1989.

Eichenberger, Jerry A. *General Aviation Law (5th ed.).* McGraw-Hill, New York, 1997.

King, E. M., and J. P. Smith, *Computing Economic Loss in Cases of Wrongful Death*. The Band Corporation, Santa Monica, California, 1988.

Landes, W. M., and R. A. Posner, *The Economic Structure of Tort Law*, Harvard University Press, Cambridge, Massachusetts, 1987.

Malecki, Donald S., and Ronald C. Horn, Eric A. Wiening, Arthur L. Flitner. *Commercial Liability Insurance and Risk Management* (3rd ed.) Volume 1., American Institute for CPCU, Malvern, Pennsylvania, 1995.

McCormic, Barnes W., and Capt. M.P. Papadakis. *Aircraft Accident Reconstruction and Litigation.* Lawyers & Judges Publishing Company, Inc., Tucson, Arizona, 1996.

Posner, R. A. *Economic Analysis of Law* (3rd ed.), Little Brown and Company Law Book Division, Boston, Massachusetts, 1986.

Shavell, S., "Strict Liability versus Negligence," *Journal of Legal Study*, 1980.

Vaughn, Emmett J., and Therese M. Vaughan. *Fundamentals of risk and insurance* (9th ed.) John Wiley & Sons, Inc., New York, 2003.

Chapter 7

Insurance Contracts

OUTLINE

Introduction
Prerequisites to an Enforceable Contract
Formation of the Contract
The Policy Layout
Characteristics of the Insurance Contract
Authority of Agents and Brokers
Waiver and Estoppel

OBJECTIVES

At the end of this chapter you should be able to:
Identify the prerequisites to an enforceable contract.
Discuss the importance of applications and binders for insurance contracts.
Describe the major components of an insurance contract.
Define the following characteristics of the insurance policy: aleatory, conditional, unilateral, personal, contract of adhesion, and contract of utmost good faith.
Differentiate between representations and warranties
Compare the causal connection concept and the contribute-to-the-loss standard in breach of warranty suits
Explain how the parol (oral) evidence rule works.
Explain concealment and the role of fraud.
Explain the Law of Agency.
Discuss the three types of authority possessed by an agent.
Describe how the doctrines of waiver and estoppel affect the powers of agents.

INTRODUCTION

The insurance contract is usually called a policy. It is generally governed by the rules of contract law and will be interpreted in the same manner as all other contracts. Policyholders sometimes forget that the insurance contract is a legal obligation both on the part of the company and also on their part. Policyholders will frequently request the company to waive minimum pilot requirements or extend territorial limits under the policy. It would be unfair to other policyholders not to enforce the insurance contract fairly and impartially.

The aspects of law most relevant to insurance are contract law and agency law because the insurance policy is a legal contract and insurance companies must carry on most of their relations with the public through their agents. A fundamental rule of contract law is that any contract will be interpreted more strongly in favor of the party that did not draw it. Since the insurance company invariably prepares the insurance contract without consultation or assistance from the insured, any ambiguities in the contract will be interpreted in favor of the policyholder. It is also noteworthy that juries have a natural tendency to favor the injured party. This prejudice exists to some extent against all large corporations, but seems to be particularly potent toward insurance companies.

PREREQUISITES TO AN ENFORCEABLE CONTRACT

As in all contracts, there are certain prerequisites before an insurance policy will be valid. These general characteristics are as follows:

1. *Offer and acceptance*. There must be a definite unqualified offer by one party, the offeror, and the offer must be accepted without change by the offeree. A

valid offer must meet the test of contractual intention, definiteness, and communication to the offeree. In insurance, the prospect for insurance makes an offer to the insurance company through either an oral or written application. The acceptance takes place when an authorized agent binds the coverage, or the policy is issued. Sometimes, the insurance company will reject the prospect's offer and make a counteroffer based on changes in coverage, limits, or rates. Coverage is not effective until accepted by the prospect. In property and liability insurance, an oral binder is an enforceable contract. Coverage starts immediately, and if a loss occurs prior to the written binder being issued, the insurance company will be liable for the loss. The risk manager should get a binder number and the name of the insurance company at the time of the acceptance. Life insurance agents have no authority to bind an insurance company.

2. *Consideration.* All contracts must be supported by a legal consideration, which means that there must be an exchange of values by the parties. The values exchanged do not have to be equal. The consideration of the insurance company is the promise to pay for losses caused by covered perils. The consideration by the insured is the payment of the premium, or the promise to pay it, plus an agreement to abide by the conditions of the policy. In life insurance, at least one-twelfth of the annual premium must be submitted with the written application to have a legal consideration.
3. *Competent parties.* An insurance company is legally competent to contract if it is licensed to do business in the state in which the policy is written and if it is licensed to write the type of insurance in question. Applicants for insurance are legally competent if they are legally of age and of sound mind. In most states, a minor is considered to be a person under the age of 18. The law concerning contracting with minors is that, except for contracts of necessities of life, the contract is voidable at the option of the minor. The courts have held that insurance does not qualify as a necessity of life. Marriage creates full contractual competence regardless of age. Most states allow persons under the legal age to enter into valid and enforceable life insurance contracts. The age limit varies from 14 1/2 to 18 years.
4. *Legal purpose.* An insurable interest must be present; otherwise the contract is a gambling contract and unenforceable. However, insurance can be written to cover property used in an illegal enterprise and still be valid. For example, insurance purchased on an aircraft used to haul contraband would still be valid, even though the use of the aircraft was illegal. Coverage would be denied if the accident occurred while committing an illegal act.

FORMATION OF THE CONTRACT

Two basic instruments used in the formation of insurance contracts are the application and the binder.

The Application

The *application* is generally required as a basis for the contract, and the insurer relies upon its statements for much of the underwriting information. The application can be looked upon as the inducement for the applicant to make an offer. There is no standard form of application and there are different applications for various lines of insurance. However, all applications follow a pattern. For example, the hull and liability application includes information that will: (1) identify the applicant; (2) give all the particulars concerning the aircraft to be insured; (3) give detailed pilot information; (4) identify previous accidents; and (5) indicate the coverages and limits desired. In addition, underwriters will usually require a completed pilot qualification report to accompany the application.

The Binder

In some cases insurance coverage may be provided while the application is being processed. This is done with a *binder*, which is a temporary contract, pending the issuance of the policy. Binders should be written with a unique binder number. This will document the understanding between the insured and the agent/broker. Major items included under a hull and liability binder are: (1) the name and address of the insured; (2) description of the aircraft; (3) leinholder in the event of an encumbrance on the aircraft; (4) coverages and limits of liability; (5) pilot warranty; and (6) any other pertinent clauses and conditions.

THE POLICY LAYOUT

The insurance policy is a contract between the insured and the insurer. It defines the rights and duties of the contracting parties and while different policies are designed to cover various risks, they all have similar components: declarations, insuring agreements, definitions, exclusions, and conditions. Most aviation insurance policies also have endorsements.

Declaration

The *declaration* makes up the first part of the insurance policy and includes the descriptive material relating to the risk. The declaration identifies the person(s) or organization(s) covered by the contract, period of coverage, policy coverage and limits, premium charged, description of the object of insurance, and any warranties or promises made by the insured regarding the nature and control of the insured risk.

Insuring Agreements

The *insuring agreements* broadly define the coverages afforded under the policy. For example, in most liability policies these agreements cover claims arising out of the insured's negligence or alleged negligence. They promise to defend any liability suit brought against the insured if the coverage applies.

Definitions

The *definitions* of important terms in the policy are usually in a separate section. Terms found in the hull and liability policy include aircraft, bodily injury, property damage, named insured, passenger, pilot-in-command, and Federal Aviation Administration.

Exclusions

Exclusions reduce the broad coverage provided in the insuring agreements. The purpose of exclusions is to:

1. Eliminate duplicate coverage in other policies the insured may have such as workers' compensation coverage.
2. Eliminate coverage not needed by the typical insured even though it may be important to some insureds.
3. Eliminate specialized coverage that the insurer is not qualified to offer or that requires special underwriting and rating, such as air meet liability.

Conditions

The *conditions* provide the ground rules by enumerating the duties of the parties to the contract. Remember that the insurance policy is a conditional contract. Before the insurance company will pay for a loss or defend an insured, the insured has certain duties to perform under the contract. Failure to do so may release the insurer from its obligations. Many conditions found in insurance policies are common to all. For example, all policies contain cancellation provisions as well as duties of the insured in the event of loss, such as giving notice to the insurer within a certain time period and filing a proof of loss. There are also requirements with regard to protecting the property against further loss and cooperation of the insured.

Endorsements

An underwriter uses *endorsements* to make changes in the policy. They may increase or decrease the coverage, change the premium, correct a statement, or make any number of other changes to the contract. The pilot warranty might be amended to include a named pilot who does not meet the minimums or the territorial limits in the policy may be extended to include a particular trip. These situations normally require an endorsement and often times an additional premium.

CHARACTERISTICS OF THE INSURANCE CONTRACT

The insurance policy is a legal contract and as such is governed by the general rules of contract law. There are, however, several features of the insurance policy, which distinguish it from most other contracts. The following represent the more important characteristics.

Aleatory Contract

Insurance is classified as an *aleatory contract,* because the values exchanged by the contracting parties are not necessarily equal. The ordinary commercial contract is known legally as a commutative contract, and each party expects to receive approximately the same value as he gives. The person who pays $80,000 for an aircraft expects that the aircraft is worth $80,000, and the seller is also satisfied with the value of the sale. In insurance, if a loss does occur during the policy period, the amount of the loss will generally exceed the annual premium. If no loss occurs, then the premium exceeds the amount the insurer pays, which is zero. The individual who pays $1,000 for hull coverage may recover $80,000 if his aircraft is destroyed or stolen.

Conditional Contract

Insurance is a *conditional contract* since the promises of the insurance company are conditioned upon the insured paying the initial and subsequent premiums and also fulfilling any requirements of the contract. Typical policy requirements include giving notice of an accident, protecting the aircraft from further damage after an accident, and filing a proof of loss statement.

Unilateral Contract

From the legal standpoint, insurance is a *unilateral contract* because only one party makes promises that are enforceable. Policyholders cannot be required to pay premiums or adhere to policy conditions. If they fail to pay the premiums, the conditional characteristic of the contract keeps them from being able to collect for losses. If the insured does what is promised, then the insurance company is legally required to carry out the provisions of the policy. The ordinary commercial contract is a *bilateral contract*, which means that the promise of one party is given in return for the promise of another. For example, the purchaser of an aircraft radio promises to pay $3,500 in return for the promise of the dealer to deliver the radio to him. In insurance, the act is on the part of the insured, namely, paying the premium on the policy. The essential duty of the insurance company is to furnish a guarantee (promise) of payment in the event a loss occurs.

Personal Contract

The insurance contract is a *personal* one, which means that its issuance depends upon such things as the personal characteristics of the applicant, his pilot qualifications, and use of the aircraft. For this reason, the insured cannot transfer the protection of his policy to another without the consent of the company. At the time of purchasing a used aircraft for cash, the new owner may assume that the existing hull and liability insurance will go with the airplane. This is obviously not the case. When title (ownership) passes, the existing insurance policy is no longer valid because the insured does not have an insurable interest in the airplane any more.

Contract of Adhesion

The standardized insurance contract is prepared entirely by the insurance company; there is no element of bargaining over the terms of the basic contract. With few exceptions, the insured must either accept or reject the contract as a whole. In other words, the insured either adheres to the contract as it has been prepared by the insurance company or else he does not accept it. It is *a contract of adhesion*. The legal importance of this is that, since the applicant for insurance has no part in preparing the policy language, any ambiguities in the contract will be resolved more strongly against the insurance company. The insured will therefore receive the benefit of any doubt in the legal interpretation of the contract. This principle is due to the fact that the insurer had the advantage of writing the terms of the contract to suit its particular purposes. Policy language and its interpretation are often argued in court. The frequency of this occurring is growing due to the willingness of insurance companies to tailor coverages for their large accounts by issuing a manuscript policy. A now well-known example of a law suit involving language interpretation in a manuscript policy involved the definition of occurrence in the World Trade Center litigation. The policy defined an occurrence as "all losses or damages that are attributable directly or indirectly to one cause or to one series of similar causes. All such losses will be added together and that total amount of such losses will be treated as one occurrence irrespective of the period of time or area over which such losses occur." On the basis of this definition, which was found to be unambiguous, insurers found to be bound by this form were deemed responsible for no more than a single occurrence. *World Trade Ctr.Props*. L.L.C. v. *Hartford Fire Ins. Co.*, 345 F.3d 154 (2d Cir. 2003) 1.

Utmost Good Faith

In ordinary commercial contracts the rule of "let the buyer beware" prevails because in most businesses the buyer can inspect the product and obtain a reasonable idea as to its quality. In insurance, the applicant is not in a good position to inspect the product; even if the insurance company furnishes specimen policies for examination, the interpretation of these is often beyond the applicants ability. However, the company may also be at a disadvantage because it is unable to determine all the facts concerning the risk. The phrase *utmost good faith* means that the insurance contract must contain a greater degree of good faith, both on the part of the insured and of the company, than is true of ordinary commercial contracts. So to protect the primary interests of the insurer, a number of formalized defense devices have evolved. These are categorized as representations and warranties, parol (oral) evidence rule, concealment, and fraud.

Representations and Warranties

In applying for insurance, the person seeking coverage makes certain statements to the insurance company or to its agent or through the broker. The company must rely to a greater or lesser extent upon the truth of these statements in deciding whether to issue the policy. In some cases, it is possible to verify these statements from other sources, such as credit reports, but in many cases it is not. The insurance company, therefore, is at the mercy of the applicant to the extent that it must rely upon these statements being true. Although most statements made to insurance companies are true, it is important to determine the impact when false statements are made, either intentionally or unintentionally. This is determined in large part by the application of the law regarding representations and warranties.

A *representation* is a statement by the applicant made prior to, or at the time of, making the contract. Its purpose is to give the insurance company information upon which to base its decision whether to underwrite the risk and to establish the proper premium for the policy. A representation is a statement of knowledge or opinion by the applicant, generally made in the application but also done orally. The answers to questions such as the following are representations: Is your aircraft normally hangared or tied down? Where? Have you had any aircraft accidents during the past five years? Do you hold a valid pilot's license and a current medical certificate? How many pilot-in-command hours do you have in the model aircraft to be insured? How many hours have you flown during the past 90 days? When and where did you first learn to fly? From a technical standpoint a representation does not become a part of the contract, but rather is an inducement to enter into the contract.

A representation which is untrue is called a *misrepresentation*, and it may be used by the company to void the contract only if the misrepresentation is material. A misrepresentation is material if the insurance company, had it known the facts at the inception of the policy, would have refused to issue the policy or would have issued it only on a different basis. The burden of proving materiality is upon the insurer. Misrepresentations concerning the insured's piloting experience is generally material since they have an important bearing upon whether the company will consider the risk and for what premium. Statements about the insured's place of birth, where and when he learned to fly, and how many driving tickets he received during the past year are usually not considered material. When the representation is merely a statement of opinion or belief on the part of the applicant, it is obvious that if the representation is false he cannot be held to be at fault. Some courts have held that there must be bad faith on the part of the applicant before the insurance company is able to cancel the contract or deny coverage on this basis. Other jurisdictions require that for materiality, the misrepresentation must have actually "increased the risk of loss." For example, a company might have a difficult time defending its denial of coverage in the event of an accident because an insured inadvertently let his medical certificate lapse for two months. Not having a valid medical certificate for two years might be another story. The best legal authority is that where the insurance company is relying upon misrepresentations of fact in underwriting the contract, it is of no concern whether a misrepresentation is made purposely or innocently. If a misrepresentation is material, the insurance company generally has the right to refuse payment under the contract.

A warranty is a statement or promise set forth in the policy, the untruth or nonfulfillment of which in any respect renders the policy voidable by the insurer, regardless of the materiality of such statement or promise. Warranties are of two types, promissory and affirmative. A *promissory warranty* makes a statement or promise about the future or continuing truth of the matter represented. For example, stating that a burglar alarm will be installed and maintained in proper working order on the aircraft while it is hangared or tied down at All American Airport would be a promissory warranty included in the contract. Another example might be a clause to the effect that a co-pilot will be utilized at all times when the aircraft is operated under instrument flight rules (IFR) or flown into high density traffic areas.

An *affirmative warranty* is the more common type and is a statement concerning a fact as of the time the contract is entered into and nothing more. If an affirmative warranty is untrue to the slightest extent, the insurance company may void the contract. A pilot warranty requiring a valid private pilot's license and current medical certificate with a minimum of 200 pilot in-command hours would be an affirmative warranty. Another example of an affirmative warranty would be an aircraft policy that states that no insurer has cancelled an aircraft insurance policy covering the insured within the last three years.

The question of materiality does not enter into a consideration of warranties since by their very definition the question of materiality is not an issue. A warranty forms an essential part of a contract and must be included in it. It will be readily seen that a warranty may sometimes work an undue hardship on the insured because a slight misstatement may allow the insurance company to refuse payment. This can be illustrated by the legal concept known as *causal connection*. The aircraft policy has an open pilot warranty which states that the policy applies only when the aircraft is being operated by a pilot with a commercial pilot's certificate, current medical certificate, 2,000 logged pilot- in-command hours, and 25 hours in make and model being flown. A pilot with an expired medical certificate has an accident that resulted from a defective aircraft part. Even though there was no causal relationship between the expired medical certificate and the accident, the insurance company might decline to pay the damages solely because there was a breach of an affirmative warranty. Other events that occur without causal connection that might result in no coverage are:

- Pilot meets the total hour's requirement but lacks the specified logged time in make and model.
- Use of the airplane for purposes not stated on the declaration page. Charging passengers when the airplane was rated industrial aid is an example.
- An accident occurring on an island off the coast of Florida when the policy specifically limits coverage to the continental United States.
- An accident where the pilot was engaged in formal flight instruction and this was not permitted in the policy.

Due to the unfairness that can arise from this concept most jurisdictions have adopted the *contribute-to-the-loss standard* when breach of warranty issues are the basis for the law suit. Under this standard the insured will only be denied coverage if there was a causal connection between the breach of the warranty and the actual loss. It is interesting to note that the loss burden of proof is placed on the insured to prove that the breach of the warranty was NOT related to the loss. South Carolina and Texas have elected to place the burden of proof on the insurer in all contribute-to-the-loss cases.
Warranties may be distinguished from representations in the following ways:

1. Warranties form a part of the contract and are agreed to be essential to it; representations are collateral inducements to a contract being formed.
2. Warranties are written into the policy; representations may be contained in other documents such as lease agreements or applications or may even be oral statements given to an agent.
3. Warranties are conclusively presumed to be material; representations must be proved to be material by the insurance company.
4. Warranties must be strictly complied with; only substantial truth is required in the case of representations.

Thus the most important differences between a warranty and a representation are the question of materiality and the requirement that a warranty must become a part of the policy. If a warranty is breached, it does not matter whether the breach is small or large; but a misrepresentation must be material before it will affect the enforceability of the contract.

Parol (Oral) Evidence Rule

An important rule in interpreting insurance contracts is what is known as the *parol (oral) evidence rule*, or the entire contract rule. This rule states that the prepared document is presumed to represent the intent of the parties, and no oral evidence will be admissible to contradict its written terms. There are a limited number of exceptions where the written terms of a contract can be modified by oral evidence. Parol evidence may be admissible in situations in which the terms of a written contract are incomplete, where the contract is ambiguous, or when there has been a mistake or fraud in the preparation of the written contract. The parol evidence rule generally prohibits the incorporation of any warranty into the policy by reference. Incorporation by reference is a legal method whereby the policy makes reference to a separate document and states that it is incorporated in the policy. Generally speaking, it is impossible to incorporate either a warranty or representation into the policy by this method. If the application is not physically attached to the policy, it is not part of the policy and warranties or statements made in the application cannot be used against the insured.

Reasonable Expectations Doctrine

This doctrine represents an extension of the general rule that ambiguities are to be interpreted against the insurance company. Under the *reasonable expectations doctrine*, the courts interpret an insurance policy to mean what a reasonable buyer would expect it to mean. When this doctrine is used, the insured's reasonable expectations will dictate policy provisions and override the actual written policy. An important corollary of this doctrine is that policy language is to be interpreted as a layperson would understand it, and not as a lawyer or other person skilled in the law of insurance might interpret it. Insurance companies continue to rewrite and modernize their policies to assist the layperson in understanding terms and policy provisions.

Concealment

Concealment may be defined as remaining silent when there is a duty to speak. Thus it involves the deliberate withholding of information which the insured is under a legal obligation to furnish to the insurance company. The question naturally arises as to what information the insured is obligated to give. Over the years, the doctrine of concealment has gradually been liberalized, so that at the present time the insured is usually required to answer only those questions that appear in the printed application form. He is not, in most lines of insurance, obligated to volunteer any additional information. It is assumed that the insurance company, in drawing up a detailed survey questionnaire or application, has asked for all the information needed to make a fair evaluation of the risk. Since the insurance company cannot be expected to inquire about everything that may be material to the subject matter of the insurance, it would be prudent for the applicant to disclose extraordinary facts within his scope of knowledge. For example, a company would not ask if the hangar that the insured is renting was also a warehouse for the storage of explosives. This is a material fact and must be disclosed to the insurance company.

The concealment of a fact which is material to the risk need not be intentional or fraudulent in order to allow the insurance company to void the policy. In a strict sense, the applicant is required to answer all of the questions in the application with complete truth. It is not necessary that there be a fraudulent intent to deceive on the part of the applicant for the policy to be voidable. As a practical measure, the more liberal insurance companies tend to interpret concealment to mean that the insured has willfully concealed facts that were known to him.

The difference between misrepresentation and concealment should be noted. A misrepresentation is a positive misstatement of fact, whereas concealment is the failure to speak when there is a legal duty to do so. Assume that an applicant is asked to provide a statement concerning his health. He mentions a number of trivial matters but neglects to mention that he is suffering from heart trouble and is flying subject to a waiver from the FAA. In this case, his silence cannot be defended, since he is under a legal duty to answer the questions fully and completely. The failure to answer the question fully is the legal equivalent of a fraudulent misrepresentation that he does not have heart trouble.

Fraud

Fraud is the deliberate attempt to mislead or cheat a third party. An innocent misstatement of fact, no matter how important, does not constitute fraud. Fraud on the part of the insured may occur either before the contract is written, while it is in force, or after a loss has occurred. Where there is fraud before the completion of a contract, it may be said that no legal contract ever came into existence, because the two parties did not contemplate the same thing when the contract was drawn up. Under contract law fraud at any stage makes a contract voidable by the injured party. This is equitable since each party is entitled to rely upon a minimum degree of honesty and fair dealing from the other party.

AUTHORITY OF AGENTS AND BROKERS

Because most insurance is placed in force through the efforts of agents and brokers, the relationships between insurance companies and their agents and between insurance agents and the general public are of considerable importance. Insurance agency relationships are based upon and governed by the *Law of Agency*, which is defined as "a relationship based upon an expressed or implied agreement whereby one person, the agent, is authorized to act for another, his principal, to transact business with third parties, the insured." Agents may possess three different types of authority: contractual, implied, and apparent.

Contractual authority of the agent is that granted to him by his contract with the insurance company. *Implied authority* is that which is necessarily granted in order for the agent to carry out his contractual duties and obligations. *Apparent authority* is that which the public believes the agent to possess and which he may or may not actually possess.

The insurer is liable for any fraud or other wrong perpetrated by its agent in the course of his employment. Consequently, insurance companies are very careful in the selection of their representatives. The *agent* is deemed to be acting for the principal, and public policy demands that acts done in the performance of regular duties should be imputed to the principal. Any important information that is known to the agent, either at the time of the formation of the contract or acquired by him prior to its completion is deemed to be known by the insurer. This rule applies even if the information was not communicated to the insurance company.

The authority of insurance agents differs considerably in the various lines of insurance. Because of the specialized nature of aviation insurance and the catastrophe exposure, most insurers restrict binding authority or changes in coverage to authorized company underwriters. All binders, policies, and endorsements are prepared and issued by the aviation insurers. To avoid misunderstanding, insurance companies make every attempt to notify the public of any limitation upon their agents' authority. Statements in the application that specifically limit the authority of the agent best accomplish this. The question of whether any given act of an agent is binding upon the insurer depends upon whether the third party had reasonable grounds for believing, in the light of all surrounding circumstances, that the insurance company had authorized the act in question. If such reasonable grounds did exist, the insurer will be bound regardless of what authority the agent possesses.

Brokers

An insurance *broker* is the legal agent of the prospective insured and is engaged to arrange insurance coverage on the best possible terms. The broker normally does business with a number of insurance companies and may have an agency agreement with some of them. Thus a broker is free to do business with any company that will write the business. Insurance brokers are particularly important in major metropolitan areas, while in rural areas and small cities there may be few, if any, brokers. The legal distinction between a broker and agent is that the broker is the agent of the insured, rather than of the insurance company. In actual practice, the distinction between the broker and agent is often slight. The broker in major metropolitan areas solicits insurance in the same manner as independent agents. The major advantages of brokers are that they generally possess specialized insurance knowledge and may place coverage with various companies. The larger brokerage firms who place insurance for air carriers and corporate accounts generally have a staff of aviation insurance specialists.

Waiver and Estoppel

The doctrines of waiver and estoppel affect the authority of agents and brokers as well as an insurer's position regarding the contract of insurance. An estimated one-third to one-half of the lawsuits between insured and insurer about the validity of enforceability of the contract involve a claim by the insured and denied by the insurer that the latter has waived a defense that he is now asserting.

Waiver

A *waiver* may be defined as the voluntary relinquishment of a known right or privilege. In most cases involving an alleged waiver, it is claimed that the insurance company has waived, or relinquished, one of its rights (provisions in the policy) and therefore must make a loss payment which it would not otherwise have had to make. Underwriters are quite often asked to waive such provisions in the policy as the territorial limits, minimum pilot requirements, or the assumed liability exclusion.

The definition of waiver as a "voluntary" relinquishment often does not describe the situation accurately, since the insurance company may insist that it has not waived a provision of the contract, whereas the insured will insist that the provision has been waived. In many cases it is claimed that the insurance company's agent has waived a provision of the policy. Consequently, where the company has agreed to waive a policy provision, agents generally require that evidence in writing be sent to them as soon as possible. A fax or letter will suffice until the endorsement to the policy arrives.

Estoppel

Estoppel may be defined as the prohibition against asserting a right because of inconsistent action or conduct. The insurance company is estopped—that is, prohibited— from asserting one of its rights because it has acted inconsistently. The doctrine of estoppel is applied in order to allow the insured to recover in those cases where the insurance company has acted inconsistently and has led the insured to assume that things were true which were untrue. It is often applied to situations involving the investigation and settlement of claims. For example, suppose the agent informed an insured that it was all right to rent his aircraft on occasion despite the fact that the policy purpose of use stated for business and pleasure only. Following an accident and investigation in which it was determined that the aircraft was rented, the company may be estopped from denying liability (asserting a right) because of the inconsistent action of the agent which led the insured to believe it was all right to rent his aircraft.

KEY TERMS

Offer and acceptance
Consideration
Competent parties
Legal purpose
Application
Binder
Declaration
Insuring agreements
Definitions
Exclusions
Conditions
Endorsements
Aleatory contract
Conditional contract
Representation
Misrepresentation
Promissory warranty
Affirmative Warranty
Causal connection
Contribute-to-the-loss standard
Parol (oral) evidence rule
Reasonable expectations doctrine
Concealment
Fraud
Law of Agency
Contractual authority
Implied authority
Apparent authority

Unilateral contract	Agent
Bilateral contract	Broker
Personal contract	Waiver
Contract of adhesion	Estoppel
Utmost good faith	

REVIEW QUESTIONS

1. Name and explain the four prerequisites of an enforceable contract.
2. Describe a binder and explain its use in aircraft insurance.
3. All insurance policies have similar components. Identify the five major components and discuss the purpose of each. Explain the role of endorsements.
4. Explain why an aircraft policy is an aleatory contract. Why are ambiguities in the insurance policy generally interpreted in favor of the policyholder? Why can't an insured assign his policy to someone else?
5. What is a representation? How is the materiality of a misrepresentation determined? What is a warranty? Give an example of a promissory and an affirmative warranty. How are warranties distinguished from representations?
6. Why is the understanding of the concept of "causal connection" important?
7. What is the significance of the parol (oral) rule? Distinguish between concealment and fraud. Distinguish between concealment and misrepresentation.
8. Describe the three different types of authority possessed by an agent. Why do insurers restrict binding authority for agents on aviation liability risks?
9. Define waiver and estoppel. How do they affect the authority of agents?

REFERENCES

[1] Stern, Jonathan M. "The Manuscript Policy: A Potential "Stuckeyville" in the Insurance World." *For The Defense,* Vol. 47, No. 2 (February 2005)

Athern, James L., and S. Travis Pritchett. *Risk and Insurance* (6th Ed.). West Publishing Company, St. Paul, Minnesota, 1989.

Gorals, Philip. *Property and Casualty Insurance* (24th Ed.). The Rough Notes Co., Inc., New York, New York, 1997.

Mehr, Robert I., and Emerson Commack. *Principles of Insurance* (5th Ed.). Richard D. Irwin, Inc., Homewood, Illinois, 1985.

Trieschmann, James S., Robert E. Hoyt and David W. Sommer. *Risk Management & Insurance* (12th Ed.). South-Western, Mason, Ohio, 2005.

Vaughn, Emmett J., and Therese M. Vaughn. *Fundamentals of Risk and Insurance* (9th Ed.). John Wiley & Sons, Inc., New York, 2003.

PART THREE
GENERAL AVIATION INSURANCE

Chapter 8

Aircraft Hull and Liability Insurance

OUTLINE

Introduction
Declarations Page
Aircraft Hull Insurance
Coverage
Exclusions
Limit of Liability—Total or Partial Loss
Conditions Applicable to Hull Coverage
Newly Acquired Aircraft
Common Endorsements Related to Hull Coverage
Aircraft Liability Insurance
Legal Liability Coverages
Limits of Legal Liability
Medical Payments
Definition of Insured
Exclusions
Special Coverage Features
Conditions Applicable to Liability Coverages
Common Endorsements Related to Liability Coverage
Other Miscellaneous Coverages
Other Conditions Applicable to Hull and Liability
Other Endorsements
Additional Considerations for Business Aircraft Operators Who Are Reimbursed for Expenses
Insurance Considerations
Insured's Responsibilities Following a Loss
Concluding Comments

OBJECTIVES

At the end of this chapter you should be able to:
Describe the purpose of the Declarations Page and identify the items included.
Distinguish between the two most common hull coverages offered.
Define the term "aircraft" as used in the hull and liability policy.
Explain how the insured value is determined.
Describe the purpose of deductibles and various types of deductibles used in aircraft hull insurance.
Summarize the common exclusions applicable to hull coverage.
Distinguish between an "actual cash value" and a "valued basis" coverage.
Identify the insured's duties in the event of loss.
Explain the appraisal provisions.
Discuss some of the common endorsements related to hull coverage.
Identify the three basic legal liability coverages.
Explain how medical payments coverage works.
Distinguish between those individuals and organizations covered and not covered under the definition of insured.
Summarize the major exclusions found under aircraft liability coverages.
Describe several of the special coverage features applicable to the liability portion of the contract.

Discuss the conditions applicable to liability coverages.
Discuss some of the common endorsements related to liability coverage.
Highlight the general conditions applicable to hull and liability coverages found in the combined aircraft policy.
Distinguish between joint ownership, interchange agreement, time-sharing agreement, exclusive dry lease, management company arrangement and fractional ownership.
Discuss the insurance considerations under the aforementioned arrangements.

INTRODUCTION

Aircraft Hull and Liability insurance has evolved into a unique field over the years since the first aircraft policy was issued by Lloyd's of London in 1911. It has become a blend of fire, auto, personal-accident, and marine insurance, having characteristics very different from its antecedents. Reliance on knowledge of other types of insurance can easily lead to false assumptions, the least penalty of which is paying for unnecessary coverages but by far the worst is being without the protection when it is needed.

Unlike other forms of insurance, aviation insurance contracts are highly individualized. There is no standard, formal aviation policy used nationwide. Each company issues its own policy, with its unique wording, that may have little similarity to an aviation contract issued by another company. All aircraft hull and liability policies provide basic liability and physical damage coverage on the aircraft; however, additional coverages can be found under one contract that are omitted under another company's form. In addition, exclusionary wording can be found in certain policies that will not be found in others.

Some insurers offer two or more basic hull and liability contracts which present another complicating factor. Policies with less restrictive wording are designed for more attractive risks while the more restrictive contract is offered to less desirable risks.

Before getting into the specifics of the aircraft hull and liability contract, it may be helpful to point out several other unique characteristics of aviation insurance which influence the basic contract. More will be said about these characteristics in chapter 10 which concerns underwriting and pricing.

1. Aviation insurance contracts are relatively unencumbered by state and federal regulation.
2. Hundreds of insurers compete for most other lines of insurance, but only a handful may offer competitive terms for a particular aviation exposure.
3. The limited number of aircraft in the civil aircraft fleet (compared to exposure units in other fields of insurance, like automobiles), prohibits aviation insurers from applying the law of large numbers, as do most other insurers.
4. Most insurers use published rates, filed with the state insurance governing body. This is neither practical nor realistic for aviation. Market size necessitates the use of judgment rating by each aviation insurer, so premiums may differ substantially from company to company.
5. Although many agents may have the authority to bind or amend ordinary insurance coverages, such authority is seldom granted for aviation insurance.
6. Operation of general aviation aircraft in the same environment with multimillion-dollar airliners, capable of carrying hundreds of passengers, creates an enormous exposure to loss far greater than almost any other activity.

The following section covers the basic aircraft hull and liability contract. A sample contract is included at the end of this chapter.

DECLARATIONS PAGE

The *Declarations page* includes statements that present information about the risk to be insured. These statements are normally taken from an application completed by the insured to provide underwriters with information from which they make their judgment on risk selection as well as the terms of the contract and appropriate premium. Consequently, these statements are made a part of the insurance contract by including much of the application information on the declarations page itself. The intent is to protect the insurer from misrepresentations or omissions by the insured. For example, if a pilot falsely represented himself or herself as having a total of 500 logged hours and the policy was written and rated based on an open pilot warranty requiring that minimum number of hours, the insurer could probably successfully deny a claim if it was determined that the pilot had less than the 500-hour minimum.

Item 1 of the declarations states the name and address of the insured(s). This might include an individual, partnership or corporation, depending upon the legal ownership of the aircraft and that particular entity being responsible for the legal liability arising out of the ownership of the aircraft.

Item 2 includes the policy period in which the contract is in force. Most aviation policies begin and end at 12:01 a.m.

Item 3 shows the basic coverages and limits of liability selected. The insured may purchase multiple limits of liability under coverages: A—Bodily Injury Excluding Passengers, B—Passenger Bodily Injury, and C—Property Damage or a single limit Bodily Injury and Property Damage including or excluding Passengers under Coverage D. Coverage E, Medical Expense Coverage, is optional and may be purchased either including or excluding the crew.

The three Physical Damage (Hull) Coverages shown under the sample form are: F—All Risks Basis, G—All Risks Basis Not in Flight, or H—All Risk Basis Not in Motion. The applicable deductibles are also indicated. Each of the coverages will be discussed in greater detail in a following section of this chapter.

Item 4 provides a description of the aircraft to be insured including the FAA registration number, passenger capacity and insured value. Under item 5, the insured must explain any financial arrangement for the aircraft other than sole and unconditional ownership. For example, a lessor or financial institution holding a mortgage or lien on the aircraft may be listed under this section.

Item 6 Aircraft Use delineates the uses of the aircraft agreed to by the insured and the insurance carrier. Normally general aviation aircraft are used for one of the following purposes:

1. *Business and Pleasure.* Primarily individually owned aircraft for the owner's personal use and for which no charge is made and no direct profit is derived.
2. *Industrial Aid (Business or Corporate Use).* For company owned aircraft usually flown by a professional pilot and used for the transportation of executives, employees, and nonpaying guests of the company in furtherance of the company's business interests and involving no direct charge or profit from such operation.

Some policies like the example in the sample policy use language like "financial profit." Other policies use wording such as "payments made by others" to remove coverage when money is paid for a flight. A further discussion of the implications of reimbursement can be found under a later section in this chapter entitled "Additional Considerations for the Business Aircraft Operator who is Reimbursed for Expenses."

3. *Limited Commercial.* Relates to those aircraft used for profit making activi-

ties such as instruction or rental to others, and also includes the uses under Business and Pleasure or Industrial Aid. It specifically excludes transporta tion of passengers or cargo for hire as well as Special Uses.

4. *Commercial*. Covers the same exposures as Limited Commercial but includes passenger carrying for hire.
5. *Special Uses*. This category includes crop dusting, spraying, hunting, seeding, fire fighting, fish restocking, banner towing or any use which requires more detailed evaluation and special rating.

Item 7 lists the approved pilots and is perhaps the most important part of the policy for an insured to read and understand. Many insureds allow their airplanes to be flown by other pilots without considering whether such use invalidates the contract. Even the most experienced and respected pilot on the field may have an expired medical certificate or lack time in the model which may invalidate the insured's coverage.

Some policies will cover a "named pilot" and set forth the minimum requirements for other pilots who may fly the insured aircraft. Commonly referred to as the "open pilot warranty" it requires approved pilots to hold a private, commercial or airline transport certificate with an appropriate rating for the flight involved (such as a multiengine or instrument rating) and a current medical certificate. Some open pilot warranties call for a minimum number of total hours (or total logged hours), number of hours in make and model of aircraft, and the type of aircraft. For example, it might state "The policy shall not apply while the aircraft is in flight unless the pilot in command has a valid and current private, commercial, or airline transport certificate with appropriate ratings for the flight involved and a valid medical certificate, as required by the Federal Aviation Regulations of the Federal Aviation Administration, and having at least 500 hours as pilot in command, of which at least 50 hours were in aircraft equipped with retractable landing gear, and 10 hours were in the model aircraft being flown." Some pilot warranties will substitute a checkout by a flight instructor in lieu of time in the model.

The premium charged depends largely upon the experience and ability of the pilot. Insureds may improve their rates based on experience by verifying total hours flown as a pilot-in-command and time in make and model. Further, the insurance company, from an underwriting standpoint may only accept a risk if certain minimal hourly requirements are met. Some aircraft requiring a copilot will also include an open pilot warranty setting forth the minimum certificate and flying hours required for this individual.

AIRCRAFT HULL INSURANCE

Aircraft hull is derived from the marine term "hull" and means physical damage to the aircraft itself. It is designed to protect the interest of owners, operators (lessor or lessee), and other parties with a direct financial interest, such as lienholders. Hull coverage does not benefit permissive users, such as borrowers, renters, maintenance or sales organizations. Coverage for physical damage to the airplane is similar to the physical damage coverage written for automobiles; however, there are several important differences. In the first place, the airplane is more susceptible to damage than an automobile. In the second place, the value of the aircraft is usually far higher than, that of an automobile. Third, depreciation and obsolescence are of greater importance in aviation physical damage. One of the reasons why rates for used aircraft are higher than those covering new aircraft is that in the event of partial loss, old parts are generally replaced with new parts without any deduction for depreciation.

COVERAGE

The two most common hull coverages are *all risks-ground and flight* and *all risks-not in motion*. Some companies still write *all risks-not in flight* which includes coverage while the aircraft is taxiing. Years ago underwriters even wrote hull coverage for specified perils such as fire, explosion, lightning, theft, vandalism, and so forth. Because of the moral hazard and the lack of spread in rates caused by a number of factors including competition and improved loss ratios, underwriters no longer offer such a wide variety of hull coverages. There is simply not enough credit in the rates to warrant the distinction in coverages.

All Risks-Ground and Flight

The broadest aircraft hull coverage, all risks-ground and flight, provides all risks protection whether or not the aircraft is in flight at the time of loss. This coverage further provides that if the aircraft disappears after takeoff and is not reported or located within 60 days, it is considered lost in flight and hence, is covered.

All Risks-Not in Motion

This coverage is applicable to physical loss or damage while the aircraft is on the ground and not moving under its power or resulting momentum. This coverage includes a loss occurring while the aircraft is being pushed into the hangar or towed by a tractor but does not insure against damage the aircraft may sustain while taxiing.

Hull Coverage Definitions

There are several important definitions applicable under the hull portion of an aircraft hull and liability policy. First of all is the *aircraft* itself which is defined as the aircraft or rotorcraft described in the declarations including the propulsion system and equipment usually installed in the aircraft, such as any operating, navigating, or radio equipment, (1) while installed in the aircraft, (2) while temporarily removed from the aircraft, and (3) while removed from the aircraft for replacement until such time as replacement by a similar item is started. Also included are tools and equipment in the aircraft which have been specially designed for the aircraft in which they are ordinarily carried.

In flight means the time commencing with the actual takeoff run of the aircraft and continuing thereafter until it has completed its landing roll. Or, if the aircraft is a rotorcraft, from the time the rotors start to revolve under power for the purpose of flight until they subsequently cease to revolve.

In motion means while the aircraft is moving under its own power or the momentum generated therefrom or while it is in flight and, if the aircraft is a rotorcraft, any time that the rotors are rotating.

Insured Value

The *insured value* is that amount which is stated in the policy as the insured value. Usually, this amount represents the purchase price of the aircraft, if new, or the current market value, if used. The insured value must be the actual cash value of the aircraft because a moral risk may be created by insuring over value and insufficient premiums developed if under valued. This is particularly important because of the absence of a coinsurance clause in aviation policies. Coinsurance refers to a participation percentage in every loss by the insured. Years ago, coinsurance was quite prevalent in hull contracts. Under such provisions, the insured paid a specified proportion of any loss that occurred, and the insurance company paid the balance.

Another past practice which is seldom found today is a set depreciation figure (approximately 12 percent). Where this provision appeared, total losses were settled subject to the depreciation factor on a pro rata basis.

Deductibles

Most aircraft hull coverages are written subject to a deductible. This is particularly true for single -engine aircraft flown for business and pleasure purposes and aircraft used for commercial purposes. The deductible means that the insured must bear a certain amount of damage in the loss. Deductible clauses excluding small losses are based on sound insurance principles. Deductibles reduce the price of insurance by eliminating numerous small claims that are relatively expensive to handle. Deductibles also decrease the moral hazard. An insured forced to pay a part of each loss may be more careful, thus encouraging loss prevention.

The common type of deductible is the *straight deductible* found in single-engine, business and pleasure policies. It is generally expressed as a specified amount (e.g., $50, $100, $250, or more) or as a percentage of the insured value (e.g ., 5 percent, 10 percent, or more). The standard deductible which most companies use for business and pleasure risks is $50 ground-no motion and $250 in flight and taxiing (in motion). Some companies apply a dollar deductible with respect to ground losses, and a percentage deductible with respect to flight losses. For example, one company applies a $50 deductible to ground losses and a 5 percent deductible to flight losses. Other combinations are possible and an insured may eliminate the deductibles for an additional premium. Similarly, a larger deductible with a commensurately lower premium is sometimes entertained if the larger deductible is not imposed at the underwriter's request.

Generally, the standard deductibles for commercial risks (aircraft used for flight instruction, rental, or charter) are higher than those for business and pleasure risks. A typical deductible for commercial operators' aircraft would be $500 "across the board" ($500 ground-no motion and $500 in motion). Multiengine aircraft flown by corporations with professional pilots (industrial aid use) are usually not subject to deductibles. The reason being, even minor claims involving multiengine aircraft can run into thousands of dollars which would circumvent the purpose of a deductible and simply become a burden to the insured.

Underwriters will sometimes impose an *ingestion deductible* on jet aircraft for damage to a turbine engine when it sucks up rocks, hail stones, birds, and other foreign objects which can damage the fan blades and other parts of the engine. For seaplanes and amphibians, there is generally a *moored deductible* which applies while the aircraft is tied in the water. Separate deductibles apply to helicopters while the rotors are in motion and not in motion.

Deductibles usually do not apply to total or partial losses caused by theft, robbery, vandalism, fire, lightning, or explosion or while the aircraft is dismantled and being transported. These losses would also not be consistent with the primary purpose of deductibles which is to eliminate petty claims.

A *franchise deductible* is similar to a straight deductible except that once the amount of loss exceeds the franchise deductible, the loss is paid in full. This deductible is used on occasion in commercial risks, although it is generally stated as a percentage of the insured value rather than a dollar amount. Assume that an aircraft has an insured value of $50,000 subject to a 5 percent franchise. If a loss amounts to less than $2,500, the insurer is free of liability, but if the loss exceeds $2,500, the insurer is liable for the full amount.

The major disadvantage with the franchise deductible from the insurer's standpoint is the moral hazard that the insured may try to inflate the claim in an effort to collect the entire loss.

Very infrequently, aviation underwriters will offer a *disappearing deductible*. The disappearing deductible combines the franchise and straight deductibles. The typical version provides that no portion of loss less than a minimum amount will be paid. Alternatively, the deductible does not apply if the loss exceeds a higher stated dollar limit. For losses falling between the minimum and the stated dollar limit, the insured receives a percentage of the amount by which the loss exceeds the minimum amount.

In the case of scheduled air carriers, companies will occasionally write hull coverage with an aggregate deductible. Whereas a straight deductible applies to each loss, an *aggregate deductible* applies to losses during a specified period of time, such as a calendar year. A policy may provide that no losses will be paid during 20XX, for example, until the insured has incurred losses in the mount of $5 million.

EXCLUSIONS

Most aircraft hull coverages have a limited number of exclusions. The major ones are as follows.

1. *Wear and tear*. There is no coverage for loss or damage to the insured aircraft which is due and confined to *wear and tear*, deterioration, freezing, mechanical, structural, or electrical breakdown or failure, unless the loss is the direct result of other physical damage covered under the policy. For example, the company will not pay for cracked windshields caused by freezing, mechanical breakdowns, or blown tires; however, if these perils cause an accident resulting in damage to the aircraft, the company will pay including these items.
2. *Tires*. No coverage applies to loss or damage to tires unless caused by theft, vandalism, or malicious mischief; or directly by other physical damage covered under the policy.
3. *Embezzlement*. There is no coverage for loss or damage to the insured aircraft caused when someone with a legal right to possess the aircraft embezzles or converts it under a lease, rental agreement, conditional sale, mortgage, or other legal agreement regarding the use, sale, or lease of the aircraft.
4. *War Confiscation*. Hull coverage excludes any loss or damage to the aircraft caused by declared or undeclared war, invasion, rebellion, hi-jacking, or by the seizure or detention of the aircraft by any government. Coverage is also excluded for any loss or damage done by or at the direction of any government or terrorist organization. Loss or damage arising out of a hi-jacking would normally be covered unless it was carried out by some governmental authority.
5. *Depreciation or loss of use.*
6. *Other Exclusions*. Some policies include additional exclusions pertaining to the type of aircraft and the airworthiness certificate applicable to it. If the aircraft has been converted from the type described in the declarations to any other type or if the air worthiness certificate has become void or has been converted or restricted or if the operations require a special permit or waiver by the FAA (even if such permit or waiver is granted), there is no coverage. Other policies specifically exclude coverage for wearing apparel and other personal effects. Change of ownership status from that shown in the declarations is normally excluded. For example, sale or mortgage not previously advised to the insurer.

LIMIT OF LIABILITY TOTAL OR PARTIAL LOSS

Total Loss

In the event of a total loss, coverage can either be provided on what is referred to as an actual cash value (ACV) basis or on a *valued basis*. If a policy is written on a valued basis, it is presumed that the insured value shown on the declarations represents the reasonable market value of the aircraft at the time coverage was written. In case of a total loss, recovery is based on the amount of insurance purchased (insured value), regardless of market value at the time of loss. If the policy is written on an actual cash value basis, a total loss is settled on the basis of actual cash value at the time of loss which may be less than the insured value. In no event will a company pay more than the insured value, even if the aircraft has appreciated as happens with some older aircraft.

Actual cash value is considered to be replacement cost new less observed depreciation. Obviously, this is much more difficult to determine and consequently valued basis policies are preferred by insureds.

Some policies provide for a return of any *unearned hull premium* in the event of a total loss. In such a case, the company would compute what it has earned based on the percentage of the policy that has expired at the time the aircraft became a total loss and would return the unearned portion to the insured.

Partial Loss

In the event of a partial loss there are two situations to be considered: (1) when repairs are made by the insured and (2) when they are made by someone other than the insured. In the first situation, the amount paid for a partial loss is the actual net cost for material and parts of like kind and quality plus the actual straight time wages (no allowance is made for overtime wages). In addition, a figure of 50 percent of the amount of wages is generally allowed for overhead and supervisory expenses and necessary and reasonable transportation costs. The amount of the deductible is then subtracted from this figure and the remainder is the liability of the company for a partial loss.

If repairs are made by someone other than the insured, the actual cost of repairs (excluding overtime wages) plus transportation expenses is paid. In other words, the bill of the repair organization will be paid, less the deductible, but the adjustor will eliminate overtime wages, if any, and, of course, satisfy himself of the fairness of the bill.

Note that in both instances regarding partial losses no specific mention is made of depreciation. This is unnecessary since the policy refers to materials of like kind and quality.

In no event can the liability of a company for a partial loss exceed the amount recoverable as computed for a total loss. This takes care of the situation of a constructive total loss, in which the cost of repairs would exceed the amount payable for a total loss of the insured aircraft. In some cases the cost of repairing an old aircraft for which parts are no longer available would exceed the value of a total loss. Therefore, policies generally contain a specific provision that in no event shall payment for a partial loss exceed what would be payable in the event of a total loss.

For a very old aircraft and those of relatively low value, it is customary to insert in the policy what is known as a *component parts schedule*. Such aircraft are often difficult or impossible to repair. The component parts provision limits the company's liability for each specified part of the aircraft to a stipulated percentage of the sum which would be paid in the event of a total loss. Thus a figure of 15 percent for the engine means that the company will not pay more than 15 percent of the total insured value of the aircraft in the event of a total loss to the aircraft's engine.

Many policies also contain a provision which states that the company, at its option, may replace the lost or damaged aircraft with another of like kind and quality. If the aircraft is replaced or if the insured is paid for a total loss, the policy provides that the company then is entitled to any remaining salvage value. However, the insured cannot abandon the aircraft to the company without the company's consent.

Transportation Costs

The reference to *transportation costs* under the settlement of partial losses is explained in the policy provision. The policy stipulates that when transportation is necessary, the least expensive means must be used whether this involves moving the damaged aircraft or securing parts or materials for repairs. Damaged parts or the damaged aircraft must be transported to the most practical place for repairs and new parts must be secured from the nearest available source. If the aircraft is transported to some location other than the place of the accident, the transportation expenses include the cost of taking it to the place of repair and returning it either to the place of the accident or the insured's home airport, whichever is nearer.

Under the hull coverage, if a loss results from theft, robbery, or pilferage the loss is considered fully paid if the stolen property is returned before payment is made by the company. Any physical damage is reimbursed.

Automatic Reinstatement

In the event of loss or damage to an insured aircraft, whether or not covered by the policy, the insurer will reduce the insured value of the aircraft by the amount of such loss. Once repairs have begun, the insured value is increased by the amount of such repairs completed until the insured value of the aircraft as shown in the declarations is fully restored or the policy terminates.

CONDITIONS APPLICABLE TO THE HULL COVERAGE

The conditions of the aircraft hull coverage are similar in most respects to those of other physical damage policies and indicate the rights and responsibilities of both the insured and the insurer in the event of loss. These conditions relate to the insured's duties in the event of a loss, appraisal, salvage, subrogation, assistance and cooperation of the insured, and action against the company.

Insured's Duties in the Event of Loss

In the event of a loss, the insured must do the following.

1. *Give notice* as soon as practicable to the company or any of its authorized agents and also, in the event of theft, robbery, or pilferage, to the police. The insured cannot offer to pay any reward for recovery of the aircraft.
2. *Protect the aircraft* from further loss or damage. Any further loss or damage resulting from failure to protect it is not covered. All reasonable expenses incurred by the insured to prevent further damage or loss are recoverable under the terms of the policy except that any payment for security services or reward cannot be offered without written authorization of the insurer, and of course, the maximum policy limit cannot be exceeded.
3. *File a sworn proof of loss* with the company within 90 days (some companies require 60 days), unless the time is extended in writing by the company. The proof of loss must include the place, time, and cause of the accident; the interest of the insured or others in the aircraft; the current value; all encumbrances; all changes in title; and a schedule of any other insurance covering the aircraft in question. Most companies also require that the damaged aircraft and the logbook or any other records be available for inspection upon request.

Appraisal Provisions

The *appraisal condition* provides that, in case the insured and insurer fail to agree on the amount of loss, each shall select a disinterested appraiser upon written demand by the other party. Some companies require that the selection of the appraiser must be given within a certain number of days (generally 20) after the demand is made and the appraisers then select a competent and disinterested umpire. If agreement as to an acceptable umpire cannot be reached, again within a certain time period (generally 15 days), a judge of a court of record in the state where the property is located selects one. The appraisers then appraise the separate damaged articles and submit estimates only on those articles where there are differences to the umpire. The written appraisal of any two then determines the amount of loss.

The insured and the company each pay for their own appraiser and equally share the expenses of the appraisal and the umpire.

Salvage

The value of all salvaged property shall inure to the benefit of the company; however, there can be no abandonment of the property without the consent of the company.

Subrogation

The company shall be subrogated to all of the insured's rights of recovery against other parties and the insured is required to do whatever is necessary to enforce such rights.

Assistance and Cooperation of the Insured

The policy requires that the insured must cooperate with the company and upon request will assist in making settlements, in the conduct of suits, and in enforcing any right of subrogation and shall attend hearings and trials and assist in securing and giving evidence and obtaining the attendance of witnesses.

Action Against the Company

No action shall lie against the company unless the insured has fully complied with all the terms of the policy. Most companies require at least 60 days after proof of loss is filed and the amount of loss is determined.

Other conditions applicable to the hull and liability portion of the policy such as changes in the policy, assignment, cancellation, and territorial limits will be taken up after the discussion of liability in the next chapter.

NEWLY ACQUIRED AIRCRAFT

Hull coverage does not apply to substitute aircraft when the insured's aircraft is temporarily out of service for repair or maintenance. However, if an insured acquires an additional or replacement aircraft, he normally has automatic hull coverage provided the aircraft is reported within 30 days from the date of delivery. Most insurers require ownership but some cover acquisition as lessee. If the new aircraft is in addition to the originally insured aircraft, most insurers insist on insuring all aircraft. The maximum value for which newly acquired aircraft are insured is limited by some insurers to the highest value previously insured, and by others to whatever it cost the insured, without limit. Some other insurers say: "whatever it cost the insured," subject usually to some upper limit.

COMMON ENDORSEMENTS RELATED TO THE HULL COVERAGE

An endorsement provides for additional provision(s) to a policy whereby the scope of its coverage is restricted or enlarged.

Loss Payable and Breach of Warranty (Lienholders Interest)

Since so many aircraft are currently being financed, underwriters do make coverage available for the financial protection of lienholders. This coverage takes the form of an endorsement (attachment) to the policy. Its purpose is to provide an inducement to lend monies, because protection of the collateral is provided for by a broadening of policy terms.

It provides that adjustment of loss shall be made with the named insured but that payment of such loss shall be to both the named insured and the lienholder as their respective interests may appear. It further provides that, with respect to the lienholder's interest only, the policy shall not be invalidated by any act or neglect of the named insured. In effect it is a contract between the company and the lienholder in the event the insured breaches his contract and thus jeopardizes the lienholder's interest. This latter protection is particularly important to the lienholder because there are several warranties made by the named insured relative to the use of the aircraft, its proper licensing, and the experience and qualifications of its pilots which if violated do void coverage.

Should the company pay the lienholder under this endorsement it has the right to recover the amount from the named insured.

Component Parts Schedule

Many makes of aircraft are in use today whose manufacturers have either ceased operations or have discontinued those particular models. In many instances this presents a problem to the underwriters in that replacement parts are either scarce or unavailable. As a consequence, the cost to repair damage to, or replace, a part of the aircraft is out of proportion to the value of the entire plane. When insuring such risks, the *component parts schedule* is used. It limits the amount that will be paid for repairs to or replacement of certain important parts of the aircraft to specified percentages of the amount of insurance. For example, if the insured value is $50,000, the maximum amount the insured could collect for loss involving the propellers might be 10 percent of the total, or $5,000.

Loss of Use

A related hull coverage, usually added by endorsement, is loss of use. This coverage is designed to reimburse the insured for extra expense of obtaining another plane when his own business-use aircraft is out of service due to damage covered by the policy. Extra expense is defined as the actual cost of leasing or renting substitute aircraft, but does not include storage charges, service fees, salaries, maintenance, or operating costs. Reimbursement commences on the seventh or eighth day following the damage to the insured aircraft and cannot exceed 25 percent of the insured value on the damaged aircraft.

Generally, this coverage is only offered to those risks for which the use of aircraft is essential. Coverage does not apply if the insured has a similar aircraft available without charge. Also excluded are extra expenses for any period the aircraft is unavailable because work is being performed that is not necessitated by the damage to the insured aircraft.

Spare Engine and Detached-Equipment Coverage

Most aircraft hull and liability policies define the aircraft as including all of the accessories and equipment that are attached to the aircraft or when temporarily removed and not replaced. This coverage extension becomes necessary if the insured owns a spare engine or other equipment not regularly installed on the aircraft, or is responsible for a replaced component during transit. Some insurers provide this extended hull coverage on request, at no additional cost.

Automatic Hull Value Increase

The maximum payable under the hull coverage is traditionally the amount set forth in the policy declarations, less any applicable deductible. Most insurers will extend the policy, on request, to allow for increased value because of additional equipment, overhaul or modification. Usually this extension is limited to 25 percent of the original value stated.

There is no additional cost for this automatic value increase provision; however, the insurer will require notice from the insured within 30 days and, of course, pay the additional premium, based on the amount of value increase.

Unearned Hull Premium

Normally the hull premium is considered fully earned should a total loss occur prior to the expiration date. The major insurers have included a provision in many policies returning the unearned portion of the hull premium in the event of a total loss. The so-called "fully earned" policies would not. Most insurers will add this provision at no cost upon request.

Conclusion

For a clear understanding of the hull coverage under a typical hull and liability contract, please turn to the sample policy following this chapter. While these policies represent examples from several leading underwriters, you should request specimen copies from other companies for comparison.

AIRCRAFT LIABILITY INSURANCE

As a rule the liability of general aviation aircraft owners and operators for injury or damage to persons or property is in accordance with the same laws applicable to other damage suits arising out of accidents. There are no federal aircraft liability statutes and unlike automobile liability, aircraft liability coverage is a legal requirement in only a few states. The basic legal principles to be applied therefore are the common law rules of negligence, that is, the burden is on the person who has been damaged to prove fault as a proximate cause of the accident. A failure to exercise the requisite degree of legal care owed to the damaged plaintiff is required before the owner or operator owes him anything.

In these days of consumerism and free-and-easy lawsuits every owner and pilot needs liability coverage. Even if they are finally proven not at fault for the accident, the cost of legal defense can be devastating.

LEGAL LIABILITY COVERAGES

Aircraft liability insurance provides the policyholder with protection against third-party claims involving bodily injury or property damage because of ownership, maintenance, or use of aircraft. Three legal liability coverages are available to the insured, each of which is written subject to its own specific limits of liability.

Bodily Injury Excluding Passengers

This coverage protects the insured from the liabilities imposed upon by law for damages for bodily injury, sickness, disease, mental anguish, or death suffered by any person or persons, other than passengers, due to an accident arising out of the ownership, maintenance, or use of any aircraft specifically described in the policy. Separate per person and per accident limits apply to this coverage.

Passenger Bodily Injury Liability

This coverage applies in the same manner as the coverage above but with respect only to passengers. *Passengers* are defined to include persons in, on, or boarding the aircraft for the purpose of flying therein or those alighting therefrom following a flight or an attempted flight. Again, separate per person and per accident limits apply.

Property Damage Liability

This coverage insures against the liability imposed upon the insured by law for damages because of injury to or destruction of property including the loss of use thereof due to an accident arising out of the ownership, maintenance, or use of the aircraft insured. The limit for this coverage is a single limit expressed on a per accident basis.

The coverages noted above can be and are often written on an *occurrence* basis. This is defined in the policy as being an accident or a continuous or repeated exposure to conditions which result in damage or injury accidentally caused.

LIMITS OF LEGAL LIABILITY

The insurer's maximum limit of legal liability for bodily injury or property damage due to any occurrence is dictated by the specific limits of liability indicated in the declarations for each of the coverages which might be provided.

In a typical policy these limits might appear as follows:

Liability Coverages	*Limits of Liability*
a. Bodily injury excluding passengers	$250,000 each person 500,000 each occurrence
b. Passenger bodily injury	$250,000 each person 750,000 each occurrence

c. Property damage $500,000 each occurrence

As an alternative to the separate limits for each coverage, single limit legal liability insurance can be written. As the name implies, this coverage provides one limit which represents the insurer's maximum liability for one claim or for any combination of claims which might arise from one accident. Generally, all three coverages are included but occasionally *single limit legal liability* will be written for coverages (a) and (c) alone. This is true where for some reason the insured has no need for passenger bodily injury coverage or where (b) is purchased as a separate coverage along with the single limit bodily injury and property damage excluding passengers.

Because of the catastrophe exposures faced by many large corporate, commercial, and airline operators, the acquisition of excess layers of liability coverage is a necessity in order to protect their multimillion dollar assets. Often the arrangement of these excess layers of liability protection has a decided influence on the limits of liability and the method of expressing these limits in their primary policy or in any one given excess policy.

Limits might typically appear as follows:

Liability Coverage	*Limit of Liability*
Either:	
Single limit bodily injury and property damage including passengers	$5,000,000 each occurrence
Or:	
Single limit bodily injury and property damage excluding passengers	$5,000,000 each occurrence

The amount of liability coverage needed largely depends upon how much the insured has to lose. A firm's primary concern is protecting its assets. For the average successful business person or executive whose airplane is registered in his name, a $5 million single limit is not excessive. Corporations typically buy from $20 million to $100 million primary coverage. A major air carrier may carry legal liability limits up to $1 billion.

As with separate limits for each coverage, single limit liability coverage can be written on either an accident or occurrence basis; occurrence, however, is considered to be a broader term.

Another school of thought argues that insureds make a mistake by simply buying enough liability protection to cover the value of their company. Instead, they should attempt to determine their maximum probable loss, starting with the value of the passengers carried.

Liability awards are based on many factors that are difficult to quantify including pecuniary damages (for financial support, loss of inheritance, family services, and funeral expenses) and nonpecuniary damages (for loss of society and companionship and grief and mental anguish). (See Chapter 6 for an in-depth discussion of these factors.)

In addition, where the aircraft is operated may affect the value of a possible liability award. If an insured operates out of a hub airport where there is potential for a midair or ground accident with a corporate jet or airliner, or if the aircraft is operated over densely populated areas, the potential catastrophe exposure is very high.

Some insureds have explored the benefits of setting up a Subchapter S corporation for ownership of the company aircraft which would limit the liability of the shareholders to the amount that they had invested in the corporation. However, because many noncommercial aviation insurance policies contain a clause that states the policy will not cover flights for which a charge is made, partners in an S corporation need to include in their policy a clause that states "payments between insureds, their shareholders or affiliates shall not constitute commercial use or a flight for which a charge is being made. Otherwise, an insurer could decline coverage in case of an accident.

MEDICAL PAYMENTS

Medical payments is a supporting coverage normally available to noncommercial insureds where passenger bodily injury liability is written. This coverage provides payment for all reasonable expense of medical, surgical, ambulance, hospital, nursing, and related services and, in the event of death, reasonable funeral expense on behalf of injured parties while riding in the insured aircraft. It may be written to specifically exclude or, for an additional premium, specifically include the pilot and other crew members. Payment is made regardless of legal liability and is limited to the specific per person and per occurrence limits appearing in the declarations for medical payments. From a practical standpoint the provision is valuable in that persons who have their medical bills paid in full are less likely to sue under the liability provision of the contract.

DEFINITION OF INSURED

The definition of *insured* not only includes the named insured (person or organization named in the declarations) but also any other person while using or riding in the aircraft described, and for any person or organization legally responsible for its use, provided such use is by or with the permission of the *named insured*. This is commonly referred to as the *omnibus clause* which picks up any liability incurred by passengers or another pilot, other than the named insured, who is flying the aircraft with the named insured's permission.

The extension of coverage does not apply, however, to bodily injury or death suffered by any person who is a named insured, or to any employee of an insured for bodily injury or death suffered by a fellow employee during the course of his employment. Further, to avoid covering those liabilities not normally contemplated by this coverage, the extension of coverage does not apply to persons or organizations engaged in the manufacture, maintenance, repair, or sale of aircraft, engines, or components, or in the operation of any airport or flight school. It is recognized that such individuals and organizations should have their own insurance.

EXCLUSIONS

The exclusions applicable to the aircraft liability coverages are similar to those found in other liability contracts. The major ones are:

1. Liability assumed by the insured, except that an incidental airport contract for the use of the airport is permitted by some insurers. Also, in many policies this exclusion does not apply to so-called "hold-harmless" agreements that government authorities require an owner to sign before using airports they operate, such as military fields.
2. Property owned, leased, occupied, controlled or under the care of the insured generally is excluded from coverage. A number of policies, however, will cover from $250 to $500 of baggage per passenger and from $1,000 to $10,000 in damage to a hangar or contents of a hangar leased by the insured.
3. Intentional injury, except to prevent a hi-jacking or interference with safe operations.
4. Any claim that is covered under workers' compensation, unemployment compensation, or disability benefits or a similar law.

5. War, hi-jacking and other enumerated perils such as strikes, riots, civil commotions, terrorist activities, confiscation, and similar acts.
6. Bodily injury and property damage arising out of noise or pollutants.

Additional exclusions found in some policies include:

1. Flights requiring a waiver or permit from the FAA, whether granted or not. These could include maintenance flights and ferry flights of damaged aircraft.
2. Bodily injury to anyone who is a named insured.
3. Flight when the aircraft's Certificate of Airworthiness is not in effect. Most policies require that the certificate must be "in full force and effect." Some insurers have denied coverage if the annual inspection is overdue, even if the loss was not caused by the lack of that inspection.
4. When used for an unlawful purpose (such as a drug flight or even bringing a case of liquor from New Jersey to Pennsylvania).
5. When flown by a pilot not properly certificated, rated, and qualified under applicable FARs, even if named to the policy under the pilot warranty.
6. Atomic or nuclear fusion or fission or radioactivity.
7. When the number of passengers carried exceeds the maximum shown in the declarations.
8. When certain specified FARs, regarding, for example, maintenance, night or instrument flying have been violated.

If medical coverage is carried, another exclusion found in all policies states that any payment made under this coverage cannot be used to satisfy any claim under a workers' compensation or similar law.

SPECIAL COVERAGE FEATURES

Defense, Settlement, and Supplementary Payments

The company agrees to defend any suit against the insured and pay all expenses incurred by the company and all costs taxed against the insured; premiums on appeal bonds required to release attachments relating to lawsuits defended by the insurer; bail bond cost up to $250 per bond; expenses incurred by the insured for first aid at the time of the accident; and reimbursement to the insured for reasonable expenses incurred at the insurer's request in assisting the company in the investigation or defense of any claim or suit.

Temporary Use of Substitute Aircraft

In the event the named insured's aircraft is withdrawn from normal use because of its breakdown, repair, servicing, loss, or destruction, the liability insurance afforded by the policy with respect to the aircraft applies with respect to another aircraft not so owned while temporarily used as the substitute for the aircraft.

Use of Other Aircraft

The liability coverages provided under the policy apply to the named insured, if an individual and his spouse, with respect to the operation of any non-owned aircraft. This provision does not apply to any aircraft owned in full or in part by, licensed in the name of, hired aircraft by, or furnished for regular use to the named insured.

Newly Acquired Aircraft

If an insured acquires an additional or replacement aircraft he normally has automatic liability coverage provided the aircraft is reported within 30 days from the date of delivery. The same coverages and limits of liability apply to the new or replacement aircraft.

CONDITIONS APPLICABLE TO THE LIABILITY COVERAGES

The conditions applicable to the liability coverages are very similar to the hull coverage with several additional items. The conditions relate to the insured's duties in the event of an accident, financial responsibility laws, medical reports, subrogation, assistance and cooperation of the insured, and action against the company.

Insured's Duties in the Event of Loss

In addition to giving notice as soon as practicable, if a claim is made or suit is brought against the insured, the insured must immediately forward to the company every demand, notice, summons, or other process received by him or his representatives.

Financial Responsibility Laws

This condition states that when the policy is certified as proof of financial responsibility for the future under the provisions of any aircraft financial responsibility law, the insurance afforded under the policy for bodily injury liability and property damage liability shall comply with the provisions of such law. However, in no event can the limits of liability be in excess of liability limits stated in the policy. The insured must reimburse the company for any payment made by the company which it would not have been obligated to make except for the financial responsibility laws.

Medical Reports

The injured person or someone on his behalf shall give the company written proof of claim and if requested from the company, execute authorization to enable the company to obtain medical reports and copies of records. The injured person is also required to submit to a physical examination by physicians selected by the company when and as often as they may require.

Subrogation

The company shall be subrogated to all of the insured's rights of recovery against other parties and the insured is required to do whatever is necessary to enforce such rights.

Assistance and Cooperation of the Insured

The insured must cooperate with the company and upon request assist in making settlement, in the conduct of suits, and in enforcing any right of subrogation, contribution or indemnity against any person or organization who may be liable to the insured because of loss, injury, or damage. The insured is also required to attend hearings and trials and assist in securing and giving evidence and obtaining the attendance of witnesses.

Action Against the Company

No action shall be against the company unless the insured has fully complied with all the terms of the policy. In addition, with respect to the liability coverages, there can be no action against the company until the amount of the insured's obligation to pay shall have been finally determined either by judgment against the insured after actual trial or by written agreement of the insured, the claimant, and the company.

COMMON ENDORSEMENTS RELATED TO THE LIABILITY COVERAGE

Aircraft Non-Ownership Liability

The aircraft liability coverages written for a business firm follow only aircraft described in the policy or while that aircraft is laid up for maintenance or repair, a temporary substitute aircraft. In addition, not every aircraft used as a temporary substitute may be covered. Some policies place restrictions on the size, seating capacity, and so forth. Unless the named insured is an individual, there is no coverage under the aircraft policy for liability arising out of any aircraft: (1) rented or chartered in the name of the firm or (2) rented, borrowed, or chartered by employees (known or unknown by their employers) and flown on company business.

The gap in protection for liability arising out of the use of non-owned aircraft can be remedied by attaching a *non-ownership liability* endorsement to the policy. Some insurers restrict the coverage to fixed- wing aircraft with a certain seating capacity. It is not designed for an insured who uses a non-owned aircraft on a regular basis such as a leased aircraft. Most *non-ownership liability* endorsements limit the consecutive number of days coverage will apply unless the insured notifies the company and pays an additional premium.

Guest Voluntary Settlement (Admitted Liability)

Guest voluntary settlement, or as it is more commonly known, admitted liability, is a supporting coverage peculiar to aviation insurance and available to selected noncommercial corporate and business and pleasure risks in conjunction with passenger bodily injury liability coverage. It provides that if a guest passenger (or crew member if included) suffers death or injury resulting in dismemberment or loss of sight, a sum up to but not exceeding a stated principal sum be offered the guest (or crew member) or his survivor. The payment is made provided that the offer is requested by the named insured and that a full release for all bodily injury is obtained from the recipient (except in an employee's case which is covered under a workers' compensation law). With few exceptions, an employee cannot sue his employer and as such, this coverage becomes a form of accident insurance for employees.

Admitted liability is designed to make it unnecessary for an insured's guest to resort to legal action to secure compensation for injury. This avoids the embarrassment of a "friendly suit" and the necessarily high cost of litigation. The named insured always has the choice of either permitting the offer of voluntary settlement or of relying upon the protection of his passenger bodily injury liability coverage and the determination of his legal liability by a court of law. The written release is necessary in order to make any voluntary settlement binding upon the recipient. A typical limit for admitted liability would be $200,000 each person. Higher or lower limits are available.

Weekly indemnity coverage can be included as part of guest voluntary settlement. It provides that in the event that a guest passenger is totally disabled from performing all duties pertaining to his occupation, the insurer will reimburse the named insured for payment made for loss of earnings up to a stated sum per week, not to exceed 80 percent of the recipient's average weekly wage, and for a period not to exceed a maximum stated number of weeks. Generally where weekly indemnity coverage is written for more than 52 weeks, coverage for that period beyond the 52nd week is contingent upon the party being totally disabled from performing the duties pertaining to any occupation.

Permanent and total disability coverage can be provided in conjunction with guest voluntary settlement whether weekly indemnity coverage is written or not. This coverage provides for the payment of a sum up to but not exceeding the stated principal sum (less any payment which might already have been made under weekly indemnity) in the event the injured party is determined to have been permanently and totally disabled. This coverage is contingent upon a full release being obtained from the recipient and again is offered only at the request of the named insured.

Use of Military Installations

For those insureds who deal with the government and need to fly into military airfields, the government requires that the insureds waive their subrogation and assume all liability for such flights. This endorsement is designed to amend the subrogation provision and assumed liability exclusion found in all policies to accommodate this requirement by the government.

Airport Premises Liability for Regular and Incidental Locations

This coverage is normally excluded from the insured's comprehensive general liability policy. It may be purchased separately or as an extension to the hull and liability contract. It must cover not only the regularly leased or owned hangar, but incidental locations as well.

A typical exposure might involve a guest being injured by an opening or closing hangar door or by straying into the path of a taxiing aircraft. Or a guest car might be damaged while parked next to the aircraft hangar.

Most leading insurers will include this extension of coverage, on request, for the same limit as applies to the aircraft for little or no additional premium.

Non-Owned Aircraft Physical Damage

This coverage provides legal liability protection for property damage to non-owned aircraft while in the care, custody, or control of the named insured. It may apply only while aircraft is on the ground or in flight or both.

Hangarkeepers Legal Liability

This coverage provides legal liability protection for property damage to non-owned aircraft at the named insured's premises and in the care, custody, or control of the named insured. It usually applies only while the aircraft is on the ground.

Property Damage for Non-Owned Hangars

Without a special extension, typical liability policy wording excludes liability for damage to property in the care, custody, or control of the insured.

An example would be an employee of the insured hitting the insured's leased hangar with a truck and setting the hangar on fire. This coverage can be negotiated as an extension of the aircraft policy. Most leading insurers grant this extension at no additional cost.

Products Liability for Sale of Insured Aircraft

In our litigious society, the crash of a previously owned aircraft could easily result in a suit for personal injuries, death and/or substantial property damage, including the value of the aircraft itself. The insured's ordinary products liability coverage normally excludes claims involving aircraft.

Protection is available from most leading aviation underwriters as an extension of the aircraft liability coverage, at no additional cost. However, like most policy extensions, it must be requested because it is not a part of the standard contract.

One major carrier includes this coverage as part of its "coverage expansion endorsement" on an occurrence basis. This means that its policy must be in force at the time of the accident, to be effective. Other companies use the "claims made" basis so caution must be taken if coverage is changed from one company to another, otherwise a loss could be missed by both insurers.

Waiver of "Fellow Employee" Exclusion

Most policies deny protection for one employee being sued by another employee who works for the same employer. This coverage extension is available from most major aviation insurers upon request, at no additional cost.

Inclusion of Cross Liability

Typically, liability policies deny protection for one named insured being sued by another named insured. This becomes a potential problem area whenever more than one named insured appears on the same policy.

For example, Black and White own an aircraft in partnership with both names in the policy as insureds. As a passenger being flown by Black, White is injured. Without a special extension of coverage, Black would be left without liability protection. Most aviation insurers will remove the exclusion, upon request of the insured, usually without additional premium.

Contractual Liability

Normally, any liability assumed by the insured is excluded under the liability coverage. Some policies have been broadened to accept certain incidental contracts or hold-harmless agreements with governmental authorities for permission to use airport facilities.

Additional "contractual liability" should be requested for contractual agreements which the insured may sign with nongovernmental parties for the use of airport storage (hangar or tie-down) facilities. Although there is seldom a charge, the insurer usually requests that copies of these contracts be submitted within 30 days.

Search and Rescue Expense

On request, most leading aviation insurers will extend the hull and liability policy to reimburse the insured for up to $2,000 for runway foaming in the event of a gear-up landing and up to $25,000 for search-and-rescue efforts, but only after discontinuance of efforts by governmental authorities. Usually, no additional charge is assessed.

Baggage Liability Coverage

Ordinarily, property damage liability excludes property that is owned, rented, controlled, or transported by the insured. Some policies, as mentioned earlier, will provide up to $250 or $500 for loss of passengers' baggage or personal effects. Most leading insurers will, on request, increase that limit to $2,500 or $5,000, usually at no additional premium.

Cargo Liability

This coverage provides legal liability protection for the goods, merchandise, and property belonging to others that is carried or transported on the insured aircraft. It does not apply to property leased to the named insured and generally requires a bill of lading.

Personal Injury Liability

This coverage provides legal liability protection for false arrest, assault or battery, defamation, libel, slander, and so forth arising out of the operation of aircraft insured under the policy. It is written on an aggregate basis with a maximum limit of $25,000,000.

Host Liquor Liability

If a guest, following a flight in the insured's aircraft, became involved in a motor vehicle accident, it could be alleged that the accident was due to the insured having served the guest one too many drinks, during the flight. Coverage is available, usually on request, as part of the aircraft liability coverage.

Operation of Mobile Equipment

This coverage provides legal liability protection for bodily injury and property damage arising out of the use of mobile equipment and other vehicles not licensed for public road use while on airport property. Vehicles would include tugs, fuel trucks, vans and so forth.

OTHER MISCELLANEOUS COVERAGES

War, Hi-Jacking, and Other Perils Coverage

Virtually all aviation insurance policies contain the "War, Hi-jacking and other Perils Exclusion Clause" applicable to all hull and liability coverages. Commonly referred to as "War Risks," the exclusion contains some 30 perils and is far more encompassing than the simple reference to war. Coverage for war risks was available from most underwriters, for little or no additional premium, to those insureds operating their aircraft outside the United States or it possessions. War risks coverage was especially important when flying into third-world countries in Central or South America and the Middle East. All of this changed after the terrorist attack on September 11, 2001. Underwriters quickly cancelled War Risks coverage. It became evident that they could no longer write the coverage for little or no premium. In the years that followed, underwriters once again offered the coverage but for an additional hull and liability premium. Hull and/or liability coverage for War Risks may be purchased separately.

In November, 2002 Congress passed the Terrorism Risk Insurance Act (TRIA) which required all insurance companies to offer each insured the opportunity to purchase terrorism coverage. Like War Risk coverage, TRIA can be applicable to both hull and liability coverages. However, TRIA offers coverage for only one peril, terrorism, as defined in the law. War Risk coverage includes a variety of perils, of which terrorism is one. TRIA is designed by the government to provide high limits of coverage. War Risk coverage is restricted to the limits of hull or liability coverage in the policy. The insurance companies' offers to purchase terrorism coverage was available at each renewal through December 31, 2005.

Rental Expense of Temporary Replacement Parts

This coverage provides reimbursement of rental costs incurred in renting parts temporarily needed to replace aircraft parts withdrawn from use due to a physical damage loss covered by the policy.

Extra Expense for Substitute Aircraft

Extra expense for substitute aircraft provides reimbursement of rental costs incurred in renting or chartering aircraft temporarily needed to replace a specified scheduled aircraft withdrawn from use due to a physical damage loss covered by the policy; limited to the differential between the operating costs of the owned aircraft and the cost of renting or chartering the temporary aircraft.

Trip Interruption

This coverage provides reimbursement of expenses incurred for food, lodging, and travel of passengers to complete a given flight to its destination or original departure point if the trip is interrupted or discontinued due to loss covered under the policy.

Lay-up Credit for Scheduled Aircraft

In the event an insured aircraft is out of service for an extended period of time, generally at least several months, this coverage provides a return premium credit.

Mexican Liability Policy

This coverage provides a Certificate of Insurance required by the government of Mexico evidencing liability coverage issued by a Mexican insurance company for operation of the insured aircraft in Mexico.

OTHER CONDITIONS APPLICABLE TO HULL AND LIABILITY

Some conditions apply to both the hull and liability portion of the contract and are found under all contracts.

1. *Two or more aircraft insured.* When two or more aircraft are insured under a policy, the terms of the policy apply separately to each.
2. *Policy period and territorial limits.* Every policy indicates that coverage applies during the policy period within a certain territorial limit. A standard territorial limit includes the United States, Canada, and Mexico. Some include the Bahama Islands. Some policies limit coverage to within a specified distance of the Mexican border and within 10 to 20 nautical miles of land for single-and multiengine aircraft respectively.

   Even the most modest business aircraft should be covered within Alaska and the Bahamas. Most turbine aircraft are capable of international flights and should, therefore, be covered for "Worldwide" or at least "Western Hemisphere."

   The territorial limits can be extended for one trip or on a blanket basis for no additional charge if the underwriter is advised of the circumstances.
3. *Changes.* No changes to the policy are allowed without approval by the

company and upon issuance of an endorsement to that effect. Further, this condition states that any notice to an agent or knowledge possessed by any agent or by any other person shall not waive or change any part of the policy or stop the company from asserting any right under the terms of the policy.

4. *Assignment*. The insurance policy is a personal contract, which means that the insurance company has a right to select its policyholders. Generally speaking, no insurance company can be compelled to issue insurance to anyone whom they do not wish to insure. As a result, there are practically no situations in which the policyholder can make the coverage of the policy apply to another person or organization without prior written consent of the company.
5. *Cancellation*. The policy may be cancelled at any time by the named insured by simply giving written notice to the company when the cancellation should take effect and subsequently returning the policy or having a lost policy receipt completed. The company may cancel the policy at any time by giving 10 days written notice. If the named insured cancels, the return premium is computed on a short rate basis which includes a penalty. If the company cancels, earned premium is computed on a pro rata basis. Both short rate and pro rata tables are generally included in the policy.
6. *Declarations*. The following clause is typical of those found in most aircraft hull and liability contracts:

   By acceptance of this policy, the Named Insured agrees that the statements in the declarations are his agreements and representations, that this policy is issued in reliance upon the truth of such representations and that this policy embodies all agreements existing between himself and the Company or any of its agents relating to this insurance.

   This statement simply means that the contract is issued upon the understanding that the statements contained in the application for insurance are correct. The legal effect is that if the insured's declarations are false and relate to some material fact, the insurer is under no obligation to make payment in the event of a loss. The latter portion of the above clause is the entire contract rule, which states that the entire agreement between the parties is embodied in the written contract and oral evidence cannot be introduced to vary the terms of the agreement.

OTHER ENDORSEMENTS

In addition to the more common endorsements found under the Business and Pleasure and Industrial Aid policies, the following listing represents a sampling of the variety found under some aircraft hull and liability policies:

Additional Insured
Air Ambulance
Banner Towing
Cancellation Change Notice
Cargo Legal Liability
Commercial Purposes
Ferry Flight
Flying Club
Hold Harmless
Leaseback
Limit of Passenger Liability
No Claims Bonus
Reimbursement for Operating Expenses
Renter Pilot Extended Liability
Sales Demonstration Defined
Seaplane Amphibious Aircraft
Territorial Amendment
Time Out of Force
Turbine Powered Aircraft
Waiver of Subrogation
Wind and Hailstorm Deductible

ADDITIONAL CONSIDERATIONS FOR BUSINESS AIRCRAFT OPERATORS WHO ARE REIMBURSED FOR EXPENSES

One of the common misconceptions held by business and pleasure and industrial aid aircraft operators is the notion that their hull and liability policy covers reimbursement by others so long as no profit is made. It was mentioned earlier under the declarations section that business and pleasure and industrial aid use exclude any operation for which a charge is made. By this definition, *any* payment for use of the aircraft would constitute a policy violation. Remuneration to the aircraft owner becomes more complicated and, paradoxically, less clear with the more liberal definitions found in the so-called "broad form policies." Consider the following examples from three leading insurers:

> ". . . (excluding) use for any purpose involving a charge intended to result in financial profit to the Insured."

> ". . . you cannot profit from your aircraft by charging others for its use, although you can accept payment to cover operating expenses."

> "You agree not to charge anyone for using your aircraft. They can, however, reimburse you for operating expenses."

In the first case, it is unclear how a court would determine "intention" and "profit." In the last two, "operating expenses" are not further defined and it is difficult to determine whether that includes not only direct costs such as fuel and oil, but also indirect costs such as insurance, depreciation, taxes, maintenance, overhaul, storage, and crew salaries and benefits.

Many insureds accept payments from friends, employers and other companies merely to recoup operating expenses. A common arrangement involves an affiliated business paying the aircraft owner (whether an individual, partnership, or corporation) enough to cover fixed expenses such as hangar and insurance and variable costs like fuel, oil and maintenance, as well as a sum to cover the amortization of debt.

Unfortunately, these careful arrangements are dangerously incomplete if the insured's aviation policy does not clearly provide for recognition of these payments. Insurers do not necessarily require actual funds to change hands to deny coverage, just the intention to charge for the flight by making an accounting entry is enough for some carriers to deny payment.

In one case involving an individual owner of a light twin-engine aircraft, a written agreement existed between him and his company whereby he would be reimbursed for trips made on behalf of his company. When he died in a crash of his airplane on a business trip, his insurance carrier refused to pay either for the aircraft or for the claims on behalf of the deceased passengers because he was on a flight for which a charge was being made.

The insurance company argued that the written reimbursement agreement the aircraft owner had with his company *would have* resulted in payments being made for the flight even though no payment had yet changed hands for the flight on which the accident occurred. The practical effects of the insurer's decision not to pay was a long and expensive litigation for the estate of the aircraft owner. The decision posed a real threat because if the insurance company was successful, the claims of the two passengers' estates would have to be paid from the estate of the owner in addition to the loss to the estate of the owner's equity in the aircraft.

Corporations have established many shared-use agreements such as joint ownership, interchange and time-sharing agreements. For companies operating large and turbojet-powered multiengine aircraft, the FAA has specifically defined these arrangements under Federal Aviation Regulations (FARs) Part 91.501, Subparts (c) and (d).

Joint ownership is an arrangement whereby one of the registered joint owners of an airplane employs and furnishes the flight crew for that airplane and each of the registered joint owners pays a share of the charges specified in the agreement. Under an *interchange agreement* one company leases its airplane to another company in exchange for equal time, when needed, on the other company's airplane, and no charge, assessment, or fee is made, except that a charge may be made not to exceed the difference between the cost of owning, operating, and maintaining the two airplanes. A *time-sharing agreement* involves the lease of an airplane with flight crew to another party, and no charge is made for the flights conducted under that arrangement other than the following:

1. Fuel, oil, lubricants, and other additives.
2. Travel expenses of the crew, including food, lodging, and ground transportation.
3. Hangar and tie-down costs away from the aircraft's base of operations.
4. Insurance obtained for the specific flight.
5. Landing fees, airport taxes, and similar assessments.
6. Customs, foreign permits, and similar fees directly related to the flight.
7. In-flight food and beverages.
8. Passenger ground transportation.
9. Flight planning and weather contract services.
10. An additional charge equal to 100 percent of the expenses listed under number one.

The above expenses may also be charged for incidental cargo flights by a business or when demonstrating its aircraft to a prospective customer when no charge is made.

INSURANCE CONSIDERATIONS

Aviation insurers reason that their limitation of coverage under conditions where reimbursement is being made is to clearly distinguish between commercial and noncommercial risks. On the one hand, it is designed to discourage air taxi and charter operations from deceptively obtaining much lower noncommercial rates and, on the other hand, to discourage business and pleasure/industrial aid risks from falling into a commercial class operation, intentionally or not. Unfortunately, like many ideas with honorable intentions, this provision was never meant to apply in instances like the example of the light twin-engine pilot.

Because any remuneration received by an aircraft owner may void the "Use" provision of the policy, full details of the arrangement should be submitted to the insurer. If additional named insureds are added to the policy, the "cross-liability" exclusion under the liability coverage must be deleted. This exclusion denies protection for one named insured being sued by another named insured. In the case of interchange agreements, each owner should be named on the other's policy. Copies of all contracts and agreements between cooperating parties should be submitted to the insurer so as not to void the "assumed liability" exclusion.

Most major aviation insurers will endorse a noncommercial policy without charge to avoid any conflict resulting from reimbursement arrangements provided they are notified in advance. Aviation underwriters are familiar with the practice of noncommercial risks receiving reimbursement for flights. Those same underwriters are also aware that many times payments made to aircraft owners can result in a technical profit. Since this arrangement is not unusual, they are rarely surprised when approached with a reimbursement situation.

The problem arises when the policy is written, an accident occurs, and then the reimbursed flight arrangement surfaces for the first time. At that time, there is obviously no incentive for the insurer to amend the Purpose of Use. The time to deal with this problem is when the coverage is being negotiated. The amendment does not, however, allow the owner to fly for hire or to accept reimbursement or payment from anyone not specified in the amendment. Any further broadening would put the risk into a commercial category.

Joint Ownership Agreement

The insurance considerations for joint ownership are the same for Company A (owner furnishing flight crew), and Company B (owner using Company A's flight crew).

1. Hull and liability coverage on the airplane, with all joint owners named as named insureds.
2. "Purpose of Use" or "Approved Use" clause in the policy amended to allow for paying a charge under the joint ownership agreement.
3. Adequate liability limits to ensure sufficient coverage if the liability limits have to be shared with the other joint owner(s)
4. All joint owners will need a Certificate of Insurance verifying coverages provided under the policy, or preferably a copy of the policy and endorsements.

Interchange Agreement

The insurance considerations for an interchange agreement are the same for Company A (owner/user) and Company B (owner/user).

1. Both companies will carry hull and liability coverage on their respective aircraft.
2. "Purpose of Use" or "Approved Use" clause in each policy must be amended to allow for interchange use of the aircraft.
3. Both companies need to be named as an additional insured with respect to liability coverage on each others' policies.
4. With respect to hull coverage, each company must waive its subrogation rights against the other company while each is using the other's aircraft.
5. Both companies will need a clause in their respective policies stating that the other company's policy is primary while using the other company's aircraft.
6. Adequate liability limits must be provided to ensure sufficient coverage if the limits have to be shared by each company.
7. Both companies need to determine whether, and the extent to which, any indemnification language in the interchange agreement will be covered by either policy.
8. Each company will need to receive advance notice of deletion, cancellation, or material changes in coverage in the other's policy.
9. Each company will need a Certificate of Insurance from the other's insurer verifying limits, coverages and special provisions.

Time-sharing Agreement

The insurance considerations for a time-sharing agreement are different for Company A (owner) and Company B (user).

Company A (owner) will:

1. Carry the hull and liability coverage on the aircraft as the named insured.
2. Need to have a "Purpose of Use" or "Approved Use" on the policy that allows for time-sharing use of the aircraft.

3. Need adequate liability limits to ensure sufficient coverage if the limits have to be shared with Company B.
4. Need to determine whether and the extent to which, any indemnification language in the time-share agreement will be covered by Company A's policy.

Company B (user) will need:

1. To be named as an Additional Insured with respect to liability coverage on Company A's insurance policy.
2. A waiver of subrogation with respect to hull coverage on Company A's insurance policy.
3. An invalidation clause with respect to liability coverage on Company A's insurance policy.
4. Adequate liability limits on Company A's policy to ensure sufficient coverage if the limits have to be shared with Company A.
5. To consider obtaining an excess liability policy for the use of the time-shared aircraft.
6. To consider obtaining a non-owned aircraft liability policy for use of other non-owned aircraft.
7. To determine whether, and the extent to which, any indemnification language in the time-share agreement will be covered by Company A's policy.
8. To advise its insurer of the time-sharing agreement if Company B owns an aircraft, and make sure that its own insurer recognizes the agreement; Company B's insurer may agree to provide Company B's liability limit as excess over the primary limits provided by Company A's policy.
9. To receive advance notice of deletion, cancellation, or material changes in coverage for Company A's aircraft on Company A's insurance policy.
10. A Certificate of Insurance from Company A's insurer verifying coverages provided under Company A's policy.

Exclusive Dry Lease

Under an *exclusive dry lease* arrangement the lessor normally only provides the aircraft. The lessee is responsible for the maintenance, crew, fuel, and so forth. The majority of the insurance considerations are on the lessor's side.

Company A (Lessor) will need:

1. To be named on Company B's insurance policy as an additional named Insured with respect to liability coverage.
2. An invalidation clause with respect to liability coverage on Company B's insurance policy.
3. A waiver of subrogation with respect to physical damage coverage on Company B's insurance policy.
4. To be named as a loss payee with a Breach of Warranty endorsement with respect to hull coverage on Company B's policy.
5. Company B to carry adequate liability limits to ensure sufficient coverage if the limits have to be shared with Company B.
6. To determine whether, and the extent to which, any indemnification language in the dry lease agreement will be covered by Company B's policy.
7. To receive advance notice of deletion, cancellation or material changes in coverage for Company B's aircraft on Company B's insurance policy.
8. A Certificate of Insurance from Company B's insurer verifying coverages provided under Company B's policy.

Company B (Lessee) will need:

1. To carry hull and liability on the airplane as the Named Insured.
2. Adequate liability limits to ensure sufficient coverage if the limits have to be shared with Company A.
3. To determine whether, and the extent to which, any indemnification language in the dry lease agreement will be covered by Company B's policy.

Management Company

Under a *management company* arrangement the aircraft owner normally turns over the responsibility of providing the crew, maintenance, ground support, insurance, record-keeping, and overall operation of the aircraft to a management company. Some of the insurance considerations for an aircraft management company and its aircraft owner clients are as follows:

Company A (Owner) will need:

1. To be named on Company B's policy as an additional named insured with respect to liability coverage for all uses of the aircraft by Company B, including use of the aircraft by Company A and FAR Part 135 use of the aircraft by Company B.
2. To be named as a loss payee with a Breach of Warranty endorsement with respect to hull coverage on Company B's policy.
3. Adequate liability limits under Company B's policy to ensure sufficient coverage if the limits have to be shared with Company B.
4. To consider obtaining an excess liability policy if the limits of liability under Company B's fleet policy are not adequate for their needs.
5. To consider obtaining a non-owned aircraft liability policy for use of non-owned aircraft that are outside the fleet of aircraft insured under Company B's policy, if such coverage is not provided by Company B's policy.
6. To determine whether, and the extent to which, any indemnification language in the management agreement is covered by Company B's policy.
7. To receive advance notice of deletion, cancellation or material changes in coverage for Company A's aircraft on Company B's insurance policy.
8. A Certificate of Insurance from Company B's insurer verifying coverages provided under Company B's policy or a copy of the policy and endorsements.

Company B (Management Company) will normally carry the hull and liability coverage on Company A's airplane under its own fleet insurance policy.

Company B will need to:

1. Have a "Purpose of Use" or "Approved Use" on the policy that allows for all uses (FAR Parts 91 and 135) of the aircraft.
2. Carry non-owned aircraft liability coverage.
3. Determine whether, and the extent to which, any indemnification language in the management agreement will be covered by Company B's policy.

Fractional Ownership

Fractional ownership offers an opportunity for a company that might not be able to justify the purchase of its own aircraft, to acquire a share of an aircraft. The management company will normally provide the crew, maintenance, ground support, insurance, record-keeping, and overall operation of the aircraft.

Company A (Management Company) will usually carry the hull and liability coverage on the fractional owners aircraft under its own fleet insurance policy.

Company A will need to:

1. Have a "Purpose of Use" or "Approved Use" on the policy that allows for all uses (FAR Parts 91 and 135) of the aircraft.
2. Have a specific provision in the policy permitting interchange use by fractional owners of other aircraft insured on the policy.
3. Adequate liability limits on its policy to ensure sufficient coverage if the limits have to be shared with the fractional owners.
4. Determine whether, and the extent to which, any indemnification language in the fractional ownership agreement will be covered by its policy.

Fractional Owners will need to:

1. Be named on Company A's insurance policy as additional insured with respect to liability coverage for all uses of the aircraft by Company A (including use of the aircraft by Company A, interchange use of other fractionally owned aircraft in the fleet, and FAR Part 135 use of the aircraft by Company A).
2. Obtain a waiver of subrogation with respect to hull coverage under Company A's policy.
3. Be named as a loss payee with a Breach of Warranty endorsement with respect to hull coverage on Company A's policy.
4. Consider obtaining an excess liability policy for the use of its fractionally owned airplane and the other fractionally owned aircraft in the fleet.
5. Consider obtaining a non-owned aircraft liability policy for use of non-owned aircraft.
6. Determine whether, and the extent to which, any indemnification language in the fractional ownership agreement will be covered by Company A's policy.
7. Receive advance notice of deletion, cancellation, or material changes in coverage for the fractionally owned aircraft on Company A's policy.
8. Obtain a Certificate of Insurance from Company A's insurer verifying coverages provided under Company A's policy or a copy of the policy and endorsements.

Although these examples do not encompass all of the varieties of alternative arrangements, they address common considerations for some typical situations, each of which is different from the other and requires a somewhat different approach. Other specific variations require their own individual analysis.

Commercial Operations

FAR Part 135 governs the operation of aircraft for carrying passengers and cargo for hire. The aircraft owner may obtain and operate under an Air Taxi Certificate issued by the Department of Transportation (DOT) or may conduct operations under the certificate held by another.

When operating under the insured's own certificate, the "Use" provision of the policy must be amended to include "carriage of passengers and cargo for hire. " If the insured is operating under another's certificate, the insurance may be arranged under the policy of the certificate holder (with the insured's interests being fully protected under that policy) or covered entirely under the insured's policy (with the interest of the Certificate holder protected under that policy). A third alternative is to cover the commercial operations under the charter operator's policy and the noncommercial use under the insured's policy. This is not recommended due to the danger of a gap between the two policies, and no coverage for a loss.

Many, if not most, commercial operators carry limits that are insufficient for the needs of the insured, and may be reluctant to increase the cost of their insurance to accommodate the higher limits. Moreover, most policy extensions available to business and pleasure and industrial aid risks are not available to commercial operators.

Compliance with DOT necessitates filing a Certificate of Insurance. The limits required are grossly inadequate for a business aircraft operator and should not be considered as a guideline for selecting proper coverage.

Holding Companies

Many business aircraft operators set up a holding company for ownership of their aircraft. This is done primarily for tax and liability exposure reasons. Liability to shareholders of a Subchapter S corporation, as in all corporations, is limited to the amount of the shareholder's investment. Typically, the business or several businesses then lease the aircraft from the holding company.

The remuneration to the holding company by the users may very well constitute "commercial" operation under the terms of the insurance contract, and thereby render it void, if written for business or pleasure or industrial aid. This distribution should be clarified with the insurer.

Depending on individual policy language, the policy issued to the holding company, especially if written to include "rental" to the actual users, could leave them without liability coverage unless specifically added as named insureds with respect to the liability coverages. The actual users, if considered to be "renters," would be subject to subrogation in the event of a hull loss.

Listing the actual users as named insureds under the liability policy issued to the holding company would still leave the users without the benefit of non-owned aircraft liability protection, should they or their employees utilize another aircraft for the user's business.

Each case involving a holding company should be carefully reviewed with the underwriter to ensure that the interests of all parties are fully covered with respect to legal liability exposures, workers' compensation, possible subrogation action, non-owned aircraft liability coverage, and cross liability.

INSURED'S RESPONSIBILITIES FOLLOWING A LOSS

The real value of any policy and the insurer's service is evident after a loss occurs. Overall, the accident statistics of general aviation aircraft continue to improve each year (see chapter 1). However, unforeseen losses still occur to even the most experienced pilots flying a variety of aircraft. If an accident occurs, the policy contains a number of procedures that must be complied with by the insured. These requirements, normally found under the conditions section, must be adhered to so that the insurance coverage is not inadvertently voided by the policyholder. Naturally, the nature of the accident should determine the steps an insured takes immediately after a loss occurs. Listed below are the major duties of an insured:

1. It is the insured's responsibility to notify the local police.
2. The insured should arrange for the aircraft to be protected, by hiring security personnel to prevent further damage or loss. The probability of recovering stolen equipment is much greater if the insured has recorded serial numbers of all equipment. If possible, photographs should be taken of the aircraft and any other damage done to third party property owners.
3. The agent, the broker or the insurer, should be contacted as soon as possible.
4. The insurer should be provided with the time and place of the loss, a description of events prior to the accident, and names and addresses of any injured persons and witnesses.
5. If sued, the insured must forward all documents to the insurer.
6. The insured must cooperate with the insurer in making settlements, in the

conduct of suits, and in the enforcement of any right of subrogation made by the insurer.
7. The insured must attend hearings, trials, give assistance in securing and presenting evidence and help the company in seeing that witnesses appear whenever they are scheduled.
8. The insured cannot, except at his own expense, make any voluntary payment, assume any obligation or incur any costs other than necessary first aid to others at the time of the loss.
9. The insured may be required to obtain medical and other records.
10. The insured must produce all pertinent records and invoices and file a sworn proof of loss statement usually within 60 to 90 days from the time of the loss.
11. The aircraft must be made available for inspection by the insurer, and the insured must cooperate in seeing that the transfer of title to any salvage, including the insured aircraft if it is a total loss, is made to the insurer or their nominee.

CONCLUDING COMMENTS

Buying aircraft hull and liability insurance is not like buying automobile insurance. Policies vary from one insurer to another, and policy forms can vary within the same company. Significant differences exist in pilot warranties, exclusions and conditions.

Each aviation insurer has different opinions about certain categories of aircraft, airmen and use, and each company has a different way of defining, describing, pricing, and controlling risks accepted. Policy terms and wording vary greatly. There is less fine print and wordiness in hull and liability contracts than there used to be, but there is still much opportunity for confusion. Comparing coverage offered by different insurers on the same risk frequently is a difficult task. This is not just a matter of style or choice of words and terms. It is also a way for underwriters to limit their exposure.

What any particular company is able to do is further limited by its own financial capacity and the terms of its reinsurance treaties, which may prescribe the types of exposures, the types of aircraft, contractual provisions, and the maximum limits of insurance that the company can underwrite.

KEY TERMS

Declarations Page
Business and Pleasure
Industrial Aid (Business or Corporate Use)
Limited Commercial
Commercial
Special Uses
All risks ground and flight
All risks not in motion
All risks not in flight
Aircraft
In flight
In motion
Insured value
Straight deductible
Ingestion deductible
Moored deductible
Franchise deductible
Disappearing deductible
Actual cash value
Unearned hull premium
Component parts schedule
Transportation costs
Appraisal condition
Aircraft liability insurance
Passengers
Occurrence
Single limit legal liability
Medical payments
Insured
Named insured
Omnibus clause
Non-ownership liability
Guest voluntary settlement
Weekly indemnity
Permanent and total disability
Joint Ownership
Interchange agreement

Aggregate deductible
Wear and tear
Valued basis
Time-sharing agreement
Exclusive dry lease
Management Company
Fractional ownership

REVIEW QUESTIONS

1. What is the purpose of the Declarations Page? Describe four common aircraft uses shown under item 6. What is an "open pilot warranty"?
2. What are the two most common hull coverages? Why do you think all risks ground (including taxiing) is a less popular coverage from an underwriting standpoint?
3. Would engines temporarily removed from the aircraft for overhaul be included under the hull coverage? When is the aircraft deemed to be "in flight"?
4. How is the insured value determined? Is coinsurance common under the hull coverage? Do underwriters today use a fixed depreciation figure in determining values in the event of total losses?
5. What is the purpose of deductibles? Distinguish between the following deductibles: straight, franchise, disappearing, and aggregate.
6. List and briefly describe the common exclusions found under the hull coverage.
7. What is the difference between "actual cash value" and "valued basis" hull coverage?
8. What expenses will the company pay in the event of a partial loss repaired by someone other than the insured? By the insured?
9. Why do underwriters use a component parts schedule when insuring some older aircraft? What is meant by "reasonable transportation costs"?
10. List the insured's duties in the event of loss or damage to the aircraft.
11. What condition under the policy addresses the problem of the insured and insurer disagreeing with regard to the amount of loss? How is the amount of loss determined in such a case?
12. Does hull coverage apply to newly acquired aircraft? What is loss of use coverage?
13. Briefly describe the following endorsements:
    a. War-risks coverage
    b. Loss payable and Breach of Warranty
    c. Spare engine and detached-equipment coverage
    d. Automatic hull value increase
14. What is aircraft liability insurance? Distinguish between the three basic coverages. Define "passengers." Why might an insured select a single-limit of liability coverage? What are the two ways a single-limit of liability can be written?
15. What is the purpose of medical payments coverage?
16. What is the omnibus clause under the definitions of insured? Who are not covered under the definition?
17. List the major exclusions found under the liability coverages. Some policies include additional exclusions. What are they?
18. Describe the following provisions: temporary use of substitute aircraft; use of other aircraft; and newly acquired aircraft.
19. Discuss some of the conditions applicable to the liability portion of the contract.
20. Briefly describe the following endorsements:
    a. Aircraft Non-ownership liability
    b. Guest Voluntary Settlement (Admitted Liability)
    c. Products Liability for sale of insured aircraft
    d. Inclusion of cross liability
    e. Contractual liability
21. Describe the following conditions found under the combined aircraft hull and

liability contract: two or more aircraft insured; policy period and territorial limits; changes; assignment; cancellation; and declarations.

22. What are some of the implications for an insured who is reimbursed for use of his aircraft? Describe the following agreements: Joint ownership; interchange; time sharing. Why are insurers so concerned about reimbursement of operating expenses?
23. List the specific insurance considerations for the lessor and lessee under an exclusive dry lease. What is a management company arrangement? What are the insurance considerations for the management company and fractional owners under fractional ownership?
24. What are the major responsibilities of the insured following a loss?

Golden Wing Policy & Endorsements

POLICY NUMBER:

THE COMPANIES

DECLARATIONS

Item 1. NAMED INSURED
AND ADDRESS:

Item 2. POLICY PERIOD:

From   to

This insurance shall commence and cease on the dates shown at 12:01 A.M. local time at the address of the **Named Insured** set forth in Item 1 (b) above.

Item 3. LIMITS OF THE COMPANY'S LIABILITY:

Insurance is provided only with respect to the following Coverages for which a limit of liability is specified, subject to all conditions of this policy.

COVERAGES	LIMITS OF LIABILITY	
LIABILITY:		
D. Single Limit **Bodily Injury** and **Property Damage** Liability Including **Passengers**	Each **Occurrence**	Each **Passenger**
MEDICAL EXPENSE:		
E. **Medical Expenses** Including Crew	Each Person	
PHYSICAL DAMAGE:		
F. All Risk Basis	The Insured Value of the **aircraft** subject to the following deductibles: While the **aircraft** is **in motion** While the **aircraft** is not **in motion**	

TOTAL PREMIUM: $
Surcharge: $

DECLARATIONS OF POLICY NUMBER (Continued)

Item 4. DESCRIPTION OF AIRCRAFT.

Year, Make and Model	Identification Number	Seating Crew	Capacity Other	Land, Sea or Amphibian	Insured Value

Item 5. OWNERSHIP AND ENCUMBERANCES. The **Named Insured** is, and shall remain, the sole and unconditional owner of the **aircraft** described in Item 4, unless otherwise indicated herein.

Item 6. AIRCRAFT USE. The Policy shall not apply to any **Insured** while the **aircraft** is being used with the knowledge and consent of such **Insured** for any purpose involving a charge intended to result in financial profit to such **Insured** unless otherwise indicated herein.

Item 7. PILOTS. The policy shall not apply while the **aircraft** is in **flight** unless

DECLARATIONS OF POLICY NUMBER (Continued)

Endorsements forming a part of this policy on its effective date:

ARRANGED BY:

IN WITNESS WHEREOF, the Company has caused this policy to be executed on its behalf by Global Aerospace, Inc., but this policy shall not be valid unless signed by a duly authorized representative of Global Aerospace, Inc.

Leonidas G. Demas, Secretary
Global Aerospace, Inc.

A. J. Medniuk, President & C.E.O.
Global Aerospace, Inc.

Countersignature (Where Required)

For Global Aerospace, Inc.

In consideration of the payment of the premium, in reliance upon the statements in the Declarations made a part hereof, subject to all of the terms of this policy including the applicable limits of liability, the Company agrees with the **Named Insured** with respect to those coverages indicated in Item 3 of the Declarations:

INSURING AGREEMENTS

I. LIABILITY COVERAGES

Coverage A - Bodily Injury Liability Excluding Passengers To pay on behalf of the **Insured** all sums which the **Insured** shall become legally obligated to pay as damages because of **bodily injury** sustained by any person excluding any **passenger**,

Coverage B - Passenger Bodily Injury Liability To pay on behalf of the **Insured** all sums which the **Insured** shall become legally obligated to pay as damages because of **bodily injury** sustained by any **passenger**,

Coverage C - Property Damage Liability To pay on behalf of the **Insured** all sums which the **Insured** shall become legally obligated to pay as damages because of **property damage**,

Coverage D - Single Limit Bodily Injury and Property Damage Liability To pay on behalf of the **Insured** all sums which the **Insured** shall become legally obligated to pay as damages because of **bodily injury** sustained by any person (excluding any **passenger** unless the words "including **passengers**" appear in Item 3 of the declarations) and **property damage**,

caused by an **occurrence** and arising out of the ownership, maintenance or use of the **aircraft**; or, only with respect to Coverages A, C and D, caused by an **occurrence** and arising out of the maintenance or use of the **premises** in or upon which the **aircraft** is stored.

II. MEDICAL EXPENSE COVERAGE

Coverage E - Medical Expenses To pay all reasonable **medical expenses** incurred within one year from the date of injury, to or for each **passenger** (excluding any crew member unless the words "including crew" appear in Item 3 of the Declarations) who sustains **bodily injury** caused by an **occurrence,** provided the **aircraft** is being used by or with the permission of the **Named Insured**.

III. PHYSICAL DAMAGE COVERAGES

Coverage F - All Risk Basis To pay for any **physical damage** loss to the **aircraft,** including **disappearance** of the **aircraft**.

Coverage G - All Risk Basis Not in Flight To pay for any **physical damage** loss to the **aircraft** sustained while the **aircraft** is not in **flight** and which is not the result of fire or explosion following crash or collision while the **aircraft** was in **flight**.

Coverage H - All Risk Basis Not in Motion To pay for any **physical damage** loss to the **aircraft** sustained while the **aircraft** is not **in motion** and which is not the result of fire or explosion following crash or collision while the **aircraft** was **in motion**.

IV. DEFENSE, SETTLEMENT AND SUPPLEMENTARY PAYMENTS
Coverages A, B, C and D

The Company shall have the right and duty to defend any suit against the **Insured** seeking damages on account of such **bodily injury** or **property damage**, even if any of the allegations of the suit are groundless, false or fraudulent, and may make such investigation and settlement of any claim or suit as it deems expedient, but the Company shall not be obligated to pay any claim or judgment or to defend any suit after the applicable limit of the Company's liability has been exhausted by payment of judgments or settlements.

During such time as the Company is obligated to defend a claim or claims under the provisions of the preceding paragraph, the Company will pay with respect to such claim, in addition to the applicable limit of liability:

(a) all expenses incurred by the Company, all costs taxed against the **Insured** in any suit defended by the Company and all interest on the entire amount of any judgment therein which accrues after entry of the judgment and before the Company has paid or tendered or deposited in court that part of the judgment which does not exceed the limit of the Company's liability thereon;

(b) premiums on appeal bonds required in any such suit, premiums on bonds to release attachments in any such suit for an amount not in excess of the applicable limit of liability of this policy, and the cost of bail bonds required of the **Insured** because of an **occurrence** or violation of law or a regulation for civil aviation arising out of the use of the **aircraft**, not to exceed $2,500 per bail bond, but the Company shall have no obligation to apply for or furnish any such bonds;

(c) expenses incurred by the **Insured** for first aid to others at the time of an accident, for **bodily injury** to which this policy applies;

(d) all reasonable expenses incurred by the **Insured** at the Company's request, other than for loss of earnings or for wages or salaries of employees of the **Insured**.

V. TEMPORARY USE OF SUBSTITUTE AIRCRAFT
Coverages A, B, C, D and E

While an **aircraft** described in Item 4 of the Declarations is withdrawn from normal use because of its breakdown, repair, servicing, loss or destruction, such insurance as is afforded under Coverages A, B, C, D and E is extended to apply with respect to the use, by or on behalf of the **Named Insured** of any other **aircraft** not owned in whole or in part by the **Named Insured**, while temporarily used as a substitute therefor.

VI. SPECIAL NON-OWNERSHIP COVERAGE
Coverages A, B, C, D and E

The coverage provided by this Agreement applies only if the **Named Insured** is one individual or one individual and spouse. Such insurance as is afforded under Coverages A, B, C, D and E with respect to the **aircraft** described in Item 4 of the Declarations, is extended to apply with respect to the use, by or on behalf of the **Named Insured**, of any other aircraft not owned in whole or in part by, or furnished for regular use to, such **Named Insured** or spouse. The insurance provided by this Agreement shall apply only to the **Named Insured** and spouse, if any, and their employers, if any.

VII. AUTOMATIC INSURANCE FOR NEWLY ACQUIRED AIRCRAFT
All Coverages

If the **Named Insured** acquires ownership of an **aircraft** in addition to the **aircraft** described in Item 4 of the Declarations and within thirty days thereafter reports such acquisition to the Company, then the insurance afforded by this policy shall apply to such additional **aircraft** as of the time of such acquisition, provided that the Company insured all other **aircraft** owned in whole or in part by the **Named Insured** on such acquisition date. Unless the **Named Insured** and the Company agree otherwise, the Coverages and limits of liability pertaining to said additional **aircraft** shall be the same as is provided for that **aircraft** which is described in Item 4 of the Declarations as having the greatest **passenger** carrying capacity, and the Insured Value of the additional **aircraft** shall be the actual cost of the **aircraft** to the **Named Insured** but not exceeding 150% of the highest Insured Value of any **aircraft** described in Item 4 of the Declarations. The **Named Insured** shall pay any additional premium required because of the application of the insurance to such other **aircraft.**

VIII. DEPARTMENT OF DEFENSE INSURANCE REQUIREMENTS
Coverages A, B, C and D

Upon issuance of a Department of Defense Certificate of Insurance DD Form 2400 or any substitute or replacement thereof by Associated Aviation Underwriters, Inc. the insurance policy provisions required by the regulations referred to in the Certificate of Insurance shall be incorporated into this policy and substituted for any conflicting policy provisions.

IX. TWO OR MORE AIRCRAFT
All Coverages

When two or more **aircraft** are insured under this policy, the terms of this policy shall apply separately to each.

X. POLICY PERIOD, TERRITORY
All Coverages

This policy applies only to **bodily injury** or **property damage** which occurs, and to **physical damage** losses to the **aircraft** which are sustained during the policy period, while the **aircraft** is within the United States of America, Canada, Mexico or the Bahama Islands or while en route between points therein.

EXCLUSIONS
(See also Items 5, 6, and 7 of the Declarations)

This policy does not apply:

(a) Under Coverages A, B, C and D, to liability assumed by the **Insured** under any contract or agreement, but this exclusion (a) does not apply to the assumption by the **Named Insured** of the liability of others for **bodily injury** or **property damage** in any written hold harmless agreement required by a military or governmental authority as a prerequisite to the use of an airport or an airport facility;

(b) Under Coverages A, B and D, to any obligation for which the **Insured** or any carrier as his insurer may be held liable under any worker's compensation, unemployment compensation or disability benefits law, or under any similar law;

(c) Under Coverages A, B, and D, to **bodily injury** to any employee of the **Insured** arising out of and in the course of his employment by such **Insured**; but this exclusion (c) does not apply to liability assumed by the **Named Insured** under any military or governmental agreement referred to in Exclusion (a) above;

(d) Under Coverages C and D, to **property damage** to property owned, occupied, rented or used by the **Insured** or in the care, custody or control of the **Insured** or as to which the **Insured** is for any purpose exercising physical control, but this exclusion (d) shall not apply to:

  (i) personal effects of passengers, but not exceeding \$3,000 for each **passenger** in each **occurrence**, or

  (ii) an aircraft hangar or contents thereof but not exceeding \$25,000 in any one **occurrence**;

(e) Under Coverage E, to **medical expense** incurred by or for any employee of the **Insured** to the extent that such expense is payable under any worker's compensation law or under any similar law;

(f) Under Coverages F, G and H, to **physical damage**

  (i) to tires other than by fire, theft, vandalism or malicious mischief, or

  (ii) caused by and confined to (a) wear and tear, (b) deterioration or (c) mechanical or electrical breakdown or failure of equipment, components or accessories installed in the **aircraft** unless such **physical damage** be coincident with and from the same cause as other loss covered by this policy;

(g) **War, Hi-Jacking and Other Perils Exclusion**.

Under all Coverages to claims caused by:

(i) war, invasion, acts of foreign enemies, hostilities (whether war be declared or not), civil war, rebellion, revolution, insurrection, martial law, military or usurped power or attempts at usurpation of power;

(ii) any hostile detonation of any weapon of war employing atomic or nuclear fission and/or fusion or other like reaction or radioactive force or matter;

(iii) strikes, riots, civil commotions or labor disturbances;

(iv) any act of one or more persons, whether or not agents of a sovereign Power, for political or terrorist purposes and whether the loss or damage resulting therefrom is accidental or intentional;

(v) any malicious act or act of sabotage;

(vi) confiscation, nationalization, seizure, restraint, detention, appropriation, requisition for title or use by or under the order of any Government (whether civil, military or de facto) or public or local authority; or

(vii) hi-jacking or any unlawful seizure or wrongful exercise of control of the aircraft or crew in flight (including any attempt at such seizure or control) made by any person or persons on board the aircraft acting without the consent of the **Named Insured**.

Furthermore this policy does not cover claims arising while the aircraft is outside the control of the **Named Insured** by reason of any of the above perils. The aircraft shall be deemed to have been restored to the control of the **Named Insured** on the safe return of the aircraft to the **Named Insured** at an airfield not excluded by the geographical limits of this policy, and entirely suitable for the operation of the aircraft (such safe return shall require that the aircraft be parked with engines shut down and under no duress);

(h) to **bodily injury** or **property damage** arising out of:

(i) noise, whether or not it is audible to the human ear, or vibration, including sonic boom or similar phenomena caused by the movement or operation of an aircraft or any of its parts; or

(ii) any interference with the quiet enjoyment of property of others caused by the operation of an aircraft or any of its parts.

(i) to **bodily injury** or **property damage** arising out of the actual, alleged or threatened discharge, dispersal, seepage, migration, release or escape of **pollutants**:

(i) that are in or upon an aircraft;

(ii) that are contained in any property that is in or upon an aircraft.

Paragraphs (h) and (i) do not apply to **bodily injury** or **property damage** caused by or resulting from an aircraft crash, fire, explosion, collision or a recorded in-flight emergency causing abnormal aircraft operation.

(j) to **bodily injury** or **property damage** arising out of the actual, alleged or threatened discharge, dispersal, seepage, migration, release or escape of **pollutants**:

(i) at or from any premises, site or location that is or was at any time owned or occupied by, or rented or loaned to, any **Insured**;

(ii) at or from any premises, site or location that is or was at any time used by or for any **Insured** or others for the handling, storage, disposal, processing or treatment of waste;

(iii) which are or were at any time transported, handled, stored, treated, disposed of, or processed as waste by or for any **Insured** or any person or organization for whom any **Insured** may be legally responsible; or

(iv) at or from any premises, site or location on which any **Insured** or any contractors or subcontractors working directly or indirectly on any **Insured's** behalf are performing operations:

(a) if the **pollutants** are brought on or to the premises, site or location in connection with such operations by such **Insured**, contractor or subcontractor; or

(b) if the operations are to test for, monitor, clean up, remove, contain, treat, detoxify or neutralize, or in any way respond to or assess the effects of **pollutants**.

Subparagraphs (j)(i) and (j)(iv)(a) do not apply to **bodily injury** or **property damage** arising out of heat, smoke or fumes from a hostile fire. In this exclusion, a hostile fire means one that becomes uncontrollable or breaks out from where it is intended to be.

(k) any loss, cost, or expense arising out of any:

(i) request, demand or order that any **Insured** or others test for, monitor, clean up, remove, contain, treat, detoxify or neutralize, or in any way respond to or assess the effects of **pollutants**; or

(ii) claim or suit by or on behalf of a governmental authority for damages because of testing for, monitoring, cleaning up, removing, containing, treating, detoxifying or neutralizing, or in any way responding to or assessing the effects of **pollutants**,

unless resulting from an **aircraft** crash, fire, explosion or collision or a recorded in-flight emergency causing abnormal **aircraft** operation.

In exclusion (k) above **"aircraft"** means the aircraft described in Item 4 of the Declarations (and when appropriate any aircraft qualifying under the provisions of the Insuring Agreements V, VI, VII or Non-owned Aircraft Endorsement, if any, attached to and forming part of the policy).

In exclusions (i), (j) and (k) above **"pollutants"** means any solid, liquid, gaseous or thermal irritant or contaminant, including smoke, vapor, soot, fumes, acids, alkalis, chemicals, and waste. Waste includes materials to be recycled, reconditioned, or reclaimed.

LIMIT OF THE COMPANY'S LIABILITY

ALL COVERAGES
(Other Insurance)

Except with respect to insurance afforded by Insuring Agreements V and VI and to insurance specifically purchased by the **Named Insured** to apply in excess of this policy, if there is other insurance in the **Insured's** name or otherwise, against loss, liability or expense covered by this policy, the Company shall not be liable under this policy for a greater proportion of such loss, liability or expense than the applicable limit of the Company's liability bears to the total applicable limit of liability of all valid and collectible insurance against such loss, liability or expense. Insurance afforded by Insuring Agreements V and VI shall be excess insurance over any other valid and collectible insurance available to the **Insured**, either as an insured under a policy applicable to the aircraft or otherwise. When the insurance afforded by this policy is excess over any other insurance, then the Company's limits of liability in this policy shall be reduced by the applicable limits of such other insurance if such other insurance shall have been written through Global Aerospace Underwriting Managers Limited or any of its subsidiaries or subsidiaries thereof.

COVERAGES A, B, C and D
(Total Liability)

Regardless of the number of (1) **Insureds** under this policy, (2) persons or organizations who sustain **bodily injury** or **property damage**, (3) claims made or suits brought on account of **bodily injury** or **property damage**, or (4) **aircraft** to which this policy applies, the Company's liability is limited as follows:

Coverages A and B. The total liability of the Company for all damages, including damages for care and loss of services, because of **bodily injury** sustained by any one person as the result of any one **occurrence** shall not exceed the limit of liability stated in the Declarations as applicable to "each person". Subject to the above provision respecting "each person," the total liability of the Company for all damages, including damages for care and loss of services, because of **bodily injury** sustained by two or more persons as the result of any one **occurrence** shall not exceed the limit of liability stated in the declarations as applicable to "each **occurrence**."

Coverage C. The total liability of the Company for all damages because of all **property damage** sustained by one or more persons or organizations as the result of any one **occurrence** shall not exceed the limit of the liability stated in the Declarations as applicable to "each **occurrence."**

Coverage D. The total liability of the Company for all damages, including damages for care and loss of services, because of **bodily injury** or **property damage** sustained by one or more persons or organizations as the result of any one **occurrence** shall not exceed the limit of liability stated in the declarations as applicable to "each **occurrence**."

For the purpose of determining the limit of the Company's liability, all **bodily injury** and **property damage** arising out of continuous or repeated exposure to substantially the same general conditions shall be considered as arising out of one **occurrence.**

COVERAGES A, B, C and D
(Severability of Interests)

The insurance afforded applies separately to each **Insured** against whom claim is made or suit is brought, except with respect to the limits of the Company's liability.

COVERAGE E
(Total Liability)

The total liability of the Company for all **medical expenses** incurred by or on behalf of each **passenger** who sustains **bodily injury** as the result of any one **occurrence** shall not exceed the limit of liability stated in the Declarations as applicable to "each person."

COVERAGES F, G and H
(Total Liability)

In the event of a **total loss** the Company shall pay the Insured Value of the **aircraft** less any applicable deductible whereupon the Company's liability with respect to such **aircraft** shall terminate. In addition, the Company shall refund the pro rata unearned premium for such **aircraft**.

In the event of a **partial loss** the Company's liability shall not exceed the "cost to repair" the **aircraft** as specified herein, less any applicable deductible, but in no event shall the Company's liability for a **partial** loss exceed the amount for which the Company would be liable if the **aircraft** were a **total loss**.

The "cost to repair" shall consist of (a) transportation charges as specified herein and (b) the actual cost to repair the damaged property with materials and parts of like kind and quality with charges for labor at straight time rates. Transportation charges shall consist of the cost, where necessary, of transporting new or damaged parts or of transporting the damaged **aircraft** to the place of repair and return to the place of accident or home airport, whichever is nearer, by the least expensive reasonable means.

The Company shall have the right to return stolen property anytime before the loss is paid with payment for any resultant **physical damage**.

The amount specified as a deductible does not apply to losses caused by fire, lightning, explosion, transportation, theft, robbery or pilferage; however, loss caused by fire or explosion resulting directly or indirectly from collision of the **aircraft** while **in motion** shall be subject to the **"in motion"** deductible, if any.

In the event that two or more **aircraft** are insured hereunder, the applicable deductible shall apply separately to each.

With respect to damage to aircraft engines and auxiliary power units insured under this policy:

(a) foreign object damage (damage caused by object(s) not a part of the engine or its accessories) whether resulting from ingestion or otherwise, shall be considered to be "wear and tear" unless such damage is the result of a single incident sustained during the policy period which is of sufficient severity, when such damage is sustained or upon its discovery, to require immediate repairs in compliance with the requirements of the engine manufacturer;

(b) damage caused by heat which results from the operation, attempted operation or shutdown of the engine shall be considered to be "wear and tear";

(c) damage which is not "wear and tear" shall be subject to the same deductible if any, as is applicable to **in motion** damage;

(d) damage caused by the breakdown, failure or malfunction of any engine component, accessory or part shall be considered to be "mechanical breakdown" of the entire engine.

DEFINITIONS

When appearing in this policy in **bold face** print:

"Aircraft" means the aircraft described in Item 4 of the Declarations (and when appropriate any aircraft qualifying under the provisions of Insuring Agreements V, VI, or VII) including the propulsion system and equipment usually installed in the aircraft (1) while installed in the aircraft, (2) while temporarily removed from the aircraft and (3) while removed from the aircraft for replacement until such time as replacement by a similar item has commenced; also tools and equipment in the aircraft which have been specifically designed for the aircraft and which are ordinarily carried therein;

"Bodily Injury" means bodily injury, sickness, disease or mental anguish sustained by any person which occurs during the policy period, including death at any time resulting therefrom;

"Disappearance" means missing and not reported for sixty days after commencing a **flight**;

"Federal Aviation Administration" means the duly constituted authority of the United States of America having jurisdiction over civil aviation, or its duly constituted equivalent in any other country;

"Flight" means the time commencing with the actual take-off run of the **aircraft** and continuing thereafter until it has completed its landing roll or, if the **aircraft** is a rotorcraft, from the time the rotors start to revolve under power for the purpose of **flight** until they subsequently cease to revolve;

"In Motion" means while the **aircraft** is moving under its own power or the momentum generated therefrom or while it is in **flight** and, if the **aircraft** is a rotorcraft, any time that the rotors are rotating;

"Insured" The unqualified word "insured" means, (1) with respect to all Coverages, the **Named Insured** and (2) with respect to Coverages A, B, C and D only (a) any person while using the **aircraft** with the permission of the **Named Insured** provided the actual use is within the scope of such permission and (b) any other person or organization, but only with respect to his or its liability because of acts or omissions of the **Named Insured** or of an Insured under (a) above, provided, however, that the insurance afforded under this subsection (2) does not apply to

(i) any person or organization, or agent or employee thereof (other than employees of the **Named Insured**) engaged in the manufacture, maintenance, repair, or sale of aircraft, aircraft engines, components or accessories, or in the operation of any airport, hangar, flying schools, flight service, or aircraft or piloting service, with respect to any **occurrence** arising out of such activity, or

(ii) any employee with respect to injury or death of another employee of the same employer injured in the course of such employment in an **occurrence** arising out of the maintenance or use of the **aircraft** or **premises** in the business of such employer, or

(iii) the owner or lessor, or any agent or employee thereof, of any **aircraft** which is the subject of the extended insurance provisions of insuring Agreements V or VI;

"Medical Expenses" means expenses for necessary medical, surgical, x-ray and dental services, including prosthetic devices, and necessary ambulance, hospital, professional nursing and funeral services;

"Named Insured" means the person or organization named in Item 1 of the Declarations;

"Occurrence" means an accident, including continuous or repeated exposure to conditions, which results in **bodily injury** or **property damage** neither expected nor intended from the standpoint of the **Insured**, but this definition shall not be construed so as to preclude coverage for **bodily injury** or **property damage** resulting from the efforts to prevent dangerous interference with the operation of the **aircraft**;

"Partial Loss" means any **physical damage** loss which is not a **total loss**;

"Passenger" means any person in, on or boarding the **aircraft** for the purpose of riding or flying therein, or alighting therefrom after a ride, **flight** or attempted **flight** therein;

"Physical Damage" means direct and accidental physical loss of or damage to the **aircraft**, hereinafter called loss, but does not include loss of use or any residual depreciation in value, if any, after repairs have been made;

"Pilot in Command" means the pilot responsible for the operation and safety of the **aircraft** during **flight**;

"Premises" means such portions of airports as are designated and used for the parking or storage of **aircraft** exclusive of premises owned by, or leased for more than thirty days to, the **Insured**;

"Property Damage" means (a) physical injury to or destruction of tangible property which occurs during the policy period, including loss of use thereof at any time resulting therefrom, or (b) loss of use of tangible property which has not been physically injured or destroyed provided such loss of use is caused by an **occurrence** during the policy period;

"Total Loss" means any **physical damage** loss for which the "cost to repair" will equal or exceed the Insured Value of the **aircraft** as set forth in Item 4 of the Declarations. **Disappearances** or theft of the entire **aircraft** shall be considered as a **total loss**.

CONDITIONS

(Applicable to all Coverages unless Otherwise Indicated)

1. INSURED'S DUTIES IN THE EVENT OF OCCURRENCE OR LOSS

(a) In the event of an **occurrence** or loss, notice containing particulars sufficient to identify the **Insured** and also reasonably obtainable information with respect to the time, place, and circumstances thereof, and the names and addresses of the injured and of available witnesses, shall be given by or for the **Insured** to Associated Aviation Underwriters, Inc. at any of the offices listed on the policy jacket as soon as reasonably possible. In the event of theft, robbery or pilferage, the **Named Insured** shall also promptly give notice to the police.

(b) If claim is made or suit is brought against the **Insured,** the **Insured** shall immediately forward to the Associated Aviation Underwriters, Inc. every demand, notice, summons, or other process received by him or his representatives.

(c) The **Insured** shall cooperate with the Company and upon request will assist in making settlements, in the conduct of suits and in enforcing any right of subrogation, contribution or indemnity against any person or organization who may be liable to the **Insured** because of loss, injury or damage with respect to which insurance is afforded under this policy; and the **Insured** shall attend hearings and trials and assist in securing and giving evidence and obtaining the attendance of witnesses. The **Insured** shall not, except at his own cost, voluntarily make any payment, assume any obligation or incur any expenses other than for first aid to others at the time of accident.

2. FINANCIAL RESPONSIBILITY LAWS
Coverages A, B, C and D

When this policy is certified as proof of financial responsibility for the future under the provisions of any aircraft financial responsibility law, such insurance as is afforded by this policy for **bodily injury** liability and **property damage** liability shall comply with the provisions of such law to the extent of the coverage and limits of liability required by such law, but in no event in excess of liability stated in this policy. The **Insured** agrees to reimburse the Company for any payment made by the Company which it would not have been obligated to make under the terms of this policy except for the agreement contained in this paragraph.

3. MEDICAL REPORTS: PROOF AND PAYMENT OF CLAIM
Coverage E

As soon as practicable the injured person or someone on his behalf shall give to the Company written proof of claim, under oath if required, and shall, after each request from the Company, execute authorization to enable the Company to obtain medical reports and copies of records. The injured person shall submit to physical examination by physicians selected by the Company when and as often as they may reasonably require.

The Company may pay the injured person or any person or organization rendering the services and such payment shall reduce the amount payable hereunder for such injury. Payment hereunder shall not constitute an admission of liability of any person or organization or of the Company.

4. ADDITIONAL DUTIES OF NAMED INSURED
Coverages F, G and H

In the event of loss, the **Named Insured** shall

(a) protect the **aircraft**, whether or not the loss is covered by this policy and any further loss due to the **Named Insured's** failure to protect shall not be recoverable under this policy; reasonable expenses incurred in affording such protection shall be deemed incurred at the Company's request;

(b) file with the Company within 91 days after loss, sworn proof of loss in such form and including such information as the Company may reasonably require and shall, upon the Company's request, submit to examination under oath, exhibit the damaged property and produce for the Company's examination all pertinent records and invoices, permitting copies thereof to be made, all at such reasonable times and places as the Company shall designate;

(c) do all things necessary to transfer title to any salvage, including the insured **aircraft** if it is a **total loss**, to the Company or its nominee.

5. APPRAISAL
Coverages F, G, and H

If the **Named Insured** and the Company fail to agree as to the amount of loss, either may, within 60 days after proof of loss is filed, demand an appraisal of the loss. In such event, the **Named Insured** and the Company shall each select a competent appraiser, and the appraisers shall select a competent and disinterested umpire. The appraisers shall appraise the amount of the loss and failing to agree shall submit their differences to the umpire. An award in writing of any two shall determine the amount of loss. The **Named Insured** and the Company shall each pay his chosen appraiser and shall bear equally the other expenses of the appraisal and the umpire. The Company shall not be held to have waived any of its rights by any act relating to appraisal.

6. SALVAGE
Coverages F, G, and H

The value of all salvaged property shall inure to the benefit of the Company, however, there shall be no abandonment without the consent of the Company.

7. AUTOMATIC REINSTATEMENT
Coverages F, G and H

In the event of a **partial loss**, whether or not such loss is covered by this policy, the Insured Value of the **aircraft** as shown in Item 4 of the Declarations shall be reduced as of the time of loss by the amount of such loss. Upon the commencement of repairs the Insured Value shall be increased by the value of the completed repairs until the Insured Value of the **aircraft** as shown in Item 4 of the Declarations is fully restored or this policy terminates whichever shall first occur.

8. NO BENEFIT TO OTHERS
Coverages F, G and H

The insurance afforded by this policy shall not inure directly or indirectly to the benefit of any carrier or bailee liable for loss to the insured **aircraft.**

9. SUBROGATION
Coverages A, B, C, D, F, G and H

In the event of any payment under this policy the Company shall be subrogated to all of the **Insured's** rights of recovery therefor against any person or organization and the **Insured** shall execute and deliver instruments and papers and do whatever else is necessary to enforce such rights. The **Insured** shall do nothing after loss to prejudice such rights.

10. ACTION AGAINST THE COMPANY

No action shall lie against the Company unless, as a condition precedent thereto, the **Insured** shall have fully complied with all of the terms of this policy.

With respect to Coverages A, B, C and D, no action shall lie against the Company until the amount of the **Insured's** obligation to pay shall have been finally determined either by judgment against the **Insured** after actual trial or by written agreement of the **Insured,** the claimant and the Company.

Any person or organization or the legal representative thereof who has secured such judgment or written agreement shall thereafter be entitled to recover under this policy to the extent of the insurance afforded by this policy. No person or organization shall have any right under this policy to join the Company as a party to any action against the **Insured** to determine the **Insured's** liability, nor shall the Company be impleaded by the **Insured** or his legal representative. Bankruptcy or insolvency of the **Insured** or of the **Insured's** estate shall not relieve the Company of any of its obligations hereunder.

With respect to Coverages F, G and H, no action shall lie against the Company until sixty days after proof of loss is filed and the amount of loss is determined as provided in this policy.

11. CHANGES

Notice to any agent or knowledge possessed by any agent or by any other person shall not effect a waiver or a change in any part of this policy or stop the Company from asserting any right under the terms of this policy; nor shall the terms of this policy be waived or changed, except by endorsement issued to form a part of this policy signed by Associated Aviation Underwriters, Inc.

12. ASSIGNMENT

Assignment of interest under this policy shall not bind the Company until its consent is endorsed hereon; if, however, the **Named Insured** shall die or be adjudged bankrupt or insolvent within the policy period, the policy unless canceled, shall, if written notice be given to the Company within 60 days after the date of such death or adjudication, cover (1) the **Named Insured's** legal representative as **Named Insured** but only while acting within the scope of his duties as such, and (2) under Coverages A, B, C and D, any person having proper temporary custody of the **aircraft** as an **Insured,** until the appointment and qualification of such legal representative but in no event for a period of more than 60 days after the date of such death or adjudication.

13. CANCELLATION

This policy may be canceled by any **Named Insured** by mailing to the Company or to Associated Aviation Underwriters, Inc. at any of the offices listed on the policy jacket, written notice stating when thereafter the cancellation shall be effective. This policy may be canceled by the Company by mailing to the **Named Insured** at the first address shown in Item 1 of the Declarations, notice stating when, not less than 30 days thereafter, such cancellation shall be effective. The mailing of notice as aforesaid shall be sufficient proof of notice. The effective date and hour of cancellation stated in the notice shall become the end of the policy period.

In the event that the **Named Insured** fails to pay any premium when due, this policy may be canceled by the Company by mailing to the **Named Insured** at the address shown in Item 1. of the Declarations, notice stating when, not less than 10 days thereafter, such cancellation shall be effective.

If the **Named Insured** cancels, earned premium shall be computed in accordance with the Company's short rate table and procedure. If the Company cancels, earned premium shall be computed pro-rata. Premium adjustments may be made either at the time cancellation is effective or as soon as practicable after cancellation becomes effective, but payment or tender of unearned premium is not a condition of cancellation.

14. DECLARATION

By acceptance of this policy, the **Named Insured** agrees that the statements in the Declarations are his agreements and representations, that this policy is issued in reliance upon the truth of such representations and that this policy embodies all agreements existing between himself and the Company or any of its agents relating to this insurance.

NON-OWNED AIRCRAFT LIABILITY AND MEDICAL EXPENSE COVERAGE

In consideration of the payment of the premium for this policy, it is agreed that such insurance as is afforded by Coverages A, B, C, D and E shall apply to **non-owned aircraft**. This insurance is subject to the following provisions which are applicable only to the insurance afforded by this endorsement and which shall be in addition to all other applicable provisions not amended in this endorsement:

1. The insurance afforded by this endorsement does not apply:

   (a) while the **non-owned aircraft** is in **flight** unless the **pilot in command** holds a currently effective pilot's certificate issued by the **Federal Aviation Administration,** or

   (b) to liability for **bodily injury** or **property damage** which arises from the manufacture, sale, handling, distribution or disposal of goods or products by the **Named Insured** or by others trading under its name or from services provided by or on behalf of the **Named Insured**, including any materials, parts or equipment furnished in connection with such services.

2. The policy definition of **Insured** is amended to read as follows:

   "**Insured**" The unqualified word "Insured" means:

   (a) the **Named Insured**, and

   (b) any director or executive officer or employee of a **Named Insured** corporation or a partner of a **Named Insured** partnership or a member or manager of a **Named Insured** limited liability company while such person is acting in such capacity provided that no person shall be an **Insured** as respects any aircraft owned in whole or in part by, registered in the name of, or leased for a period in excess of thirty (30) days by such person or any member of that person's household.

3. The following definition is added to the policy:

   "**Non-Owned Aircraft**" means any aircraft used by or on behalf of the **Named Insured** provided a Standard Airworthiness Certificate has been issued for the aircraft by the **Federal Aviation Administration**. Non-owned aircraft does not include:

   (a) aircraft described in Item 4. DESCRIPTION OF AIRCRAFT of the Declarations,

   (b) aircraft for which insurance is afforded by Insuring Agreement V. TEMPORARY USE OF SUBSTITUTE AIRCRAFT,

   (c) aircraft owned in whole or in part by or registered in the name of the **Named Insured**,

   (d) aircraft which are the subject of a lease or service agreement with the **Named Insured** for a period in excess of thirty (30) days unless such lease or service agreement is reported to Global Aerospace, Inc. and an additional premium paid if required by the Company, or

   (e) aircraft having a seating capacity (including crew seats) in excess of

Endorsement No.

4. The Other Insurance provision set out in the LIMIT OF THE COMPANY'S LIABILITY section of the policy is amended to read as follows:

   Except as respects insurance specifically purchased by the **Named Insured** to apply in excess of this insurance, the insurance afforded by this endorsement shall be excess insurance over any other valid and collectible insurance available to the **Insured**, either as an insured under a policy applicable to **non-owned aircraft** or otherwise. When the insurance afforded by this policy is excess over any other insurance, then the Company's limits of liability in this policy shall be reduced by the applicable limits of such other insurance if such other insurance shall have been written through Global Aerospace Underwriting Managers Limited or any of its subsidiaries or subsidiaries thereof.

ALL OTHER TERMS AND CONDITIONS REMAIN UNCHANGED.

This endorsement is effective: Endorsement Premium:

Attached to and made part of Policy No.:

Issued to:

Global Aerospace, Inc.

BY: Endorsement No.

Page 2 of 2

LIABILITY AND MEDICAL EXPENSES COVERAGE
(Applicable to the War, Hi-Jacking and Other Perils Exclusion)

In consideration of the payment of the premium for this policy, it is agreed that sub-paragraphs (i), (iii), (iv), (v), (vi) and (vii) of exclusion (g), the War, Hi-Jacking and Other Perils Exclusion, of this policy are deleted as respects the Liability and Medical Expense Coverages afforded by this policy. This insurance is subject to the following provisions which are applicable only to the insurance afforded by this endorsement and which shall be in addition to all other applicable provisions not amended in this endorsement:

1. Exclusion applicable only to any insurance afforded as respects the deletion of sub-paragraph (i) of exclusion (g), the War, Hi-Jacking and Other Perils Exclusion:

   This insurance shall not include liability for damage to any form of property on the ground situated outside Canada and the United States of America unless caused by or arising out of the use of aircraft.

2. Limitation of Liability:

   The limit of the Company's liability as respects the insurance afforded by this endorsement shall be a sub-limit of $50,000,000 or the applicable policy limit whichever the lesser any one **occurrence** and in the annual aggregate except with respect to **passengers** to whom the full policy limit(s) shall apply. This sub-limit shall apply within the full policy limit and not in addition thereto.

3. Automatic Termination:

   To the extent provided below, insurance afforded by this endorsement shall terminate automatically in the following circumstances:

   (a) All insurance
   - upon the outbreak of war (whether there be a declaration of war or not) between any two or more of the following states: the United Kingdom, the United States of America, France, the Russian Federation, the People's Republic of China.

   (b) Any insurance afforded in respect of the deletion of sub-paragraph (i) of exclusion (g), the War, Hi-Jacking and Other Perils Exclusion
   - upon the hostile detonation of any weapon of war employing atomic or nuclear fission and/or fusion or other like reaction or radioactive force or matter wheresoever or whensoever such detonation may occur and whether or not an aircraft may be involved.

   (c) All insurance in respect of any aircraft requisitioned for either title or use
   - upon such requisition.

   provided that if an aircraft is in the air when (a), (b) or (c) occurs, then the insurance afforded by this endorsement (unless otherwise canceled, terminated or suspended) shall continue in respect of such aircraft until completion of its first landing thereafter and any crew members and **passengers** have disembarked.

Endorsement No.

4. Review and Cancellation:

(a) Review of Premium and/or Geographical Limits (7 days)

The Company may give notice to review premium and/or geographical limits - such notice to become effective on the expiry of seven (7) days from 12:01 A.M. local time at the address of the **Named Insured** set forth in the policy on the day after which notice is given.

(b) Limited Cancellation (48 hours)

Following a hostile detonation as specified in 3 (b) above, the Company may give notice of cancellation of one or more parts of the insurance afforded by this endorsement by reference to sub-paragraphs (iii), (iv), (v), (vi) and/or (vii) of exclusion (g), the War, Hi-Jacking and Other Perils Exclusion - such notice to become effective on the expiry of forty-eight (48) hours from 12:01 A.M. local time at the address of the **Named Insured** set forth in the policy on the day after which notice is given.

(c) Cancellation (7 days)

The insurance afforded by this endorsement may be canceled by either the Company or the **Named Insured** giving notice to become effective on the expiry of seven (7) days from 12:01 A.M. local time at the address of the **Named Insured** set forth in the policy on the day after which notice is given.

(d) Notices

All notices referred to in this endorsement shall be in writing.

ALL OTHER TERMS AND CONDITIONS REMAIN UNCHANGED.

This endorsement is effective: Endorsement Premium:

Attached to and made part of Policy No.:

Issued to:

Global Aerospace, Inc.

BY: Endorsement No.

Page 2 of 2

PHYSICAL DAMAGE COVERAGE
(Applicable to the War, Hi-Jacking and Other Perils Exclusion)

In consideration of the payment of the premium for this policy, and solely as respects the aircraft described in the schedule of this endorsement, it is agreed that sub-paragraphs (i), (iii), (iv), (v), (vi) and (vii) of exclusion (g), the War, Hi-Jacking and Other Perils Exclusion, of this policy are deleted as respects the Physical Damage Coverage afforded by this policy. This insurance is subject to the following provisions which are applicable only to the insurance afforded by this endorsement and which shall be in addition to all other applicable provisions not amended in this endorsement:

1. This insurance shall only apply to the extent that the loss or damage is not otherwise excluded by sub-paragraph (ii) of exclusion (g), the War, Hi-Jacking and Other Perils Exclusion.

2. The limits of the Company's liability as respects the insurance afforded by this endorsement shall not exceed, in the aggregate during the policy period, the lesser of:

   (a) the sum of the Insured Values of the aircraft described in the schedule of this endorsement on the date of loss, or

   (b) $300,000,000.

3. (a) Amendment of Terms or Cancellation:

   The Company may give notice, effective on the expiry of seven (7) days from 12:01 A.M. local time at the address of the **Named Insured** set forth in the policy on the day after which notice is issued, to review the rate of premium and/or the geographical limits. In the event of the review of the rate of premium and/or the geographical limits not being accepted by the **Named Insured** then at the expiry of the said seven (7) days, this endorsement shall become canceled at that date.

   (b) Automatic Review of Terms or Cancellation:

   Notwithstanding 3 (a) above, this endorsement is subject to automatic review by the Company of the rate of premium and/or conditions and/or geographical limits effective on the expiry of seven (7) days from the time of any hostile detonation of any weapon of war employing atomic or nuclear fission and/or fusion or other like reaction or radioactive force or matter wheresoever or whensoever such detonation may occur and whether or not an aircraft described in the schedule of this endorsement may be involved. In the event of the review of the rate of premium and/or conditions and/or the geographical limits not being accepted by the **Named Insured** then at the expiry of the said seven (7) days, this endorsement shall become canceled at that date.

   (c) Cancellation by Notice:

   This endorsement may be canceled by the Company or the **Named Insured** giving notice not less than seven (7) days prior to the end of each period of three (3) months from inception.

Endorsement No.

4. Automatic Termination:

Whether or not such notice of cancellation has been given, this endorsement shall terminate automatically upon the outbreak of war (whether there be a declaration of war or not) between any of the following states: the United Kingdom, the United States of America, France, the Russian Federation, the People's Republic of China. Provided that if an aircraft described in the schedule of this endorsement is in **flight** when such outbreak of war occurs then this endorsement, subject to its terms and conditions and provided it is not otherwise canceled, terminated or suspended, will be continued as respects such aircraft until such aircraft has completed its first landing thereafter.

Schedule

Year, Make, Model and Identification Number

ALL OTHER TERMS AND CONDITIONS REMAIN UNCHANGED.

This endorsement is effective: Endorsement Premium:

Attached to and made part of Policy No.:

Issued to:

Global Aerospace, Inc.

BY: Endorsement No.

Page 2 of 2

RADIOACTIVE CONTAMINATION EXCLUSION

This policy does not apply to:

1. (a) loss or destruction of or damage to any property (including aircraft) whatsoever or any loss or expense whatsoever resulting or arising therefrom

   (b) any legal liability or medical expense of whatsoever nature

   directly or indirectly caused or contributed to by or arising from ionizing radiations or contamination by radioactivity from any source whatsoever.

2. Loss, destruction, damage, expense or legal liability which, but for the provisions of paragraph 1. of this Exclusion, would be covered by this policy, and is directly or indirectly caused or contributed to by or arises from ionizing radiations or contamination by radioactivity from any radioactive materials in the course of carriage as cargo under International Air Transport Association regulations or the regulations of the duly constituted governmental authority having jurisdiction over the transportation of radioactive materials, shall (subject to all the other provisions of this policy) be covered, provided that:

   (a) it shall be a condition precedent to the liability of the Company that the carriage of any radioactive materials shall in all respects comply with the current regulations issued by the International Air Transport Association or the duly constituted governmental authority having jurisdiction relating to the carriage of restricted articles by air;

   (b) this policy shall only apply to any claim made against the **Insured** arising out of any accident or incident occurring during the period of this insurance and any such claim by the **Insured** against the Company or by any claimant against the **Insured** shall have been made within three years after the date of the **occurrence** giving rise to the claim;

   (c) in the case of any claim by virtue of this paragraph 2 under Insuring Agreement III. PHYSICAL DAMAGE COVERAGES of this policy, the level of contamination shall have exceeded the maximum permissible level set out in the following scale:

EMITTER (IAEA Health and Safety Regulations in accordance with the current ICAO Technical Instructions for the Safe Transport of Dangerous Goods by Air)	**MAXIMUM PERMISSIBLE LEVEL OF NONFIXED RADIOACTIVE SURFACE CONTAMINATION** (Averaged over 300 cm^2)
Beta, gamma and low toxicity alpha emitters	Not exceeding 4 Becquerels/cm^2 (10^{-4}microcuries/cm^2)
All other alpha emitters	Not exceeding 0.4 Becquerels/cm^2 (10^{-5}microcuries/cm^2)

   (d) the coverage afforded by this paragraph 2 may be cancelled at any time by the Company giving seven days notice of cancellation.

ALL OTHER TERMS AND CONDITIONS REMAIN UNCHANGED.

This endorsement is effective: Endorsement Premium: Included

Attached to and made part of Policy No.:

Issued to:

Global Aerospace, Inc.

BY: Endorsement No.

Page 1 of 1

PASSENGER VOLUNTARY SETTLEMENTS COVERAGE

1. In consideration of the payment of premium for Passenger Bodily Injury Liability Coverage, it is agreed that the following coverage is added to Insuring Agreement I. LIABILITY COVERAGES:

   COVERAGE J - PASSENGER VOLUNTARY SETTLEMENTS

   Irrespective of legal liability, the Company shall offer to pay on behalf of the **Insured**, at the request of the **Named Insured**, benefits set forth in paragraph 2 below, to or for the benefit of each **passenger** who sustains **bodily injury** caused by an **occurrence** arising out of the ownership, maintenance or use of aircraft described in the schedule of this endorsement.

2. If such **bodily injury**, directly and independently of all other causes, results:

   (a) within one year of the **occurrence**, in the death of the **passenger** or, if not in the death of the **passenger**, in injury involving two or more of the following: (1) severance of a hand at or above the wrist, (2) severance of a foot at or above the ankle, or (3) entire and irrecoverable loss of sight in an eye, then the Company shall offer to pay the sum requested by the **Named Insured** but not exceeding the applicable Coverage J Settlement Limit for Each Crew Member or Each Non-Crew Member set forth in the schedule of this endorsement. Should injury (as described in either (1), (2) or (3) above) be limited to only one hand, foot or eye, then the Company shall offer to pay the sum requested by the **Named Insured** but not exceeding one-half (1/2) of the applicable Coverage J Settlement Limit for Each Crew Member or Each Non-Crew Member set forth in the schedule of this endorsement.

   (b) in the injured **passenger** becoming completely disabled from performing each and every duty pertaining to their occupation, the Company shall, within thirty (30) days of payment, reimburse the **Named Insured** for payments made to the injured **passenger** for loss of earnings as a result of such disability, but not exceeding:

      (1) eighty (80) percent of the average weekly wage of the injured **passenger** based upon the twelve (12) month period immediately preceding the date of **occurrence**, or

      (2) one-half (1/2) of one (1) percent of the applicable Coverage J Settlement Limit for Each Crew Member or Each Non-Crew Member set forth the schedule of this endorsement,

      whichever is the least, per week, for the period of such continuous and complete disability from performing each and every duty pertaining to their occupation up to a maximum of one hundred four (104) consecutive weeks.

   (c) in the inability of the injured **passenger** after twelve (12) months of being continuously and completely disabled from performing each and every duty pertaining to their occupation, to perform each and every duty pertaining to any occupation or employment for wage or profit for the rest of their life, then the Company shall offer to pay the sum requested by the **Named Insured** but not exceeding the applicable Coverage J Settlement Limit for Each Crew Member or Each Non-Crew Member set forth in the schedule of this endorsement.

3. The amount otherwise due and payable as benefits set forth in paragraph 2 above shall be reduced by the amount of any payments previously made in accordance with the provisions of Coverage J to or for the same **passenger** as a result of any one **occurrence**.

4. Coverage J is subject to the following provisions, which are in addition to all other applicable provisions not amended in this endorsement:

   EXCLUSION (Applicable to Coverage J)

   This insurance does not apply to or for the benefit of any person who is in, on or boarding the aircraft for the purpose of operating or assisting in the operation of the aircraft unless the words "Coverage for crew members is included" appear in the schedule of this endorsement.

Endorsement No.

LIMITS OF LIABILITY (Applicable to Coverage J)

The Coverage J Settlement Limits set forth in the schedule of this endorsement are included in and are a part of the Company's Limits of Liability set forth in Item 3 of the Declarations for Coverage B or D as applicable, and are not in addition thereto.

The Company's Limit of Liability, if any, set forth in Coverage B or D for each **passenger** shall be reduced by the amount of payments made in accordance with the provisions of this Coverage J to or for each **passenger** as the result of each **occurrence** and the Company's Limit of Liability set forth in Coverage B or D, as applicable, for each **occurrence** shall be reduced by the amount of payments made in accordance with the provisions of this Coverage J to or for all **passengers** as the result of each **occurrence**.

The total amount which the Company shall offer to pay to or for the benefit of any one injured **passenger** shall not exceed the amount set forth in the schedule of this endorsement as the Coverage J Settlement Limit applicable to Each Crew Member or Each Non-Crew Member respectively. The total amount which the Company shall offer to pay to or for the benefit of two (2) or more injured **passengers** in each **occurrence** shall not exceed the amount set forth in the schedule of this endorsement as the Coverage J Settlement Limit applicable to Each **Occurrence**. Payment of any amount to or for any injured **passenger** in accordance with the provisions of Coverage B or D, as applicable, shall operate to terminate the Company's obligations set out in this Coverage J as respects such **passenger**.

If any other Voluntary Settlement insurance (or Crew Member, Passenger or Guest Voluntary Settlement insurance) is available to or for the benefit of the injured **passenger** and shall have been written through Global Aerospace Underwriting Managers Limited or any of its subsidiaries or subsidiaries thereof, the Coverage J Settlement Limits specified in the schedule of this endorsement shall be reduced by the amount of such other insurance.

CONDITIONS (Applicable to Coverage J)

1. Liability Release Required.

   Except as respects benefits payable in accordance with the provisions of paragraph 2 (b) above, no payment shall be made until the injured **passenger** and all persons claiming by, through or under said **passenger** shall have executed, in a form acceptable to the Company, a full and final release for damages for which insurance is afforded by Coverage B or D.

2. No Admission.

   No offer, payment or acceptance of benefits in accordance with the provisions of Coverage J shall constitute an admission of liability or any other type of admission whatsoever on the part of the Company or of the **Insured**.

3. Physical Examinations and Reports.

   The injured **passenger** or someone on that person's behalf shall, at the request of the Company, furnish reasonably obtainable information pertaining to the injuries and execute authorization to enable the Company to obtain medical reports and copies of records. The injured **passenger** shall submit to physical examination by physicians selected by the Company when and as often as the Company may reasonably require.

4. Provisions Applicable.

   All policy provisions applicable to Coverage B or D shall apply to the insurance afforded by this Coverage J except the LIMIT OF THE COMPANY'S LIABILITY and Exclusion (c).

5. Refusal to Accept Offer.

   If the injured **passenger** and all persons having a claim by, through or under such **passenger** refuse to accept the sum offered, or fail to execute the required release within ninety (90) days of the date of the offer, or if claim is made or if suit is brought against an **Insured** for such **bodily injury**, then this Coverage J shall become null and void as respects such **passenger** and the provisions of Coverage B or D shall apply.

Endorsement No.

Schedule

1. Coverage for crew members is included.
2. Aircraft and Settlement Limits:

	Settlement Limits		
	Each **Passenger**		
Year, Make, Model and Identification Number	Each Crew Member	Each Non-Crew Member	Each **Occurrence**

and

Aircraft for which insurance is afforded by Insuring Agreement V. TEMPORARY USE OF SUBSTITUTE AIRCRAFT or Insuring Agreement VII. AUTOMATIC INSURANCE FOR NEWLY ACQUIRED AIRCRAFT	Regardless of the seating capacity of such aircraft, the Coverage J Settlement Limits shall be the same as the highest of any Coverage J Settlement Limit for Each Crew Member, Each Non-Crew Member or Each **Occurrence** shown above. However, if any such Coverage J Settlement Limit for Each Crew Member, Each Non-Crew Member or Each **Occurrence** is shown as NOT COVERED, it shall likewise be NOT COVERED for any aircraft used as a temporary substitute for that aircraft.

ALL OTHER TERMS AND CONDITIONS REMAIN UNCHANGED.

This endorsement is effective:

Endorsement Premium:

Attached to and made part of Policy No.:

Issued to:

Global Aerospace, Inc.

BY:

Endorsement No.

Page 3 of 3

PHYSICAL DAMAGE ADDITIONAL INTEREST
(Applicable To Coverage F)

Subject to the following provisions which apply only to the insurance afforded by this endorsement and which shall be in addition to all other applicable provisions not amended in this endorsement, it is agreed that as respects Coverage F - All Risk Basis of Insuring Agreement III. PHYSICAL DAMAGE COVERAGES of this policy:

1. Subject to the terms of a mortgage, lease or other agreement, the person(s) or organization(s) described in paragraph 10 below hereinafter referred to as the lienholder has a financial interest in the aircraft specified in paragraph 10 below hereinafter referred to as the encumbered aircraft.

2. If:

   (a) the Company denies coverage for the **Named Insured's** claim for **physical damage** because of the **Named Insured's** acts or because the **Named Insured** has failed to comply with the terms of this policy, and

   (b) the **physical damage** does not result from conversion, embezzlement or secretion of the encumbered aircraft by the **Named Insured**,

   the lienholder shall still have a right to receive payment for **physical damage** in accordance with the provisions of Coverage F if the lienholder:

   (1) at the request of the Company, pays any premium due for Coverage F if the **Named Insured** has failed to do so;

   (2) submits to Global Aerospace, Inc. a signed, sworn proof of loss within sixty (60) days after receiving notice from the Company of the **Named Insured's** failure to do so; and

   (3) has notified Global Aerospace, Inc. of any change in ownership or substantial change in risk known to the lienholder.

   All of the terms of the policy applicable to Coverage F will then apply directly to the lienholder. The **physical damage** loss shall be adjusted with and payable solely to the lienholder in an amount not to exceed the lesser of either the Insured Value of the encumbered aircraft less any applicable deductible, or the net amount owing to the lienholder by the **Named Insured** in accordance with the terms of such mortgage, lease or other agreement, as of the date the **physical damage** is sustained, if any balance remains after the lienholder has used all reasonable means to collect the amount due from the **Named Insured**, less (i) installments more than thirty (30) days overdue, (ii) penalties, and (iii) unearned charges.

3. If the Company pays the lienholder for **physical damage** in accordance with the provisions of Coverage F and denies payment therefor to the **Named Insured** because of the **Named Insured's** acts or because the **Named Insured** has failed to comply with the terms this policy:

   (a) the lienholder's rights under the mortgage, lease or other agreement and all related securities held as collateral to the debt will be transferred to the Company to the extent of the amount the Company pays; and

Endorsement No.

(b) the lienholder's right to recover the full amount of the lienholder's claim will not be impaired.

At its option, the Company may pay to the lienholder the whole principal due on the mortgage, lease or other agreement plus any accrued interest. In this event, the mortgage, lease or other agreement and all related securities will be transferred to the Company. The **Named Insured** will pay its remaining mortgage debt, rents or other obligations to the Company.

4. The **Named Insured** agrees, upon demand of the Company, to reimburse the Company for the full amount of any payment made that is subject to the provisions of paragraph 2 of this endorsement.

5. Any payment for **physical damage**, other than payment that is subject to the provisions of paragraph 2 of this endorsement, shall be made after the **physical damage** loss has been adjusted with the **Named Insured** and shall be made payable to:

   (a) the **Named Insured**,

   (b) the lienholder, and

   (c) if any, other persons or organizations having a financial interest in the encumbered aircraft who are described elsewhere in this policy,

   jointly for the account of all interests.

6. If the Company cancels this policy, it will give written notice to the lienholder at least:

   (a) ten (10) days before the effective date of cancellation if the Company cancels for non-payment of premium; or

   (b) thirty (30) days before the effective date of cancellation if the Company cancels for any other reason.

7. The provisions of this endorsement shall apply only as respects the financial interest of the lienholder, and not as respects any other interest the lienholder may have or have had in the encumbered aircraft relating to the design, manufacture, sale, modification, maintenance, service or operation of the encumbered aircraft, other than operation by the **Named Insured**. In the event of **physical damage** to which Coverage F applies, payment made by the Company to the lienholder shall not prejudice the Company's right to recover such payment from the lienholder for any interest, other than financial, the lienholder may have in the encumbered aircraft.

8. The lienholder's rights and duties set forth in this endorsement may not be transferred without the written consent of the Company.

9. As used in this endorsement, **Named Insured** means only

Endorsement No.

10. ENCUMBERED AIRCRAFT AND LIENHOLDER:

Year, Make, Model and Identification Number	Lienholder

ALL OTHER TERMS AND CONDITIONS REMAIN UNCHANGED.

This endorsement is effective: Endorsement Premium:

Attached to and made part of Policy No.:

Issued to:

Global Aerospace, Inc.

BY: Endorsement No.

Chapter 9

Airport Premises Liability and Other Aviation Coverages

OUTLINE

Airport Premises Liability
Other Airport Liability Coverages
Other Aviation Liability Coverages

OBJECTIVES

At the end of this chapter you should be able to:
Recognize the purpose of the airport premises liability coverage and describe the basic information included under the declarations.
List the exclusions found in a typical airport premises liability policy and explain why they are included.
Discuss the unique conditions found in an airport premises liability policy.
Explain the following extensions in coverage under the airport premises liability policy: medical payments, contractual liability, alterations and/or new construction liability, and elevator liability.
Identify the products and services sold by a fixed base operator.
Describe the coverage provided under products and completed operations liability and hangarkeepers liability.
Distinguish between personal injury liability and advertising injury liability.
Explain why air meet liability is not covered under the basic airport premises liability policy.
Explain why an individual or company not owning an aircraft might want to purchase an aircraft non-ownership liability policy.
Highlight the coverage found under the following policies: aerial application, manufacturers product liability, excess liability and umbrella liability, loss of use, loss of license, pilot accident, and ultralight aircraft insurance.

AIRPORT PREMISES LIABILITY

The owner or operator of an airport or portions thereof such as a fixed base operator has the same general type and degree of liability exposure as the operator of most public premises. People sustain injuries and damage their clothing when they fall over obstructions or trip over concealed obstacles. Their automobiles get damaged when struck by airport service vehicles on the airport premises. Claims from such accidents can be for large amounts but claims stemming from aircraft accidents have even greater catastrophe potential. The occupants of aircraft may be killed or severely injured and expensive aircraft damaged or destroyed, not to mention injury to other persons or other property at or near an airport. Liability in such instances may stem from a defect in the surface of the runway, from the failure of the airport operator or owner to mark obstructions properly, or from failure to send out the necessary warnings and to close the airport when it is not in usable condition.

Airport operators owe a duty to a wide range of people and litigation may arise from a variety of events occurring on, and off, the airport premises. The principal sources of litigation may be summarized under two headings: (1) aircraft operations such as aircraft accidents, fueling, aircraft in the care, custody or control of the operator, and maintenance and service work; and (2) premises operations such as automobile parking lots, elevators and escalators, police and security, slipping and falling, special events, tenants and contractors, and vehicular traffic.

The purpose of *airport premises liability* coverage is to protect the owner or operator of an airport against loss because of legal liability due to maintenance or use of the airport and all operations at or away from it, including elevators and escalators which are necessary or incidental to airport activities. This coverage comprises all ordinary premises hazards, including those caused by aircraft except: (1) aircraft owned by, hired or loaned to the insured; (2) aircraft in flight by or for the account of the insured; and (3) air meets, contests or exhibitions.

Among the many exposures airport owners and operators may incur are unmarked obstacles left on airports, creating safety hazards for guests. The courts have consistently held the operator responsible for the safety of aircraft and the public as well as for issuing proper warning of hazards. In many cases, municipalities have not been immune, with the courts determining that the operation of an airport is a proprietary or corporate function rather than a governmental responsibility.

If an insured is not the owner, but a tenant, his limited operations are covered under an airport premises liability policy. For example, fixed base operators, aircraft sales agencies, aircraft repair shops, restaurants, and concessionaires may occupy only a small part of an airport area, but accidents for which they may be held liable may occur anywhere on the airport.

Aviation insurers offer a wide variety of airport premises liability policies designed to fit the particular needs of airport owners, operators, and lessees, whether they are individuals, partnerships, corporations, municipalities, or governmental organizations. The airport premises liability policy generally follows one of the two basic liability forms designed for most businesses. The owners', landlords', and tenants' (OL&T) form is considered more restrictive and has diminished in importance in recent years. It is usually purchased by smaller airports, small to medium sized FBOs and concessionaires at airports. The more popular comprehensive general liability (CCL) form is more inclusive in that it covers any newly acquired exposure eligible for coverage under the contract occurring after the policy's inception. It is this feature providing coverage for the "unknown hazard" that distinguishes the CGL from the OL&T, making it the most complete airport liability policy available.

In addition to encompassing all the coverage provided under the OL&T, the CGL adds coverage for the following exposures: products and completed operations liability, independent contractors liability (construction and demolition coverage), contractual liability, personal and advertising liability, and hangarkeepers' liability. The OL&T form can be endorsed to provide these separate coverages. Both forms can also be endorsed to provide additional coverages such as air meet liability. All of these aforementioned extensions to the basic policy will be discussed later in the chapter.

Declarations

The declarations under the airport premises liability include the following.

1. Name and address of the insured and whether this is an individual, partnership, corporation, or joint venture.
2. The policy period-generally one or three years.
3. Coverages and limits of liability. Insurance is afforded only with respect to coverages for which a premium is indicated. In establishing the limits of liability, an insured normally considers the hull value and passenger liability of the largest aircraft using the airport.
4. Description of premises and purpose of use.
5. Whether the insured is conducting any other operations at the insured location or any other location.
6. A schedule of coverages including premium basis and advance premiums.

7. Whether the insured occupies the entire premises.
8. Whether the insured's interest in the premises is that of owner or general lessee or tenant.

Insuring Agreements

The basic coverage includes bodily injury and property damage liability arising out of the ownership, maintenance, or use of the airport premises described in the declarations. Both coverages are generally written on an occurrence basis. As in the aircraft liability policy, the coverages can be written with separate limits for the bodily injury (BI) and property damage (PD), or a single-limit BI and PD.

Definition of Insured

The insured under the airport premises liability policy includes the named insured and any partner, executive officer, director, stockholder, or employee while acting within the scope of their duties as such.

Exclusions

The OL&T and CGL forms used by many of the aviation insurers share many common exclusions to liability coverage. With respect to premises operations coverage, most airport liability contracts include the following exclusions:

1. Liability assumed by the insured under any contract or agreement except incidental contracts such as a lease of premises, easement agreement, sidetrack agreement, or elevator maintenance agreement.
2. Liability arising out of the maintenance or use of any aircraft owned by, hired by or for, or loaned to the insured, or any aircraft in flight by or for the account of the insured.
3. Any liability arising from the ownership or operation of automobiles or other vehicles away from the premises.
4. Any air meet, air race, demonstration, or show for which an admission charge or an automobile parking charge is made.
5. Any grandstand or group seating structure of any kind.
6. Watercraft while away from the premises, or power-driven land vehicles and vehicles attached, including loading and unloading, while away from the premises or the ways immediately adjoining.
7. Any elevator, other than an elevator which is not operated, maintained, or controlled by the insured and is located in a building of which the insured is not the owner, general lessee, or sole tenant.
8. Operations on or from other premises which are owned, rented, or controlled by the insured.
9. Bodily injury liability coverage does not apply to injury of an employee of the insured or to any obligation for which the insured may be held liable under any workers' compensation law.
10. Property damage liability does not apply to injury to or destruction of any property owned, occupied, rented, or in the care, custody, or control of the insured.
11. Any sickness or injury incurred by employees which is not covered by state workers' compensation law.
12. Injury by products manufactured or sold by the insured or work which has been completed by the insured out of which the accident arises, unless specifically assumed.
13. Liability due to work of independent contractors or as a result of structural alterations, unless specifically assumed.
14. Contractual liability, unless specifically assumed.
15. Liability imposed as a result of liquor laws (so-called dram shop liability).
16. Intentional injury or damage.

17. Any war, civil insurrection, or rebellion.

Several of the exclusions are present because the risk is expected to be covered by other insurance policies, as in the case of 2, 3, 4, 6, 7, 9, 10, 12, 13, 14, and 15 above. The war hazard is excluded in all types of insurance contracts, as is intentionally caused injury or damage. Damage to property in the care, custody, or control of the insured is excluded in almost all liability policies, since it is considered to be in the same category as property owned by the insured.

Conditions

A number of the conditions in the airport premises liability contract are similar to those which have been previously noted in connection with the combined aircraft hull and liability policy. Specifically, most airport liability policies contain the following provisions:

1. Assignment. The policy cannot be assigned without the written consent of the company.
2. Subrogation. Upon payment of a loss, the company will be subrogated to all of the insured's rights of recovery against negligent third parties.
3. Changes. No change may be made in the policy without the written consent of the company. No agent may waive any provision of the policy.
4. Cancellation. The policy may be cancelled by giving 10 days written notice to the insured. The insured has the right to cancel his policy at any time, in which case the premium will be returned on a short-rate basis.
5. Notice of accident. The insured is expected to give written notice of accident to the company as soon as possible.
6. Other insurance. If the insured has other insurance, each company will pay only its pro rata share of any loss.

Other conditions relate to premium, inspection and survey, assistance and cooperation of the insured, and automatic coverage.

Premium

Airport premises liability policies generally contain a specific description of how the premises premium will be computed. The following are among the most common methods: area of the premises; sales; number of admissions; and number of objects insured. The exact method used will vary with the coverage. In some cases a uniform premium is applied. Here the premium is the same for all eligible insureds regardless of their personal characteristics. This is usually the case with smaller airports or tenants on an airport.

Inspection and Surveys

The inspection and survey clause gives the company the right to inspect the insured's premises and to audit his books. The reason for the inspection privilege is to enable the company to determine the hazards present and to charge a correct premium. It is also to benefit the insured, since companies are often able to make recommendations which will enable the insured to reduce his accidents. The right to audit the insured's books is necessary because many airport liability contracts are written with only a deposit premium. The exact premium is determined after the expiration of the policy from an audit of the insured's books.

Assistance and Cooperation

This clause requires the insured's assistance and cooperation and is especially important in airport liability contracts. Often the company's only defense against a claim is the insured's testimony.

Automatic Coverage

Most airport liability contracts provide automatic coverage for new premises and operations for 30 days. Naturally, if an additional premium is due, the insured must notify the company within this 30-day period and pay such additional premium as is required.

OTHER AIRPORT LIABILITY COVERAGES

Additional coverages are included under the basic airport premises liability contract by checking the appropriate boxes under the schedule of coverages in the declarations and by the addition of coverage endorsements. These additional coverages include medical payments, contractual liability, alterations and/or new construction, products and completed operations, hangarkeepers' liability, personal and advertising injury liability, and air meet liability.

Medical Payments

Medical payments can be provided to cover all reasonable medical expenses incurred by the insured arising out of injuries to members of the public while on the premises. The medical payments coverage is applicable regardless of whether the insured is legally responsible for injuries which are sustained. Coverage applies only to members of the public.

There is no coverage with respect to: the insured, his partners, or employees; any injury covered by a workers' compensation law; or any independent contractors employed by the insured.

Medical expenses are normally defined as all necessary medical, surgical, x-ray, and dental services, including prosthetic devices, and necessary ambulance, hospital, professional nursing, and funeral services. A separate limit of liability applies to each person and each accident.

Contractual Liability

While the basic OL&T and CGL forms cover liability assumed under certain types of incidental contracts, liability assumed under other types requires special contractual liability coverage. Coverage is afforded the insured for the liability he assumes under the provisions of hold harmless agreements in leases or contracts with others, such as the airport owner and/or lessor, the gasoline or oil supplier, fuel equipment supplier, and others.

Since contracts in the aviation field are so diversified and often involve such substantial liabilities, underwriters will normally only approve designated contracts and not offer the coverage on a blanket basis.

Alterations and/or New Construction Liability

Operations by independent contractors for the insured may be covered for the extension of runways, installation of new landing strips, demolition or alterations of existing structures, and the construction of hangars, administration buildings, or repair shops. Underwriters require information on the extent and duration of the contracted operation as well as contract Costs.

With this coverage the insured is protected against liability for actions of independent contractors, including liability due to the insured's failure in supervising independent contractors' work. No matter how carefully the insured selects a contractor and how tight the contract, the insured could be brought into a lawsuit because of the contractor's actions. Some obligations, such as the insured's obligation to protect the public, cannot be transferred or delegated to the contractor. The insured may be sued even though the contractor uses great care as well as when the contractor fails to provide appropriate safety measures. Thus, for example, the airport operator may be held responsible for the contractor's failure to provide proper protection of sidewalks during a terminal building expansion.

Products and Completed Operations

Liability coverage for the sale of products and completed operations hazard is available to the supplier of aircraft products and to the airport owner and fixed base operator in relation to the manufacture, sale, and distribution of products; repairs and modification to aircraft; and to the performance of services relating to aircraft products. Specifically, aircraft products coverage includes: (1) sale of new and used aircraft; (2) sale of aircraft parts and accessories; and (3) sale of fuel and oil. *Completed operations* is defined as aircraft repairs and servicing, including installation of parts and accessories.

Products liability protects the insured for liability incurred as a result of injury to members of the public which may result from defective products or from completed operations. In essence, the coverage is designed to pay for occurrences caused by mistakes in the manufacture or preparation of products or the rendering of service work.

Coverage

Products liability covers sums which the insured becomes legally obligated to pay as damages if the accident occurs: (1) away from the insured's premises and (2) after the insured has relinquished the product to others. Accidents which occur on the premises of the insured because of defective products would be covered by the basic airport premises liability contract. For example, suppose a customer had contaminated fuel pumped into his aircraft resulting in engine damage and inability to take off. The airport premises liability policy would cover such an accident, since the customer was still on the premises. If the accident took place after takeoff and was incurred while in flight away from the airport, the products liability coverage would come into play. The products coverage is basically an off- premises coverage since the basic airport premises liability policy provides protection for accidents occurring on the premises.

The coverage afforded by the products and completed operations sections of the policy is often considered to be two different types. It is in the sense that the coverage of each generally applies to a different type of insured. The products liability coverage is applicable to those who manufacture or market aircraft products and components to be sold to others. The completed operations section is applicable primarily to firms engaged in servicing, installation, and repair work, such as fixed base operations.

Products liability is also purchased by restaurants and fast food establishments located at airports. The coverage would protect an insured for claims arising out of such things as food poisoning and foreign substances in food products.

Limits of Liability

The products liability coverage contains three limits of liability: a per person, a per accident, and an *aggregate policy limit*. A major problem in the writing of products liability has been that of catastrophe losses. Products which are widely distributed may cause tremendous losses before a mistake is discovered. The very nature of the coverage lends itself to covering losses which may run into very large figures. This is true both with respect to bodily injury and also property damage. Companies have limited their liability for catastrophe losses by imposing an aggregate limit of liability with respect to BI and PD.

Products liability for the aircraft and engine manufacturers as well as the thousands of component parts manufacturers is a specialized line of aviation insurance and large volumes of it are written by only a few of the markets, most notably Global Aerospace, USAIG, and Lloyd's of London. Because of the catastrophe exposure, most markets sell this coverage only after careful inspection of all the insured's operations.

Hangarkeepers' Liability

Hangarkeepers' liability protection, basically a form of bailee insurance, covers the insured's liability for loss or damage to aircraft which are the property of others and in the custody of the insured for safekeeping, storage, or repairs and while in or on the described premises. Basic hangarkeepers' coverage excludes aircraft while in flight. Coverage, however, can be arranged for in flight hangarkeepers' coverage.

While this form of protection, like most aviation contracts, is not a standard form, it is written on approximately the same terms by most insurers who write it, usually as an endorsement to the airport premises liability policy. The need for hangarkeepers' liability coverage arises because of the airport liability policy exclusion of liability for property in the care, custody, or control of the insured. Airport owners and operators including FBOs who provide hangarage or operate a maintenance and repair facility need hangar keepers' coverage. Once a charge is made, a bailee-bailor relationship is established and the airport owner or FBO is responsible for a high degree of care of the property in his control. Hence, he can be held liable for damage caused by any neglect or failure to exercise this care by himself or his employees.

Coverage

The hangarkeepers' liability coverage assumes the insured's legal obligations for injury to or destruction of aircraft. Aircraft means any aircraft including component parts and tools and repair equipment, operating and navigation instruments, and radio equipment including parts temporarily detached and not replaced by other similar parts. Coverage applies only to property in or on the premises described in the policy.

The hangarkeepers' liability coverage contains a limited number of exclusions. The most noteworthy of these relates to the product hazard of the insured's operation. Damage to materials furnished or faulty work performed by the insured which cause the accident is not covered. Obviously the purpose of this exclusion is to keep the policy from covering the obligation of the insured to correct defective or unsatisfactory workmanship or to replace defective materials. For example, if the insured had repaired the electrical system of a customer's aircraft and because the work was done carelessly, the system failed and caused a fire, the exclusion would free the insurer of any responsibility for the cost of repairing the electrical system a second time. It would not affect the insured's liability for other damage to the aircraft.

There is no coverage of aircraft owned, rented, or loaned to the insured, a member of his family, or any of his employees. If the insured is a partnership or corporation the same exclusion applies to any partner, officer, or member of his family. Coverage in these situations is available, of course, through the hull coverage under a combined aircraft hull and liability policy.

Limits of Liability

Hangarkeepers' liability coverage is written with a limit per aircraft and a limit per occurrence for each location for which the insured has operations. Normally an insured will carry limits sufficient to protect him against loss or damage to an average aircraft and average total aircraft in his care, custody, or control at any one time.

Most endorsements contain a deductible clause which requires at least $50 be deducted from every loss. The amount of deductible can vary up to $1,000 and generally does not apply to fire, lightning, or explosion losses.

Personal and Advertising Injury Liability

Personal injury liability coverage protects against liability claims for other than physical harm and property damage allegations. It covers claims alleging intentional torts such as false arrest, detention, malicious prosecution, libel, slander, wrongful entry, eviction, or invasion of privacy. This coverage, available only to major airports for many years, is now available as part of the CGL form or by endorsement under the OL&T form.

Advertising injury liability provides coverage for such offenses as oral or written publication of material that slanders or libels a person or organization or its products or services or violates the right to privacy. It also protects an insured against misappropriation of advertising ideas or style or infringement upon another's copyright, title, or slogan.

Air Meet Liability

The airport premises liability policy excludes liability for accidents occurring during air meets or aerial exhibitions for which an admission charge is made. The reason for this exclusion is that the hazards during air meets and aerial exhibitions are much greater than those usually encountered in connection with the operation of an aircraft.

During the summer months in particular, many airports are the scene of an air meet that involves the serious additional hazards of grandstand or bleacher collapse and stunting or racing at high speeds and low altitudes near a crowd of spectators. Although the show may be conducted with strict adherence to federal regulations, aircraft can lose control with disastrous results. Consequently, this insurance requires extremely careful underwriting and inspection. When the risk is accepted, the air meet liability endorsement is attached to the airport premises liability policy.

The coverage, which is usually written for a very short term, protects only the sponsor; it does not cover the liability of participants; nor does it respond for injury to the participants. Premiums vary tremendously depending on the nature, size, and duration of the show.

One of the main attractions at many air meets in the past few years has been an aerobatic team from one of the branches of the armed services. Before such a team will perform, however, the U. S. government must be presented with a certificate of insurance showing that the sponsor is covered by the necessary liability insurance and that the contract has been endorsed to hold the service team and the U.S. government harmless from any liability arising out of the team's participation.

A copy of Global's Comprehensive General Liability policy for airports is included at the end of this chapter.

OTHER AVIATION LIABILITY COVERAGES

Owners, operators, and manufacturers of aircraft represent a diverse group of risks which require a number of unique coverages tailored to meet their individual needs. The following list, although by no means inclusive, identifies some of the coverages anyone entering the aviation insurance profession should be aware of.

Aerial Application

An area of particular specialization and growing importance within the field of aviation insurance is aerial application. *Aerial application* is defined as those activities that involve the discharge of materials from aircraft in flight for food and fiber production and health control. This is an inherently dangerous activity requiring special techniques and approaches, but with the technological developments of recent years, one that is becoming more essential to the economy. Rapid advances in agricultural technology with better techniques in manufacturing aircraft for this work have combined to make it a profitable insurance line. Growth of this business has made insurance coverage for these businesses a matter of more popular interest. Phoenix Aviation Managers is one of the leading domestic insurers of this line of insurance.

Coverage

Coverage of aerial application aircraft is divided into three distinct segments: third-party liability coverage *excluding chemical liability insurance*; *chemical liability* coverage; and hull coverage. Hull coverage was discussed in chapter 8 and is basically the same for aerial application aircraft.

Liability insurance needs of aerial applicators differ somewhat from those of the regular aircraft owner or operator. Coverages can be written *excluding chemical drift (XC), restricted (or limited) chemical drift (RC)*, or *comprehensive chemical drift (CC)*. Chemical drift liability protects the named insured from claims arising out of the application of crop protection products which drift from the target site onto other persons or their property

XC only offers aircraft liability coverages for the agricultural aircraft. Some policies include liability coverage for the application of fertilizers and seeds under the XC coverage. However, this should be verified by reviewing the policy. One of the greatest hazards seems to be with transmission lines, which, if broken may cause substantial *consequential loss* (losses to company customers as a result of the downed lines). Because this exposure is so great, policies exclude any consequential loss. RC coverage applies to insecticides, fungicides, fertilizers or seeds only. No herbicides are covered under RC coverage including defoliants and desiccants.

CC or Comprehensive Chemical Drift coverage is the most inclusive and most commonly written. It includes coverage for all crop protection products appropriately labeled for application by air. The only exception being (in some cases) Picloram. This exclusion can be purchased by the aerial applicator if they need to apply any herbicide which includes Picloram as an active ingredient. Insurers often go through phases where they may or may not exclude specific herbicides such as glyphosates or some trendy new chemical to the market which does not perform as expected from the CC drift coverage lists so it is often wise to ask for clarification when placing this coverage with an insurance company. However, Picloram is consistently excluded.

Most state law requires a commercial aerial application company to carry a minimum liability of $100,000 BI / $300,000 BI per occurrence / $100,000 property damage per occurrence. Some states have lower requirements; however, this limit is practically universal in acceptance. It is possible to provide higher limits of liability on a combined single limit basis but most companies will not offer such limits above $500,000 combined single limit for CC liability. Also note that there is no passenger liability included on an Ag policy unless specifically requested. Ninety-nine percent of all Ag planes are single seat aircraft with only a few exceptions.

If the aerial applicator sprays the wrong field or chemicals drift onto an adjacent field owned by the same farmer he is working for, there is no coverage. These exclusions can be bought back as *crops being treated* and *adjacent fields coverage*. The policy excludes drift which occurs when applying a crop protection product from an application site onto another crop owned by the same farmer. Adjacent fields coverage provides coverage for drift onto crops owned by the same farmer the applicator is contracted to spray for. Crops being treated protects the named insured when the operator causes damage to a crop that the operator is intentionally spraying. The operator must purchase adjacent fields coverage to have crops being treated. In other words, an operator can have adjacent fields coverage alone, but cannot purchase crops being treated alone since it is impossible to intentionally spray a field with the wrong chemical that is owned by the farmer the operator is contracted to spray for.

By endorsement, the owner of the land, the farmer, or the grower of a crop may be included as an additional insured under the crop duster's policy for damages done by the crop duster.

The aerial applicator is subject to a special short-rate table in the event of cancellation. It is simply a way in which the insurance company can accelerate the rate at which a policy becomes fully earned. A policy is fully earned in 120 days which is the typical length of a crop-dusting season. From 1 to 30 days, 33.3% of the premium is fully earned; 31-60 days, 60% is fully earned; 61-90 days, 75% is fully earned; 91-120 days, 85% is fully earned; and 121 days and longer, 100% is fully earned. The purpose of the table is to prevent an aerial applicator from using an aircraft for the entire spraying season, during the period of greatest risk, and then dropping the coverage having paid only four months' premium.

Individual and Corporate Non-Ownership

By virtue of the definition of insured, the coverages provided an aircraft owner through his aircraft liability policy are generally available to those who are permitted to use the aircraft or in whose interest the aircraft is used. These parties, however, may be reluctant to rely upon the owner's insurance and therefore prefer to purchase their own coverage. Such coverage is available to them through an *aircraft non-ownership liability policy*.

The need for aircraft non-ownership liability protection is great because of the tremendous amount of travel by air today. Individual businessmen, salesmen, and executives of large corporations have found flying an airplane enables them to cover a wider area of operation in less time, economically, and with a minimum amount of personal energy. These savings are accomplished by point-to-point travel in a rented or chartered airplane and by being able to designate the most convenient times of departure or arrival, not possible with scheduled means of transportation. The necessity for insurance in most lines is usually apparent. With non-ownership liability, this is not always true. Corporate management is frequently unaware that some of its personnel are flying on company business. Furthermore the limits of liability carried under the owner's policy may not be adequate for the corporation.

An aircraft non-ownership liability policy can be written to cover the liabilities arising out of the use of a particular non- owned aircraft, or it may cover liabilities arising out of the use of any non -owned aircraft. In the case of a particular non-owned aircraft, underwriters will normally treat the risk similar to an owned aircraft for rating purposes. Most non-ownership exposures contemplate infrequent usage whether anticipated exposures are known or unknown. The coverage is always written as excess insurance over any other valid and collectible insurance available to the insured.

Up to this point stress has been placed on the need which a business may have for this coverage. Equally in need of such insurance is any individual who flies or charters aircraft which he does not own. If he flies a friend's aircraft, it may be uninsured or have inadequate limits of liability. If he flies an airplane rented from an FBO, the FBO's aircraft liability policy may not extend to cover the liability of a renter pilot. In any event, those who rent aircraft usually do not actually see the owner's liability policy and they are exposing themselves to uncertainty both as to coverage and amount.

Underwriters also make available coverage for damage to the non-owned aircraft being used by the insured. In effect, this is subrogation coverage which would respond in the event the owner's carrier comes after the negligent party following loss or damage to the owner's aircraft. This coverage is particularly important for a free-lance flight instructor.

Hangar keepers often buy a variation of this coverage called *hangarkeepers' in-flight* coverage which protects them for loss or damage to non-owned aircraft while in-flight and in their care, custody, or control. Instead of a separate policy, the coverage is normally provided under his owned aircraft liability coverage by amending the care, custody, and control exclusion. Again, infrequent use is contemplated and if such exposure were a long term arrangement such as a leased aircraft, it would be treated similarly to an owned aircraft.

Manufacturer's Product Liability

Many different products are manufactured for the aviation industry. These products include airframe and component assemblies, engines and control surfaces, seating, food service equipment, and often non- operational comfort and convenience items. The number of airframe and engine manufacturers is quite limited; however, the number of suppliers of aircraft components runs into the thousands. While only a small likelihood exists that a product from one of the suppliers will fail, there is a good chance in today's legal climate that the supplier will be sued anyway whenever his product is involved in an aviation accident. Most product liability insurance policies exclude all aviation exposures. Consequently many suppliers of aircraft components turn to the aviation insurance market for a separate manufacturer's product liability policy. The major markets for this specialized coverage are Global Aerospace, USAIG, and AIG.

The policy provides coverage for damage arising out of the use of goods or products manufactured, sold, handled, or distributed by the insured. *Grounding coverage* can also be provided should, in the interests of safety, an aircraft be withdrawn from service because of the existence or alleged or suspected existence of a fault, defect, or condition in two or more such aircraft.

Substantial limits of liability for bodily injury and property damage are available subject to an annual aggregate limit and a sublimit with respect to the grounding liability mentioned above.

Excess Liability

Excess liability insurance adds coverage above a specific amount up to a specified limit. For example, a corporate insured may require $50 million in legal liability protection from third party suits, but the primary aviation insurer only has the capacity to provide $20 million. One solution to this problem is to purchase an excess liability policy which provides a limit of $30 million excess of $20 million. The excess liability underwriter only participates if the claim exceeds the primary limit.

Another variation of excess liability insurance that is designed for self-insurers is called *excess aggregate insurance*. Popular among some of the aircraft and component manufacturers in recent years because of the rising number of products liability claims, this coverage provides protection up to an aggregate amount for all losses over a stated amount for the policy year. The insured must pay all liability claims (including loss adjustment expense) until the specified amount is reached. Then the excess aggregate policy assumes payment. This coverage applies the principle of insuring catastrophic loss only rather than first-dollar coverage for all claims.

Finally, there is *umbrella liability insurance* that is designed to fill the gaps in liability protection associated with basic coverages or self- insured retentions. Typically, the insured must buy airport premises liability (OL&T or CGL forms), automobile liability insurance, hangar keepers' liability, and employers' liability insurance with certain minimum limits of liability. The umbrella liability policy covers above these amounts. It also provides coverage on all but a few specified excluded exposures which are not covered under the standard liability policy, but such coverage is subject to a stated retention (deductible) by the insured. Most insurers require the insured to absorb at least $25,000 of the loss on uninsured or self-insured exposures. Finally, the umbrella liability policy provides automatic replacement for underlying liability which is reduced or exhausted by losses.

Loss of Use Coverage

Loss of use coverage is designed to reimburse the insured for the cost of renting a substitute aircraft while the insured's aircraft is undergoing repairs following an accident. While this coverage can be purchased by a corporate aircraft operation it is particularly beneficial for a commercial operator who will lose revenue while his aircraft is out of service.

Most coverage is written with a deductible in the form of a waiting period from 1 to 14 days after the accident. In addition, the coverage normally has a time limitation on it, whereby benefits only apply for a specific number of days, or up to a maximum dollar amount. Coverage only applies while the insured's aircraft is undergoing repairs following an accident, and does not apply in case of a total loss.

Loss of License Insurance

In accordance with Federal Aviation Regulations, a pilot must hold a private, commercial, or airline transport pilot license with appropriate ratings for the flight involved along with a valid and current medical certificate. If, for some reason, an accident or illness caused a disabling physical condition that prevented a pilot from passing a medical exam required for the certificate, he or she would be unable to fly. Consequently, many pilots who fly commercially and depend upon flying as a primary source of income purchase *loss of license insurance*. As the name implies, coverage is afforded in the event an accident or an illness causes a disabling physical condition which prevents a pilot from passing the medical requirements necessary to obtain a medical certificate. The policy will usually pay the pilot a predetermined amount per month after a waiting period, which serves as a deductible, until the pilot recovers and is able to resume flight duties.

If, after a predetermined number of months (normally between 8 to 12 months), the pilot is still disabled, and it appears the condition will continue, the company will pay a preselected lump sum of money (the principal sum of the policy less the amount paid out in monthly payments) to the pilot.

Pilot Accident Insurance

Accident policies in today's insurance market are readily available; however, in many such policies protection for pilots and crew members is excluded. The *pilot accident policy* is a limited exposure, covering only those accidents resulting from exposure to aircraft. The policy provides protection for pilots and crew members while flying, servicing, or repairing any aircraft. Benefits provide for loss of life, limb or sight as well as total disability, payable weekly up to 52 weeks. Medical expense is also payable up to the limit purchased.

Experimental Aircraft

A number of aircraft operating today do not fall within the "standard" airworthiness certificate issued by the FAA. A special *"experimental airworthiness certificate"* is issued to owners of these aircraft to designate that they do not have a type certificate or do not conform to its type certificate and is in a condition for safe operation. Examples would include vintage aircraft, warbirds, aircraft flown for research and development, exhibition, such as air shows, motion pictures and television, air racing, and light sport aircraft.

Commonly referred to as ultralight aircraft, it is estimated that there are over 45,000 light-sport aircraft operating today. They include aircraft whose major portion has been fabricated and assembled by individuals for their own recreation or manufactured by the holder of a production certificate for that kit, without the supervision and quality control of the production certificate holder. Presently, there are over 100 kit manufacturers.

For operational simplicity, light-sport aircraft are limited to a single engine if powered, and fixed landing gear. They are small, simple-to-operate, low performance aircraft that are generally defined by their limitations: two occupants; takeoff weight of 1,232 pounds; a stalling speed in the landing configuration of 39 knots; and, a speed in straight and level flight of 115 knots. Light-sport aircraft include conventional aircraft such as fixed-wing, gliders, lighter-than-air aircraft, powered parachutes, and weight-shift-control aircraft (sometimes referred to as trikes).

Experimental aircraft owners purchase aircraft hull and liability coverage but more often purchase liability only coverage because of the difficulty in establishing an insured value for the aircraft itself. The number of insurers writing experimental aircraft is quitelimited and not all of them will entertain all of the classes of risks within this category. Avemco, AIG, Global Aerospace, and the U.S. Specialty Insurance Company are some of the markets for this class of business.

KEY TERMS

Airport premises liability
Medical payments
Completed operations
Products liability
Aggregate policy limit
Hangarkeepers' liability
Personal injury liability
Advertising injury liability
Aerial application
Excluding chemical liability
Chemical liability
Excluding chemical drift (XC)
Restricted (or limited) chemical drift (RC)
Comprehensive chemical drift (CC)
Consequential Loss
Crops being treated
Adjacent fields' coverage
Aircraft non-ownership liability
Hangarkeepers' in flight
Grounding coverage
Excess liability insurance
Excess aggregate insurance
Umbrella liability insurance
Loss of use coverage
Loss of license insurance
Pilot accident policy
Experimental airworthiness certificate

REVIEW QUESTIONS

1. What is the purpose of the airport premises liability policy? Give some examples of accidents which would be covered under this policy. Describe some of the basic items found under the declarations. Who is covered as an insured? List 10 exclusions found under the policy. What is the purpose of many of the exclusions?
2. Which conditions are found in most liability contracts? Which ones are unique to the airport premises liability policy?
3. What is the purpose of medical payments coverage? contractual liability? alterations and or new construction liability?
4. What are the typical products and services sold by a fixed base operator? What is meant by completed operations? Why does an airport operator or FBO need products liability coverage? Why does the coverage apply away from the insured's premises? Why is products liability written with an aggregate limit?
5. A fixed base operator who has aircraft of others in his care, custody, or control for storage or repair should consider which coverage? What coverage is needed for airports that sponsor air shows? What is the purpose of personal injury liability? advertising injury liability?
6. Distinguish between the following aerial applicator coverages: excluding chemical drift (XC), restricted (or limited) chemical drift (RC), and comprehensive chemical drift (CC)
7. Should a large corporation with facilities throughout the country and no known aircraft exposure consider aircraft non-ownership liability? Why? If an individual pilot is covered under the "omnibus" provisions of an owner's aircraft hull and liability policy, why would he consider an individual aircraft non- ownership liability policy?
8. Many small aircraft component suppliers purchase manufacturer's product liability coverage even though the likelihood of their being proven negligent in the event of an accident is very small. What is the reason for this?
9. Distinguish between the following coverages: excess liability; excess aggregate; and, umbrella liability.
10. What is the purpose of loss of use coverage? Who might be a likely prospect for such coverage? Under what circumstances would loss of license insurance apply? Describe the coverages available for ultralight aircraft owners.
11. Describe the aircraft falling within the experimental airworthiness certificate. Identify the insurance markets for these aircraft.

Airport Liability Insurance Policy & Endorsements

AIRPORT LIABILITY INSURANCE

THROUGH

GLOBAL AEROSPACE, INC.

HOME OFFICE: 51 JOHN F. KENNEDY PARKWAY
SHORT HILLS, NEW JERSEY 07078

BRANCH OFFICE:

FOR

ARRANGED BY:

GUIDE TO THE PROVISIONS OF YOUR POLICY

This guide (and divider tabs, if any) has been prepared to help you in reading your policy. They are not a part of the policy nor do they make reference to all the provisions which might affect your insurance. You are therefore urged to read the entire policy carefully.

SECTION IV – POLICY CONDITIONS

SECTION V – DEFINITIONS

SECTION VI – GENERAL POLICY EXCLUSIONS

ENDORSEMENTS

AIRPORT LIABILITY INSURANCE POLICY

POLICY NUMBER:

THE COMPANIES

DECLARATIONS

Item 1. Named Insured
and Address:

Item 2. Policy Period

From:

To:

12:01 AM Standard Time at your mailing address shown under Item 1.

Item 3. In return for payment of the premium and subject to all of the terms of the policy, we agree with you to provide the insurance as stated in this policy.

LIMITS OF INSURANCE

General Aggregate Limit (Other than Products-Completed Operations and Hangarkeepers')

Products-Completed Operations Aggregate Limit

Personal & Advertising Injury Aggregate Limit

Each Occurrence Limit

Fire Damage Limit (Any One Fire)

Medical Expense Limit (Any One Person)

Hangarkeepers' Each Loss Limit
Hangarkeepers' Each Aircraft Limit

Deductibles, if any, will be described in an endorsement entitled DEDUCTIBLE ENDORSEMENT.

Item 4. Location of airport premises owned, rented to or occupied by the Named Insured at the beginning of the policy period:

Item 5. Form of Business:

Item 6. Policy Premium:
Total Premium at Inception: $
Surcharge: $

DECLARATIONS OF POLICY NUMBER (Continued)

Endorsements forming a part of this policy on its effective date:

IN WITNESS WHEREOF, the Company has caused this policy to be executed on its behalf by Global Aerospace, Inc., but this policy shall not be valid unless signed by a duly authorized representative of Global Aerospace, Inc.

Leonidas G. Demas, Secretary
Global Aerospace, Inc.

A. J. Medniuk, President & C.E.O.
Global Aerospace, Inc.

Countersignature (Where Required)

For Global Aerospace, Inc.

Various provisions in this policy restrict coverage. Read the entire policy carefully to determine rights, duties and what is and is not covered.

Throughout this policy the words **you** and **your** refer to the Named Insured shown in the Declarations and any other person or organization qualifying as a Named Insured under this policy. The words **we**, **us** and **our** refer to the Company providing this insurance.

The word **insured** means any person or organization qualifying as such under **SECTION II - WHO IS AN INSURED**.

Other words and phrases that appear in ***bold italicized*** type have special meaning. Refer to **SECTION V - DEFINITIONS**.

SECTION I - COVERAGES

COVERAGE A - BODILY INJURY AND PROPERTY DAMAGE LIABILITY

1. **Insuring Agreement.**

(a) We will pay those sums that the insured becomes legally obligated to pay as damages because of ***bodily injury*** or ***property damage*** to which this insurance applies resulting from your ***airport operations***. We will have the right and duty to defend any ***suit*** seeking those damages. We may at our discretion investigate any ***occurrence*** and settle any claim or ***suit*** that may result. But:

(1) The amount we will pay for damages is limited as described in **SECTION III - LIMITS OF INSURANCE**; and

(2) Our right and duty to defend end when we have used up the applicable limit of insurance in the payment of judgments or settlements under Coverages A or B or medical expenses under Coverage C.

No other obligation or liability to pay sums or perform acts or services is covered unless explicitly provided for under **SUPPLEMENTARY PAYMENTS** - COVERAGES A, B and D.

(b) This insurance applies to ***bodily injury*** and ***property damage*** only if:

(1) The ***bodily injury*** or ***property damage*** is caused by an ***occurrence*** and takes place in the ***coverage territory***, and

(2) The ***bodily injury*** or ***property damage*** occurs during the policy period.

(c) Damages because of ***bodily injury*** include damages claimed by any person or organization for care, loss of services or death resulting at any time from the ***bodily injury.***

2. **Exclusions.**

This insurance does not apply to:

(a) ***Bodily injury*** or ***property damage*** expected or intended from the standpoint of the insured. This exclusion (a) does not apply to ***bodily injury*** resulting from the use of reasonable force to protect persons or property.

(b) ***Bodily injury*** or ***property damage*** for which the insured is obligated to pay damages by reason of the assumption of liability in a contract or agreement. This exclusion (b) does not apply to liability for damages:

(1) Assumed in a contract or agreement that is an ***insured contract***, provided the ***bodily injury*** or ***property damage*** occurs subsequent to the execution of the contract or agreement; or

(2) That the insured would have in the absence of the contract or agreement.

(c) ***Bodily injury*** or ***property damage*** for which any insured may be held liable by reason of:

(1) Causing or contributing to the intoxication of any person;

(2) The furnishing of alcoholic beverages to a person under the legal drinking age or under the influence of alcohol; or

(3) Any statute, ordinance or regulation relating to the sale, gift, distribution or use of alcoholic beverages.

This exclusion (c) applies only if you are in the business of manufacturing, distributing, selling, serving or furnishing alcoholic beverages.

(d) Any obligation of the insured under a workers' compensation, disability benefits or unemployment compensation law or any similar law.

(e) ***Bodily injury*** to:

(1) An employee of the insured arising out of and in the course of employment by the insured; or

(2) The spouse, child, parent, brother or sister of that employee as a consequence of (e)(1) above.

This exclusion (e) applies:

(3) Whether the insured may be liable as an employer or in any other capacity; and

(4) To any obligation to share damages with or repay someone else who must pay damages because of the injury.

This exclusion (e) does not apply to liability assumed by the insured under an ***insured contract***.

(f) The conduct of any contest or exhibition permitted, sponsored or participated in by the insured other than static displays in public access areas.

(g) ***Bodily injury*** or ***property damage*** arising out of the ownership, maintenance, use or entrustment to others of any ***aircraft***, ***auto*** or watercraft owned or operated by or rented or loaned to any insured. Use includes operation and ***loading or unloading***. With respect to ***aircraft***, operated by includes operation on behalf of any ***insured.***

This exclusion (g) does not apply to:

(1) A watercraft while ashore on premises you own or rent;

(2) A watercraft you do not own that is:

(i) Less than 26 feet long; and

(ii) Not being used to carry persons or property for a charge;

(3) Parking an ***auto*** on, or on the ways next to, premises you own or rent, provided the ***auto*** is not owned by or rented or loaned to you or the insured;

(4) Liability assumed under any ***insured contract*** for the ownership, maintenance or use of watercraft;

(5) ***Bodily injury*** or ***property damage*** arising out of the operation of any of the equipment listed in paragraph (f)(1) or (f)(2) of the definition of ***mobile equipment*** (Section V. 13.); or

(6) An ***auto*** an insured operates on airport premises exclusive of public roadways and parking areas.

(h) ***Bodily injury*** or ***property damage*** arising out of:

(1) The transportation of ***mobile equipment*** by an ***auto*** owned or operated by or rented or loaned to any insured; or

(2) The use of ***mobile equipment*** in, or while in practice or preparation for, a prearranged racing, speed or demolition contest or in any stunting activity.

(i) ***Bodily injury*** or ***property damage*** arising out of the ownership, maintenance or use of:

(1) Grandstands, bleachers or observation platforms other than observation decks or promenades that are part of permanent structures on the premises;

(2) Swimming pools;

(3) Lodging accommodations for the general public; or

(4) Schools other than flight crew and aircraft maintenance schools.

(j) ***Property damage*** to:

(1) Property you own, rent, or occupy;

(2) Premises you sell, give away or abandon, if the ***property damage*** arises out of any part of those premises;

(3) Property loaned to you;

(4) Personal property in the care, custody or control of the insured;

(5) That particular part of real property on which you or any contractors or subcontractors working directly or indirectly on your behalf are performing operations, if the ***property damage*** arises out of those operations; or

(6) That particular part of any property that must be restored, repaired or replaced because ***your work*** was incorrectly performed on it.

Paragraph (j)(2) of exclusion (j) does not apply if the premises are ***your work*** and were never occupied, rented or held for rental by you.

Paragraphs (j)(3), (j)(4), (j)(5) and (j)(6) of exclusion (j) do not apply to liability assumed under a sidetrack agreement.

Paragraph (j)(6) of exclusion (j) does not apply to ***property damage*** included in the ***products-completed operations hazard***.

(k) ***Property damage*** to ***your product*** arising out of it or any part of it.

(l) ***Property damage*** to ***your work*** arising out of it or any part of it and included in the ***products-completed operations hazard***.

This exclusion (l) does not apply if the damaged work or the work out of which the damage arises was performed on your behalf by a subcontractor.

(m) ***Property damage*** to ***impaired property*** or property that has not been physically injured, arising out of:

(1) A defect, deficiency, inadequacy or dangerous condition in ***your product*** or ***your work***; or

(2) A delay or failure by you or anyone acting on your behalf to perform a contract or agreement in accordance with its terms.

This exclusion (m) does not apply to the loss of use of other property arising out of sudden and accidental physical injury to ***your product*** or ***your work*** after it has been put to its intended use.

(n) Damages claimed for any loss, cost or expense incurred by you or others for the loss of use, withdrawal, recall, inspection, repair, replacement, adjustment, removal or disposal of:

(1) ***Your product,***
(2) ***Your work,*** or
(3) ***Impaired property***

if such product, work, or property is withdrawn or recalled from the market or from use by any person or organization because of a known or suspected defect, deficiency, inadequacy or dangerous condition in it.

(o) ***Bodily injury*** or ***property damage*** arising out of ***aircraft noise*** or interference with the quiet enjoyment of property by overflight or other operation of ***aircraft***.

(p) ***Bodily injury*** or ***property damage*** arising out of the taking of or exercising of the property rights of others by overflight or other operation of ***aircraft***.

(q) ***Bodily injury*** or ***property damage*** arising out of aircraft traffic control operations.

Exclusions (c) through (q) do not apply to damage by fire to premises rented to you. A separate limit of insurance applies to this coverage as described in **SECTION III - LIMITS OF INSURANCE**.

COVERAGE B - PERSONAL AND ADVERTISING INJURY LIABILITY

1. **Insuring Agreement.**

(a) We will pay those sums that the insured becomes legally obligated to pay as damages because of ***personal injury*** or ***advertising injury*** to which this insurance applies resulting from your ***airport operations***. We will have the right and duty to defend any ***suit*** seeking those damages. We may at our discretion investigate any ***occurrence*** or offense and settle any claim or ***suit*** that may result. But:

(1) The amount we will pay for damages is limited as described in **SECTION III - LIMITS OF INSURANCE**; and

(2) Our right and duty to defend end when we have used up the applicable limit of insurance in the payment of judgments or settlements under Coverages A or B or medical expenses under Coverage C.

No other obligation or liability to pay sums or perform acts or services is covered unless explicitly provided for under **SUPPLEMENTARY PAYMENTS** - COVERAGES A, B and D.

(b) This insurance applies to:

(1) ***Personal injury*** caused by an offense arising out of your ***airport operations***, excluding advertising, publishing, broadcasting or telecasting done by or for you;

(2) ***Advertising injury*** caused by an offense committed in the course of advertising your goods, products or services;

but only if the offense was committed in the ***coverage territory*** during the policy period.

2. **Exclusions.**

This insurance does not apply to:

(a) ***Personal injury*** or ***advertising injury***:

(1) Arising out of oral or written publication of material, if done by or at the direction of the insured with knowledge of its falsity;

(2) Arising out of oral or written publication of material whose first publication took place before the beginning of the policy period;

(3) Arising out of the willful violation of a penal statute or ordinance committed by or with the consent of the insured; or

(4) For which the insured has assumed liability in a contract or agreement. This exclusion (a)(4) does not apply to liability for damages that the insured would have in the absence of the contract or agreement.

(5) Arising out of ***aircraft noise***, or interference with the quiet enjoyment of property by overflight or other operation of ***aircraft***;

(6) Arising out of the taking of or exercising of the property rights of others by overflight or other operation of ***aircraft***.

(b) ***Advertising injury*** arising out of:

(1) Breach of contract, other than misappropriation of advertising ideas under an implied contract;

(2) The failure of goods, products or services to conform with advertised quality or performance;

(3) The wrong description of the price of goods, products or services; or

(4) An offense committed by an insured whose business is advertising, broadcasting, publishing or telecasting.

COVERAGE C - MEDICAL PAYMENTS

1. **Insuring Agreement.**

(a) We will pay medical expenses as described below for ***bodily injury*** caused by an accident and resulting from your ***airport operations*** provided that:

(1) The accident takes place in the ***coverage territory*** and during the policy period;

(2) The expenses are incurred and reported to us within one year of the date of the accident; and

(3) The injured person submits to examination, at our expense, by physicians of our choice as often as we reasonably require.

(b) We will make these payments regardless of fault. These payments will not exceed the applicable limit of insurance. We will pay reasonable expenses for:

(1) First aid at the time of an accident;

(2) Necessary medical, surgical, X-ray and dental services, including prosthetic devices; and

(3) Necessary ambulance, hospital, professional nursing and funeral services.

2. **Exclusions.**

We will not pay expenses for ***bodily injury***:

(a) To any insured.

(b) To a person hired to do work for or on behalf of any insured or a tenant of any insured.

(c) To a person injured on that part of premises you own or rent that the person normally occupies.

(d) To a person, whether or not an employee of any insured, if benefits for the ***bodily injury*** are payable or must be provided under a workers' compensation or disability benefits law or a similar law.

(e) To a person injured while taking part in athletics.

(f) Included within the ***products-completed operations hazard***.

(g) Excluded under Coverage A.

SECTION I (Continued)

COVERAGE D - HANGARKEEPERS' LIABILITY

1. **Insuring Agreement.**

(a) We will pay those sums that the insured becomes legally obligated to pay as damages because of ***loss*** to ***aircraft*** (subject to the deductible shown in the Deductible Endorsement if applicable unless such ***loss*** results from fire or explosion or while the ***aircraft*** is dismantled and being transported) occurring while such ***aircraft*** is in the care, custody or control of the insured for safekeeping, storage, service or repair. We will have the right and duty to defend any ***suit*** seeking those damages. We may at our discretion investigate any ***loss*** and settle any claim or ***suit*** that may result. But:

(1) The amount we will pay for damages is limited as described in **SECTION III - LIMITS OF INSURANCE** and

(2) Our right and duty to defend end when we have used up the applicable limit of insurance in the payment of judgments or settlements under Coverage D.

No other obligation or liability to pay sums or perform acts or services is covered unless explicitly provided for under **SUPPLEMENTARY PAYMENTS** - COVERAGES A, B and D.

(b) This insurance applies to damages because of ***loss*** to ***aircraft*** only if:

(1) The ***loss*** takes place in the ***coverage territory***; and

(2) The ***loss*** occurs during the policy period.

2. **Exclusions.**

This insurance does not apply to:

(a) The insured's liability under any agreement to be responsible for ***loss***.

(b) ***Loss*** to robes, wearing apparel, personal effects or merchandise.

(c) ***Loss*** to ***aircraft*** owned by or rented or leased to any insured.

(d) ***Loss*** due to theft or conversion caused in any way by you, your employees or by your shareholders.

(e) ***Loss*** to ***your work*** arising out of it or any part of it.

(f) ***Loss*** to ***aircraft*** while ***in flight***.

SUPPLEMENTARY PAYMENTS - COVERAGES A, B and D

We will pay, with respect to any claim or ***suit*** we defend:

1. All expenses we incur.

2. Up to $2,500 for cost of bail bonds required because of accidents or traffic law violations arising out of the use of any vehicle to which the Bodily Injury Liability Coverage applies. We do not have to furnish these bonds.

3. The cost of bonds to release attachments, but only for bond amounts within the applicable limit of insurance. We do not have to furnish these bonds.

4. All reasonable expenses incurred by the insured at our request to assist us in the investigation or defense of the claim or ***suit***, including actual loss of earnings up to $100 a day because of time off from work.

5. All costs taxed against the insured in the ***suit***.

6. Pre-judgment interest awarded against the insured on that part of the judgment we pay. If we make an offer to pay the applicable limit of insurance, we will not pay any pre-judgment interest based on that period of time after the offer.

7. All interest on the full amount of any judgment that accrues after entry of the judgment and before we have paid, offered to pay, or deposited in court the part of the judgment that is within the applicable limit of insurance.

These payments will not reduce the limits of insurance.

SECTION II - WHO IS AN INSURED

1. If you are designated in the Declarations as:

   (a) An individual, you and your spouse are insureds, but only with respect to the conduct of a business of which you are the sole owner.

   (b) A partnership or joint venture, you are an insured. Your members, your partners, and their spouses are also insureds, but only with respect to the conduct of your business.

   (c) An organization other than a partnership or joint venture, you are an insured. Your executive officers and directors are insureds, but only with respect to their duties as your officers or directors. Your stockholders are also insureds, but only with respect to their liability as stockholders.

2. Each of the following is also an insured:

   (a) Your employees, other than your executive officers, but only for acts within the scope of their employment by you. However, no employee is an insured for:

      (1) ***Bodily injury*** or ***personal injury*** to you or to a co-employee while in the course of his or her employment, or the spouse, child, parent, brother or sister of that co-employee as a consequence of such ***bodily injury*** or ***personal injury***, or for any obligation to share damages with or repay someone else who must pay damages because of the injury; or

      (2) ***Bodily injury*** or ***personal injury*** arising out of his or her providing or failing to provide professional health care services; or

      (3) ***Property damage*** to property owned or occupied by or rented or loaned to that employee, any of your other employees, or any of your partners or members (if you are a partnership or joint venture).

   (b) Your airport manager, but only for acts within the scope of his or her duties.

   (c) Any person (other than your employee), or any organization while acting as your real estate manager.

   (d) Any person or organization having proper temporary custody of your property if you die, but only:

      (1) With respect to liability arising out of the maintenance or use of that property; and

      (2) Until your legal representative has been appointed.

   (e) Your legal representative if you die, but only with respect to duties as such. That representative will have all your rights and duties under this policy.

3. With respect to ***mobile equipment*** registered in your name under any motor vehicle registration law, any person is an insured while driving such equipment along a public highway with your permission. Any other person or organization responsible for the conduct of such person is also an insured, but only with respect to liability arising out of the operation of the equipment, and only if no other insurance of any kind is available to that person or organization for this liability. However, no person or organization is an insured with respect to:

   (a) ***Bodily injury*** to a co-employee of the person driving the equipment; or

   (b) ***Property damage*** to property owned by, rented to, in the charge of, or occupied by you or the employer of any person who is an insured under this provision.

4. Any organization you newly acquire or form, other than a partnership or joint venture, and over which you maintain ownership or majority interest, will qualify as a Named Insured if there is no other similar insurance available to that organization. However:

   (a) Coverage under this provision is afforded only until the 90th day after you acquire or form the organization or the end of the policy period, whichever is earlier.

   (b) Coverage A does not apply to ***bodily injury*** or ***property damage*** that occurred before you acquired or formed the organization.

   (c) Coverage B does not apply to ***personal injury*** or ***advertising injury*** arising out of an offense committed before you acquired or formed the organization.

   (d) Coverage C does not apply to medical expenses arising out of ***bodily injury*** that occurred before you acquired or formed the organization.

   (e) Coverage D does not apply to ***loss*** to ***aircraft*** before you acquired or formed the organization.

   No person or organization is an insured with respect to the conduct of any current or past partnership or joint venture that is not shown as a Named Insured in the Declarations.

SECTION III – LIMITS OF INSURANCE

1. The Limits of Insurance shown in the Declarations and the rules below fix the most we will pay regardless of the number of:

    (a) Insureds;

    (b) Claims made or ***suits*** brought;

    (c) Persons or organizations making claims or bringing ***suits***; or

    (d) ***Aircraft*** to which Coverage D applies.

2. The General Aggregate Limit is the most we will pay for the sum of:

    (a) Damages under Coverage A, except damages because of ***bodily injury*** or ***property damage*** included in the ***products-completed operations hazard***;

    (b) Damages under Coverage B; and

    (c) Medical expenses under Coverage C.

3. The Products-Completed Operations Aggregate Limit is the most we will pay under Coverage A for damages because of ***bodily injury*** and ***property damage*** included in the ***products-completed operations hazard***.

4. Subject to 2. above, the Personal and Advertising Injury Aggregate Limit is the most we will pay under Coverage B for the sum of all damages because of all ***personal injury*** and all ***advertising injury.***

5. Subject to 2. or 3. above, whichever applies, the Each Occurrence Limit is the most we will pay for the sum of:

    (a) Damages under Coverage A; and

    (b) Medical expenses under Coverage C

    because of all ***bodily injury*** and ***property damage*** arising out of any one ***occurrence***.

6. Subject to 5. above, the Fire Damage Limit is the most we will pay under Coverage A for damages because of ***property damage*** to premises rented to you arising out of any one fire.

7. Subject to 5. above, the Medical Expense Limit is the most we will pay under Coverage C for all medical expenses because of ***bodily injury*** sustained by any one person.

8. The Hangarkeepers' Each Loss Limit is the most we will pay for the sum of damages under Coverage D because of any one ***loss***.

9. Subject to 8. above, the Hangarkeepers' Each Aircraft Limit is the most we will pay for the sum of damages under Coverage D because of ***loss*** to any one ***aircraft*** in any one ***loss***.

The limits of this policy apply separately to each consecutive annual period and to any remaining period of less than 12 months, starting with the beginning of the policy period shown in the Declarations, unless the policy period is extended after issuance for an additional period of less than 12 months. In that case, the additional period will be deemed part of the last preceding period for purposes of determining the Limits of Insurance.

SECTION IV – POLICY CONDITIONS

1. **Bankruptcy.**

   Bankruptcy or insolvency of the insured or of the insured's estate will not relieve us of our obligations under this policy.

2. **Cancellation.**

   (a) The first Named Insured shown in the Declarations may cancel this policy by mailing or delivering to us advance written notice of cancellation.

   (b) We may cancel this policy by mailing or delivering to the first Named Insured written notice of cancellation at least:

   (1) days before the effective date of cancellation if we cancel for nonpayment of premium; or

   (2) days before the effective date of cancellation if we cancel for any other reason.

   (c) We will mail or deliver our notice to the first Named Insured's last mailing address known to us.

   (d) Notice of cancellation will state the effective date of cancellation. The policy period will end on that date.

   (e) If this policy is cancelled, we will send the first Named Insured any premium refund due. If we cancel, the refund will be pro rata. If the first Named Insured cancels, the refund may be less than pro rata. The cancellation will be effective even if we have not made or offered a refund.

   (f) If notice is mailed, proof of mailing will be sufficient proof of notice.

3. **Changes.**

   This policy contains all the agreements between you and us concerning the insurance afforded. The first Named Insured shown in the Declarations is authorized to make changes in the terms of this policy with our consent. This policy's terms can be amended or waived only by endorsement issued by Global Aerospace, Inc. and made a part of this policy.

4. **Duties in the Event of Occurrence, Loss, Claim or Suit.**

   In this Policy Condition 4, the words **we**, **us** and **our** refer to Global Aerospace, Inc.

   (a) You must see to it that we are notified promptly of an ***occurrence,*** offense or ***loss*** that may result in a claim. Notice should include:

   (1) How, when and where the ***occurrence***, offense or ***loss*** took place;

   (2) The names and addresses of any injured persons and witnesses; and

   (3) The nature and location of any injury or damage arising out of the ***occurrence***, offense or ***loss.***

   (b) If a claim is made or ***suit*** is brought against any insured, you must:

   (1) Immediately record the specifics of the claim or ***suit*** and the date received; and

   (2) Notify us as soon as practicable.

   You must see to it that we receive written notice of the claim or ***suit*** as soon as practicable.

(c) You and any other involved insured must:

(1) Immediately send us copies of any demands, notices, summonses or legal papers received in connection with the claim or ***suit***;

(2) Authorize us to obtain records and other information;

(3) Cooperate with us in the investigation, settlement or defense of the claim or ***suit***; and

(4) Assist us, upon our request, in the enforcement of any right against any person or organization that may be liable to the insured because of injury or damage to which this insurance may also apply.

(d) No insureds will, except at their own cost, make any payment, assume any obligation, or incur any expense, other than for first aid, without our consent.

5. **Examination of Your Books and Records.**

We may examine and audit your books and records as they relate to this policy at any time during the policy period and up to three years afterward.

6. **Inspections and Surveys.**

We have the right but are not obligated to:

(a) Make inspections and surveys at any time;

(b) Give you reports on the conditions we find; and

(c) Recommend changes.

Any inspections, surveys, reports or recommendations relate only to insurability and the premiums to be charged. We do not make safety inspections. We do not undertake to perform the duty of any person or organization to provide for the health or safety of workers or the public. And we do not warrant that conditions:

(1) Are safe or healthful; or

(2) Comply with laws, regulations, codes or standards.

This condition applies not only to us, but also to any rating, advisory, rate service or similar organization that makes insurance inspections, surveys, reports or recommendations.

7. **Legal Action Against Us.**

No person or organization has a right under this policy:

(a) To join us as a party or otherwise bring us into a ***suit*** asking for damages from an insured; or

(b) To sue us on this policy unless all of its terms have been fully complied with.

A person or organization may sue us to recover on an agreed settlement or on a final judgment against an insured obtained after an actual trial; but we will not be liable for damages that are not payable under the terms of this policy or that are in excess of the applicable limit of insurance. An agreed settlement means a settlement and release of liability signed by us, the insured and the claimant or the claimant's legal representative. Service of process may be made upon Global Aerospace, Inc. on behalf of the Company. However, we do not waive our right to commence an action in any court of competent jurisdiction or to seek a transfer to another court as permitted by law.

8. **Other Insurance.**

If other valid and collectible insurance is available to the insured for a loss we cover under Coverages A, B or D of this policy, our obligations are limited as follows:

(a) Primary Insurance

This insurance is primary except when (b) below applies. If this insurance is primary, our obligations are not affected unless any of the other insurance is also primary. Then we will share with all that other insurance by the method described in (c) below.

(b) Excess Insurance

This insurance is excess over any of the other insurance, whether primary, excess, contingent or on any other basis:

(1) That is Fire, Extended Coverage, Builder's Risk, Installation Risk or similar coverage for ***your work***;

(2) That is Fire Insurance for premises rented to you;

(3) If the loss arises out of the maintenance or use of ***aircraft***, ***autos*** or watercraft to the extent not subject to Exclusion (g) of Coverage A (Section I); or

(4) If the loss is included within the ***products-completed operations hazard***.

When this insurance is excess, we will have no duty under Coverage A, B or D to defend any claim or ***suit*** that any other insurer has a duty to defend. If no other insurer defends, we will undertake to do so, but we will be entitled to the insured's rights against all those other insurers.

When this insurance is excess over other insurance, we will pay only our share of the amount of the loss, if any, that exceeds the sum of:

(1) The total amount that all such other insurance would pay for the loss in the absence of this insurance; and

(2) The total of all deductible and self-insured amounts under all that other insurance.

We will share the remaining loss, if any, with any other insurance that is not described in this Excess Insurance provision and was not bought specifically to apply in excess of the Limits of Insurance shown in the Declarations of this policy.

(c) Method of Sharing

If all of the other insurance permits contribution by equal shares, we will follow this method also. Under this approach each insurer contributes equal amounts until it has paid its applicable limit of insurance or none of the loss remains, whichever comes first.

If any of the other insurance does not permit contribution by equal shares, we will contribute by limits. Under this method, each insurer's share is based on the ratio of its applicable limit of insurance to the total applicable limits of insurance of all insurers.

9. **Premiums.**

The first Named Insured shown in the Declarations:

(a) Is responsible for the payment of all premiums; and

(b) Will be the payee for any return premiums we pay.

10. **Premium Audit.**

(a) We will compute all premiums for this policy in accordance with our rules and rates.

(b) Premium shown in this policy as advance premium is a deposit premium only. At the close of each audit period we will compute the earned premium for that period. Audit premiums are due and payable on notice to the first Named Insured. If the sum of the advance and audit premiums paid for the policy term is greater than the earned premium, we will return the excess to the first Named Insured.

(c) The first Named Insured must keep records of the information we need for premium computation and send us copies of those records at such times as we may request.

11. **Representations.**

By accepting this policy, you agree:

(a) The statements in the Declarations are accurate and complete;

(b) Those statements are based upon representations you made to us; and

(c) We have issued this policy in reliance upon your representations.

12. **Separation of Insureds.**

Except with respect to the Limits of Insurance and any rights or duties specifically assigned in this policy to the first Named Insured, this insurance applies:

(a) As if each Named Insured were the only Named Insured; and

(b) Separately to each insured against whom claim is made or ***suit*** is brought.

13. **State Statutes.**

    If the terms of this policy are in conflict with or inconsistent with the statutes of any state where this policy is in effect, we will conform to those state statutes.

14. **Titles of Paragraphs.**

    The titles of the various paragraphs of this policy, amendments, if any, attached to this policy and divider tabs, if any, are inserted solely for reference and are not to be deemed in any way to limit or affect the provisions to which they relate.

15. **Transfer of Rights of Recovery Against Others to Us.**

    If the insured has rights to recover all or part of any payment we have made under this policy, those rights are transferred to us. The insured must do nothing after loss to impair them. At our request, the insured will bring ***suit*** or transfer those rights to us and help us enforce them.

16. **Transfer of Your Rights and Duties Under This Policy.**

    Your rights and duties under this policy may not be transferred without our written consent except in the case of the death of an individual named insured.

    If you die, your rights and duties will be transferred to your legal representative but only while acting within the scope of duties as your legal representative. Until your legal representative is appointed, anyone having proper temporary custody of your property will have your rights and duties but only with respect to that property.

SECTION V - DEFINITIONS

1. ***Advertising injury*** means injury arising out of one or more of the following offenses:

   (a) Oral or written publication of material that slanders or libels a person or organization or disparages a person's or organization's goods, products or services;

   (b) Oral or written publication of material that violates a person's right of privacy;

   (c) Misappropriation of advertising ideas or style of doing business; or

   (d) Infringement of copyright, title or slogan.

2. ***Aircraft*** means any aircraft including components attached to or carried on the aircraft or components that are detached and not replaced by other similar components and tools specifically designed for the make and model of aircraft.

3. ***Aircraft noise*** means the noise of ***aircraft*** and associated vibration including the phenomenon called sonic boom.

4. ***Airport operations*** means all operations arising from the ownership, maintenance or use of locations for an airport or heliport including that portion of roads or other accesses that adjoin these locations. ***Airport operations*** also include all operations necessary or incidental to the activities of an airport or heliport.

5. ***Auto*** means a land motor vehicle, trailer or semitrailer designed for travel on public roads, including any attached machinery or equipment. But ***auto*** does not include ***mobile equipment***.

6. ***Bodily injury*** means bodily injury, sickness, mental anguish or disease sustained by a person, including death resulting from any of these at any time.

7. ***Coverage territory*** means:

   (a) The United States of America (including its territories and possessions), Puerto Rico and Canada;

   (b) International waters or airspace, provided the injury or damage does not occur in the course of travel or transportation to or from any place not included in 7(a) above; or

   (c) All parts of the world if:

      (1) The injury or damage arises out of:

         (i) ***Your product*** or ***your work*** made, sold or performed in the territory described in 7(a) above; or

         (ii) The activities of a person whose home is in the territory described in 7(a) above, but who is away for a short time on your business; and

      (2) The insured's responsibility to pay damages is determined in a ***suit*** on the merits, in the territory described in 7(a) above or in a settlement we agree to.

8. ***Impaired property*** means tangible property, other than ***your product*** or ***your work***, that cannot be used or is less useful because:

   (a) It incorporates ***your product*** or ***your work*** that is known or thought to be defective, deficient, inadequate or dangerous; or

(b) You have failed to fulfill the terms of a contract or agreement;

if such property can be restored to use by:

(c) The repair, replacement, adjustment or removal of ***your product*** or ***your work***; or

(d) Your fulfilling the terms of the contract or agreement.

9. ***In flight*** means the time commencing with the actual take-off run of the ***aircraft*** until it has completed its landing roll, or if the ***aircraft*** is a rotorcraft, from the time the rotors start to rotate under power until they cease to rotate.

10. ***Insured contract*** means:

(a) A lease of premises;

(b) A sidetrack agreement;

(c) An easement or license agreement, except in connection with construction or demolition operations on or within 50 feet of a railroad;

(d) An obligation, as required by ordinance, to indemnify a municipality, except in connection with work for a municipality;

(e) An elevator maintenance agreement; or

(f) That part of any other contract or agreement pertaining to your ***airport operations*** (including an indemnification of a municipality in connection with work performed for a municipality) under which you assume the tort liability of another party to pay for ***bodily injury*** or ***property damage*** to a third person or organization. Tort liability means a liability that would be imposed by law in the absence of any contract or agreement.

An ***insured contract*** does not include that part of any contract or agreement:

(a) That indemnifies any person or organization for ***bodily injury*** or ***property damage*** arising out of construction or demolition operations within 50 feet of any railroad property and affecting any railroad bridge or trestle, tracks, roadbeds, tunnel, underpass or crossing;

(b) That indemnifies an architect, engineer or surveyor for injury or damage arising out of:

(1) Preparing, approving or failing to prepare or approve maps, drawings, opinions, reports, surveys, change orders, designs or specifications; or

(2) Giving directions or instructions, or failing to give them, if that is the primary cause of the injury or damage;

(c) Under which the insured, if an architect, engineer or surveyor, assumes liability for injury or damage arising out of the insured's rendering or failing to render professional services, including those listed in (b) above and supervisory, inspection or engineering services; or

(d) That indemnifies any person or organization for damage by fire to premises rented or loaned to you.

11. ***Loading or unloading*** means the handling of property:

    (a) After it is moved from the place where it is accepted for movement into or onto an ***aircraft***, watercraft or ***auto***;

    (b) While it is in or on an ***aircraft***, watercraft or ***auto***; or

    (c) While it is being moved from an ***aircraft***, watercraft or ***auto*** to the place where it is finally delivered;

    but ***loading or unloading*** does not include the movement of property by means of a mechanical device, other than a hand truck, that is not attached to the ***aircraft***, watercraft or ***auto***.

12. ***Loss*** means an accident resulting in direct damage to tangible property, including continuous or repeated exposure to substantially the same general harmful conditions. ***Loss*** includes any resulting loss of use.

13. ***Mobile equipment*** means any of the following types of land vehicles, including any attached machinery or equipment:

    (a) Bulldozers, farm machinery, forklifts and other vehicles designed for use principally off public roads;

    (b) Vehicles maintained for use primarily on or next to premises you own or rent including special use vehicles designed for operation on airports;

    (c) Vehicles that travel on crawler treads;

    (d) Vehicles, whether self-propelled or not, maintained primarily to provide mobility to permanently mounted:

        (1) Power cranes, shovels, loaders, diggers or drills; or

        (2) Road construction or resurfacing equipment such as graders, scrapers or rollers;

    (e) Vehicles not described in 13(a), 13(b), 13(c) or 13(d) above that are not self-propelled and are maintained primarily to provide mobility to permanently attached equipment of the following types:

        (1) Air compressors, pumps and generators, including spraying, welding, building cleaning, geophysical exploration, lighting and well servicing equipment; or

        (2) Cherry pickers and similar devices used to raise or lower workers;

    (f) Vehicles not described in 13(a), 13(b), 13(c) or 13(d) above maintained primarily for purposes other than the transportation of persons or cargo.

        However, self-propelled vehicles with the following types of permanently attached equipment are not ***mobile equipment*** but will be considered ***autos***:

        (1) Cherry pickers and similar devices mounted on automobile or truck chassis and used to raise or lower workers; and

        (2) Air compressors, pumps and generators, including spraying, welding, building cleaning, geophysical exploration, lighting and well servicing equipment.

14. ***Occurrence*** means an accident, including continuous or repeated exposure to substantially the same general harmful conditions.

15. ***Personal injury*** means injury, other than ***bodily injury***, arising out of one or more of the following offenses:

    (a) False arrest, detention or imprisonment;

    (b) Malicious prosecution;

    (c) The wrongful eviction from, wrongful entry into or invasion of the right of private occupancy of a room, dwelling or premises that a person occupies by or on behalf of its owner, landlord or lessor;

    (d) Oral or written publication of material that slanders or libels a person or organization or disparages a person's or organization's goods, products or services;

    (e) Oral or written publication of material that violates a person's right of privacy; or

    (f) Misdirection of a person to an ***aircraft*** or other conveyance.

16. (a) ***Products-completed operations hazard*** includes all ***bodily injury*** and ***property damage*** occurring away from premises you own or rent and arising out of ***your product*** or ***your work*** except:

    (1) Products that are still in your physical possession; or

    (2) Work that has not yet been completed or abandoned.

    (b) ***Your work*** will be deemed completed at the earliest of the following times:

    (1) When all of the work called for in your contract has been completed.

    (2) When all of the work to be done at the site has been completed if your contract calls for work at more than one site.

    (3) When that part of the work done at a job site has been put to its intended use by any person or organization other than another contractor or subcontractor working on the same project.

    Work that may need service, maintenance, correction, repair or replacement, but which is otherwise complete, will be treated as completed.

    (c) This hazard does not include ***bodily injury*** or ***property damage*** arising out of:

    (1) The transportation of property, unless the injury or damage arises out of a condition in or on a vehicle created by the ***loading or unloading*** of it;

    (2) The existence of tools, uninstalled equipment or abandoned or unused materials.

SECTION V (Continued)

17. ***Property damage*** means:

    (a) Physical injury to tangible property, including all resulting loss of use of that property. All such loss of use shall be deemed to occur at the time of the physical injury that caused it; or

    (b) Loss of use of tangible property that is not physically injured. All such loss shall be deemed to occur at the time of the ***occurrence*** that caused it.

18. ***Suit*** means a civil proceeding in which damage because of ***bodily injury***, ***property damage***, ***personal injury*** or ***advertising injury*** to which this insurance applies are alleged. ***Suit*** includes:

    (a) An arbitration proceeding in which such damages are claimed and to which you must submit or do submit with our consent; or

    (b) Any other alternative dispute resolution proceeding in which such damages are claimed and to which you submit with our consent.

19. ***Your product*** means:

    (a) Any goods or products, other than real property, manufactured, sold, handled, distributed or disposed of by:

        (1) You;

        (2) Others trading under your name; or

        (3) A person or organization whose business or assets you have acquired; and

    (b) Containers (other than vehicles), materials, parts or equipment furnished in connection with such goods or products.

    Your product includes:

    (c) Warranties or representations made at any time with respect to the fitness, quality, durability, performance or use of ***your product;*** and

    (d) The providing of or failure to provide warnings or instructions.

    Your product does not include vending machines or other property rented to or located for the use of others but not sold.

20. ***Your work*** means:

    (a) Work or operations performed by you or on your behalf; and

    (b) Materials, parts or equipment furnished in connection with such work or operations.

    Your work includes:

    (c) Warranties or representations made at any time with respect to the fitness, quality, durability, performance or use of ***your work***; and

    (d) The providing of or failure to provide warnings or instructions.

SECTION VI - GENERAL POLICY EXCLUSIONS

Other provisions of this policy may limit or exclude insurance coverage. You are therefore urged to read the entire policy carefully.

This insurance does not apply to:

1. **Pollution**

   (a) ***Bodily injury***, ***property damage***, ***personal injury*** or ***advertising injury*** arising out of the actual, alleged or threatened discharge, dispersal, seepage, migration, release or escape of **pollutants**:

   (1) At or from any premises, site or location that is or was at any time owned or occupied by, or rented or loaned to, any insured;

   (2) At or from any premises, site or location that is or was at any time used by or for any insured or others for the handling, storage, disposal, processing or treatment of waste;

   (3) Which are or were at any time transported, handled, stored, treated, disposed of, or processed as waste by or for any insured or any person or organization for whom you may be legally responsible; or

   (4) At or from any premises, site or location on which any insured or any contractors or subcontractors working directly or indirectly on any insured's behalf are performing operations:

   (i) if the **pollutants** are brought on or to the premises, site or location in connection with such operations by such insured, contractor or subcontractor; or

   (ii) if the operations are to test for, monitor, clean up, remove, contain, treat, detoxify or neutralize, or in any way respond to, or assess the effects of **pollutants**.

   Subparagraphs (a)(1) and (a)(4)(i) do not apply to ***bodily injury*** or ***property damage*** arising out of heat, smoke or fumes from a hostile fire.

   As used in this exclusion 1., a hostile fire means one that becomes uncontrollable or breaks out from where it was intended to be.

   (b) Any loss, cost, or expense arising out of any:

   (1) Request, demand or order that any insured or others test for, monitor, clean up, remove, contain, treat, detoxify or neutralize, or in any way respond to or assess the effects of **pollutants**; or

   (2) Claim or ***suit*** by or on behalf of a governmental authority for damages because of testing for, monitoring, cleaning up, removing, containing, treating, detoxifying or neutralizing, or in any way responding to or assessing the effects of **pollutants**.

As used in **GENERAL POLICY EXCLUSION 1. Pollution:**

"Pollutants" means any solid, liquid, gaseous or thermal irritant or contaminant, including smoke, vapor, soot, fumes, acids, alkalis, chemicals and waste. Waste includes materials to be recycled, reconditioned or reclaimed.

2. **War, Hi-Jacking and Other Perils**

Bodily injury, ***property damage***, ***personal injury***, ***advertising injury*** or ***loss*** to ***aircraft*** due to:

(a) War, invasion, acts of foreign enemies, hostilities (whether declared or not), civil war, rebellion, insurrection, martial law, military or usurped power or attempts at usurpation of power.

(b) Any hostile detonation of any weapon of war employing atomic or nuclear fission and/or fusion or other like reaction or radioactive force or matter.

(c) Strikes, riots, civil commotions or labor disturbances.

(d) Any act of one or more persons, whether or not agents of a sovereign power, for political or terrorist purposes and whether the loss or damage resulting therefrom is accidental or intentional.

(e) Any malicious act or act of sabotage.

(f) Confiscation, nationalization, seizure, restraint, detention, appropriation, requisition for title or use by or under the order of any government (whether civil, military or de facto) or public or local authority.

(g) Hi-jacking or any unlawful seizure or wrongful exercise of control of an ***aircraft*** or crew (including any attempt at such seizure or control) made by any person or persons, whether such ***aircraft*** or crew are ***in flight*** or not.

3. **Nuclear Energy Liability**

(a) ***Bodily injury*** or ***property damage***:

(1) With respect to which an insured under the policy is also an insured under a nuclear energy liability policy issued by Nuclear Energy Liability Insurance Association, Mutual Atomic Energy Liability Underwriters, Nuclear Insurance Association of Canada or any of their successors, or would be an insured under any such policy but for its termination upon exhaustion of its limit of liability; or

(2) Resulting from the **hazardous properties** of **nuclear material** and with respect to which (a) any person or organization is required to maintain financial protection pursuant to the Atomic Energy Act of 1954, or any law amendatory thereof, or (b) the insured is, or had this policy not been issued would be, entitled to indemnity from the United States of America, or any agency thereof, under any agreement entered into by the United States of America, or any agency thereof, with any person or organization.

(b) Expenses incurred under Medical Payments coverage with respect to ***bodily injury*** resulting from the **hazardous properties** of **nuclear material** and arising out of the operation of a **nuclear facility** by any person or organization.

(c) ***Bodily injury*** or ***property damage*** resulting from the **hazardous properties** of **nuclear material**, if:

(1) The **nuclear material** (a) is at any **nuclear facility** owned by, or operated by or on behalf of, an insured or (b) has been discharged or dispersed therefrom;

(2) The **nuclear material** is contained in **spent fuel** or **waste** at any time possessed, handled, used, processed, stored, transported or disposed of by or on behalf of an insured, or

(3) The ***bodily injury*** or ***property damage*** arises out of the furnishing by an insured of services, materials, parts or equipment in connection with the planning, construction, maintenance, operation or use of any **nuclear facility**, but if such facility is located within the United States of America, its territories or possessions or Canada, this exclusion (3) applies only to ***property damage*** to such **nuclear facility** and any property thereat.

As used in **GENERAL POLICY EXCLUSION 3. Nuclear Energy Liability:**

"Hazardous properties" include radioactive, toxic or explosive properties;

"Nuclear material" means **source material**, **special nuclear material** or **by-product material**;

"Source material", **"special nuclear material"**, and **"by-product material"** have the meanings given them in the Atomic Energy Act of 1954 or in any law amendatory thereof;

"Spent fuel" means any fuel element or fuel component, solid or liquid, which has been used or exposed to radiation in a **nuclear reactor**;

"Waste" means solely with respect to this exclusion 3., any waste material (a) containing **by-product material** other than the tailings or wastes produced by the extraction or concentration of uranium or thorium from any ore processed primarily for its **source material** content, and (b) resulting from the operation by any person or organization of any **nuclear facility** included under the first two paragraphs of the definition of **nuclear facility**.

"Nuclear facility" means:

(a) Any **nuclear reactor**;

(b) Any equipment or device designed or used for (1) separating the isotopes of uranium or plutonium, (2) processing or utilizing **spent fuel**, or (3) handling, processing or packaging ***waste***;

(c) Any equipment or device used for the processing, fabricating or alloying of **special nuclear material** if at any time the total amount of such material in the custody of the insured at the premises where such equipment or device is located consists of or contains more than 25 grams of plutonium or uranium 233 or any combination thereof, or more than 250 grams of uranium 235;

(d) Any structure, basin, excavation, premises or place prepared or used for the storage or disposal of **waste**;

and includes the site on which any of the foregoing is located, all operations conducted on such site and all premises used for such operations;

"Nuclear reactor" means any apparatus designed or used to sustain nuclear fission in a self-supporting chain reaction or to contain a critical mass of fissionable material;

"Property damage" includes all forms of radioactive contamination of property.

Chapter 10

Underwriting and Pricing General Aviation Risks

OUTLINE

The Function of Underwriting
Evaluating Aircraft Hull and Liability Risks
A closer look: 4 key elements of aircraft underwriting
Underwriting Industrial Aid, Commercial, P&B and Special Use risks
Underwriting Rotorcraft Risks
Evaluating and Underwriting Ground Risks:
Airport Liability Risks
Fixed Based Operator Risks
Pricing Various Aviation Risks

OBJECTIVES

At the end of this chapter you should be able to:
Understand the purpose, function, and need for underwriting.
Describe the unique nature of aviation exposures faced by underwriters.
Define and discuss the underwriting processes of preselection and postselection.
Explain the conflict which may arise between the production and the underwriting staffs.
List the basic information needed by underwriters to provide an aircraft hull and liability quotation.
Discuss the importance of age, construction, and configuration in underwriting the type of aircraft.
Explain the importance of pilot requirements in underwriting the aircraft risk.
Describe the five purpose of use categories.
Identify the two primary factors underwriters consider in evaluating helicopter risks.
Summarize the major factors taken into consideration by underwriters in evaluating airport risks.
Give some examples of rating aviation risks.

THE FUNCTION OF UNDERWRITING

Underwriting is the process of selecting and pricing risks (prospective insureds) which are presented to the insurer. The purpose of underwriting is to maximize profits by accepting a favorable distribution of risks. Underwriting success is simply measured by an underwriter's ability to collect enough money from the masses so as to be able to pay the unfortunate losses of the few while at the same time successfully covering underwriting expenses and returning a fair profit to the underwriting company shareholders. The process is based primarily on selection, so this part of the definition of underwriting is discussed first. Pricing, which also impacts underwriting success, will also be covered in detail.

The Need for Underwriting

Applicants for insurance are not selected randomly, neither do they have the same loss expectancies. A newly rated private pilot flying a high-performance single-engine aircraft presents a completely different risk from an instrument-rated private pilot with 1000 total hours including 100 hours in the particular model. Those applicants with loss expectancies substantially higher than are provided for in the premium charged for a particular class of risks should either be charged a higher premium or declined coverage.

If a company were to refrain from discriminating against applicants failing to meet underwriting standards contemplated in the rate level, it would be forced to charge all insureds rates higher than those charged by competitors in order to remain profitable. This higher rate would cause a loss of attractive risks who would insure at the lower rates charged by competing companies practicing selective underwriting. Only those not eligible for coverage by the selective underwriters would buy protection from the nonselective one. The result would be that the nonselective company would have to charge even higher rates, producing a vicious cycle of high rates that could not attract sufficient numbers or a spread of risks sufficient to enable the company to remain in business. There is an expression in the insurance business, "Select or be selected against."

Another need for underwriting is equity in the rate structure, which means that, within a broad range or classification of risks, an insured should be charged a premium commensurate with loss expectancy. Classifications that differentiate among exposures are used for rating purposes. Of necessity, these classifications must be broad enough to include an adequate number of exposure units so that the law of averages will work, yet not too broad so that substantially different risks are lumped together. On the other hand there will be a loss of credibility in the rates if there are too many classifications and not enough risks in each classification for the law of averages to work.

Insurers must have a workable selection process for assigning all acceptable exposures to their correct classification and for assuring that there will be a sufficient number of insureds with below-average loss expectancies to offset those with loss expectancies above the class average.

As noted, the primary purpose of underwriting (risk selection) is to obtain a profitable distribution of risks. If underwriting is to produce a profitable distribution of risks, it must produce an adequate distribution of them. An adequate distribution of risks requires their diversification among many types of aircraft, purposes of use, pilots, coverages, and geographical areas. Overconcentration of exposures is poor underwriting practice. Underwriting companies can jeopardize their distribution by writing too many units of particular aircraft type or writing too many units of a particular risk profile such as single-pilot turbine aircraft. Overconcentration can adversely impact underwriting financial results because spread of risk is compromised.

Aviation Exposures

Catastrophe Loss

Aircraft and the perils of flight present many unique problems for aviation underwriters, but none is more fundamental than the constant exposure to *catastrophe loss*. The threat of this type of loss exists to some degree in every form of insurance but nowhere must it be given such positive consideration or be more carefully underwritten than where aircraft are involved.

Of the many reasons for this condition the most significant is the physical properties of aircraft themselves. Because of the environment in which they operate, they must be of relatively light construction and intricate design. Airplanes simply cannot be engineered in the same manner as trailer trucks or trains and made to accommodate the impacts of collision or the stresses and strains associated with other accidents to which they might be exposed. With specific design, weight, and speed requirements to be met, aircraft must be accepted by underwriters as being considerably more susceptible to substantial damage and total loss than any other type of vehicle.

Substantial damage or total loss alone, of course, does not necessarily constitute catastrophe loss but with aircraft there always exists the possibility of bodily injury, property damage, and loss of life. A review of some of the more recent aircraft accidents shows how quickly these factors can turn airplane accidents into major disasters receiving front page headlines. As speeds, size of equipment, fuel load, and passenger capacities increase, the probability of this type of catastrophe will also increase. The dollar payouts associated with catastrophe losses continue to rise today with increased hull values, higher liability awards, and growing legal defense costs.

Limited Spread

Complicating this exposure to catastrophe loss is a situation which provides the aviation underwriter with a *very limited spread of risks*. The combined fleets of all the certificated U.S. scheduled airlines include only about 7,000 aircraft. The total of all active U.S. civil aircraft is only approximately 200,000. The significance of these figures is twofold. In the first place there are fewer units at risk compared to other lines of insurance for as successful an operation of the law of large numbers, upon which insurers traditionally rely for ability to predict losses. Secondly, numbers for any one insurer are too few to permit the development of credible statistics upon which actuarially sound rating formulas can be based. This absence of credible statistics places the underwriter in the position of having to rely to a large extent upon personal judgment in selecting risks and determining rates. There is no industry rating bureau in aviation as there is in other fire and casualty fields which develop rating manuals based on statistics reported by the various member companies.

In recent years, more advanced methods of statistical analysis have been employed by some underwriting companies. These advanced techniques center on predicting losses in spite of lower unit counts found in the aviation insurance industry. These techniques rely on good underlying data. Underwriting companies are becoming acutely aware of the importance of managing data internally, and this task is made easier by advances in computer software.

Diversification

Though spread is limited and catastrophe loss a threatening possibility, the aviation underwriter's task would not be nearly so difficult if each risk could be conveniently categorized, dealt with as a unit of a class, and underwritten in a manner similar to automobiles. Unfortunately, this treatment is not possible. Even aircraft of identical make and model present insuring problems which make it impossible to rate them by class. For example, their values may differ signigicantly depending upon the radios, navigational aids, or other avionics equipment on board, and these value differences could lead to significant premium differences and payout possibilities. Additionally, aircraft of the same make and model could be used for different purposes which would lead to a different rating approach based on the particular risk profile. The possible loss scenario changes with the purpose of use as well.

Even more important to the underwriters than the varying factors which determine the amount of possible loss are those which have a bearing on the probability of loss. Factors such as prevailing weather conditions, the use for which an aircraft is flown, and the experience and abilities of the pilots are as fundamental to this problem as are the number of hours flown and the quality of maintenance received. For larger risks, the management personnel and their experience levels become a key factor. There exist so many variables vital to the proper analysis of every risk that underwriters must treat each case in accordance with its own particular merits. They cannot rely on broad identification with a class to justify insurability or to act as anything but the most general basis for their rating.

Rapidity of Change

Having to shoulder the burden of prudent risk selection, underwriters must be more than just able insurance people. Such individuals must be technically versed in the structural and aerodynamic problems associated with flight as well as the operational and physiological problems encountered by the pilot. They must have an understanding and appreciation of aircraft power plants and, most importantly, they must be able to keep abreast of the developments and changes which take place almost daily within the industry. New aircraft types continue to be introduced to the market and each one poses unique underwriting challenges. Underwriters must also be aware of loss/accident trends so they can be addressed in the appropriate manner. Aviation is a dynamic field and underwriters cannot afford to find themselves lagging behind. They must be constantly aware of new hazards which arise as speeds increase and the state of the art of flying becomes more sophisticated. They must be equally aware of the declining importance of hazards which may have been serious at one time but which now have been reduced or eliminated by advancing technology or other changes.

Selection of Risks

The agent or broker who sells the business generally makes a preliminary appraisal of the exposure. The major part of underwriting, however, is done by full-time underwriters in home or branch offices. Most companies also have internal loss control or safety departments that assist in risk evaluation. To some extent, groups outside the company, such as engineering firms, auditing firms, and credit-rating organizations, supplement the underwriters by furnishing information and recommendations upon which underwriting decisions are based.

Methods of Selecting Insureds

In selecting new insureds, underwriters have two problems. One is how to select new insureds; that is, how to decide whether to accept or reject an application for insurance. This procedure may be called *preselection*. The other problem is how to get rid of undesirable insureds and is called *postselection*.

The rules governing the preselection of insureds are generally defined as an opinion about a particular area of aviation risk, and often this opinion is shaped by a combination of items or events. These opinions tend to be fluid and can be heavily influenced by such things as the market experience (overall experience of all underwriting companies) on the particular type of risk being considered, the individual experience of the particular underwriting company being approached, and the individual technical knowledge of the individual underwriters themselves. For example, coverage may be difficult to obtain on a particular subclass of general aviation risk across all companies because of a recent proliferation of losses on similar risks. Likewise, company A may choose to abstain from a particular type of risk due to a recent large loss. Alternatively, a particular underwriter may simply have a strong negative opinion about a particular area of General Aviation based on something other than underwriting experience.

The application of preselection rules generally begin with instructions to the agent or broker, who may be told to refrain from presenting certain types of applicants to the underwriting company. For example, brokers may be advised that a particular underwriting company may not wish to increase its exposure to low-time private pilots in light twin-engine aircraft or experimental aircraft. Likewise, they may also be advised of a maximum insured value or limits of liability the company can consider. Other factors, such as their general underwriting practice with regard to amending pilot warranties, extending territorial limits, and so forth may simply become apparent by virtue of their underwriting track record.

Rather than simply reject an application for insurance, underwriters may choose to quote alternative, for example, agreeing to cover a twin-engine aircraft provided the PIC agrees to use a copilot on all flights until he or she meets the under writers experience requirements. The company is free to charge whatever rate it wishes and may accept or reject the risk at that rate, or make a counter-offer at a higher rate. The underwriter might also offer insureds restricted coverage, or require them to use special protective measures or install specific loss prevention devices. For example, an underwriter might require an insured to hangar the aircraft if it is located in an area of the country that is prone to hailstorms.

It is usually easier for underwriters to refuse an application than face the difficulty of dealing with an insured who is considered undesirable. However, a company can be too conservative, and literally underwrite itself out of business by virtue of having limited spread of risk if it refuses too many applicants. Consider the underwriting results of company A that has 100 insured customers versus those of company B that has 1,000. While it can be argued that Company A may have endeavored to select only the best of risks, we all know that even the best risks sometimes suffer fortuitous losses. Should one of company A's risks suffer such a loss, it is likely that it would have limited premium resources as compared with company B to cover the event; hence, there is a balance between production and selection that underwriters often most manage. The art of selection is also impacted by other production-related pressures. Consider the underwriting company that finds itself dealing with a particular agent who represents a significant volume of his or her business. It is understandable that an underwriter is going to have accept some below average risks in order to continue to attract the agent's better risks. One of the keys to successful underwriting is managing relationships with brokers and agents. Most aviation insurance is broker/agent produced, so underwriting companies have a vested interest in maximizing their relationships to the greatest extent possible.

Eliminating undesirable risks is known as postselection. The easiest method of eliminating an undesirable risk is simply waiting until the expiration of the policy when the company can notify the agent or broker that it does not wish to renew the contract. The circumstances, however, may be of a nature that the underwriter does not want to wait until the end of the policy term but must terminate the policy as soon as possible. If, for example, a follow-up inspection of an FBO's premises reveals undesirable physical conditions or unsound operational practices and procedures, the underwriter might recommend immediate cancellation of the policy.

Underwriting and Production

One of the unique problems faced by insurers compared to other businesses is the conflict which often arises between underwriting and production. The production (or marketing) people are charged with the responsibility of developing new business and in most cases underwriters bear significant responsibility for developing new, profitable business. The underwriters primary task, however, revolves around obtaining a profitable distribution of exposure units.

In most companies, however, **both** production and underwriting are responsibilities of the underwriting staff. This apparent conflict requires underwriters to carefully balance production and underwriting forces and this is not easily accomplished. Depending on the business cycle or market climate at a particular point in time and depending on a company's particular focus, internal pressures may cause the company to lean in a certain direction at any given time. For example, if a company has had poor loss experience, it might decide to tighten underwriting requirements while sacrificing production. A company can never focus or stray too far in one direction because in time it will face inadequate production or unacceptably high loss ratios. The production and underwriting conflict creates a dynamic environment where striking the right balance is an ever-present challenge.

EVALUATING THE AIRCRAFT HULL AND LIABILITY RISK

Agents or brokers who submit a completed application for hull and liability insurance (see samples at the end of this chapter) generally include all the information needed by the underwriter to make a firm quotation. If an application is not available or time does not permit the completion of one, an underwriter will often give a quotation in writing or over the phone subject to his or her receiving a completed application within a stated period of time. The basic information needed to offer a quotation includes the following.

1. Name and address of the applicant. This would include the individual(s), corporation or partnership that have an insurable interest in the aircraft. An insurable interest is one that, should the event insured against take place, the insured might suffer a financial loss. If the happening of the event insured against does not result in a financial loss to the insured there can be no insurable interest in the property.
2. Business of the applicant. The business of the applicant is helpful in determining how the aircraft is going to be used. If the individual is an accountant, it can be assumed that the aircraft will be used for business and pleasure. If the applicant is a construction company the aircraft might be used to fly personnel and/or supplies to job sites and the usage would be considered industrial aid.
3. Effective time and date of coverage. The normal time of day for inception and expiration of aviation policies is 12:01 AM. If there is a current policy in force, care must be given that there is no gap or overlap in coverage.
4. The type(s) and limit(s) of liability coverage desired. This item was covered under the hull and liability policy in chapter 8.
5. The type of aircraft physical damage (hull) coverage desired and deductibles. This item was covered under the hull and liability policy in chapter 8. However, the importance of having an amount of insurance which reflects the current market value of the aircraft cannot be overstated. Neither under-insurance nor over-insurance is acceptable.
6. Description of the aircraft. Underwriters need a complete description of the aircraft including the following items:
   a. Year, make and model of the aircraft.
   b. FAA identification number (Aircraft "N" number).
   c. Seating capacity crew and passengers. On most four-place aircraft this is no prob-lem as there is normally a pilot and three passenger seats. However, in the case of some multiengine aircraft that are operated with or without a copilot depending upon the flight involved, some confusion might arise. In such a case it is best to assume that there might be an occasion for the crew seat to be occupied by a passenger and as such rated accordingly. On larger multiengine aircraft a rest room seat with a lid and cushion is often provided as an additional place to sit. If this rest room seat has been approved to serve as an additional passenger seat, and is supplied a seat belt, then it should be counted as an additional seat in the aircraft.
   d. Land, sea or amphibian aircraft. Underwriters must be advised if an aircraft, normally manufactured with wheels, for land use, is converted to a float plane by removing the wheels and installing floats. There are other types of aircraft which need to be identified such as a rotorcraft.
   e. Purchased new or used and the date.
   f. Price paid including avionics equipment. Avionics equipment can often represent up to a third of the aircraft value.
   g. Current market value. Underwriters will often check this value against similar aircraft in the *Aircraft Bluebook Price Digest* or similar publication, which lists current values on used and new aircraft.
   h. Engine hours since new, or since the last major overhaul.
   i. Number of hours the aircraft was flown during the last 12 months and

estimated number of hours to be flown in the next 12 months.

7. Whether the aircraft is normally hangared or tied down and the name of the airport. This information can be very important particularly for those aircraft that are tied down in parts of the country subject to hail, windstorm, tornadoes and general exposure to weather. Quite often underwriters will require insureds to carry higher deductibles if the aircraft is normally tied down. A surcharge on the hull rate is also typical for tied-down aircraft. Another problem with tied-down aircraft is the higher incidence of theft of aircraft and avionics equipment. In certain locations where drug traffic has grown, underwriters have encouraged owners to install alarm systems and special locks on their aircraft to make them more difficult to steal. Underwriters are also concerned about the number of risks insured at a particular location because of the potential catastrophe exposure should the area be subjected to some natural disaster such as a flood or tornado. Finally, the physical description of the airport itself is very important to the underwriter. Questions concerning the airport facilities, runway length and width, paved or grass, lighted or unlighted, service hours, control tower operated, and obstructions are important factors in determining whether or not a particular aircraft, given its flight characteristics, can operate safely out of the airport.
8. Purposes of use. The aircraft use plays an important role in underwriting and pricing risks. Some of the more common uses include business and pleasure, corporate transportation, instruction, rental and charter. Some less common uses include flying clubs, crop dusting, banner towing and low altitude photography. The risks inherent in each of these uses vary considerably and consequently, so does the pricing. Some of the exposures may be uninsurable or at least not attractive at a reasonable price by certain carriers.
9. Territorial limits. Underwriters are concerned if there are any flights con templated outside of the continental United States. Each policy has specific territorial limits set forth where coverage will apply. If an accident occurred outside the approved geographic area, no coverage would apply. Consequently, if the insured is going to fly outside the country, underwriters must be apprised of the particulars so that the limits can be extended or, if that is not possible, the insured must be made aware of the limitation in coverage.
10. Pilots who will operate the aircraft. Because this is such a critical area in the operation of any aircraft, underwriters require a great deal of information. In fact, the information in the application is generally supplemented by a completed pilot questionnaire. Information includes:
    a. Name and age of the pilot(s). Age is an important underwriting criterion since some companies are reluctant to underwrite pilots who are in their sixties or seventies because of the known physical effects of advanced age. Companies usually consider exceptions on a case-by-case basis. When the carrier agrees to insure an older pilot it may require a first or second class physical exam as a condition of the policy.
    b. Pilot certification and ratings. The four classes of FAA licenses are student pilot, private pilot, commercial pilot, and airline transport pilot. Some of the more common ratings are: aircraft single-engine land, aircraft multiengine land, instrument, aircraft single-engine sea, aircraft multiengine sea, glider, balloon, various rotorcraft ratings, and a rating for each type of aircraft weighing in excess of 12,500 pounds.
    c. Medical certificate, date of last physical and class. Most insurers require that the medical certificate be current for coverage to be in effect. Whether a certificate is current or not depends on how many months have elapsed

since the examination, and under what circumstances the pilot is flying the aircraft. There are three classes of physicals: (1) first class, which expires every six months and is required by an airline transport pilot acting as pilot-in-command (PIC) of an aircraft which is carrying passengers for hire on a scheduled basis, (2) second class, which expires every 12 months, and is required by a commercial pilot who receives compensation for his or her services, and (3) third class, which expires every 24 months and is used by a pilot who is not receiving direct compensation for his or her piloting skills. Interestingly, a pilot who holds a first or second class certificate which has expired, may continue to fly, provided the individual exercises only the privileges of the medical certificate who's time has not yet expired. For example, a pilot holding an expired second class certificate may continue to fly, provided he or she receives no compensation for flying, until a total of 24 months has elapsed; in other words after the expiration of 12 months, the second class certificate, in effect, lapses into a second class physical.

d. Hours logged as a pilot-in-command. Underwriters are particularly concerned knowing the total hours, hours in the aircraft model to be insured, retractable hours, multiengine hours and hours flown during the last 90 days. The Federal Aviation Administration only requires that a pilot's hours be logged in order to qualify for certain licenses and ratings. Consequently, not all pilots take the time to log all of their flying time. As a result it is possible that a pilot might have flown 2,000 hours but only recorded 1,500 in his or her log book. This information becomes important to an aviation underwriter who normally will base acceptance of the risk and pricing on logged flying time. Underwriters are typically interested in how much time the pilot has logged as pilot-in-command. In accordance with Federal Aviation Regulations, a private or commercial pilot can only log time as PIC while being the sole manipulator of an aircraft that he or she is properly rated for, or while an airline transport pilot is acting as PIC, or while a certified flight instructor is acting as a flight instructor. Many pilots mistakenly give incorrect PIC hours that do not qualify under the FAA's definition. The log book provides a breakdown of hours by aircraft type. This information becomes important when an underwriter needs to determine the pilot's experience in a particular aircraft. For example, if the insured aircraft has retractable landing gear, the underwriter will most certainly request the pilot's logged hours in retractable gear aircraft as well as time in the particular make and model. If the pilot has sufficient time in retractable gear aircraft, but none in the make and model for which insurance is sought, the underwriter may require the prospective insured to receive a check ride in the aircraft by a certified flight instructor. If the pilot has no time in retractable gear aircraft, the company may elect not to approve the individual as a pilot for this aircraft. If the individual is approved, the underwriter may require a minimum number of hours of dual instruction before allowing the pilot to fly solo. All of these provisions are spelled out in the pilot warranty.

e. Date of the last FAA flight (biennial) review and the name of the examiner. Every two years a pilot is required by the FAA to take a check ride with a certified flight instructor in order to insure that the pilot has minimum acceptable skills and knowledge to continue exercising the privileges of the certificate in a safe manner.

11. Pilot's physical and flight history. Before accepting the risk underwrit-

ers will request personal physical and flight history from the applicant. This information includes questions such as: Do any of the prospective pilots have any physical impairments or a medical waiver from the FAA? Have any prospective pilots ever had their FAA or Military Pilot certificate suspended or revoked? Have there been any citations for any violation of Federal Aviation Regulations? Has any pilot been involved in an aircraft accident? Have any of the pilots been convicted of or pleaded guilty to a felony or for drunken driving?

12. Loss payee in addition to the named insured. With respect to the hull coverage, underwriters want to know if there is any outstanding encumbrance and if so, how much and to whom? The most common mortgagee is a bank, or other financial institution that lends the aircraft owner the money to buy the aircraft. Another might be a lessor who owns the aircraft but has leased the aircraft to the named insured. Mortgagees and lessors require that they be shown on the policy as a loss payee in the event of a hull loss. In the event of a total loss, payment would be made to the named insured and mortgagee or lessor as their interest may appear. The underwriter will also ask if breach of warranty coverage is required by the lienholder. This was covered under hull endorsements in chapter 8; however, the breach of warranty coverage basically protects the lienholder's interest in the event that the insured breaches his insurance contract by some violation.
13. Loss history. Underwriters are very interested in an insured's prior loss record. From an operational standpoint, loss records can provide valuable insight into an aircraft operator's past and they can provide a basis on which to set future expectations. Loss history is another valuable tool that helps the underwriter in risk assessment.
14. Other questions. Some applications ask if the insured is a member of the National Business Aircraft Association (NBAA). Because of the safety and professional aircraft management services provided by NBAA for its members, evidence of membership clearly demonstrates a concern by the insured for these areas of operation. Underwriters will normally request the name of the last insurance carrier, if any, and whether or not any carrier has declined to cover the insured or refused to renew.
15. The last section of any application always contains a paragraph wherein the applicants warrant that the information supplied on the application is true and complete to the best of their knowledge. Carriers will potentially deny claims in the event the insured has misrepresented material information on the application.

A Closer Look at Evaluating Aircraft Hull and Liability Risks

Since so much depends upon the aviation underwriters' ability to carefully and knowingly select and rate risks, it will be helpful to discuss the major factors upon which they make their evaluation. Underwriters are concerned with four principal areas: (1) the type of aircraft to be insured, (2) pilot qualifications , (3) geographical considerations and (4) the purpose for which the aircraft is to be used

Type of Aircraft and Equipment

The specific aircraft to be flown determines the insured value which will be placed upon it and the number of crew members and passengers it can accommodate. This information provides the underwriters with the loss potential of the risk in terms of dollars by defining the top limit of loss to which the company is exposed with respect to physical damage to the aircraft and to some degree the maximum possible third party legal liability. They must consider this maximum loss potential before going on to the more important task of determining the probabilities of loss.

An aircraft's susceptibility to loss can be a function of any number of factors relative to its age, construction, and general configuration.

Age

The problem of age is largely one of gradual airframe deterioration and power plant weariness. After a period of time and after extensive exposure to the rigors of flight and the impact of numerous landings, all aircraft show signs of wear and tear. Often it is a decrease in performance by virtue of dents in the airfoils, corrosion of the skin, nicks in the propeller blades, or a dropping off of the rated horsepower of the engine. Most aircraft are designed with a sufficient margin built into their performance/weight ratio so that this decrease in performance has little effect on their airworthiness. With others, however, it is much more critical and any performance lag poses a serious problem.

Each type of airplane has its own effective lifespan ranging from a few years to several decades and many have inherent weaknesses which must be recognized. The underwriter must be aware of all of these characteristics and give them consideration in arriving at an underwriting decision. This consideration is particularly important since it has been estimated that about half of all active U.S. civil aircraft were manufactured more than 30 years ago.

Construction

Though an airplane's construction has a bearing upon frequency of loss, it is far more meaningful to the underwriter as a guide to how expensive repairs will be. With airplanes there is considerable variety in the complexity of construction and in the materials used, with the result that each presents its own peculiar repair problems. They are not like automobiles where a dented fender is a dented fender regardless of make or model. Older aircraft made of tubular steel or wood frame covered by doped fabric are particularly susceptible to the hazards of hail, windstorm, and general deterioration; but they are relatively easy to repair. Many maintenance facilities are available and rigged to recover or patch damaged skin and to repair or replace broken ribs and spars. These aircraft are quite different from aircraft of more traditional all- metal construction. Here, even most superficial damage requires the talents of an experienced sheet metal worker and the facilities of a specially equipped repair shop. With aircraft of particularly complex construction, underwriters must recognize that relatively minor damage can necessitate the replacement of an entire structural member at considerable expense. They must also be concerned with the possibility of a constructive total loss and face the inordinately high costs of repair.

Configuration

Aircraft *configuration* holds its own particular complications for the underwriter. For example, those airplanes having *conventional landing gear* (two main wheels mounted forward of the center of gravity with a balancing wheel in the rear) sit with a nose high attitude on the ground which detracts from the pilot's forward visibility and increases the hazards associated with ground operations. On the other hand, the more common *tricycle landing gear* aircraft (two main wheels aft of the center of gravity and a third wheel up under the nose) promotes better visibility on the ground but is considerably less forgiving of landings on rough or soft terrain or taxiing collisions with low obstacles. Seaplanes and amphibians face a full range of marine hazards as well as those of flight. Multiengine aircraft, though they enjoy the added reliability of multiple power plants, present an asymmetrical thrust and drag problem when one engine fails which requires more advanced pilot skills to handle properly. Virtually every aircraft has some characteristic basic to its configuration which creates its own particular set of problems.

One of the biggest problems facing corporate pilots in the last 30 years is the transition from prop to prop-jet and pure-jet aircraft. The principal problem here is that of pilot retraining and the added exposure presented during the period of transition. The prop-jet and pure-jet aircraft are not more difficult to fly but pilots do have to adjust their thinking and change some of their flying habits.

Pilots

The old adage, "Aviation, like the sea, is not inherently dangerous, just mercilessly unforgiving of human error," is a truism which indicates the importance to the underwriters of pilot experience and ability in the evaluation of an aircraft risk.

In this area the underwriters are fortunate to have operating in their behalf a rather intricate pilot licensing and rating system supervised by the Federal Aviation Administration. This system gives them at least some of the necessary assurances that the aircraft the company is insuring is operated by a qualified pilot. This assurance alone, however, is not enough. The FAA is not putting up thousands of dollars in protection against losses which the insured may incur. In addition, the underwriters must investigate the pilot's background, experience, and accident record to make sure the pilot's qualifications are adequate. Often, an underwriter will find it necessary to impose restrictions on the operation of an aircraft beyond those demanded by normal federal licensing regulations. Such restrictions may be imposed when a pilot first flies under the authority of a newly acquired rating or certificate or when he makes a transition from one type of aircraft to another. These restrictions are normally included in the wording of the pilot warranty in the policy and take the form of specific minimum flying hour requirements. Sometimes they are drafted to require that a pilot obtain so many additional hours of dual instruction before flying solo, or that he always be accompanied by a qualified copilot. Occasionally, they specify that flying be limited to fair weather and daylight hours.

In addition to minimum flying hour requirements, formal initial and recurrent training in a particular make and model aircraft are considered essential requirements by underwriting companies, especially when larger, more sophisticated aircraft are involved. Formal training programs usually involve flight simulators where different types of emergencies can be simulated in a controlled environment which cannot be safely duplicated in the actual aircraft. By practicing different flight situations involving emergencies, the crew will be better prepared in the real world for those situations and as a result underwriters look very favorably on these training programs.

The disturbing fact that over 70 percent of the non-airline accidents involve some degree of pilot error is evidence of the importance of the human factor in aviation. It justifies the utmost care taken by the underwriter in evaluating that aspect of each risk.

Surprisingly, there is no industry standard nor does there seem to be much agreement between insurance companies on minimum pilot requirements except in the broadest terms. Each carrier has its own idea of minimum pilot or crew qualifications that the insured must have to qualify for coverage.

The following *minimum pilot requirements* are often used by underwriters for privately owned and operated aircraft; however, they are merely a guide and can be raised or lowered depending upon the limits of liability carried and other underwriting factors.

		Minimum Total Logged Hours		
Aircraft	*Certificate*	*Total*	*In Type*	*In Model*
SE–Fixed Gear	Student or better	None	None	None
SE–Retractible Gear	Private or better	200	50	10
ME–LightTwin	Private or better	500	100	10
ME–MediumTwin	Private or better	1,000	200	10
Turboprop or jet	Commercial	2,000	500	10

Co-pilots having a commercial pilot's certificate are generally required for all turboprop or jet aircraft.

The thing to keep in mind about these pilot minima is that they are not inflexible. For example, an underwriter may offer a quotation to a corporate customer based on the PIC of a medium-twin having 1,500 total hours, 500 hours multiengine, and 50 hours in the model. The insured may counter that his pilot has only 1,000 hours total time but all 500 hours of his multiengine experience is in the model aircraft to be insured. Under these circumstances, the underwriter may agree to insure this pilot at the same rate and limits of liability as he would insure the higher-time pilot.

Most underwriters agree that recency of experience and experience in the model are more important than total time in evaluating a pilot. This assumes that the pilot has a good safety record and appropriate FAA ratings for the operation involved. Underwriters also generally prefer professional pilots (whose only responsibility is flying the company airplane) than pilots who have other duties (a corporate vice president who also flies). Pilots who have other responsibilities in addition to flying generally are not as experienced as full-time professional pilots, and they also pose a unique exposure in that their piloting judgment might be compromised due to a corporate priority that must be met. In other words, pressure may be exerted in order to get to a particular destination in spite of bad weather or some other hazardous condition such as a short, wet runway or lack of a precision instrument approach at that particular airport.

Often a pilot warranty will include high minimum requirements and several named pilots who do not meet the conditions of the blanket requirement but may qualify by virtue of other factors. In such cases, the underwriter has examined the credentials of these pilots separately, and in some cases, charged an additional premium or added conditions to their use of the aircraft.

Geographic Considerations

The terrain, prevailing weather conditions, and other elements of the geography of airports used and areas of most concentrated flying also have a decided effect upon an underwriter's evaluation of a risk.

Airport location is of particular significance for it has an important bearing on the safe operation of the aircraft insured. Every airplane has minimum required runway lengths determined by the distance necessary for its takeoff and landing rollout. Each minimum is predicated upon the airfield being at sea level and its runway temperature being a constant 59°F. As the elevation of the field and/or the temperature of the runway increases, the minimum also increases. An increase of 1000 feet of elevation or 15°F. of temperature, for example, increases the required minimum runway length by 10 percent. Clearly, one airport in the cool coastal areas of New England might be entirely adequate whereas its twin located 5000 feet above sea level near Denver, Colorado, or on the Mojave Desert of California, where runway temperatures reach 120°F., would be totally unacceptable from an underwriting standpoint.

Other concerns relative to airport location are the probability of exposure to hail and severe windstorm, or other local conditions which result in usually frequent periods of restricted visibility. These factors increase the hazards associated with flight operations and must be considered by the underwriters.

Purpose of Use

Every aircraft risk is unique in its susceptibility to loss by virtue of the type of equipment flown, the attitude and aptitude of its pilots, and the geography of its particular part of the world. Still, each risk must be classified relative to some denominator common to a number of others to permit the insurer to make comparisons. In aviation insurance the purpose for which the aircraft is to be flown is employed as that common denominator. It permits risks exposed to the same general types of perils to be compared with one another and provides the starting point from which the underwriters can proceed in exercising their underwriting judgment. It also provides a basis for rating a particular risk given the unique exposures associated with the different use categories. Many underwriting companies also rely on these categories to study and compare financial results within the general aviation sector of use categories. Each use category presents its own unique set of exposures.

Generally speaking, four *purpose of use categories* are used within the general aviation industry: (1) business and pleasure, (2) industrial aid, (3) commercial, and (4) special use. Each use category contains unique characteristics and exposures, and each category requires its own underwriting approach.

UNDERWRITING B&P, INDUSTRIAL AID, COMMERCIAL, AND SPECIAL USE RISKS

Business and Pleasure

Business and pleasure applies to those risks which involve individually owned aircraft used for the owner's personal purposes for which no charge is made and no direct profit is derived. A number of underwriting challenges are common to risks within this category; pilots of limited experience (many of whom might be transitioning to a more sophisticated aircraft), flying clubs with multiple ownership of aircraft, aircraft which are of low value and marginally equipped, and the exposures associated with operation from airfields having limited facilities. Another challenge in the business and pleasure segment is pilots of limited flying experience upgrading to single-engine and multiengine turbine aircraft. These exposures must be underwritten carefully as the hull values can be several million dollars. Even new single-engine or multiengine piston aircraft are valued above $500,000 in many cases so the exposures to underwriting companies continues to increase.

Industrial Aid

The term *industrial aid* applies to corporate-owned aircraft which are used for the transportation of employees, business associates, and executives and which are flown by professional pilots hired on a full-time basis specifically for that purpose. These pilots normally are well qualified, commercially rated, and at the controls many hours every month. Normally a considerable degree of control is exercised over the nature and conduct of the flights by either the corporate owner or a chief pilot. Consequently, industrial aid is considered a preferred type of business in aviation insurance and the rate structure is lower than business and pleasure. The accident record for this class compares favorably with that of the airlines. Key underwriting considerations in this segment include average load factors, percentage of passengers who are company guests, geographical area of operations and formal initial and recurrent training programs undertaken by the pilots. Underwriters are also interested in the flight department management team as well for larger industrial aid risks.

Commercial Use

The term *commercial use* refers to charter operators, air taxi operators, and others who operate aircraft under part 135 of the Federal Aviation Regulations for general profit in transporting persons and cargo for hire, undertaking high altitude photography, and conducting similar operations not requiring a special waiver from the Federal Aviation Administration. This use category also includes leasing aircraft to renter pilots and giving flight instruction to student pilots and others. This latter category including rental and instruction is commonly referred to as *limited commercial use.*

In underwriting and rating risks in this category, two important factors must be considered. First, commercial aircraft are flown for many more hours a year than are business and pleasure or industrial aid aircraft and these extra hours increase the exposure at least proportionately. This is particularly true when we consider the number of pilots with varying levels of experience who may operate a particular aircraft. This can vary from an experienced pilot on a cross-country charter flight to a student pilot practicing touch and go's. This factor has an important bearing on the rates for the hull coverage. With the increased usage associated with commercial risks comes increased attritional losses, which are those partial hull losses involving bird strikes, prop strikes, foreign object damage to engines, and lightning strikes just to name a few. These losses increase the costs of insurance for commercial operators.

Second, and more important, a very strong obligation exists on the part of the commercial operator to ensure the safety and well-being of the members of the public he serves. This obligation is recognized by the courts as being considerably higher than the obligation of a private owner to a guest and is reflected in the comparative size of awards granted in legal liability cases (see chapter 6). For these two reasons, rates for commercial exposures are generally much higher than are rates for other noncommercial categories.

Special Use

Special use is reserved for unusual purposes, several of which require waivers from the Federal Aviation Administration. Included within this class are crop dusting, low altitude photography, banner towing, pipeline patrol, flight testing, hunting, fire fighting, law enforcement, and many others. The only common denominator which exists between risks in this category is that each represents exposure to some of aviation's more serious perils. As a use classification it is of little assistance to the underwriter in providing a framework for developing rates, but it does serve to identify those risks which require special and detailed underwriting attention.

UNDERWRITING ROTORCRAFT

Underwriting rotorcraft has changed appreciably since the mid-1970s. Several important underlying factors have contributed to this situation: (1) safety, and the implementation of professional operating standards among the operators; (2) recurrent training, done either in-house or through professional centers has expanded greatly in scope; (3) turbine-powered rotorcraft are statistically 4.5 times less accident prone than their piston counterparts; and (4) technological improvements in rotorcraft construction and in cockpit avionics .

Underwriters are particularly concerned with two factors when evaluating helicopter risks: (1) Purpose of use. Because of the helicopter's operational versatility and limited total production units, helicopters are difficult to rate as opposed to fixed-wing aircraft. They may be used for executive transportation, pipeline patrol, offshore oil rig supply, sling cargo, police patrol, air ambulance, and other operations. Additional factors related to the purpose of use is the extent to which the operator flys in IFR conditions. The type of helicopter, particularly whether it is single-engine or multiengine, has an important bearing on the underwriting decision and ultimately the rating for a given risk. It is important to note the different exposure dynamics involved with the different purposes of use. Depending on the usage, operators could be landing on rooftop helipads in an urban environment, engaging in long over water flights, or flying over empty fields in a rural setting. Obviously the exposures can vary dramatically. (2) Pilot qualifications. Helicopters can be very unforgiving in an emergency, demanding the highest degree of skill from the pilot. A pilot's overall qualifications total flying hours, rotary-wing flight time, and experience in the make and model are key elements in the underwriting selection process. Formal initial or recurrent pilot training programs are also an important factor in the rotorcraft underwriting process.

EVALUATING AND UNDERWRITING GROUND RISKS – AIRPORT LIABILITY RISKS AND FIXED BASED OPERATOR RISKS

Airport Liability Risks

Owners and operators of airports are liable for all damage caused by their failure to exercise reasonable care. Their liability extends not only to lessees, airplane passengers, or other persons using the facilities of the airport, but also to spectators, visitors, and other members of the public who may be on or about the premises. Underwriters investigate all aspects of an airport's operation before entertaining the risk. The airport risk spectrum ranges from a grass strip in a small town to a large international airport in a major metropolitan region. All must show evidence of experienced personnel, careful maintenance, and adherence to regulations.

Medium to large airport risks are typically put out to bid each year or every few years. In recent years the market has been very competitive in the airport segment, especially for some of the larger airports in major U.S. cities. Liability limits can reach $500 million for the larger airports and in some cases the limits are even higher. Most insurance companies set up reinsurance to handle these larger limits. In the aftermath of September 11, special attention is now paid by underwriters to airport security measures. One of the key factors in underwriting airports is the extent to which the airport engages in service operations, which are those operations involving aircraft fueling, hangaring, maintenance, and other related activities. Most airports outsource service operations functions to fixed based operators and these types of exposures are discussed in the next section. Another important factor is total passenger movement at a given airport. Passenger movement data indicates important exposure details that form the basis on which underwriters can price the account based on expected losses. Generally speaking, higher passenger movement indicate higher claim frequency (primarily slip and fall claims) and increased chances of a high severity loss that might arise in a heavy airline operations environment.

An airport liability policy is written subject to the careful completion and approval of a detailed application (see the samples following this chapter). To properly assess the risk, underwriters need the following information:

1. Name, address, and business of the applicant.
2. Name and location of the airport and the extent of the applicant' s occupancy. Total acreage of the airport and estimated miles of roads.
3. Complete description of all hangars and other buildings on the airport occupied by the applicant. Elevators, escalators, moving sidewalks, and sprinkler system if any, must be identified.
4. Type and description of runways. Type includes sod, blacktop, grave], ce-= ment. Length, width, overrun area, clear zone, and obstructions must be identified (Airport Layout Plan).
5. Height of airport above sea level.
6. FAA classification (under the National Plan of Integrated Airport Systems).
7. Annual airline and general aviation operations (local and itinerant). Also, the number of airline enplanements.
8. Airport crash, fire and rescue capability including a description of facilities, equipment, vehicles, hydrants, and water sources.
9. Airport organizational structure including police and security protection (airport fencing and television monitoring).
10. A copy of all agreements between the applicant and others involving any assumption of liability.
11. Description of any new construction, repairs and alterations including a list of the independent contractors and the cost.
12. Whether the airport has a control tower and the extent of the applicant's jurisdiction over airport traffic control.
13. Operations of the applicant including estimated annual gross receipts.

14. List of all airport vehicles, aircraft, and helicopters.
15. List of all sublessees and their operations on the airport including their insurance requirements.
16. Particulars concerning the applicants responsibility for tie down and hangaring aircraft. Complete description of the area including maximum value of any one aircraft and of all aircraft in the applicant's custody at any one time.
17. Type of fueling operation and the applicant's participation.
18. Safety program to protect the public from accidents.
19. Loss experience over the past 3 to 5 years including dates, type of claim and the cost or reserve. Underwriters are interested in evaluating the severity and frequency of airport claims. Airports generally have higher claim frequency (resulting from slips and falls by airport passengers) than other aviation risks and as a result underwriting companies may impose a deductible to avoid the smaller payouts. Underwriters must be aware that high claim frequency will create increased loss adjusting expenses and this must be taken into consideration when developing the pricing for airport liability policies.

Fixed Based Operator Risks

Fixed based operators engage in a variety of aviation service functions and must be carefully underwritten because of the scope of their potential exposures. Fixed based operators typically sell fuel, move and store aircraft, sell aircraft and related parts, and perform various aircraft maintenance functions. The primary exposure areas for FBOs involve premises, products/completed operations, and hangarkeepers liability.

Premises exposures consist primarily of office, ramp, and ongoing operations exposures. Products/completed operations exposures involve products sales such as fuel and work performed by the FBO such as aircraft maintenance. Products/completed operations exposures are measured estimating gross receipts for the next 12 months. Gross receipt projections are normally required for fuel and lubricants, new and used aircraft, aircraft parts, and aircraft repairs and servicing. To measure hangarkeepers' exposures, underwriters must know the number of planes hangared or tied down and the average value of any one aircraft as well as the aggregate value of all aircraft. Tie-down facilities, if used, should be described in detail. Information concerning the average value of aircraft hangared or tied down is important in determining the limits of liability to be written. Ordinarily underwriters require that the limits of liability can not be less than the average value for each aircraft and the average aggregate value of all aircraft. From an underwriting standpoint, acceptance of hangar keepers' liability coverage depends to a large extent upon the housekeeping practices of the insured. Moving expensive aircraft on the ramp and in and out of hangars represents significant exposures. Management experience and oversight as well as proper training of line personnel are keys to minimizing these exposures. Fire is another hangarkeepers peril and proper maintenance of hangars is vital. Fire suppression systems are an important underwriting consideration. Furthermore, since aircraft repairs generally require use of dopes, paints, washing of engines with inflammables, and welding parts, it is necessary to know where these inflammables are stored and whether the repairs are made in the hangar where aircraft are stored. Of equal importance are the construction of hangars and repair shops and the location of repair shops in relation to storage hangars.

In recent years, FBO insurance has been impacted by a couple of factors. First, hangarkeepers' losses sustained by insurance carriers that result in an FBO's negligence in moving aircraft have become greater on the severity scale. Increased hull values and increased loss adjusting costs have dramatically increased the severity of many hangarkeepers' losses. This has resulted in insurance companies losing money in this class of business. Many insurance companies have imposed significant hangarkeepers' deductibles (some as high as $50,000 per aircraft) to help improve underwriting results. Many insurance companies now require standardized training of line personnel in order to help minimize hangarkeepers' losses.

Secondly, aircraft maintenance performed by FBOs has become another problem area from an underwriting standpoint. With the enactment of the General Aviation Revitalization Act in 1994, FBOs have found themselves on the wrong side of the equation. The act prohibits lawsuits against aircraft manufacturers when the aircraft involved is more than 18 years old. This has created a situation where FBOs are becoming the targets of lawsuits because of past maintenance or other service operations performed on aircraft.

Although it is becoming more and more important for FBOs to have adequate coverage, it is becoming increasingly expensive and in some cases it may not be available.

PRICING VARIOUS AVIATION RISKS

The pricing of insurance is called *ratemaking*. It is the calculation of the contribution that each policyholder shall make in order to bear his or her fair share of losses and expenses. The price a person pays for insurance is called a premium and is the rate per unit of coverage times the units purchased. The rate is the cost per unit of protection purchased. The unit of protection varies with the line of insurance. In hull insurance, the rate is for each $100 of protection; in workers' compensation, the unit of exposure is each $100 of payroll; and in products liability, it is for each $1,000 of gross receipts.

The pricing problem in insurance is complicated because rates have to be established before all costs are known. Ratemakers have to forecast the probable losses from a study of past experience. Thus an element of guesswork is involved. Furthermore, since insurance is a regulated industry, its rates are subject to a degree of state control, and companies may be frequently called upon to justify a certain rate.

Aviation Rates

In contrast to other property and casualty fields no rating schedule exists showing rates applicable to different classes of aviation risk. In the aviation field there is an open market. Rates, therefore, are not standard and are to a large degree based upon judgment. Some states require that companies file "rate spreads." Such a filing indicates a minimum and a maximum rate but leaves the actual rate for a specific risk to the judgment of the underwriter. The rates charged are influenced to a great extent by the company's own experience and the current economic cycle.

Some companies furnish rate sheets that provide an average rate for an average risk of a particular class. These rates are not firm, and the final rate quotation is made only after the underwriter has been given an opportunity to appraise the particular risk. Competition also influences rates.

Rates are ordinarily quoted on an annual basis. There are risks that do not lend themselves to annual quotations predicated upon the number of aircraft owned. FBOs that have an active turnover of owned aircraft may secure a policy requiring periodic reporting of aircraft, usually monthly or quarterly. Premiums are determined from these reports which show the aircraft at risk during a particular time.

Hull and Liability Rates

Hull rates are generally annual and expressed either as a percentage of the insured value or as a dollar amount applicable to each $100 of insured value. A base rate is determined for the class of business largely based upon the value of the hull. To this premium are added debit or credit percentages because of usage, pilot experience, policy modifications, and numerous other items that enter into the negotiations of an aircraft premium under any rating scheme.

The following examples demonstrate a typical premium quotation for a single-engine and multiengine aircraft operator:

1. Aircraft: Single-engine fixed gear
   Owner: Individual with business included as named insured
   Seating: Three passengers and one pilot
   Coverage: All Risks Ground and Flight
   Insured Value: $40,000
   Deductibles: $50 ground—no motion and $250 in flight and taxiing
   Use: Business and Pleasure
   Pilot Warranty: Any Private Pilot or better
   Territorial Limits: United States of America, Canada, Mexico, or the Bahama Islands

Hull (base rate)	*Annual Premium*
2% (or $2/$100 value)	$800

   Debits and Credits (example only)
   a. 15% credit off base rate for open pilot warranty with minimum of 300 hours.
   b. 20% surcharge on base rate to include a named student pilot.
   c. 10% credit off base for named private with 150 hours.
   d. For multiple ownership above basic two pilots add 5% for each additional private pilot and 10% for each additional student.
   e. 10% surcharge on base rate if aircraft is tied down.
   f. $40 credit off annual premium to increase in flight and taxiing deductible to $500.

Liability Coverage	*Limits of Liability*	*Annual Base Premium*
Bodily Injury and Property Damage including passengers	$1,000,000 each occurrence	$560

   Similar to the hull coverage, debits and credits are added to the base premium depending upon a multitude of underwriting factors.

   Medical payments coverage is also generally written with a limit of $5,000 or $10,000 per seat and can include or exclude crew members. The premium per seat is quoted on a flat annual basis.
2. Aircraft: Multiengine turbo-prop
   Owner: Corporation
   Seating: Seven passengers and two crew
   Coverage: All Risks Ground and Flight
   Insured Value: $1,300,000
   Deductibles: Nil
   Use: Industrial Aid
   Pilot Warranty: PIC 3,000 hours TT, 1,000 hours ME and 250 hours in make and model, ATP Certificate, Copilot 500 hours TT, 100 hours ME and 25 hours in make and model, Commercial Certificate.
   Territorial Limits: Western hemisphere including Caribbean Basin, Central and South America

Hull (base rate)	*Annual Premium*
.55% (or .55/$100 value)	$7,150

In the case of large aircraft used for industrial aid, there are no debits and credits to the rate because it is contemplated that the aircraft is operated by a professional crew who receive recurrent training. In addition, the loss experience is much more favorable for industrial aid risks, making it a preferred class of business.

Liability Coverage	*Limits of Liability*	*Annual Premium*
a. Bodily Injury and Property Damage including Passengers	$20,000,000 each occurrence	$4,000
b. Guest Voluntary Settlement (Admitted Liability Coverage)	$250,000 each person including crew	included

Guest voluntary settlement coverage is generally quoted on a per seat basis but can also be quoted as a rate per $1 ,000 of coverage. Crew members can be included or excluded, and the coverage follows the number of seats on the aircraft. The admitted liability rate generally depends upon two factors: (1) the average number of passengers carried (load factor) and (2) the average mix of employees versus guests. Remember that employees cannot sue their employer and so their only recourse would be to accept the admitted payment.

Liability Coverage	*Limits of Liability*	*Annual Premium*
c. Non-Ownership Liability Coverage	$20,000,000 each occurrence	included
d. Medical Payments Coverage	$10,000 each occurrence including crew	included
Other Policy Extensions		
e. Premises/hangar keepers' liability including damage to non-owned hangars		included
f. Products liability coverage on sale of insured aircraft		included
g. Waiver of "Fellow Employee" exclusion and coverage for "Cross Liability" included		included
h. Spare engine and equipment while detached and/or in transit		$200
i. Contractual liability included for incidental contracts or as required for operations		included

j.	Baggage liability including crew	$2,500 each person	included
k.	Breach of Warranty in favor of the First National Bank		included
I.	War Risks coverage		$450

Airport Liability Rates

Airports and the liability exposures they represent can vary considerably, from a Chicago O'Hare which is literally a city unto itself handling all types of aircraft activity, to a small grass strip on the outskirts of a rural town which serves as the base for several general aviation aircraft. Consequently, when the underwriter considers the factors which affect premises liability rates, the annual premium can vary from hundreds of thousands of dollars to several thousand dollars. Many larger airports will carry limits up to $500 million while a $1 million single limit of liability protection may suffice for the small grass strip. Pricing is highly dependent on the limit purchased and generally speaking the bulk of the premium charge comes from the premises rate. Airport liability rates are also a function of current market conditions, an airport's loss history, passenger movements, and the airport's involvement in service operations. If the airport engages in service operations then the rating process begins to resemble that of an FBO which is discussed in the next section. The following illustrates how a typical airport liability quotation would work:

Rating assumptions: assumes < 500,000 passenger movements annually, airport does not engage in service operations

Coverages	Limit of Liability	Premium
General Aggregate Limit	$50,000,000	$42,000
Personal & Advertising Injury	$50,000,000	$Included
Products-Completed Operations	$50,000,000	$Included
Each Occurrence Limit	$50,000,000	$Included
Fire Damage Limit	$250,000 any one fire	$Included
Medical Expense	$5,000 any one person	$Included
Hangarkeepers' Limit	$50,000,000 per aircraft/per loss	$Included
War Liability	$50,000,000	$4,200
Non-Owned Aircraft Liability (limited to 12 seats)	$50,000,000	$2,500
Applicable Hangarkeepers' Deductible:	$25,000 Each aircraft	

Note: if the airport was engaged in service operations then there would most likely be premium charges for products/completed operations and hangarkeepers and would be calculated in accordance with the methods described in the next section

FBO ratemaking

Fixed base operators and other commercial risks that have a fleet of aircraft (at least five) that change during the year as aircraft are bought and sold, often have their hull and liability coverages written under a reporting form policy. Under this arrangement, the insured normally pays a deposit premium at inception and is required to report his aircraft monthly including (1) year, make, and model of the insured aircraft, (2) FAA registration "N" number, (3) insured value, and (4) number of days the aircraft was at risk during the month. The hull and liability coverages can be written on a rate per diem or per flying hour or a combination of both. For example, the hull rate for an aircraft flown commercially (instruction, rental and charter) may be $6 per $100 insured value for all of the FBO's aircraft with reported values from $25,000 to $35,000. A $30,000 aircraft would generate an annual premium of $1,800. Based on an annual hourly exposure of 1,200 hours the monthly rate and premium would be as follows:

Rate / flying hour		*Hrs. flown / mo.*		*Insured Value*	*Monthly Premium*
$6/$100 = .005 X 1,200 hrs.		100	X	$30,000 =	$150

If the actual hours flown during the year exceed the estimate (1,200 hrs. in this case) the additional premium in considered fully earned. On the other hand, if the hours do not materialize, the insured is generally subject to a minimum premium of at least 60 percent of the estimated annual premium.

FBOs generally prefer reporting form policies because premiums (subject to a deposit and minimums) are paid on a monthly pay as-you-go basis which yields important cash flow benefits. In addition, higher premiums are paid during months of increased flight activity and lower premiums during inactive periods when revenues are lower.

FBO insurance (excluding hull and liability exposures) is usually priced with three components—premises, products, and hangarkeepers. Premises is largely a function of the limit and number of locations. Products liability rates vary according to the product classification and limit of liablity. For example, based on limits of $1,000,000 each occurrence for bodily injury and r property damage, the following rates might apply:

Classification	*Rate per $1,000 of Gross Receipts*
Sale of New Aircraft	$ 1.00
Sale of Aircraft Parts	2.50
Sale of Used Aircraft	3.50
Sale of Gas and Oil	4.35
Aircraft Servicing and Repair	15.78

Basic hangarkeepers' liability rates largely depend upon the limits required and can be affected by the deductibles applicable to this coverage. Hangarkeepers' rates can also depend on whether or not the insured is simply storing aircraft or does repair and servicing work in the hangar facility. Geography can also play a role since rates might be higher in climates producing ice and snow on a regular basis. As an example, pricing for hangarkeepers' coverage of $1,000,000 per aircraft/ $1,000,000 per loss with a $25,000 per aircraft deductible can range from $5,000 to $6,000 annually.

This brief discussion of aviation rates was merely intended to highlight some examples of rating used in the aviation insurance industry. A complete analysis would require a working knowledge of aviation underwriting and a complete review of a company's underwriting manuals which are continually revised and updated.

KEY TERMS

Underwriting
Catastrophe loss
Limited spread of risks
Preselection
Postselection
Configuration
Conventional landing gear
Tricycle landing gear
Minimum pilot requirements
Purpose of use categories
Business and pleasure
Industrial aid
Commercial use
Limited commercial use
Special use
Ratemaking

REVIEW QUESTIONS

1. What is the purpose of underwriting? How does underwriting serve to provide equity in the rating structure?
2. Discuss the unique nature of aviation exposures as distinguished from other lines of insurance. Why is the limited spread of risks such a difficult problem for underwriters? How does diversification of aircraft and rapidity of change complicate this problem?
3. Give some examples of how underwriters preselect risks. What is meant by postselection? Describe the conflict which often arises between production and underwriting.
4. Describe the basic information required by underwriters in order to offer an aircraft hull and liability quotation.
5. Discuss the major consideration taken by underwriters in reviewing the following areas: type of aircraft and equipment; pilots; geographical considerations; and purpose of use.
6. Distinguish between "business and pleasure" and "industrial aid." Why do you think hull rates for an aircraft used exclusively for charter operations are relatively low compared with an aircraft used for student instruction and rental (limited commercial)? On the other hand liability rates for an aircraft used exclusively for charter operations are relatively high compared to aircraft used for student instruction and rental purposes. Why? Describe what is meant by special use.
7. What are the two factors that underwriters are particularly concerned with in evaluating helicopter risks?
8. What is the basic information underwriters require in evaluating the airport liability risk? What underwriting information is needed for products and hangar keepers' liability?
9. Obtain a quotation for a single and multiengine aircraft used for business and pleasure. Determine the underwriting details including value, limits of liability, territorial limits, pilots, and so forth.
10. What is the big advantage of reporting form policies?

Applications

G L O B A L   A E R O S P A C E

APPLICATION FOR AIRCRAFT HULL AND LIABILITY INSURANCE

(Check which is desired) ☐ A QUOTATION ☐ INSURANCE POLICY ☐ RENEWAL POLICY

NAME OF APPLICANT ______________________________

ADDRESS ______________________________

____

BUSINESS OR OCCUPATION OF APPLICANT ______________________________

APPLICANT IS: ☐ INDIVIDUAL(S) ☐ CORPORATION ☐ PARTNERSHIP ☐ OTHER ______________

INSURANCE IS REQUESTED FROM 12:01 A.M. ______________ 20 ______ to 12:01 A.M. ______________ 20 ______

Liability Coverage	LIMITS OF LIABILITY DESIRED	
	Each Person	Each Occurrence
☐ SINGLE LIMIT BODILY INJURY AND PROPERTY DAMAGE LIABILITY: Passengers: ☐ included, ☐ excluded	$ Each Passenger	$
☐ OTHER LIABILITY ______________	$	$

☐ MEDICAL EXPENSE Crew ☐ included ☐ excluded	$ Each Person

Physical Damage Coverage	AMOUNT OF INSURANCE DESIRED (attach explanation if other than current market value).	DEDUCTIBLES	
		IN MOTION	NOT IN MOTION
AIRCRAFT 1. ☐ ALL RISK BASIS ☐ ALL RISK BASIS NOT IN FLIGHT ☐ ALL RISK BASIS NOT IN MOTION	$ ______________	☐ $1,000 ☐ $500 ☐ $______ ☐ ______%	☐ $100 ☐ $______ ☐ ______%
AIRCRAFT 2. ☐ ALL RISK BASIS ☐ ALL RISK BASIS NOT IN FLIGHT ☐ ALL RISK BASIS NOT IN MOTION	$ ______________	☐ $1,000 ☐ $500 ☐ $______ ☐ ______%	☐ $100 ☐ $______ ☐ ______%

Aircraft: If Airworthiness Certificate is other than Standard, please explain ______________

If engine is being operated beyond TBO, please explain ______________

Year, Make and Model	FAA Registration Number	Seating Capacity		Land (L) Sea (S) Amph (A)	PURCHASED		Current Market Value (Incl. Extras)	No. of Hours Aircraft Flown In Last 12 Mos.	Est. No. of Hours Next 12 Mos.
		Crew	Other		New or Used	Date			
1.									
2.									

Aircraft usually based at ______________ ☐ Hangared; ☐ Tied-down

(Name of Home Airport, If Private Airport, give detailed location.)

ARE ANY FLIGHTS CONTEMPLATED OUTSIDE CONTINENTAL U.S.? ☐ YES ☐ NO

IF "YES," where: ______________

PURPOSES OF USE (Check all applicable uses)

☐ Pleasure or ☐ Business (not flown by professional pilots employed for this purpose)

☐ Instruction of ______________ (Name of Student)

☐ Corporate-Executive (flown by professional pilots employed for this purpose)

☐ Flying Club

☐ Low Altitude Photography

☐ Patrol Flights ☐ Banner Towing ☐ Crop Dusting

☐ Air Ambulance

☐ Air Hearse

☐ Other Uses not indicated above (explain) ______________

☐ Use for which a charge is made (explain) ______________

____

PILOTS: COMPLETE THIS SECTION (INCLUDING ITEMS 1.-5. BELOW) FOR EVERY PILOT WHO WILL OPERATE AN AIRCRAFT DURING THE POLICY TERM UNLESS A PILOT QUESTIONNAIRE IS COMPLETED BY THE PILOT.

NAME OF PILOT	Date of Birth	Pilot Certification and Ratings								Medical Certificate		Hours Logged as Pilot in Command							
												All Aircraft					In Aircraft Model To Be Insured		
		Stud.	Pvt.	Com'l.	ASEL	AMEL	Instrumt.	ATP	Other	Date of Last Physical	Class	Total	Last 90 Days	Last 12 Mos.	Retract. Gear	Multi-Engine	Total	Last 90 Days	Last 12 Mos.
1.																			
2.																			
3.																			
4.																			

	Pilot No. 1	Pilot No. 2	Pilot No. 3	Pilot No. 4
FAA Certificate No.				
Date of Last Biennial Flight Review:				
Details of other proficiency training:				
Name and address of pilot's employer if other than applicant:				

Explain circumstances if:

1. Any pilots named above have any: (a) physical impairments__________
   (b) waivers, limitations, conditions on their medical certificates or on their airman certificates__________
2. An FAA, Military, or other pilot certificate held by any pilot named above has ever been suspended or revoked__________
3. Any pilot named above has ever been cited for violation of any aviation regulation in any country__________
4. Any pilot named above has ever been involved in any aircraft accident__________
5. Any pilot named above has ever been convicted of or pleaded guilty to a felony or driving while intoxicated__________

APPLICANT is: ☐ Sole owner ☐ Owner subject to mortgage or conditional sales contract. ☐ Lessee ☐ Other - explain__________

If aircraft is encumbered, name and address of lienholder or lessor__________

Amount of encumbrance (excluding interest and finance charges) $__________ Will Breach of Warranty Coverage be required by lienholder? ☐ Yes ☐ No

Member of NBAA? ☐ Yes ☐ No Type Membership: ☐ Corporate ☐ Business ☐ Associate

Name of last aviation insurance carrier (if none so state)__________

To the Applicant's knowledge no damage has been sustained to, nor claims by others have arisen out of the operation of, any aircraft owned by or in the custody of the Applicant except:__________

Has any insurance company or underwriter at any time declined an application submitted by or canceled or refused to renew a policy held by the applicant or any of the pilots names herein in regard to any type of insurance? ☐ Yes ☐ No If so, explain circumstances:__________

All particulars herein are declared to be true and complete to the best of my/our knowledge and no information has been withheld or suppressed and I/we agree that this application and the terms and conditions of the policy in use by the insurer shall be the basis of any contract between me/us and the insurer. I hereby authorize the insurer to investigate all or any qualifications or statements contained herein.

Date__________ **Applicant's Signature(s)**__________

THIS APPLICATION DOES NOT COMMIT THE INSURER TO ANY LIABILITY NOR MAKE THE APPLICANT LIABLE FOR ANY PREMIUM UNLESS AND UNTIL THE INSURER AGREES TO EFFECT THIS INSURANCE.

Name of Agent or Broker__________

Address__________

☐ Broker ☐ Agent

Global Aerospace insurance company in which agency license held __________ __________

G L O B A L   A E R O S P A C E

APPLICATION FOR HELICOPTER HULL AND LIABILITY INSURANCE

GLOBAL AEROSPACE

(Check which is desired) ☐ A QUOTATION ☐ INSURANCE POLICY ☐ RENEWAL POLICY

NAME OF APPLICANT ____________________

ADDRESS ____________________

BUSINESS OR OCCUPATION OF APPLICANT ____________________

APPLICANT IS: ☐ **INDIVIDUAL(S)** ☐ **CORPORATION** ☐ **PARTNERSHIP** ☐ **OTHER** ____________________

INSURANCE IS REQUESTED FROM 12:01 A.M. ____________ 20______ to 12:01 A.M. ____________ 20______

Liability Coverage	LIMITS OF LIABILITY DESIRED	
	Each Person	Each Occurrence
☐ SINGLE LIMIT BODILY INJURY AND PROPERTY DAMAGE LIABILITY: Passengers – ☐ included, ☐ excluded	$ Each Passenger	$
☐ OTHER LIABILITY____________	$	$
☐ MEDICAL EXPENSE Crew – ☐ included, ☐ excluded	$ Each Person	

Physical Damage Coverage

AMOUNT OF HULL INSURANCE

Aircraft 1. $ ____________

Aircraft 2. $ ____________

DEDUCTIBLES ☐ $ ☐ %

Rotors not in motion: ____________

Rotors in motion: ____________

Aircraft Year, Make and Model	FAA REGISTRATION NUMBER	SEATING CAPACITY CREW	SEATING CAPACITY PASS	PURCHASED NEW OR USED	PURCHASED Date	PRICE PAID BY APPLICANT (INCLUDING EXTRAS)	PRESENT ESTIMATED VALUE (INCL. EXTRAS)	ENGINE HRS. SINCE NEW OR SINCE LAST MAJOR OVERHAUL	NO. OF HOURS FLOWN LAST 12 MOS.	EST. FLIGHT HOURS NEXT 12 MOS.
1.										
2.										

Description of special or extra equipment installed on aircraft and spares inventory
Aircraft 1. ____________ Value $ ______
Aircraft 2. ____________ Value $ ______
Spare parts inventory ____________ Value $ ______

APPLICANT IS: ☐ Sole owner ☐ Owner subject to mortgage or conditional sales contract ☐ Lessee ☐ Other - explain ____________

If aircraft is encumbered, name and address of lienholder or lessor____________

Amount of encumbrance (excluding interest and finance charges) $____________ Will Breach of Warranty Coverage be required by lienholder? ☐ Yes ☐ No

AIRCRAFT USE: CHECK USE(S) TO WHICH POLICY IS TO APPLY:

- ☐ Pleasure (Non-Professional Pilots)
- ☐ Business (Non-Professional Pilots)
- ☐ Corporate - Executive (Flown by professional pilots hired for this purpose)
- ☐ Instruction - Initial
- ☐ Instruction - Check-out
- ☐ Instruction - Pilot Upgrade
- ☐ Charter ☐ Passenger ☐ Cargo
- ☐ Air Ambulance, Medvac
- ☐ Police Operations
- ☐ Traffic Watch or News
- ☐ Other Uses Not Listed: ____________
- ☐ Search and Rescue
- ☐ Patrol Flights (describe below)
- ☐ Slash Burning
- ☐ Fire Control, Water Bucket, Fire Support
- ☐ Crop Dusting, Spraying, Seeding
- ☐ External Load - Slung Cargo
- ☐ Pole/Inflight Pick Up and Delivery
- ☐ Logging
- ☐ Heliskiing

Is Airworthiness Certificate other than standard? ☐ Yes ☐ No If yes, explain ____________

Is engine being operated beyond TBO? ☐ Yes ☐ No If yes, explain ____________

Aircraft usually based at____________ Hangared? ☐ Yes ☐ No
(Name of Home Airport or Heliport)

If private heliport, describe facilities and security:____________

Are landing sites not approved by the FAA used?________ If yes, how often?________ Identify sites ____________

Are building top landing pads used?________ If yes, how often? ________ Give location and description ____________

G-31H (8/03)

Areas of Operation: ____ FAR licenses held: ____
Are floats installed? ____ Percentage of time: ____ Value: ____
Are flights at night contemplated? ____ How frequently? ____ Are landing sites lighted? ____
Who performs maintenance? ____

Pilots: COMPLETE THIS SECTION (INCLUDING ITEMS 1.-9. BELOW) FOR EVERY PILOT WHO WILL OPERATE AN AIRCRAFT DURING THE POLICY TERM UNLESS A PILOT QUESTIONNAIRE IS COMPLETED BY THE PILOT.

NAME OF PILOT	Date of Birth	Helicopter Certificate and Ratings					Medical Certificate		Pilot in Command Hours - Logged					Estimated helicopter flight hours next 12 mos.:
									Helicopter					
		Pvt.	Com'l	IFR	ATP	Type Ratings (List)	Date of Last Physical	Class	Total All Aircraft	Total Recip.	Total Turbine	In Model To Be Insured	Total Last 12 Months	
1.														
2.														
3.														
4.														

PILOT	1	2	3	4
1.				
2.				
3.				
4.				
5.				
6.				
7.				
8.				
9.				

1. Has the pilot successfully completed the manufacturer's approved pilot's ground and flight training school for any helicopter? (Yes or No) Specify make and model: ____ Date: ____
2. Does the pilot participate in a formal recurrent training program? (Yes or No)*
3. Was pilot's original rotorcraft rating obtained through the military? (Yes or No)
4. Does the pilot have any physical impairments? (Yes or No)*
5. Does the pilot have an waivers, restrictions, limitations or conditions attached to your medical certificate? (Yes or No)*
6. Has any pilot's FAA, Transport Canada, military or other pilot certificate ever been suspended or revoked? (Yes or No)*
7. Has any pilot ever been cited for any violation of any aviation regulation in any country? (Yes or No)*
8. Has any pilot ever been involved in any aircraft accident? (Yes or No)*
9. Has any pilot ever been convicted or pleaded guilty to a felony or driving while intoxicated? (Yes or No)*

Explain all "yes" answers to these questions: ____

Member of NBAA? ☐ Yes ☐ No Type Membership: ☐ Corporate ☐ Business ☐ Associate
HAI? ☐ Yes ☐ No

Name of last aviation insurance carrier (if none so state) ____

To the Applicant's knowledge no damage has been sustained to, nor claims by others have arisen out of the operation of, any aircraft owned by or in the custody of the Applicant except: ____

Has any insurance company or underwriter at any time declined an application submitted by or canceled or refused to renew a policy held by the applicant or any of the pilots names herein in regard to any type of insurance? ____
If so, explain ____

All particulars herein are declared to be true and complete to the best of my/our knowledge and no information has been withheld or suppressed and I/we agree that this application and the terms and conditions of the policy in use by the insurer shall be the basis of any contract between me/us and the insurer. I hereby authorize the insurer to investigate all or any qualifications or statements contained herein.

Date ____ **Applicant's Signature(s)** ____

THIS QUESTIONNAIRE DOES NOT COMMIT THE INSURER TO ANY LIABILITY NOR MAKE THE APPLICANT LIABLE FOR ANY PREMIUM UNLESS AND UNTIL THE INSURER AGREES TO EFFECT THIS INSURANCE.

Name of Agent or Broker ____
Address ____
☐ Broker ☐ Agent Global Aerospace Member insurance company in which agency license held ____
Are you the holding producer? ☐ Yes ☐ No For how many years? ____

PILOT QUESTIONNAIRE

NAME OF POLICYHOLDER/AIRCRAFT OWNER ______

NAME OF PILOT ______ Date of Birth ______

Address ______

Present Employer ______ Date Employed ______

Address ______ Position Held ______

Previous Employers	Position	Dates

Have you ever been discharged or asked to resign? ______ If so, explain ______

PILOT CERTIFICATE AND RATINGS CURRENTLY HELD

☐ STUDENT	☐ SINGLE ENGINE LAND	☐ CENTER LINE THRUST	☐ MECHANIC AIRCRAFT
☐ PRIVATE	☐ SINGLE ENGINE SEA	☐ OTHER (Specify)	☐ MECHANIC POWER PLANT
☐ COMMERCIAL	☐ MULTI-ENGINE LAND	______	☐ INSTRUMENT RATING, OBTAINED BY
☐ AIRLINE TRANSPORT	☐ MULTI-ENGINE SEA	☐ TYPE RATING (Specify aircraft)	☐ FAA FLIGHT CHECK
☐ INSTRUCTOR	☐ HELICOPTER	______	☐ MILITARY INSTRUMENT CARD

FAA Certificate No. ______ Date first certificated as pilot ______

If student, (a) name of instructor or/FBO ______

(b) airport at which instruction is given ______

Class of medical certificate held ______ Date of last FAA physical examination ______

Physical impairments, if any ______

Waivers, limitations, or conditions specified on medical certificate, if any ______

Date of last Biennial Flight Review ______ Type of aircraft used ______ Date of last simulator instruction ______

Biennial Flight Review conducted by ______ How often? ______

Make and model of aircraft on which approval is sought ______

Have you attended aircraft manufacturer's ground and flight training course or its equivalent? ☐ Yes ☐ No

Type of aircraft: ______ ______ ______

Name of facility: ______ ______ ______

Date: ______ ______ ______

FLYING EXPERIENCE — LOGGED HOURS ONLY

	Make and Model of Aircraft	Dates Flown (By Years)	Pilot in Command	Co-Pilot*	Dual	Total Time	Total Last 90 Days	Total Last 12 Months
SINGLE ENGINE AIRCRAFT								
	TOTAL SINGLE ENGINE							
MULTI-ENGINE & JET AIRCRAFT								
	TOTAL MULTI-ENGINE							
SEAPLANES AND HELICOPTERS								
					GRAND TOTAL			

*Show co-pilot time only if co-pilot is required by aircraft type certificate or is required by regulation under which flight is conducted

EDUCATION

Circle highest year completed: High School 1 2 3 4: College 1 2 3 4: Graduate School 1 2 3 4

	Name of School	Attended From: To:	Did you graduate/complete course?
COLLEGE			
GRADUATE SCHOOL			
BUSINESS OR TECHNICAL SCHOOL			

AIRCRAFT ACCIDENTS

Have you ever been involved in any aircraft accident?_______________ If yes, explain all accidents.

Location	Date:	Make and Model of Aircraft	Registration Number of Aircraft	Probable Cause and Remarks

Explain circumstances if:

1. You have any: (a) physical impairments _______________

(b) waivers, limitations, or conditions on your medical certificate or on your pilot certificate_______________

2. Any FAA, Transport Canada or military pilot certificate held by you has ever been suspended or revoked _______________

____

3. You have ever been cited for violation of any aviation regulation in any country _______________

____

____

4. You have ever been convicted of or pleaded guilty to a felony or driving while intoxicated _______________

____

All particulars herein are declared to be true and complete to the best of my/out knowledge and no information has been withheld or suppressed and I/we agree that this questionnaire and the terms and conditions of the policy in use by the insurer shall be the basis of any contract between me/us and the insurer. I hereby authorize the insurer to investigate all or any qualifications or statements contained herein.

Date _______________ Pilot's Signature _______________

Policyholder's or Applicant's Signature(s) _______________

THIS APPLICATION DOES NOT COMMIT THE INSURER TO ANY LIABILITY NOR MAKE THE APPLICANT LIABLE FOR ANY PREMIUM UNLESS AND UNTIL THE INSURER AGREES TO EFFECT THIS INSURANCE.

Name of Agent or Broker _______________

Address _______________

☐ Broker ☐ Agent

Global Aerospace member insurance company in which agency license held. _______________

APPLICATION FOR FIXED BASE OPERATOR AIRCRAFT HULL AND LIABILITY INSURANCE

Name of Applicant: ______________________________

Address: ______________________________

Form of Business: ☐ Corporation ☐ Individual ☐ Partnership ☐ Joint Venture ☐ Other (Describe) ______________

FBO manager's name: ______________________________

FBO manager's length of experience in aviation operations: ______________ How long has manager been employed by applicant?: ______________

Applicant's aircraft will be operated for the following purposes:

Yes	No	Purpose	Estimated Annual Flight Hours
☐	☐	Rental of aircraft	______
☐	☐	Instruction by flight instructors employed by applicant	______
☐	☐	Instruction by independent flight instructors	______
☐*	☐	Passenger or property carriage for compensation or hire	______
☐	☐	Cargo, package or check operations	______
☐	☐	Sales demonstration of aircraft	______
☐	☐	Private business of applicant/aircraft owner	______
☐	☐	Air ambulance or air hearse	______
☐	☐	Local sightseeing	______
☐	☐	Crop dusting, seeding or spraying	______

*If "Yes," attach copy of applicant's air taxi certificate and operations specifications.

Yes	No	Purpose	Estimated Annual Flight Hours
☐	☐	Transportation of hazardous materials	______
☐	☐	Sky diving	______
☐	☐	Banner towing	______
☐	☐	Aerial photography and survey	______
☐	☐	ROTC flight training	______
☐	☐	Glider towing	______
☐	☐	Air shows, contests or exhibitions	______
☐	☐	Powerline or pipeline patrol	______
Other		______________	______
Other		______________	______
Other		______________	______
Other		______________	______

Attach a description of the minimum ratings and flight experience that you require for pilots to operate each type of aircraft.

Are there any employed or renter pilots or leaseback owner pilots who do not meet your regular minimums for ratings or flight experience for a specific aircraft? ☐ Yes ☐ No

If "Yes," describe: ______________________________

____

____

Do renter pilots complete a written test for each make and model rented? ☐ Yes ☐ No

Do you use written checkout forms to record maneuvers and pilot performance during the rental flight checkout? ☐ Yes ☐ No

Are copies of pilot's license, medical and ground and flight checkout forms maintained on file? ☐ Yes ☐ No

Do all renters sign a rental agreement for each flight? ☐ Yes ☐ No If "Yes," attach copy of agreement.

Describe aircraft key control and dispatching procedures: ______________________________

____

____

____

What procedures do you use to monitor the location, of your aircraft? ______________________________

____

____

____

How many pilots does the applicant employ full time? ______________ part time? ______________

Are charter operations single pilot or dual pilot?

☐ All charter operations have dual pilot crews. ☐ Other (Describe) ______________________________

☐ Dual pilot crews are used only when required by regulation. ______________________________

Applicant will operate aircraft NOT OWNED by the applicant for the following purposes:

Yes	No		Estimated Annual Flight Hours	Yes	No		Estimated Annual Flight Hours
☐	☐	Dual instruction in customer's aircraft	______	☐	☐	Furnishing crew to operate aircraft owned by others	______
☐	☐	Delivery or ferrying of non-owned aircraft	______	☐	☐	Sales demonstration of aircraft on consignment	______
☐	☐	Test flying of non-owned aircraft after maintenance	______				

Other (describe): ______

Do you require customers of these services to include you as an insured on their aircraft insurance and supply a certificate of insurance? ☐ Yes ☐ No

Do you require customers of these services to hold you harmless by written agreement for damage to their aircraft? ☐ Yes ☐ No

Do you have a standard pilot services agreement? ☐ Yes ☐ No If "Yes," attach copy.

Do you charter aircraft for company business? ☐ Yes ☐ No If "Yes," describe usage or attach Non-Owned Aircraft Application ______

Do you use or anticipate using any non-owned aircraft with 25 or more seats? ☐ Yes ☐ No

General Information

How many years has the applicant been in business under the same ownership and management? ______

Does applicant operate lease-back aircraft? ☐ Yes ☐ No If "Yes," attach copy of standard leaseback agreement.

Does applicant operate any aircraft on a long term basis (over 30 days) which are not listed in the following Schedule of Aircraft? ☐ Yes ☐ No If "Yes," describe: ______

Is the applicant's flight school certified in accordance with FAR Part 141? ☐ Yes ☐ No

Does applicant have business operations or aircraft positioned at other airports or locations? ☐ Yes ☐ No If "Yes," describe: ______

Will applicant's aircraft be operated outside the U.S. or Canada? ☐ Yes ☐ No If "Yes," describe type of operation, aircraft and area: ______

Who performs maintenance on applicant's aircraft? ______

Is there any other pertinent information, or any potential change in exposure which materially affect this risk? ☐ Yes ☐ No If "Yes," describe: ______

Aircraft liability and hull insurance now in effect:

Insurance company: ______ Expiration Date: ______

Coverages, limits, and deductibles: ______

Number of years applicant has been insured by current insurance company: ______

Has any insurer cancelled or refused to renew the applicant' insurance? ☐ Yes ☐ No

Loss experience: List all aircraft hull and liability claims for the last five years. Attach separate sheet if necessary. Attach insurance company loss run if available.

Date	Description	Losses: Paid	Reserved	Expenses	Total

Coverages and deductibles requested

Aircraft liability limit $______________ Combined single limit each occurrence

Renter pilot liability limit $______________________________

In flight hangarkeeper's liability limit $______________ Each aircraft $______________ Aggregate

In flight hangerkeeper's deductible $______________ Deductible

Aircraft physical damage deductibles $______________ Deductible in motion

$______________ Deductible not in motion

Are any alternate quotes requested for: ☐ Coverages? ☐ Limits? ☐ Deductibles? If so, describe: ____________________

____

____

What is the maximum value of any one aircraft likely to be covered under the policy during the next twelve months? $____________

Insurance is requested from 12:01 A.M. ______________ 20 ________ to 12:01 A.M. ______________ 20 ________

(standard time at address of applicant)

All particulars herein are declared to be true and complete to the best of my/our knowledge and no information has been withheld or suppressed and I/We agree that this application and the terms and conditions of the policy in use by the insurer shall be the basis of any contract between Me/Us and the insurer. I hereby authorize the insurer to investigate all or any qualifications statements contained herein.

Date__________ Applicants's signature and title ______________________________

This application does not commit the insurer to any liability nor make the applicant liable for any premium unless and until the company agrees to effect this insurance.

Name of agent or broker ______________________________

Address ______________________________________

☐ Broker ☐ Agent Are you the holding producer? ☐ Yes ☐ No If "Yes," for how many years?

Global Aerospace member insurance company in which agency license is held ______________________________

NORTH AMERICAN HOME OFFICE

51 John F. Kennedy Parkway, Short Hills, New Jersey 07078 (973) 379-0800 FAX (973) 379-0900

SCHEDULE OF AIRCRAFT OWNED BY APPLICANT

Aircraft Year, Make & Model	Aircraft Registration	Total Seats	Insured Value	Name and address of Lienholder	Amount of Lien	Hours Flown Last 12 Months	Estimated Percentages Flown			
							Rental	Charter	Instruction	Other

SCHEDULE OF AIRCRAFT LEASED BY APPLICANT

Aircraft Year, Make & Model	Aircraft Registration	Total Seats	Insured Value	Lessor's/Owners Name and Address	Lienholder's Name and Address, Amount of Lien	Hours Flown Last 12 Months	Estimated Percentages Flown				
							By owner	Rental	Charter	Instruction	Other

List all employed and independent contractor pilots, independent flight instructors and leaseback owners operating aircraft:

Name of Pilot	Age	Pilot Certificate and ratings	Pilot is:*	Hours Logged as Pilot in command Total	Retrac. Gear	Multi Eng.	Makes and Models Aircraft pilot will be operating. Indicate if as pilot-in-command or as copilot.
			E IC LBO				
			E IC LBO				
			E IC LBO				
			E IC LBO				
			E IC LBO				
			E IC LBO				
			E IC LBO				
			E IC LBO				
			E IC LBO				
			E IC LBO				
			E IC LBO				
			E IC LBO				

***E=Employee IC=Independent contractor pilot or flight instructor LBO=Leaseback owner**

APPLICATION FOR NON-OWNED AIRCRAFT LIABILITY INSURANCE

NAME OF APPLICANT ______

ADDRESS ______

BUSINESS OR OCCUPATION OF APPLICANT ______

APPLICANT IS: ☐ INDIVIDUAL(S) ☐ CORPORATION ☐ PARTNERSHIP ☐ OTHER______

INSURANCE IS REQUESTED FROM 12:01 A.M. ______20______ to 12:01 A.M.______20______

Liability Coverage		LIMITS OF LIABILITY DESIRED	
		Each Person	Each Occurence
☐	SINGLE LIMIT BODILY INJURY AND PROPERTY DAMAGE LIABILITY: Passengers - ☐ included, ☐ excluded	$	$
☐	OTHER COVERAGE ______	$	$
☐	MEDICAL EXPENSE	$	

DOES APPLICANT HAVE DIRECTIVES REGARDING RENTAL OR CHARTER OF AIRCRAFT, OR USE OF EMPLOYEE'S PERSONAL AIRCRAFT? ☐ YES ☐ NO

IF "YES" ATTACH COPIES OF SUCH DIRECTIVES, BULLETINS, MEMOS, ETC., AND BRIEFLY OUTLINE APPLICANT'S POLICY:______

DESCRIBE ALL RENTAL OR CHARTER OF AIRCRAFT BY APPLICANT, OR APPLICANT'S EMPLOYEES, AND DESCRIBE USAGE INCLUDING PURPOSE OF USE, NAMES OF CHARTER OPERATORS, TYPES OF AIRCRAFT, DESTINATIONS, NUMBER OF FLIGHTS, AND NUMBER OF HOURS FLOWN:______

DO YOU USE OR ANTICIPATE USING ANY NON-OWNED AIRCRAFT WITH 25 OR MORE SEATS? ☐ YES ☐ NO

ARE ANY FLIGHTS CONTEMPLATED OUTSIDE THE UNITED STATES ☐ YES ☐ NO IF "YES," WHERE:______

DO YOU OBTAIN A CERTIFICATE OF INSURANCE FROM EACH AIRCRAFT OPERATOR NAMING YOU AN ADDITIONAL INSURED? ☐ YES ☐ NO

DO YOU REQUIRE A MINIMUM LIMIT OF LIABILITY FROM THE AIRCRAFT OPERATOR? ☐ YES ☐ NO IF "YES", AMOUNT: $______

ARE EMPLOYEE'S PERSONAL AIRCRAFT USED ON APPLICANTS BEHALF? ☐ YES ☐ NO. IF "YES," DESCRIBE USAGE:______

IS THE APPLICANT INCLUDED AS AN INSURED ON EMPLOYEE'S AIRCRAFT INSURANCE AND REQUIRE A CERTIFICATE OF INSURANCE? ☐ YES ☐ NO

DOES APPLICANT OWN OR LEASE ANY AIRCRAFT? ☐ YES ☐ NO IF "YES," DESCRIBE:______

PILOTS: COMPLETE THIS SECTION (INCLUDING ITEMS 1.-5. BELOW) FOR EVERY PILOT WHO WILL OPERATE AN AIRCRAFT DURING THE POLICY TERM UNLESS A PILOT QUESTIONNAIRE IS COMPLETED BY THE PILOT. THIS SECTION NEED NOT BE COMPLETED FOR AIRLINE, CHARTER OR AIR TAXI PILOTS NOT EMPLOYED BY THE APPLICANT.

NAME OF PILOT	Date of Birth	Pilot Certification and Ratings								Medical Certificate		Hours Logged as Pilot in Command				
		Stud.	Pvt.	Com'l.	ASEL	AMEL	Instrumt.	ATP	Other	Date of Last Physical	Class	Total	Retract. Gear	Multi-Engine	Last 90 Days	Last 12 Mos.
1.																
2.																
3.																
4.																

Pilot No.	Hours Flown on Applicants Business		FAA Certificate No.	Date of Last Biennial Flight Review
	Last 12 Mos.	Est. Next 12 Mos.		
1.				
2.				
3.				
4.				

Explain circumstance if:

1. Any pilots named above have any: (a) physical impairments__________
   (b) waivers, limitations, or conditions attached to their medical certificates__________
2. An FAA, Military, or other pilot certificate held by any pilot named above has ever been suspended or revoked__________
3. Any pilot above has ever been cited for violation of any aviation regulation in any country__________
4. Any pilot named above has ever been involved in any aircraft accident__________
5. Any pilot named above has ever convicted of or pleaded guilty to a felony or driving while intoxicated__________

PLEASE COMPLETE THE FOLLOWING ON THE AVIATION INSURANCE CURRENTLY IN FORCE FOR THE APPLICANT:

COVERAGE	NAME OF COMPANY	LIMIT OF LIABILITY	EXPIRATION DATE
Applicant's Aircraft Liability/Hull			
Employee's Aircraft Liability/Hull (if known)			

THE FOLLOWING INFORMATION IS TO BE FURNISHED BY APPLICANT WHO IS NOT AN INDIVIDUAL:

Total number of employees __________ How many of these employees regularly travel in the course of their employment?__________

List location of applicant's branch offices and subsidiaries__________

All particulars herein are declared to be true and complete to the best of my/our knowledge and no information has been withheld or suppressed and I/we agree that this application and the terms and conditions of the policy in use by the insurer shall be the basis of any contract between me/us and the insurer. I hereby authorize the insurer to investigate all or any qualifications or statements contained herein.

Date__________ Applicant's Signature(s)__________

THIS APPLICATION DOES NOT COMMIT THE INSURER TO ANY LIABILITY NOR MAKE THE APPLICANT LIABLE FOR ANY PREMIUM UNLESS AND UNTIL THE INSURER AGREES TO EFFECT THIS INSURANCE.

Name of Agent or Broker__________

Address__________

☐ Broker ☐ Agent

Global Aerospace Member insurance company in which agency license held__________

G L O B A L A E R O S P A C E

APPLICATION FOR AIRPORT LIABILITY INSURANCE

GLOBAL AEROSPACE

Name of Applicant: ______

Address: ______

Business of Applicant: ______

Form of Business: ☐ Public entity ☐ Individual ☐ Partnership ☐ Joint Venture ☐ Other (Describe) ______

Applicant's interest in premises: ☐ Owner ☐ Lessee ☐ Other (Describe) ______

Applicant's occupancy is: ☐ Entire ☐ Part (Describe)

Name and Location of all Airport(s) to be insured: ______

Description and location of other premises or facilities used permanently, occasionally or on a temporary basis in conjunction with airport or business described above: ______

Airport Manager's Name: ______

Manager's length of experience in airport operations: ______ How long has manager been employed by applicant?: ______

Is airport certified under Federal Aviation Regulation Part 139? ☐ Yes ☐ No If "No", is airport completely fenced? ☐ Yes ☐ No

Does the applicant engage in:

If applicable, please provide annual sales receipts for:

	Yes	No	Last Year (Actual)	This Year (Est./Act.)	Next Year (Estimated)
Aircraft fueling?	☐	☐	$______	$______	$______
Aircraft maintenance?	☐	☐	$______	$______	$______
Hangaring of aircraft?	☐	☐	$______	$______	$______
Rental of premises for retail stores or services?	☐	☐	$______	$______	$______
Rental or lease of hangars?	☐	☐			
Rental or lease of land or buildings?	☐	☐			
Operation of aircraft?	☐	☐			
Airline passenger security screening?	☐	☐			
Operation of control tower?	☐	☐			
Operation of Unicom?	☐	☐			
Towing or moving of aircraft?	☐	☐			
Ownership and/or maintenance of navaids, windshear detectors, or aviation communications equipment?	☐	☐			

Other **aviation activities** on or off airport premises? ☐ ☐ If "yes," describe: ______

Any **non-aviation activities** on or off airport premises? ☐ ☐ If "yes," describe: ______

Value of aircraft in applicant's care, custody or control at any one time: Maximum all aircraft $______ Maximum any one aircraft $______

Do airlines use airport? ☐ Yes ☐ No

List all air carriers using the airport including commuter, charter, overnight, and cargo airlines: ______

Largest type of aircraft using the airport: ______

	Last Year (Actual)	This Year (Actual/Estimated)	Next Year (Estimated)
Total annual number of airline passenger enplanements and deplanements:	______	______	______
Total annual number of aircraft movements:	______	______	______

Describe airport crash, fire and rescue protection, EMS and ambulance service. If fire service is off airport, state location and distance. ______

______

______ Who employs CFR and EMS staff? ______

Who provides general security and police services? ______

______ Who employs security guards and police? ______

Who provides airline passenger security screening? ______

______ Who employs security screening staff? ______

Does the applicant operate any medical facilities? ☐ Yes ☐ No Does the applicant employ or contract any medical personnel? ☐ Yes ☐ No

If "yes," describe: ______

______

Does applicant operate auto parking facilities? ☐ Yes ☐ No Name of independent operator of auto parking facility, if applicable: ______

Is applicant held harmless by auto parking operator? ☐ Yes ☐ No Annual revenues from auto parking: $______ Number of parking spaces: ______

Does applicant:

	Yes	No
Have in force a bird strike prevention plan?	☐	☐
Maintain an air crash emergency plan?	☐	☐
Maintain other emergency plan?	☐	☐

If "yes," describe: ______

______

Describe all vehicles and mobile equipment operated by applicant (that are not insured elsewhere): Attach separate sheet if necessary.

Are any vehicles or mobile equipment licensed for use on or used on public roads? ☐ Yes ☐ No

If "yes," describe: ______

Type	Special Equipment	Quantity	Type	Special Equipment	Quantity

Who is responsible for inspection and maintenance of ramps, taxiways and runways? ______

______

Who is responsible for snow removal (if applicable)? ______

______

Who provides janitorial service? ______

Who employs janitorial staff? ______

Who owns fuel tank farms? ______

Who is responsible for their operation and maintenance? ______

Tanks are located: ☐ Above ground Name of Underground Storage Tank (UST) insurance company ______

☐ Below ground Name of Environmental Impairment Liability insurance company: ______

UST and pollution insurance coverages provided ______

Are there any active, inactive or abandoned dumps, landfills or aircraft salvage yards on, adjacent to, or near airport? ☐ Yes ☐ No If "yes," describe: ______

______

______

Do airport premises contain:

			Quantity	Maintained by
Elevators?	☐ Yes	☐ No	______	______
Escalators?	☐ Yes	☐ No	______	______
Moving sidewalks?	☐ Yes	☐ No	______	______
Electric doors?	☐ Yes	☐ No	______	______
Passenger trams?	☐ Yes	☐ No	______	______

During the next 12 months will the applicant be involved in:

If applicable, estimated costs of work performed by:

			Applicant	Contractor
New construction?	☐ Yes	☐ No	$________	$________
Structural Alterations?	☐ Yes	☐ No	$________	$________

Are there any:

Airshows, contests or exhibitions held at the airport? ☐ Yes ☐ No If "Yes", please describe: ____________

Who provides airshow insurance? ____________ Is Applicant an Insured under policy? ☐ Yes ☐ No

What coverages and limits are provided? ____________

Uses of non-owned aircraft on airport business, either chartered or piloted by airport employees? ☐ Yes ☐ No If "Yes", please describe usage or attach non-owned aircraft application: ____________

Insurance requirements for tenants or other parties:

	Minimum liability limits you require them to carry:	Are you an additional insured under their policy?		Are you "held harmless" in your contract with them?	
Airlines	$________	☐ Yes	☐ No	☐ Yes	☐ No
Police, Fire, EMS	$________	☐ Yes	☐ No	☐ Yes	☐ No
Fixed base operators	$________	☐ Yes	☐ No	☐ Yes	☐ No
Contractors	$________	☐ Yes	☐ No	☐ Yes	☐ No
Food/Liquor services	$________	☐ Yes	☐ No	☐ Yes	☐ No
Other tenants	$________	☐ Yes	☐ No	☐ Yes	☐ No
Other vendors*	$________	☐ Yes	☐ No	☐ Yes	☐ No

*including security, parking, and janitorial services.

Attach samples of applicant's standard agreements/contracts with the tenants or other parties.

Does applicant require all tenants and vendors to show proof of insurance (as appropriate) holding applicant harmless? ☐ **Yes** ☐ **No**

Are certificates of insurance maintained on file by applicant? ☐ **Yes** ☐ **No**

Has applicant signed any agreements assuming liability of others? ☐ **Yes** ☐ **No** **If "Yes" attach copies of agreements.**

Airport liability insurance now in effect:

Carrier: ____________ Expiration Date: ________

Coverages, limits, and deductibles: ____________

Loss experience: List all claims for the last five years. Attach separate sheet if necessary. Attach insurance company loss run if available.

Date	Description	Losses: Paid	Reserved	Expenses	Total

Total ________

Workers Compensation insurance now in effect:

Carrier: ______________________________ Expiration Date: ______________

Limits ______________________________

Has any insurer cancelled or refused to renew the applicant's insurance? ☐ Yes ☐ No

Is insurance being requested by public bid? ☐ Yes ☐ No If "Yes", attach complete bid specifications

Insurance is requested from 12:01 A.M. ______________ 20______ to 12:01 A.M. ______________ 20______
(standard time at address of applicant)

Coverages requested Limits of Insurance

Bodily injury and property damage liabilty: $______________ Aggregate

Personal and advertising injury liability: $______________ Aggregate

Medical payments: $______________ Each person

Hangarkeeper's liability: $______________ Each loss

Deductibles requested: $______________ Each occurrence: $______________ Aggregate

Other requested coverages: ______________________________

____

Additional insureds: ______________________________

____

All particulars herein are declared to be true and complete to the best of my/our knowledge and no information has been withheld or suppressed and I/We agree that this application and the terms and conditions of the policy in use by the insurer shall be the basis of any contract between Me/Us and the insurer. I hereby authorize the insurer to investigate all or any qualifications or statements contained herein.

Date__________ Applicant's signature and title ______________________________

This application docs not commit the insurer to any liability nor make the applicant liable for any premium unless and until the company agrees to effect this insurance.

Name of agent or broker ______________________________

Address ______________________________

☐ Broker ☐ Agent Are you the holding producer? ☐ Yes ☐ No For how many years? __________

Global Aerospace Member Insurance Company in which agency license held ______________________________

NORTH AMERICAN HOME OFFICE
51 John F. Kennedy Parkway, Short Hills, New Jersey 07078
(973) 379-0800 FAX (973) 379-0900

G L O B A L   A E R O S P A C E

APPLICATION FOR FIXED BASE OPERATOR AVIATION GENERAL LIABILITY INSURANCE

Name of Applicant: ______

Address: ______

Business of Applicant: ______

Form of Business: ☐ Corporation ☐ Individual ☐ Partnership ☐ Joint Venture ☐ Other (Describe) ______

Description and Location of premises to be insured: ______

Applicant's interest in premises: ☐ Owner ☐ Lessee ☐ Other (Describe) ______

Applicant's occupancy is: ☐ Entire ☐ Part (Describe) ______

Description and location of premises or facilities used on a permanent, occasional or temporary basis in conjunction with the premises or business described above: ______

Premises manager's name: ______

Manager's length of experience in aviation operations: ______ How long has manager been employed by applicant?: ______

Does the applicant engage in:

If applicable, please provide annual sales receipts and/or fuel gallonage for:

	Yes	No	Last Year (Actual)	This Year (Estimated/Actual)	Next Year (Estimated)
Fueling or servicing of airlines?	☐	☐	$ ____ / ____ gals.	$ ____ / ____ gals.	$ ____ / ____ gals.
Fueling of other aircraft?	☐	☐	$ ____ / ____ gals.	$ ____ / ____ gals.	$ ____ / ____ gals.
Fuel storage, wholesaling or flowage arrangements?	☐	☐	$ ____ / ____ gals.	$ ____ / ____ gals.	$ ____ / ____ gals.
Operation or ownership of fuel trucks, tanks or fuel hydrant system?	☐	☐			
Aircraft service or maintenance?	☐	☐	$ ______	$ ______	$ ______
Sale of new aircraft?	☐	☐	$ ______	$ ______	$ ______
Sale of used aircraft?	☐	☐	$ ______	$ ______	$ ______
Sale of parts or equipment (not installed)?	☐	☐	$ ______	$ ______	$ ______
Manufacture of any products?	☐	☐	$ ______	$ ______	$ ______
Rental or lease of hangars or tie downs?	☐	☐	If "Yes," supply specimen copies of lease or rental contracts.		
Hangaring of aircraft?	☐	☐	If "Yes," supply specimen copies of hangaring contract.		
Towing, moving or parking of aircraft?	☐	☐			
Value of aircraft in applicant's care, custody or control at any one time:			Maximum any one aircraft $ ______	Total all aircraft $ ______	
Operation of UNICOM?	☐	☐			
Rental or lease to others of land or buildings?	☐	☐			
Rental of premises to others for retail stores or services?	☐	☐			
Other **aviation activities** on or off airport premises	☐	☐	If "Yes," describe ______		
Any **non-aviation activities** on or off airport premises?	☐	☐	If "Yes," describe ______		

Are non-owned aircraft used on applicant's business, either chartered or piloted by applicant's employees? ☐ Yes ☐ No If "Yes," describe usage or attach non-owned aircraft application: ______

Do you use or anticipate using any non-owned aircraft with 25 or more seats? ☐ Yes ☐ No

Does applicant sponsor or participate in any airshows, contests or exhibitions? ☐ Yes ☐ No If "Yes," please describe: ______________________

____

____

Who provides airshow insurance? ______________________ Is applicant an insured under the airshow policy? ☐ Yes ☐ No

What coverages and limits are provided? ______________________

Is applicant responsible for inspection and maintenance of ramps, taxiways or runways? ☐ Yes ☐ No If "Yes," please describe: ______________________

____

____

Who is responsible for snow removal (if applicable)? ______________________

____

Describe all vehicles (including mobile equipment and automobiles) operated by the applicant on airport premises. Indicate which have coverage on the applicant's auto policy.

Vehicle	Auto coverage?	Vehicle	Auto coverage?	Vehicle	Auto coverage?
__________	☐ Yes ☐ No	__________	☐ Yes ☐ No	__________	☐ Yes ☐ No
__________	☐ Yes ☐ No	__________	☐ Yes ☐ No	__________	☐ Yes ☐ No
__________	☐ Yes ☐ No	__________	☐ Yes ☐ No	__________	☐ Yes ☐ No

Does the applicant's auto insurance policy have any restrictions on vehicle operations on airports? ☐ Yes ☐ No

Are any of applicant's vehicles or mobile equipment which are not covered on the applicant's auto insurance policy operated off the applicant's premises? ☐ Yes ☐ No

Is there a training or licensing program for drivers operating in aircraft movement areas? ☐ Yes ☐ No

Who owns fuel tank farms? ______________________

Who is responsible for their operation and maintenance? ______________________

Who is responsible for fuel testing and quality assurance? ______________________

____

Is there a formal training program in fuel handling and aircraft fueling procedures? ☐ Yes ☐ No If "Yes," describe: ______________________

____

____

Fuel tanks are located: ☐ Above ground Name of Underground Storage Tank (UST) insurance company: ______________________

☐ Below ground Name of Environmental Impairment Liability insurance company: ______________________

Are there any active, inactive or abandoned dumps, landfills or aircraft salvage yards on, adjacent to, or near premises? ☐ Yes ☐ No If "yes," describe: __________

____

Does the applicant's premises contain:

			Quantity	Maintained by
Elevators?	☐ Yes	☐ No	______	______________________
Escalators?	☐ Yes	☐ No	______	______________________
Moving sidewalks?	☐ Yes	☐ No	______	______________________
Electric doors?	☐ Yes	☐ No	______	______________________
Passenger trams?	☐ Yes	☐ No	______	______________________

If applicable, estimated costs of work performed by:

During the next 12 months will the applicant be involved in:

			Applicant	Contractor
New construction?	☐ Yes	☐ No	$ __________	$ __________
Structural Alterations?	☐ Yes	☐ No	$ __________	__________ $

Insurance requirements for sub-tenants, vendors and other parties:

	Minimum liability limits you require them to carry:	Are you an additional insured under this policy?	Are you "held harmless" in your contract with them?
Fuel supplier	$ __________	☐ Yes ☐ No	☐ Yes ☐ No
Name of fuel supplier ______________________			
Contractors	$ __________	☐ Yes ☐ No	☐ Yes ☐ No
Food/Liquor services	$ __________	☐ Yes ☐ No	☐ Yes ☐ No
Sub-tenants	$ __________	☐ Yes ☐ No	☐ Yes ☐ No
Other vendors*	$ __________	☐ Yes ☐ No	☐ Yes ☐ No

*including security, parking, and janitorial services.

Attach samples of applicant's standard agreements or contracts with the sub-tenants or other parties.

Does applicant require all tenants and vendors to show proof of insurance (as appropriate)? ☐ Yes ☐ No

Are certificates of insurance maintained on file by applicant? ☐ Yes ☐ No

Has applicant signed any agreements assuming liability of others? ☐ Yes ☐ No If "Yes," attach copies of agreements.

Is there any other pertinent information, or any potential changes in exposure which materially affect this risk? ☐ Yes ☐ No If "yes," describe: ______________

____

____

____

____

____

General liability insurance now in effect:

Carrier: ______________________________ Expiration Date: ______________

Coverages, limits, and deductibles: ______________________________

____

Number of years applicant has been insured by current insurance company: ______________

Workers Compensation insurance now in effect:

Insurance company: ______________________________ Expiration Date: ______________

Loss experience: List all claims for the last five years **other than** Workers' Compensation claims. Attach separate sheet if necessary. Attach insurance company loss run if available.

Date	Description	Losses			
		Paid	Reserved	Expenses	Total

Total ______________

Are loss amounts shown above reduced by a deductible? ☐ Yes ☐ No If "Yes," describe deductible ______________

Are loss amounts shown above reduced by a self-insured retention (SIR)? ☐ Yes ☐ No If "Yes," describe SIR program ______________

Has any insurer cancelled or refused to renew the applicant's insurance? ☐ Yes ☐ No

Insurance is requested from 12:01 A.M. ______________ **20** ________ **to 12:01 A.M.** ______________ **20** ________

(standard time at address of applicant)

Coverages and deductibles requested	**Limits of Insurance**		**Deductibles**			
Bodily injury and property damage liability:	$ ________	Each occurrence	$ ________	Per claim	$ ________	Per occurrence
including Products-Completed Operations	☐ Yes ☐ No					
Personal and advertising injury liability:	$ ________	Aggregate	$ ________	Per claim	$ ________	Per offense
Fire Damage:	$ ________	Any one fire				
Medical payments:	$ ________	Each person				
Hangarkeepers' liability:	$ ________	Each loss	$ ________	Per loss		
	$ ________	Each aircraft	$ ________	Per aircraft		

What additional insureds, waivers, indemnifications, hold harmlesses or other contractual provisions are required? ______________

____

____

____

Are any alternate quotes requested for: ☐ Coverages? ☐ Limits? ☐ Deductibles? If so, describe: ______________________________

____

____

All particulars herein are declared to be true and complete to the best of my/our knowledge and no information has been withheld or suppressed and I/We agree that this application and the terms and conditions of the policy in use by the insurer shall be the basis of any contract between Me/Us and the insurer. I hereby authorize the insurer to investigate all or any qualifications or statements contained herein.

Date __________ Applicant's signature and title ______________________________

This application does not commit the insurer to any liability nor make the applicant liable for any premium unless and until the company agrees to effect this insurance.

Name of agent or broker ______________________________

Address ______________________________

☐ Broker ☐ Agent Are you the holding producer? ☐ Yes ☐ No If "Yes," for how many years? __________

AAU member insurance company in which agency license is held ______________________________

USAIG All-Clear Aircraft Insurance Application

Name of Applicant ______

Address ______

You are ☐ Individual ☐ Corporation ☐ Partnership ☐ Other, explain ______

Your business is ______

Your present aircraft insurance company is ______ Policy Expires ______

Has Applicant had any accidents or incidents? ☐ No ☐ Yes (Explain "Yes" on reverse side)

Has any insurer canceled or refused to renew any aviation insurance for you or any of your pilots? ☐ No ☐ Yes (Explain "Yes" on reverse side)

Aircraft Information

Year ______ Make and Model ______ FAA "N" No. ______

Capacity: Pass. ______ Crew ______ Standard Airworthiness Category ☐ No ☐ Yes

Is aircraft equipped with any modifications not provided by manufacturer (STOL kit, performance devices, etc.) ☐ No ☐ Yes

Explain "Yes" answer ______

Aircraft is a landplane ☐ Yes ☐ No (describe) ______ is it usually hangared? ☐ No ☐ Yes

Aircraft is usually based at ______

Purchase date ______ Purchase price (with equipment) $______ Current Value $______

Engine Hours Single ______ Twin (L) ______ (R) ______ Airframe Hours ______

Explain "Yes" answers on reverse side of application.

Will any charge (other than operating expenses) be made for the use of the aircraft? ☐ No ☐ Yes
Will the aircraft be used for anything other than transporting people? ☐ No ☐ Yes
Will the aircraft be used anyplace other than at paved runway airports? ☐ No ☐ Yes
Will the aircraft be used outside the continental United States? ☐ No ☐ Yes
Do you own or exclusively lease any other aircraft? ☐ No ☐ Yes
Do you use non-owned aircraft? ☐ No ☐ Yes
Will the aircraft be used for student or pilot instruction? ☐ No ☐ Yes
Name of Instructor ______ Flight School ______

Pilot Information Data required on all pilots who will operate the aircraft.

Pilot No. 1

Name ______
Birthdate / / Soc. Sec. No. ______
Occupation ______
Year learned to fly ______ Last Medical / /
Last BFR / / In Make/Model A/C ______
FAA Pilot Certificates held ☐Stu. ☐Pvt. ☐Comm. ☐ATP ☐CFI ☐ ______

Pilot-in-Command Hours

All Aircraft			This Make & Model		S.E.	Multi
Total	Last 12 Mo.	Last 90 Days	Total	Last 90 Days	Ret. Gr.	Eng

Total Jet	Total Turbo Prop	Helicopters		Seaplanes	
		Piston Total	Turbine Total	S/E Total	Multi Eng. Total

Recurrent/Transition Courses: Describe and give dates of last courses attended ______

- Current FSI Pro Card or Simuflite Card ______
- FAA Pilot Proficiency Award Program participant? ______
  If "Yes", what phase have you completed? ______
  For what type aircraft? ______
  Date completed ______

Pilot No. 2

Name ______
Birthdate / / Soc. Sec. No. ______
Occupation ______
Year learned to fly ______ Last Medical / /
Last BFR / / In Make/Model A/C ______
FAA Pilot Certificates held ☐Stu. ☐Pvt. ☐Comm. ☐ATP ☐CFI ☐ ______

Pilot-in-Command Hours

All Aircraft			This Make & Model		S.E.	Multi
Total	Last 12 Mo.	Last 90 Days	Total	Last 90 Days	Ret. Gr.	Eng Total

Total Jet	Total Turbo Prop	Helicopters		Seaplanes	
		Piston Total	Turbine Total	S/E Total	Multi Eng. Total

Recurrent/Transition Courses: Describe and give dates of last courses attended ______

- Current FSI Pro Card or Simulflite Card ______
- FAA Pilot Proficiency Award Program participant? ______
  If "Yes", what phase have you completed? ______
  For what type aircraft? ______
  Date completed ______

390 AC Rev. (10/96) (Page 1 of 2) See reverse side

EXPLAIN EACH "YES" ANSWER – With respect to each pilot...

	PILOT NO. 1	PILOT NO. 2
As pilot, any incidents, accidents; any citations for FAR violations or license limitations?	☐ No ☐ Yes	☐ No ☐ Yes
Any physical impairments or limitations or waivers on Medical Certificate?	☐ No ☐ Yes	☐ No ☐ Yes
Any felony convictions or license suspensions arising out of operation of a motor vehicle?	☐ No ☐ Yes	☐ No ☐ Yes
Any arrests for operation of a motor vehicle recklessly or under influence of alcohol or drugs?	☐ No ☐ Yes	☐ No ☐ Yes
Will anyone, other than you or the pilots shown above, use your aircraft?	☐ No ☐ Yes	☐ No ☐ Yes

Aircraft Ownership

I do not own the aircraft by myself ☐ Names and addresses of: ☐ Co-owner(s) ☐ Mortgagee(s) ☐ Lessor(s)

______________________________ ______________________________

______________________________ ______________________________

______________________________ ______________________________

Amount of any lien or loan, excluding interest and/or finance charges $____________________

Does your lienholder require lienholder's interest insurance (Breach of Warranty)? ☐ No ☐ Yes

Indicate the coverages desired.

Coverage	***Limits of Coverage***	
Combined Liability Coverage for bodily injury and property damage	$	Each Occurrence
Medical Coverage	$	Each Person
Aircraft Physical Damage Coverage $ Not in-motion deductible	$ In-motion deductible	$ Limit

Use this space for answering questions.

____

____

____

____

____

____

____

____

____

____

I/We authorize the following agent/broker to represent me/us in the placing of this insurance:

NAME AND ADDRESS OF AGENT/BROKER: ______________________________

____

I/We represent that all information provided in this application is true and complete to the best of my/our knowledge and that no relevant information has been withheld, I/We understand that no insurance is in force unless and until United States Aviation Underwriters, Incorporated (Managers of the USAIG) effects a binder of insurance or issues a policy. It is understood, however, that if insurance is ordered from and accepted by United States Aviation Underwriters, Incorporated, the full amount of premium becomes due and payable immediately. I/We authorize United States Aviation Underwriters, Incorporated to investigate all or any qualifications or statements contained herein.

Date ________________ Signature of Applicant ______________________________

NEW YORK • ATLANTA • CHICAGO • DALLAS • DENVER • HOUSTON
LOS ANGELES • MEMPHIS • MINNEAPOLIS • PITTSBURGH • SAN FRANCISCO
ST. LOUIS • SEATTLE • TOLEDO • WICHITA

390 AC Rev. (10/96) (Page 2 of 2)

AIRPORT INSURANCE APPLICATION

NAME OF APPLICANT ______________________________

ADDRESS ______________________________

APPLICANT IS: ☐ Individual ☐ Corporation ☐ Partnership (name each partner) ______________

whose business is: ______________________________

Quotation for Airport Liability insurance is requested for an annual period beginning ______________ ______

Name of airport ______________ located ________ miles ________ (north, east, south, west) of ______________ (city)

APPLICANT IS: ☐ Tenant ☐ General Lessee ☐ Airport owner Present Insurance Expires ______________

OPERATIONS of APPLICANT Indicate all operations and estimated annual gross receipts.

				List all other sources and receipts below. Use separate sheet if necessary.	
Fuel & Lubricants	$______	Aircraft Repair	$______		
Tiedowns & Hangaring	$______	Aircraft Charter	$______	______________	$______
Landing Fees	$______	Rental & Instruction	$______	______________	$______
New Aircraft	$______	Helicopter Repairs	$______	______________	$______
Used Aircraft	$______	Restaurant	$______	______________	$______
Aircraft Parts	$______	Auto Parking	$______	Total ---	$______

FUELING: On premises ☐ YES ☐ NO Done by applicant ☐ YES ☐ NO

FUELING is by: ☐ Truck ☐ Hydrant ☐ Gas pump ☐ Gas pit ☐ ______________ (other)

Annual Gallonage: Airline ______________ gallons; General Aviation ______________ gallons; Military ______________ gallons.

Type of fuel sold: AVGAS ☐ JET FUEL ☐

Fuel Storage Facilities: Underground ______________ gallons; Above ground ______________ gallons.

Annual Gallonage of Turbine Engine Fuel: ______________ gallons.

TIE DOWN & HANGARING by APPLICANT -- are aircraft of others taxied, towed or moved by applicant? ☐ NO ☐ YES

Number of: tiedown spaces ______________; T-hangars ______________; multiple aircraft hangars ______________

Number of aircraft: tied down ______________; in T-hangars ______________; in multiple aircraft hangars ______________

Highest value a/c: tied down $ ______________; in T-hangars $______________; in multiple aircraft hangars $______________

Total value all a/c: tied down $ ______________; in T-hangars $______________; in multiple aircraft hangars $______________

APPLICANTS VEHICLES-ELEVATORS and AIRCRAFT

Indicate the number and type of vehicles maintained for use exclusively on the airport premises:

Fuel Trucks ________, Sweepers ________, Snow Removal ________, Fire Engines ________, Tugs ________

Hydrant Carts ________, Pickup Trucks ________, Passenger Cars ________, Other ________

State number of: Elevators ______________, Escalators ______________, Moving Sidewalks ______________

State number of Aircraft owned or operated by applicant ______________; number of Helicopters ________

CONTRACTS --- Has applicant entered into any written agreements assuming the liability of others,

such s lease of premises, fuel supplier, equipment lease, etc? .... ☐ NO ☐ YES (attach copies)

Does applicant use uniform customer contracts for hangaring, service, etc? ☐ NO ☐ YES (attach sample)

CONSTRUCTION by Independent Contractors – show estimated cost by type of construction---

Runways & taxiways .... $______________ next year; $______________ next three years.

All others (describe) ______________ $______________ next year; $______________ next three years.

F-137 3/77

Aircraft traffic is controlled -- .... ☐ NO ☐ YES – by ☐ Tower ☐ Unicom – Operated by: ____________________

Is there an airport manager? .... ☐ NO ☐ YES Employed by: ____________________

Is manager on premises during hours of operation? .... ☐ YES ☐ NO Hours of operation __________ to _____

Fire station located at airport .... ☐ YES ☐ NO It is __________ miles from the airport.

Is airport fenced? .... ☐ NO ☐ YES Who maintains the airport? ____________________

Does the insured own, operate or maintain any aids to navigation? ☐ NO ☐ YES (describe)

If applicant is Owner or General Lessee – complete the following and enclose a map or FAA Form 5010-I

Airport manager is: ☐ Employee of applicant; ☐ Independent Contractor (furnish copy of contract)

Any recreational or other Non-Aviation facilities or use of Airport premises? ☐ NO ☐ YES (describe)

List Airlines and Scheduled Air Taxis that will serve this airport during next three years:

Total Estimated Arrivals & Departures:	PRESENT YEAR	NEXT YEAR (EST.)	FOLLOWING YEAR (EST.)
Revenue Passengers			
Airline Aircraft			
General Aviation Aircraft			
Military Aircraft			

LIABILITY COVERAGE – state limits of liability desired	EACH PERSON	EACH OCCURRENCE
Bodily Injury Liability	$	$
Property Damage Liability	X X X	$
Single Limit Bodily Injury and Property Damage	X X X	$
Ground Hangarkeepers Liability	EACH AIRCRAFT $	$

LOSS HISTORY and PREVIOUS AVIATION INSURANCE	Explain each "YES" answer
Has applicant had any airport/aviation losses/claims during last five years?	☐ NO ☐ YES
Has insurer canceled, declined or refused to renew any airport/aviation insurance?	☐ NO ☐ YES
Name of last or present airport/aviation insurance company:	

I/We authorize the following agent or broker to represent me/us in the placing of this insurance:

.... name and address of agent or broker ....

I/We warrant that all information provided in this application is true and complete to the best of my/our knowledge and that no relevant information has been withheld. I/We understand that no insurance is in force unless and until United States Aviation Underwriters, Incorporated (Managers of the USAIG) effects a binder of insurance or issues a policy. It is understood, however, that if insurance is ordered from and accepted by the United States Aviation Underwriters, Incorporated, the full amount of premium becomes immediately due and payable. I/We authorize the United States Aviation Underwriters, Incorporated to investigate all or any qualifications or statements contained herein.

Date .... 19....... X ....

PERSONAL SIGNATURE OF APPLICANT OR AUTHORIZED EXECUTIVE IS REQUIRED

Agent represents following member company(ies) of USAIG: ....

Agent or broker --- please send to:

NEW YORK • ATLANTA • CHICAGO • DALLAS • DENVER • HOUSTON • LOS ANGELES MEMPHIS • MINNEAPOLIS • PITTSBURGH • SAN FRANCISCO • ST. LOUIS • SEATTLE • TOLEDO • WICHITA

USAIG Pilot Record

Name ______________________________

Address ______________________________

____

Birthdate ______________ Social Security No. ______________

Certificate No. ______________________________

Occupation ______________________________

Employer ______________________________

Marital Status ______________ No. of Dependents ________

FAA PILOT CERTIFICATES NOW HELD AND YEAR OBTAINED

Student .... ________
Private .... ________
Commercial .... ________
ATP .... ________
Flight Instructor ..... ________

FAA PILOT RATINGS NOW HELD AND YEAR OBTAINED

ASEL .... ________
AMEL .... ________
ASES .... ________
AMES .... ________
Instrument .... ________
Rotorcraft .... ________

FAA MEDICAL CERTIFICATE

Date Issued ______________ Class ______________

Waivers (If none, write none) ______________________________

TRAINING AND RECURRENT TRAINING

Year of first solo flight ________ Type rated in following aircraft ______________________________

____

Describe Flight Training (School, location, equipment, instructor, etc.) ______________________________

____

Date of last Biennial Flight Review or equivalent ______________ Date of last instrument competency check ______________

Do you participate in FAA Pilot Proficiency Awards Program? ☐ No ☐ Yes. If "Yes," what phase have you completed? ________

For what type aircraft? ______________________ Date completed ______________________

Recurrent/Transition Courses: Describe and give details of last courses attended:

____

____

School or instructor ______________________________

Do you hold a current FSI Pro Card or Simuflite Card? ☐ Yes Date ______________ ☐ No

PILOT-IN-COMMAND EXPERIENCE

AIRCRAFT MAKE/MODEL	TOTAL HOURS	TOTAL LAST 12 MONTHS	TOTAL LAST 90 DAYS	TOTAL INSTRUMENT	TOTAL NIGHT

Please explain fully any "Yes" answers to the following questions on reverse side.

As pilot-in-command or as co-pilot have you had or been involved in any aircraft incidents or accidents? ☐ No ☐ Yes

As pilot-in-command or as co-pilot have you been found guilty of any Federal Air Regulations violations? ☐ No ☐ Yes

Has your automobile drivers license ever been suspended or revoked? ☐ No ☐ Yes

Have you ever been arrested for operating an automobile under the influence of alcohol or drugs? ☐ No ☐ Yes

Have you had any automobile accidents within the last five years? ☐ No ☐ Yes

I represent that the answers given are true and complete to the best of my knowledge and belief and that no material information has been withheld.

Date ______________ Signed ______________________________

(Pilot's Personal Signature Required)

This pilot record is filed in connection with the Insurance Application of ______________________________

F-104 (REV. 1/97)

UNITED STATES AVIATION UNDERWRITERS, INCORPORATED

AIRCRAFT INSURANCE BINDER

*Agent Name and Address * * *	Date: July 11, 2005 Policyholder: * * * *

Description of Aircraft: *

This is to confirm we are providing coverages, shown below, for which a dollar amount has been filled in. If no dollar amount appears, that coverage is not provided. These limits or coverages may be altered by the policy or its endorsements.

The coverages shown below will begin **/**/** at *12:01 A.M., and they will terminate, without further notice **/**/** at *12:01 A.M., unless continued by written notice from us. This binder will be replaced by our *400AC policy form.

COVERAGE	LIMITS OF COVERAGE		
Combined Liability Coverage for bodily injury (except to passengers) and property damage	$	*.00	Each Occurrence
Liability Coverage for bodily injury to passengers only	$ $	*.00 *.00	Each Person Each Occurrence
Medical Coverage	$	*.00	Each Person
*	$	*.00	Each Occurrence

Aircraft Physical Damage Coverage	Not In-Motion Deductible	In-Motion Deductible	Limit
	$ *.00	$ *.00	$ *.00

Policyholder is (*) Sole Owner (*) Mortgagor (*) Lessee (*) Other

Aircraft Use. Policyholder agrees not to charge anyone for using the aircraft. The policyholder may be reimbursed for operating expenses.

Pilots: (*) Named Pilot(s): *

(*) Others: Any *Private - Commercial Pilot with ** rating and a minimum of *** hours, including *** hours in **

Payments for loss covered under Your Aircraft Physical Damage Coverage will be made to the Policyholder and *.

Total Annual Premium $ *

United States Aviation Underwriters, Incorporated

By ______________________________

*Underwriter

(*) Application attached must be completed and returned to us before binder expires.
(*) Confirming policy is being issued.

All premiums are due upon delivery of the policy. Flat cancellations are not permitted.

USAIG Certificate of Insurance

This is to certify to: *
*

whose address is: *
*
*

that: *PH

whose address is: *add1
*add2
*add3

is at this date insured with the Several Participating Companies of the United States Aircraft Insurance Group, for the Limits of Coverage stated below, at the following locations: *the United States of America, its territories and possessions, Canada, Mexico, the Bahamas and the islands of the West Indies or while enroute between these places.

Descriptive Schedule of Coverages

*(Aircraft Description)

Kind of Insurance	Policy Number	Policy Term	Limits of Coverage	
AIRCRAFT LIABILITY Combined Liability Coverage for bodily injury and property damage	*PN	*eff - *exp	Each Person	Each Occurrence $ *
Medical Coverage			$ *	
AIRCRAFT PHYSICAL DAMAGE - ALL RISKS	*PN	*eff - *exp		

	Not In-Motion Deductible	In-Motion Deductible	Amount of Insurance
*(Aircraft Description)	$ *	$ *	$ *
*(Aircraft Description)	$ *	$ *	$ *

			Each Aircraft	Each Occurrence
AIRPORT LIABILITY Combined Liability Coverage for bodily injury and property damage	*ALOPN	*eff - *exp		$ *
Hangarkeeper's Liability			$ *	$ *
Property Damage Deductible				$ *

*Only with respect to operations by, for or on behalf of the "Policyholder":

*

<u>*Please see the attached endorsement(s).</u>

This certificate or verification of insurance is not an insurance policy and does not amend, extend or alter the coverage afforded by the policies listed herein. Notwithstanding any requirement, term or condition of any contract or other document, with respect to which this certificate or verification of insurance may be issued or may pertain, the insurance afforded by the policies described herein is subject to all terms, exclusions and conditions of such policies.

The ***Aviation Managers*** of the USAIG (United States Aircraft Insurance Group) agree that in the event of cancellation of the policy(ies), they will endeavor to give the party to whom this certificate is issued * days advance notice of such cancellation, but the ***Aviation Managers*** shall not be liable in any way for failure to give such notice.

UNITED STATES AVIATION UNDERWRITERS, INC., ***Aviation Managers***

Address: *

By ______________________________ date: *_____
*

PART FOUR
OTHER LINES OF INSURANCE

Chapter 11

Airline and Space Insurance

OUTLINE

Airline Insurance
Space Insurance

OBJECTIVES

At the end of this chapter you should be able to:
Distinguish between the various classes of airline service in the United States.
Identify three major criteria used in the process of airline risk selection
Describe the major elements that are considered by underwriters in determining airline pricing. Define "quota share" or "vertical" placement.
Summarize the history of space insurance from the mid-1960s.
Describe several of the important uses of satellites.
Distinguish between launch providers and launch vehicles.
Distinguish between in-orbit coverage and in-orbit third party liability coverage.
Define launch risk guarantee insurance.
Explain the purpose of the 1972 Space Treaty.
Discuss some of the factors taken into consideration in underwriting space insurance.
Highlight the following space insurance design considerations: Sum Insured, Policy Period, Attachment of Risk, Termination of Risk, Definitions and Deductibles.
Explain how space insurance premium rates move in cycles based upon supply and demand.
Discuss several future space underwriting issues.

AIRLINE INSURANCE

A Brief History of the Airline Industry

In the decade that followed World War I, the first use of aircraft in support of commerce appeared and the precursors of today's major air carriers, both cargo and passenger, were formed. Advances were made and more modern aircraft were introduced during the 1930s and flights across the Atlantic Ocean were initiated via flying boats or "Clippers."

Further advancement of the industry took place as a result of a second world war. Following World War II, a surplus of military aircraft such as the Douglas DC-3 and a large cadre of trained pilots greatly expanded the scope of airline operations.

The dawn of a more modern jet transport era occured in 1958, marked by the first jet service across the Atlantic operated by Pan American and BOAC in Boeing 707s and DeHavilland Comet 4s respectively. Jet equipment became more prevalent as more and more of the major airlines of the day replaced their piston engine aircraft with jet transports. Wide-body aircraft (DC 10s, L1011s and Boeing 747s), second generation airliners (Boeing 737s and Airbus 300's) and supersonic aircraft (the Concorde) were introduced in the 1970s.

As airlines evolved over the course of the last Century and at the dawn of a new millennium, the risk to life and property has also grown. Airline insurance has developed along with the airline industry during this entire period to protect the financial viability of airlines and respond to loss events, both catastrophic and those that are more routine or attritional in nature.

The Airline Industry Today

There are more than 300 airlines operating around the world today and they play a vital role in the global economy. Of this total, 270 of them are members of the International Air Transport Association (IATA) and represent the vast majority of the world's air transport capacity. This group carries almost 2 billion passengers annually to innumerable destinations. At any given time, depending upon regionally varying economic and geo-political conditions, growth rates are between 5 and 6 percent annually. Any number of factors can make these figures vary widely. The greatest impact has been felt in recent years from concerns over war, terrorism, and the effects of Severe Acute Respiratory Syndrome (SARS). Even with these setbacks, traffic, or the movement of passengers and cargo, continues to grow at a fairly strong rate, but the yields or margins on airline revenues are a different story altogether. Profits have come under great pressure in this hyper-competitive industry and this puts great pressure on all suppliers to the airline industry, including providers of aviation insurance coverage. (Source: IATA 2004 Annual Report)

The U.S. Airline Segment

The U.S. airline industry operates within this worldwide group in a $100 billion market annually, growing by some 4 to 5 percent per annum and employing more than a half a million people. It is an industry that is considered vital to the national interest moving more than 600 million passengers and 22.5 million metric tons of cargo each year with a fleet of almost 5,000 aircraft conducting more than 10 million scheduled departures each year.
(Source: Air Transport Association)

It is a highly elastic and cyclical industry as well. In many ways it is not unlike our insurance marketplace in that capacity, defined by available seats in the airline business and by available share participations in the airline insurance market, are rarely at equilibrium with demand. Later in this chapter we will discuss issues of quota share insurance capacity and its effect upon price.

Approximately 1/3 of the world's passenger traffic is concentrated in the U.S. air transportation system and this will be the primary focus of the chapter.

Classify, Select and Rate

The task of underwriting this class of business is not unlike that which is undertaken in other lines of casualty insurance. The risk must first be classified. Next, underwriting standards and minimums must be met for risk selection. And once selected, rating is promulgated. The way that rate and premium levels are developed warrants its own separate discussion and this will be presented in greater detail later in the chapter. For purposes of this section, suffice to say that if the prevailing market rate is at a level considered to be unacceptable, then this will determine whether or not the risk is selected. Another way to look at this is if too many underwriters are willing to write the risk at a premium level which does not meet basic rating guidelines, then the selection decision is made before any other risk qualities are considered by the underwriter.

Classifications

Within the airline segment there are several classifications to consider. The largest and most obvious segment is the Major Airline class. This group comprises some of the largest air carriers in the world and includes American Airlines, United Airlines, Delta Air Lines, Northwest Airlines and Continental Airlines. These five carriers represent approximately 2/3 of the U.S. market in terms of passenger traffic and departures. The class includes widebody aircraft, with high aircraft values and extensive liability exposures. As a result their policies carry the highest limits of liability available in the market.

The next class to consider is one with major carriers operating mainly narrowbody aircraft and having more regional focus, with very little if any long-haul international service. These carriers include Southwest Airlines, JetBlue Airways, Alaska Air Group, Aloha Airlines, Hawaiian Airlines, Midwest Airlines, US Airways and Spirit Airlines amongst others.

A third classification is the Regional Airline segment. This classification has seen enormous growth in recent years as larger carriers have shifted some of their shorter, "thinner" routes over to regional affiliates and code share partners operating smaller, more economical regional jets and turboprops.

A fourth classification is the charter airline, which operates airline equipment but does not use a published schedule.

And a fifth and final classification is the cargo segment There are almost 800 aircraft in the U.S. cargo fleet alone and they conduct over 600,000 departures a year but the liability exposure stemming from these operations is obviously not as severe as that of passenger carriers, although third party exposure is just as significant.

Selection

There are numerous criteria used in the process of airline risk selection but the three that stand out as most important are those found to be a part of any venture capitalist model:

1. Management—the strength and stability of the management team are important considerations in the selection process. Airlines are capital-intensive entities operating in highly cyclical and extremely competitive markets and requiring a very skilled labor force. This creates challenging work and requires strong management teams to ensure a well-run operation.
2. Capital—As mentioned above, airlines are capital-intensive entities. The purchase of aircraft, gates and other supporting infrastructure requires large capital outlays and the highly skilled workforce that includes pilots, mechanics and flight attendants involves a large payroll under long-term contracts.
3. Business Plan—It is not always easy to get this right, but the plan must make sense. If a new carrier expects to simply enter a market dominated by established air carriers, there must be a well thought out plan and of course there must be adequate capital to give it staying power.

Rating

What determines the right rate for an airline?

First of all, the methods that are commonly used when pricing airline risks are not very different when compared with other hull and liability programs in the aviation market. An airline may operate several hundred aircraft of various types and values. The two elements of airline pricing are 1) the individual and combined fleet value of hulls at risk and 2) the liability exposure presented, this being a matrix of liability limit, exposure of that limit to maximum probable loss (MPL) and other risk factors as depicted in Figure 11.1. In the case of hull coverage, Underwriters will generally set rates on the average fleet value for a particular type of aircraft. For example, a rate of 0.05 percent on the average fleet value for B737s during the policy period. Airline deductibles can vary considerably and are dictated mainly by the size and category of aircraft.

The lower end of the range is 1 percent of Insured Value for smaller turboprops and the higher end is as follows: $500,000 for narrow-body jetliner category (i.e., B727, B737-100/200), $750,000 for Hybrid category (i.e., B737-300 series and higher, A319/320/321) and $1,000,000 for widebody aircraft (i.e., B747/757/767/777, A300/310/330/340). These deductibles function on an occurrence basis and are considered to be industry standard. In addition to these deductibles, there are varying aggregate deductible schemes that can be used limited only by creativity and the willingness and financial ability of the insured to share in the risk taking.

Passenger legal liability coverage is generally quoted on a basis of a rate per 1,000 Revenue Passenger Miles or RPMs. The volume of passenger miles flown,

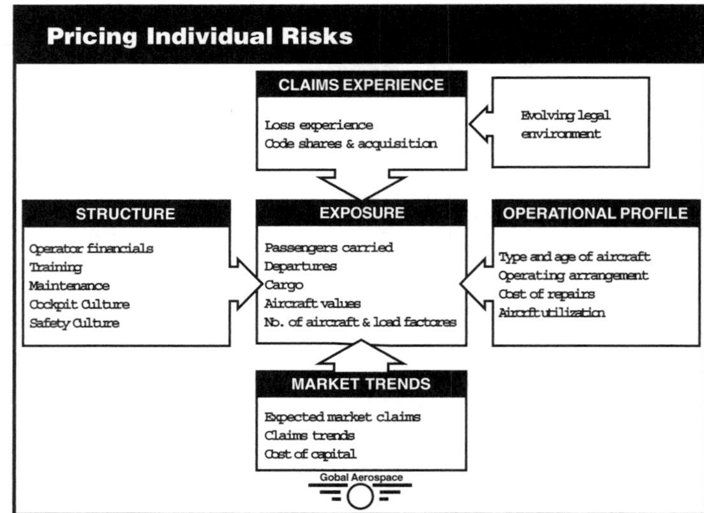

Figure 11.1 Pricing Individual Airline Risk

seating capacity of the Insured's aircraft and limit of liability required will all affect the final rate. Third Party Bodily Injury (excluding passengers) and Property Damage coverages are rated either on a basis of any one aircraft for a certain period (usually 12 months) or according to the revenue miles flown during a given period.

These elements of exposure are rated using the following rating bases and metrics:

1. Hull Rate per $100 of Insured Value coupled with;
2. One or more of the following Liability rating bases / metrics:
    - Projected Revenue Passenger Miles or RPMs
    - Projected Passengers Enplaned
    - Projected Number of Departures
    - Total Number of Aircraft in the Fleet at inception and pro-rata for the year
    - Total Number of Available Passenger Seats for the year
    - Average Hull Value
    - Average Seats per Aircraft
    - Enplanements per Departure
    - Average Trip Segment Length

With rates set for the program, underwriters will then establish a deposit premium amount for the program which can be anywhere from 75 to 100 percent of projected earned premium. The deposit premium is often paid on a quarterly basis and is adjusted upon expiration.

Because of the size of the hull and liability premium of a large air carrier and the fact that loss distribution is so varied, underwriters have also devised various forms of profit sharing and no-claims bonus schemes. Under the former, a percentage of the earned premium less claims paid or outstanding during the year is paid at the end of the policy term. A no-claims bonus is similar but normally applies to hull only.

The rates set for an airline placement are affected primarily by two factors—the first is supply of capital, and in turn, the amount of capacity underwriters can make available for airline risk transfer in the marketplace. The second is loss activity in the segment. These factors are always subject to swift and sudden change as experienced in 2001.

Following the terrorist attacks in the United States on September 11, 2001 Federal Reserve Chairman Alan Greenspan, stated before the Joint Economic Committee of Congress:

> *The shock of the tragedies at the World Trade Center and the Pentagon has reshaped those assessments of risk and required an abrupt realignment of prices in many markets to reflect the expected costs of operating in what we now recognize as a more hostile world.*

Many policyholders often ask insurers why their premiums are increasing when they haven't had any claims. The answer is not always readily apparent unless you take a broad view of the larger population of risks.

Insurance, by simple definition, is the loss sustained by the few, shared by the many—guaranteed by others. Typically, small losses are contained within specialty market segments within the insurance industry, such as aviation insurance. However, insurance companies protect themselves and their policyholders from catastrophic losses by purchasing reinsurance.

Reinsurance is insurance purchased by an insurance company to protect its assets beyond a certain limit or retention. When a catastrophic loss does occur the loss is spread across many other lines of insurance through channels of reinsurance placements designed to spread the risk of one market segment through many related and unrelated market segments. While many policyholders think of themselves as part of a small insurance market segment, such as aviation insurance, in reality we all participate in a much broader worldwide market.

It is important to understand that certain specialty insurance lines, such as aviation, that insure operators who have the potential for catastrophic loss, depend on large capital commitments from both direct and reinsurance companies. As the cost of capital and reinsurance increases, so does the cost of insurance for policyholders. Since the terrorist attacks of 2001, capital investors, realizing the extent of catastrophic exposures facing air carriers today, are seeking better returns on their capital investment. Capital markets will exit high risk, high exposure markets to deploy their capital where the potential for catastrophic loss is greatly diminished, if returns are inadequate. This loss of capital, or supply, has a direct impact on the availability of reinsurance and demonstrates the characteristics of supply and demand in the marketplace.

The above elements must be in place for underwriters to select airline risk for addition to a portfolio of similar risks. There must be assurances that business philosophies are aligned and that a long-term partnership can be established. When these criteria are satisfied, it is all the more likely that the air carrier will be in business for the long term and there will be stability in the relationship with aviation insurers which is essential for the underwriting process to yield good results. Underwriters cannot predict when or where large losses will occur. The best way to fund and spread large losses is over as many accounts as possible and over a period of time, which permits funding of large losses, a core principle of insurance.

Structure of an Airline Insurance Placement

Due to the catastrophic exposure associated with airline risks and the financial capacity needed to secure that risk, several coinsurers are involved in each airline insurance placement. This arrangement is known as a "quota share" or "vertical" placement. A significant portion of the aviation insurance market is based in Europe; therefore, a United States-based broker may partner with a London broker for negotiation in the London market. After an airline's broker delivers a submission identifying exposures and specifications to several insurers, rate and coverage negotiations take place. Each potential coinsurer negotiates for a percentage of the placement. Shares may range from as little as 1 to as much 25 percent or more. Because the lead coinsurer is the primary service provider and is responsible for policy issuance, claims management and emergency response support, the lead coinsurer may receive higher rates. The other coinsurers or "following market," collect their respective shares of premium and pay their respective shares of claim costs. The lead insurer is responsible for establishing claim procedures with the insured and communicating with the following market regarding large losses.

Financial Security

There are four principal elements of an aviation insurance product, three of which have been discussed above. They are Capacity or the ability for a company to accept the transfer of risk, Service in the form of underwriting and claims management, a Price which is fair for all involved and lastly, Financial Security. When approaching the market, a broker and a client must seek underwriters with superior financial positions. The quality of security behind the companies that are involved in the aviation insurance market is paramount and is necessary in order to secure payment of losses and ensure an airline's financial viability, to live up to the promise.

In Closing

The challenge facing insurers in this segment of the industry involves maintaining a stable and viable insurance market. Airline insurers must continue to provide comprehensive service, the capacity to accept enormous risk transfer, contain losses inherent in the air transport environment and safeguard the balance sheet of air carriers. There are very few alternative financial products that can match this undertaking.

SPACE INSURANCE

INTRODUCTION

Space Insurance involves indemnifying the insured for the ownership, operation or use of spacecraft providing first party hull coverage for the asset itself and third party liability coverage where required. This is much easier said than done as space insurance is a relatively young market that involves expensive hardware and high liability requirements. Space risks by their nature introduce new technologies that have never been tested before.

The space underwriting market is generally thought of solely with respect to covering the hull value of the satellite or the operation of transponders on a satellite. There are specialist brokers, underwriters and their respective consultants that address this exposure. Third party liability exposures associated with the space risk are also unique but often handled by aviation liability underwriters rather than the space market specifically, but there is crossover. Related risk areas including builders' risk, transit risk and third party liability outside the launch and in-orbit phase are typically handled by traditional property casualty markets.

This section will provide an introduction to space insurance. A brief history and description of satellites and launch vehicles will introduce some important concepts. This will be followed by a review of peripheral insurance closely tied to the space risks including pre-launch, transponder coverage, launch risk guarantee and third party liability insurance. The space insurance section will then describe the underwriting process and some unique features of space policies and the market. To close, a few thoughts on future issues and how the satellite risk profile is changing will be presented.

HISTORY

The first space insurance policy was written in 1965 for *Intelsat I*, known as *Early Bird*, which was the first commercial geostationary communication satellite.

Being the first, the policy had limitations and only covered pre-launch for a value of $5 million and third party liability for a limit of $25 million. Today, every phase of the space risk can be insured from the manufacturer's builder's risk through launch, commissioning, in-orbit and all related third party liabilities. Standard exclusions do apply, but insurance is available.

Space insurance is typically purchased by commercial entities and not by governmental agencies. Commercial entities that make large upfront investments have to answer to capital markets, banks and shareholders so they must protect their assets. Government exposures including the Shuttle, the International Space Station, spy satellites, global positioning systems (GPS), NASA and weather monitoring satellites historically have not been insured. Today, the government may test the markets for insurability of its satellites or occasionally put a subcontractor at risk, but this is not typical.

Space is a new frontier and going forward there will be more to consider than simply sending satellites into orbit. Richard Branson of Virgin Airlines is planning to start a space tourism business using the technology of *Space Ship One* by 2008. *Space Ship One* was the first privately funded operation putting man on the edge of space. It carried liability insurance only with no hull coverage. The expansion of commercial enterprises into space will increase demand for higher hull values and limits of liability as these new enterprises will require insurance for their very high valued spacecraft and the people who travel in them. NASA is also looking for a replacement for the Shuttle within the decade and this could be privatized. The space market is already at its capacity limit with respect to higher valued satellites so additional capital will be required in the future to meet increased demand.

Historical Space Insurance Events

- 1965: *Early Bird* was first insured commercial geostationary communications satellite.
- 1968: Comsat insured seven Intelsat satellites for launch but included a two failure deductible.
- 1975: The first in-orbit policy was written for RCA for Satcom series of satellites.
- 1984: Underwriters funded the Shuttle rescue mission of *Westar VI* and *Palapa B2* which were repaired and relaunched to their intended orbit.
- 1986: The *Challenger* failure saw the end to commercial use of the Shuttle.
- 1990: *Asiasat 1* was the first insured Chinese Long March launch vehicle.
- 1994: *Ariane* failure generated the largest insured loss to date at $356 million.
- 1997: A Delta II failed launch of a GPS satellite led to the first third party liability claims made during a non-commercial launch.
- 1998 the maiden flight of Delta III failed causing total loss of a PanAmSat satellite.
- 2000–2001: Six Boeing 702 model satellites suffered in-orbit generic solar array degradation costing insurers $800 million.
- 2003: *Columbia* failed upon entering the atmosphere killing the crew and spreading debris over three states. No insurance claims were made.
- 2004: Scaled Composite's *Space Ship One* spacecraft won the X-Prize of $10 million being the first private company to launch the same vehicle to orbit within 14 days.

SATELLITES

A *satellite* is any object orbiting another in space such as a planet or for our purposes a man-made object orbiting the earth for a commercial purpose. In 1945, the futurist Arthur C. Clarke wrote that communication signals could be transmitted to and from earth by placing a relay station in space over the earth's equator at a distance of about 22,300 miles. That object in space would appear to remain fixed over the same location on earth as the planet rotated, thereby providing a stationary platform for the continuous relay of communications signals. Geostationary (GEO) satellites, as they are called, can cover vast areas of the earth for with as few as three satellites placed strategically over the equator, coverage of the entire earth can be achieved. Geostationary communication satellites have become the most valuable space assets and the arc over the equator has become populated.

Today satellites have many applications that make them commercially viable. The first uses included telecommunications delivery internationally. Television broadcasters used them to acquire signals anywhere in the world and today only require a ground station the size of a minivan to beam signals to satellites to be distributed anywhere. Because of the increase in power capabilities of satellites, they are now able to deliver direct to home television or direct to car digital radio. Meteorology, messaging, telephone and digital imaging services are well served by satellites and Internet access may be the next market.

Each satellite is unique and effectively manufactured by hand, taking years to create. The only exceptions to this are those used in low earth orbit constellations that can be mass produced as they are identical. Satellite manufacturers in an effort to standardize manufacturing use like models as the platform for a satellite. Think of a model or platform as an auto chassis that includes standard items required to launch, maneuver and power the satellite. The platform has set locations for integral components including batteries, radiators, motors for station keeping, momentum wheels for steerage and solar panels.

Listed below are some of the common satellite models and their manufacturers. Some manufacturers not mentioned below currently cater only to government programs and they include Ball Aerospace, General Dynamics and Northrop Grumman (TRW).

Satellite Manufacturers & Satellite Models

Alcatel	Spacebus 3000, Meteosat
Boeing Satellite Systems (Hughes)	BSS 376, BSS 601, BSS 702
EADS Astrium	Eurostar 3000
Lockheed Martin	Satcom 7000, A2100
Motorola (LEO)	Iridium
NPO PM (Russia)	Express M, 2000
Orbital Science	Microstar, Star 2
Space Systems Loral (LEO/GEO)	Globalstar / FS1300

On the platform is placed the communications payload consisting of all the parts required to meet the specific needs of the mission. The communications payload accesses, amplifies and retransmits the signal. It is made up of multiple transponders which independently beam signals to earth over a specific geographic area. The power levels of the beams dictate the amount of information that can be carried over that signal and the size of ground antenna required for signal reception. A combination of high transmission power and a large antenna on the satellite typically translates into the use of smaller dishes to receive the signal. Small antennas on the ground lower cost and facilitate use.

Geostationary satellites are large with high power requirements. There is constant pressure to build larger satellites that can generate more power to support the higher number of transponders and to power larger antenna. The power capabilities today have reached over 10,000 watts. This requires large solar arrays and the use of batteries for times a satellite is in the earth's shadow. Satellite antenna size has also increased with the largest now being made of mesh that can expand to the size of football fields. They also must have motors to power the satellite so it can maintain its position within a specified area (called station keeping) over the equator. Satellites today can be over 5 tons in weight. The higher the weight the larger and more expensive the launch vehicle must be.

Geostationary satellites are the most prominent satellites but medium and low earth orbit (LEO) satellites can offer similar functionality at a lower cost. The satellite is smaller, weighs less and doesn't have to be pushed as high to orbit. However, the tradeoff is that they are not stationary above the earth so multiple satellites (a constellation) is needed to maintain continuous contact with a specific ground station. Some LEO satellites are small enough that many can be launched at the same time on the same launch vehicle further reducing costs.

Following is a brief description of some existing commercial satellite systems that have become well known to the public due to the popularity of their services.

Satellite Application Examples

Direct TV uses powerful geostationary satellites with large antenna to provide programmed television direct to the home competing against cable providers. Users have satellite dishes setup on or near their home at a fixed position pointed toward the satellite. The higher your latitude location, the smaller the angle to the south the antenna will have to be pointed. From New York City the angle above the southern horizon is about 23 degrees.

Iridium is a constellation of 66 satellites in low earth orbit (LEO) that cross over the earth at different angles to cover the world with telephone service provided to handheld Iridium phones. Manufacturing costs of the satellites were reduced because of mass production. Launch costs were reduced due to smaller satellite size with up to 12 satellites being launched at one time. There is speculation that had Iridium come to market prior to the increased popularity of cell phones, we might all be using Iridium today and would not have to contend with the mass proliferation of cell towers.

XM and Sirius Satellite Radio. These two companies are competitors in the same market of delivering digital radio direct to automobiles and homes but they each have different satellite configurations. XM has two satellites located in GEO providing coverage for North America. Line of sight is required so there is degradation at higher latitudes but this is only a factor in Northern Canada. Sirius used a different approach with three satellites in Medium Earth Orbit (MEO) that travel a figure 8 pattern over North and South America. These satellites cost less as they are smaller and don't have to be as powerful being closer to earth. Both systems use omni-directional receiving antenna that do not have to be pointed and they are as small as a deck of cards.

LAUNCH VEHICLES

The launch vehicle for spacecraft provides the critical path to reaching orbit. Depending on the mission requirements spacecraft can be launched to different orbits around earth. The optimum point to launch a geostationary satellite is from the equator as the initial velocity of the rocket resulting from the rotation of the earth is greatest at this point. Additionally, the farther a satellite is launched from the equator the greater the angle correction (inclination angle) required to return it to an equatorial orbit. Launch vehicles will inject satellites into an elliptical orbit called a transfer orbit. The satellite has a motor (Apogee Kick Motor or AKM) that will fire when the satellite is farthest from earth to round out its desired GEO orbit. This is then called the drift orbit stage until the satellite finds its home in the geostationary ring at a specific degree of longitude.

Non-geostationary satellites don't have as far to travel and are typically smaller so their launch mission is less complicated. Smaller launch vehicles without multiple stages may be used to place the satellites directly into their desired orbits possibly eliminating the need for an AKM as well. A revolutionary launch vehicle to launch small satellites to LEO was developed by Orbital Science Corporation. The Pegasus rocket drops from the belly of a transport size aircraft (L-1011) at 30,000 feet then ignites and transports its cargo to LEO. In 2004 Burt Rutan used this same concept of a mother ship dropping the launch vehicle with his *Space Ship One*. Unlike traditional launch vehicles, the Shuttle and *Space Ship One* are referred to as Reusable Launch Vehicles (RLVs) because after launch they return to earth and can be refurbished for additional launches, hence reusable.

There is a constant push to launch higher weights with less expensive launch vehicles. This is measured as reducing cost per pound to orbit. Many new concepts are on the drawing board and in early stages of development. In 2005, a company called SpaceX launched an entirely new launch vehicle. The purpose was to get the cost of launching half ton LEO satellites to $6 million per launch competing with Orbital Science that charges about $20 million. The cost of the large launch vehicles for geostationary satellites can be from $70-90 million a launch. The exhibit below lists the most common launch vehicles and the companies that provide them.

Launch Providers and Launch Vehicles

Arianespace	*Ariane 4, Ariane 5*
Boeing Launch Services (McDonnell Douglas)	Delta II/III/IV
China	Long March 3
Khrunichev State Research (ILS – Russia)	Proton K/M
Lockheed Martin (ILS-International Launch Services)	Titan, Atlas III, V
Israel	Shavit
ISRO (India)	PSLV
NASA (United Space Alliance)	STS – Space Shuttle
NASDA (Japan)	H-2/3/5
Orbital Science Corp.	Pegasus, Taurus
Russia	*Soyuz, Cosmos*
Sea Launch (Boeing, Kvaerner, Yuzhmash & Energia)	Zenit 3SL

Most launch providers started as government-sponsored programs and have evolved into the commercial area. A few of the vehicles are still struggling to become viable such as the Japanese H-2, India's PSLV or Israel's Shavit. Some do not cater to the commercial market such as Soyuz, Space Shuttle, Taurus and Lockheed's Titan. The most popular vehicles for geostationary satellites are the Ariane, ILS Atlas or Proton, Delta and Sea Launch rockets. With respect to low earth orbit the Delta II and Pegasus are more likely to be used. The Chinese Long March is available commercially and has competitive pricing but the United States has an embargo on its use.

The field is full of joint ventures between launch providers and this trend will likely continue. ILS is a joint venture between Lockheed Martin and Russia where their rockets are marketed jointly. Boeing has its own Delta rockets but is a major supporter of Sea Launch which is a joint venture. United Space Alliance which maintains the Shuttle is a joint venture between Boeing and Lockheed Martin. In 2005 Boeing and Lockheed Martin formed a joint venture called United Launch Alliance to create efficiencies for the Air Force's Evolved Expendable Launch Vehicle (EELV) program worth $32 billion. However, the government did not award the contract to one provider but decided to keep the only two competitors in place which reduced the ability for either to recoup its research and development costs. Both companies will continue to compete against each other on commercial launches using the same launch vehicles, Boeings Delta IV and Lockheed Martin's Atlas V.

INSURANCE COVERAGE OVERVIEW

The Space Insurance market consisting of underwriters and brokers specializing in space risks focuses on the hull coverage of the satellite itself from the launch phase through its life which can be up to 15 years. Prior to launch the satellite asset is no different from any other piece of high value property and is managed by the property market and inland-marine market when transported. This section will review the different kinds of insurance available while the space hull aspect will be covered in the next section.

The underwriting process starts with a view to the insureds and their insurable interest. Pre-launch, the manufacturer is typically the insured who has an interest in the satellite. The satellite purchaser can be required to carry insurance from the start of manufacture but that is not typical. Often the manufacturer may be providing the launch as well as manufacturing the satellite. In this situation it is not uncommon for the manufacturer under a turn-key contract to retain the risk until delivery of an operational satellite after all check outs have been complete in-orbit. All of the terms are spelled out in the purchase agreement and will be reviewed by the underwriters.

Pre-Launch and Manufacturers' Coverage

Pre-Launch and Manufacturers' Coverage indemnifies the insured for physical loss or damage to the asset. Loss or damage during manufacture, testing, shipping and integration with the launch vehicle are covered. Delay or termination coverage protects the insured for financial losses caused by covered perils which delay or terminate a satellite program. Insurance is provided by traditional property and inland-marine markets.

Satellites are very high value assets taking from two to three years to manufacture. The components alone can be very expensive. However, because these assets are no different from a supercomputer, for example, they can be managed by the property markets. They are inventory that will increase in value over time so a builder's risk policy is appropriate with valuations specified during the build process should there be a loss. Damage can occur in the factory from a testing failure or a physical event to the satellite. The customer will not accept an impaired satellite. Unlike other land-based equipment a satellite cannot be repaired in-orbit so it must meet all specifications within limits at launch.

The transport of the satellite to the launch pad is covered with the marine markets. Integration of the satellite on the launch vehicle is covered as well. Coverage usually ceases at intentional ignition of the launch vehicle. However, in the event of a terminated ignition (launch abort) coverage can be re-attached and will cease again at the next launch attempt. Depending on the launch provider and the launch vehicle being used each transfer of the risk from one policy to another must be clearly defined. The launch could start at ignition or at the point the launch vehicle lifts off the pad. In the case of a Pegasus rocket does it attach when the aircraft departs the runway with the rocket attached or at 30,000 feet when the rocket drops and fires? Space and property underwriters will have to review all contracts to be very clear on these points as a launch loss can occur at a millisecond between any of these events.

Launch and In-Orbit Insurance

Launch and in-orbit are the essence of space insurance, and it will be reviewed in detail in the next section.

Transponder Insurance

The insured is not the satellite owner/operator but typically a company that purchases or leases the use of a transponder on a satellite. Think of a transponder as one of many channels (repeaters) on a satellite. The typical insured is a television station or a multinational business. *Transponder* coverage provides protection against the loss of use of the transponder. The lease agreement for the transponder between the operator and insured must be reviewed as to what protections the insured has. There are three possible scenarios.

1. Protected Service is when the insured will receive the use of a replacement transponder on the same satellite or another satellite should his transponder fail.
2. Unprotected Service is when the insured will not receive a replacement in the event his transponder fails.
3. Pre-emptible Service is when the insured can loose his transponder to another should someone else's transponder fail.

Underwriting and pricing of the insurance depend on which of these scenarios exist as well as the health of a satellite and the amount of extra capacity on it. This insurance is written in the space market but can also be handled by traditional business interruption insurance markets. A space underwriter may not be willing to write transponders on satellites they already insure as they must watch accumulation of risk. If an underwriter already has a $10 million line on a satellite in orbit and that is the maximum capacity, the underwriter would decline to cover any further exposure on the same satellite.

Launch Risk Guarantee Insurance

Launch providers prior to the mid-1980s did not provide *Launch Risk Guarantee insurance* to their clients. It was solely up to the satellite owner to purchase an all risk launch policy. Because of availability of insurance, launch providers are now able to offer the coverage to their clients for a replacement launch in the event the satellite is not placed in the proper orbit, if it is destroyed or if it is damaged by the launch vehicle. The contract with the satellite owner will charge an additional fee for this protection and it often mirrors the cost of insurance.

This insurance is written in the space market and is addressed and written the same way as traditional launch insurance only the insured is the launch provider. An advantage to the launch provider may be that insurance can be purchased for multiple launches under one policy based on his launch record and the cost could be more competitive than a satellite owner could get for a single launch. Historically, the launch phase has been the most at risk phase of space insurance, so the cost of insurance for this phase can be significant. This would translate to quite a savings for the satellite buyer should he take advantage of a launch provider's program if competitive.

The satellite owner will have to weigh the advantages to purchasing this through the launch provider and covering all risk on his satellite on his own. If the satellite owner does take advantage of the launch provider's guarantee he will still likely be purchasing satellite hull insurance at the point of separation from the launch vehicle. There is the possibility of a gap being created in this situation should there be question as to when an anomaly (loss event) occurs. The nature of launch failures leaves little or no debris to examine with respect to cause of loss as the satellite either reached an incorrect orbit or exploded. This gap could be remote but it is another item to place in the equation when the satellite buyer is weighing the advantages to purchasing launch risk guarantee insurance from the launch provider or covering it under his own program.

Third Party Liability Insurance

Third party liability coverage is written in the aviation market by liability underwriters and in some cases it includes space underwriters depending on the insurer. Third party liability exposure exists for the period from launch until all pieces of the vehicle or satellite fall back down to earth. Satellites in geostationary orbit would take hundreds of years to fall through the atmosphere but typically never will because when they reach end of life they use remaining fuel to boost themselves a few hundred miles above the geostationary altitude to a useless orbit. In-orbit liability exposure may be considered remote by many satellite owner/operators but the exposure exists as long as they have an asset in space. Should a satellite fail and spin out of control any resulting damage it causes to another object (satellite, space station, etc.) could result in a claim.

Liability exposure is governed by the launching state (country) and there are international treaties addressing who will be declared at fault in the event of damages. Commonly referred to as the *Space Treaty* the 1972 Convention on International Liability for Damages Caused by Space Objects provides a body of law governing space liability.

The Space Treaty establishes:

- Definition of "launching state" and "space object"
- Absolute liability of launching state for damages on ground or to aircraft in flight
- Fault based liability for damages caused to objects in space.
- Joint and several liability of launching states which cause damage to third party state on earth or to aircraft in flight (absolute liability). If third party damage in space, liability based on fault (proportional fault or equal apportionment if undetermined)
- Does not apply to damages to nationals of launching state, or participating foreign nationals.

With respect to the launch liability exposures, the underwriting is different from space hull insurance as it typically is not the purchase agreement between the buyer and manufacturer that dictates exposure but the contract between the launch provider and the governing body. In the United States all launches must be licensed by the Federal Aviation Administration (FAA) and the application for license includes a maximum possible loss analysis. The FAA will require a specified limit of liability be carried by the launch provider based on this analysis which looks at location of launch, size of vehicle, etc. Currently, the government will provide an excess layer of coverage above this required limit. The regulations also require that all parties to a launch (including the satellite owner, manufacturer, subcontractors and the government) agree to cross-waiver of liability against all other parties. This makes each responsible for his own loss and keeps litigation to a minimum in this inherently dangerous activity. Europe and other countries have similar regulations.

Third party liability coverage is typically purchased by the launch provider for the launch. The major launch providers in the United States purchase this under their comprehensive aviation products liability program that covers all their launch activity within an annual policy period. In Russia the satellite owner may be required to purchase the coverage for a launch and it is typically a per launch coverage. The cost of insurance is based on the limit required, the loss experience of the launch vehicle and the remoteness of the launch from populated areas. Limits of liability may range from $10 to $400 million.

The last type of insurance is *in-orbit third party liability coverage* that covers any damage a satellite might cause to another satellite should it go out of control. This in-orbit coverage has become a bit more popular as operators with low earth orbit constellations have a higher likelihood of an occurrence. There is also de-orbit coverage that can be purchased and is typically found with regard to large objects such as *Skylab*, the *Mir* Space Station or the Hubble space telescope but it could apply to a mass de-orbit of a constellation of LEO satellites.

The FAA is currently reviewing how to structure new liability regulations to apply to space tourism companies as the exposure is unique and requires special treatment compared with existing exposures. Privatizing the industry and attempting to protect civilian astronauts will likely increase liability requirements. The question will be how will the insurance industry react to it and will enough capacity be available to meet the new requirements.

UNDERWRITING SPACE INSURANCE

Space insurance is unlike other lines of insurance as the law of large numbers is difficult if not impossible to apply. Even the aviation market appears large when compared to the space market as there are hundreds of thousands of aircraft but during a given year there are only 30 to 60 commercial launches. To go further the group of launches is not homogenous as there are five or six different major launch providers and as many satellite manufacturers building different satellites. Therefore, it is most important that the underwriting expertise be as competent as possible.

Space underwriters and brokers develop the expertise for the business through previous space industry experience or are self-educated. This is rocket science and consultants from the industry are relied on to advise underwriters and satellite buyers. The technologies constantly change and it is important to understand it in great detail in order to evaluate the risk. Even after underwriters are on risk they may require further consultants after a loss. This is particularly true with partial losses as the calculation of the extent of the loss can be complicated. This is not such a large concern for launch failures as a total loss will be obvious.

The space underwriting process is a lengthy one and may start years before a satellite is ordered from a manufacturer. Not only do the underwriters have to understand the technical aspects of the satellite configuration and ability to meet its specifications, but they must build some confidence in the business plan in order to avoid any moral hazards.

Because the sum insured of satellites can range from $200 to $400 million or more for a geostationary satellite or $50 to $200 for a low earth orbit satellite, insurance is written on a quota share basis. This is similar to how the aviation market handles airlines or large aviation product liability programs. Each insurer takes only a percentage of the risk because no one company has the capacity to manage the entire risk. Unlike the airlines or products markets, space underwriters each underwrite on their own behalf instead of having a "lead" underwriter who agrees to the policy wording and manages any claims on behalf of the other underwriters. The space markets each write their own policy and manage claims independently of the others adding complexity to the brokers' job. The broker will have to be sure that any differences in policy language is kept to a minimum and will push for consistency.

Space underwriters are often briefed simultaneously with group meetings taking place. A new start-up satellite organization may come to underwriters while still working on financing to be sure the insurance will be available when required. Initial underwriter briefings will take place to present an overview of the business plan. Once the prospective insured has signed a purchase agreement for a satellite, the underwriters will again be briefed by the manufacturer on the mission requirements and technical specifications of the satellite. Underwriters will go back and forth with the brokers, insured and manufacturers getting questions answered until they are satisfied they have enough information to rate the risk.

The insurance product, the "policy," is the culmination of the study of the satellite project by the broker, the technical consultants and the underwriters and can represent as much as three years' work. Once a launch provider and launch vehicle have been identified the underwriters will receive copies of purchase agreements and launch agreements allowing them to evaluate the risk, design a policy that fits and provide premium quotes. The space broker will get input from a majority of the underwriters then come up with a rating scheme that all can agree to. All insurance markets are on a quota-share basis and quote on their own but at the end of the day each market will receive the same premium rate as there can be no favoritism. If that final premium number is unacceptable to a market then they will decline to accept it and not take a share on the risk.

Insurance Program Design Considerations

- Sum Insured
- Policy Period
- Attachment of Risk
- Termination of Risk
- Deductibles
- Definitions

Sum Insured

The sum insured in the policy goes beyond what we think of as hull insurance for an aircraft. An aircraft value is based on an agreed sum insured the underwriter and broker discuss and agree on after the underwriter has had a chance to review bluebook value and equipment onboard, etc. Satellite insured value is much broader and includes more that the satellite itself. The agreed value includes replacement costs including the cost to manufacture, launch, finance and insure. This may appear to be overly generous but remember a satellite takes years to manufacture and a launch vehicle must be procured. The financing and insurance costs could be unknown as future pricing swings cannot be predicted. The underwriter will ask to quantify each of these values by the insured prior to coverage being placed.

To provide a monetary example, the cost to manufacture the satellite could be $200 million with the launch costing $70 million. The insurance and financing costs add another $80 million providing a total insured value of $350 million. Once the value has been set it is up to the broker to complete the placement. The ability to insure it depends on the availability of market capacity. There is always the possibility that insurance cannot be completed based on a less reliable satellite or launch vehicle. In such a case, underwriters may only want to put a portion of their capacity at risk. In such a case there are two outcomes, either the premium is increased to attract more capacity or the insured must accept a lower insured value than desired in effect taking a share of the risk himself.

Policy Period

A space policy is unique as it does not incept like a standard occurrence policy. The policy is often underwritten and bound by the broker and underwriters but the launch (attachment of risk) under the policy may not take place for up to three years after the policy has been bound. There is a specified time period wherein the launch must take place (from 24 to 36 months after policy inception) and the risk period takes place thereafter. A typical risk period is from time of launch plus one year. Thus, underwriters must manage the long-tail exposures under space insurance as their capital can be exposed anywhere from one to four years after policy inception.

Perhaps an example will help to understand the point. A policy is written and effective at July 1, 2005 for a launch taking place anytime from July 1, 2005 to July 1, 2008. The underwriters are not exposed until the launch takes place. If the launch does not take place until June 30, 2008 and the risk period is one year the underwriter will be at risk until June 30, 2009. This is four years after the policy is written. These long-tail issues have historically been even more severe as there was a time in the late 1990s where underwriters were agreeing to insure satellites for a risk period from launch plus three or five years. In such an event if the launch doesn't take place until the end of the three year policy period the underwriter could be at risk up to eight years after the policy inception.

Premium payments are made with a deposit premium of 10 percent of the full premium due at policy inception. The remainder is then due 30 days prior to the launch date. Material changes that take place prior to the launch will require underwriter approval and if significant enough may lead an underwriter to re-rate the risk or even retract their participation. Such a change could include switching to a different launch vehicle or the realization that similar model satellites are having in-orbit anomalies requiring modification prior to launch.

Attachment of Risk depends on contractual conditions and two possible examples are:

- At Intentional Ignition: The time when the automatic sequence control system indicates that the intentional ignition of the first main engines of the launch vehicle has occurred.
- At Lift-off: Intentional ignition of the launch vehicle propulsion systems causing upward acceleration of the launch vehicle following the intentional removal of all mechanical restraints, if any, designed to prevent such upward acceleration

Termination of Risk is negotiated with the insured and can be as early as end of launch or cover an in-orbit period thereafter. Common options are:

- In-orbit acceptance, or
- 180 days following launch, or
- 12, 24, 36, 48 or 60 months following launch depending on various factors, including the business plan, complexity of the satellite and/or mission life.

The first option suggests the coverage is only for launch vehicle flight only and the insured is willing to take on the risk once the satellite has been injected by the launch vehicle to a given orbit. This can be as little as 25 minutes after launch. The second option suggests that coverage will run until the satellite has run through all of its checkouts or the end of what is called the commissioning period. These two options may be of interest if the satellite owner has a fleet in-orbit policy that the satellite might attach to once injection in-orbit or commissioning is complete.

Lastly, the launch plus one year or more covers the launch and in-orbit exposure. This is the most popular option as operators usually have an interest in insurance for the life of their asset. If launch plus one year is taken they will then purchase one year policies there after to cover the in-orbit life of the satellite. Again, periods in excess of one year was an option, but due to the long tail and increase in in-orbit failures these options are no longer available. After the year 2000 risk periods of more than one year have not been available.

Definitions and Deductibles

Definitions guide space policies by clarifying terms and conditions. As noted with attachment of risk the point of launch can be defined differently under different launch contracts. Partial loss definitions are likely the most complex definitions you will find anywhere. A partial loss can come about from infinite factors that affect the satellite operation. If the satellite is not able to survive its predetermined life or meet its operational requirements set out in the specifications then a partial loss has occurred. How that is measured is very difficult. If it is due to power reduction it might be from solar array degradation or battery cell failure. If signals are not reaching the correct geographic area on the ground there could be problems with the antenna or the transponders. If there is a leak in the satellite's engines, it may not be able to keep its position in orbit for the specified life time. All of these factors must be addressed in the loss definition to define how a dollar amount can be placed on each type of degradation. How to determine the useful life left in an operational satellite can lead to long negotiations.

Deductibles for space programs may not be of the nature often thought of in other areas of insurance. If a fleet of satellites is to be launched and the insured wants to reduce his costs he may take a deductible of one launch failure. Another example may be within the definition of partial loss where it may specify that a total loss does not occur until 75 percent of a satellites operational life has been lost. Lastly, a deductible can take the form of a straight exclusion. There may be components on a satellite that have failed on other satellites of the same model that create an increased chance of failing on any like satellites. These failures are referred to as generic failures (anomalies). To protect themselves on renewal, underwriters may simply exclude that component from coverage. Solar arrays, motors or communication payload components have all been excluded at one point or another from space policies due to these generic failures.

Policy Summary

To sum up the policy issuance process, the policy is drafted and agreed to between the insured, broker and underwriters. A premium of 10 percent of the policy premium is paid to hold the policy bound. The policy will state a coverage period, typically launch plus one year, for a launch taking place within three years of the date of policy issuance. Thus, the policy period has no relationship to the risk period other than holding the underwriters to the risk when launch eventually does happen. If a satellite gets delayed outside the policy period the policy can be extended or will be completely renegotiated depending on circumstances. Thirty days prior to the launch the remaining 90 percent of the premium is paid and underwriters are at risk from the launch date for the risk period. Once the launch policy expires, the insured purchases an in-orbit policy in annual increments for the life of the satellite.

The insured may have only purchased a launch policy that expires after separation from the launch vehicle or after commissioning. Or, the insured may have purchased launch risk guarantee coverage from the launch provider and only needs to purchase insurance at separation and for commissioning and in-orbit thereafter. The commissioning phase starts when the ground controllers acquire the satellite and start the process of turning the satellite on (booting it up) and testing all functions. This takes anywhere from 30 to 90 days. The risk is highest for the launch period then reduces for commissioning. The in-orbit phase was thought to be the lowest risk phase but that is currently up for debate due to many in-orbit and generic failures taking place over the past decade. Once a satellite is in orbit the likelihood of a total loss is less likely than a partial loss scenario.

In-Orbit coverage indemnifies the Insured for physical loss of, damage to, or failure of the satellite in-orbit. Coverage starts following expiry of the launch policy and continues for the life of the satellite with policies being issued in annual periods. Some space markets do not participate on in-orbit coverage because it is felt the rates are not adequate and recently there have been increases in the in-orbit exposure as new technologies have failed to meet specifications. Also, not all operators buy coverage particularly those with large fleets of satellites who have an inherent spread of risk.

In-Orbit Partial Loss Costs

- Business Interruption
- Increased cost of operating the satellite
- Reduction in revenues

- Purchase or lease of additional capacity from third parties
- Increase in the use (and cost) of terrestrial links

Satellites are thought of in the industry as coming to life once the solar arrays are deployed and the power is turned on. Once the satellite has completed commissioning the health status is monitored for the rest of its life which can be 15 years. Health status reports are provided at a minimum to underwriters on an annual basis. Reports include full status of payload performance, attitude, telemetry command, power, solar array, battery, thermal situation, propulsion, previous anomaly updates, new anomalies, prognosis and estimated life calculations. In the space business because everything is in engineering terms when there is any unexpected, event it is referred to as an anomaly. An anomaly can be as minor as an adjustment in antenna pointing or as catastrophic as a complete shutdown of a satellite. Regardless of the degree, in the industry all anomalies are treated very seriously and investigated thoroughly to reduce the chance for any future surprises.

Market, Supply and Demand

Like all nonregulated property casualty insurance, space insurance premium rates move in cycles based on supply and demand. Space insurance has been written since the 1960s but it did not mature until the 1970s when coverage became available for the launch phase. The loss history of launch vehicles was of the greatest concern through the mid-1990s and inaugural vehicles had particularly poor results. In the mid-1990s the market had some good years and looked as though over the long term it would become profitable.

In the late 1990s, in-orbit failures, including generic failures, became more frequent and raised underwriting concerns particularly as launch plus five year policies were being written at the time. A recent study by United States Aviation Insurance Underwriters for the 11 years 1994-2004 shows the space underwriters made only a 1 percent cumulative profit. This is not a show of confidence to capital providers for this market. Since 1999, reinsurance for the space market is basically non-existent and all underwriters capacity is truly their own.

It is estimated that today the available capacity for a launch is $425 million. This may not cover the largest geostationary satellites and the total in-orbit capacity per satellite is limited to $240 million. As noted many markets offer less capacity or no capacity for in-orbit exposures. When the launch vehicle is not proven such as a new derivative or the satellite is pushing technology limits the launch capacity available may be reduced to below the insured's valuation. Recently a satellite operator was only able to secure $175 million of capacity for a satellite valued at $250 million.

Launch premium rates over the years for a standard launch plus one year coverage have ranged from 9 to 25 percent of the sum insured value net of commissions. Launch rates since 2000 have remained at a high point of 16 to 25 percent range. This is due to recently high loss years due to the generic fleet component failures. In-orbit premium rates have ranged from 1-4 percent of value for an annual policy. These rates have also increased in recent years and are currently in the 2.5 -3.5 percent range for an average risk.

Space Brokers and Underwriters

The list below represents major space brokers and underwriters active as of 2006.

Brokers

AON	Paris, London and Washington D.C.
Benfield (ISB)	London
International Space Brokers (ISB)	Washington D.C., France
Marsh	New York, London

Willis	New York, London, Bethesda, MD, Singapore

Underwriters

AGF	France
LRS	France
SCOR	France
Hannover Re	Germany
Munich Re	Germany
SATEC	Italy
Tokyo Marine	Japan
AIG/Redholm	London
Amlin	London
Brit	London
Catlin	London
Global Aerospace	London & New Jersey
Hayward	London
Hiscox	London
Liberty	London
Watkins	London
Swiss Re	Switzerland
ACE	Philadelphia
AXA Space	Washington, D.C.
USAIG	New York
XL Aerospace	Santa Barbara

FUTURE UNDERWRITING ISSUES

Space risks continue to evolve as does the political environment surrounding them. There has always been a push to manufacturer larger more powerful satellites with more capabilities. Competition for new launch vehicles will continue as manufactures push to reduce the cost per pound to orbit. Underwriters will have to watch these new developments closely and will always be skeptical of new vehicles as the track record of inaugural launchers is poor.

The mid-1990s saw increases in launches per year, and with the advent of LEO constellations there was an expectation that 30 satellite launches a year would become the norm. This would provide the space underwriters with a better spread of risk although the law of large numbers remains illusive. Unfortunately, the bankruptcy of Iridium sent shock waves through the financial markets and financing for any new space projects became very scarce. The launches dropped back to the 15 launches per year range by 2000 and LEO constellation growth saw an end. Launches today, in 2006, are starting to increase once again but the underwriters are still recovering from the in-orbit failures of 1999 and 2000. Thus, the pricing pressures continue as underwriters struggle to maintain long-term profitability.

Political forces have caused great concern in the underwriting markets with the strict regulations of the United States State Department of International Traffic in Arms Regulations (ITAR). In 1999 regulation of ITAR moved from the Commerce Department to the State Department. All launch vehicle and satellite information must be approved and "cleaned" prior to export from the United States. Therefore, any buyer of United States satellites or launch vehicles or underwriters evaluating such information who are located outside the United States may not get necessary details and if they do, likely not in a timely manner. The real downside to this is that the U.S. manufacturers have lost valuable satellite business as foreign owner/operators are seeking the technology outside the United States to avoid such restrictions. This will continue to be a huge drain on U.S. manufacturers and launch providers.

Lastly, underwriters must take into account environmental hazards. Satellites are built to protect their payload against the environment as much as possible but space is a hostile environment. Space debris is a problem that gets worse with each launch because spent launch vehicle stages continue in low orbit for years. Other factors are meteors with annual peaks in showers taking place from August to October. The Leonid storms are trailing debris from the comet Temple-Tuttle that orbits the sun once every 33 years. These unknowns can be the cause of catastrophic in-orbit failures that may never be understood. In the event satellite operators can predict high meteor activity or track debris they can make evasive maneuvers or repoint solar arrays away from the obstacles, but these practices have limitations.

Solar flares present another type of space event that can negatively affect satellites. The sun solar max occurs on an 11-year cycle with the last peak in 2000. The effect solar flares have on satellites is on the electronics. A flare sends out a wave of highly charged particles that can send a power surge or disruption through the electronics of a satellite with the worst case being a shut down of the satellite. Other than placing a satellite in what is called a "safe mode" there is little evasive maneuvering that can be done. A safe mode is comparable to turning your computer off for a period of time and then once the solar wave has passed it can be rebooted. This is not a popular tactic as few operators are willing to shut down a perfectly working satellite with the remote chance that it will not reboot.

The satellite risk profile below describes areas of concern for the underwriters. Two related issues concern the industries push to reduce manufacturing times and the heritage of components. Manufacturers in marketing efforts attempt to reduce the time it takes to manufacture a satellite. The underwriting concern is that corners may be cut such as eliminating component testing. Will reliability suffer because of the rush to complete a satellite on schedule? Heritage of components is somewhat related in that if a component has not been tested in space before or has no track record (heritage) then how can its performance in space truly be judged. The profile below also exemplifies the constant push in the technology to increase power and mass.

Satellite Risk Profile

• Satellite Mass Increasing	Over 5 Tons
• Satellites are more Complex	Digital compression, on-board Computers, interconnectivity
• Satellites Require More Power	Over 10,000 Watts
• Satellite Manufacturing Cycle	From 36 Months to 15
• Satellite Engine Technology Evolving	New engines for in-orbit propulsion
• Heritage of Components	New untested technology
• ITAR Restrictions	Limits Underwriting Data
• Environmental Issues	Space Debris, Solar Flares

The study of space risks is ongoing and volumes of material can be found on the issues raised in this chapter. A reference section is provided at the end of the chapter for those wishing to further their space insurance studies.

Key Terms

Airline classifications
Airline risk selection
Airline rating
Space insurance
Satellite
Pre-launch and manufacturers' coverage
Transponder coverage
Launch risk guarantee
Space Treaty
In-orbit third party liability coverage
In-orbit coverage

Review Questions

1. How would you classify the hundreds of airlines operating around the world today? Why is it said that the airline industry is highly elastic and very cyclical?
2. What are the three most important criteria in airline risk selection? How are rates determined? Why might an air carrier experience an increase in rates when it has had no claims?
3. Why is reinsurance so important in airline placements? Describe the arrangement known as "quota share" or "vertical" placement?
4. Briefly summarize the history of space insurance from the mid 1960s. What are some of the commercial uses of satellites? Distinguish between geostationary satellites and low earth orbit (LEO) satellites. Distinguish between launch providers and launch vehicles.
5. What is pre-launch and manufacturers coverage? How has launch risk guarantee insurance changed over the years?
6. What is the purpose of the 1972 Space Treaty? In-orbit third party liability coverage?
7. Discuss some of the factors underwriters take into consideration in evaluating a space insurance risk. How does the sum insured differ between satellites and aircraft? How does the policy differ? When does the risk terminate?
8. Why is it so difficult to determine partial losses to satellites? How might in-orbit coverage be broadened? Space insurance premiums move in cycles based upon supply and demand . Explain.
9. Identify some of the largest brokerages and underwriters of space insurance. What are some of the issues regarding space risks faced by underwriters in the future?

References

The Air Force Role in Developing International Outer Space Law, Delbert R. Terrill Jr., Colonel, USAFR, Air University Press, Maxwell Air Force Base, Alabama. May 1999.

Airclaims–The Space Review: Airclaims, Space Department, Cardinal Point, Newall Road, Heathrow Airport, London TW6 2AS – UK. Website: www.airlcaims.co.uk

Annual Report, Air Transport Association, Washington, D.C., 2004.

Annual Report, International Air Transport Association, Montreal, Canada, 2004.

Commercial Space Transportation Competitiveness Act of 2000, Public Law 106-405 referred to as Space Competitiveness Act.

49 U.S.C. Subtitle IX, Chapter 701, (know as the CSLA (Commercial Space Launch Act)

Liability Risk-Sharing Regime for U.S. Commercial Space Transportation: Study and Analysis, April 2002, U.S. Department of Transportation and Federal Aviation Administration. Available from website: http://ast.faa.gov/

PL 85-804: Public Law 52.250-1: Indemnification under Public Law 85-804

Research and Invention in Outer Space, Liability and Intellectual Property Rights. Editor Sa'idMosteshar. Martinus Nijhoff Publishers and International Bar Association. 1995.

Space Flight and Insurance, Second Edition (Revised), a publication of the Munich Reinsurance Company. 1993 Munchener Ruckversicherungs-Gesellschat.

Space News International, publisher Imaginova Corp., 6883 Commercial Drive, Springfield, VA 22159-0500.

Space Risks I/II and III- The Pocket Guide (1995, 1996 and 1997 respectively) by Willis Corroon Inspace and Mark Williamson, Space Technology Consultant.

2003 Commercial Space Transportation Forecasts, May 2003, Federal Aviation Administration's Associate Administrator for Commercial Space Transportation (AST) and the Commercial Space Transportation Advisory Committee (COMSTAC). Available for download at website: http://ast.faa.gov/

2002 U.S. Commercial Space Transportation Developments and Concepts: Vehicles, Technologies, and Spaceports. Associate Administrator for Commercial Space Transportation, Federal Aviation Administration. Available for download at website: http://ast.faa.gov/

Chapter 12

Aviation Business Property Insurance and Transportation Insurance

OUTLINE

Commercial Property Policy
Property Insurance Rates
Business Income, Extra Expense and Rental Value Coverage Forms
Risk Management Decision Areas
Miscellaneous Property Coverages
Crime Insurance
Inland Marine Insurance
Transportation Insurance

OBJECTIVES

At the end of this chapter you should be able to:
Identify and explain five common policy conditions in the commercial property form.
Explain types of business property covered, and give examples of property that is excluded.
Explain the vacancy restriction endorsement and the windstorm and hail endorsement.
Explain and give examples of business income, extra expense, and rental value coverages.
Briefly explain how property coverage rates are determined.
Explain the following risk management decisions areas:
named peril versus all risk coverage; replacement cost versus actual cash value; coinsurance versus full value; and specific versus blanket insurance.
Explain pollution liability insurance for underground fuel storage tanks.
Explain the various crime coverages available to the aviation risk manager.
Identify three types of property that would be covered by inland marine insurance.
Differentiate the liability of common carriers and contract carriers.
Explain the cargo liability coverage endorsement, inland transit policy, and the spares endorsement.

In addition to pure aviation risk exposures, aviation risk managers must also deal with potential financial losses associated with ownership of or responsibility for real and personal business property. Airport buildings, FBO maintenance and repair facilities, and hangars along with their contents are important risk exposures. Losses may be direct, consisting of loss of the asset itself, or indirect, resulting from the loss of use of the asset.

Commercial insurance has evolved from a hodgepodge of separate policies and endorsements into a packaged format that combines appropriate coverages into a single policy. In January 1986, the Insurance Services Office (ISO), a trade association of insurers, introduced its *portfolio program*. Most insurers have adopted the portfolio program but because ISO is a statistical and advisory body, the adoption of the portfolio program by individual insurers is voluntary. The portfolio program was designed to eliminate the redundancy in coverage provisions, and incorporate updated, simplified language. The commercial lines described in this chapter will be confined to a discussion of property, crime, and inland marine coverages.

COMMERCIAL PROPERTY POLICY

Policy Structure

The commercial property policy has the following coverage parts:

- Common Policy Declarations
- Common Policy Conditions
- Building and Personnel Property Coverage Form
- Insuring Clause or Agreement
- Exclusions
- Definitions
- Selected Endorsements

Common Policy Declarations

The common policy declaration page shows the policy period, usually one year, and the name, mailing address, and business description of the insured. Coverage parts forming part of the policy with limits of coverage selected, appropriate deductibles, and the insuring company are listed. A number of forms and endorsements that the insured has selected along with any supplemental policies follow. A summary of premiums is listed usually by coverage area.

Common Policy Conditions

Policy conditions set provisions, rules of conduct, duties, and obligations for the parties. A number of common insurance conditions describe such things as the policy period and coverage territory, the insured's obligation in the event of loss, how settlements are handled when other insurance is involved, and the right of each party to cancel. Depending on the kind of policy, conditions may be found in a "Conditions" section, or spread throughout the policy form. Other common conditions are:

- Changes in the policy terms can be made by a written endorsement issued by the insurance company.
- The insurer is granted the right to audit books and records of the insured in connection with the policy during the policy period and during the three years following policy expiration.
- Insurer has the right but not the obligation to make inspections and surveys of the insured's property.
- Responsibility for payment of premiums rests with the first named insured on the declaration page.
- The insured's rights and duties under this policy can be transferred to an other only with the written consent of the insurer. In the event of the insured's death, rights and duties are automatically transferred to the insured's legal representative.
- If the insurer decides not to renew the policy, the insurer will mail to the first named insured written notice of the nonrenewal not less than 60 days before the end of the policy period.

Building and Personnel Property Coverage Form

The building and personnel property coverage form is designed to protect the insured's real property, business personal property, and property of others in the care, custody, and control of the insured. The building coverage defines building to include the structure described, completed additions, fixtures, machinery, and equipment which are permanently installed. Owned personal property used to service the building and premises, additions under construction, and repairs to the building are also included. Business personal property includes furniture and fixtures, machinery and equipment, stock, value of work performed or arranged by the insured on personal property of others, and all other personal property owned by the insured and used in the business. Coverage for personal property of others applies to such property in the insured's care, custody, and control, and located on the designated premises or within a specified area (usually within 1000 feet of the premises. Some policies include fuel farms, fences, Visual Approach Slope Indicator (VASI) and radar equipment, and lights in the property section designated as "yard property." Other coverage forms will write these items under the inland marine section which will be addressed later in this chapter.

There are two approaches available to the risk manager to protect the firm's property: named perils and all risk policies. *Named perils policy* specifies the perils covered. This policy form lists 16 perils like: fire, lightning, windstorm and hail, smoke, vandalism, sprinkler leakage, and theft. In addition to listing the perils, the policy will define what is actually meant by the stated covered peril. For example, smoke is a covered peril and the policy states that smoke coverage extends only to sudden and accidental smoke damage. The *all risk policy* covers all perils not otherwise excluded. This is the policy form discussed in this chapter and it will provide broader coverage and give the risk manager a better understanding of exposures not covered. Because of the broader coverage, an all risk policy will cost more than the named perils policy. An important advantage of the all risk approach is that it is more difficult for the insurance company to deny coverage. This is because the burden of proof is on the insurer to show that coverage does not apply to a particular loss, whereas with a named perils policy the insurance company must show that the loss was caused by a peril specifically listed in the policy.

Additional Coverages and Coverage Extensions

In addition to direct damage to covered property, the typical property policy includes coverage extensions at specified limits. Some of these extensions include:

- Debris removal made necessary by loss to covered property by a covered peril. This coverage is limited to a maximum of 25 percent of the direct damage loss, plus the amount of the deductible. For example, if direct damage to insured property is $60,000, and the deductible is $500, the insurer will pay up to $15,500 for debris removal. If this is inadequate, the policy provides an additional $250,000 under the limit of insurance provision.
- Pollutant cleanup and removal coverage will pay up to $100,000 to extract pollutants from land or water, provided that the release of the pollutant is caused by a covered peril.
- Fire department service charges.
- The policy will pay 25 percent of the covered loss, not to exceed $25,000 for rewards paid to secure stolen property.
- Policy provides coverage of up to $250,000 for additional expenses due to the changes in building codes or ordinances.
- Up to $25,000 for temporary repairs to protect property after a loss.
- Reimbursement for repairs of faulty fire protective equipment that accidentally discharges.
- Up to $25,000 for business personal property that is damaged while temporarily out of the country and in the possession of an employee.
- Coverage extensions are available and the following represents the variety of choices:

    - Newly constructed or acquired property
    - Personal effects
    - Valuable papers and records
    - Outdoor property
    - Theft damage to rented property
    - Water damage
    - Accounts receivable

Property and Costs Not Covered

The property coverage form typically excludes coverage for several items including, but not limited to:

- Accounts and bills
- Currency, deeds, money, notes, checks, drafts, or securities.
- Contraband
- Water, land, growing crops, or standing timber
- The cost of excavating, grading, backfilling, reclaiming, or restoring land or water
- The cost to research, replace, or restore the information on valuable papers and records
- Fine arts
- Personal property sold under an installment after delivery to the purchaser
- Vehicles or self-propelled machines that are licensed for use on public roads
- Aircraft or watercraft
- Animals or birds
- Automobiles held for sale
- Bulkheads, pilings, piers, wharves, docks, dikes, or dams
- Underground tanks, pipes, flues, drains, tunnels
- The following property while outside of covered buildings: bridges, roadways, walks, patios, or other paved surfaces, retaining walls, fences, trees, shrubs, plants, or lawns, harvested grain, hay, straw, or other crops.

Some of these items can be specifically covered by attaching an endorsement or writing a separate policy while others are considered “uninsurable,” i.e., contraband.

A typical property form excludes certain coverages that are either considered “uninsurable” under the insurance definition, or available under a separate policy or an endorsement. Some of these include:

Exclusions

- Enforcement of any ordinance or law that requires that the building be torn down
- Any earth movement other than “sinkhole collapse”
- Seizure or destruction of property by orders of governmental authority
- Nuclear reaction or radiation
- War, including undeclared or civil war
- Failure or fluctuation of power or other utility service supplied to the described premises
- Flood or mudslide
- Neglect of the insured to use reasonable means to save and preserve property from further damage at the time of the loss
- Dishonest or criminal acts
- Explosion of steam boilers, steam pipes, steam engines, or steam turbines

The commercial property policy will include certain additional coverages with limited coverage. It should be noted that each company’s policy form varies. Some standard limitations include:

Limitations

- $10,000 for furs, fur garments, and garments trimmed with fur
- $10,000 for jewelry, watches, watch movements, jewels, pearls, precious stones, bullion, gold, silver, and platinum. This limit is raised to $50,000 if these metals are used as a raw material in the insured’s business.
- $1,000 for stamps, tickets and letters of credit.

Definitions

Definitions define important terms used in the policy language. Definitions do not provide or exclude coverage, they simply clarify coverage. The placement of definitions varies by policy. In some cases the definitions will be in the conditions sections, while other policy forms will include an exclusive section. Most policies will put quotations around specific terms where a definition is available.

Selected Endorsements

The risk manager and the insurance company have a large number of endorsements available to add, modify, or delete coverages. Endorsements are used to tailor coverages to the needs of an insured and they permit the insurance company to modify risks to better conform to underwriting standards. The *vacancy restriction endorsement* is used to protect the insurer from the added risks associated with a building that is empty. After being vacant for 60 days, the policy excludes loss from vandalism, sprinkler leakage, building glass breakage, water damage, theft, and attempted theft. All other covered losses would be reduced by 15 percent.

Windstorm or hail endorsement is frequently used in high-risk areas like coastal areas and known hail regions. The declaration page would indicate a deductible expressed as either a dollar amount, or a percentage that would be subtracted from each windstorm or hail claim. The percentages run from 1 percent to 5 percent. A unique feature of this endorsement is that the deductible applies to each building and to personal property if damaged rather than the normal single deductible per occurrence.

Reporting Form Coverage

Reporting forms are specifically designed for aviation businesses which have widely fluctuating levels of parts and other inventory, or wide ranging values of hangared aircraft. The commercial property policy to which this form may be attached is written with a maximum limit adequate to cover the highest exposure anticipated during the policy year. The insurer's risk moves up and down as the firm reports each month the actual values exposed to loss. A provisional premium is paid at the inception of the policy and is adjusted at the end of the policy year to reflect the true cost of the protection provided.

BUSINESS INCOME, EXTRA EXPENSE, AND RENTAL VALUE COVERAGE FORMS

In addition to the cost of a direct loss to business property, risk managers must also analyze the potential loss of revenue and profits due to a direct loss. An FBO may have to shut down its maintenance facility until the property is repaired or replaced. The inability to service maintenance customers under contract may increase loss potential. Another concern is the necessity to pay fixed costs while the property is unusable. The commercial property policy allows the risk manager to select the following coverages: (1) business income, (2) rental value, and (3) extra expense.

Business income coverage indemnifies a business for losses during the time the business is unable to operate while the property is being repaired or replaced. The losses would be the net profit before income taxes the business would have earned if there had been no interruption and the expenses that continue despite the interruption. Ongoing expenses include payroll of management staff, maintenance services provided under contract, and fixed expenses like interest, insurance, and mortgage payments. Coverage is written subject to a coinsurance provision that requires coverage equal to 50, 60, 70, 80, 90, or 100 percent of the firm's annual earnings for the 12-month period of the policy. The following five conditions must be met for the coverage to apply:

1. Property loss from a covered peril must have occurred.
2. The business must have been totally or partially shut down because of the loss.

Business Income Worksheet
Manufacturing Operations

	Actual values for year ending 200_	Estimated values for year ending 200_
A. Net Income Before Taxes		
B. Add Total Operating Expenses		
C. Add Direct Labor		
D. Add Factory Overhead		
Sub-Total		
If Ordinary Payroll is to be excluded or limited:		
E. Deduct any or all Ordinary Payroll Expense		
F. Business Income Basis		
G. Number of months required to recover from a total destruction of property (Show the # of months as a percentage of a year. Example: 6 months = .5; 9 months = .75, etc.)		
H. Estimated Business Income Exposure Amount (F) x (G)		
I. If Extra Expense is to be covered, show the Estimated Total amount from Line 5 of the Extra Expense Worksheet		
J. Estimated Business Income and Extra Expense Exposure Amount (H + I)		

Figure 12.1

3. It must be established that if the loss had not occurred the business would have continued to operate.
4. Loss must have occurred during the policy period.
5. It must be shown that the business would have continued to earn at least enough to pay fixed costs.

Extra expense coverage is an alternative method of protecting a firm from the losses incurred as a result of a covered direct loss. Some businesses, particularly those that are service oriented, believe they must continue to operate to maintain customer relations and to prevent their customers from turning to competitors. Consequently, these firms would incur additional expenses to continue as near normal operations as possible. Extra expense coverage does not provide protection against just an interruption of business activities. It also does not cover loss of income or profits, nor does it cover continuing normal business expenses. Examples of reimbursable extra expenses are the cost of moving to temporary quarters; the cost of renting these quarters and necessary business equipment; higher prices for rush orders from suppliers and the additional transportation expenses, and higher labor cost due to inefficiencies.

EXTRA EXPENSE WORKSHEET

If your business were to suffer an insured loss but you most stay open for business, you could incur costs above and beyond regular expenses. The purpose of this worksheet is to estimate the potential expsoure/expenses incurred as your business continues operations while trying to get back to normal after a loss. Business Income insurance covers what the business would have earned if no loss had occurred. Extra Expense covers the cost related to maintaining the market share and reducing the duration and severity of the loss.

	Column A 1st month	**Column B** Each subsequent month
Temporary Location Expenses:		
- Temporary location (rent)		
- Temporary fixtures, machinery & equipment		
Moving & hauling		
Installation of operations		
Light, heat & power at temporary location		
Insurance at temporary location		
Employee expenses:		
- Transportation		
- Overtime		
- Travel allowance		
- Incentives		
- Additional staff		
Other Expenses:		
Advertising		
Telephone and communications (installation and maintenance at temporary location		
Engineering & administrative costs		
Emergency facilities		
Net amount paid to others for services and manufacturing		
Additional freight and shipping costs due to temporary location		
Automobile rentals		
Other.		
TOTAL	$	$

TOTAL EXTRA EXPENSE
Calculations should be based on the largest foreseeable recovery period in order to ensure adequate coverage.

Total extra expense per month, for each subsequent month following loss **(Column B Total)**	**(Line 1)**	$__________
Number of months required to recover from total destruction of property *excluding first month if Extra Expense dollars are spent*	**(Line 2)**	__________
Total extra expense for all months after 1st month **(Line 1 x Line 2)**	**(Line 3)**	$__________
Total extra expense for first month following loss **(Column A Total)**	**(Line 4)**	$__________
Estimated Total Extra Expense (Line 3 + Line 4)	**(Line 5)**	$

Figure 12.2

GLOSSARY

Net Income Before Taxes

Net income before taxes is listed on your income statement under "Net Income Before Taxes."

Don't include other types of income listed on your statement, such as "Other Income," "Extraordinary Gain or Loss," or other income sources that aren't related to the primary operation of your business.

Total Operating Expenses

Operating expenses are annual expenses you have that relate to the primary operation of your business. It includes items such as your rent, lease payment on property or equipment, wages and salaries, payroll taxes, benefits, insurance premiums, property taxes, utilities, administrative expenses, depreciation and professional services.

Don't include items listed in your income statement under "Cost of Goods Sold" - the expenses you incur in order to manufacture, create or sell your product - in this section.

Direct Labor Costs

Direct Labor Costs are listed in your latest income statement under "Cost of Goods Sold" section.

Factory Overhead Costs

Factory Overhead costs are listed in your latest income statement under "Cost of Goods Sold" section and includes items such as indirect labor, depreciation, insurance and taxes and repairs and maintenance.

Ordinary Payroll Expense Deduction

In this section, you must estimate whether you want to continue to pay your employees if your business is shut down and your property is destroyed. For example, during a shutdown, if you plan to continue to pay all employees, deduct nothing (enter $0).

If you do not plan to pay all your employees during a shutdown, you'll exclude the cost of their pay here. When you enter this deduction, you can include payroll, benefits, FICA, union dues and worker's compensation insurance costs.

Don't include payroll for officers, executives, department managers and others designated as key employees in your Income Statement. That compensation is not considered part of your "Ordinary Payroll."

Recovery Time

In this section, enter the number of months you believe it would take your business to rebuild your property and return to your current revenue level if your business property were totally destroyed'

For most companies, it takes six months to a year to return to pre-loss revenue levels and for businesses operating specialized fields or in a highly competitive industry, it can take even longer.
Factors to consider include the time it will take to clear debris from your site, get permits, rebuild your property or select a new location, replace equipment and machinery, become fully operational and regain customers. Some businesses such as retailer, contractors, and out door services experience seasonal changes in income levels. There fluctuations should be considered when determining your insurance needs.

Note: Every business is different. Before purchasing coverage, you should discuss these issues with your financial advisor or independent agent.

Disclaimer

The accuracy and completeness of the results is based upon the information you provide. Safeco does not guarantee or warrant that the results will meet an insured's business requirements and the estimated Business Income and Extra Expense amounts calculated are not a formal or final recommendation of coverage limits to be purchased.

Figure 12.3

Calculating a limit for Business Income and /or Extra Expense coverage is extremely important in the risks management process. If inadequate coverage is purchased, the insured will be forced to bear part of the risk. If too much coverage is purchased, the insured is paying an excessive premium for coverage that is not needed. The worksheets illustrated in Figures 12.1 and 12.2 are good tools to use in determining the exact amount of coverage an individual business may need.

Rental value coverage is designed to cover the loss of income due to a covered peril making the rental property uninhabitable. Most leases relieve the tenant from the monthly rent until the building can be occupied again. This coverage reimburses the landlord the amount of rent the property could have produced. The reimbursement will continue for the shortest period of time required to restore or replace the building.

PROPERTY INSURANCE RATES

Property insurance rates are developed by *rating bureaus* that gather statistical and actuarial data for rate making purposes. State laws prohibit rates which are excessive, inadequate or unfairly discriminatory. These guidelines are designed to promote competition, protect the public interest and create stability within the insurance industry. An inadequate rate structure can result in company insolvencies. Preventing excessive rates protects the consumer against overpaying for insurance. Preventing unfair discrimination means that an insurer cannot unfairly discriminate between risks having the same exposure and characteristics. This does not mean that a company cannot underwrite against risk exposures. For example, a metal hangar that does not do spray painting will carry a lower rate than a similar building that has a painting operation. In addition to actuarial and statistical data. rates are also based on building construction as defined by Insurance Services Offices (ISO):

Frame (Code 1)

Buildings where the exterior walls are wood or other combustible materials including construction where combustible materials are combined with other materials such as brick veneer, stone veneer, wood iron-clad, stucco on wood.

Joisted Masonry (Code 2)

Buildings where the exterior walls are constructed of masonry materials such as adobe, brick, concrete, gypsum block, hollow concrete block, stone, tile or similar materials, and where the floors and roof are combustible.

Non-Combustible (Code 3)

Buildings where the exterior walls are constructed of and supported by metal, asbestos, gypsum, or other non-combustible materials.

Masonry Non-Combustible (Code 4)

Buildings where the exterior walls are constructed of masonry materials as described in Code 2 with the floors and roof of metal or other non-combustible material.

Modified Fire Resistive (Code 5)

Buildings where the exterior walls and the floors and roof are constructed of masonry or fire resistive material with a fire resistance rating of one hour or more but less than two hours.

Modified Fire Resistive (Code 6)

Buildings where the exterior walls and the floors and roof are constructed of masonry or fire resistive materials having a fire resistance rating of not less than two hours.

The loss experience in a given area plays a major role in the cost of property coverage. All cities with a population of more than 25,000 are surveyed periodically and rated in classes in descending order from 1 to 10 known as protection classes. The classes assigned reflect the cities ability to prevent and fight fires and considers the adequacy of water supply, fire departments, alarm systems, structural conditions, hazard ordinances, and the like. In each area, the rate, which the insured pays, will reflect the rating class assigned.

RISK MANAGEMENT DECISION AREAS

Replacement Cost versus Actual Cash Value

It is the responsibility of the risk manager to determine the value of the firm's property and how much insurance to purchase. Insurance can be purchased on either replacement cost basis or on actual cash value basis. *Replacement cost* is defined as the cost to replace the property today with new materials of like kind and quality. *Actual cash value* is usually defined as that amount of money required to replace the damaged or destroyed property with new materials at present-day prices, less depreciation (ACV = R - D). The only difference between the two methods of valuation is whether there is coverage for depreciation. Finance persons often speak of *book value* of an asset as a measure of worth. This is an accounting term and is determined by subtracting the accumulated depreciation expense from the purchase price of the asset. The term has no relevance in determining property values for buying insurance. A professional appraisal is the best way to determine current value of real property. Appraisal firms can provide the risk manager with accurate data. Three methods of determining market value are used: the income approach, the market approach, and the cost replacement approach. The cost replacement approach is the only one appropriate for insurance because it provides a dollar figure to replace the building with new materials at today's labor and materials costs. If appraisal services are not used, a good estimate of replacement cost can be determined by using square footage data and cost of replacing the existing construction. A general contractor in the area could be consulted for this information.

Replacement value and market value are usually not the same. For example, a 10-year-old building was purchased for $400,000. Is that market value or replacement value? It is probably market value and will not serve as a guide for the purchase of property insurance. Selling price of older buildings will reflect wear and tear and age of major components, like roofs and heating and air conditioning systems. It is important always to subtract the value of the land since there is no coverage for any damage to land or pavements. The cost of foundations and any other underground property should also not be included in the property valuation.

Coinsurance versus Full Value

Statistics gathered by fire-rating bureaus indicate that about 85 percent of all building losses are for less than 20 percent of the value of the property. Only 5 percent of the losses result in damages that exceed 50 percent of the property value. These statistics provide evidence of a high degree of probability that losses suffered to property will be partial. Thus, risk managers might carry insurance equal to only a small portion of property value. If everyone did this, the insurer, in order to collect sufficient premiums, would have to charge a higher rate per $1,000 of exposed value than it would if everyone insured 100 percent of value. To make sure that a high percentage of value is insured, insurance companies permit risk managers to select a coinsurance percentage and receive a reduction in the premium rate. Under the provision of the *coinsurance clause*, the insured agrees to maintain insurance equal to some selected percentage of value. The required amount is usually 80 or 90 percent of replacement value of the property. It is important to note that if an 80 percent coinsurance clause is selected, and it does represent 80 percent of true value, the insured will receive 100 percent reimbursement for covered losses up to the face amount of the insurance. It does not mean that the insured will have to pay 20 percent of all losses. If the insured agrees to a coinsurance clause and fails to maintain the required percentage to value, a penalty will be assessed on all partial losses. At the time of the loss, the insurance company will make payment on the basis of the following formula:

$$\frac{\text{amount of insurance carried}}{\text{amount of insurance required}} \text{ X amount of loss = amount paid - deductible}$$

To illustrate, suppose Ace Flying Service purchased a hangar and the replacement value was determined to be $400,000. Since the company agreed to an 80 percent coinsurance clause they purchased $320,000 of insurance with a $500 per occurrence deductible. Covered fire damage of $80,000 was suffered and the insurance company paid $79,500. ($320,000/$320,000 X $80,000 = $80,000 - $500)

The possibility of a penalty can be illustrated with the above example but making the loss occur two years later with no changes in coverage. In applying the formula at time of the loss the insurance company found that the replacement value of the building had risen to $440,000 due to increased construction and labor costs. Because the required 80 percent of value was not maintained, Ace Flying Service will only receive $72,227 ($320,000/$352,000 X $80,000 = $72,727 - $500). Risk managers must remember that the insurance company only measures the amount of coverage required for compliance with the selected coinsurance clause at the time of the loss. It is also the risk manager's responsibility to maintain the proper percentage level over time. High inflation makes this task more difficult.

To assist risk managers in high inflationary times, an *inflation guard endorsement* can be attached. This endorsement automatically increases the limit of insurance for the coverage to which it applies on a quarterly basis. The amount of increase is a percent of the original face amount. Risk managers must select 1, 2, or 3 percent and so on, with the premium for the endorsement varying with the percentage selected. This will prevent the insured from being penalized for not maintaining the required level of coverage during the policy year.

It is possible to suspend the coinsurance clause by activating the optional *agreed value coverage* provision. Essentially, the insurer waives the requirement that the insured must maintain a certain percentage of value. The insurer accepts the amount on the declaration page as full value and will not use the standard formula at time of loss to determine the amount paid.

Most insurers will require a current statement of property values as a condition for granting and renewing the agreed value provision. A current appraisal may also be required.

Specific versus Blanket Insurance

Up to this point, property coverage limits have been in a form known as *specific insurance*. This approach applies a definite dollar amount of coverage to each stated property. *Blanket insurance* is an alternative approach for stating dollar coverage. Under this form, one amount of insurance covers all property located at multiple locations. For example, an FBO has facilities at three different airports in Florida. Instead of writing specific insurance for each location, the risk manager might insure them on a blanket basis, with a single amount of insurance applicable to all three locations. Most insurers require a 90 percent coinsurance clause when coverage is written on a blanket basis.

The advantages of the blanket approach can be illustrated by using the Florida-based FBO. Suppose each of the three locations has replacement-valued buildings of $125,000. If the buildings are insured on a blanket basis, with a 90 percent coinsurance clause, $337,500 of insurance will be bought. In the event of a loss, coverage will apply up to the full $125,000 of value. If the same three buildings were insured for $112,500 each on a specific basis, recovery would be limited to the $112,500 applicable to each. Blanket insurance is also appropriate for contents. This form is especially advantageous when inventory is frequently moved between two or more locations while the total value at risk remains relatively constant. If specific basis is used, imbalances in inventory value may occur with loss potential exceeding an individual location's personal property limits.

MISCELLANEOUS PROPERTY COVERAGES

Additional property coverages can be purchased to tailor an account based on specific coverage needs. For example, an FBO in California may need protection against earthquake losses while an FBO located in Florida has catastrophic exposures related to hurricanes and flood. Additional coverage can be attached via an endorsement or written on a stand alone policy.

Systems Protection or Boiler and Machinery insurance includes property and liability coverages and is highly specialized because it requires underwriters with a technical knowledge of electrical systems, loss control engineers who are qualified to perform state mandated boiler inspections, and claims adjusters that understand the unique technicalities of this coverage. The standard property policy excludes coverage for explosion of steam boilers, steam pipes, steam turbines, or steam engines if owned, leased, or operated by the insured. Property coverages often commonly exclude loss by mechanical breakdown. The systems protection coverage form provides coverage for these exposures.

Tenants Improvements and Betterments insurance covers the insured's interest in a building that is occupied, but not owned by the insured. The insured has an insurable interest in any additions or improvements they make to the structure. i.e., addition of a spray painting booth that adds value to the property.

Fire Legal Liability insurance protects an insured that leases a building but does not have an insurable interest in the property except for legal liability that may be incurred due to loss or damage to the property owner. An example is a fire in a hangar that is leased by the insured.

Earthquake insurance protects an insured from losses resulting directly from damage caused by earth movement including landslide, mudflow, earth sinking, rising or shifting, and earthquake. This coverage is typically excluded in the commercial property policy and can be purchased as an endorsement to the policy or as a stand alone policy.

Pollution Liability insurance - During the last decade, more than 330,000 releases from substandard fuel tanks have been reported in the United States. Many of these releases have caused serious environmental damage as well as harming human population. In December 1998, the Environmental Protection Agency (EPA) adopted the rules and a 10-year compliance schedule that have been the cornerstone of the underground storage tank (UTS) compliance and cleanup programs which are managed by the states. The state programs have focused on improvements in four key areas:

1. Prevention of releases from tanks and piping by the use of corrosion protection on steel tanks and piping or the use of corrosion resistant material.
2. Prevention of spills and overfills during transfer of product into the tank.
3. Monitoring of the tank and piping to detect system failures and ensure early repairs to equipment and cleanup of environmental contamination from releases.
4. Buying insurance or arranging equivalent financial protection for environmental cleanup and third party damages.

Pollution liability insurance for underground fuel storage tanks has become a vital risk management concern due to the federal financial responsibility rules which went into effect on December 22. 1998. Tank owners must now demonstrate financial responsibility of at least $1 million for cleanup in the event of an underground fuel tank spill or leak. The purchase of insurance and the use of state cleanup funds can demonstrate financial responsibility. Firms with a net worth of $10 million or more can also use self-insurance programs to demonstrate financial responsibility. The EPA has outlined exactly what insurance policies must cover to meet the financial responsibility regulations. A policy's limit of liability must be dedicated to storage-tank pollution losses and cannot be shared with any other exposure. This requirement prevents the packaging of UTS coverage with other pollution exposures. Over and above the stated limits of liability the policy must provide for the cost of defending the insured. EPA further dictates that an insurer must provide "first dollar" coverage and then seek reimbursement for any deductible from the insured. Approved policies must also cover pollution losses associated with the loading and unloading of fuel from underground storage tanks. Cost of insurance depends on liability limits, number of tanks, and the age of the tanks. New storage tanks with advanced lead-detection systems can be written for less than $300 per tank. Older upgraded systems that still rely on manual inventory for their leak detection may be rated at $500 to $600 per tank.

CRIME INSURANCE

Crime insurance or dishonesty insurance insures the FBO or airport owner for the loss of property due to the wrongful taking by someone else. Commercial crime coverage is part of the portfolio program and provides a menu of fourteen crime forms. Those crime forms, which are important for aviation risk managers, include:

- Employee dishonesty coverage
- Theft, disappearance, and destruction coverage
- Robbery and safe burglary coverage
- Premises burglary coverage

Employee dishonesty coverage will be described in detail in chapter 14. Theft, disappearance, and destruction coverage covers money and securities for loss by theft and loss by "disappearance and destruction." In effect, this is all risk coverage for money and securities. Coverage is available for losses on premises and for losses off premises. The insured may select either or both, and separate limits apply to each. Exclusions include losses resulting from the giving or surrendering of property in any exchange or purchase, loss or damage to the interior of the premises resulting from fire, however caused, and loss from damage to the premises or to containers of covered property by vandalism or malicious mischief. Also excluded are dishonest acts of employees, directors, trustees, or authorized representatives. The policy limit stated on the declaration page is the maximum amount the insurer will pay per occurrence.

Robbery and safe burglary coverage covers robbery of property other than money and securities that occurs inside or outside of the premises. *Robbery* means the taking of property by a person causing or threatening to cause bodily harm. A coverage extension obligates the insurer to pay also for damages to the premises caused by the robbery. Limits of coverage and appropriate deductibles are stated on the declaration page and apply to each occurrence. There is a special $1,000 limit for the loss of precious metals and stones, pearls, furs, or related articles, and to manuscripts, drawings, and records. Losses from fire and vandalism are excluded as are losses of or to motor vehicles.

Premises burglary coverage covers actual or attempted burglary of inventory, furniture, fixtures, and equipment inside the premises. Money and securities are not covered. *Burglary* is defined as the taking of property from inside the premises by a person unlawfully entering or leaving the premises as evidenced by marks of forcible entry or exit. This coverage has the same exclusions as robbery and safe burglary. A special condition of this coverage is that if a covered loss occurs, the coverage is suspended. Coverage is restored when the premises are brought back to the prior security condition or are protected by a security guard.

INLAND MARINE COVERAGES

Inland Marine insurance is a diverse and very flexible type of property coverage. There are a variety of coverage forms that can be used to customize coverage. Following are examples of property that can be covered by inland marine insurance:

- Cargo
- Accounts Receivable
- Fine Arts
- Buildings under construction
- Installation of Building Materials
- Electronic Data Processing
- Miscellaneous Tools and Equipment
- Bridges, Tunnels, and Piers

You will note that in all of these examples coverage principally involves property being transported, property of a movable or floating nature, or property instrumental in transportation and communication. Inland marine rates can either be filed or non-filed and offers a wide range of flexibility in coverage forms and pricing. Because of this lack of regulation, inland marine exposures historically have caused intense competition, and in some cases inadequate rates. In the late 1920s the National Convention of Insurance Commissioners, now called the National Association of Insurance Commissioners, (NAIC) drafted a "Nationwide Definition and Interpretation of the Insuring Powers of Marine and Transportation Underwriters." This document limited the insuring powers of insurance companies underwriting marine risks by defining those risks and coverages which they could and could not write. The document has been revised twice since its inception and the current adopted definition is referred to as the "1976 Nationwide Definition." Although the NAIC only makes recommendations and each state insurance commissioner is free to decide whether or not to implement part or all of the definition. NAIC's document has helped stabilize inland marine and transportation underwriting in states where it has been adopted.

NAIC's document defines six classes of covered property. Two are covered by ocean marine insurance and the other four by inland marine insurance.

- Imports (Ocean Marine)
- Exports (Ocean Marine)
- Domestic Shipments (Inland Marine)
- Means of Transportation and Communication (Inland Marine)
- Personal Property Floater Risks (Inland Marine)
- Commercial Property Floater Risks (Inland Marine)

TRANSPORTATION INSURANCE

Sharing the risk of transporting goods is one of the oldest forms of insurance. The early Greek merchants issued bottomry contracts and respondentia contracts, which assisted merchants that borrowed money to finance voyages. Under these contracts, the lender took a lien on the ship itself, in the case of bottomery contracts, and the cargo in the case of respondentia contracts. If the ship or cargo were lost at sea, the loan was cancelled. A substantial interest charge was made for the loan and for the possibility that the loan might be cancelled. Whether cargo is shipped by water, land, or air, it is subjected to many perils that may cause a loss. Owners and operators of the various modes of transportation realize their inability to control adequately or completely acts of nature or to prevent human failure as it affects the safe movement of cargo.

The liability of the carrier depends on the mode of transportation. In the field of ocean shipping the carrier is only responsible for failure to exercise ordinary care and is governed by the United States Carriage of Goods by Sea Act (COGSA). Basically, the act imposes liability on the carrier only if the carrier failed to make the vessel seaworthy and suitable for carrying the cargo when the voyage began and the loss resulted from the unseaworthy condition. In addition, COGSA limits recovery to $500 per package or customary freight unit. Under common law, the liability for a land or air carrier is considerably greater but is not absolute. These carriers are responsible for all loss or damage to cargo except:

- Acts of God. Acts of nature like floods, tornadoes, and earthquakes that are neither preventable nor controllable. Fire is not considered an act of God.
- Acts of a public enemy. The action by forces at war with a domestic government, not acts of gangsters, mobs, or rioters.
- Order of a public authority. Confiscation for drug involvement is an example.
- Neglect of the shipper. Improper packaging which causes loss.
- Inherent nature of the goods. Spoilage of perishable goods, and other special qualities of a product which cause it to damage or destroy itself.

Air cargo insurance is a form of both ocean marine and inland marine insurance because it protects cargo shipped domestically as well as internationally. A *cargo liability coverage endorsement* is available to cover the legal liability of the air cargo carrier against negligent damage or loss of cargo entrusted to it for safe delivery. A second type of coverage, known as the *inland transit policy* (sometimes called the *annual transit floater*), is available to a firm (shipper) that chooses to insure its own cargo while it is in the possession of a third party carrier rather than relying exclusively on the cargo carrier.

The owner of property (shipper) has three choices when its cargo must be transported: engage the services of a common carrier or a contract carrier, or use the firm's own airplane. *Common carriers* are carriers engaged in the transport of goods for the public according to regular time schedules, defined routes, and established rates. When common carriers receive goods for shipment, they become a bailee and assume certain levels of care for the goods in their care, custody, and control. An *air waybill of lading* (AWB) is a written contract setting forth the terms and conditions of the bailment.

It would appear that a common carrier becomes an insurer of goods, thus relieving the owner of any responsibility. This is not totally true since the liability of common carriers is not absolute. Risk managers may purchase an inland transit policy because it provides coverage door to door; there are no tariff limitations, claims are settled promptly, and the possibility of having to sue the carrier if the insured is unable to clearly establish carrier negligence is eliminated. Another reason to purchase an inland transit policy is that there is often no clear-cut responsibility for *freight forwarders* who assemble and consolidate shipments or independent truckers hired by the carrier to pick up the cargo for the carrier. Most carriers have contracts with truckers to handle the consigned service of customer goods. If damage to cargo occurs while in the possession of the trucker, is the trucker responsible, or is the cargo carrier? The answer lies in where the charge for the pickup and delivery is billed. If the charge appears in the air tariff, the carrier is responsible. If charged directly to the customer, the trucker is responsible. This is an important question since theft accounts for roughly 75–80 percent of all cargo losses.

Contract carriers do not offer their services to the public at large but operate under a contract with individual shippers. Risk managers have an opportunity to negotiate the carrier's liability and have it included within the terms of the contract. The necessity for risk transfer will be dictated by the extent of the liability assumed by the carrier. For businesses that only ship occasionally, the trip transit policy is available.

The limit of liability for common air cargo carriers is stated by published tariffs. Most scheduled domestic and international carriers limit their responsibility to $9.07 per pound. FedEx's Express Freight published liability is limited to $100 or $1.00 per pound, whichever is greater. All carriers offer the shipper the opportunity to purchase increased liability limits through the additional charge of $0.50 for every $100 of additional declared value. The key to adequate coverage for damaged or lost cargo is correctly calculating insured value of the cargo. The recommended way is to take the current value of the cargo, add the cost of airfreight, and then add a buffer of 10 percent to the total. Thus, a shipment valued at $10,000 with $1,000 airfreight would have an insured value of $12,100.

Using company-owned airplanes to transport business property eliminates any third party responsibility. Risk managers evaluate the potential loss per occurrence and decide either to retain the risk or to transfer it to an insurance company by adding an endorsement to their aviation hull and liability policy.

Since air cargo common carriers and contract carriers may be held legally responsible for loss of or damage to the property in their custody and control, they can transfer this liability exposure by purchasing a cargo liability coverage endorsement. It is not uncommon for larger air cargo carriers and airlines to retain their cargo liability exposures rather than purchase the endorsement. This endorsement, when added to their aircraft liability policy, will pay on behalf of the insured all sums that the insured shall become legally obligated to pay as a carrier or bailee for damages because of damage or destruction of tangible personal property of others. Coverage is provided only when a charge under an air waybill (AWB) or shipping receipt is issued by the insured. Property is covered only while in or on, or being loaded on or unloaded from an aircraft insured under the policy or while located at the insured's terminal. Terminal coverage, however, is usually limited to a certain number of hours, such as 72 hours. This endorsement gives the insured all risk coverage, but there are claims that the insurer will not cover. Exclusions are as follows:

- Any loss of market because of any delay, whether or not this delay is caused by an occurrence covered under this policy.
- Any consequential loss of any nature; however, the insurer will pay for the cost of reconstruction of data contained in documents carried.
- Any loss caused by the insured, employees, directors, or agents due to infidelity.
- Any loss caused by wear, tear, deterioration, or freezing or due to the perishable nature of the property.
- Any loss or damage of any accounts, bills, jewelry, currency, deeds, evidences of debt, letters of credit, passports, documents, money, notes, securities, or airline or other tickets.
- Any physical loss of or damage to cargo which is considered dangerous or harmful and for which the insured must secure a specific permit or waiver

from federal, state, county, or municipal authority.

The cargo liability coverage endorsement will have a separate single limit of liability coverage per occurrence and the selected flat deductible will apply.
The inland transit policy covers the following property in transit:

- Personal property owned by the insured.
- Personal property shipped to customers on a Free On Board (F.O.B.) point of destination basis

Excluded property includes samples in the custody of salespersons; property insured under import or export ocean marine policies; airborne shipments to and from Alaska, Puerto Rico, and Hawaii; shipments made by air unless via regularly scheduled airlines; property shipped by mail; and property of others if the insured is acting as a common or contract carrier. This all risk coverage is purchased with a single limit of liability per occurrence. Protection is afforded from the time the property leaves the original point of shipment until delivered at the destination.

Many FBOs need to provide physical damage coverage for spare parts while in transit. A *spares endorsement* is available to provide all risk coverage for physical damage or loss to spare parts which are owned, leased, consigned, or in the care, custody, or control of the insured under a written agreement. Spare parts are defined as engines, spare parts, and equipment intended solely for attachment to an aircraft or designed exclusively for use with an aircraft. Coverage takes place during the policy period while the spare parts are in the care, custody, or control of the insured or while in transit by land, sea, or air (including the insured's own aircraft) anywhere in the world. Limits of liability per occurrence must be selected as well as a flat deductible. Under this endorsement, the insurer won't cover the following loss or damage:

- Done to property that has been attached to an aircraft and is intended to be used on the aircraft.
- Caused by and confined to wear and tear, deterioration, freezing, mechanical or electrical breakdown or failure, unless the loss is a direct result of other physical damage covered under this endorsement.
- Caused when someone with a legal right to possess the spare parts, embezzles, or converts them.
- Caused by declared or undeclared war, invasion, rebellion or by seizure or detention of the spare parts by any government; nor will the insurer cover damage done to spare parts by or at the direction of any government.
- Arising out of mysterious disappearance or unexplained loss or shortage disclosed upon taking inventory.
- Any consequential loss of any nature.
- Any loss of market or profit because of any delay whether or not the delay is caused by an occurrence covered by this policy.

KEY TERMS

Portfolio program
Named perils policy
All risk policy
Vacancy restriction endorsement
Windstorm or hail endorsement
Reporting forms
Business income coverage
Extra expense coverage
Tenants improvements and betterments insurance
Fire legal liability insurance
Earthquake insurance
Pollution liability coverage
Crime insurance
Robbery
Burglary

Rental value coverage
Rating bureaus
Replacement cost
Actual cash value
Book value
Coinsurance clause
Inflation guard endorsement
Agreed value coverage
Specific insurance
Blanket insurance
Systems protection or boiler and machineryinsurance
Inland marine insurance
Cargo liability coverage endorsement
Inland transit policy
Common carriers
Air waybill of lading (A WB)
Freight forwarder
Contract carriers
Spares endorsement

REVIEW QUESTIONS

1. Explain the major objectives of the ISO portfolio program.
2. Specifically state the types of property that are covered under the commercial property form.
3. When a commercial property policy is purchased in joint name, which insured is responsible for the payment of premiums?
4. What role does loss experience play in determining property insurance rates?
5. In addition to broader coverage, explain another major benefit to the insured that purchases all risk coverage.
6. Which valuation method is best: replacement cost or actual cash value?
7. Explain why insurance companies usually require a coinsurance warranty.
8. State the major advantage of blanket insurance.
9. What risk exposures are a risk manager transferring when business income coverage is added?
10. State how the windstorm/hail endorsement deductible differs from the normal straight or flat commercial property deductible.
11. Identify three types of property that are written using inland marine insurance.
12. Differentiate between robbery and burglary.
13. Is the liability of a common carrier absolute? Explain.
14. Explain the coverage afforded by a cargo liability coverage endorsement, an inland transit policy, and a spares endorsement.

REFERENCES

Badger, Dennis, and Geoffery Whitehead. Elements of Cargo Insurance. Woodhead-Faulkner Ltd. Cambridge, England, 1983.

McCormick, Roy C. Coverages Applicable. The Rough Notes Co., Inc. Indianapolis, Indiana, 1989

Property Insurance Account Handling Guide. International Risk Management Institute, Inc. Dallas, Texas, 1988.

Vaughn, Emmett J., and Therese Vaughan. Fundamentals of Risk and Insurance (9th Ed.). John Wiley & Sons. New York, 2003.

Williams, C. Arthur Jr., and Richard M. Heins. Risk Management and Insurance (6th Ed.). McGraw-Hill Book Company. New York, 1989.

COMMERCIAL PROPERTY POLICY

COMMON POLICY CONDITIONS

All Coverage Parts included in this policy are subject to the following conditions.

A. Cancellation

1. The first Named Insured shown in the Declarations may cancel this policy by mailing or delivering to us advance written notice of cancellation.

2. We may cancel this policy by mailing or delivering to the first Named Insured written notice of cancellation at least:

a. 10 days before the effective date of cancellation if we cancel for nonpayment of premium; or

b. 30 days before the effective date of cancellation if we cancel for any other reason.

3. We will mail or deliver our notice to the first Named Insured's last mailing address known to us.

4. Notice of cancellation will state the effective date of cancellation. The policy period will end on that date.

5. If this policy is cancelled, we will send the first Named Insured any premium refund due. If we cancel, the refund will be pro rata. If the first Named Insured cancels, the refund may be less than pro rata. The cancellation will be effective even if we have not made or offered a refund.

6. If notice is mailed, proof of mailing will be sufficient proof of notice.

B. Changes

This policy contains all the agreements between you and us concerning the insurance afforded. The first Named Insured shown in the Declarations is authorized to make changes in the terms of this policy with our consent. This policy's terms can be amended or waived only by endorsement issued by us and made a part of this policy.

C. Examination Of Your Books And Records

We may examine and audit your books and records as they relate to this policy at any time during the policy period and up to three years afterward.

D. Inspections And Surveys

1. We have the right to:

a. Make inspections and surveys at any time;

b. Give you reports on the conditions we find; and

c. Recommend changes.

2. We are not obligated to make any inspections, surveys, reports or recommendations and any such actions we do undertake relate only to insurability and the premiums to be charged. We do not make safety inspections. We do not undertake to perform the duty of any person or organization to provide for the health or safety of workers or the public. And we do not warrant that conditions:

a. Are safe or healthful; or

b. Comply with laws, regulations, codes or standards.

3. Paragraphs 1. and 2. of this condition apply not only to us, but also to any rating, advisory, rate service or similar organization which makes insurance inspections, surveys, reports or recommendations.

4. Paragraph 2. of this condition does not apply to any inspections, surveys, reports or recommendations we may make relative to certification, under state or municipal statutes, ordinances or regulations, of boilers, pressure vessels or elevators.

E. Premiums

The first Named Insured shown in the Declarations:

1. Is responsible for the payment of all premiums; and

2. Will be the payee for any return premiums we pay.

F. Transfer Of Your Rights And Duties Under This Policy

Your rights and duties under this policy may not be transferred without our written consent except in the case of death of an individual named insured.

If you die, your rights and duties will be transferred to your legal representative but only while acting within the scope of duties as your legal representative. Until your legal representative is appointed, anyone having proper temporary custody of your property will have your rights and duties but only with respect to that property.

IL 00 17 11 98

COMMERCIAL PROPERTY CONDITIONS

This Coverage Part is subject to the following conditions, the Common Policy Conditions and applicable Loss Conditions and Additional Conditions in Commercial Property Coverage Forms.

A. CONCEALMENT, MISREPRESENTATION OR FRAUD

This Coverage Part is void in any case of fraud by you as it relates to this Coverage Part at any time. It is also void if you or any other insured, at any time, intentionally conceal or misrepresent a material fact concerning:

1. This Coverage Part;

2. The Covered Property;

3. Your interest in the Covered Property; or

4. A claim under this Coverage Part.

B. CONTROL OF PROPERTY

Any act or neglect of any person other than you beyond your direction or control will not affect this insurance.

The breach of any condition of this Coverage Part at any one or more locations will not affect coverage at any location where, at the time of loss or damage, the breach of condition does not exist.

C. INSURANCE UNDER TWO OR MORE COVERAGES

If two or more of this policy's coverages apply to the same loss or damage, we will not pay more than the actual amount of the loss or damage.

D. LEGAL ACTION AGAINST US

No one may bring a legal action against us under this Coverage Part unless:

1. There has been full compliance with all of the terms of this Coverage Part; and

2. The action is brought within 2 years after the date on which the direct physical loss or damage occurred.

E. LIBERALIZATION

If we adopt any revision that would broaden the coverage under this Coverage Part without additional premium within 45 days prior to or during the policy period, the broadened coverage will immediately apply to this Coverage Part.

F. NO BENEFIT TO BAILEE

No person or organization, other than you, having custody of Covered Property will benefit from this insurance.

G. OTHER INSURANCE

1. You may have other insurance subject to the same plan, terms, conditions and provisions as the insurance under this Coverage Part. If you do, we will pay our share of the covered loss or damage. Our share is the proportion that

the applicable Limit of Insurance under this Coverage Part bears to the Limits of Insurance of all insurance covering on the same basis.

2. If there is other insurance covering the same loss or damage, other than that described in 1. above, we will pay only for the amount of covered loss or damage in excess of the amount due from that other insurance, whether you can collect on it or not. But we will not pay more than the applicable Limit of Insurance.

H. POLICY PERIOD, COVERAGE TERRITORY

Under this Coverage Part:

1. We cover loss or damage commencing:

   a. During the policy period shown in the Declarations; and

   b. Within the coverage territory.

2. The coverage territory is:

   a. The United States of America (including its territories and possessions);

   b. Puerto Rico; and

   c. Canada.

I. TRANSFER OF RIGHTS OF RECOVERY AGAINST OTHERS TO US

If any person or organization to or for whom we make payment under this Coverage Part has rights to recover damages from another, those rights are transferred to us to the extent of our payment. That person or organization must do everything necessary to secure our rights and must do nothing after loss to impair them. But you may waive your rights against another party in writing:

1. Prior to a loss to your Covered Property or Covered Income.

2. After a loss to your Covered Property or Covered Income only if, at time of loss, that party is one of the following:

   a. Someone insured by this insurance;

   b. A business firm:

      (1) Owned or controlled by you; or

      (2) That owns or controls you; or

   c. Your tenant.

This will not restrict your insurance.

BUILDING AND PERSONAL PROPERTY COVERAGE FORM

Various provisions in this policy restrict coverage. Read the entire policy carefully to determine rights, duties and what is and is not covered.

Throughout this policy the words “you” and “your” refer to the Named Insured shown in the Declarations. The words “we”, “us” and “our” refer to the Company providing this insurance.
Other words and phrases that appear in quotation marks have special meaning.Refer to Section **H. – Definitions.**

A. Coverage

We will pay for direct physical loss of or damage to Covered Property at the premises described in the Declarations caused by or resulting from any Covered Cause of Loss.

1. Covered Property

Covered Property, as used in this Coverage Part, means the type of property described in this Section, **A.1.,** and limited in **A.2. ,** Property Not Covered, if a Limit of Insurance is shown in the Declarations for that type of property.

a. Building, meaning the building or structure described in the Declarations, including:

(1) Completed additions;

(2) Fixtures, including outdoor fixtures;

(3) Permanently installed:

(a) Machinery and

(b) Equipment;

(4) Personal property owned by you that is used to maintain or service the building or structure or its premises, including:

(a) Fire extinguishing equipment;

(b) Outdoor furniture;

(c) Floor coverings; and

(d) Appliances used for refrigerating, ventilating, cooking, dishwashing or laundering;

(5) If not covered by other insurance:

(a) Additions under construction, alterations and repairs to the building or structure;

(b) Materials, equipment, supplies and temporary structures, on or within 100 feet of the described premises, used for making additions, alterations or repairs to the building or structure.

b. Your Business Personal Property located in or on the building described in the Declarations or in the open (or in a vehicle) within 100 feet of the described premises, consisting of the following unless otherwise specified in the Declarations or on the Your Business Personal Property – Separation of Coverage form:

(1) Furniture and fixtures;

(2) Machinery and equipment;

(3) "Stock";

(4) All other personal property owned by you and used in your business;

(5) Labor, materials or services furnished or arranged by you on personal property of others;

(6) Your use interest as tenant in improvements and betterments. Improvements and betterments are fixtures, alterations, installations or additions:

(a) Made a part of the building or structure you occupy but do not own; and

(b) You acquired or made at your expense but cannot legally remove;

(7) Leased personal property for which you have a contractual responsibility to insure, unless otherwise provided for under Personal Property of Others.

c. Personal Property Of Others that is:

(1) In your care, custody or control; and

(2) Located in or on the building described in the Declarations or in the open (or in a vehicle) within 100 feet of the described premises.

However, our payment for loss of or damage to personal property of others will only be for the account of the owner of the property.

2. Property Not Covered

Covered Property does not include:

a. Accounts, bills, currency, food stamps or other evidences of debt, money, notes or securities. Lottery tickets held for sale are not securities;

b. Animals, unless owned by others and boarded by you, or if owned by you, only as "stock" while inside of buildings;

c. Automobiles held for sale;

d. Bridges, roadways, walks, patios or other paved surfaces;

e. Contraband, or property in the course of illegal transportation or trade;

f. The cost of excavations, grading, backfilling or filling;

g. Foundations of buildings, structures, machinery or boilers if their foundations are below:

(1) The lowest basement floor; or

(2) The surface of the ground, if there is no basement;

h. Land (including land on which the property is located) , water, growing crops or lawns;

i. Personal property while airborne or waterborne;

j. Bulkheads, pilings, piers, wharves or docks;

k. Property that is covered under another coverage form of this or any other policy in which it is more specifically described, except for the excess of the amount due (whether you can collect on it or not) from that other insurance;

l. Retaining walls that are not part of a building;

m. Underground pipes, flues or drains;

n. Electronic data, except as provided under Additional Coverages – Electronic Data. Electronic data means information, facts or computer programs stored as or on, created or used on, or transmitted to or from computer software (including systems and applications software) , on hard or floppy disks, CD-ROMs, tapes, drives, cells, data processing devices or any other repositories of computer software which are used with electronically controlled equipment. The term computer programs, referred to in the foregoing description of electronic data, means a set of related electronic instructions which direct the operations and functions of a computer or device connected to it, which enable the computer or device to receive, process, store, retrieve or send data.This Paragraph n. , does not apply to your "stock" of prepackaged software.

o. The cost to replace or restore the information on valuable papers and records, including those which exist as electronic data. Valuable papers and records include but are not limited to proprietary information, books of account, deeds, manuscripts, abstracts, drawings and card index systems. Refer to the Coverage Extension for Valuable Papers And Records (Other Than Electronic Data) for limited coverage for valuable papers and records other than those which exist as electronic data.

p. Vehicles or self-propelled machines (including aircraft or watercraft) that:

(1) Are licensed for use on public roads; or

(2) Are operated principally away from the described premises.

This paragraph does not apply to:

(a) Vehicles or self-propelled machines or autos you manufacture, process or warehouse;

(b) Vehicles or self-propelled machines, other than autos, you hold for sale;

(c) Rowboats or canoes out of water at the described premises; or

(d) Trailers, but only to the extent provided for in the Coverage Extension for Non-Owned Detached Trailers.

q. The following property while outside of buildings:

(1) Grain, hay, straw or other crops;

(2) Fences, radio or television antennas (including satellite dishes) and their lead-in wiring, masts or towers, signs (other than signs attached to buildings) , trees, shrubs or plants (other than "stock" of trees, shrubs or plants) , all except as provided in the Coverage Extensions.

3. Covered Causes Of Loss

See applicable Causes of Loss Form as shown in the Declarations.

4. Additional Coverages

a. Debris Removal

(1) Subject to Paragraphs (3) and (4) , we will pay your expense to remove debris of Covered Property caused by or resulting from a Covered Cause of Loss that occurs during the policy period. The expenses will be paid only if they are reported to us in writing within 180 days of the date of direct physical loss or damage.

(2) Debris Removal does not apply to costs to:

(a) Extract "pollutants" from land or water; or

(b) Remove, restore or replace polluted land or water.

(3) Subject to the exceptions in Paragraph (4) , the following provisions apply:

(a) The most we will pay for the total of direct physical loss or damage plus debris removal expense is the Limit of Insurance applicable to the Covered Property that has sustained loss or damage.

(b) Subject to (a) above, the amount we will pay for debris removal expense is limited to 25% of the sum of the deductible plus the amount that we pay for direct physical loss or damage to the Covered Property that has sustained loss or damage.

(4) We will pay up to an additional $10,000 for debris removal expense, for each location, in any one occurrence of physical loss or damage to Covered Property, if one or both of the following circumstances apply:

(a) The total of the actual debris removal expense plus the amount we pay for direct physical loss or damage exceeds the Limit of Insurance on the Covered Property that has sustained loss or damage.

(b) The actual debris removal expense exceeds 25% of the sum of the deductible plus the amount that we pay for direct physical loss or damage to the Covered Property that has sustained loss or damage. Therefore, if **(4) (a)** and/or **(4) (b)** apply, our total payment for direct physical loss or damage and debris removal expense may reach but will never exceed the Limit of Insurance on the Covered Property that has sustained loss or damage, plus $10,000.

b. Preservation Of Property

If it is necessary to move Covered Property from the described premises to preserve it from loss or damage by a Covered Cause of Loss, we will pay for any direct physical loss or damage to that property:

(1) While it is being moved or while temporarily stored at another location; and

(2) Only if the loss or damage occurs within 30 days after the property is first moved.

c. Fire Department Service Charge

When the fire department is called to save or protect Covered Property from a Covered Cause of Loss, we will pay up to $1,000 for your liability for fire department service charges:

(1) Assumed by contract or agreement prior to loss; or

(2) Required by local ordinance.

No Deductible applies to this Additional Coverage.

d. Pollutant Clean Up And Removal

We will pay your expense to extract "pollutants" from land or water at the described premises if the discharge, dispersal, seepage, migration, release or escape of the "pollutants" is caused by or results from a Covered Cause of Loss that occurs during the policy period. The expenses will be paid only if they are reported to us in writing within 180 days of the date on which the Covered Cause of Loss occurs.

This Additional Coverage does not apply to costs to test for, monitor or assess the existence, concentration or effects of "pollutants". But we will pay for testing which is performed in the course of extracting the "pollutants" from the land or water.

The most we will pay under this Additional Coverage for each described premises is $10,000 for the sum of all covered expenses arising out of Covered Causes of Loss occurring during each separate 12 month period of this policy.

e. Increased Cost Of Construction

(1) This Additional Coverage applies only to buildings to which the Replacement Cost Optional Coverage applies.

(2) In the event of damage by a Covered Cause of Loss to a building that is Covered Property, we will pay the increased costs incurred to comply with enforcement of an ordinance or law in the course of repair, rebuilding or replacement of damaged parts of that property, subject to the limitations stated in e. (3) through e. (9) of this Additional Coverage.

(3) The ordinance or law referred to in e. (2) of this Additional Coverage is an ordinance or law that regulates the construction or repair of buildings or establishes zoning or land use requirements at the described premises, and is in force at the time of loss.

(4) Under this Additional Coverage, we will not pay any costs due to an ordinance or law that:

(a) You were required to comply with before the loss, even when the building was undamaged; and

(b) You failed to comply with.

(5) Under this Additional Coverage, we will not pay for:

(a) The enforcement of any ordinance or law which requires demolition, repair, replacement, reconstruction, remodeling or remediation of property due to contamination by "pollutants" or due to the presence, growth, proliferation, spread or any activity of "fungus", wet or dry rot or bacteria; or

(b) Any costs associated with the enforcement of an ordinance or law which requires any insured or others to test for, monitor, clean up, remove, contain, treat, detoxify or neutralize, or in any way respond to, or assess the effects of "pollutants", "fungus", wet or dry rot or bacteria.

(6) The most we will pay under this Additional Coverage, for each described building insured under this Coverage Form, is $10,000 or 5% of the Limit of Insurance applicable to that building, whichever is less. If a damaged building is covered under a blanket Limit of Insurance which applies to more than one building or item of property, then the most we will pay under this Additional Coverage, for that damaged building, is the lesser of: $10,000 or 5% times the value of the damaged building as of the time of loss times the applicable coinsurance percentage.

The amount payable under this Additional Coverage is additional insurance.

(7) With respect to this Additional Coverage:

(a) We will not pay for the Increased Cost of Construction:

(i) Until the property is actually repaired or replaced, at the same or another premises; and

(ii) Unless the repairs or replacement are made as soon as reasonably possible after the loss or damage, not to exceed two years. We may extend this period in writing during the two years.

(b) If the building is repaired or replaced at the same premises, or if you elect to rebuild at another premises, the most we will pay for the Increased Cost of Construction, subject to the provisions of e. (6) of this Additional Coverage, is the increased cost of construction at the same premises.

(c) If the ordinance or law requires relocation to another premises, the most we will pay for the Increased Cost of Construction, subject to the provisions of e. (6) of this Additional Coverage, is the increased cost of construction at the new premises.

(8) This Additional Coverage is not subject to the terms of the Ordinance or Law Exclusion, to the extent that such Exclusion would conflict with the provisions of this Additional Coverage.

(9) The costs addressed in the Loss Payment and Valuation Conditions, and the Replacement Cost Optional Coverage, in this Coverage Form, do not include the increased cost attributable to enforcement of an ordinance or law. The amount payable under this Additional Coverage, as stated in e. (6) of this Additional Coverage, is not subject to such limitation.

f. Electronic Data

(1) Under this Additional Coverage, electronic data has the meaning described under Property Not Covered – Electronic Data.

(2) Subject to the provisions of this Additional Coverage, we will pay for the cost to replace or restore electronic data which has been destroyed or corrupted by a Covered Cause of Loss. To the extent that electronic data is not replaced or restored, the loss will be valued at the cost of replacement of the media on which the electronic data was stored, with blank media of substantially identical type.

(3) The Covered Causes of Loss applicable to Your Business Personal Property apply to this Additional Coverage – Electronic Data, subject to the following:

(a) If the Causes Of Loss – Special Form applies, coverage under this Additional Coverage – Electronic Data is limited to the "specified causes of loss" as defined in that form, and Collapse as set forth in that form.

(b) If the Causes Of Loss – Broad Form applies, coverage under this Additional Coverage – Electronic Data includes Collapse as set forth in that form.

(c) If the Causes Of Loss Form is endorsed to add a Covered Cause of Loss, the additional Covered Cause of Loss does not apply to the coverage provided under this Additional Coverage – Electronic Data.

(d) The Covered Causes of Loss include a virus, harmful code or similar instruction introduced into or enacted on a computer system (including electronic data) or a network to which it is connected, designed to damage or destroy any part of the system or disrupt its normal operation. But there is no coverage for loss or damage caused by or resulting from manipulation of a computer system (including electronic data) by any employee, including a temporary or leased employee, or by an entity retained by you or for you to inspect, design, install, modify, maintain, repair or replace that system.

(4) The most we will pay under this Additional Coverage – Electronic Data is $2,500 for all loss or damage sustained in any one policy year, regardless of the number of occurrences of loss or damage or the number of premises, locations or computer systems involved. If loss payment on the first occurrence does not exhaust this amount, then the balance is available for subsequent loss or damage sustained in but not after that policy year. With respect to an occurrence which begins in one policy year and continues or results in additional loss or damage in a subsequent policy year(s) , all loss or damage is deemed to be sustained in the policy year in which the occurrence began.

5. Coverage Extensions

Except as otherwise provided, the following Extensions apply to property located in or on the building described in the Declarations or in the open (or in a vehicle) within 100 feet of the described premises.
If a Coinsurance percentage of 80% or more or, a Value Reporting period symbol, is shown in the Declarations, you may extend the insurance provided by this Coverage Part as follows:

a. Newly Acquired Or Constructed Property

(1) Buildings

If this policy covers Building, you may extend that insurance to apply to:

(a) Your new buildings while being built on the described premises; and

(b) Buildings you acquire at locations, other than the described premises, intended for:

(i) Similar use as the building described in the Declarations; or

(ii) Use as a warehouse.

The most we will pay for loss or damage under this Extension is $250,000 at each building.

(2) Your Business Personal Property

(a) If this policy covers Your Business Personal Property, you may extend that insurance to apply to:

(i) Business personal property, including such property that you newly acquire, at any location you acquire other than at fairs, trade shows or exhibitions;

(ii) Business personal property, including such property that you newly acquire, located at your newly constructed or acquired buildings at the location described in the Declarations; or

(iii) Business personal property that you newly acquire, located at the described premises.

The most we will pay for loss or damage under this Extension is $100,000 at each building.

(b) This Extension does not apply to:

(i) Personal property of others that is temporarily in your possession in the course of installing or performing work on such property; or

(ii) Personal property of others that is temporarily in your possession in the course of your manufacturing or wholesaling activities.

(3) Period Of Coverage

With respect to insurance on or at each newly acquired or constructed property, coverage will end when any of the following first occurs:

(a) This policy expires;

(b) 30 days expire after you acquire the property or begin construction of that part of the building that would qualify as covered property; or

(c) You report values to us.

We will charge you additional premium for values reported from the date you acquire the property or begin construction of that part of the building that would qualify as covered property.

b. Personal Effects And Property Of Others

You may extend the insurance that applies to Your Business Personal Property to apply to:

(1) Personal effects owned by you, your officers, your partners or members, your managers or your employees.This extension does not apply to loss or damage by theft.

(2) Personal property of others in your care, custody or control.

The most we will pay for loss or damage under this Extension is $2,500 at each described premises. Our payment for loss of or damage to personal property of others will only be for the account of the owner of the property.

c. Valuable Papers And Records (Other Than Electronic Data)

(1) You may extend the insurance that applies to Your Business Personal Property to apply to the cost to replace or restore the lost information on valuable papers and records for which duplicates do not exist. But this Extension does not apply to valuable papers and records which exist as electronic data. Electronic data has the meaning described under Property Not Covered – Electronic Data.

(2) If the Causes Of Loss – Special Form applies, coverage under this Extension is limited to the "specified causes of loss" as defined in that form, and Collapse as set forth in that form.

(3) If the Causes Of Loss – Broad Form applies, coverage under this Extension includes Collapse as set forth in that form.

(4) Under this Extension, the most we will pay to replace or restore the lost information is $2,500 at each described premises, unless a higher limit is shown in the Declarations. Such amount is additional insurance. We will also pay for the cost of blank material for reproducing the records (whether or not duplicates exist) , and (when there is a duplicate) for the cost of labor to transcribe or copy the records. The costs of blank material and labor are subject to the applicable Limit of Insurance on Your Business Personal Property and therefore coverage of such costs is not additional insurance.

d. Property Off-Premises

(1) You may extend the insurance provided by this Coverage Form to apply to your Covered Property while it is away from the described premises, if it is:

(a) Temporarily at a location you do not own, lease or operate;

(b) In storage at a location you lease, provided the lease was executed after the beginning of the current policy term; or

(c) At any fair, trade show or exhibition.

(2) This Extension does not apply to property:

(a) In or on a vehicle; or

(b) In the care, custody or control of your salespersons, unless the property is in such care, custody or control at a fair, trade show or exhibition.

(3) The most we will pay for loss or damage under this Extension is $10,000.

e. Outdoor Property

You may extend the insurance provided by this Coverage Form to apply to your outdoor fences, radio and television antennas (including satellite dishes) , signs (other than signs attached to buildings) , trees, shrubs and plants (other than "stock" of trees, shrubs or plants) , including debris removal expense, caused by or resulting from any of the following causes of loss if they are Covered Causes of Loss:

(1) Fire;

(2) Lightning;

(3) Explosion;

(4) Riot or Civil Commotion; or

(5) Aircraft.

The most we will pay for loss or damage under this Extension is $1,000, but not more than $250 for any one tree, shrub or plant. These limits apply to any one occurrence, regardless of the types or number of items lost or damaged in that occurrence.

f. Non-Owned Detached Trailers

(1) You may extend the insurance that applies to Your Business Personal Property to apply to loss or damage to trailers that you do not own, provided that:

(a) The trailer is used in your business;

(b) The trailer is in your care, custody or control at the premises described in the Declarations; and

(c) You have a contractual responsibility to pay for loss or damage to the trailer.

(2) We will not pay for any loss or damage that occurs:

(a) While the trailer is attached to any motor vehicle or motorized conveyance, whether or not the motor vehicle or motorized conveyance is in motion;

(b) During hitching or unhitching operations, or when a trailer becomes accidentally unhitched from a motor vehicle or motorized conveyance.

(3) The most we will pay for loss or damage under this Extension is $5,000, unless a higher limit is shown in the Declarations.

(4) This insurance is excess over the amount due (whether you can collect on it or not) from any other insurance covering such property.

Each of these Extensions is additional insurance unless otherwise indicated. The Additional Condition, Coinsurance, does not apply to these Extensions.

B. Exclusions And Limitations

See applicable Causes of Loss Form as shown in the Declarations.

C. Limits Of Insurance

The most we will pay for loss or damage in any one occurrence is the applicable Limit of Insurance shown in the Declarations.

The most we will pay for loss or damage to outdoor signs attached to buildings is $1,000 per sign in any one occurrence.

The limits applicable to the Fire Department Service Charge and Pollutant Clean Up and Removal Additional Coverages are in addition to the Limits of Insurance.

Payments under the Preservation of Property Additional Coverage will not increase the applicable Limit of Insurance.

D. Deductible

In any one occurrence of loss or damage (hereinafter referred to as loss) , we will first reduce the amount of loss if required by the Coinsurance Condition or the Agreed Value Optional Coverage. If the adjusted amount of loss is less than or equal to the Deductible, we will not pay for that loss. If the adjusted amount of loss exceeds the Deductible, we will then subtract the Deductible from the adjusted amount of loss, and will pay the resulting amount or the Limit of Insurance, whichever is less.

When the occurrence involves loss to more than one item of Covered Property and separate Limits of Insurance apply, the losses will not be combined in determining application of the Deductible. But the Deductible will be applied only once per occurrence.

E. Loss Conditions

The following conditions apply in addition to the Common Policy Conditions and the Commercial Property Conditions.

1. Abandonment

There can be no abandonment of any property to us.

2. Appraisal

If we and you disagree on the value of the property or the amount of loss, either may make written demand for an appraisal of the loss. In this event, each party will select a competent and impartial appraiser. The two appraisers will select an umpire. If they cannot agree, either may request that selection be made by a judge of a court having jurisdiction. The appraisers will state separately the value of the property and amount of loss. If they fail to agree, they will submit their differences to the umpire. A decision agreed to by any two will be binding. Each party will:

a. Pay its chosen appraiser; and

b. Bear the other expenses of the appraisal and umpire equally.

If there is an appraisal, we will still retain our right to deny the claim.

3. Duties In The Event Of Loss Or Damage

a. You must see that the following are done in the event of loss or damage to Covered Property:

(1) Notify the police if a law may have been broken.

(2) Give us prompt notice of the loss or damage. Include a description of the property involved.

(3) As soon as possible, give us a description of how, when and where the loss or damage occurred.

(4) Take all reasonable steps to protect the Covered Property from further damage, and keep a record of your expenses necessary to protect the Covered Property, for consideration in the settlement of the claim. This will not increase the Limit of Insurance. However, we will not pay for any subsequent loss or damage resulting from a cause of loss that is not a Covered Cause of Loss. Also, if feasible, set the damaged property aside and in the best possible order for examination.

(5) At our request, give us complete inventories of the damaged and undamaged property. Include quantities, costs, values and amount of loss claimed.

(6) As often as may be reasonably required, permit us to inspect the property proving the loss or damage and examine your books and records.

Also permit us to take samples of damaged and undamaged property for inspection, testing and analysis, and permit us to make copies from your books and records.

(7) Send us a signed, sworn proof of loss containing the information we request to investigate the claim.You must do this within 60 days after our request. We will supply you with the necessary forms.

(8) Cooperate with us in the investigation or settlement of the claim.

b. We may examine any insured under oath, while not in the presence of any other insured and at such times as may be reasonably required, about any matter relating to this insurance or the claim, including an insured's books and records. In the event of an examination, an insured's answers must be signed.

4. Loss Payment

a. In the event of loss or damage covered by this Coverage Form, at our option, we will either:

(1) Pay the value of lost or damaged property;

(2) Pay the cost of repairing or replacing the lost or damaged property, subject to b. below;

(3) Take all or any part of the property at an agreed or appraised value; or

(4) Repair, rebuild or replace the property with other property of like kind and quality, subject to b. below.

We will determine the value of lost or damaged property, or the cost of its repair or replacement, in accor dance with the applicable terms of the Valuation Condition in this Coverage Form or any applicable provision which amends or supersedes the Valuation Condition.

b. The cost to repair, rebuild or replace does not include the increased cost attributable to enforcement of any ordinance or law regulating the construction, use or repair of any property.

c. We will give notice of our intentions within 30 days after we receive the sworn proof of loss.

d. We will not pay you more than your financial interest in the Covered Property.

e. We may adjust losses with the owners of lost or damaged property if other than you. If we pay the owners, such payments will satisfy your claims against us for the owners' property. We will not pay the owners more than their financial interest in the Covered Property.

f. We may elect to defend you against suits arising from claims of owners of property. We will do this at our expense.

g. We will pay for covered loss or damage within 30 days after we receive the sworn proof of loss, if you have complied with all of the terms of this Coverage Part and:

(1) We have reached agreement with you on the amount of loss; or

(2) An appraisal award has been made.

5. Recovered Property

If either you or we recover any property after loss settlement, that party must give the other prompt notice. At your option, the property will be returned to you. You must then return to us the amount we paid to you for the property. We will pay recovery expenses and the expenses to repair the recovered property, subject to the Limit of Insurance.

6. Vacancy

a. Description Of Terms

(1) As used in this Vacancy Condition, the term building and the term vacant have the meanings set forth in (1) (a) and (1) (b) below:

(a) When this policy is issued to a tenant, and with respect to that tenant's interest in Covered Property, building means the unit or suite rented or leased to the tenant. Such building is vacant when it does not contain enough business personal property to conduct customary operations.

(b) When this policy is issued to the owner or general lessee of a building, building means the entire building. Such building is vacant unless at least 31% of its total square footage is:

(i) Rented to a lessee or sub-lessee and used by the lessee or sub-lessee to conduct its customary operations; and/or

(ii) Used by the building owner to conduct customary operations.

(2) Buildings under construction or renovation are not considered vacant.

b. Vacancy Provisions

If the building where loss or damage occurs has been vacant for more than 60 consecutive days before that loss or damage occurs:

(1) We will not pay for any loss or damage caused by any of the following even if they are Covered Causes of Loss:

(a) Vandalism;

(b) Sprinkler leakage, unless you have protected the system against freezing;

(c) Building glass breakage;

(d) Water damage;

(e) Theft; or

(f) Attempted theft.

(2) With respect to Covered Causes of Loss other than those listed in b. (1) (a) through b. (1) (f) above, we will reduce the amount we would otherwise pay for the loss or damage by 15%.

7. Valuation

We will determine the value of Covered Property in the event of loss or damage as follows:

a. At actual cash value as of the time of loss or damage, except as provided in b. , c., d. and e. below.

b. If the Limit of Insurance for Building satisfies the Additional Condition, Coinsurance, and the cost to repair or replace the damaged building property is $2,500 or less, we will pay the cost of building repairs or replacement.

The cost of building repairs or replacement does not include the increased cost attributable to enforcement of any ordinance or law regulating the construction, use or repair of any property. However, the following property will be valued at the actual cash value even when attached to the building:

(1) Awnings or floor coverings;

(2) Appliances for refrigerating, ventilating, cooking, dishwashing or laundering; or

(3) Outdoor equipment or furniture.

c. "Stock" you have sold but not delivered at the selling price less discounts and expenses you otherwise would have had.

d. Glass at the cost of replacement with safety glazing material if required by law.

e. Tenant's Improvements and Betterments at:

(1) Actual cash value of the lost or damaged property if you make repairs promptly.

(2) A proportion of your original cost if you do not make repairs promptly. We will determine the proportionate value as follows:

(a) Multiply the original cost by the number of days from the loss or damage to the expiration of the lease; and

(b) Divide the amount determined in (a) above by the number of days from the installation of improvements to the expiration of the lease.

If your lease contains a renewal option, the expiration of the renewal option period will replace the expiration of the lease in this procedure.

(3) Nothing if others pay for repairs or replacement.

F. Additional Conditions

The following conditions apply in addition to the Common Policy Conditions and the Commercial Property Conditions.

1. Coinsurance

If a Coinsurance percentage is shown in the Declarations, the following condition applies.

a. We will not pay the full amount of any loss if the value of Covered Property at the time of loss times the Coinsurance percentage shown for it in the Declarations is greater than the Limit of Insurance for the property.

Instead, we will determine the most we will pay using the following steps:

(1) Multiply the value of Covered Property at the time of loss by the Coinsurance percentage;

(2) Divide the Limit of Insurance of the property by the figure determined in Step (1) ;

(3) Multiply the total amount of loss, before the application of any deductible, by the figure determined in Step (2) ; and

(4) Subtract the deductible from the figure determined in Step (3) .

We will pay the amount determined in Step **(4)** or the limit of insurance, whichever is less. For the remainder, you will either have to rely on other insurance or absorb the loss yourself.

2. Mortgageholders

a. The term mortgageholder includes trustee.

b. We will pay for covered loss of or damage to buildings or structures to each mortgageholder shown in the Declarations in their order of precedence, as interests may appear.

c. The mortgageholder has the right to receive loss payment even if the mortgageholder has started foreclosure or similar action on the building or structure.

d. If we deny your claim because of your acts or because you have failed to comply with the terms of this Coverage Part, the mortgageholder will still have the right to receive loss payment if the mortgageholder:

(1) Pays any premium due under this Coverage Part at our request if you have failed to do so;

(2) Submits a signed, sworn proof of loss within 60 days after receiving notice from us of your failure to do so; and

(3) Has notified us of any change in ownership, occupancy or substantial change in risk known to the mortgageholder.

All of the terms of this Coverage Part will then apply directly to the mortgageholder.

e. If we pay the mortgageholder for any loss or damage and deny payment to you because of your acts or because you have failed to comply with the terms of this Coverage Part:

(1) The mortgageholder's rights under the mortgage will be transferred to us to the extent of the amount we pay; and

(2) The mortgageholder's right to recover the full amount of the mortgageholder's claim will not be impaired. At our option, we may pay to the mortgageholder the whole principal on the mortgage plus any accrued interest. In this event, your mortgage and note will be transferred to us and you will pay your remaining mortgage debt to us.

f. If we cancel this policy, we will give written notice to the mortgageholder at least:

(1) 10 days before the effective date of cancellation if we cancel for your nonpayment of premium; or

(2) 30 days before the effective date of cancellation if we cancel for any other reason.

g. If we elect not to renew this policy, we will give written notice to the mortgageholder at least 10 days before the expiration date of this policy.

G. Optional Coverages

If shown as applicable in the Declarations, the following Optional Coverages apply separately to each item.

1. Agreed Value

a. The Additional Condition, Coinsurance, does not apply to Covered Property to which this Optional Coverage applies. We will pay no more for loss of or damage to that property than the proportion that the Limit of Insurance under this Coverage Part for the property bears to the Agreed Value shown for it in the Declarations.

b. If the expiration date for this Optional Coverage shown in the Declarations is not extended, the Additional Condition, Coinsurance, is reinstated and this Optional Coverage expires.

c. The terms of this Optional Coverage apply only to loss or damage that occurs:

(1) On or after the effective date of this Optional Coverage; and

(2) Before the Agreed Value expiration date shown in the Declarations or the policy expiration date, whichever occurs first.

2. Inflation Guard

a. The Limit of Insurance for property to which this Optional Coverage applied will automatically increase by the annual percentage shown in the Declarations.

b. The amount of increase will be:

(1) The Limit of Insurance that applied on the most recent of the policy inception date, the policy anniversary date, or any other policy change amending the Limit of Insurance, times

(2) The percentage of annual increase shown in the Declarations, expressed as a decimal (example: 8% is .08) , times

(3) The number of days since the beginning of the current policy year or the effective date of the most recent policy change amending the Limit of Insurance, divided by 365.

3. Replacement Cost

a. Replacement Cost (without deduction for depreciation) replaces Actual Cash Value in the Loss Condition, Valuation, of this Coverage Form.

b. This Optional Coverage does not apply to:

(1) Personal property of others;

(2) Contents of a residence;

(3) Works of art, antiques or rare articles, including etchings, pictures, statuary, marbles, bronzes, porcelains and bric-a-brac; or

(4) "Stock", unless the Including "Stock" option is shown in the Declarations.
Under the terms of this Replacement Cost Optional Coverage, tenants' improvements and betterments are not considered to be the personal property of others.

c. You may make a claim for loss or damage covered by this insurance on an actual cash value basis instead of on a replacement cost basis. In the event you elect to have loss or damage settled on an actual cash value basis, you may still make a claim for the additional coverage this Optional Coverage provides if you notify us of your intent to do so within 180 days after the loss or damage.

d. We will not pay on a replacement cost basis for any loss or damage:

(1) Until the lost or damaged property is actually repaired or replaced; and

(2) Unless the repairs or replacement are made as soon as reasonably possible after the loss or damage.

With respect to tenants' improvements and betterments, the following also apply:

(3) If the conditions in d.(1) and d. (2) above are not met, the value of tenants' improvements and betterments will be determined as a proportion of your original cost, as set forth in the Valuation Condition of this Coverage Form; and

(4) We will not pay for loss or damage to tenants' improvements and betterments if others pay for repairs or replacement.

e. We will not pay more for loss or damage on a replacement cost basis than the least of (1) , (2) or (3) , subject to f. below:

(1) The Limit of Insurance applicable to the lost or damaged property;

(2) The cost to replace the lost or damaged property with other property:

(a) Of comparable material and quality; and

(b) Used for the same purpose; or

(3) The amount actually spent that is necessary to repair or replace the lost or damaged property.

If a building is rebuilt at a new premises, the cost described in **e. (2)** above is limited to the cost which would have been incurred if the building had been rebuilt at the original premises.

f. The cost of repair or replacement does not include the increased cost attributable to enforcement of any ordinance or law regulating the construction, use or repair of any property.

4. Extension Of Replacement Cost To Personal Property Of Others

a. If the Replacement Cost Optional Coverage is shown as applicable in the Declarations, then this Extension may also be shown as applicable. If the Declarations show this Extension as applicable, then Paragraph 3.b. (1) of the Replacement Cost Optional Coverage is deleted and all other provisions of the Replacement Cost Optional Coverage apply to replacement cost on personal property of others.

b. With respect to replacement cost on the personal property of others, the following limitation applies:
If an item(s) of personal property of others is subject to a written contract which governs your liability for loss or damage to that item(s) , then valuation of that item(s) will be based on the amount for which you are liable under such contract, but not to exceed the lesser of the replacement cost of the property or the applicable Limit of Insurance.

H. Definitions

1. "Fungus" means any type or form of fungus, including mold or mildew, and any mycotoxins, spores, scents or by-products produced or released by fungi.

2. "Pollutants" means any solid, liquid, gaseous or thermal irritant or contaminant, including smoke, vapor, soot, fumes, acids, alkalis, chemicals and waste. Waste includes materials to be recycled, reconditioned or reclaimed.

3. "Stock" means merchandise held in storage or for sale, raw materials and in-process or finished goods, including supplies used in their packing or shipping.

CP 00 10 04 02

BUSINESS INCOME (WITHOUT EXTRA EXPENSE) COVERAGE FORM

Various provisions in this policy restrict coverage. Read the entire policy carefully to determine rights, duties and what is and is not covered.

Throughout this policy the words "you" and "your" refer to the Named Insured shown in the Declarations. The words "we", "us" and "our" refer to the Company providing this insurance.

Other words and phrases that appear in quotation marks have special meaning.Refer to Section **G. – Definitions.**

A. Coverage

1. Business Income

Business Income means the:

a. Net Income (Net Profit or Loss before income taxes) that would have been earned or incurred; and

b. Continuing normal operating expenses incurred, including payroll.

For manufacturing risks, Net Income includes the net sales value of production.

Coverage is provided as described and limited below for one or more of the following options for which a Limit of Insurance is shown in the Declarations:

a. Business Income including "Rental Value".

b. Business Income other than "Rental Value".

c. "Rental Value".

If option **a.** above is selected, the term Business Income will include "Rental Value".If option **c.** above is selected, the term Business Income will mean "Rental Value" only.

If Limits of Insurance are shown under more than one of the above options, the provisions of this Coverage Part apply separately to each.

We will pay for the actual loss of Business Income you sustain due to the necessary "suspension" of your "operations" during the "period of restoration". The "suspension" must be caused by direct physical loss of or damage to property at premises which are described in the Declarations and for which a Business Income Limit of Insurance is shown in the Declarations. The loss or damage must be caused by or result from a Covered Cause of Loss. With respect to loss of or damage to personal property in the open or personal property in a vehicle, the described premises include the area within 100 feet of the site at which the described premises are located.

With respect to the requirements set forth in the preceding paragraph, if you occupy only part of the site at which the described premises are located, your premises means:

a. The portion of the building which you rent, lease or occupy; and

b. Any area within the building or on the site at which the described premises are located, if that area services, or is used to gain access to, the described premises.

2. Covered Causes Of Loss, Exclusions And Limitations

See applicable Causes of Loss Form as shown in the Declarations.

3. Additional Limitation – Interruption Of Computer Operations

a. Coverage for Business Income does not apply when a "suspension" of "operations" is caused by destruction or corruption of electronic data, or any loss or damage to electronic data, except as provided under the Additional Coverage – Interruption Of Computer Operations.

b. Electronic data means information, facts or computer programs stored as or on, created or used on, or transmitted to or from computer software (including systems and applications software) , on hard or floppy disks, CD-ROMs, tapes, drives, cells, data processing devices or any other repositories of computer software which are used with electronically controlled equipment. The term computer programs, referred to in the foregoing description of electronic data, means a set of related electronic instructions which direct the operations and functions of a computer or device connected to it, which enable the computer or device to receive, process, store, retrieve or send data.

4. Additional Coverages

a. Expenses To Reduce Loss

In the event of a covered loss of Business Income, we will pay necessary expenses you incur, except the cost of extinguishing a fire, to avoid further loss of Business Income. The total of our payment for Business Income loss and Expenses to Reduce Loss will not be more than the Business Income loss that would have been payable under this Coverage Form (after application of any Coinsurance penalty) if the Expenses to Reduce Loss had not been incurred. This coverage does not increase the Limit of Insurance.

The Coinsurance condition does not apply specifically to such Expenses to Reduce Loss, but it is used as described above to determine the total amount payable.

b. Civil Authority

We will pay for the actual loss of Business Income you sustain caused by action of civil authority that prohibits access to the described premises due to direct physical loss of or damage to property, other than at the described premises, caused by or resulting from any Covered Cause of Loss. This coverage begins 72 hours after the time of that action, and will apply for a period of up to three consecutive weeks from the date on which the coverage begins.

c. Alterations And New Buildings

We will pay for the actual loss of Business Income you sustain due to direct physical loss or damage at the described premises caused by or resulting from any Covered Cause of Loss to:

(1) New buildings or structures, whether complete or under construction;

(2) Alterations or additions to existing buildings or structures; and

(3) Machinery, equipment, supplies or building materials located on or within 100 feet of the described premises and:

(a) Used in the construction, alterations or additions; or

(b) Incidental to the occupancy of new buildings.

If such direct physical loss or damage delays the start of "operations", the "period of restoration" will begin on the date "operations" would have begun if the direct physical loss or damage had not occurred.

d. Extended Business Income

(1) Business Income Other Than "Rental Value"

If the necessary "suspension" of your "operations" produces a Business Income loss payable under this policy, we will pay for the actual loss of Business Income you incur during the period that:

(a) Begins on the date property (except "finished stock") is actually repaired, rebuilt or replaced and "operations" are resumed; and

(b) Ends on the earlier of:

(i) The date you could restore your "operations", with reasonable speed, to the level which would generate the business income amount that would have existed if no direct physical loss or damage had occurred; or

(ii) 30 consecutive days after the date determined in (1) (a) above.

However, Extended Business Income does not apply to loss of Business Income incurred as a result of unfavorable business conditions caused by the impact of the Covered Cause of Loss in the area where the described premises are located.

Loss of Business Income must be caused by direct physical loss or damage at the described premises caused by or resulting from any Covered Cause of Loss.

(2) "Rental Value"

If the necessary "suspension" of your "operations" produces a "Rental Value" loss payable under this policy, we will pay for the actual loss of "Rental Value" you incur during the period that:

(a) Begins on the date property is actually repaired, rebuilt or replaced and tenantability is restored; and

(b) Ends on the earlier of:

(i) The date you could restore tenant occupancy, with reasonable speed, to the level which would generate the "Rental Value" that would have existed if no direct physical loss or damage had occurred; or

(ii) 30 consecutive days after the date determined in (2) (a) above.

However, Extended Business Income does not apply to loss of "Rental Value" incurred as a result of unfavorable business conditions caused by the impact of the Covered Cause of Loss in the area where the described premises are located.

Loss of "Rental Value" must be caused by direct physical loss or damage at the described premises caused by or resulting from any Covered Cause of Loss.

e. Interruption Of Computer Operations

(1) Under this Additional Coverage, electronic data has the meaning described under Additional Limitation – Interruption Of Computer Operations.

(2) Subject to all provisions of this Additional Coverage, you may extend the insurance that applies to Business Income to apply to a "suspension" of "operations" caused by an interruption in computer operations due to destruction or corruption of electronic data due to a Covered Cause of Loss.

(3) With respect to the coverage provided under this Additional Coverage, the Covered Causes of Loss are subject to the following:

(a) If the Causes Of Loss – Special Form applies, coverage under this Additional Coverage – Interruption Of Computer Operations is limited to the "specified causes of loss" as defined in that form, and Collapse as set forth in that form.

(b) If the Causes Of Loss – Broad Form applies, coverage under this Additional Coverage – Interruption Of Computer Operations includes Collapse as set forth in that form.

(c) If the Causes Of Loss Form is endorsed to add a Covered Cause of Loss, the additional Covered Cause of Loss does not apply to the coverage provided under this Additional Coverage – Interruption Of Computer Operations.

(d) The Covered Causes of Loss include a virus, harmful code or similar instruction introduced into or enacted on a computer system (including electronic data) or a network to which it is connected, designed to damage or destroy any part of the system or disrupt its normal operation. But there is no coverage for an interruption related to manipulation of a computer system (including electronic data) by any employee, including a temporary or leased employee, or by an entity retained by you or for you to inspect, design, install, maintain, repair or replace that system.

(4) The most we will pay under this Additional Coverage – Interruption Of Computer Operations is $2,500 for all loss sustained in any one policy year, regardless of the number of interruptions or the number of premises, locations or computer systems involved. If loss payment relating to the first interruption does not exhaust this amount, then the balance is available for loss sustained as a result of subsequent interruptions in that policy year. A balance remaining at the end of a policy year does not increase the amount of insurance in the next policy year. With respect to any interruption which begins in one policy year and continues or results in additional loss in a subsequent policy year(s) , all loss is deemed to be sustained in the policy year in which the interruption began.

(5) This Additional Coverage – Interruption in Computer Operations does not apply to loss sustained after the end of the "period of restoration", even if the amount of insurance stated in (4) above has not been exhausted.

5. Coverage Extension

If a Coinsurance percentage of 50% or more is shown in the Declarations, you may extend the insurance provided by this Coverage Part as follows:

NEWLY ACQUIRED LOCATIONS

a. You may extend your Business Income Coverage to apply to property at any location you acquire other than fairs or exhibitions.

b. The most we will pay for loss under this Extension is $100,000 at each location.

c. Insurance under this Extension for each newly acquired location will end when any of the following first occurs:

(1) This policy expires;

(2) 30 days expire after you acquire or begin to construct the property; or

(3) You report values to us.

We will charge you additional premium for values reported from the date you acquire the property.

This Extension is additional insurance. The Additional Condition, Coinsurance, does not apply to this Extension.

B. Limits Of Insurance

The most we will pay for loss in any one occurrence is the applicable Limit of Insurance shown in the Declarations.

The limit applicable to the Coverage Extension is in addition to the Limit of Insurance.

Payments under the following Additional Coverages will not increase the applicable Limit of Insurance:

1. Alterations and New Buildings;

2. Civil Authority;

3. Extended Business Income;

4. Expenses to Reduce Loss.

C. Loss Conditions

The following conditions apply in addition to the Common Policy Conditions and the Commercial Property Conditions.

1. Appraisal

If we and you disagree on the amount of Net Income and operating expense or the amount of loss, either may make written demand for an appraisal of the loss. In this event, each party will select a competent and impartial appraiser.

The two appraisers will select an umpire. If they cannot agree, either may request that selection be made by a judge of a court having jurisdiction. The appraisers will state separately the amount of Net Income and operating expense or amount of loss. If they fail to agree, they will submit their differences to the umpire. A decision agreed to by any two will be binding. Each party will:

a. Pay its chosen appraiser; and

b. Bear the other expenses of the appraisal and umpire equally.

If there is an appraisal, we will still retain our right to deny the claim.

2. Duties In The Event Of Loss

a. You must see that the following are done in the event of loss:

(1) Notify the police if a law may have been broken.

(2) Give us prompt notice of the direct physical loss or damage. Include a description of the property involved.

(3) As soon as possible, give us a description of how, when, and where the direct physical loss or damage occurred.

(4) Take all reasonable steps to protect the Covered Property from further damage, and keep a record of your expenses necessary to protect the Covered Property, for consideration in the settlement of the claim. This will not increase the Limit of Insurance. However, we will not pay for any subsequent loss or damage resulting from a cause of loss that is not a Covered Cause of Loss. Also, if feasible, set the damaged property aside and in the best possible order for examination.

(5) As often as may be reasonably required, permit us to inspect the property proving the loss or damage and examine your books and records.

Also permit us to take samples of damaged and undamaged property for inspection, testing and analysis, and permit us to make copies from your books and records.

(6) Send us a signed, sworn proof of loss containing the information we request to investigate the claim.You must do this within 60 days after our request. We will supply you with the necessary forms.

(7) Cooperate with us in the investigation or settlement of the claim.

(8) If you intend to continue your business, you must resume all or part of your "operations" as quickly as possible.

b. We may examine any insured under oath, while not in the presence of any other insured and at such times as may be reasonably required, about any matter relating to this insurance or the claim, including an insured's books and records. In the event of an examination, an insured's answers must be signed.

3. Loss Determination

a. The amount of Business Income loss will be determined based on:

(1) The Net Income of the business before the direct physical loss or damage occurred;

(2) The likely Net Income of the business if no physical loss or damage had occurred, but not including any Net Income that would likely have been earned as a result of an increase in the volume of business due to favorable business conditions caused by the impact of the Covered Cause of Loss on customers or on other businesses;

(3) The operating expenses, including payroll expenses, necessary to resume "operations" with the same quality of service that existed just before the direct physical loss or damage; and

(4) Other relevant sources of information, including:

(a) Your financial records and accounting procedures;

(b) Bills, invoices and other vouchers; and

(c) Deeds, liens or contracts.

b. Resumption Of Operations

We will reduce the amount of your Business Income loss to the extent you can resume your "operations", in whole or in part, by using damaged or undamaged property (including merchandise or stock) at the described premises or elsewhere.

c. If you do not resume "operations", or do not resume "operations" as quickly as possible, we will pay based on the length of time it would have taken to resume "operations" as quickly as possible.

4. Loss Payment

We will pay for covered loss within 30 days after we receive the sworn proof of loss, if you have complied with all of the terms of this Coverage Part and:

a. We have reached agreement with you on the amount of loss; or

b. An appraisal award has been made.

D. Additional Condition

COINSURANCE

If a Coinsurance percentage is shown in the Declarations, the following condition applies in addition to the Common Policy Conditions and the Commercial Property Conditions.

We will not pay the full amount of any loss if the Limit of Insurance for Business Income is less than:

a. The Coinsurance percentage shown for Business Income in the Declarations; times

b. The sum of:

(1) The Net Income (Net Profit or Loss before income taxes) , and

(2) Operating expenses, including payroll expenses,

that would have been earned or incurred (had no loss occurred) by your "operations" at the described premises for the 12 months following the inception, or last previous anniversary date, of this policy (whichever is later) .

Instead, we will determine the most we will pay using the following steps:

1. Multiply the Net Income and operating expense for the 12 months following the inception, or last previous anniversary date, of this policy by the Coinsurance percentage;

2. Divide the Limit of Insurance for the described premises by the figure determined in Step 1; and

3. Multiply the total amount of loss by the figure determined in Step 2.

We will pay the amount determined in Step **3** or the limit of insurance, whichever is less. For the remainder, you will either have to rely on other insurance or absorb the loss yourself.

In determining operating expenses for the purpose of applying the Coinsurance condition, the following expenses, if applicable, shall be deducted from the total of all operating expenses:

1. Prepaid freight – outgoing;

2. Returns and allowances;

3. Discounts;

4. Bad debts;

5. Collection expenses;

6. Cost of raw stock and factory supplies consumed (including transportation charges) ;

7. Cost of merchandise sold (including transportation charges) ;

8. Cost of other supplies consumed (including transportation charges) ;

9. Cost of services purchased from outsiders (not employees) to resell, that do not continue under contract;

10. Power, heat and refrigeration expenses that do not continue under contract (if Form CP 15 11 is attached) ;

11. All ordinary payroll expenses or the amount of payroll expense excluded (if Form CP 15 10 is attached) ; and

12. Special deductions for mining properties (royalties unless specifically included in coverage; actual depletion commonly known as unit or cost depletion – not percentage depletion; welfare and retirement fund charges based on tonnage; hired trucks) .

E. Optional Coverages

If shown as applicable in the Declarations, the following Optional Coverages apply separately to each item.

1. Maximum Period Of Indemnity

a. The Additional Condition, Coinsurance, does not apply to this Coverage Form at the described premises to which this Optional Coverage applies.

b. The most we will pay for loss of Business Income is the lesser of:

(1) The amount of loss sustained during the 120 days immediately following the beginning of the "period of restoration"; or

(2) The Limit of Insurance shown in the Declarations.

2. Monthly Limit Of Indemnity

a. The Additional Condition, Coinsurance, does not apply to this Coverage Form at the described premises to which this Optional Coverage applies.

b. The most we will pay for loss of Business Income in each period of 30 consecutive days after the beginning of the "period of restoration" is:

(1) The Limit of Insurance, multiplied by

(2) The fraction shown in the Declarations for this Optional Coverage.

3. Business Income Agreed Value

a. To activate this Optional Coverage:

(1) A Business Income Report/Work Sheet must be submitted to us and must show financial data for your "operations":

(a) During the 12 months prior to the date of the Work Sheet; and

(b) Estimated for the 12 months immediately following the inception of this Optional Coverage.

(2) The Declarations must indicate that the Business Income Agreed Value Optional Coverage applies, and an Agreed Value must be shown in the Declarations. The Agreed Value should be at least equal to:

(a) The Coinsurance percentage shown in the Declarations; multiplied by

(b) The amount of Net Income and operating expenses for the following 12 months you report on the Work Sheet.

b. The Additional Condition, Coinsurance, is suspended until:

(1) 12 months after the effective date of this Optional Coverage; or

(2) The expiration date of this policy;

whichever occurs first.

c. We will reinstate the Additional Condition, Coinsurance, automatically if you do not submit a new Work Sheet and Agreed Value:

(1) Within 12 months of the effective date of this Optional Coverage; or

(2) When you request a change in your Business Income Limit of Insurance.

d. If the Business Income Limit of Insurance is less than the Agreed Value, we will not pay more of any loss than the amount of loss multiplied by:

(1) The Business Income Limit of Insurance; divided by

(2) The Agreed Value.

4. Extended Period Of Indemnity

Under Paragraph **A.4.d. , Extended Business Income,** the number "30" in Subparagraphs **(1) (b)** and **(2) (b)** is replaced by the number shown in the Declarations for this Optional Coverage.

F. Definitions

1. "Finished Stock" means stock you have manufactured.

"Finished stock" also includes whiskey and alcoholic products being aged, unless there is a Coinsurance percent age shown for Business Income in the Declarations.

"Finished stock" does not include stock you have manufactured that is held for sale on the premises of any retail outlet insured under this Coverage Part.

2. "Operations" means:

a. Your business activities occurring at the described premises; and

b. The tenantability of the described premises, if coverage for Business Income including "Rental Value" or "Rental Value" applies.

3. "Period of Restoration" means the period of time that:

a. Begins 72 hours after the time of direct physical loss or damage caused by or resulting from any Covered Cause of Loss at the described premises; and

b. Ends on the earlier of:

(1) The date when the property at the described premises should be repaired, rebuilt or replaced with reason able speed and similar quality; or

(2) The date when business is resumed at a new permanent location.

"Period of restoration" does not include any increased period required due to the enforcement of any ordinance or law that:

(1) Regulates the construction, use or repair, or required the tearing down of any property; or

(2) Requires any insured or others to test for, monitor, clean up, remove, contain, treat, detoxify or neutralize, or in any way respond to, or assess the effects of "pollutants".

The expiration date of this policy will not cut short the "period of restoration".

4. "Pollutants" means any solid, liquid, gaseous or thermal irritant or contaminant, including smoke, vapor, soot, fumes, acids, alkalis, chemicals and waste. Waste includes materials to be recycled, reconditioned or reclaimed.

5. "Rental Value" means Business Income that consists of:

a. Net Income (Net Profit or Loss before income taxes) that would have been earned or incurred as rental income from tenant occupancy of the premises described in the Declarations as furnished and equipped by you, including fair rental value of any portion of the described premises which is occupied by you; and

b. Continuing normal operating expenses incurred in connection with that premises, including:

(1) Payroll; and

(2) The amount of charges which are the legal obligation of the tenant(s) but would otherwise be your obligations.

6. "Suspension" means:

a. The slowdown or cessation of your business activities; or

b. That a part or all of the described premises is rendered untenantable, if coverage for Business Income including "Rental Value" or "Rental Value" applies.

EXTRA EXPENSE COVERAGE FORM

Various provisions in this policy restrict coverage. Read the entire policy carefully to determine rights, duties and what is and is not covered.

Throughout this policy the words "you" and "your" refer to the Named Insured shown in the Declarations. The words "we", "us" and "our" refer to the Company providing this insurance.

Other words and phrases that appear in quotation marks have special meaning.Refer to Section **D. – Definitions.**

A. Coverage

We will pay the actual and necessary Extra Expense you sustain due to direct physical loss of or damage to property at premises which are described in the Declarations and for which an Extra Expense Limit of Insurance is shown in the Declarations. The loss or damage must be caused by or result from a Covered Cause of Loss. With respect to loss of or damage to personal property in the open or personal property in a vehicle, the described premises include the area within 100 feet of the site at which the described premises are located.
With respect to the requirements set forth in the preceding paragraph, if you occupy only part of the site at which the described premises are located, your premises means:

a. The portion of the building which you rent, lease or occupy; and

b. Any area within the building or on the site at which the described premises are located, if that area services, or is used to gain access to, the described premises.

1. Extra Expense

Extra Expense means necessary expenses you incur during the "period of restoration" that you would not have incurred if there had been no direct physical loss or damage to property. Coverage pertains to expenses (other than the expense to repair or replace property) which are incurred to:

a. Avoid or minimize the "suspension" of business and to continue "operations" at the described premises or at replacement premises or temporary locations, including relocation expenses and costs to equip and operate the replacement location or temporary location.

b. Minimize the "suspension" of business if you cannot continue "operations".

We will also pay Extra Expense to repair or replace property, but only to the extent it reduces the amount of loss that otherwise would have been payable under this Coverage Form.

2. Covered Causes Of Loss, Exclusions And Limitations

See applicable Causes of Loss Form as shown in the Declarations.

3. Additional Limitation – Interruption Of Computer Operations

a. Coverage for Extra Expense does not apply when action is taken to avoid or minimize a "suspension" of "operations" caused by destruction or corruption of electronic data, or any loss or damage to electronic data, except as provided under the Additional Coverage – Interruption Of Computer Operations.
b. Electronic data means information, facts or computer programs stored as or on, created or used on, or transmitted to or from computer software (including systems and applications software) , on hard or floppy disks, CD-ROMs, tapes, drives, cells, data processing devices or any other repositories of computer software which are

used with electronically controlled equipment. The term computer programs, referred to in the foregoing description of electronic data, means a set of related electronic instructions which direct the operations and functions of a computer or device connected to it, which enable the computer or device to receive, process, store, retrieve or send data.

4. Additional Coverages

a. Alterations And New Buildings

We will pay for the actual and necessary Extra Expense you incur due to direct physical loss or damage at the described premises caused by or resulting from any Covered Cause of Loss to:

(1) New buildings or structures, whether complete or under construction;

(2) Alterations or additions to existing buildings or structures; and

(3) Machinery, equipment, supplies or building materials located on or within 100 feet of the described premises and:

(a) Used in the construction, alterations or additions; or

(b) Incidental to the occupancy of new buildings.

b. Civil Authority

We will pay for the actual and necessary Extra Expense you incur caused by action of civil authority that prohibits access to the described premises due to direct physical loss of or damage to property, other than at the described premises, caused by or resulting from any Covered Cause of Loss. This coverage will apply for a period of up to three consecutive weeks from the date of that action.

c. Interruption Of Computer Operations

(1) Under this Additional Coverage, electronic data has the meaning described under Additional Limitation – Interruption Of Computer Operations.

(2) Subject to all provisions of this Additional Coverage, you may extend the insurance that applies to Extra Expense to apply to a "suspension" of "operations" caused by an interruption in computer operations due to destruction or corruption of electronic data due to a Covered Cause of Loss.

(3) With respect to the coverage provided under this Additional Coverage, the Covered Causes of Loss are subject to the following:

(a) If the Causes Of Loss – Special Form applies, coverage under this Additional Coverage – Interruption Of Computer Operations is limited to the "specified causes of loss" as defined in that form, and Collapse as set forth in that form.

(b) If the Causes Of Loss – Broad Form applies, coverage under this Additional Coverage – Interruption Of Computer Operations includes Collapse as set forth in that form.

(c) If the Causes of Loss Form is endorsed to add a Covered Cause of Loss, the additional Covered Cause of Loss does not apply to the coverage provided under this Additional Coverage – Interruption Of Computer Operations.

(d) The Covered Causes of Loss include a virus, harmful code or similar instruction introduced into or enacted on a computer system (including electronic data) or a network to which it is connected, designed to damage or destroy any part of the system or disrupt its normal operation. But there is no coverage for an interruption related to manipulation of a computer system (including electronic data) by any employee, including a temporary or leased employee, or by an entity retained by you or for you to inspect, design, install, maintain, repair or replace that system.

(4) The most we will pay under this Additional Coverage – Interruption Of Computer Operations is $2,500 for all loss sustained in any one policy year, regardless of the number of interruptions or the number of premises, locations or computer systems involved. If loss payment relating to the first interruption does not exhaust this amount, then the balance is available for loss sustained as a result of subsequent interruptions in that policy year. A balance remaining at the end of a policy year does not increase the amount of insurance in the next policy year. With respect to any interruption which begins in one policy year and continues or results in additional loss in a subsequent policy year(s) , all loss is deemed to be sustained in the policy year in which the interruption began.

(5) This Additional Coverage – Interruption Of Computer Operations does not apply to loss sustained after the end of the "period of restoration", even if the amount of insurance stated in (4) above has not been exhausted.

5. Coverage Extension

You may extend the insurance provided by this Coverage Part as follows:

NEWLY ACQUIRED LOCATIONS

a. You may extend your Extra Expense Coverage to apply to property at any location you acquire other than fairs or exhibitions.

b. The most we will pay for loss under this Extension is $100,000 at each location.

c. Insurance under this Extension for each newly acquired location will end when any of the following first occurs:

(1) This policy expires;

(2) 30 days expire after you acquire the property; or

(3) You notify us of how you want this coverage to apply to that location.

We will charge you additional premium from the date you acquire the property.

This Extension is additional insurance.

B. Limits Of Insurance

The most we will pay for loss in any one occurrence is the applicable Limit of Insurance shown in the Declarations.

The limit applicable to the Coverage Extension is in addition to the Limits of Insurance.

Payments under the following Additional Coverages will not increase the applicable Limit of Insurance:

1. Alterations and New Buildings; or

2. Civil Authority.

C. Loss Conditions

The following conditions apply in addition to the Common Policy Conditions and the Commercial Property Conditions.

1. Appraisal

If we and you disagree on the amount of loss, either may make written demand for an appraisal of the loss. In this event, each party will select a competent and impartial appraiser. The two appraisers will select an umpire. If they cannot agree, either may request that selection be made by a judge of a court having jurisdiction. The appraisers will state separately the amount of loss. If they fail to agree, they will submit their differences to the umpire.A decision agreed to by any two will be binding. Each party will:

a. Pay its chosen appraiser; and

b. Bear the other expenses of the appraisal and umpire equally.

If there is an appraisal, we will still retain our right to deny the claim.

2. Duties If You Incur Extra Expense

a. You must see that the following are done if you incur Extra Expense:

(1) Notify the police if a law may have been broken.

(2) Give us prompt notice of the direct physical loss or damage. Include a description of the property involved.

(3) As soon as possible, give us a description of how, when, and where the direct physical loss or damage occurred.

(4) Take all reasonable steps to protect the Covered Property from further damage, and keep a record of your expenses necessary to protect the Covered Property, for consideration in the settlement of the claim. This will not increase the Limit of Insurance. However, we will not pay for any subsequent loss or damage resulting from a cause of loss that is not a Covered Cause of Loss. Also, if feasible, set the damaged property aside and in the best possible order for examination.

(5) As often as may be reasonably required, permit us to inspect the property proving the loss or damage and examine your books and records.

Also permit us to take samples of damaged and undamaged property for inspection, testing and analysis, and permit us to make copies from your books and records.

(6) Send us a signed, sworn proof of loss containing the information we request to investigate the claim. You must do this within 60 days after our request.We will supply you with the necessary forms.

(7) Cooperate with us in the investigation or settlement of the claim.

(8) If you intend to continue your business, you must resume all or part of your "operations" as quickly as possible.

b. We may examine any insured under oath, while not in the presence of any other insured and at such times as may be reasonably required, about any matter relating to this insurance or the claim, including an insured's books and records. In the event of an examination, an insured's answers must be signed.

3. Limits On Loss Payment

We will not pay more for Extra Expense than the percentages shown in the Declarations times the Limit of Insurance.

When the "period of restoration" is:

a. 30 days or less, the first percentage applies.

b. 60 days or less, but more than 30 days, the second percentage applies.

c. More than 60 days, the third percentage applies.

4. Loss Determination

a. The amount of Extra Expense will be determined based on:

(1) All expenses that exceed the normal operating expenses that would have been incurred by "operations" during the "period of restoration" if no direct physical loss or damage had occurred. We will deduct from the total of such expenses:

(a) The salvage value that remains of any property bought for temporary use during the "period of restoration", once "operations" are resumed; and

(b) Any Extra Expense that is paid for by other insurance, except for insurance that is written subject to the same plan, terms, conditions and provisions as this insurance; and

(2) Necessary expenses that reduce the Extra Expense otherwise incurred.

b. We will reduce the amount of your Extra Expense loss to the extent you can return "operations" to normal and discontinue such Extra Expense.

c. If you do not resume "operations", or do not resume "operations" as quickly as possible, we will pay based on the length of time it would have taken to resume "operations" as quickly as possible.

5. Loss Payment

We will pay for any loss within 30 days after we receive the proof of loss, if you have complied with all of the terms of this Coverage Part and:

a. We reach agreement with you on the amount of loss; or

b. An appraisal award has been made.

D. Definitions

1. "Operations" means your business activities occurring at the described premises.

2. "Period of Restoration" means the period of time that:

a. Begins with the date of direct physical loss or damage caused by or resulting from any Covered Cause of Loss at the described premises; and

b. Ends on the earlier of:

(1) The date when the property at the described premises should be repaired, rebuilt or replaced with reasonable speed and similar quality; or

(2) The date when business is resumed at a new permanent location.

"Period of restoration" does not include any increased period required due to the enforcement of any ordinance or law that:

(1) Regulates the construction, use or repair, or requires the tearing down of any property; or

(2) Requires any insured or others to test for, monitor, clean up, remove, contain, treat, detoxify or neutralize, or in any way respond to, or assess the effects of "pollutants".

The expiration date of this policy will not cut short the "period of restoration".

3. "Pollutants" means any solid, liquid, gaseous or thermal irritant or contaminant, including smoke, vapor, soot, fumes, acids, alkalis, chemicals and waste. Waste includes materials to be recycled, reconditioned or reclaimed.

4. "Suspension" means the slowdown or cessation of your business activities.

LEGAL LIABILITY COVERAGE FORM

Various provisions in this policy restrict coverage. Read the entire policy carefully to determine rights, duties and what is and is not covered.

Throughout this policy the words "you" and "your" refer to the Named Insured shown in the Declarations. The words "we", "us" and "our" refer to the Company providing this insurance.
Other words and phrases that appear in quotation marks have special meaning.Refer to Section **F. – Definitions.**

A. Coverage

We will pay those sums that you become legally obligated to pay as damages because of direct physical loss or damage, including loss of use, to Covered Property caused by accident and arising out of any Covered Cause of Loss. We will have the right and duty to defend any "suit" seeking those damages. However, we have no duty to defend you against a "suit" seeking damages for direct physical loss or damage to which this insurance does not apply. We may investigate and settle any claim or "suit" at our discretion. But:

(1) The amount we will pay for damages is limited as described in Section C. Limits Of Insurance; and

(2) Our right and duty to defend end when we have used up the Limit of Insurance in the payment of judgments or settlements.

1. Covered Property And Limitations

Covered Property, as used in this Coverage Form, means tangible property of others in your care, custody or control that is described in the Declarations or on the Legal Liability Coverage Schedule.

Covered Property does not include electronic data. Electronic data means information, facts or computer programs stored as or on, created or used on, or transmitted to or from computer software (including systems and applications software) , on hard or floppy disks, CD-ROMs, tapes, drives, cells, data processing devices or any other repositories of computer software which are used with electronically controlled equipment. The term computer programs, referred to in the foregoing description of electronic data, means a set of related electronic instructions which direct the operations and functions of a computer or device connected to it, which enable the computer or device to receive, process, store, retrieve or send data.

2. Covered Causes Of Loss

See applicable Causes of Loss Form as shown in the Declarations.

3. Additional Coverage

SUPPLEMENTARY PAYMENTS

We will pay, with respect to any claim or any "suit" against you we defend:

a. All expenses we incur.

b. The cost of bonds to release attachments, but only for bond amounts within our Limit of Insurance.We do not have to furnish these bonds.

c. All reasonable expenses incurred by you at our request, including actual loss of earnings up to $250 a day because of time off from work.

d. All costs taxed against you in the "suit".

e. Prejudgment interest awarded against you on that part of the judgment we pay. If we make an offer to pay the Limit of Insurance, we will not pay any prejudgment interest based on that period of time after the offer.

f. All interest on the full amount of any judgment that accrues after entry of the judgment and before we have paid, offered to pay, or deposited in court the part of the judgment that is within our Limit of Insurance.

4. Coverage Extensions

a. Additional Insureds

If the Named Insured shown in the Declarations is a partnership, limited liability company or corporation, throughout this Coverage Form, the words "you" and "your" include:

(1) Partners, members, executive officers, trustees, directors and stockholders of such partnership, limited liability company or corporation, but only with respect to their duties as such; and

(2) Managers of a limited liability company, but only with respect to their duties as such.

b. Newly Acquired Organizations

Throughout this Coverage Form, the words "you" and "your" also include any organization (other than a partnership, joint venture or limited liability company) you newly acquire or form and over which you maintain ownership or majority interest if there is no other similar insurance available to that organization.

This Coverage Extension ends:

(1) 90 days after you acquire or form the organization; or

(2) At the end of the policy period shown in the Declarations;

whichever is earlier.

This Extension does not apply to direct physical loss or damage that occurred before you acquired or formed the organization.

c. Newly Acquired Property

(1) You may extend the insurance that applies to Covered Property, as used in this Coverage Form, to apply to your liability for tangible property of others that comes under your care, custody or control after the beginning of the current policy period. This Extension is subject to the following:

(a) All terms and Conditions of this Coverage Form.

(b) Buildings must be intended for:

(i) Similar use as the building described in the Declarations or on the Legal Liability Coverage Schedule; or

(ii) Use as a warehouse.

The most we will pay as the result of any one accident for loss or damage to buildings covered under this Extension is $250,000 at each building.

(c) Personal property must be at a location:

(i) That you own; or

(ii) That is or comes under your care, custody or control;

other than at fairs or exhibitions.

The most we will pay as the result of any one accident for loss or damage to personal property covered under this Extension is $100,000 at each building.

(2) Insurance under this Extension for each item of property of others will end when any of the following first occurs:

(a) This policy expires;

(b) 30 days expire after the property has come under your care, custody or control; or

(c) You report values to us.

We will charge you additional premium for values reported from the date the property comes under your care, custody or control.

This Extension does not apply to direct physical loss or damage that occurred before the property came under your care, custody or control.

B. Exclusions And Limitations

See applicable Causes of Loss Form as shown in the Declarations.

C. Limits Of Insurance

The most we will pay in damages as the result of any one accident is the applicable Limit of Insurance shown on the Legal Liability Coverage Schedule, or in the Declarations.

Payments under the Additional Coverage and the Newly Acquired Property Coverage Extension are in addition to the Limits of Insurance.

The existence of one or more:

1. Additional Insureds, or

2. Newly Acquired Organizations,

does not increase the Limit of Insurance.

D. Loss Conditions

The following conditions apply in addition to the Commercial Property Conditions:

1. Duties In The Event Of Accident, Claim Or Suit

a. You must see to it that we are notified promptly of any accident that may result in a claim. Notice should include:

(1) How, when and where the accident took place; and

(2) The names and addresses of any witnesses.

Notice of an accident is not notice of a claim.

b. If a claim is made or "suit" is brought against you, you must see to it that we receive prompt written notice of the claim or "suit".

c. You must:

(1) Immediately send us copies of any demands, notices, summonses or legal papers received in connection with the claim or "suit";

(2) Authorize us to obtain records and other information;

(3) Cooperate with us in the investigation, settlement or defense of the claim or "suit"; and

(4) Assist us, upon our request, in the enforcement of any right against any person or organization that may be liable to you because of damage to which this insurance may also apply.

d. You will not, except at your own cost, voluntarily make a payment, assume any obligation, or incur any expense without our consent.

2. Legal Action Against Us

No person or organization has a right under this Coverage Form:

a. To join us as a party or otherwise bring us into a "suit" asking for damages from you; or

b. To sue us on this Coverage Form unless all of its terms have been fully complied with.

A person or organization may sue us to recover on an agreed settlement or on a final judgment against you obtained after an actual trial; but we will not be liable for damages that are not payable under the terms of this Coverage Form or that are in excess of the Limit of Insurance. An agreed settlement means a settlement and release of liability signed by us, you and the claimant or the claimant's legal representative.

3. Other Insurance

You may have other insurance covering the same loss as the insurance under this Coverage Form. If you do, we will pay our share of the covered loss. Our share is the proportion that the Limit of Insurance under this Coverage Form covering such loss bears to the Limits of Insurance of all insurance covering the loss.

4. Transfer Of Rights Of Recovery Against Others To Us

If you have rights to recover all or part of any payment we have made under this Coverage Form, those rights are transferred to us. You must do nothing after loss to impair them. At our request, you will bring "suit" or transfer those rights to us and help us enforce them.

E. Additional Conditions

The following conditions apply in addition to the Common Policy Conditions.

1. Amendment Of Commercial Property Conditions

None of the Commercial Property Conditions apply to this Coverage Form, except:

a. Condition A. , Concealment, Misrepresentation Or Fraud;

b. Condition C. , Insurance Under Two Or More Coverages; and

c. Condition E. , Liberalization.

2. Bankruptcy

Bankruptcy or insolvency of you or your estate will not relieve us of our obligations under this Coverage Form.

3. Policy Period, Coverage Territory

Under this Coverage Form:

a. We will pay for loss or damage caused by an accident that occurs:

(1) During the policy period shown in the Declarations; and

(2) Within the coverage territory.

b. The coverage territory is:

(1) The United States of America;

(2) Puerto Rico; and

(3) Canada.

4. Separation Of Insureds

The insurance under this Coverage Form applies separately to you and each additional insured, except with respect to the Limits of Insurance.

F. Definition

"Suit" includes an arbitration proceeding to which you must submit or submit with our consent.

CP 00 40 04 02

POLICY NUMBER:
COMMERCIAL PROPERTY **CP 04 05 04 02**

THIS ENDORSEMENT CHANGES THE POLICY.PLEASE READ IT CAREFULLY.

ORDINANCE OR LAW COVERAGE

This endorsement modifies insurance provided under the following:

BUILDING AND PERSONAL PROPERTY COVERAGE FORM
CONDOMINIUM ASSOCIATION COVERAGE FORM
STANDARD PROPERTY POLICY

A. Each Coverage – Coverage A, Coverage B and Coverage C – is provided under this endorsement only if that Coverage(s) is chosen by entry in the above Schedule and then only with respect to the building identified for that Coverage(s) in the Schedule.

B. Application Of Coverage(s)

The Coverage(s) provided by this endorsement apply only if both **B.1.** and **B.2.** are satisfied and are then subject to the qualifications set forth in **B.3.**

1. The ordinance or law:

a. Regulates the demolition, construction or repair of buildings, or establishes zoning or land use requirements at the described premises; and

b. Is in force at the time of loss.

But coverage under this endorsement applies only in response to the minimum requirements of the ordinance or law. Losses and costs incurred in complying with recommended actions or standards that exceed actual requirements are not covered under this endorsement.

2.a. The building sustains direct physical damage that is covered under this policy and such damage results in enforcement of the ordinance or law; or

b. The building sustains both direct physical damage that is covered under this policy and direct physical damage that is not covered under this policy, and the building damage in its entirety results in enforcement of the ordinance or law.

c. But if the building sustains direct physical damage that is not covered under this policy, and such damage is the subject of the ordinance or law, then there is no coverage under this endorsement even if the building has also sustained covered direct physical damage.

3. In the situation described in B.2.b. above, we will not pay the full amount of loss otherwise payable under the terms of Coverages A,B, and/or C of this endorsement. Instead, we will pay a proportion of such loss; meaning the proportion that the covered direct physical damage bears to the total direct physical damage.

(Section **H.** of this endorsement provides an example of this procedure.)

However, if the covered direct physical damage, alone, would have resulted in enforcement of the ordinance or law, then we will pay the full amount of loss otherwise payable under the terms of Coverages **A, B** and/or **C** of this endorsement.

C. We will not pay under Coverage A,B or C of this endorsement for:

1. Enforcement of any ordinance or law which requires the demolition, repair, replacement, reconstruction, remodeling or remediation of property due to contamination by "pollutants" or due to the presence, growth, proliferation, spread or any activity of "fungus", wet or dry rot or bacteria; or

2. The costs associated with the enforcement of any ordinance or law which requires any insured or others to test for, monitor, clean up, remove, contain, treat, detoxify or neutralize, or in any way respond to, or assess the effects of "pollutants", "fungus", wet or dry rot or bacteria.

D. Coverage

1. Coverage A – Coverage For Loss To The Undamaged Portion Of The Building

With respect to the building that has sustained covered direct physical damage, we will pay under Coverage **A** for the loss in value of the undamaged portion of the building as a consequence of enforcement of an ordinance or law that requires demolition of undamaged parts of the same building.

Coverage **A** is included within the Limit of Insurance shown in the Declarations as applicable to the covered building. Coverage **A** does not increase the Limit of Insurance.

2. Coverage B – Demolition Cost Coverage

With respect to the building that has sustained covered direct physical damage, we will pay the cost to demolish and clear the site of undamaged parts of the same building, as a consequence of enforcement of an ordinance or law that requires demolition of such undamaged property.

The Coinsurance Additional Condition does not apply to Demolition Cost Coverage.

3. Coverage C – Increased Cost Of Construction Coverage

a. With respect to the building that has sustained covered direct physical damage, we will pay the increased cost to:

(1) Repair or reconstruct damaged portions of that building; and/or

(2) Reconstruct or remodel undamaged portions of that building, whether or not demolition is required;

when the increased cost is a consequence of enforcement of the minimum requirements of the ordinance or law.

However:

(1) This coverage applies only if the restored or remodeled property is intended for similar occupancy as the current property, unless such occupancy is not permitted by zoning or land use ordinance or law.

(2) We will not pay for the increased cost of construction if the building is not repaired, reconstructed or remodeled.

The Coinsurance Additional Condition does not apply to Increased Cost of Construction Coverage.

b. When a building is damaged or destroyed and Coverage C applies to that building in accordance with 3.a. above, coverage for the increased cost of construction also applies to repair or reconstruction of the following, subject to the same conditions stated in 3.a. :

(1) The cost of excavations, grading, backfilling and filling;

(2) Foundation of the building;

(3) Pilings; and

(4) Underground pipes, flues and drains.

The items listed in **b. (1)** through **b. (4)** above are deleted from Property Not Covered, but only with respect to the coverage described in this Provision, **3.b.**

E. Loss Payment

1. All following loss payment Provisions, E.2. through E.5. , are subject to the apportionment procedures set forth in Section B.3. of this endorsement.

2. When there is a loss in value of an undamaged portion of a building to which Coverage A applies, the loss payment for that building, including damaged and undamaged portions, will be determined as follows:

a. If the Replacement Cost Coverage Option applies and the property is being repaired or replaced, on the same or another premises, we will not pay more than the lesser of:

(1) The amount you would actually spend to repair, rebuild or reconstruct the building, but not for more than the amount it would cost to restore the building on the same premises and to the same height, floor area, style and comparable quality of the original property insured; or

(2) The Limit of Insurance shown in the Declarations as applicable to the covered building.

b. If the Replacement Cost Coverage Option applies and the property is not repaired or replaced, or if the Replacement Cost Coverage Option does not apply, we will not pay more than the lesser of:

(1) The actual cash value of the building at the time of loss; or

(2) The Limit of Insurance shown in the Declarations as applicable to the covered building.

3. Unless Paragraph E.5. applies, loss payment under Coverage B – Demolition Cost Coverage will be determined as follows:

We will not pay more than the lesser of the following:

a. The amount you actually spend to demolish and clear the site of the described premises; or

b. The applicable Limit of Insurance shown for Coverage B in the Schedule above.

4. Unless Paragraph E.5. applies, loss payment under Coverage C – Increased Cost of Construction Coverage will be determined as follows:

a. We will not pay under Coverage C:

(1) Until the property is actually repaired or replaced, at the same or another premises; and

(2) Unless the repairs or replacement are made as soon as reasonably possible after the loss or damage, not to exceed two years. We may extend this period in writing during the two years.

b. If the building is repaired or replaced at the same premises, or if you elect to rebuild at another premises, the most we will pay under Coverage C is the lesser of:

(1) The increased cost of construction at the same premises; or

(2) The applicable Limit of Insurance shown for Coverage C in the Schedule above.

c. If the ordinance or law requires relocation to another premises, the most we will pay under Coverage C is the lesser of:

(1) The increased cost of construction at the new premises; or

(2) The applicable Limit of Insurance shown for Coverage C in the Schedule above.

5. If a Combined Limit of Insurance is shown for Coverages B and C in the Schedule above, Paragraphs E.3. and E.4. of this endorsement do not apply with respect to the building that is subject to the Combined Limit, and the following loss payment provisions apply instead:

The most we will pay, for the total of all covered losses for Demolition Cost and Increased Cost of Construction, is the Combined Limit of Insurance shown for Coverages **B** and **C** in the Schedule above. Subject to this Combined Limit of Insurance, the following loss payment provisions apply:

a. For Demolition Cost, we will not pay more than the amount you actually spend to demolish and clear the site of the described premises.

b. With respect to the Increased Cost of Construction:

(1) We will not pay for the increased cost of construction:

(a) Until the property is actually repaired or replaced, at the same or another premises; and

(b) Unless the repairs or replacement are made as soon as reasonably possible after the loss or damage, not to exceed two years. We may extend this period in writing during the two years.

(2) If the building is repaired or replaced at the same premises, or if you elect to rebuild at another premises, the most we will pay for the increased cost of construction is the increased cost of construction at the same premises.

(3) If the ordinance or law requires relocation to another premises, the most we will pay for the increased cost of construction is the increased cost of construction at the new premises.

F. The terms of this endorsement apply separately to each building to which this endorsement applies.

G. Under this endorsement we will not pay for loss due to any ordinance or law that:

1. You were required to comply with before the loss, even if the building was undamaged; and

2. You failed to comply with.

I. The following definition is added:

"Fungus" means any type or form of fungus, including mold or mildew, and any mycotoxins, spores, scents or by-products produced or released by fungi.

POLICY NUMBER:
COMMERCIAL PROPERTY

CP 10 54 06 95

THIS ENDORSEMENT CHANGES THE POLICY. PLEASE READ IT CAREFULLY.

WINDSTORM OR HAIL EXCLUSION

This endorsement modifies insurance provided under the following:

CAUSES OF LOSS – BASIC FORM
CAUSES OF LOSS – BROAD FORM
CAUSES OF LOSS – SPECIAL FORM
STANDARD PROPERTY POLICY

A. The following is added to the EXCLUSIONS section and is therefore not a Covered Cause of Loss:

WINDSTORM OR HAIL

We will not pay for loss or damage:

1. Caused directly or indirectly by Windstorm or Hail, regardless of any other cause or event that contributes concurrently or in any sequence to the loss or damage; or

2. Caused by rain, snow, sand or dust, whether driven by wind or not, if that loss or damage would not have occurred but for the Windstorm or Hail.

But if Windstorm or Hail results in a cause of loss other than rain, snow, sand or dust, and that resulting cause of loss is a Covered Cause of Loss, we will pay for the loss or damage caused by such Covered Cause of Loss. For example, if the Windstorm or Hail damages a heating system and fire results, the loss or damage attributable to the fire is covered subject to any other applicable policy provisions.

B. Under ADDITIONAL COVERAGE – COLLAPSE, in the Causes of Loss – Broad Form, Windstorm or Hail is deleted from paragraph a.(1).

C. In the Causes of Loss – Special Form, Windstorm or Hail is deleted from the "specified causes of loss".

D. Under ADDITIONAL COVERAGE EXTENSIONS – PROPERTY IN TRANSIT, in the Causes of Loss – Special Form, Windstorm or Hail is deleted from paragraph b.(1).

CAUSES OF LOSS – SPECIAL FORM

Words and phrases that appear in quotation marks have special meaning.Refer to Section **F.** – Definitions.

A. Covered Causes Of Loss

When Special is shown in the Declarations, Covered Causes of Loss means Risks Of Direct Physical Loss unless the loss is:

1. Excluded in Section B. , Exclusions; or

2. Limited in Section C. , Limitations;

that follow.

B. Exclusions

1. We will not pay for loss or damage caused directly or indirectly by any of the following. Such loss or damage is excluded regardless of any other cause or event that contributes concurrently or in any sequence to the loss.

a. Ordinance Or Law

The enforcement of any ordinance or law:

(1) Regulating the construction, use or repair of any property; or

(2) Requiring the tearing down of any property, including the cost of removing its debris.

This exclusion, Ordinance Or Law, applies whether the loss results from:

(1) An ordinance or law that is enforced even if the property has not been damaged; or

(2) The increased costs incurred to comply with an ordinance or law in the course of construction, repair, renovation, remodeling or demolition of property, or removal of its debris, following a physical loss to that property.

b. Earth Movement

(1) Earthquake, including any earth sinking, rising or shifting related to such event;

(2) Landslide, including any earth sinking, rising or shifting related to such event;

(3) Mine subsidence, meaning subsidence of a man-made mine, whether or not mining activity has ceased;

(4) Earth sinking (other than sinkhole collapse) , rising or shifting including soil conditions which cause settling, cracking or other disarrangement of foundations or other parts of realty. Soil conditions include contraction, expansion, freezing, thawing, erosion, improperly compacted soil and the action of water under the ground surface.

But if Earth Movement, as described in **b. (1)** through **(4)** above, results in fire or explosion, we will pay for the loss or damage caused by that fire or explosion.

(5) Volcanic eruption, explosion or effusion. But if volcanic eruption, explosion or effusion results in fire, building glass breakage or Volcanic Action, we will pay for the loss or damage caused by that fire, building glass breakage or Volcanic Action.

Volcanic action means direct loss or damage resulting from the eruption of a volcano when the loss or damage is caused by:

(a) Airborne volcanic blast or airborne shock waves;

(b) Ash, dust or particulate matter; or

(c) Lava flow.

All volcanic eruptions that occur within any 168 hour period will constitute a single occurrence.

Volcanic action does not include the cost to remove ash, dust or particulate matter that does not cause direct physical loss or damage to the described property.

c. Governmental Action

Seizure or destruction of property by order of governmental authority.

But we will pay for loss or damage caused by or resulting from acts of destruction ordered by governmental authority and taken at the time of a fire to prevent its spread, if the fire would be covered under this Coverage Part.

d. Nuclear Hazard

Nuclear reaction or radiation, or radioactive contamination, however caused.

But if nuclear reaction or radiation, or radioactive contamination, results in fire, we will pay for the loss or damage caused by that fire.

e. Utility Services

The failure of power or other utility service supplied to the described premises, however caused, if the failure occurs away from the described premises. Failure includes lack of sufficient capacity and reduction in supply.

But if the failure of power or other utility service results in a Covered Cause of Loss, we will pay for the loss or damage caused by that Covered Cause of Loss.

This exclusion does not apply to the Business Income coverage or to Extra Expense coverage. Instead, the Special Exclusion in Paragraph **B.4.a. (1)** applies to these coverages.

f. War And Military Action

(1) War, including undeclared or civil war;

(2) Warlike action by a military force, including action in hindering or defending against an actual or expected attack, by any government, sovereign or other authority using military personnel or other agents; or

(3) Insurrection, rebellion, revolution, usurped power, or action taken by governmental authority in hindering or defending against any of these.

g. Water

(1) Flood, surface water, waves, tides, tidal waves, overflow of any body of water, or their spray, all whether driven by wind or not;

(2) Mudslide or mudflow;

(3) Water that backs up or overflows from a sewer, drain or sump; or

(4) Water under the ground surface pressing on, or flowing or seeping through:

(a) Foundations, walls, floors or paved surfaces;

(b) Basements, whether paved or not; or

(c) Doors, windows or other openings.

But if Water, as described in **g.(1)** through **g. (4)** above, results in fire, explosion or sprinkler leakage, we will pay for the loss or damage caused by that fire, explosion or sprinkler leakage.

h. "Fungus", Wet Rot, Dry Rot And Bacteria

Presence, growth, proliferation, spread or any activity of "fungus", wet or dry rot or bacteria.

But if "fungus", wet or dry rot or bacteria results in a "specified cause of loss", we will pay for the loss or damage caused by that "specified cause of loss".

This exclusion does not apply:

1. When "fungus", wet or dry rot or bacteria results from fire or lightning; or

2. To the extent that coverage is provided in the Additional Coverage – Limited Coverage For "Fungus", Wet Rot, Dry Rot And Bacteria with respect to loss or damage by a cause of loss other than fire or lightning.

Exclusions **B.1.a.** through **B.1.h.** apply whether or not the loss event results in widespread damage or affects a substantial area.

2. We will not pay for loss or damage caused by or resulting from any of the following:

a. Artificially generated electrical current, including electric arcing, that disturbs electrical devices, appliances or wires.

But if artificially generated electrical current results in fire, we will pay for the loss or damage caused by that fire.

b. Delay, loss of use or loss of market.

c. Smoke, vapor or gas from agricultural smudging or industrial operations.

d. (1) Wear and tear;

(2) Rust or other corrosion, decay, deterioration, hidden or latent defect or any quality in property that causes it to damage or destroy itself;

(3) Smog;

(4) Settling, cracking, shrinking or expansion;

(5) Nesting or infestation, or discharge or release of waste products or secretions, by insects, birds, rodents or other animals.

(6) Mechanical breakdown, including rupture or bursting caused by centrifugal force. But if mechanical breakdown results in elevator collision, we will pay for the loss or damage caused by that elevator collision.

(7) The following causes of loss to personal property:

(a) Dampness or dryness of atmosphere;

(b) Changes in or extremes of temperature; or

(c) Marring or scratching.

But if an excluded cause of loss that is listed in **2.d. (1)** through **(7)** results in a "specified cause of loss" or building glass breakage, we will pay for the loss or damage caused by that "specified cause of loss" or building glass breakage.

e. Explosion of steam boilers, steam pipes, steam engines or steam turbines owned or leased by you, or operated under your control. But if explosion of steam boilers, steam pipes, steam engines or steam turbines results in fire or combustion explosion, we will pay for the loss or damage caused by that fire or combustion explosion. We will also pay for loss or damage caused by or resulting from the explosion of gases or fuel within the furnace of any fired vessel or within the flues or passages through which the gases of combustion pass.

f. Continuous or repeated seepage or leakage of water, or the presence or condensation of humidity, moisture or vapor, that occurs over a period of 14 days or more.

g. Water, other liquids, powder or molten material that leaks or flows from plumbing, heating, air conditioning or other equipment (except fire protective systems) caused by or resulting from freezing, unless:

(1) You do your best to maintain heat in the building or structure; or

(2) You drain the equipment and shut off the supply if the heat is not maintained.

h. Dishonest or criminal act by you, any of your partners, members, officers, managers, employees (including leased employees) , directors, trustees, authorized representatives or anyone to whom you entrust the property for any purpose:

(1) Acting alone or in collusion with others; or

(2) Whether or not occurring during the hours of employment.

This exclusion does not apply to acts of destruction by your employees (including leased employees) ; but theft by employees (including leased employees) is not covered.

i. Voluntary parting with any property by you or anyone else to whom you have entrusted the property if induced to do so by any fraudulent scheme, trick, device or false pretense.

j. Rain, snow, ice or sleet to personal property in the open.

k. Collapse, except as provided below in the Additional Coverage for Collapse. But if collapse results in a Covered Cause of Loss at the described premises, we will pay for the loss or damage caused by that Covered Cause of Loss.

l. Discharge, dispersal, seepage, migration, release or escape of "pollutants" unless the discharge, dispersal, seepage, migration, release or escape is itself caused by any of the "specified causes of loss". But if the dis charge, dispersal, seepage, migration, release or escape of "pollutants" results in a "specified cause of loss", we will pay for the loss or damage caused by that "specified cause of loss".

This exclusion, **l.** **,** does not apply to damage to glass caused by chemicals applied to the glass.

m. Neglect of an insured to use all reasonable means to save and preserve property from further damage at and after the time of loss.

3. We will not pay for loss or damage caused by or resulting from any of the following, 3.a. through 3.c. But if an excluded cause of loss that is listed in 3.a. through 3.c. results in a Covered Cause of Loss, we will pay for the loss or damage caused by that Covered Cause of Loss.

a. Weather conditions. But this exclusion only applies if weather conditions contribute in any way with a cause or event excluded in Paragraph 1. above to produce the loss or damage.

b. Acts or decisions, including the failure to act or decide, of any person, group, organization or governmental body.

c. Faulty, inadequate or defective:

(1) Planning, zoning, development, surveying, siting;

(2) Design, specifications, workmanship, repair, construction, renovation, remodeling, grading, compaction;

(3) Materials used in repair, construction, renovation or remodeling; or

(4) Maintenance;

of part or all of any property on or off the described premises.

4. Special Exclusions

The following provisions apply only to the specified Coverage Forms.

a. Business Income (And Extra Expense) Coverage Form, Business Income (Without Extra Expense) Coverage Form, Or Extra Expense Coverage Form

We will not pay for:

(1) Any loss caused directly or indirectly by the failure of power or other utility service supplied to the described premises, however caused, if the failure occurs outside of a covered building. Failure includes lack of sufficient capacity and reduction in supply.

But if the failure of power or other utility service results in a Covered Cause of Loss, we will pay for the loss resulting from that Covered Cause of Loss.

(2) Any loss caused by or resulting from:

(a) Damage or destruction of "finished stock"; or

(b) The time required to reproduce "finished stock".

This exclusion does not apply to Extra Expense.

(3) Any loss caused by or resulting from direct physical loss or damage to radio or television antennas (including satellite dishes) and their lead-in wiring, masts or towers.

(4) Any increase of loss caused by or resulting from:

(a) Delay in rebuilding, repairing or replacing the property or resuming "operations", due to interference at the location of the rebuilding, repair or replacement by strikers or other persons; or

(b) Suspension, lapse or cancellation of any license, lease or contract. But if the suspension, lapse or cancellation is directly caused by the "suspension" of "operations", we will cover such loss that affects your Business Income during the "period of restoration" and any extension of the "period of restoration" in accordance with the terms of the Extended Business Income Additional Coverage and the Extended Period Of Indemnity Optional Coverage or any variation of these.

(5) Any Extra Expense caused by or resulting from suspension, lapse or cancellation of any license, lease or contract beyond the "period of restoration".

(6) Any other consequential loss.

b. Leasehold Interest Coverage Form

(1) Paragraph B.1.a. Ordinance Or Law, does not apply to insurance under this Coverage Form.

(2) We will not pay for any loss caused by:

(a) Your cancelling the lease;

(b) The suspension, lapse or cancellation of any license; or

(c) Any other consequential loss.

c. Legal Liability Coverage Form

(1) The following exclusions do not apply to insurance under this Coverage Form:

(a) Paragraph B.1.a. , Ordinance Or Law;

(b) Paragraph B.1.c. , Governmental Action;

(c) Paragraph B.1.d. , Nuclear Hazard;

(d) Paragraph B.1.e. , Utility Services; and

(e) Paragraph B.1.f. , War And Military Action.

(2) The following additional exclusions apply to insurance under this Coverage Form:

(a) Contractual Liability

We will not defend any claim or "suit", or pay damages that you are legally liable to pay, solely by reason of your assumption of liability in a contract or agreement. But this exclusion does not apply to a written lease agreement in which you have assumed liability for building damage resulting from an actual or attempted burglary or robbery, provided that:

(i) Your assumption of liability was executed prior to the accident; and

(ii) The building is Covered Property under this Coverage Form.

(b) Nuclear Hazard

We will not defend any claim or "suit", or pay any damages, loss, expense or obligation, resulting from nuclear reaction or radiation, or radioactive contamination, however caused.

C. Limitations

The following limitations apply to all policy forms and endorsements, unless otherwise stated.

1. We will not pay for loss of or damage to property, as described and limited in this section. In addition, we will not pay for any loss that is a consequence of loss or damage as described and limited in this section.

a. Steam boilers, steam pipes, steam engines or steam turbines caused by or resulting from any condition or event inside such equipment. But we will pay for loss of or damage to such equipment caused by or resulting from an explosion of gases or fuel within the furnace of any fired vessel or within the flues or passages through which the gases of combustion pass.

b. Hot water boilers or other water heating equipment caused by or resulting from any condition or event inside such boilers or equipment, other than an explosion.

c. The interior of any building or structure, or to personal property in the building or structure, caused by or resulting from rain, snow, sleet, ice, sand or dust, whether driven by wind or not, unless:

(1) The building or structure first sustains damage by a Covered Cause of Loss to its roof or walls through which the rain, snow, sleet, ice, sand or dust enters; or

(2) The loss or damage is caused by or results from thawing of snow, sleet or ice on the building or structure.

d. Building materials and supplies not attached as part of the building or structure, caused by or resulting from theft.

However, this limitation does not apply to:

(1) Building materials and supplies held for sale by you, unless they are insured under the Builders Risk Coverage Form; or

(2) Business Income coverage or Extra Expense coverage.

e. Property that is missing, where the only evidence of the loss or damage is a shortage disclosed on taking inventory, or other instances where there is no physical evidence to show what happened to the property.

f. Property that has been transferred to a person or to a place outside the described premises on the basis of unauthorized instructions.

2. We will not pay for loss of or damage to the following types of property unless caused by the "specified causes of loss" or building glass breakage:

a. Animals, and then only if they are killed or their destruction is made necessary.

b. Fragile articles such as statuary, marbles, chinaware and porcelains, if broken. This restriction does not apply to:

(1) Glass; or

(2) Containers of property held for sale.

c. Builders' machinery, tools and equipment owned by you or entrusted to you, provided such property is Covered Property.

However, this limitation does not apply:

(1) If the property is located on or within 100 feet of the described premises, unless the premises is insured under the Builders Risk Coverage Form; or

(2) To Business Income coverage or to Extra Expense coverage.

3. The special limit shown for each category, a. through d. , is the total limit for loss of or damage to all property in that category. The special limit applies to any one occurrence of theft, regardless of the types or number of articles that are lost or damaged in that occurrence. The special limits are:

a. $2,500 for furs, fur garments and garments trimmed with fur.

b. $2,500 for jewelry, watches, watch movements, jewels, pearls, precious and semi-precious stones, bullion, gold, silver, platinum and other precious alloys or metals. This limit does not apply to jewelry and watches worth $100 or less per item.

c. $2,500 for patterns, dies, molds and forms.

d. $250 for stamps, tickets, including lottery tickets held for sale, and letters of credit.

These special limits are part of, not in addition to, the Limit of Insurance applicable to the Covered Property.

This limitation, **C.3. ,** does not apply to Business Income coverage or to Extra Expense coverage.

4. We will not pay the cost to repair any defect to a system or appliance from which water, other liquid, powder or molten material escapes. But we will pay the cost to repair or replace damaged parts of fire extinguishing equipment if the damage:

a. Results in discharge of any substance from an automatic fire protection system; or

b. Is directly caused by freezing.

However, this limitation does not apply to Business Income coverage or to Extra Expense coverage.

D. Additional Coverage – Collapse

The term Covered Cause of Loss includes the Additional Coverage – Collapse as described and limited in **D.1.** through **D.5.** below.

1. With respect to buildings:

a. Collapse means an abrupt falling down or caving in of a building or any part of a building with the result that the building or part of the building cannot be occupied for its intended purpose;

b. A building or any part of a building that is in danger of falling down or caving in is not considered to be in a state of collapse;

c. A part of a building that is standing is not considered to be in a state of collapse even if it has separated from another part of the building;

d. A building that is standing or any part of a building that is standing is not considered to be in a state of collapse even if it shows evidence of cracking, bulging, sagging, bending, leaning, settling, shrinkage or expansion.

2. We will pay for direct physical loss or damage to Covered Property, caused by collapse of a building or any part of a building that is insured under this Coverage Form or that contains Covered Property insured under this Coverage Form, if the collapse is caused by one or more of the following:

a. The "specified causes of loss" or breakage of building glass, all only as insured against in this Coverage Part;

b. Decay that is hidden from view, unless the presence of such decay is known to an insured prior to collapse;

c. Insect or vermin damage that is hidden from view, unless the presence of such damage is known to an insured prior to collapse;

d. Weight of people or personal property;

e. Weight of rain that collects on a roof;

f. Use of defective material or methods in construction, remodeling or renovation if the collapse occurs during the course of the construction, remodeling or renovation. However, if the collapse occurs after construction, remodeling or renovation is complete and is caused in part by a cause of loss listed in 2.a. through 2.e. , we will pay for the loss or damage even if use of defective material or methods, in construction, remodeling or renovation, contributes to the collapse.

The criteria set forth in **1.a.** through **1.d.** do not limit the coverage otherwise provided under this Causes of Loss Form for the causes of loss listed in **2.a. , 2.d.** and **2.e.**

3. With respect to the following property:

a. Outdoor radio or television antennas (including satellite dishes) and their lead-in wiring, masts or towers;

b. Awnings, gutters and downspouts;

c. Yard fixtures;

d. Outdoor swimming pools;

e. Fences;

f. Piers, wharves and docks;

g. Beach or diving platforms or appurtenances;

h. Retaining walls; and

i. Walks, roadways and other paved surfaces;

if the collapse is caused by a cause of loss listed in **2.b.** through **2.f. ,** we will pay for loss or damage to that property only if:

a. Such loss or damage is a direct result of the collapse of a building insured under this Coverage Form; and

b. The property is Covered Property under this Coverage Form.

4. If personal property abruptly falls down or caves in and such collapse is not the result of collapse of a building, we

will pay for loss or damage to Covered Property caused by such collapse of personal property only if:

a. The collapse was caused by a Cause of Loss listed in 2.a. through 2.f. above;

b. The personal property which collapses is inside a building; and

c. The property which collapses is not of a kind listed in 3. above, regardless of whether that kind of property is considered to be personal property or real property.

The coverage stated in this Paragraph **4.** does not apply to personal property if marring and/or scratching is the only damage to that personal property caused by the collapse.

Collapse of personal property does not mean cracking, bulging, sagging, bending, leaning, settling, shrinkage or expansion.

5. This Additional Coverage, Collapse, will not increase the Limits of Insurance provided in this Coverage Part.

E. Additional Coverage – Limited Coverage For "Fungus", Wet Rot, Dry Rot And Bacteria

1. The coverage described in E.2. and E.6. only applies when the "fungus", wet or dry rot or bacteria is the result of one or more of the following causes that occurs during the policy period and only if all reasonable means were used to save and preserve the property from further damage at the time of and after that occurrence.

a. A "specified cause of loss" other than fire or lightning; or

b. Flood, if the Flood Coverage Endorsement applies to the affected premises.

2. We will pay for loss or damage by "fungus", wet or dry rot or bacteria. As used in this Limited Coverage, the term loss or damage means:

a. Direct physical loss or damage to Covered Property caused by "fungus", wet or dry rot or bacteria, including the cost of removal of the "fungus", wet or dry rot or bacteria;

b. The cost to tear out and replace any part of the building or other property as needed to gain access to the "fungus", wet or dry rot or bacteria; and

c. The cost of testing performed after removal, repair, replacement or restoration of the damaged property is completed, provided there is a reason to believe that "fungus", wet or dry rot or bacteria are present.

3. The coverage described under E.2. of this Limited Coverage is limited to $15,000. Regardless of the number of claims, this limit is the most we will pay for the total of all loss or damage arising out of all occurrences of "specified causes of loss" (other than fire or lightning) and Flood which take place in a 12-month period (starting with the beginning of the present annual policy period) . With respect to a particular occurrence of loss which results in "fungus", wet or dry rot or bacteria, we will not pay more than a total of $15,000 even if the "fungus", wet or dry rot or bacteria continues to be present or active, or recurs, in a later policy period.

4. The coverage provided under this Limited Coverage does not increase the applicable Limit of Insurance on any Covered Property. If a particular occurrence results in loss or damage by "fungus", wet or dry rot or bacteria, and other loss or damage, we will not pay more, for the total of all loss or damage, than the applicable Limit of Insurance on the affected Covered Property.

If there is covered loss or damage to Covered Property, not caused by "fungus", wet or dry rot or bacteria, loss payment will not be limited by the terms of this Limited Coverage, except to the extent that "fungus", wet or dry rot or bacteria causes an increase in the loss. Any such increase in the loss will be subject to the terms of this Limited Coverage.

5. The terms of this Limited Coverage do not increase or reduce the coverage provided under Paragraph F.2. (Water Damage, Other Liquids, Powder Or Molten Material Damage) of this Causes Of Loss Form or under the Additional Coverage – Collapse.

6. The following, 6.a. or 6.b. , applies only if Business Income and/or Extra Expense coverage applies to the described premises and only if the "suspension" of "operations" satisfies all terms and conditions of the applicable Business Income and/or Extra Expense coverage form.

a. If the loss which resulted in "fungus", wet or dry rot or bacteria does not in itself necessitate a "suspension" of "operations", but such "suspension" is necessary due to loss or damage to property caused by "fungus", wet or dry rot or bacteria, then our payment under Business Income and/or Extra Expense is limited to the amount of loss and/or expense sustained in a period of not more than 30 days.The days need not be consecutive.

b. If a covered "suspension" of "operations" was caused by loss or damage other than "fungus", wet or dry rot or bacteria but remediation of "fungus", wet or dry rot or bacteria prolongs the "period of restoration", we will pay for loss and/or expense sustained during the delay (regardless of when such a delay occurs during the "period of restoration") , but such coverage is limited to 30 days. The days need not be consecutive.

F. Additional Coverage Extensions

1. Property In Transit

This Extension applies only to your personal property to which this form applies.

a. You may extend the insurance provided by this Coverage Part to apply to your personal property (other than property in the care, custody or control of your salespersons) in transit more than 100 feet from the described premises. Property must be in or on a motor vehicle you own, lease or operate while between points in the coverage territory.

b. Loss or damage must be caused by or result from one of the following causes of loss:

(1) Fire, lightning, explosion, windstorm or hail, riot or civil commotion, or vandalism.

(2) Vehicle collision, upset or overturn. Collision means accidental contact of your vehicle with another vehicle or object. It does not mean your vehicle's contact with the road bed.

(3) Theft of an entire bale, case or package by forced entry into a securely locked body or compartment of the vehicle.There must be visible marks of the forced entry.

c. The most we will pay for loss or damage under this Extension is $5,000.

This Coverage Extension is additional insurance. The Additional Condition, Coinsurance, does not apply to this Extension.

2. Water Damage, Other Liquids, Powder Or Molten Material Damage

If loss or damage caused by or resulting from covered water or other liquid, powder or molten material damage loss occurs, we will also pay the cost to tear out and replace any part of the building or structure to repair damage to the system or appliance from which the water or other substance escapes.This Coverage Extension does not increase the Limit of Insurance.

3. Glass

a. We will pay for expenses incurred to put up temporary plates or board up openings if repair or replacement of damaged glass is delayed.

b. We will pay for expenses incurred to remove or replace obstructions when repairing or replacing glass that is part of a building. This does not include removing or replacing window displays.

This Coverage Extension, **F.3.,** does not increase the Limit of Insurance.

G. Definitions

1. "Fungus" means any type or form of fungus, including mold or mildew, and any mycotoxins, spores, scents or by-products produced or released by fungi.

2. "Specified Causes of Loss" means the following: Fire; lightning; explosion; windstorm or hail; smoke; aircraft or vehicles; riot or civil commotion; vandalism; leakage from fire extinguishing equipment; sinkhole collapse; volcanic action; falling objects; weight of snow, ice or sleet; water damage.

a. Sinkhole collapse means the sudden sinking or collapse of land into underground empty spaces created by the action of water on limestone or dolomite. This cause of loss does not include:

(1) The cost of filling sinkholes; or

(2) Sinking or collapse of land into man-made underground cavities.

b. Falling objects does not include loss or damage to:

(1) Personal property in the open; or

(2) The interior of a building or structure, or property inside a building or structure, unless the roof or an outside wall of the building or structure is first damaged by a falling object.

c. Water damage means accidental discharge or leakage of water or steam as the direct result of the breaking apart or cracking of a plumbing, heating, air conditioning or other system or appliance (other than a sump system including its related equipment and parts) , that is located on the described premises and contains water or steam.

Chapter 13

Workers' Compensation, Automobile, and Bonds

OUTLINE

Workers' Compensation
Business Auto Policy
Fidelity, Surety, and Customs Bonds

OBJECTIVES

At the end of this chapter you should be able to:
Discuss employer liability during the early 1900s.
Explain the philosophy of workers' compensation laws.
Name and explain the four types of benefits available to an injured worker.
Describe the role of second injury funds.
Identify the major components of a workers' compensation cost control program.
Describe the four insuring agreements available in a business auto policy.
Explain personal injury protection (PIP).
Define fidelity, surety, and customs bonds and explain their use in risk management.

WORKERS' COMPENSATION

It is a basic principle of law that a person who is injured through negligence of another has a right to be compensated for damages. The law does require that the injured person must prove negligence in a court of law. Workers' compensation laws were passed by the states to modify this principle by imposing liability upon the employer for on-the-job accidents without regard to the question of fault. Because of this no-fault concept, risk managers shift this liability exposure to an insurance company or establish a self-insurance program. These laws also provide benefits for dependents of those workers who are killed because of work-related accidents or illnesses. Some laws also protect employers and fellow workers by limiting the amount an injured employee can recover from an employer and by eliminating the liability of co-workers in most accidents.

Historical Background

Under English common law, a worker injured on the job had no more right against the employer than a member of the public. Later in the mid-1800s, common law considered minimum work requirements which employers must meet. These were known as common law obligations. An injured worker could bring suit against the employer if the employer failed to keep the following requirements:

1. Provide a safe working place
2. Provide proper tools and machinery for the job
3. Provide suitable safety rules
4. Provide reasonably competent fellow workers
5. Warn of any dangers inherent in the work place that the worker could not be reasonably expected to know about

Even if one or more of these conditions were violated, certain legal defenses were developed for the employers' protection. The three main defenses available were:

1. *Assumption of risk:* A worker is presumed to accept the normal risks associated with the job, even though hazardous.

2. *Fellow servant rule:* An employer is not responsible for injuries caused by another worker. The injured worker would have to seek damages from the fellow worker, not the employer.
3. *Contributory negligence:* If a worker is in any way negligent in causing the injury, the worker could not collect from the employer even though the employer was grossly negligent.

In addition to these defenses, common law also stated that only the injured worker had the right to sue the employer for damages. If the worker died, the right of claim against the employer also died.

Because the harshness of these principles resulted in injured workers being unable to transfer their burdens of financial loss, they were modified during the latter half of the nineteenth century. The modifications improved the workers' success rate, but as long as the system relied on the law of negligence (requiring proof of negligence on the part of the employer) the worker was at a decided disadvantage. State legislatures recognized this imbalance and beginning in 1902, started enacting workers' compensation laws to guarantee adequate compensation to workers injured on the job. These state laws were based upon the principle that injuries are inherent in production of goods and services, and because society benefits from the consumption of this production, it should bear the burden of the costs associated with industrial accidents. The basic philosophy of these laws was: "Employers will be absolutely liable for worker injuries regardless of fault because the cost of industrial accidents should be considered a cost of production and passed on to the purchaser." The first state to pass a workers' compensation law was Maryland, in 1902. It was later declared unconstitutional, so the first effective law was passed in Wisconsin, in 1911. This state law set a pattern for most statutes that followed, and with the passage of a Mississippi Workers' Compensation Act in 1948, compensation laws were operative in all states.

Even though there are 50 different compensation laws, their basic principles are sufficiently similar to allow a discussion as a unit. There are four principles upon which all the laws are based. First, the laws are no-fault laws. Absolute liability is imposed upon the employer for injury suffered by the worker that arises out of and in the course of employment. Generally, injuries sustained at work are considered due to the work, and the worker is entitled to the benefits allowed by law regardless of who was at fault. Since contributory negligence is not a defense in worker compensation claims, the worker is entitled to benefits even if the accident was caused by his own negligence. However, no compensation is due to the injured worker if the injury was occasioned primarily by the:

- Intoxication of the worker, by the influence of narcotic drugs, barbiturates or stimulants not prescribed by a physician;
- Willful intention of the worker to injure or kill himself or another; and
- Willful disregard of safety rules and regulations.

The second common principle states that injured workers are entitled to the stated schedule of benefits as a matter of right, without having to use the court system to prove negligence. For this privilege, the worker gives up the right to sue the employer. In some cases, the total benefits received might be less than the worker could have received through the courts since benefits are intended as an income supplement and by design, create an incentive to return to work. The third principle assumes that workers are poor managers of money so benefits are paid periodically, rather than in a lump sum. This payment schedule ensures a greater degree of security for the injured worker by eliminating the risks associated with the management of large sums of money. The fourth and last principle requires all employers to show financial responsibility. The most common method of meeting this requirement is through the purchase of insurance from private insurance companies. In six states, insurance must be purchased from a monopolistic state insurance fund. Most states will allow companies to self-insure their workers' compensation risk, provided they have a sufficient number of employees and can demonstrate sufficient resources to pay anticipated losses. A bond may be required to guarantee payment of benefits. So the goal of the workers' compensation system is to benefit both employees and employers by:

- Replacing uncertain remedies with certain ones;
- Avoiding the expenses and risk of tort litigation; and
- Channeling workers' compensation disputes through the cheaper administrative system.

Workers' Compensation Policy

A new simplified language policy was introduced in 1984. This new policy includes two standard coverages: workers' compensation and employers' liability. The *workers' compensation insuring agreement* obligates the insurance company to pay sums that the insured is legally obligated to pay under the worker compensation laws of the state(s) where the insured is conducting business. There are no exclusions under this coverage, and there is no maximum limit on the insurers' liability. If the employer is liable to the workers under the law, the insurer makes direct payment to the workers or their dependents.

The second part of the policy, *employers' liability insuring agreement*, is designed to cover the liability of the employer to workers with standard limits of \$100,000 each accident, \$100,000 for occupational disease for each worker, and a \$500,000 occupational disease aggregate. This liability coverage is desired because employers are exposed to suits due to illegal employment of minors, losses claimed by spouses of injured workers, and in some states, suits by injured workers for gross negligence.

An additional coverage is available to risk managers and is frequently needed when business operations involve multiple states. Other states' insurance coverage is designed to protect against liability under the workers' compensation laws of states in which the employer does not expect to have employees, but where a workers' compensation obligation might be incurred. This exposure is brought about when workers travel interstate on company business and are injured. A corporate pilot is an example. Rather than listing probable states individually, it is common to use a blanket designation, stipulating that coverage applies to all states except.... For foreign travel many workers' compensation underwriters will add to the policy a "foreign voluntary compensation" endorsement. This endorsement extends the statutory benefits to include work-related injury and disease occurring outside the United States. In addition to the normal statutory coverage that is extended under this endorsement, a specified limit of repatriation coverage can be added. Repatriation costs are those expenses incurred in moving a patient home from a foreign location or to a medical facility that can better meet the patient's needs.

Persons Covered

Workers' compensation coverage is compulsory for all employees except for a few classifications like casual day labor. Generally, corporate officers are considered employees and are covered under the act. They can file a written election to be excluded from coverage. If a business is operated as a proprietorship or partnership, the owners are not usually covered, but may elect to be covered if desired. For a worker to be covered, all acts require an employer-employee relationship. Workers who are independent contractors do not come under the provisions of the law since they are not considered employees. Pilots who moonlight by flying single trips for a fee would not be entitled to benefits for injuries suffered on that trip. The following criteria are often used to classify a worker as an independent contractor rather than an employee:

- Employer has no control over work hours
- Workers use their own equipment
- Employer does not withhold income or social security taxes

Benefits

According to the National Safety Council's *Report on Injuries in America*, 2003, there were 4,500 workplace fatalities, 3.4 million disabling injuries and the total cost of these incidents was $156.2 billion. There are generally four types of benefits provided by workers' compensation laws:

1. Medical expenses—In most states, medical expenses incurred by the injured worker are covered 100 percent and without limit. Covered expenses not only include doctor and hospital costs, but also any expense incurred at home that is medically necessary. However, if there are no medical expenses incurred and submitted to the insurance carrier for a period of three years, the medical benefit entitlement ceases.
2. Wage replacement—After a waiting period, normally three days to seven days, injured workers are provided a weekly income until they are able to return to work. The amount and duration of the income depends upon the worker's average weekly wage, and the classification of disability. The size of the weekly income is generally two-thirds of the worker's average weekly wage up to a dollar maximum. For example, the 2004 maximum weekly benefit in North Dakota was $577 per week. Total temporary disability is the most common type of disability and exists when the worker is unable to work because of an injury but will clearly return to work. Weekly payments for this category may not exceed 312 weeks nor continue more than eight (8) years after the date of the injury in the state of Utah. A worker who suffers an injury, which prevents him or her from engaging in gainful employment, is classified as totally and permanently disabled. Weekly income will be paid for life, but after six months, the level of wages is integrated with social security so the total weekly payments do not exceed 80 percent of average weekly wage. In 15 states, replacement wages are automatically increased with the rise in cost-of-living, and in many others, there is an annual increase in the maximum dollar limit of weekly payments.

   When an injury results in the loss of a member or sight, or loss of full use of some part of the body, the disability is classified as a partial permanent disability. Since the time away from work would generate inadequate compensation, the worker receives a lump sum equal to X number of weeks times the average weekly wage. For example, the loss of a thumb is 60 weeks, and the loss of an arm is 230 weeks. This benefit is payable in addition to all other benefits the worker is entitled to under the law.
3. Survivor compensation—Benefits may be paid to eligible survivors when a worker is killed as a result of a work-related accident. Funds for a funeral typically amount from $5,000 to $7,500. Dependents may be eligible to receive weekly income. The usual formula is 50 percent of the deceased worker's average weekly wage up $150,000 which is the current average stated dollar limit. Eligible spouses receive benefits for life or until remarriage, while dependent children are covered until they reach 18, or marry.

4. Rehabilitation—The largest percentage of workers who are disabled make a complete recovery and return to work promptly. Many workers, however, suffer serious injuries that require rehabilitation to restore them to a meaningful and productive life. Rehabilitation involves the following activities:

   - Physical therapy to restore injured workers as nearly as possible to their state of health prior to the accident;
   - Vocational training to match their reduced level of occupational capacity; and
   - Psychological evaluations to assist them in adjusting to their new situation and be able to perform a useful function for society.

   The funds for payment of rehabilitation benefits may or may not come from the employer or an insurance company. In some states, the costs are paid by the state, and in others, a pool is developed by taxing all insurance companies writing worker compensation insurance in the state. Finally, the Federal Vocational Rehabilitation Act provides federal funds to assist states in this most important humanitarian function.

Second-Injury Funds

Second injury funds have been established in most states to facilitate employment of physically handicapped workers. Employers are not reluctant to hire the physically handicapped because they will not be exposed to any additional worker liability. Under all compensation laws, employers are liable for disability incurred in employment, except preexisting handicaps. When a worker suffers an injury, which qualifies only as a partial disability, but due to a previous injury, the worker is permanently disabled; the second-injury fund pays the difference. This fund is supported by required contributions based upon total compensation paid during the year, or on premiums collected.

Cost of Workers' Compensation Insurance

The annual premium for workers' compensation insurance is typically based upon a percentage of the employer's payroll. The percentage per $100 of payroll varies with the type of industry and the degree of hazard of the various occupations within the business firm. An employer in a relatively dangerous profession like crop dusting would pay a much higher premium per dollar of payroll than one in a relatively safe field such as pipeline patrol. The following aviation examples illustrate this relationship between the occupation and the percentage:

Charter pilot in Alaska 13%
Scheduled Alaskan pilot 7-8%
Scheduled domestic pilot 3-4 %
Airline baggage handler 6-8%

The actual percentage rate paid by a particular employer is influenced not only by the degree of hazard of the industry classification, but also by the level of benefits in the law and how often injured workers use the system.

The *Federal Employment Compensation Act* provides workers' compensation for non-military federal employees. Many of its provisions are typical of most state workers' compensation laws. Benefits are limited to "disability or death" sustained while in the performance of the employee's duties but not caused willfully by the employee or by intoxication. The act covers medical expenses due to the disability and may require the employee to undergo job retraining. A disabled employee receives two thirds of normal monthly salary during the disability and may receive more for permanent physical injuries, or if he has dependents. The act provides for compensation for the survivors of an employee who is killed. The office of Workers' Compensation Programs administers the act.

Risk Management Implications

Workers' compensation premium expense may be quite significant for employers because the rates are sensitive to the frequency and severity of injuries suffered by their workers. It is not unusual for premium costs to run between 10 and 30 percent of payroll, and the rates have been rising on the average of 5 to 9 percent per year. Large firms and small firms that belong to a group plan can benefit from an *experience rating system*. Under this rating system, a modification is made in the manual rate to reflect the insured's past claim experience. When it is favorable, a reduction will apply to the worker compensation rate for the next policy year. An aggressive workers' compensation *cost control program* will pay large dividends through future rate reductions. A cost control program would include the following:

1. Informing executives of the firm about the actual costs of industrial accidents. Hidden costs from production delays, decreased worker morale, additional training, property damage, and reduced productivity are all associated with worker injuries. One study indicated that for every $1,000 of direct cost you have in workers' compensation, you are paying up to $4,000 more in indirect costs. These expenses are not line items on the operating statement, and are rarely itemized for management's evaluation. With full knowledge of the real costs of worker injuries, executives will pay more than lip service to risk managers' cost reduction proposals by participating in their communication to the work force and providing necessary resources.
2. Installing loss control incentive programs. Tangible rewards to supervisors for managing a safe work environment and to workers for claim-free work performance are important in any program. Rewards can be in the form of cash, time off with pay, prizes of merchandise, savings bonds, etc.
3. Inviting workers to participate. Establish safety committees, with worker and management membership, to promote the upward flow of communication as to ways to make the work environment safer. Through active participation, the level of worker commitment to safer work practices increases.
4. Investigating all accidents and incidents promptly. A great deal can be learned about accident prevention by investigating all accidents, and then taking corrective action. Even "near misses" should be examined to make sure policies are in place to reduce the possibility that future accidents may occur causing serious injury.
5. Conducting a safety program audit. A thorough survey of the firm's safety program will assure that on the job injuries will be kept to a minimum. The risk management staff can conduct this survey or it can be contracted to independent engineering/consulting firms, and insurance company staffs whose services are available to non-policyholders. A typical safety program audit will investigate the following areas:

    - An evaluation of accident investigation procedures
    - A critique of record-keeping procedures
    - Measuring compliance with Occupational Safety and Health Act (OSHA) requirements
    - Plant inspections to judge individual worker safety
    - An examination of safety committee activities
    - Assessment of worker/supervisor safety training programs
    - Recommendations for improving the safety program and the firm's loss

experience, including an assignment of individual responsibilities for accomplishing stated objectives.

6. Increasing pre-hiring requirements. Many injuries can be avoided if the following preventive steps are taken prior to employment: (1) administer pre-employment physicals and drug testing to uncover preexisting health problems and to document past health history; (2) carefully checking the employee's background to discover the extent of any prior claim history; and (3) testing the employee to better match job specifications with job descriptions.
7. Establishing an aggressive "return-to-work" program. Research shows that employees heal faster and get back to their regular jobs faster if they can participate in transitional work.
8. Physician selection and management. Identify medical providers who specialize and understand occupational injuries and illnesses. Such providers understand the importance of treating work-related illnesses quickly, and are committed to returning workers to useful employment as soon as it is medically feasible.
9. Cracking down on fraud. Fraud costs billions of dollars every year. Many studies show that fraud adds more than 10 percent to workers' compensation costs. Let the employees know that falsely reporting a claim is a crime.
10. Establishing employee assistance programs (EAP) and wellness programs. Today's enlightened employers realize that healthier employees are more productive and less accident-prone on the job. The objective of an EAP program is to reduce stress, increase productivity, reduce absenteeism, and reduce the likelihood of accidents. Employees utilize the program for personal issues, such as divorces or legal issues. At other times they use it for physical concerns, such as medical problems they might have, or for information on substance abuse.

Aggressive workers' compensation cost control programs are successful because they attack the problem from many different aspects. The essential components will include incentives to motivate employees at all levels, safety and training programs, policies and procedures which will reduce the severity and frequency of injuries, and well thought out administrative procedures which will be efficient and further reduce costs.

BUSINESS AUTO POLICY

Automobile exposure is often overlooked by the risk manager when developing a plan to manage the physical property. This is due partly because automobile values are low compared to aircraft values and may seem insignificant. Also, it is sometimes assumed that this coverage should be placed on the Inland Marine (IM) equipment form when in fact this may not be the best way to handle this exposure. Any automobile that is licensed for road use, regardless of its use, should be covered under an automobile policy. If the vehicle is not licensed for road use, it can be covered on the IM form. Private passenger automobiles, which are owned or leased by individuals and used in a business organized as a sole proprietorship, may be insured under a personal auto policy. Private passenger automobiles, trucks, and specialty vehicles (fire trucks) owned or leased to partnerships and corporations must be insured under a *business auto policy*. This policy can be purchased either as a separate policy, or included as a part of a package policy, depending on your insurance company. Insurers use the business auto policy to insure automobile exposures of almost any type of organization, with two major exceptions:

1. Auto businesses, such as auto dealerships, repair facilities, and parking lots. These types of businesses can insure their automobile exposures under the ISO garage form.
2. Motor carriers for hire. Business that use automobiles to transport property of others.

Persons Insured

The business auto policy includes coverage for the named insured (XYZ Air Inc.), its employees, other persons driving owned or leased vehicles with permission, and other persons and organizations who may be vicariously liable for acts or omissions of the named insured or permissive users.

Covered Vehicles

The broad definition of automobile in the policy reads: "Auto" means a land motor vehicle; trailer or semi-trailer designed for travel on public roads but does not include "mobile equipment." This definition would include a motorcycle and an eighteen-wheel tractor-trailer. The area of concern for airports and FBOs is the lack of coverage for mobile equipment. Examples of mobile equipment are: bulldozers, farm equipment, forklifts and other vehicles designed for use principally off public roads; vehicles maintained for use solely on or next to premises the insured owns or rents; and vehicles that travel on crawler treads. However, self-propelled vehicles with the following types of permanently attached equipment are not "mobile equipment" but would be considered "autos;" equipment designed primarily for snow removal, road maintenance, and street cleaning. Three classes of automobiles are recognized in the policy:

1. Owned automobiles
2. Hired automobiles leased, hired, rented, or borrowed, excluding autos owned by employees.
3. Non-owned automobiles leased, hired, rented, or borrowed from employees.

Risk managers must select coverage symbols that are used to identify "covered auto" under the business auto policy. Careful selection should be used to ensure that the correct vehicles are picked up for coverage.

Symbol	Description of Covered Auto Designation Symbols	
1.	Any "Auto"	
2.	Owned "Autos" Only	Only those "autos" you own (and for liability coverage of any "trailers" you don't own while attached to power units you own). This includes those "autos" you acquire ownership of after the policy begins.
3.	Owned Private Passenger "Autos" Only	Only the private passenger "autos" you own. This includes those private passenger "autos" you acquire ownership of after the policy begins.
4.	Owned "Autos" Other Than Private Passenger "Autos" Only	Only those "autos" you own that are not of the private passenger type (and for liability coverage any "trailers" you don't own while attached to power units you own). This includes those "autos" not of the private passenger type you aquire ownership of after the policy begins.

5.	Owned "Autos" Subject To No-Fault	Only those "autos" you own that are required to have no-fault benefits in the state where they are licensed or principally garaged. This includes those "autos" you acquire ownership of after the policy begins provided they are required to have no-fault benefits in the state where they are licensed or principally garaged.
6.	Owned "Autos" Subject To Compulsory Uninsured Motorist Law	Only those "autos" you own that because of the law A in the state where they are licensed or principally garaged are required to have and cannot reject uninsured motorists coverage. This includes those "autos" you acquire ownership of after the policy begins provided they are subject to the same state uninsured motorist's requirement.
7.	Specifically Described "Autos"	Only those "autos" described in Item 3 of the declarations for which a premium charge is shown (and for liability coverage any "trailers" you don't own while attached to any power unit described in Item 3).
8.	Hired "Autos" Only	Only those "autos" you lease, hire, rent, or borrow. This does not include any "auto" you lease, hire, rent, or borrow from any of your "employees", partners (if you are a partnership), members (if you are a limited liability company) or members of their households.
9.	Non-owned "Autos" Only	Only those "autos" you do not own, lease, hire, rent or borrow that are used in connection with your business. This includes "autos" owned by your "employees," partners (if you are a partnership), members (if you are a limited liability company), or members of their households but only while used in your business or your personal affairs.
10.	Company Manuscript Form	Used when company wants to specifically cover certain vehicles or operations.

The numerical designation selected appears on the declaration page opposite the various coverages, indicating the classes of autos covered under the policy. If symbols 1, 2, 3, 4, 5 or 6 are entered next to a coverage in item two of the Declaration, then you have coverage for "autos" that you acquire of the type described. Although automatic coverage is provided, most underwriters will require that vehicles are added to the policy throughout the term to ensure that they are getting premium for the exposure.

Liability Insuring Agreements

The commercial automobile policy has policy language referred to as insuring agreements. These agreements clarify coverage and define what the insurer will and will not do. There are four major sections in the standard automobile policy: liability, medical payments, uninsured/underinsured motorists, and property damage to owned or leased vehicles.

The *liability insuring agreement* states that the insurance company will pay, up to the policy limit, damages for bodily injury and property damage of others, which any insured becomes legally responsible because of an occurrence. Limits of liability can be written on either a split liability basis, or a combined single limits basis. If a risk manager purchased the following liability limits: $250,000/ $500,000/$50,000, the firm would be covered up to $250,000 for bodily injury per person, per occurrence; $500,000 for bodily injury per occurrence; and $50,000 for property damage of others, per occurrence. These liability limits apply to each vehicle insured individually, and are automatically reinstated when the vehicle is repaired and in operation again.

The insurer has the right and the duty to defend the insured against a lawsuit asking for damages covered under the liability insuring agreement. The insurer reserves the right to investigate and settle any claim or suit as the insurer deems appropriate. The insurer's duty to defend or settle ends when the limit of insurance has been exhausted by payment of judgments or settlements. In addition to the stated limits of liability on the declaration page, this insuring agreement also provides coverage for the following:

1. Cost of defending suits
2. Premiums on appeal bonds and bonds to release attachments in suits covered under the policy are covered in full
3. Cost of bail bonds up to a limit of $250
4. Interest on judgments after the judgment has been entered
5. Loss of earnings up to $50 per day for attending hearings and trials

Medical Payments Insuring Agreement

The *medical payments insuring agreement* states that the insurer will pay to the named insured and invited non-paying guests all reasonable expenses incurred for necessary medical and funeral services because of bodily injury occurring while occupying (in, upon, getting in, on, out, or off) a covered vehicle up to the limits stated on the declaration page. Named insureds are also covered up to the same stated limits for bodily injury caused by an auto while a pedestrian. Coverage is limited to those expenses incurred within 3 years of the accident. The basic limit of liability for medical payments coverage is $1,000 per person per occurrence, with no aggregate limit per occurrence. Because this coverage is inexpensive, limits of $5,000 to $10,000 are common. One of the unique features of this coverage is that it is no-fault. There is no requirement to prove negligence to receive payments.

Uninsured/Underinsured Motorist Insuring Agreement

The *uninsured/underinsured motorists insuring agreement* promises to pay the amount that an injured insured could have collected from the insurer of a negligent uninsured/underinsured driver if the driver had carried adequate automobile liability insurance. The limits of liability are written on a per person per occurrence basis and generally match the limits of liability selected for liability to third parties. In most states, this coverage applies to bodily injury only, but in 14 states, property damage to the insured's auto is also included. Insureds receive payments under this agreement only when they are injured by uninsured/underinsured motorists. The definition of an uninsured/underinsured vehicle includes:

1. An automobile which is not covered by bodily injury liability insurance or has inadequate limits to pay the damages;
2. A hit-and-run automobile; and

3. An automobile that was insured at the time of the accident, but subsequently the insurer becomes unable to pay.

Subject to the policy limits, the insurer agrees to put the insured in the same position that he or she would be in if the motorist responsible for the accident had carried adequate auto liability insurance or in the case of a hit-and-run incident the motorist could be identified. The actual amount the policy will pay is to be decided by agreement between the injured party and the insurer. If agreement cannot be reached, the policy states that each party selects an arbitrator and the arbitrators select an umpire, and these three parties settle the matter. Each party is responsible for the cost of the arbitrator he selected, and one-half of the cost of the umpire.

Even though employees are covered under workers' compensation and would generally not receive benefits under this coverage, business firms frequently carry uninsured/underinsured motorist coverage for the following reasons:

1. Some insuring agreements will provide excess coverage for employees when workers' compensation is inadequate.
2. Employees may be injured by an uninsured motorist while driving a company automobile for personal use.
3. An uninsured motorist may injure business guests.
4. Some business owners choose not to be covered under workers' compensation.

Physical Damage Insuring Agreement

There is now a single *physical damage insuring agreement* that provides coverage on an all risk basis. This agreement is preferred over the traditional specified peril approach that listed coverage against named perils. Under this agreement, the insurer promises to pay for direct and accidental loss to a covered automobile, or any non-owned automobile, including their equipment, minus any applicable deductible shown on the declaration page. The insurer will pay for loss to the covered auto caused by:

- collision, and
- other than collision (commonly referred to as comprehensive coverage).

These two coverages can be purchased separately or together, but they each have an individual premium rate and deductible.

Collision is defined as the upset, or collision with another object with a covered automobile. The following perils are specifically identified as perils not considered a collision: breakage of glass, loss by missiles, falling objects, fire, theft, or larceny, explosion, earthquake, windstorm, hail, water, flood, malicious mischief or vandalism, riot or civil commotion, or contact with a bird or animal. Coverage for *loss other than collision* applies to all losses except those that are specifically excluded. If the risk manager chooses not to purchase loss other than collision coverage, property damage coverage is still available on a named peril basis. For example, fire and theft coverage can be bought at rates below those for loss other than collision coverage.

When an accident occurs, damages are paid regardless of who was at fault. This no-fault provision facilitates having the car repaired; thereby reducing the time the automobile is out of service. When the damage to an automobile was caused by a negligent motorist, the driver's liability coverage will pay for the damages, and generally will pay for a substitute automobile. If the accident did not involve a negligent third party, the insurer will pay for repairs minus the stated deductible. The insurer's liability under the physical damage coverage is limited to the lesser of

(1) the actual cash value of the damaged or stolen automobile, or (2) the cost to repair or replace the automobile. *Actual cash value* (ACV) is defined as the replacement cost of the automobile minus its depreciation. Since this is not an agreed value policy, the insured is uncertain as to the payment in the event of a total loss. You can get a rough idea of the auto's ACV by consulting the *Kelly Blue Book*. The National Automobile Dealers Association also publishes the *Official Used Car Guide*, which is updated each month.

According to Information Services Office (ISO), a company that tracks auto claims for the insurance industry, about 10 percent of collision claims in the United States result in a car's being totaled. When an auto is considered totaled by the insurance company depends upon the type and age of the automobile. Minor damage to a 15-year old Buick might result in the car's being totaled while major damage to a brand new Saab might not. If the cost of repair exceeds approximately 80 percent of the auto's actual cash value, then the car is considered a total loss. The insurance company will pay the insured the car's actual cash value, minus the deductible. Then the car goes to a salvage yard, where it's auctioned off to the highest bidder and usually chopped up for parts. The insurance company keeps whatever money it received for the car in salvage. The decision to repair or total the automobile contractually rests with the insurance company.

Rates for automobile physical damage insurance will vary widely depending upon geographical area, annual mileage, type of vehicle, age of vehicle, and in some cases, the age of the drivers. Larger firms, operating a fleet of automobiles, may qualify for experience rates. These rates evaluate all vehicles (for better or worse) based upon the loss experience over a period of several years. Small business firms can receive favorable rate treatment by qualifying for a safe driver plan and by having drivers without traffic citations.

Personal Injury Protection (No-Fault)

Many states have laws that either require auto owners to carry personal injury protection coverage or require insurers to offer the coverage to all motorists. *Personal injury protection (PIP)* varies from state to state. PIP in the state of Florida is a no-fault type of coverage that pays the insured, relatives living in the insured's home, passengers other than family members, and licensed persons who drive the car with the insured's permission for certain accident-related medical expenses regardless of who caused the accident. Basic PIP covers these items, up to the $10,000 policy limit per accident:

- 80 percent of reasonable medical expenses
- 60 percent of lost wages and replacement services, such as child care
- $5,000 for death benefits

For higher premiums, the firm can increase the amounts of coverage and the percentages of qualified expenses that are covered. Different insurers may offer different PIP packages. Deductibles are an important element of PIP coverage. Increasing the amount of the deductible will substantially reduce the premium of PIP. Most insurers offer PIP deductibles of $250, $500, $1,000, and $2,000. First dollar protection is available if the insured does not desire a deductible.

The decision to purchase all four insuring agreements for business vehicles is far from automatic. The automobile exposure offers a risk manager an opportunity to manage the risk in multiple ways. Obviously, the liability exposure should always be transferred because of the catastrophic loss potential, and the inability to predetermine the extent of loss. Uninsured/ underinsured motorist coverage and medical payments coverage duplicates some existing coverages like workers' compensation, group hospitalization and surgery plans, long -term disability, and even some provisions of social security. Thus, this elective coverage should be analyzed very carefully to determine its real merits to the business. Physical damage coverage for the vehicle fleet will usually require prioritizing based upon current actual cash value. Older vehicles would be candidates for risk retention, while newer and more expensive vehicles would probably benefit from coverage. Even when physical damage coverage is purchased, higher deductibles, especially for collision, will reduce total premiums appreciably.

Major Exclusions

The business auto policy lists the following 12 exclusions from liability coverage: (1) intentional injury; (2) assumed liability through a contract; (3) workers' compensation claims; (4) employers' liability; (5) fellow employee; (6) bailee; (7) handling of property; (8) movement of property by mechanical device; (9) operation of mobile equipment; (10) completed operations; (11) pollution; and (12) war.

Medical payments coverage is subject to its own specific list of exclusions, and the major one for risk managers to be aware of is the elimination of coverage for employees who are injured in an automobile accident while engaged in company business. Injured employees will be covered by workers' compensation. If the principal occupants of covered autos are employees; this coverage does not have much value. However, many firms purchase medical payments coverage on private passenger autos furnished to the executives or key persons of the firm, as well as on autos used to transport customers of the firm and other non-employees.

The following exclusions for physical damage coverage are of particular interest to the risk manager:

1. Automobiles used to carry persons or property for hire
2. Damage due to wear and tear, freezing, mechanical or electrical breakdown or failure, and road damage to tires
3. Damage caused by radioactive contamination or by the discharge of a nuclear weapon and by war in all of its forms
4. Damage to equipment designed for reproduction of sound unless permanently installed in the automobile
5. Damage to sound receiving and transmitting equipment such as CB radios, cellular telephones, and their accessories unless installed in the opening in the dash or console where the radio is normally located.

FIDELITY AND SURETY BONDS

A *bond* is a contract under which one party is bound financially for the performance by another of an agreed upon obligation. Thus a contract of suretyship involves three parties: the principal, who promises to act in a certain way: the surety, who guarantees to be bound with the first party to fulfill the obligation; and a third party, the obligee, to whom these promises are made. If the principal does not perform as promised, the surety is forced to indemnify the obligee.

Each year, thefts by employees probably amount to several times the loss from individuals outside the firm. Employees often steal small amounts of money or inventory over a period of years, which can add up to enormous sums. Many times, discovery of the missing funds is delayed because of poorly designed checks and balances and inadequate inventory control methods. To illustrate the point, on February 26, 1999, *The News-Journal*, a Daytona Beach, Florida newspaper, carried the story of a former Port Orange finance department employee who admitted that she stole $258,000 over the previous six years. *Fidelity bonds* protect employers from loss caused by dishonest acts of employees. The employee is the principal who owes a duty of honest performance to the obligee, the employer. The bond covers loss of money, securities, or other property resulting from acts of fraud, forgery, embezzlement, and theft by an employee, up to the face amount of the bond, which is called the penalty. There are three types of fidelity bonds available to risk management: individual, scheduled, and blanket. Individual bonds name a specific employee whom the employer wants covered, while the scheduled bond lists all the names of the employees or their positions. The most popular form of fidelity bond is the *blanket bond*. The major advantage of this broad form of coverage is that individual employees or positions don't need to be listed. All existing employees, regardless of position, are covered and new employees are covered automatically. The employee who steals is often the least suspected and might not be bonded if the FBO is using the other types of bonds. The blanket bond is issued for a $10,000 minimum but may be increased to meet specific company needs. The selected limit of liability is per occurrence, and is immediately restored for other losses caused by other employees. The bond is written for a one- year period, covers all dishonesty losses occurring during the policy year, and may also cover all dishonesty losses discovered from the previous year if the loss would have been covered by insurance. Some policies have a non-cumulation of limits clause which states that regardless of the number of years this insurance remains in force or the number of premiums paid, the limit of liability in the policy does not cumulate from year to year or period to period. This clause can present a major problem when employee theft is discovered and the theft has been going on for multiple years and the total far exceeds the limits of the policy. The policy excludes coverage for losses caused by employees when the employer knew of previous dishonesty. An additional exclusion states that losses that are only provable by an inventory shortage are not covered.

Surety bonds, as distinguished from fidelity bonds, guarantee the performance of the principal. Airports and FBOs most commonly use surety bonds when engaging the services of independent contractors. By requiring a surety bond from the contractor who is building a hangar, resurfacing a runway, or supplying fuel, the firm is assured that if the terms of the contract are not satisfactorily met, all resulting losses will be reimbursed by the insurance company. These surety bonds are often referred to as performance bonds. Other examples of surety bonds include labor and material bonds, supply contract bonds, completion bonds, bid bonds, and court bonds. *Customs Bonds are* required by the U. S. Customs Service (Title 19 USC section 1623) as a means to ensure that importers guarantee payment in the event that liquidated damages are assessed against shipments imported into the country. A bond is intended to protect the U.S. government in the event the importer cannot or will not fulfill their obligation to pay. There are two types of Customs Bonds:

- A *Single Transaction Entry Bond* (SEB) is used by companies that import infrequently and have no need for continuous coverage.
- A *Continuous Bond* is used by companies that import on a regular basis.

KEY TERMS

Assumption of risk
Fellow servant rule
Contributory negligence
Workers' compensation insuring agreement
Employers' liability insuring agreement
Second-injury funds
Federal Employment Compensation Act
Experience rating systems
Cost control program
Business auto policy
Liability insuring agreement
Uninsured/underinsured motorist insuring agreement
Physical damage insuring agreement
Collision
Loss other than collision
Actual cash value
Personal injury protection (PIP)
Bond
Fidelity bond
Blanket bond
Surety bond
Customs bonds

Medical payments insuring agreement

Single transaction entry bond (SEB)
Continuous Bond

REVIEW QUESTIONS

1. Explain the philosophy of the workers' compensation law, and describe the circumstances in the late 1800s that brought worker injuries into focus.
2. Identify and explain the four benefit areas available to an eligible injured worker.
3. Explain the social value of second-injury funds.
4. Explain how workers' compensation rates are determined, and state the importance to the risk manager of an experience rating system.
5. Describe the typical components of a workers' compensation cost control program.
6. Explain the four insuring agreements available to a risk manager to transfer the risk of automobile ownership.
7. Explain the following statement: "Physical damage coverage is really no-fault insurance."
8. Only one of the four business automobile policy insuring agreements is essential coverage. Name the insuring agreement and explain why?
9. Explain personal injury protection (PIP) coverage.
10. Describe and differentiate between fidelity bonds, surety bonds, and custom bonds.

CA 00 01 10 01

BUSINESS AUTO POLICY

BUSINESS AUTO COVERAGE FORM

Various provisions in this policy restrict coverage. Read the entire policy carefully to determine rights, duties and what is and is not covered.

Throughout this policy the words "you" and "your" refer to the Named Insured shown in the Declarations. The words "we", "us" and "our" refer to the Company providing this insurance.

Other words and phrases that appear in quotation marks have special meaning. Refer to Section **V** – Definitions.

SECTION I – COVERED AUTOS

Item Two of the Declarations shows the "autos" that are covered "autos" for each of your coverages. The following numerical symbols describe the "autos" that may be covered "autos". The symbols entered next to a coverage on the Declarations designate the only "autos" that are covered "autos".

A. Description Of Covered Auto Designation Symbols

Symbol	Description Of Covered Auto Designation Symbols	
1	Any "Auto"	
2	Owned "Autos" Only	Only those "autos" you own (and for Liability Coverage any "trailers" you don't own while attached to power units you own) . This includes those "autos" you acquire ownership of after the policy begins.
3	Owned Private Passenger "Autos" Only	Only the private passenger "autos" you own. This includes those private passenger "autos" you acquire ownership of after the policy begins.
4	Owned "Autos" Other Than Private Passenger "Autos" Only	Only those "autos" you own that are not of the private passenger type (and for Liability Coverage any "trailers" you don't own while attached to power units you own) . This includes those "autos" not of the private passenger type you acquire ownership of after the policy begins.
5	Owned "Autos" Subject To No-Fault	Only those "autos" you own that are required to have No-Fault benefits in the state where they are licensed or principally garaged. This includes those "autos" you acquire ownership of after the policy begins provided they are required to have No-Fault benefits in the state where they are licensed or principally garaged.
6	Owned "Autos" Subject To A Compulsory Uninsured Motorists Law	Only those "autos" you own that because of the law in the state where they are licensed or principally garaged are required to have and cannot reject Uninsured Motorists Coverage. This includes those "autos" you acquire ownership of after the policy begins provided they are subject to the same state uninsured motorists requirement.
7	Specifically Described "Autos"	Only those "autos" described in Item Three of the Declarations for which a premium charge is shown (and for Liability Coverage any "trailers" you don't own while attached to any power unit described in Item Three) .

8	Hired "Autos" Only	Only those "autos" you lease, hire, rent or borrow. This does not include any "auto" you lease, hire, rent, or borrow from any of your "employees", partners (if you are a partnership) , members (if you are a limited liability company) or members of their households.
9	Nonowned "Autos" Only	Only those "autos" you do not own, lease, hire, rent or borrow that are used in connection with your business. This includes "autos" owned by your "employees", partners (if you are a partnership) , members (if you are a limited liability company) , or members of their households but only while used in your business or your personal affairs.

B. Owned Autos You Acquire After The Policy Begins

1. If Symbols 1, 2, 3, 4, 5 or 6 are entered next to a coverage in Item Two of the Declarations, then you have coverage for "autos" that you acquire of the type described for the remainder of the policy period.

2. But, if Symbol 7 is entered next to a coverage in Item Two of the Declarations, an "auto" you acquire will be a covered "auto" for that coverage only if:

a. We already cover all "autos" that you own for that coverage or it replaces an "auto" you previously owned that had that coverage; and

b. You tell us within 30 days after you acquire it that you want us to cover it for that coverage.

C. Certain Trailers, Mobile Equipment And Temporary Substitute Autos

If Liability Coverage is provided by this Coverage Form, the following types of vehicles are also covered "autos" for Liability Coverage:

1. "Trailers" with a load capacity of 2,000 pounds or less designed primarily for travel on public roads.

2. "Mobile equipment" while being carried or towed by a covered "auto".

3. Any "auto" you do not own while used with the permission of its owner as a temporary substitute for a covered "auto" you own that is out of service because of its:

a. Breakdown;

b. Repair;

c. Servicing;

d. "Loss"; or

e. Destruction.

SECTION II – LIABILITY COVERAGE

A. Coverage

We will pay all sums an "insured" legally must pay as damages because of "bodily injury" or "property damage" to which this insurance applies, caused by an "accident" and resulting from the ownership, maintenance or use of a covered "auto".

We will also pay all sums an "insured" legally must pay as a "covered pollution cost or expense" to which this insurance applies, caused by an "accident" and resulting from the ownership, maintenance or use of covered "autos". However, we will only pay for the "covered pollution cost or expense" if there is either "bodily injury" or "property damage" to which this insurance applies that is caused by the same "accident".

We have the right and duty to defend any "insured" against a "suit" asking for such damages or a "covered pollution cost or expense". However, we have no duty to defend any "insured" against a "suit" seeking damages for "bodily injury" or "property damage" or a "covered pollution cost or expense" to which this insurance does not apply. We may investigate and settle any claim or "suit" as we consider appropriate. Our duty to defend or settle ends when the Liability Coverage Limit of Insurance has been exhausted by payment of judgments or settlements.

1. Who Is An Insured

The following are "insureds":

a. You for any covered "auto".

b. Anyone else while using with your permission a covered "auto" you own, hire or borrow except:

(1) The owner or anyone else from whom you hire or borrow a covered "auto". This exception does not apply if the covered "auto" is a "trailer" connected to a covered "auto" you own.

(2) Your "employee" if the covered "auto" is owned by that "employee" or a member of his or her household.

(3) Someone using a covered "auto" while he or she is working in a business of selling, servicing, repairing, parking or storing "autos" unless that business is yours.

(4) Anyone other than your "employees", partners (if you are a partnership) , members (if you are a limited liability company) , or a lessee or borrower or any of their "employees", while moving property to or from a covered "auto".

(5) A partner (if you are a partnership) , or a member (if you are a limited liability company) for a covered "auto" owned by him or her or a member of his or her household.

c. Anyone liable for the conduct of an "insured" described above but only to the extent of that liability.

2. Coverage Extensions

a. Supplementary Payments

In addition to the Limit of Insurance, we will pay for the "insured":

(1) All expenses we incur.

(2) Up to $2,000 for cost of bail bonds (including bonds for related traffic law violations) required because of an "accident" we cover.We do not have to furnish these bonds.

(3) The cost of bonds to release attachments in any "suit" against the "insured" we defend, but only for bond amounts within our Limit of Insurance.

(4) All reasonable expenses incurred by the "insured" at our request, including actual loss of earnings up to $250 a day because of time off from work.

(5) All costs taxed against the "insured" in any "suit" against the "insured" we defend.

(6) All interest on the full amount of any judgment that accrues after entry of the judgment in any "suit" against the "insured" we defend, but our duty to pay interest ends when we have paid, offered to pay or deposited in court the part of the judgment that is within our Limit of Insurance.

b. Out-Of-State Coverage Extensions

While a covered "auto" is away from the state where it is licensed we will:

(1) Increase the Limit of Insurance for Liability Coverage to meet the limits specified by a compulsory or financial responsibility law of the jurisdiction where the covered "auto" is being used. This extension does not apply to the limit or limits specified by any law governing motor carriers of passengers or property.

(2) Provide the minimum amounts and types of other coverages, such as no-fault, required of out-of-state vehicles by the jurisdiction where the covered "auto" is being used.

We will not pay anyone more than once for the same elements of loss because of these extensions.

B. Exclusions

This insurance does not apply to any of the following:

1. Expected Or Intended Injury

"Bodily injury" or "property damage" expected or intended from the standpoint of the "insured".

2. Contractual

Liability assumed under any contract or agreement.

But this exclusion does not apply to liability for damages:

a. Assumed in a contract or agreement that is an "insured contract" provided the "bodily injury" or "property damage" occurs subsequent to the execution of the contract or agreement; or

b. That the "insured" would have in the absence of the contract or agreement.

3. Workers' Compensation

Any obligation for which the "insured" or the "insured's" insurer may be held liable under any workers' compensation, disability benefits or unemployment compensation law or any similar law.

4. Employee Indemnification And Employer's Liability

"Bodily injury" to:

a. An "employee" of the "insured" arising out of and in the course of:

(1) Employment by the "insured"; or

(2) Performing the duties related to the conduct of the "insured's" business; or

b. The spouse, child, parent, brother or sister of that "employee" as a consequence of Paragraph a. above.

This exclusion applies:

(1) Whether the "insured" may be liable as an employer or in any other capacity; and

(2) To any obligation to share damages with or repay someone else who must pay damages because of the injury.

But this exclusion does not apply to "bodily injury" to domestic "employees" not entitled to workers' compensation benefits or to liability assumed by the "insured" under an "insured contract". For the purposes of the Coverage Form, a domestic "employee" is a person engaged in household or domestic work performed principally in connection with a residence premises.

5. Fellow Employee

"Bodily injury" to any fellow "employee" of the "insured" arising out of and in the course of the fellow "employee's" employment or while performing duties related to the conduct of your business.

6. Care, Custody Or Control

"Property damage" to or "covered pollution cost or expense" involving property owned or transported by the "insured" or in the "insured's" care, custody or control. But this exclusion does not apply to liability assumed under a sidetrack agreement.

7. Handling Of Property

"Bodily injury" or "property damage" resulting from the handling of property:

a. Before it is moved from the place where it is accepted by the "insured" for movement into or onto the covered "auto"; or

b. After it is moved from the covered "auto" to the place where it is finally delivered by the "insured".

8. Movement Of Property By Mechanical Device

"Bodily injury" or "property damage" resulting from the movement of property by a mechanical device (other than a hand truck) unless the device is attached to the covered "auto".

9. Operations

"Bodily injury" or "property damage" arising out of the operation of any equipment listed in Paragraphs **6.b.** and **6.c.** of the definition of "mobile equipment".

10. Completed Operations

"Bodily injury" or "property damage" arising out of your work after that work has been completed or abandoned.

In this exclusion, your work means:

a. Work or operations performed by you or on your behalf; and

b. Materials, parts or equipment furnished in connection with such work or operations.

Your work includes warranties or representations made at any time with respect to the fitness, quality, durability or performance of any of the items included in Paragraphs **a.** or **b.** above.

Your work will be deemed completed at the earliest of the following times:

(1) When all of the work called for in your contract has been completed.

(2) When all of the work to be done at the site has been completed if your contract calls for work at more than one site.

(3) When that part of the work done at a job site has been put to its intended use by any person or organization other than another contractor or subcontractor working on the same project.

Work that may need service, maintenance, correction, repair or replacement, but which is otherwise complete, will be treated as completed.

11. Pollution

"Bodily injury" or "property damage" arising out of the actual, alleged or threatened discharge, dispersal, seepage, migration, release or escape of "pollutants":

a. That are, or that are contained in any property that is:

(1) Being transported or towed by, handled, or handled for movement into, onto or from, the covered "auto";

(2) Otherwise in the course of transit by or on behalf of the "insured"; or

(3) Being stored, disposed of, treated or processed in or upon the covered "auto";

b. Before the "pollutants" or any property in which the "pollutants" are contained are moved from the place where they are accepted by the "insured" for movement into or onto the covered "auto"; or

c. After the "pollutants" or any property in which the "pollutants" are contained are moved from the covered "auto" to the place where they are finally delivered, disposed of or abandoned by the "insured".

Paragraph **a.** above does not apply to fuels, lubricants, fluids, exhaust gases or other similar "pollutants" that are needed for or result from the normal electrical, hydraulic or mechanical functioning of the covered "auto" or its parts, if:

(1) The "pollutants" escape, seep, migrate, or are discharged, dispersed or released directly from an "auto" part designed by its manufacturer to hold, store, receive or dispose of such "pollutants"; and

(2) The "bodily injury", "property damage" or "covered pollution cost or expense" does not arise out of the operation of any equipment listed in Paragraphs 6.b. and 6.c. of the definition of "mobile equipment".

Paragraphs **b.** and **c.** above of this exclusion do not apply to "accidents" that occur away from premises owned by or rented to an "insured" with respect to "pollutants" not in or upon a covered "auto" if:

(1) The "pollutants" or any property in which the "pollutants" are contained are upset, overturned or damaged as a result of the maintenance or use of a covered "auto"; and

(2) The discharge, dispersal, seepage, migration, release or escape of the "pollutants" is caused directly by such upset, overturn or damage.

12. War

"Bodily injury" or "property damage" due to war, whether or not declared, or any act or condition incident to war. War includes civil war, insurrection, rebellion or revolution. This exclusion applies only to liability assumed under a contract or agreement.

13. Racing

Covered "autos" while used in any professional or organized racing or demolition contest or stunting activity, or while practicing for such contest or activity. This insurance also does not apply while that covered "auto" is being prepared for such a contest or activity.

C. Limit Of Insurance

Regardless of the number of covered "autos", "insureds", premiums paid, claims made or vehicles involved in the "accident", the most we will pay for the total of all damages and "covered pollution cost or expense" combined, resulting from any one "accident" is the Limit of Insurance for Liability Coverage shown in the Declarations.

All "bodily injury", "property damage" and "covered pollution cost or expense" resulting from continuous or repeated exposure to substantially the same conditions will be considered as resulting from one "accident".

No one will be entitled to receive duplicate payments for the same elements of "loss" under this Coverage Form and any Medical Payments Coverage Endorsement, Uninsured Motorists Coverage Endorsement or Underinsured Motorists Coverage Endorsement attached to this Coverage Part.

SECTION III – PHYSICAL DAMAGE COVERAGE

A. Coverage

1. We will pay for "loss" to a covered "auto" or its equipment under:

a. Comprehensive Coverage

From any cause except:

(1) The covered "auto's" collision with another object; or

(2) The covered "auto's" overturn.

b. Specified Causes Of Loss Coverage

Caused by:

(1) Fire, lightning or explosion;

(2) Theft;

(3) Windstorm, hail or earthquake;

(4) Flood;

(5) Mischief or vandalism; or

(6) The sinking, burning, collision or derailment of any conveyance transporting the covered "auto".

c. Collision Coverage

Caused by:

(1) The covered "auto's" collision with another object; or

(2) The covered "auto's" overturn.

2. Towing

We will pay up to the limit shown in the Declarations for towing and labor costs incurred each time a covered "auto" of the private passenger type is disabled. However, the labor must be performed at the place of disablement.

3. Glass Breakage – Hitting A Bird Or Animal – Falling Objects Or Missiles

If you carry Comprehensive Coverage for the damaged covered "auto", we will pay for the following under Comprehensive Coverage:

a. Glass breakage;

b. "Loss" caused by hitting a bird or animal; and

c. "Loss" caused by falling objects or missiles.

However, you have the option of having glass breakage caused by a covered "auto's" collision or overturn considered a "loss" under Collision Coverage.

4. Coverage Extensions

a. Transportation Expenses

We will pay up to $20 per day to a maximum of $600 for temporary transportation expense incurred by you because of the total theft of a covered "auto" of the private passenger type. We will pay only for those covered "autos" for which you carry either Comprehensive or Specified Causes of Loss Coverage. We will pay for temporary transportation expenses incurred during the period beginning 48 hours after the theft and ending, regardless of the policy's expiration, when the covered "auto" is returned to use or we pay for its "loss".

b. Loss Of Use Expenses

For Hired Auto Physical Damage, we will pay expenses for which an "insured" becomes legally responsible to pay for loss of use of a vehicle rented or hired without a driver, under a written rental contract or agreement. We will pay for loss of use expenses if caused by:

(1) Other than collision only if the Declarations indicate that Comprehensive Coverage is provided for any covered "auto";

(2) Specified Causes Of Loss only if the Declarations indicate that Specified Causes Of Loss Coverage is provided for any covered "auto"; or

(3) Collision only if the Declarations indicate that Collision Coverage is provided for any covered "auto".

However, the most we will pay for any expenses for loss of use is $20 per day, to a maximum of $600.

B. Exclusions

1. We will not pay for "loss" caused by or resulting from any of the following. Such "loss" is excluded regardless of any other cause or event that contributes concurrently or in any sequence to the "loss".

a. Nuclear Hazard

(1) The explosion of any weapon employing atomic fission or fusion; or

(2) Nuclear reaction or radiation, or radioactive contamination, however caused.

b. War Or Military Action

(1) War, including undeclared or civil war;

(2) Warlike action by a military force, including action in hindering or defending against an actual or expected attack, by any government, sovereign or other authority using military personnel or other agents; or

(3) Insurrection, rebellion, revolution, usurped power or action taken by governmental authority in hindering or defending against any of these.

2. We will not pay for "loss" to any covered "auto" while used in any professional or organized racing or demolition contest or stunting activity, or while practicing for such contest or activity. We will also not pay for "loss" to any covered "auto" while that covered "auto" is being prepared for such a contest or activity.

3. We will not pay for "loss" caused by or resulting from any of the following unless caused by other "loss" that is covered by this insurance:

a. Wear and tear, freezing, mechanical or electrical breakdown.

b. Blowouts, punctures or other road damage to tires.

4. We will not pay for "loss" to any of the following:

a. Tapes, records, discs or other similar audio, visual or data electronic devices designed for use with audio, visual or data electronic equipment.

b. Any device designed or used to detect speed measuring equipment such as radar or laser detectors and any jamming apparatus intended to elude or disrupt speed measurement equipment.

c. Any electronic equipment, without regard to whether this equipment is permanently installed, that receives or transmits audio, visual or data signals and that is not designed solely for the reproduction of sound.

d. Any accessories used with the electronic equipment described in Paragraph c. above.

Exclusions **4.c.** and **4.d.** do not apply to:

a. Equipment designed solely for the reproduction of sound and accessories used with such equipment, provided such equipment is permanently installed in the covered "auto" at the time of the "loss" or such equipment is removable from a housing unit which is permanently installed in the covered "auto" at the time of the "loss", and such equipment is designed to be solely operated by use of the power from the "auto's" electrical system, in or upon the covered "auto"; or

b. Any other electronic equipment that is:

(1) Necessary for the normal operation of the covered "auto" or the monitoring of the covered "auto's" operating system; or

(2) An integral part of the same unit housing any sound reproducing equipment described in a. above and

permanently installed in the opening of the dash or console of the covered "auto" normally used by the manufacturer for installation of a radio.

5. We will not pay for "loss" to a covered "auto" due to "diminution in value".

C. Limit Of Insurance

1. The most we will pay for "loss" in any one "accident" is the lesser of:

a. The actual cash value of the damaged or stolen property as of the time of the "loss"; or

b. The cost of repairing or replacing the damaged or stolen property with other property of like kind and quality.

2. An adjustment for depreciation and physical condition will be made in determining actual cash value in the event of a total "loss".

3. If a repair or replacement results in better than like kind or quality, we will not pay for the amount of the betterment.

D. Deductible

For each covered "auto", our obligation to pay for, repair, return or replace damaged or stolen property will be reduced by the applicable deductible shown in the Declarations. Any Comprehensive Coverage deductible shown in the Declarations does not apply to "loss" caused by fire or lightning.

SECTION IV – BUSINESS AUTO CONDITIONS

The following conditions apply in addition to the Common Policy Conditions:

A. Loss Conditions

1. Appraisal For Physical Damage Loss

If you and we disagree on the amount of "loss", either may demand an appraisal of the "loss". In this event, each party will select a competent appraiser. The two appraisers will select a competent and impartial umpire. The appraisers will state separately the actual cash value and amount of "loss". If they fail to agree, they will submit their differences to the umpire. A decision agreed to by any two will be binding. Each party will:

a. Pay its chosen appraiser; and

b. Bear the other expenses of the appraisal and umpire equally.

If we submit to an appraisal, we will still retain our right to deny the claim.

2. Duties In The Event Of Accident, Claim, Suit Or Loss

We have no duty to provide coverage under this policy unless there has been full compliance with the following duties:

a. In the event of "accident", claim, "suit" or "loss", you must give us or our authorized representative prompt notice of the "accident" or "loss". Include:

(1) How, when and where the "accident" or "loss" occurred;

(2) The "insured's" name and address; and

(3) To the extent possible, the names and addresses of any injured persons and witnesses.

b. Additionally, you and any other involved "insured" must:

(1) Assume no obligation, make no payment or incur no expense without our consent, except at the "insured's" own cost.

(2) Immediately send us copies of any request, demand, order, notice, summons or legal paper received concerning the claim or "suit".

(3) Cooperate with us in the investigation or settlement of the claim or defense against the "suit".

(4) Authorize us to obtain medical records or other pertinent information.

(5) Submit to examination, at our expense, by physicians of our choice, as often as we reasonably require.

c. If there is "loss" to a covered "auto" or its equipment you must also do the following:

(1) Promptly notify the police if the covered "auto" or any of its equipment is stolen.

(2) Take all reasonable steps to protect the covered "auto" from further damage. Also keep a record of your expenses for consideration in the settlement of the claim.

(3) Permit us to inspect the covered "auto" and records proving the "loss" before its repair or disposition.

(4) Agree to examinations under oath at our request and give us a signed statement of your answers.

3. Legal Action Against Us

No one may bring a legal action against us under this Coverage Form until:

a. There has been full compliance with all the terms of this Coverage Form; and

b. Under Liability Coverage, we agree in writing that the "insured" has an obligation to pay or until the amount of that obligation has finally been determined by judgment after trial. No one has the right under this policy to bring us into an action to determine the "insured's" liability.

4. Loss Payment – Physical Damage Coverages

At our option we may:

a. Pay for, repair or replace damaged or stolen property;

b. Return the stolen property, at our expense. We will pay for any damage that results to the "auto" from the theft; or

c. Take all or any part of the damaged or stolen property at an agreed or appraised value.

If we pay for the "loss", our payment will include the applicable sales tax for the damaged or stolen property.

5. Transfer Of Rights Of Recovery Against Others To Us

If any person or organization to or for whom we make payment under this Coverage Form has rights to recover damages from another, those rights are transferred to us. That person or organization must do everything necessary to secure our rights and must do nothing after "accident" or "loss" to impair them.

B. General Conditions

1. Bankruptcy

Bankruptcy or insolvency of the "insured" or the "insured's" estate will not relieve us of any obligations under this Coverage Form.

2. Concealment, Misrepresentation Or Fraud

This Coverage Form is void in any case of fraud by you at any time as it relates to this Coverage Form. It is also void if you or any other "insured", at any time, intentionally conceal or misrepresent a material fact concerning:

a. This Coverage Form;

b. The covered "auto";

c. Your interest in the covered "auto"; or

d. A claim under this Coverage Form.

3. Liberalization

If we revise this Coverage Form to provide more coverage without additional premium charge, your policy will automatically provide the additional coverage as of the day the revision is effective in your state.

4. No Benefit To Bailee – Physical Damage Coverages

We will not recognize any assignment or grant any coverage for the benefit of any person or organization holding, storing or transporting property for a fee regardless of any other provision of this Coverage Form.

5. Other Insurance

a. For any covered "auto" you own, this Coverage Form provides primary insurance. For any covered "auto" you don't own, the insurance provided by this Coverage Form is excess over any other collectible insurance. However, while a covered "auto" which is a "trailer" is connected to another vehicle, the Liability Coverage this Coverage Form provides for the "trailer" is:

(1) Excess while it is connected to a motor vehicle you do not own.

(2) Primary while it is connected to a covered "auto" you own.

b. For Hired Auto Physical Damage Coverage, any covered "auto" you lease, hire, rent or borrow is deemed to be a covered "auto" you own. However, any "auto" that is leased, hired, rented or borrowed with a driver is not a covered "auto".

c. Regardless of the provisions of Paragraph a. above, this Coverage Form's Liability Coverage is primary for any liability assumed under an "insured contract".

d. When this Coverage Form and any other Coverage Form or policy covers on the same basis, either excess or primary, we will pay only our share. Our share is the proportion that the Limit of Insurance of our Coverage

Form bears to the total of the limits of all the Coverage Forms and policies covering on the same basis.

6. Premium Audit

a. The estimated premium for this Coverage Form is based on the exposures you told us you would have when this policy began. We will compute the final premium due when we determine your actual exposures. The estimated total premium will be credited against the final premium due and the first Named Insured will be billed for the balance, if any. The due date for the final premium or retrospective premium is the date shown as the due date on the bill. If the estimated total premium exceeds the final premium due, the first Named Insured will get a refund.

b. If this policy is issued for more than one year, the premium for this Coverage Form will be computed annually based on our rates or premiums in effect at the beginning of each year of the policy.

7. Policy Period, Coverage Territory

Under this Coverage Form, we cover "accidents" and "losses" occurring:

a. During the policy period shown in the Declarations; and

b. Within the coverage territory.

The coverage territory is:

a. The United States of America;

b. The territories and possessions of the United States of America;

c. Puerto Rico;

d. Canada; and

e. Anywhere in the world if:

(1) A covered "auto" of the private passenger type is leased, hired, rented or borrowed without a driver for a period of 30 days or less; and

(2) The "insured's" responsibility to pay damages is determined in a "suit" on the merits, in the United States of America, the territories and possessions of the United States of America, Puerto Rico, or Canada or in a settlement we agree to.

We also cover "loss" to, or "accidents" involving, a covered "auto" while being transported between any of these places.

8. Two Or More Coverage Forms Or Policies Issued By Us

If this Coverage Form and any other Coverage Form or policy issued to you by us or any company affiliated with us apply to the same "accident", the aggregate maximum Limit of Insurance under all the Coverage Forms or policies shall not exceed the highest applicable Limit of Insurance under any one Coverage Form or policy. This condition does not apply to any Coverage Form or policy issued by us or an affiliated company specifically to apply as excess insurance over this Coverage Form.

SECTION V – DEFINITIONS

A. "Accident" includes continuous or repeated exposure to the same conditions resulting in "bodily injury" or "property damage".

B. "Auto" means a land motor vehicle, "trailer" or semitrailer designed for travel on public roads but does not include "mobile equipment".

C. "Bodily injury" means bodily injury, sickness or disease sustained by a person including death resulting from any of these.

D. "Covered pollution cost or expense" means any cost or expense arising out of:

1. Any request, demand, order or statutory or regulatory requirement; or

2. Any claim or "suit" by or on behalf of a governmental authority demanding that the "insured" or others test for, monitor, clean up, remove, contain, treat, detoxify or neutralize, or in any way respond to, or assess the effects of "pollutants".

"Covered pollution cost or expense" does not include any cost or expense arising out of the actual, alleged or threatened discharge, dispersal, seepage, migration, release or escape of "pollutants":

a. That are, or that are contained in any property that is:

(1) Being transported or towed by, handled, or handled for movement into, onto or from the covered "auto";

(2) Otherwise in the course of transit by or on behalf of the "insured";

(3) Being stored, disposed of, treated or processed in or upon the covered "auto";

b. Before the "pollutants" or any property in which the "pollutants" are contained are moved from the place where they are accepted by the "insured" for movement into or onto the covered "auto"; or

c. After the "pollutants" or any property in which the "pollutants" are contained are moved from the covered "auto" to the place where they are finally delivered, disposed of or abandoned by the "insured".

Paragraph **a.** above does not apply to fuels, lubricants, fluids, exhaust gases or other similar "pollutants" that are needed for or result from the normal electrical, hydraulic or mechanical functioning of the covered "auto" or its parts, if:

(1) The "pollutants" escape, seep, migrate, or are discharged, dispersed or released directly from an "auto" part designed by its manufacturer to hold, store, receive or dispose of such "pollutants"; and

(2) The "bodily injury", "property damage" or "covered pollution cost or expense" does not arise out of the operation of any equipment listed in Paragraphs 6.b. or 6.c. of the definition of "mobile equipment".

Paragraphs **b.** and **c.** above do not apply to "accidents" that occur away from premises owned by or rented to an "insured" with respect to "pollutants" not in or upon a covered "auto" if:

(1) The "pollutants" or any property in which the "pollutants" are contained are upset, overturned or damaged as a result of the maintenance or use of a covered "auto"; and

(2) The discharge, dispersal, seepage, migration, release or escape of the "pollutants" is caused directly by such upset, overturn or damage.

E. "Diminution in value" means the actual or perceived loss in market value or resale value which results from a direct and accidental "loss".

F. "Employee" includes a "leased worker". "Employee" does not include a "temporary worker".

G. "Insured" means any person or organization qualifying as an insured in the Who Is An Insured provision of the applicable coverage. Except with respect to the Limit of Insurance, the coverage afforded applies separately to each insured who is seeking coverage or against whom a claim or "suit" is brought.

H. "Insured contract" means:

1. A lease of premises;

2. A sidetrack agreement;

3. Any easement or license agreement, except in connection with construction or demolition operations on or within 50 feet of a railroad;

4. An obligation, as required by ordinance, to indemnify a municipality, except in connection with work for a municipality;

5. That part of any other contract or agreement pertaining to your business (including an indemnification of a municipality in connection with work performed for a municipality) under which you assume the tort liability of another to pay for "bodily injury" or "property damage" to a third party or organization. Tort liability means a liability that would be imposed by law in the absence of any contract or agreement;

6. That part of any contract or agreement entered into, as part of your business, pertaining to the rental or lease, by you or any of your "employees", of any "auto". However, such contract or agreement shall not be considered an "insured contract" to the extent that it obligates you or any of your "employees" to pay for "property damage" to any "auto" rented or leased by you or any of your "employees".

An "insured contract" does not include that part of any contract or agreement:

a. That indemnifies a railroad for "bodily injury" or "property damage" arising out of construction or demolition operations, within 50 feet of any railroad property and affecting any railroad bridge or trestle, tracks, roadbeds, tunnel, underpass or crossing; or

b. That pertains to the loan, lease or rental of an "auto" to you or any of your "employees", if the "auto" is loaned, leased or rented with a driver; or

c. That holds a person or organization engaged in the business of transporting property by "auto" for hire harmless for your use of a covered "auto" over a route or territory that person or organization is authorized to serve by public authority.

I. "Leased worker" means a person leased to you by a labor leasing firm under an agreement between you and the labor leasing firm, to perform duties related to the conduct of your business. "Leased worker" does not include a "temporary worker".

J. "Loss" means direct and accidental loss or damage.

K. "Mobile equipment" means any of the following types of land vehicles, including any attached machinery or equipment:

1. Bulldozers, farm machinery, forklifts and other vehicles designed for use principally off public roads;

2. Vehicles maintained for use solely on or next to premises you own or rent;

3. Vehicles that travel on crawler treads;

4. Vehicles, whether self-propelled or not, maintained primarily to provide mobility to permanently mounted:

a. Power cranes, shovels, loaders, diggers or drills; or

b. Road construction or resurfacing equipment such as graders, scrapers or rollers.

5. Vehicles not described in Paragraphs 1.,2. , 3., or 4. above that are not self-propelled and are maintained primarily to provide mobility to permanently attached equipment of the following types:

a. Air compressors, pumps and generators, including spraying, welding, building cleaning, geophysical exploration, lighting and well servicing equipment; or

b. Cherry pickers and similar devices used to raise or lower workers.

6. Vehicles not described in Paragraphs 1., 2. , 3. or 4. above maintained primarily for purposes other than the transportation of persons or cargo. However, self-propelled vehicles with the following types of permanently attached equipment are not "mobile equipment" but will be considered "autos":

a. Equipment designed primarily for:

(1) Snow removal;

(2) Road maintenance, but not construction or resurfacing; or

(3) Street cleaning;

b. Cherry pickers and similar devices mounted on automobile or truck chassis and used to raise or lower workers; and

c. Air compressors, pumps and generators, including spraying, welding, building cleaning, geophysical exploration, lighting or well servicing equipment.

L. "Pollutants" means any solid, liquid, gaseous or thermal irritant or contaminant, including smoke, vapor, soot, fumes, acids, alkalis, chemicals and waste. Waste includes materials to be recycled, reconditioned or reclaimed.

M. "Property damage" means damage to or loss of use of tangible property.

N. "Suit" means a civil proceeding in which:

1. Damages because of "bodily injury" or "property damage"; or

2. A "covered pollution cost or expense",

to which this insurance applies, are alleged.

"Suit" includes:

a. An arbitration proceeding in which such damages or "covered pollution costs or expenses" are claimed and to which the "insured" must submit or does submit with our consent; or

b. Any other alternative dispute resolution proceeding in which such damages or "covered pollution costs or expenses" are claimed and to which the insured submits with our consent.

O. "Temporary worker" means a person who is furnished to you to substitute for a permanent "employee" on leave or to meet seasonal or short-term workload conditions.

P. "Trailer" includes semitrailer.

THIS ENDORSEMENT CHANGES THE POLICY. PLEASE READ IT CAREFULLY.

AUTO MEDICAL PAYMENTS COVERAGE

This endorsement modifies insurance provided under the following:

BUSINESS AUTO COVERAGE FORM
GARAGE COVERAGE FORM
MOTOR CARRIER COVERAGE FORM
TRUCKERS COVERAGE FORM

With respect to coverage provided by this endorsement, the provisions of the Coverage Form apply unless modified by the endorsement.

A. Coverage

We will pay reasonable expenses incurred for necessary medical and funeral services to or for an "insured" who sustains "bodily injury" caused by "accident". We will pay only those expenses incurred, for services rendered within three years from the date of the "accident".

B. Who Is An Insured

1. You while "occupying" or, while a pedestrian, when struck by any "auto".

2. If you are an individual, any "family member" while "occupying" or, while a pedestrian, when struck by any "auto".

3. Anyone else "occupying" a covered "auto" or a temporary substitute for a covered "auto". The covered "auto" must be out of service because of its breakdown, repair, servicing, loss or destruction.

C. Exclusions

This insurance does not apply to any of the following:

1. "Bodily injury" sustained by an "insured" while "occupying" a vehicle located for use as a premises.

2. "Bodily injury" sustained by you or any "family member" while "occupying" or struck by any vehicle (other than a covered "auto") owned by you or furnished or available for your regular use.

3. "Bodily injury" sustained by any "family member" while "occupying" or struck by any vehicle (other than a covered "auto") owned by or furnished or available for the regular use of any "family member".

4. "Bodily injury" to your "employee" arising out of and in the course of employment by you. However, we will cover "bodily injury" to your domestic "employees" if not entitled to workers' compensation benefits. For the purposes of this endorsement, a domestic "employee" is a person engaged in household or domestic work performed principally in connection with a residence premises.

5. "Bodily injury" to an "insured" while working in a business of selling, servicing, repairing or parking "autos" unless that business is yours.

6. "Bodily injury" caused by declared or undeclared war or insurrection or any of their consequences.

7. "Bodily injury" to anyone using a vehicle without a reasonable belief that the person is entitled to do so.

8. "Bodily Injury" sustained by an "insured" while "occupying" any covered "auto" while used in any professional racing or demolition contest or stunting activity, or while practicing for such contest or activity. This insurance also does not apply to any "bodily injury" sustained by an "insured" while the "auto" is being prepared for such a contest or activity.

D. Limit Of Insurance

Regardless of the number of covered "autos", "insureds", premiums paid, claims made or vehicles involved in the "accident", the most we will pay for "bodily injury" for each "insured" injured in any one "accident" is the Limit Of Insurance for Auto Medical Payments Coverage shown in the Declarations.

No one will be entitled to receive duplicate payments for the same elements of "loss" under this coverage and any Liability Coverage Form, Uninsured Motorists Coverage Endorsement or Underinsured Motorists Coverage Endorsement attached to this Coverage Part.

E. Changes In Conditions

The Conditions are changed for Auto Medical Payments Coverage as follows:

1. The Transfer Of Rights Of Recovery Against Others To Us Condition does not apply.

2. The reference in Other Insurance in the Business Auto and Garage Coverage Forms and Other Insurance – Primary And Excess Insurance Provisions in the Truckers and Motor Carrier Coverage Forms to "other collectible insurance" applies only to other collectible auto medical payments insurance.

F. Additional Definitions

As used in this endorsement:

1. "Family member" means a person related to you by blood, marriage or adoption who is a resident of your household, including a ward or foster child.

2. "Occupying" means in, upon, getting in, on, out or off.

THIS ENDORSEMENT CHANGES THE POLICY. PLEASE READ IT CAREFULLY.

CHANGES IN COMMERCIAL AUTO COVERAGE FORMS

This endorsement modifies insurance provided under the following:

BUSINESS AUTO COVERAGE FORM
BUSINESS AUTO PHYSICAL DAMAGE COVERAGE FORM
GARAGE COVERAGE FORM
MOTOR CARRIER COVERAGE FORM
TRUCKERS COVERAGE FORM

SECTION I – LOSS OF USE

Changes In Physical Damage Coverage

Coverage Extension under Physical Damage Coverage is replaced by the following:

Coverage Extensions

A. Transportation Expenses

We will pay up to $15 per day to a maximum of $450 for temporary transportation expense incurred by you because of the total theft of a covered "auto" of the private passenger type. We will pay only for those covered "autos" for which you carry either Comprehensive or Specified Causes Of Loss Coverage. We will pay for temporary transportation expenses incurred during the period beginning 48 hours after the theft and ending, regardless of the policy's expiration, when the covered "auto" is returned to use or we pay for its "loss".

B. Loss Of Use Expenses

For Hired Auto Physical Damage, we will pay expenses for which an "insured" becomes legally responsible to pay for loss of use of a vehicle rented or hired without a driver, under a written rental contract or agreement. We will pay for loss of use expenses if caused by:

1. Other than collision only if the Declarations indicate that Comprehensive Coverage is provided for any covered "auto";

2. Specified Causes Of Loss only if the Declarations indicate that Specified Causes Of Loss Coverage is provided for any covered "auto"; or

3. Collision only if the Declarations indicate that Collision Coverage is provided for any covered "auto".

However, the most we will pay for any expenses for loss of use is $15 per day, to a maximum of $450.

SECTION II – LIMITED WORLDWIDE COVERAGE FOR HIRED AUTOS

Paragraph **7. Policy Period, Coverage Territory** of the **General Conditions** is amended by the addition of the following:

The coverage territory is extended to anywhere in the world if:

a. A covered "auto" of the private passenger type is leased, hired, rented or borrowed without a driver for a period of 30 days or less; and

b. The "insured's" responsibility to pay damages is determined in a "suit" on the merits, in the United States of America, the territories and possessions of the United States of America, Puerto Rico, or Canada or in a settlement we agree to.

SECTION III – CHANGES IN DEFINITIONS

A. The definition of "insured contract" contained in Section V – Definitions of the Business Auto Coverage Form and Section VI – Definitions of the Motor Carrier and Truckers Coverage Forms is replaced by the following:

"Insured contract" means:

1. A lease of premises;

2. A sidetrack agreement;

3. Any easement or license agreement, except in connection with construction or demolition operations on or within 50 feet of a railroad;

4. An obligation, as required by ordinance, to indemnify a municipality, except in connection with work for a municipality;

5. That part of any other contract or agreement pertaining to your business (including an indemnification of a municipality in connection with work performed for a municipality) under which you assume the tort liability of another to pay for "bodily injury" or "property damage" to a third party or organization. Tort liability means a liability that would be imposed by law in the absence of any contract or agreement;

6. That part of any contract or agreement entered into, as part of your business, pertaining to the rental or lease, by you or any of your "employees", of any "auto". However, such contract or agreement shall not be considered an "insured contract" to the extent that it obligates you or any of your "employees" to pay for "property damage" to any "auto" rented or leased by you or any of your "employees".

An "insured contract" does not include that part of any contract or agreement:

a. That indemnifies a railroad for "bodily injury" or "property damage" arising out of construction or demolition operations, within 50 feet of any railroad property and affecting any railroad bridge or trestle, tracks, roadbeds, tunnel, underpass or crossing; or

b. That pertains to the loan, lease or rental of an "auto" to you or any of your "employees", if the "auto" is loaned, leased or rented with a driver; or

c. That holds a person or organization engaged in the business of transporting property by "auto" for hire harmless for your use of a covered "auto" over a route or territory that person or organization is authorized to serve by public authority.

B. The definition of "insured contract" contained in Section VI – Definitions of the Garage Coverage Form is replaced by the following:

"Insured contract" means:

1. A lease of premises;

2. A sidetrack agreement;

3. Any easement or license agreement, except in connection with construction or demolition operations on or within 50 feet of a railroad;

4. An obligation, as required by ordinance, to indemnify a municipality, except in connection with work for a municipality;

5. That part of any other contract or agreement pertaining to your garage business (including an indemnification of a municipality in connection with work performed for a municipality) under which you assume the tort liability of another to pay for "bodily injury" or "property damage" to a third party or organization. Tort liability means a liability that would be imposed by law in the absence of any contract or agreement;

6. An elevator maintenance agreement;

7. That part of any contract or agreement entered into, as part of your garage business, pertaining to the rental or lease, by you or any of your "employees", of any "auto". However, such contract or agreement shall not be considered an "insured contract" to the extent that it obligates you or any of your "employees" to pay "property damage" to any "auto" rented or leased by you or any of your "employees".

An "insured contract" does not include that part of any contract or agreement:

1. That indemnifies an architect, engineer or surveyor for injury or damage arising out of:

   a. Preparing, approving or failing to prepare or approve maps, drawings, opinions, reports, surveys, change orders, designs or specifications; or

   b. Giving directions or instructions, or failing to give them, if that is the primary cause of the injury or damage.

2. That indemnifies any person or organization for damage by fire to premises rented or loaned to you.

3. That pertains to the loan, lease or rental of an "auto", to you or any of your "employees" if the "auto" is loaned, leased or rented with a driver; or

4. That holds a person or organization engaged in the business of transporting property by "auto" for hire harmless for your use of a covered "auto" over a route or territory that person or organization is authorized to serve by public authority; or

5. That indemnifies a railroad for "bodily injury" or "property damage" arising out of construction or demolition operations, within 50 feet of any railroad property and affecting any railroad bridge or trestle, tracks, roadbeds, tunnel, underpass or crossing.

Chapter 14

Employee Benifits and Business Use of Life Insurance

OUTLINE

Employee Benefits
Group Insurance Compared with Individual Insurance
Life Insurance
Group Disability Income Insurance
Group Medical Care Insurance
Pension Plans
Savings Plans
Business Uses of Life Insurance

OBJECTIVES

At the end of this chapter you should be able to:
Differentiate group insurance from individual insurance on the basis of underwriting, administration, and pricing.
Describe the following employee group insurance coverages: life, medical care, and disability income.
Explain the major provisions of the Employment Retirement Insurance Security Act (ERISA).
Name and describe qualified and nonqualified retirement plans.
Explain Individual Retirement Accounts (IRA), Roth IRA, 401(k), SIMPLE-IRA, and KEOGH plans.
Explain the following business uses of life insurance: business continuation, key person, split-dollar life insurance and deferred compensation plans.

EMPLOYEE BENEFITS

The following findings are from the Summary, "National Compensation Survey: Employee Benefits in the United States, March 2004," and give an overview of the availability and usage of the major employee benefits used in private industry today.

> Paid leave was the most commonly provided employee benefit in the private sector: Paid vacations and holidays were available to 77 percent of employees. Paid jury duty leave was also common, available to 70 percent of workers. Half of the workers had paid military leave benefits.
>
> The large majority of employees covered by medical care plans were in plans requiring employee contributions for both single coverage and family coverage. Employee contributions to medical care premiums averaged $264.59 per month for family coverage; for single coverage, employee contributions averaged $67.57 per month.
>
> Twenty-one percent of employees were in defined benefit retirement plans, and 42 percent were covered by defined contribution plans. (Some employees participated in both types.) The overall coverage of retirement plans has held relatively steady for the last few years.
>
> Fifty-one percent of workers had access to life insurance, and nearly as many, 48 percent, participated. Short- and long-term disability benefits were available to 39 and 30 percent of workers, respectively, and nearly all partici pated.

Employee benefit plans may be defined as any plan, sponsored or started unilaterally or jointly by employers and employees, which provides benefits that stem from the employment relationship and is not underwritten or paid directly by government. The cost of employee benefits increased at an average annual rate of 3.5 percent from March 1991 to September 2004. In March 1991, benefit cost were $6.79 per hour worked, or 30.4 percent of total compensation. In September of 2004, benefit costs were $10.89, or 31.4 percent of total compensation. [1] On an annualized basis, the average cost per employee for a benefits package is $ 22,651. Risk managers are taking positive action to reverse the trend my modifying plan designs in the medical and pension areas. Some of the increased cost is being shifted to the employee through required payroll contributions and copayments for medical services.

Most employers have accepted this major expense as an integral part of the cost of doing business. Today's workers expect their employer to provide protection against medical expenses, loss of income due to accident or illness, death benefits, and retirement income. A large number of employees could not, or would not purchase these insurance coverages on an individual basis due to their high cost. Even though law does not require these types of benefits, employers recognize that their cost is a part of the total compensation package. Benefit packages are required in firms that have a negotiated collective bargaining agreements.

Risk managers are involved in managing only those benefit programs that are insurance based. Human resource departments are responsible for benefits like vacations, sick leave policy, and other non-insurance benefit programs. This chapter will cover the following personnel loss exposures: group life insurance, group disability income, group medical expense coverage, group personal accident insurance, pension plans, and thrift and savings plans. Small business firms cannot afford to provide all of these voluntary coverages because of their cost. They should pick and choose the benefits to offer carefully for maximum results. Benefit plans in general should accomplish the following three objectives:

1. Generate a profit for the firm, not cut into it. The benefits should lead to enhanced profitability through reduced turnover and training expenses, retention of high-productivity employees, and increased morale.
2. Represent a genuine value to the employees.
3. Benefit the employees and their families through tax advantages, and reduce personal expenses that would have to be paid otherwise.

The two most popular coverages are group life insurance and group medical expenses. An employee benefits report published by Employee Benefit Research Institute (EBRI) stated in April 2006, that 61 percent of employees in private industry were offered health care benifits in 2004. In that same year, 51 percent of employees participated in employer provided life insurance protection.) U.S. Department of Labor, 2004).

GROUP INSURANCE COMPARED WITH INDIVIDUAL INSURANCE

Group insurance differs from insurance written on one person in three ways: (1) underwriting, (2) administration, and (3) pricing. Individuals desiring to purchase insurance must submit an application, take a physical examination, and wait until the underwriter decides if the risk is acceptable and at what premium rate. Group underwriting eliminates the individual application and physical exam because the group is selected as a whole. Groups that are most acceptable to insurance companies will have the following characteristics:

- The acquisition of insurance is incidental to the major purpose of the group;
- 10 or more employees with a minimum of 15 percent participating in the plan;
- Employee mix which is not concentrated by age, sex, or nationality, and has

enough turnover to allow younger persons into the group; and
- Some physical qualifications required for employment.

Employers offer group coverages to all full-time employees who are actively at work on the initial start- up date of the plan. Future full-time employees receive coverage after they fulfill a probationary period if any. Employees are not required to show evidence of insurability thus the need to fill out lengthy health histories or take physical exams is eliminated.

The administration of group insurance differs from individual insurance in that a master policy is issued to the employer, and each covered employee receives a certificate along with a booklet describing the coverage. Employers perform most of the day-to-day administrative procedures for the insurance company, and pay the premium once a month. In some cases, the employer may also become involved in the claims process.

Group life insurance is less expensive than individual life insurance because the wholesale method of distributing the coverage permits savings in underwriting and administrative costs. In addition, sales commissions are lower and employers help control misuse and fraudulent claims. Employers with 100 or more employees are usually eligible for experience-rated premiums. Under this arrangement, each firm's claims experience influences the cost of coverage. Risk managers can favorably influence the firm's cost by having aggressive loss control programs. *Noncontributory plans* are ones where the employer pays the total cost of the benefits. If the employee shares in the cost of the coverage through payroll deductions, it is a *contributory plan.*

LIFE INSURANCE

Group Term Insurance

A large percentage of employers in private industry provide group life insurance for their employees. In addition, some have found it helpful to move a step beyond this and sponsor a program that allows employees to purchase individual policies. These voluntary programs require no direct cash contribution from the employer. They give the employee the privilege of buying term insurance and various forms of cash value insurance at lower prices, through payroll deduction. Employers prefer one-year renewable term for insuring employees. *Group term insurance* is economical for it is intended purely for death protection and does not accumulate cash value for the covered employee. The coverage is automatically renewed each year the employee remains employed. If death occurs while covered by the plan, the face amount of the policy is paid to the appointed beneficiary either in a lump sum or in installments. The policy limit is payable for death caused by work-related accidents as well as off the job accidents and illnesses. A typical group life insurance plan would have the following features:

- Provides a death benefit equal to two- times base annual salary, up to a maximum of $50,000;
- At age 65, the death benefit is reduced to 1.3 times base annual salary, to the maximum of $50,000;
- Provides an Accidental Death and Dismemberment benefit equal to the amount of the basic life insurance;
- Provides life insurance for eligible dependents ($5,000 for spouse, $2,000 for each child);
- Offers living choices—an accelerated death benefit that allows terminally ill employees and their dependents the opportunity to collect all or part of their life insurance prior to death.

If the employee terminates employment, the plan allows the employee, without showing any evidence of insurability, to purchase within 31 days an individual permanent life insurance policy. The new policy cannot exceed the limits of the group term, and the premium rate is based upon the attained age of the employee. This conversion benefit would be especially important for persons who have health problems, dangerous occupations, or hazardous avocations. Each of these would preclude them from purchasing individual life insurance at standard rates. Private flying by low-time pilots is an example of a hobby that may cause an insurance company either to increase the premium, or exclude coverage while flying, when a person applies for an individual life insurance policy.

The cost of providing group term insurance is quite low per employee. Even though the cost of insuring an employee goes up each year due to increasing mortality costs, the total cost of the plan remains fairly constant because the age composition tends to remain level due to attrition and replacement with younger employees. Traditionally, group term insurance plans are noncontributory which means that the employer pays 100 percent of the cost. This practice has become the norm because the total contribution by the employer is tax deductible as a business expense. Employees can exclude from personal income tax that portion of the employer's contribution used to purchase the first $50,000 of term insurance protection. To illustrate this favorable tax treatment, an employee in the 28 percent income tax bracket, is as well off with a $72 annual contribution by the employer to a group life insurance plan as with a $100 salary increase.

Non-group Life Insurance

Individual policies of life insurance are often offered to employees. Additional term insurance is offered in multiples of annual income. This supplemental life coverage is illustrated by the following choices:

- Option 1 – One times base salary to a maximum of $250,000
- Option 2 – Two times base salary to a maximum of $500,000
- Option 3 – Three times base salary to a maximum of $750,000
- Option 4 – Four times base salary to a maximum of $1,000,000

The employee pays the total cost of this supplemental term life insurance. Some employers choose to enhance the quality of their life insurance program by offering their employees a type of insurance that not only pays a death benefit but also accumulates savings during their working years. Cash value insurance that is used for individual policies are whole life and universal life and differs from term insurance in the following ways:

- Individual policies are issued rather than a master policy with individual certificates;
- For a stated dollar amount of death benefit, premiums remain constant for the life of the policy;
- Some evidence of insurability required when death benefits exceed certain limits; and
- The covered employee must report any contributions by employers as income each year.

Whole life insurance delivers a set death benefit for a premium that remains constant from the time the policy is issued. The policy often is called *straight life insurance* and premiums are required for as long as the face amount of the policy is in effect or to age 85. As table 14.1 illustrates, a straight life policy is designed as a combination of decreasing term (the pure-protection portion) and an increasing savings portion that equals the face amount of the policy at age 100. Because the annual

Table 14.1 $50,000 Straight Life Insurance Male Age 35 (Annual premium) $686.50 (non-participating)

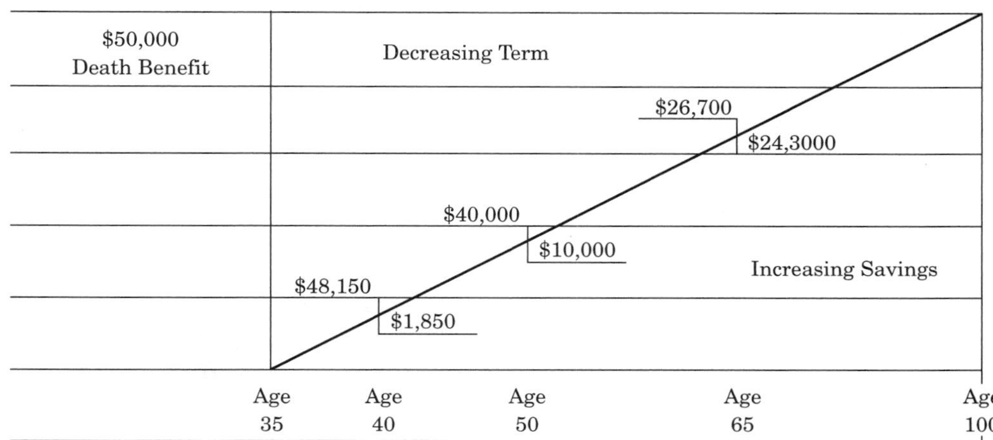

cost of straight life insurance exceeds the cost of term protection during the early years, the surplus funds are used to set up a savings account that earns interest. With each increase in the savings portion, there is a corresponding decrease in the pure-protection portion. If death should occur, the beneficiary will only receive the face amount of the policy ($50,000). At age 50, for example, the insurance company only has $40,000 of risk, because $10,000 of the death benefit comes from over-charges in premiums plus investment interest. The savings portion is available at any time on a loan basis at an interest rate stated in the policy. If death occurs while a loan is outstanding, the death benefit is reduced by the amount of the loan. When premiums are voluntarily stopped, the value of the savings portion is available to the insured, and the insurance company has no further obligations. In the above example, an employee age 65 would have $24,300 to take in cash or purchase an annuity for lifetime income.

Universal life insurance is an alternative to whole life and has had exceptional acceptance since its introduction in 1979. Even though there is no standard form of this policy, most varieties share the same basic characteristics. The composition is similar to whole life in that there is a savings element and a decreasing term element. Beyond this, the similarities cease. The key advantage of this form of cash value insurance is flexibility. The savings portion offers a low interest guarantee (usually 4 to 5 percent) but the funds are more aggressively invested by the insurance company so the insured enjoys competitive rates of return that accumulate on a tax deferred basis. Some plans even allow the insured to self-direct the selection of the investments. Additional flexibility comes in the ability to increase or decrease the death benefit, as needs change and to increase, reduce, or even skip premium payments. Each year, insurers send a disclosure statement that clearly prorates the premium between the cost of death protection, expenses, and changes in savings. This is a vast improvement over whole life insurance where there is no annual communication between the insurer and the policyholder. Will universal life insurance provide higher rates of return on the savings portion than whole life policies? This depends upon how well the universal life investment benefits from the more aggressive management when compared with the long-run returns on the conservative investments from whole life portfolios.

GROUP DISABILITY INCOME INSURANCE

Risk managers and individual wage earners often underestimate the need for income replacement insurance. Total and permanent disability has been called economic death because the person is unable to generate an income through working but still requires financial support. A paper prepared by the American College entitled "The Economics of Disability," points out: At age 35, the chance of experiencing total disability of three months or more before age 65 is about 33 percent. The average length of the disability will exceed five years. Moreover, nearly 30 percent of all disability cases will be permanent.

Group disability income insurance complements and enhances workers' compensation and social security programs that partially replace income when employees are unable to work. Risk managers provide this insurance when they desire to protect employees' personal resources from being eroded due to their inability to work over extended periods. Disability income insurance is broken down into (1) group temporary disability income insurance and (2) long-term disability (LTD) insurance.

Group temporary disability income insurance provides replacement income at a 60 to 75 percent level to an employee who is unable to work due to an accident or illness for a maximum of 13 to 26 weeks. There is a one- to two-week waiting period because sick leave policies will often continue wages at existing levels during this time. Since all employees are covered by workers' compensation insurance, disabilities caused by occupational accidents may be excluded from coverage. This first type of disability income insurance is a candidate for risk retention in some firms because risk managers can predict quite accurately the financial loss for the number of weeks that were selected for payment.

Group long-term disability insurance (LTD) picks up where temporary disability ends, and continues income to a disabled worker for either a specific number of years or to age 65. This type of risk exposure is generally transferred to an insurance company through the purchase of a group long-term disability policy. The quality of the LTD policy will be determined by how "disability" is defined. Most definitions will fall into one of the following categories:

1. The inability of the employee to engage in his or her own occupation.
2. The inability of the employee to engage in any reasonable occupation for which he or she is or might easily become qualified.
3. The inability of the employee to engage in any occupation.

From the employee perspective, the first category is the best and would result in a greater number of employees being judged totally and permanently disabled. The third category is best for the business firm if the goal is to reduce the total cost of long-term disability. The middle definition is the one most used by insurance companies.

The income received by disabled workers will be a percentage of their actual wages at the time of the disability, up to some maximum dollar amount. Income from the plan is reduced when employees become eligible for replacement income from workers' compensation, social security, and other public programs. Total and permanently disabled employees are eligible for retirement income from social security after a six-month waiting period. Because the definition of disability in the Social Security Act—inability to engage in any substantially gainful activity—is usually more restrictive than long-term disability policies, many disabled employees would not qualify, thus no reduction in income from the LTD policy. The firm's cost of a LTD program will depend upon the age and sex composition of the employees, the nature of the business, the definition of disability, the length of time disability income is payable, and in larger firms the influence of experience rating.

GROUP MEDICAL CARE INSURANCE

Many business firms today provide *group medical care insurance* along with group life insurance. Medical care plans protect employees and their families from extensive hospital, surgical, nursing, and related medical expenses. A survey of 1,883 employers by Mercer Human Resource Consulting found employers anticipate average cost increases of nearly 10 percent for their medical plans in 2006, or about three times the rate of inflation.[2] With the escalating cost of medical care today, individuals are unable to pay the cost for adequate medical services from their own resources. Thus, risk managers are continuing to research ways medical expenses can be transferred to commercial insurance companies and Health Maintenance Organizations (HMO). Self-insurance, using a third party administrator (TPA) to handle utilization review and claims is receiving more attention. To eliminate the cost burden of unusual medical cases like organ transplants or AIDS, self-insuring employers will purchase stop loss coverage to assume these types of expenses when they exceed $100,000 per year per insured.

Risk managers do have various options available for providing medical care coverage for their employees, but all plans will have the following characteristics:

1. Coverage is provided immediately for accidents and non-preexisting illness or disease. Coverage for preexisting conditions usually has a one- to three-year waiting period.
2. Annual deductible of $250 to $1,000 per person per calendar year is required, along with a coinsurance clause that requires some participation by the employee up to a specified dollar limit. A popular arrangement is the 80/20 coinsurance clause that requires the employee to pay 20 percent of the claim, after the deductible, up to an annual limit of $1, 500. With an annual deductible of $500, the maximum out of pocket cost for any employee would be 2,000 per year.
3. The employer usually pays the annual cost for employee coverage. The tax deductibility of the premiums by the employer encourages this noncontributory format. As with group life insurance, the employer contributions are not taxable to the employee. Employees pay for dependent coverage if desired.
4. A 1985 federal law, *Consolidated Omnibus Budget Reconciliation Act (COBRA)*, requires employers with 20 or more employees to allow employees who terminate to continue their medical coverage by paying 102 percent of the group premium. The length of COBRA coverage is between 18 and 36 months, depending on the circumstances. Employees have a right to choose COBRA benefits when coverage is lost due to:

   - Reduction in work hours, or
   - Termination of employment (other than for gross misconduct) including retirement.

Covered dependents also have a right, independent of the employee's right, to COBRA coverage. The covered dependent may elect COBRA even if the employee does not. A spouse or dependent child covered under an employee's health plan has the right to elect COBRA continuation coverage if they lose coverage due to:

- The employee's death
- The employee's termination (other than gross misconduct), or reduction in work hours
- Divorce or legal separation from the employee
- The employee's entitlement to Medicare
- If a covered individual ceases to meet the definition of a dependent.

5. Typical exclusions include workers' compensation claims; self-inflicted injuries, medical expenses as the result of committing a felony, war, cosmetic or plastic surgery, ordinary vision or dental care, and expenses that are not medically necessary.
6. Some limitations exist for expenses involved with long-term nursing care, mental illness, and treatment for drug and alcohol addiction.

Comprehensive Medical Care Plan Design

Group medical care insurance through commercial insurance companies have undergone major changes in plan design in an attempt to provide adequate coverage at affordable rates. Plan designs today pay the following medical expenses that are reasonable and customary: hospital semiprivate room and board, hospital miscellaneous charges, ambulance, anesthesia, surgery, emergency room care, physician fees in office and hospital, diagnostic procedures, and other medically necessary services. This basic coverage may be enhanced by the addition of major medical provisions that increase the limits of dollar coverage to $1 million or more. Current plans include the following cost containment features that encourage employees and their families to use medical services more responsibly:

1. Annual deductibles along with a coinsurance clause;
2. Preauthorization of non-emergency surgery and hospital stays;
3. Requirement of second opinions for major surgery;
4. Elimination or reduction of deductibles and coinsurance for out-patient surgery and birthing centers;
5. Copayments of $15 to $35 by employee for doctor office visits and prescrip= tion drugs; and
6. Hospice care included as any other hospital

Health Maintenance Organizations

Health Maintenance Organizations (HMOs) have become an important alternative in the delivery of health care for employees. The concept originated in 1929, but had little acceptance by employers until the rising medical costs in the 1970s encouraged risk managers to seek viable alternatives to the traditional plans. An HMO is often a freestanding facility that offers comprehensive health care for a flat monthly fee. Medical services are provided by a team of salaried physicians and technicians and the patient will be referred to specialists and other hospitals when their expertise is required. Proponents of HMOs cite the following advantages:

1. Employee receives all medical care under one roof.
2. Reduction of administrative costs due to limited required paper work.
3. Encourages preventive health care that reduces total medical expenses.
4. Staff is salaried, thus no incentive to order unnecessary services.
5. Facilities are efficiently run because of high use.

Critics argue that:

1. Employees desire freedom of choice in selecting health care providers.
2. The better professionals choose to be in private practice and not be tied to a salary.
3. Overuse by the employee is encouraged since there is little or no dollar participation.

HMOs will continue to be important providers of health care. Current law requires that if there is a certified HMO in the area of the business firm that has not closed its enrollment, employers of 25 or more people *must* offer their employees the option of joining that HMO if the HMO desires to participate.

Blue Cross and Blue Shield Plans

The early days of *Blue Cross and Blue Shield Plans* mark the birth of prepaid health care coverage in America. Originally, Blue Cross plans were formed to cover the cost of hospital care while Blue Shield Plans were established to cover physicians' services. Now, both brands represent the full spectrum of health care coverage. Together, 40 independent Blue Cross and Blue Shield Member Plans make up the Blue Cross and Blue Shield System. One in four Americans is enrolled in a Blue Cross and Blue Shield managed care plan. This system is coordinated by the Blue Cross and Blue Shield Association; however, all Member Plans function as independent, locally operated companies. Blue Cross and Blue Shield Member Plans provide several types of health care coverage including health maintenance organizations (HMOs), preferred provider organizations (PPOs), point of service (POS) programs and fee-for-service coverage.

PENSION PLANS

One of the benefits valued by employees in any organization is a retirement plan. As companies compete more and more aggressively for top quality employees, they are focusing on attractive retirement plans, as drawing cards. Findings from the Summary, "National Compensation Survey: Employee Benefits in the United States," March 2005 (http://www.bls.gov/ncs/ebs/sp/ebsm00.pdf) stated that 21 percent of employees participated in defined benefit retirement plans and 42 percent in defined contribution plans. This explains why almost 40 percent of workers must rely exclusively on Social Security and personal savings to provide income after retirement. Traditional pension plans provide retirement income for the life of the employee at a level that is predetermined by plan design, or is a factor of contributions as a percentage of salary plus investment return. The funds to support the retirement income are accumulated during the employee's working years by either the employer alone, or by a combination of employer and employee contributions. Risk managers use Social Security income as a base upon which to build retirement income equaling 65 to 75 percent of the employee's average last five years annual pay.

Employee Retirement Income Security Act of 1974 *(ERISA)*

Congress passed the *Employee Retirement Income Security Act of 1974 (ERISA)* in response to a growing concern over the viability of private pensions and the discrimination being practiced in areas of eligibility, coverage, vesting, and benefit levels. The primary focus of this act was to establish standards for pension plans that would provide better guarantees and more equal treatment to the employees they covered. Major provisions of ERISA which risk managers need to aware of include:

- Reporting and Disclosure—Employees and beneficiaries must be informed of their benefits and rights. Regular reports must be filed with the Department of Labor, Internal Revenue Service, and the Pension Benefit Guaranty Corporation.
- Plan Participation Rules—An employee, who is at least 21 years of age and has completed one year of service, must be permitted to participate within the next six months. One year of service means 1,000 hours or more of service during a 12-month period.
- *Vesting*—Vesting rights guarantee that an employee gains ownership to all or some portion of employer contributions even if employment terminates before retirement. Prior to ERISA, employees terminated just before their normal retirement date would lose all rights to their retirement income. ERISA requires that vesting provisions must follow one of the following or

any schedule granting vesting more quickly:

1. Cliff vesting—100 percent vesting after five years of service.
2. Graded vesting—20 percent vesting after three years of service, plus 10 percent for each additional year of service up to seven years.

Pension plans in smaller organizations where key employees (generally owners and certain officers) receive more than 60 percent of the plan asset are considered "top heavy" plans and must accelerate vesting. For these plans, the following or any schedule granting vesting more quickly, must be followed:

1. Cliff vesting—100 percent after three years of service, or
2. Graded vesting—20 percent after two years of service and 20 percent for each year thereafter.

Most FBOs and small airports would fall into this "top heavy" category.

Types of Pension Plans

Pension plans which cover a broad class of employees and meet the requirements of the Internal Revenue Code that allows all parties to receive favorable tax treatment are called *qualified pension plans*. There are two major types of qualified pension plans that tend to identify with an organization's management philosophy. Paternalistic firms that provide predictable, secure, and continuing income for their employees in retirement favor *defined benefit plans*. Firms which are aggressive and willing to take risks tend to favor *defined contribution plans* that rely upon investment returns for income adequacy and the actual level of benefit is unknown until retirement starts. Defined benefit plans continue to be the most dominant, but due to the increasing cost of funding retirement income, a high proportion of new pension plans each year are of the defined contribution type. Defined benefit plans specify in dollar amounts what the employee will receive in monthly income starting at age 65, the normal retirement date. Plan provisions do allow early retirement at reduced income levels. The target income level is usually 65 to 75 percent of the employee's average last five years wages. These plans are usually noncontributory, the annual expense is tax deductible by the employer, and tax deferred to the employee. To help reduce the employer costs of funding retirement benefits, the plan will subtract from the target income level the amount of the employee's Social Security retirement benefit. This is called offset integration.

In defined contribution plans, employers make fixed and regular contributions for their employees on a percentage of pay bases. A popular contribution rate is 8 percent of employee gross pay, with a provision that allows employees to match the amount with their own funds. The employer contributions are tax deductible and tax deferred to the employee. Any voluntary contributions paid by the employee are treated as an income reduction. This favorable tax treatment defers income taxes until the dollars are actually received. Some employers prefer this funding method because the level of contributions is fixed, and all inflation and investment risks are shifted to the employee. Retirement planning is more difficult with this type of plan because the actual retirement income received will depend upon growth in wages and investment results.

Both of these plans are *funded*. Dollars are set aside in advance of the date they will be required to pay retirement income. The opposite of a funded plan is a pay-as-you -go plan that is unsatisfactory. There is no security if the employer is not in business when the employee reaches retirement age or is unable to pay out of current operations. ERISA now requires full funding for currently incurred liabilities. Two types of funding agencies are available: trusteed and insurance companies. With trusteed plans, all contributions are held in trust funds that are conservatively invested. At retirement, accumulated funds provide annuities for the employee and if elected, to the spouse. Greater choices are available if an insurance company is used as the funding agency. Group permanent life insurance may be used as a funding vehicle, along with group deferred annuities. Deposit administration plans are becoming more popular because contributions are not assigned to specific employees until retirement. The insurance company guarantees a minimum interest rate. The money is invested at competitive market rates to give employees a higher rate of return. Lump sum distributions are available in some plan designs that allow the employee the freedom of choice between an annuity and a cash settlement. If the employee leaves before retirement, ownership of employer contributions will depend upon the vesting provisions selected by the employer. If the employee dies before retirement, the designated beneficiary will receive the accumulated funds in one lump sum. These pension funds will be subject to income tax unless the beneficiary puts them into an Individual Retirement Account (IRA) within 60 days of receipt.

401(k) Salary Reduction Agreement Plan

401(k) plans are retirement vehicles that allow employees to save for their own retirements. They were named for section 401(k) of the Internal Revenue Code, which permits employees of qualifying companies to set aside tax-deferred funds. By making this change to the Code in 1978, the government opened the door for more efficient retirement planning for a majority of Americans. Not all employers make matching contributions, and those who do contribute at different levels. A typical match might be 25 to 50 percent of employees' contributions up to a certain level. Your contributions to your 401(k) plan are automatically yours to keep, but you may have to be "vested" before you are entitled to your employer's matching contributions. This means having a certain level of service with your company, often three years. Some plans have graduated scales for vesting. For example, you may be 50 percent vested after two years and 100 percent vested after three years. With other plans, you may be entitled to your employer's contributions immediately, without waiting to be vested.

Key limitations imposed by the Internal Revenue Code include:

- The maximum annual salary deferral allowed for any employee as of 2005 was $14,000. This limit is subject to annual cost-of-living adjustments.
- Plans must meet special nondiscrimination deferred tests that are designed to prevent highly paid employees from taking substantially greater advantage of this tax shelter than lower-paid employees take.
- Employees can be required to complete one year of service to participate in the plan.

SIMPLE-IRA

Small businesses like FBOs and privately owned airports can become overwhelmed by high administrative costs and paperwork required with qualified plans. Without adequate resources and staff support, small firms are faced with offering employees no retirement benefits. One viable solution is to offer the SIMPLE-IRA that was created by Congress on January 1, 1997. A *SIMPLE-IRA* is a tax deferred retirement plan provided by employers with fewer than 100 employees who do not maintain or contribute to any other retirement plan. Every eligible employee who meets the requirements of the plan as established by the employer must be offered access to the plan. Eligible employees must include those who have earned at least $5,000 in compensation in the prior two years and who are reasonably expected to receive $5,000 during the coming year. Contributions are made by both the employee and the employer. In a SIMPLE-IRA, contributions and the investment earnings can grow tax-deferred until withdrawal, at which time they are taxed as ordinary income. Annually, the maximum employee pre-tax (reduces taxable income) contribution is $10,000 for 2005 plus any cost-of-living adjustments for later years. Employees age 50 or over can make a catch-up contribution of up to $2,000 for 2005, $2,500 for 2006 and $2,500 plus any cost-of-living adjustments for later years. Employer contribution must be either:

- 100 percent match for all employees (up to 3 percent of employee's total compensation), or
- 2 percent for all eligible contributions.

Participants are always vested immediately. This means that 100 percent of the employer contributions belong to the employee. Generally, 100 percent of the contributions are placed into mutual funds or variable annuities which the employee self direct. Withdrawals from SIMPLE-IRA plans are subject to a 25 percent tax penalty during the first two years if under age 59 1/2; 10 percent after two years and under age 59 ½.

Keogh Plans

Congress passed the Self-Employed Individuals Tax Retirement Act of 1962 so self-employed individuals could have retirement plans with the same tax benefits as qualified pension plans. This act has become better known as the *Keogh Act.* The provisions of this act allow a sole proprietor or an incorporated professional with earned income from personal services conducted in a business or trade to establish a self-employment retirement plan and make tax deferred contributions in a government-approved account that is managed by a financial institution, such as an insurance company, bank or mutual fund. In addition, the income tax on the investment income is also deferred until received. The maximum amount one can contribute to a Keogh depends on whether it is a defined contribution or a defined benefit plan. For 2005, the annual benefit for a defined benefit plan participant cannot exceed the lesser of 100 percent of the participant's average compensation for his or her highest three consecutive years or $170,000. If it is a defined contribution plan, annual contributions and other additions in 2005 (except for earnings) to an account cannot exceed the lesser of 100 percent of the compensation actually paid to the participant or $42,000.

SAVINGS PLANS

Individual Retirement Accounts

A traditional *Individual Retirement Account* (IRA) is a tax-deferred investment and savings account that acts as a personal retirement fund for people with employment income. Earnings grow tax-deferred until withdrawal, at which time they are taxed as ordinary income. These plans have no employer involvement. Prior to 1986, all contributions to IRAs were on an income reduction basis. This deductibility of the $2,000 IRA contribution saved an individual in the 28 percent tax bracket up to $560 in taxes. The Tax Revision Act of 1986 restricted the deductibility of contributions for persons who were covered under a pension plan and or exceeded the total income guidelines. Individuals have the flexibility of making contributions each year in any amount up to $2,000. After 1998, employees with spouses that did not have earned income could establish a spousal IRA and contribute up to $2,000 per year. So a family could save $4,000 per year toward their retirement on a tax preference basis. If less than the maximum is contributed in any year, the deficiency cannot be made up in future years. The law does allow individuals access to their contributions, but there is a 10 percent tax penalty on any funds taken out prior to age 59 ½.

Employees establishing an IRA have complete control over the management of their contributions. Funds can be placed with various financial institutions depend-

Table 14.2 IRA Contribution Limits –Tax Years 2005-2008

Year	Maximum Contribution (under Age 50)	Maximum Contribution (Age 50 and Older)
2005	$ 4,000	$ 4,500
2006	$ 4,000	$ 5,000
2007	$ 4,000	$ 5,000
2008	$ 5,000	$ 6,000

ing upon the employee's investment philosophy and willingness to accept risk. IRAs can be moved from one institution to another when investment changes are desired. A small annual fee is charged by the institution to manage the IRA account.

Congress signed into law in August 1997 the Taxpayer Relief Act that created a new form of IRA called the *Roth IRA.* To most people, the Roth IRA is an improvement over the traditional IRA because even though the contribution is made with after-tax income, all earnings from the IRA are completely tax-free after age 59 ½. To be eligible for the maximum contribution, the annual income limits are $95,000 for single individuals and $150,000 for married individuals filing joint returns. The amount one contributes is reduced gradually and then completely eliminated when your modified adjusted gross income exceeds $110,000 (single) or $160,000 (married filing jointly). Table 14.2 illustrates the current legislation guidelines concerning the maximum annual IRA contributions per taxpayer.

BUSINESS USE OF LIFE INSURANCE

Individual life insurance policies are used to facilitate transfer of ownership at the death of an owner, and to protect the firm from loss of profits when a key person dies. Additional uses of individual policies include helping key employees purchase adequate life insurance protection for their dependents and deferring compensation until the employee retires.

Business Continuation Life Insurance

Small firms use life insurance to fund *cross-purchase agreements*. Under these agreements, each owner agrees that at death his or her share of the business is to be sold to the remaining owners, and the business or the other owners agree to buy a deceased owner's share. A formula to determine the value of an owner's share at death is included in the agreement. Owners buy sufficient life insurance on each other's lives to retire each other's equity in case of death. For example, three stockholders who own equal shares of a $240,000 business would purchase $40,000 of life insurance on each of the other two. If one stockholder dies, the estate of the deceased received $80,000 and the remaining stockholders each have a 50 percent ownership in the corporation. This arrangement benefits all parties. The estate of the deceased receives a fair price for the owner's equity in cash, and the surviving owners have control of the business.

Key Person Insurance

In a small business, the loss of a key person can have major impacts on the future viability of the firm. This potential loss can be transferred by the purchase of *key person insurance*. The business buys a life insurance policy on the life of the employee with the premiums paid by the firm and the firm is the beneficiary. One approach to determining the amount of insurance is to capitalize the profit contribution of the key person. For example, a $100,000 per year profit contribution would be capitalized by three to reflect the length of time required for a new employee to replace the lost profits. In this case, a $300,000 policy would be purchased. Term insurance is often used because the primary purpose of the insurance is death protection. If there is also a need for cash accumulation, then a permanent form of insurance like whole life is purchased. The premiums would not be tax deductible by the business, but the death proceeds would be income tax free.

Split- Dollar Plan of Life Insurance and Deferred Compensation

Split-dollar life insurance is used to recruit and retain top-performing employees. This plan will increase the employee's financial security by increasing death benefits to surviving dependents and providing savings for future use. To illustrate how the plan works, a $100,000 whole life policy is bought on a key person. The annual premium at age 35 is $1,373. The first year, the employee would pay the entire premium. Each year thereafter, the employer would help the employee by paying premiums that equal the increase in cash value. Assuming the cash value for the second year is $500, the employee would only pay $873. The employee's annual cost will continue to drop, and will disappear after 10 to 12 years. Employers may retain control of the cash value and if the employee dies, the death benefit, which goes to the employee's beneficiary, is reduced by the accumulated cash value. In this case, the employer is treating premium contributions as a loan to the employee. Some employers will use the cash value to fund a *deferred compensation plan*. If this is done, the employer's premium payments are not taxed to the employee. At retirement, all proceeds paid to the employee would be fully taxed.

KEY TERMS

Employee benefit plans
Noncontributory plans
Contributory plans
Group term insurance
Whole life insurance
Straight life insurance
Universal life insurance
Group temporary disability income insurance
Group long-term disability insurance (LTD)
Group medical care insurance
Consolidated Omnibus Budget Reconciliation Act (COBRA)
Health Maintenance Organizations (HMOs)
Blue Cross and Blue Shield Plans
Employee Retirement Income Security Act of 1974 (ERISA)
Vesting
Qualified pension plans
Defined benefit plans
Defined contribution plans
Funded
401(k) plans
SIMPLE-IRA
Keogh Act
Individual Retirement Account (IRA)
Roth IRA
Cross-purchase agreements
Key person insurance
Split-dollar life insurance
Deferred compensation plan

REVIEW QUESTIONS

1. Describe the major reasons for the growth in employee benefits.
2. Explain how underwriting is different for group insurance when compared with individual insurance.
3. Why is one-year renewable term the most popular type of life insurance for insuring employee groups?
4. Describe temporary disability and long -term disability and explain why one of them is a candidate for risk retention.
5. Explain the major components of a comprehensive medical plan, and state the rationale for deductibles and coinsurance clauses.
6. State the major advantages and disadvantages of HMOs.
7. Define vesting and state the two vesting provisions in ERISA, which apply to "top heavy" plans.
8. Differentiate between defined contribution and defined benefit pension plans.
9. Explain the advantages to the employer of a 401(k) retirement plan.
10. Briefly describe the following savings plans designed for the self-employed and

or small businesses: SIMPLE-IRA plans and Keogh plans.

11. Identify the major advantages of using the Roth IRA rather than the traditional IRA.
12. Describe the three principal business uses of life insurance.

REFERENCES

[1]U.S. Department of Labor, Bureau of Labor Statistics, "Employee Compensation-September 2004." USDL,: Press release 04-2490, December 15, 2004, www.bls.gov/ncs/ect/home.htm

[2] "Trends to watch in'06: "Future of health, pension benefits looks cloudy." Boselovid, Len and Christopher Snowbeck. December 29, 2005. www.post-gazette.com/pg/05363/629210.stm

McCaffery, Robert M. *Employee Benefit Programs: A Total Compensation Perspective*. PWS Kent Publishing Company, Boston, Massachusetts, 1988.

Williams, C. Arthur, Jr., Peter C. Young and Michael L. Smith. *Risk Management and Insurance* (8th ed.). McGraw-Hill Book Company, New York, 1997.

Glossary

This glossary includes all key terms appearing at the end of the chapters, as well as many others in the text of significance in the insurance and the legal professions. The definitions are meant to be brief and straight forward rather than technically precise and all inclusive.

Abandonment: The relinquishing of a thing or a property without necessarily designating who shall take possession of it.

Absolute Liability: A doctrine that states certain persons are to be held liable for damages, regardless of whether fault or negligence can be proved against them.

Accident: An unexpected, unforeseen event. It may be a mishap or fortuitous occurrence.

Accident, Pure: An accident caused by an unavoidable event. In other words, no party to the accident was negligent or at fault.

Accident, Unavoidable: An accident that could not have been avoided despite all parties having exercised due care and diligence.

Accidental Death Benefit: The benefit (amount of insurance settlement) paid to an insured's surviving heirs following death from an accident.

Accommodation Line: The writing of an insurance contract that normally would not have been acceptable to the insurer. Such coverage is usually issued as an accommodation to the insured in view of the company's desire to obtain additional new business from the insured at some future date.

ACE USA International & Specialty Aerospace: Focuses primarily on underwriting airports, special risks, and sattelites. ACE USA is a member of USAIG where it participates in a broad range of aviation products.

Action: A legal action; a proceeding in a court in which a plaintiff claims against a defendant; a prosecution in a court by one party against another.

Active Risk Retention: The risk has been identified and measured and a decision made to absorb any losses out of the company resources or self-insurance.

Act of God: A happening resulting purely from nature, without the interference or participation of humans.

Actual Cash Value: Regarding property, actual cash value is replacement cost new less observed depreciation. The objective is repayment for the real loss sustained by the insured. The computed amount may be "book value" or "market value," but often is not.

Additional Insured: A person or persons other than the original named insured, who are protected under the terms of a policy.

Adjacent fields' coverage; Provides coverage for chemical drift onto crops owned by the same farmer the applicator is contracted to spray for.

Adjudication: The determination of issues in a lawsuit; the judgment of a court, settling a matter deliberately and finally.

Adjuster: The individual who acts as a representative of the insurance company when settling claims with the insured or third parties who may believe that they have cause for filing a claim.

Administrative Law: Rules and regulations developed by governmental agencies such as the FAA who have been given the authority to interpret legislation which they enforce.

Admitted Liability: *See* Guest Voluntary Settlement.

Adverse Selection: The inclination of poor insurance risks to purchase more insurance coverage versus those considered better risks. The term also refers to the tendency of some insureds to attempt to take advantage of favorable options in their policies.

Advertising Injury Liability: Provides coverage for such offenses as oral or written publication of material that slanders or libels a person or organization or its products or services or infringes on the right to privacy.

Aerial Application: Those activities that involve the discharge of materials from aircraft in flight for food and fiber production and health control.

Aerospace Industries Association (AIA): An industry organization representing aviation/aerospace manufacturers.
Affirmative Warranty: A guarantee of accuracy of some statement or condition.
Agency System: A marketing system whereby most capital stock and many mutual insurers accept business from authorized, independent agents who may represent several different companies simultaneously.
Agent: An individual authorized by a principal (insurance company), or an individual who acts on behalf of others regarding their business affairs. Most agents secure, negotiate, and service insurance contracts as an employee or representative of a company or companies.
Aggregate Deductible: Applies to all losses during a specified period of time, such as a calendar year.
Aggregate Policy Limit: The maximum amount an insurance company will pay under the terms of a policy during the term covered by that policy.
Agreed Value Coverage: The insurer waives the requirement that the insured must maintain a certain percentage of value. The amount shown on the declaration page is considered full value.
AIG Aviation, Inc.: Headquarters in Atlanta, AIG is part of the American International Croup of companies. It underwrites all classes of aviation business but primarily is a market for general aviation aircraft.
Aircraft: The aircraft or rotorcraft described in the declarations including the propulsion system and equipment usually installed in the aircraft, such as operating, navigating, or radio equipment.
Aircraft Liability Insurance: This form of coverage protects the insured from claims fort bodily injury or death by members of the public, and passengers if included under the terms of the insurance. This kind of insurance is normally written with limits per injured person, and another limit per occurrence. Other policies may be issued with a combined single limit, or total aggregate amount with no limit per person, or for each passenger. Protection against loss from claims filed by any third party for damage to property, including the use of that property is a part of this coverage.
Aircraft Non-Ownership Liability: Coverage that protects the exposure from use of aircraft not owned by or regularly provided to the named insured.
Airline: Refers to that class of business involving the operation of major, national, and regional air carriers.
Airline Classifications: Refers to the legacy air carriers, the newer airlines primarily operating narrow-body aircraft and having a more regional focus, regional airlines operating shorter routes and serving as feeders to the major carriers, charter carriers, and cargo airlines.
Airline Pricing: Those factors taken into consideration in determining premiums to be charged. They include the individual and combined fleet value of hulls at risk and the liability limit, including the exposure of that limit to maximum probable loss (MPL).
Airline Risk Selection: Those factors that underwriters consider in selecting airline risks. The most important are the carriers' management philosophy and success, including profitability, capital structure, and business plan.
Airport Premises Liability: Designed to protect the owner or operator of an airport against losses arising out of use of the airport.
Air Taxi and Charter Operators: Nonscheduled air carriers operating on- demand commercial service for passengers and cargo shippers.
Airway Bill of Lading (AWB): A written contract setting forth the terms and conditions for the shipment of cargo.
Aleatory Contracts: Contracts in which a person may receive back a greater amount of money than he or she has put into the transaction.
All Risk Policy: A commercial property policy which covers all perils not otherwise excluded.
All Risks Ground and Flight: *See* Insurance (All Risk).
All Risks Not in Flight: *See* Insurance (All Risk).
All Risks Not in Motion: *See* Insurance (All Risk).
Annuitant: The person to whom an annuity is payable, usually the person to receive the annuity.
Annuity: A contract that provides a periodic income at regular intervals for a specified period of time, such as for a number of years or for life.
Apparent Authority: The authority that the public believes the agent to possess, and which he or she may or may not actually possess.
Appeal: The request for a review by a higher court of a verdict, or decision made by a lower court.
Appellant: The party who appeals a case from a lower court to a higher one.
Appellee: The respondent; the party against whom an appeal is taken.

Application: A request; a statement signed by a person(s) applying for insurance. From this information, the company is able to decide the degree of risk, the acceptability of the applicant, and the amount of premium required for the risk.

Appraisal: An evaluation of the worth of a property (an aircraft and its equipment). An assessment of the extent of damage or loss resulting from an accident or theft, sometimes determined; should a disagreement occur, by independent experts.

Appraisal Condition: A policy provision that provides for appraisal by an independent professional should a disagreement develop concerning the relative value of a loss.

Assault: Threatened battery. An attempt at or a physical threat of violence to another.

Assignment: The legal transfer of one person's interest in an insurance policy to another person. An assignment may be absolute, in which case all rights are transferred and may not be reacquired except by action of the assignee, or collateral, in which case the assignment is only for the purpose of covering an indebtedness and rights are restored to the assignor when the debt is satisfied.

Associated Aviation Underwriters (AAU): Formed in 1929, AAU wrote all classes of aviation insurance business including the major air carriers, airports and manufacturers. *See* Global Aerospace.

Assumed Liability: A party, who by contract agrees to be responsible for loss or damage whether or not the liability is one that is imposed by law.

Assumption of Risk: The risk a worker assumes by accepting a particular job; normal risks associated with the job, even though hazardous. It also can be used as a defense in a negligence suit in which the defendant argues that the plaintiff either expressly or by implication assumed the risk. (For example, tying down one's own aircraft.)

Assurance: *See* Insurance.

Assured: *See* Insured.

Attractive Nuisance Doctrine: A principle stating that people who have on their premises something that is attractive to children, but which also has inherent dangers connected with it, are expected to take reasonable care that no harm come to said children should they trespass or utilize the attractive nuisance.

Automatic Reinstatement: A policy provision which automatically restores the prior insured value of an aircraft after completion of repairs.

Avemco Insurance Company: A direct-writing company that focuses primarily on general aviation aircraft operated by individuals and businesses including FBOs. Acquired in 1997 by HCC Insurance Holdings, Inc.

Aviation/Aerospace Manufacturers: Includes those companies engaged in research, development, and manufacture of aerospace systems, including manned and unmanned aircraft; space-launch vehicles and spacecraft; propulsion, guidance, and control units for all of the foregoing; and a variety of airborne and ground-based equipment.

Aviation Disaster Family Assistance Act of 1996: This act delineates the responsibilities of the National Transportation Safety Board (NTSB), other governmental agencies, and the airlines in the event of an aircraft accident resulting in major loss of life.

Aviation Insurance: Insurance which covers the hazards associated with aviation.

Aviation Insurance Association (AIA): An organization of underwriters, brokers, agents and lawyers engaged in aviation insurance. Based in Kansas City, MO.

Bailee: A person (or organization) to whom goods are delivered to be held in trust.

Bailment: The giving of personal property by one person to another in trust. Usually the property is held until a contract is fulfilled.

Bailor: Someone who delivers goods (bails) to another (bailee). He or she may or may not own the goods.

Battery: Unlawfully striking or touching another person.

Beneficiary: The person named in the policy to receive the insurance proceeds at the death of the insured. The first person named is the primary beneficiary, subsequent persons are contingent beneficiaries. If the beneficiary designation may be changed, it is revocable; if it may not be changed, the designation is irrevocable.

Benefits: The monies to be paid under the terms of a policy by an insurance company.

Best's Insurance Reports: ***Property-Liability***: An annual publication that rates insurance companies based on underwriting results, management efficiency, adequacy of reserves, and soundness of investments.

Bilateral Contract: An ordinary commercial contract in which a promise by one party is given in return for the promise of another.

Binder: A temporary insurance contract entered into while the actual policy is being written. The terms of such a binder are the same as those in the final policy.

Blanket Insurance: One amount of insurance covers all property located at multiple locations.

Blue Cross and Blue Shield Plans: Blue Cross and Blue Shield managed care plans provide medical care coverage to one out of every seven Americans. The system consists of 53 independent organizations that function as locally operated companies.

Bodily Injury: Injury to the body of a person including sickness, disease or death.

Bodily Injury Liability: *See* Liability Insurance, Bodily Injury.

Bond: An obligation; a written document that states a certain amount of money is owed and will be paid on a certain date.

Bond, Appeal: Money that must be set aside by the party making an appeal; should the appeal to a higher court fail, the monies go to pay costs and damages of the unsuccessful appeal.

Bond, Bail: The posting of a bond to release an individual who is being held in legal custody. The bond assures the court that the accused will appear at the proper time to answer charges against him.

Bond, Blanket: A broad form fidelity bond that does not require employees or positions to be separately listed.

Bond, Fidelity: Protects employers from loss caused by dishonest acts of employees.

Bond, Surety: Guarantees the performance of the principal, in most cases an independent contractor. Often referred to as a performance bond.

Book Value: The purchase price of an asset less accumulated depreciation.

Bound: Being controlled by an obligation; an applicant is bound by the insuring company as an insured when a binder is issued to implement coverage.

Breach of Contract: One party to a contract refuses to fulfill part of the bargain.

Breach of Warranty (Lienholder's Interest): Provides physical damage (hull) coverage by endorsement for a lender in the event that the insured invalidates or breaches the contract and the company would otherwise not be obligated to pay.

British Aviation Insurance Group (BAIG): One of the world's oldest aviation insurers, which traces its roots back to 1924, joined the former Associate Aviation Underwriters in 2001 to form Global Aerospace.

Broker: A broker represents the insured in placing insurance with insurance companies. Though he represents the insured, he is paid a commission by the insurance company. He is legally responsible for the collection of premiums and the delivery of policies to the insured.

Burden of Proof: The duty of establishing the truth of a contention in a lawsuit. Normally, this burden lies upon the plaintiff or prosecutor who has instituted the action.

Burglary: Taking property from inside the premises by a person unlawfully entering or leaving the premises as evidenced by marks of forcible entry or exit.

Business and Pleasure: Any personal, pleasure, family or business use of an aircraft excluding any operation for which a charge is made.

Business Auto Policy: An auto policy designed to protect a business firm against loss or damage to owned or leased automobiles, trucks, and specialty vehicles, and for damages for bodily injury and property damage of others that an insured becomes legally obligated to pay.

Business Interruption Insurance: Indemnifies a business for losses during the time the business is unable to operate while the property is being repaired or replaced.

Business Life Insurance: Life insurance purchased by a business enterprise on the life of a member of the firm. It is often bought by a partnership to protect the surviving partners against loss caused by the death of a partner, or by a corporation to reimburse it for loss caused by the death of a key person.

Cancellation: A stipulation in property and liability contracts that gives the insurer or the insured the right to cancel the policy before its expiration date. Premium adjustments, if any, which are to be made in the event of cancellation are usually delineated in the contract of insurance.

Cancellation, Flat: The termination of an insurance contract preceding its actual inception or effective date. Should a flat cancellation occur, there is no premium charged against the applicant.

Cancellation, Pro rata: The cancellation of an insurance contract, usually at the request of the insurer, prior to its expiration. The insured normally receives a refund of that portion of the premium coinciding with the percentage of the unexpired term of the policy.

Cancellation, Short-rate: At the request of the insured, cancellation of a policy prior to its expiration will involve a return to the insured, of less than the proportion of the premium that would have been refunded under the pro rata procedure.

Care, Ordinary: The degree of diligence one must exercise in order to avoid injury or damage to others. The exercise of less than ordinary care may lead to a charge of negligence.

Cargo Insurance: Insurance against the loss of or damage to cargo carried on aircraft (or other means of transportation).

Cargo Legal Liability Endorsement: Covers the insured carrier or bailee for injury or destruction to tangible property of others.

Cash Surrender Value: The amount available in cash upon voluntary termination of a policy by its owner before it becomes payable by death or maturity.

Casualty Insurance: Protection for a loss or damage occasioned by an accident. It often pays medical expenses, loss of time from work, and most important compensation for suffering and physical injuries.

Catastrophe Loss: A major disaster; something greater than the normal casualty.

Causal Connection: Refers to the direct cause of the loss. Some courts have held that a misrepresentation such as an expired medical certificate cannot void coverage by an insurance company because there was no causal connection with the loss.

Cause, Probable: A reasonable cause, one that has a good chance of being true; a good ground for suspicion that a crime has been committed.

Cause of Action: The legal basis for a lawsuit by one person against another.

Ceding Company: In reinsurance to denote the primary company who cedes a portion of the risk to a reinsurer.

Certified Aviation Insurance Professional (CAIP): A professional designation for individuals who complete a series of courses and a national exam covering aviation insurance.

Chance of Loss: The long-run relative frequency of a loss.

Charter: Commercial use of an aircraft for which a charge is made or compensation (consideration) in some form is received by the insured, while either carrying passengers and/or cargo, or performing some other service under a written or oral agreement (contract).

Chartered Life Underwriter (CLU): A professional designation for individuals who have passed 10 examinations covering all aspects of life, health, and accident insurance.

Chartered Property and Casualty Underwriter (CPCU): A professional designation for individuals who have passed 10 examinations covering all aspects of property and casualty insurance.

Civil Law: (1) Written Law. (2) Law prevailing as the result of acts or statutes. (3) Law dealing with civil rather than criminal matters. Also known as municipal law in contrast to common law which has a universal application.

Civil Liability: A sum of money assessed against a defendant. It may be single, double, or triple the original amount of the actual damages.

Civil Wrong: A wrong against a specific person that constitutes an invasion of the rights of this third party. Civil wrongs are divided into two types: torts and breach of contract.

Claim: A demand for property or money, or its equivalent; an assertion that one is entitled to something or that one owns something.

Claimant: Someone who asserts a right; a person making a claim.

Clause, Deductible: Policy conditions that state what amount the insured will pay in the event of a loss, before the insurance company agrees to pay for costs in excess of that amount.

Clause, Omnibus: A policy clause which provides coverage to others than the named insured, if certain requirements are complied with as stated in the insurance contract.

Coinsurance: Two or more policies issued by different insurance companies covering the same risk. Also, a sharing of a risk by the insurer and the insured on a percentage basis.

Coinsurance Clause: A provision that requires an insured to maintain insurance equal to some selected percentage of value, normally 80 or 90 percent of actual cash value or replacement value of the property.

Collision: The upset or collision with another object by an automobile.

Commercial Use: Use of an aircraft for which a charge is made while providing instruction, rental, charter, or other services.

Commissions: Monies paid to an agent or broker for his services. Such monies are usually a percentage of the total amounts involved in the transaction.

Common Carriers: Companies engaged in the transport of goods for the public according to regular time schedules, defined routes, and for established rates.

Common Law: Referred to as "unwritten law" and as "judge-made law," since it consists of the great body of past court decisions.

Comparative Negligence: *See* Negligence, Comparative.

Compensatory damages: These damages represent the combined total of monetary losses that can be inferred from the facts and circumstances of the case.

Completed Operations: In products liability, used to describe aircraft repairs and servicing, including installation of parts and accessories.

Component Parts Schedule: An endorsement on policies covering older aircraft that limits the company's liability for each specified part of the aircraft to a stipulated percentage of the total value in the event of a total loss.

Comprehensive Chemical Drift (CC): It includes coverage for all crop protection products appropriately labeled for application by air.

Comprehensive Major Medical Insurance: A policy designed to give the protection offered by both a basic and a major medical health insurance policy. It is characterized by a low deductible amount, a coinsurance feature and high maximum benefits.

Concealment: The active suppression of facts, or a neglect to disclose facts that a person knows and is duty-bound to communicate.

Conditional Contract: The promise of one party is conditioned upon the act of another. For example, the promise by an insurance company to cover an insured provided the insured fulfills the requirements of the policy, including paying the premium.

Conditions: Provisions of a policy which, along with the Insuring Agreements and Exclusions, complete a contract for insurance.

Configuration: Whether the aircraft has conventional landing gear or tricycle landing gear.

Consequential Loss: A loss caused only indirectly by a risk against which insurance is in force. For example, losses to power company customers as a result of downed lines. *See also* Indirect Loss.

Consideration: One of the legal requirements for most contracts to be completed. The consideration provided by the insurance company is its series of promises under the policy. The consideration provided by the insured is the application and the initial premium.

Consolidated Omnibus Budget Reconciliation Act (COBRA): Requires employers with 20 or more employees who terminate to continue their medical coverage by paying 102 percent of the group premium. The length of COBRA coverage is between 18 and 36 months.

Constructive Total Loss: A situation in which the repair of property (the aircraft) would be equal to or greater in cost than replacement.

Contingent Business Interruption Insurance: Covers business losses which are caused by an important supplier's or customer's plant being damaged or destroyed by fire or other peril.

Continuous Bond: This bond is used by companies that import on a regular basis.

Contract: An agreement between two or more people, one party (or parties) agreeing to perform certain acts, the other party (or parties) agreeing to pay for or give other consideration for said performance. A contract places an obligation on one party to do something and an obligation upon the other party to reward the doer.

Contract Carriers: Companies that do not offer their services to the public at large but operate under a contract with individual shippers.

Contract of Adhesion: Any ambiguities in policy wording are held in favor of the insured because the company prepared the contract.

Contractual Authority: The authority given an agent by the insurance company under a contract.

Contractual Liability: A contractual obligation to pay damages for which another is legally liable.

Contractual Transfer: A risk handling technique that uses contractual agreements to shift the loss exposure associated with an asset or activity from one firm to another.

Contribute-to-the-Loss Standard: When their standard is involved in breach of warranty suits, insureds can be denied coverage only when there was a causal relationship between the breach and the accident.

Contributory Negligence: This means both parties contributed to an accident by their negligence. *See* Negligence, Contributory.

Contributory Plan: A type of group insurance plan in which the employee shares the cost of the coverage.

Conventional Landing Gear: The two main wheels are mounted forward of the center of gravity with the balancing wheel in the rear. The aircraft sits with a nose high altitude while on the ground.

Conversion: (1) The taking of another's property without permission or cause. (2) To change or transform the use of property in a secretive manner without the knowledge of the legal owner.

Convertible Term Insurance: Term insurance which can be exchanged, at the option of the policyholder and without evidence of insurability, for another plan of insurance, most frequently permanent insurance.

Cost Control Program: An aggressive approach by risk managers to reduce the severity and frequency of workers' compensation claims through improved communications, motivation, safety programs, and personnel practices.

Coverage: The scope of insurance provided under the terms of the Declarations, Insuring Agreements, Exclusions, and Conditions of the policy.

Credit Life Insurance: Term life insurance issued through a lender or lending agency to cover payment of a loan, installment purchase, or other obligation, in case of death.

Crew Member: A person assigned to perform duty in an aircraft during flight time.

Crime Insurance: Covers the insured for the loss of property due to the wrongful taking by someone else.

Criminal Act: A crime against society and the perpetrator can be punished by the state, for example, arson or theft.

Crops Being Treated: Protects the named insured when the operator causes damage to a crop that the operator is intentionally spraying.

Cross-purchase Agreements: Each owner of a business agrees that his or her share of the business is to be sold to the remaining owners, and the business or the other owners agree to buy a deceased owner's share.

Customs Bonds: This type of bond is required by the U.S. Customs Service (Title 19 USC Section 1623) as a means to ensure that importers guarantee payment in the event that liquidated damages are assessed against a shipment imported into this country.

Damages: Compensation that the law awards to someone who has been injured or has suffered a loss because of the action of another.

Damages, Actual: Money awarded to a complainant equal to his actual loss or injury as distinguished from punitive damages which are awarded in excess of the actual damages.

Damages, Compensatory: The precise loss suffered by a plaintiff, as distinguished from punitive damages, which are over and above the actual losses sustained.

Damages, Consequential: Loss or injury that results indirectly.

Damages, Punitive: Damages in excess of the actual loss that has already occurred. Punitive damages are usually ordered as a punishment to the defendant for poor or bad conduct that caused the damage.

Declarations Page: Statements that present information about the risk to be insured. Items such as policy period, amounts and types of coverage, and a description of the insured property.

Deductible: Amount of expense to be paid by the insured after a loss, and prior to or in conjunction with payment of any policy benefits.

Defamation: Actions which injure a person's reputation. Defamatory acts may be either libel (written) or slander (oral).

Deferred Compensation Plan: The employer's premium payments are not taxed to the employee. Upon retirement, all proceeds paid to the employee would be fully taxed.

Defined Benefit Plans: Provides a predictable, secure, and continuing income for employees in retirement.

Defined Contribution Plan: A pension plan that relies on investment returns for income adequacy and the actual level of benefit is unknown until retirement begins.

Definitions: Important terms used in the policy and found under a separate section.

Degree of Risk: The likelihood of an occurrence; the accuracy with which losses can be predicted.

Depreciation: In relation to a fixed asset, depreciation is defined as the inevitable decrease in value resulting from wear, tear, and the lapse of time.

Direct Loss: Physical loss or damage to an object that is not foreseen.

Direct Writing Companies: Insurance companies that offer their coverage through employed service representatives or captive agents, who represent their interests exclusively.

Disability: (1) The state of being legally incapable of performing an act; a lack of competence or power to perform. (2) An injury or illness which incapacitates one from carrying out his usual duties. Such disability may be physical or mental, total or partial, temporary or permanent.

Disability, Partial: The inability to perform one's normal duties, or the partial loss of earning power.

Disability, Permanent: Disability which is expected to continue for the lifetime of the person involved. Can be included as part of the guest voluntary settlement coverage.

Disability, Temporary: Disability from which a person is expected to recover.

Disability, Total: A condition resulting in the inability to perform one's duties or occupation, creating a total loss of earning power.

Disability Benefit: A feature added to some life insurance policies providing for waiver of premium, and sometimes for payment of monthly income, if the policyholder becomes totally and permanently disabled.

Disability Income Insurance: A form of health insurance that provides periodic payments to replace income when an insured person is unable to work as a result of illness, injury or disease.

Disappearing Deductible: Combines the franchise and straight deductibles. No losses are paid under a certain minimum. Once the minimum is exceeded, the insured receives a percentage of the amount by which the loss exceeds the minimum amount. Once the loss exceeds a stated amount, the insurer pays the entire amount.

Dismemberment: Loss of body members (limbs), or use thereof, or loss of sight due to injury.

Dynamic Risks: Risks that are associated with changes, especially changes in human wants and improvements due to technology.

Earned Premium: That portion of a premium for which the policy protection has already been given during the now-expired portion of the policy term.

Earthquake Insurance: Protects the insured from losses resulting directly from damage caused by earth movement.

Effective Date: The date on which an insurance contract takes effect, and from which coverage under the policy is in force.

Electronic Data Processing Coverage: Provides coverage for electrical and magnetic injury, mechanical break down, and temperature and humidity changes.

Eligible Employees: Those members of a group who have met the eligibility requirements under a group life or health insurance plan.

Embezzlement: The fraudulent appropriation of money or goods by one to whom they have been entrusted.

Employee Benefit Plans: Any type of plan, sponsored or started unilaterally or jointly by employers and employees, which provides benefits that stem from the employment relationship and is not underwritten or paid directly by government.

Employers' Liability Insuring Agreement: A part of the workers' compensation policy which is designed to cover the liability of the employer to workers who can sue their employers under certain conditions such as gross negligence on the part of the employer.

Employment Retirement Income Security Act of 1974 (ERISA): Establishes standards for pension plans that provide better guarantees and more equal treatment to the employees they cover.

Encumbrance: A liability that lowers the value of a piece of property, such as a lien or a mortgage.

Endorsements: Amendments or changes, in writing, to an insurance policy, and agreed to by both parties.

Endowment Insurance: Life insurance payable to the policyholder if he is living, on the maturity date stated in the policy, or to a beneficiary if the policyholder dies prior to that date.

Escrow: When two parties make an agreement or contract that will take a certain amount of time to perform, they may agree that the monies to be paid for the performance of the contract shall be held by a third person. Upon completion of the terms of the agreement of contract, the third person turns over the money or property to the person who has fulfilled the contract.

Estoppel: Being prevented, or "stopped" from denying the existence of coverage, or a contract under certain circum stances. For example, after a company allows an agent to write business he is not authorized to write.

Excess Aggregate Insurance: Provides coverage up to an aggregate amount for all losses over a stated amount for the policy year. The insured must pay all liability claims until the specified amount is reached.

Excess Liability Insurance: Additional limits of liability above a specific amount up to a specified limit; for example, $20 million excess of $20 million.

Excess of Loss Reinsurance: An arrangement whereby a reinsurer becomes liable to pay only when the losses incurred by the ceding company exceed some predetermine figure.

Excluding Chemical Drift (XC): Only offers aircraft liability coverages for agricultural aircraft. Some policies include liability coverage for the application of fertilizers and seeds under the XC coverage

Exclusions: Certain clauses in a policy that specify situations or special conditions in which insurance coverage would be invalidated.
Exclusive Dry Lease: An arrangement whereby the lessor normally provides only the aircraft. The lessee is responsible for the maintenance, crew, fuel and so forth.
Expense Ratio: The ratio of underwriting expenses (including commissions) to net premiums written, expressed as a percent. This ratio measures the company's operational efficiency in underwriting its book of business.
Experience Rating Systems: A modification from the manual rates for firms who belong to a group to reflect their past claim experience in determining their premium for the current policy.
Experimental Airworthiness Certificate: Is issued to owners of these aircraft to designate that they do not have a type certificate or do not conform to its type certificate and is in a condition for safe operation.
Expiration Date: The date on which an insurance policy terminates, unless it has been renewed by the insured.
Express Warranty: *See* Warranty, Expressed.
Extended Term Insurance: A form of insurance available as a non-forfeiture option. It provides the original amount of insurance for a limited period of time.
Extra Expense Insurance: Is an alternative method of protecting a firm from the losses incurred as a result of a covered direct loss. Examples include the cost of moving to temporary quarters or the cost of renting these quarters and necessary equipment.
Facultative Reinsurance: An agreement between the ceding company and the reinsurer, in which the reinsurer becomes involved in underwriting the risk, and reserves the right to accept or reject before coverage is granted.
False Arrest, Detention: The unprivileged restriction of another's freedom of movement.
Federal Employment Compensation Act: Provides workers' compensation for nonmilitary federal employees.
Federal Tort Claims Act: A law passed by the federal government which gives Federal District Courts the authority to hear claims for damages against the United States.
Fellow Servant Rule: An employer's defense in a workers' compensation claim in which injuries were caused by a fellow worker.
Fiduciary: One who holds a position of trust and has rights and powers which he or she must exercise for the benefit of others.
Financial Responsibility Laws: Laws structured to make it impossible for the reckless and financially irresponsible operator (one who has become involved in an accident) of a conveyance (transport vehicle) to secure an operator's license unless there is a guarantee that he is able to pay, and will pay, within the limits established by the statutes, damages for which he becomes liable.
Fire Insurance: This coverage provides indemnity for loss or damage to property (an aircraft) that is caused by fire, fire resulting from explosion or lightning, and windstorm damage.
Fire Legal Liability Insurance: Protects an insured that leases a building but does not have an insurable interest in the property except for legal liability.
Fixed Base Operators: Airport-based commercial operators who provide some or all of the following activities: line services, aircraft and engine maintenance, sale of parts and accessories, aircraft sales, charter and rental of aircraft, corporate flight services and flight training.
Fleet: A group of aircraft usually insured under one policy, and commonly owned by the same individual or company.
Floater Policy: A policy which covers property in any location within a given territory, such as avionics, regardless of whether in the airplane or in the maintenance shop.
Flying Club: An aircraft owned or operated by three or more individuals. Flying clubs can be incorporated or non-incorporated organizations generally formed for the purpose of operating aircraft at a reasonable cost per capita.
Foreign Sovereign Immunities Act: Passed by Congress in 1976 to resolve the problems inherent in deciding whether to subject a foreign nation to liability in the courts of this country.
Fortuitous Event: An unforeseen event; something happening by chance; an accidental occurrence.

401 (K) Plans: Added to the Internal Revenue Code in 1980 to allow employees to voluntarily save money on a tax favored basis. These employee savings could be matched by the employer up to a specified limit.
Fractional Ownership: Several companies jointly purchase an aircraft to reduce costs. A management company normally provides the crew, maintenance, ground support, insurance, record keeping and overall operation of the aircraft.

Franchise Deductible: Similar to a straight deductible except that once the amount of loss exceeds the franchise deductible, the entire loss is paid in full.

Fraud: An intentional distortion of the truth perpetrated upon someone in order to convince him to give up money, property, or other things rightfully belonging to him; deception; deceit; trickery.

Freight Forwarder: Consolidates small shipments prior to their transfer to a common carrier.

Frequency: A measure of how often a particular type of loss will occur.

Front Companies: Insurance companies that reinsure virtually 100 percent of their business.

Fundamental Risks: Are group risks which are impersonal in origin and effect. They are primarily caused by social, political, or natural occurrences. Examples include war, unemployment, drought, and natural disasters like floods.

Funded: Pension plans are funded when monies are set aside in advance of the date when they will be needed to pay retirement benefits.

General Aviation Manufacturers Association (GAMA): An organization based in Washington, D.C. representing manufacturers of general aviation aircraft, engines, and component parts.

General Aviation Revitalization Act of 1994 (GARA): An 18-year statute of repose that was passed to help revitalize the general aviation manufacturing industry.

General Damages: Include many intangible losses in addition to the loss of financial support such as loss of society, companionship, consortium, love, care and protection.

Global Aerospace: Largest of the multi-company pools, it was formed in 2001 by combining the strengths of the former Associated Aviation Underwriters and British Aviation Insurance Group (BAIG).

Government Contractor Defense: May shield military contractors from liability for design defects when the design is in compliance with the specifications required under a government contract.

Grace Period: A specified period of time following the premium due date during which payment of the premium may be made without penalty or suspension of the coverage. Grace periods are rare in aviation insurance policies.

Graded Premium Plan: A form of whole life insurance where the annual premium increases over a number of years, usually five or ten years.

Grandfather Clause: An exception to a new restriction or new statute which permits those already doing something to continue doing it even though the activity is contrary to the new restriction or statute.

Great American Insurance Companies—Aviation Division: One of the oldest group of companies in the United States. The Aviation Division was formed in 1997 following the acquisition of aviation insurance from the former Aviation Office of America (AOA). The Aviation Division primarily focuses on all classes of general aviation business.

Gross Negligence: *See* Negligence, Gross.

Grounding Coverage: Written in conjunction with manufacturers' product liability to protect the manufacturer in the event that aircraft are grounded by federal authorities.

Group Annuity: A pension plan providing annuities at retirement to a group of people under a master contract. It is usually issued to an employer for the benefit of employees. The individual members of the group hold certificates as evidence of their annuities.

Group Life Insurance: Life insurance usually without medical examination, on a group of people under a master policy. It is typically issued to an employer for the benefit of employees. The individual members of the group hold certificates as evidence of their insurance.

Group Long-Term Disability (LTD): *See* Disability Permanent.

Group Medical Expense Insurance: Provides medical expense coverage to protect employees and their families from extensive hospital, surgical, nursing, and related medical expenses.

Group Temporary Disability Income Insurance: Provides replacement income at a 60 to 10 percent level to an employee who is unable to work due to an accident or illness for a maximum of 13 to 26 weeks. There is normally a one-or two-week waiting period before coverage commences.

Group Term Insurance: Life insurance payable to a beneficiary only when an insured dies within a specified period.

Guaranteed Insurability Option: A provision which may be added to a permanent insurance policy which gives the policy holder the right to purchase additional policies of a limited amount at specified dates in the future without evidence of insurability.

Guest: A person who does not pay for transportation.

Guest Statutes: A law, in some states, prohibiting a guest riding in a friend's vehicle or aircraft from suing that friend if there is an accident. However, the guest can sue if the driver or pilot has shown unusual (gross) negligence.

Guest Voluntary Settlement: Also known as admitted liability coverage. In the event of bodily injury to a passenger, the insurer offers a settlement on a definitely determined basis regardless of whether the insured is legally liable. A release must be obtained from the injured party prior to settlement.

Hail Insurance: Insurance against damage from hail. In aviation, included in all-risk hull insurance.

Hangarkeepers' In flight: Protects the insured hangarkeeper for loss or damage to non-owned aircraft while in-flight and in the hangarkeeper's care, custody, or control.

Hangarkeepers' Liability: A form of bailee insurance that covers the insured hangarkeepers' liability for loss or damage to aircraft which are the property of others and in the insured's custody for storage, repair, or safekeeping.

Hazard: A condition, operation, or activity that has the net effect of increasing the possibility of incurring a loss.

Hazard, Design Induced: A hazard resulting from a peculiarity in the design of an aircraft or other manufactured product.

Hazard, Moral: An individual who is noted for taking unfair advantage of legal technicalities, or who has repudiated contracts in the face of possible financial loss.

Hazard, Morale: An attitude of carelessness and lack of concern that increases the chance of loss occurring.

Hazard, Physical: Location, construction (in the case of a building) and their use such as poor housekeeping can represent physical hazards. An aircraft tied down at an airport located near a high crime area would certainly be subject to theft.

HCC Aviation Insurance Group: A wholly owned subsidiary of HCC Insurance Holdings, Inc. Formed in 1997 after the acquisition of a number of smaller aviation insurers, including Southern Aviation Underwriters, Continental Insurance Underwriters and Signal Aviation Underwriters. Primarily focuses on all classes of general aviation business.

Health Insurance: Protection that provides payment of benefits for covered sickness or injury. Included under this heading are various types of insurance such as accident insurance, disability income insurance, medical expense insurance, and accidental death and dismemberment insurance.

Health Maintenance Organization (HMO): An organization that provides a wide range of comprehensive health care services for a specified group at a fixed periodic payment. The HMO can be sponsored by the government, medical schools, hospitals, employers, labor unions, consumer groups, insurance companies, and/or hospital--medical plans.

Hold-harmless Agreement: An agreement under which the legal liability of one party for damages or injury is assumed by the other party to the agreement. Such hold-harmless agreements between pilots and passengers virtually never stand up in court.

Hull Insurance: Insurance covering the aircraft, including the engine, propeller, and all other systems and equipment permanently attached to the aircraft (though it may be removable for maintenance), including avionics. Hull insurance is usually issued with a deductible clause ranging from $50 to $250. Hull insurance may be written for aircraft on the ground, not in motion; for aircraft on the ground and in motion (meaning under its own power), or for aircraft in flight. When specified as all-risk coverage it covers the aircraft under all circumstances, regardless of the reason for damage or loss.

Imminent Danger: A situation so dangerous and life threatening that one must take immediate action, not awaiting help from others or from authorities.

Impact Rule: A common-law provision which permits a cause of action for the negligent cause of emotional distress only where it is accompanied by some physical injury.

Implied: Intended, but not expressed in words. An implied agreement is one that the parties intend to implement but have not declared in a written document.

Implied Authority: The authority granted an agent by an insurance company in order for the agent to carry out his or her contractual duties and obligations.

Implied Warranty: *See* Warranty, Implied.

Indemnify: To protect and secure against damage or loss; to make good; to compensate for loss.

Indemnity: Insurance against possible loss; replacement, repair or payment of the value represented by the damage to or loss of property.

Indirect Loss: Loss of net income resulting from the inability to use the services of damaged property. Indirect loss, and consequential loss are terms that are interchangeable. *See also* Loss of Use Insurance.

Individual Retirement Account or Annuity (IRA): A qualified retirement plan which permits income tax deductible contributions of a limited amount for retirement purposes.

Industrial Aid: A term that applies to corporate-owned aircraft that are used for the transportation of executives, employees, customers, and guests, which are flown by professional pilots.

Inflation Guard Endorsement: Designed to automatically and continuously increase the limit of insurance for the coverage to which it applies on a quarterly basis.

In Flight: The time commencing with the actual takeoff run of the aircraft and continuing thereafter until it has completed its landing roll.

Ingestion Deductible: A deductible for jet aircraft which applies to damage done to a turbine engine due to the engine sucking up foreign objects.

Injury or Damage: Bodily and other personal injuries, loss of income due to disability, pain and suffering, disfigurement, or any other loss for which negligence is the proximate cause.

Inland Marine Insurance: A diverse and very flexible type of property coverage that includes air cargo.

Inland Transit Policy: Covers the insured for loss or damage to owned personal property while being transported by others.

In Motion: While the aircraft is moving under its own power or the momentum generated therefrom or while it is in flight and, if the aircraft is a rotorcraft, any time that the rotors are rotating.

In-Orbit Coverage: Indemnifies the insured for physical loss of damage to, or failure of the satellite in orbit.

In-Orbit Third Party Liability Coverage: Covers any damage a satellite might cause to another satellite should it lose control.

Insurable Interest: In property insurance an insurable interest is any financial interest based on some legal right in the preservation of the property. An exposure to a financial loss must exist for there to be an insurable interest in the occurrence of some event. In life insurance, it is usually because the insured or a beneficiary has a financial interest in the continued existence of the insured life or the expectancy of loss in the ending of the insured life. It must be present in life insurance before the contract goes into effect.

Insurance: A pooling of hazards in order to indemnify those who experience losses. Also, the contractual relationship between the insurance company and the insured, based on the payment of premiums by the insured and the agreement by the insurance company to indemnify the insured for certain specified losses and to perform such services as the defense of the insured in litigation arising from certain specified occurrences.

Insurance, All Risk: A term used to describe broad forms of coverage in property and liability insurance. An all-risk policy automatically includes all perils (causes of risk) that it does not specifically exclude. Most aviation all- risk hull policies include: (a) all risk while not in motion, (b) all risk except while in flight (including taxi), and (c) all-risk ground coverage extended to include all risk while in flight.

Insurance Carrier: Insurance company.

Insurance Company: A company acting as the insurer. It may, in fact, represent groups of insurance markets.

Insurance Manager: An individual who purchases insurance for his or her firm.

Insured: The party to an insurance contract whom the insurer agrees to indemnify under given conditions.

Insured Value: The amount which is stated in the policy as the insured value. Usually, this amount represents the purchase price of the aircraft, if new, or the current market value, if used.

Insurer: The party to the insurance contract who agrees to pay losses or render certain services.

Insuring Agreements: The part of a policy that describes how the insurance company will protect the policyholder against specific instances of loss or damage.

Intentional Torts: Intentional interference with a person or with property. Examples include battery, assault, mental distress, defamation, false arrest, or detention and trespass.

Interchange Agreement: One company leases its airplane to another company in exchange for equal time, when needed, on the other company's airplane and no charge or assessment is made.

Invitee: A person on the property of another by actual or implied invitation.

Joint Liability: Equal responsibility, so that if one person in a joint enterprise is sued, the other(s) are similarly sued and liable.

Joint Life and Joint Annuities: A life insurance or annuity policy issued on two or more lives.

Joint Ownership: An arrangement whereby one of the registered joint owners of an airplane employs and furnishes the flight crew for that airplane and each of the registered joint owners pays a share of the charges specified in the agreement.

Jurisdiction: The power and right to administer justice; the geographic area in which a judge or a court has the right to try and decide a case.

Keogh Plan: Allows a self-employed person with earned income from personal services conducted in a business or trade to establish a self-employment retirement plan and make tax deferred contributions to the plan. In addition, the income tax on the investment income is also deferred until received.

Key-person Insurance: Insurance that provides adequate compensation for the loss of services by disability or death of a vital employee, and resources with which to secure in a competitive market the services of a successor. Such insurance may be written to pay the employee if disabled, his heirs in the event of death, or his employer.

Last-clear-chance: An exception to the doctrine of contributory negligence. Even though the injured party was negligent, the defendant may be held responsible if he did not take any last clear chance of avoiding an accident.

Launch Risk Guarantee: Provides coverage for a replacement launch in the event the satellite is not placed in the proper orbit, if it is destroyed or is damaged by the launch vehicle.

Law: The rules, regulations, ordinances, and statutes, created by the legislative bodies of governments, under which people are expected to live.

Law of Agency: A relationship based upon an expressed or implied agreement whereby one person, the agent, is authorized to act for another, his principal, to transact business with third parties, the insured.

Law of Large Numbers: A device for reducing risk by combining a sufficient number of homogeneous exposure units to make their individual losses collectively predictable.

Law of Torts: Laws permitting individuals to recover damages for injuries.

Legacy Air Carriers: The major airlines that got started in the 1920s and 1930s and who have survived since the inception of deregulation.

Legal Duty: The duty to act or not. Whether or not a legal duty is owed to someone else is decided by the courts, and many factors may determine the degree of care required. (For example, a bystander has no legal duty to prevent a robbery .)

Legal Liability: The responsibility that two opposing parties in a lawsuit have toward each other, as recognized and enforced by the court.

Legal Reserve: The minimum reserve an insurance company must keep to meet future claims and obligations as they are calculated under the state insurance code.

Liability: A legal responsibility; the obligation to do or not to do something; an obligation to pay a debt; the responsibility to behave in a certain manner.

Liability Insurance: Insurance against the cost arising from the liability of the insured to pay for damage or injury to third parties.

Liability Insurance, Bodily Injury: Insurance to cover the cost stemming from bodily injury or death to persons other than the insured. In aviation, this type of insurance is usually issued with limits per injured person and another limit per occurrence, though other policies are written with a single limit.

Liability Insurance, Property Damage: Insurance against loss due to claims for damage to another's property.

Liability Insuring Agreement: *See* Liability Insurance, Bodily Injury and Property Damage.

License: (1) A right granted by one person (or Company) to another giving permission to the other person to do something that he could not legally do without such permission. (2) Unrestrained conduct. (3) A special privilege, such as a license to pilot an aircraft after having met certain requirements.

Licensee: One who enters upon the premises of another, with the owner's express or implied consent, principally for his own benefit.

Lien: A claim against another's property.

Lien, Mechanic's: The right of maintenance personnel to retain property in their control until services rendered have been paid for in full.

Life Insurance: Insurance providing payment of a specified amount upon the death of the insured to his beneficiaries. Aircraft owners and pilots should examine existing life policies for exclusions related to the use of non-airline aircraft.

Life Insurance in Force: The sum of the face amounts, plus dividend additions, of life insurance policies outstanding at a given time. Additional amounts payable under accidental death or other special provisions are not included.

Limited Commercial Use: Use of an aircraft for which a charge is made while providing instruction and rental services.

Limited Spread of Risks: Refers to the relatively low number of active civil aircraft compared to other lines of insurance such as automobile and homeowner insurance.

Limit of Liability: The maximum limit of liability (damages) that an insurance company assumes or is obligated to pay under the terms of any individual insurance contract.

Line: A kind of insurance or the amount of insurance.

Line Limits: The maximum amount of insurance an insurer will write on any one exposure (risk).

Litigant: A person engaged in a lawsuit.

Litigation: A lawsuit; a legal action; a suit.

Lloyd's Association: An unincorporated group of individuals, who write insurance and proportion liability for their own respective accounts in accordance with an agreement under which all parties of the Association submit.

Lloyd's Brokers: A member of Lloyd's of London who brings risks that have been funneled from all over the world to Lloyd's underwriters (agents).

Lloyd's of London: A corporation that neither underwrites (Subscribes) policies of insurance nor directly issues them itself. Insurance is written by individual "underwriting members" who must be elected to membership within the Lloyd's Association. The actual insurer then is not Lloyd's but instead the various underwriters at Lloyd's. The exchange (Lloyd's) provides underwriting quarters for its members and a place for transaction of insurance business by member underwriters, as well as risk management support services.

Lloyd's Syndicate: An organized group of Lloyd's members which is managed by a single agent (underwriter). The syndicate members furnish the capital; the syndicate agent manages the business of risk-management for the group. Liability is divided among members in accordance with agreed -to proportions for each risk assumed.

Lloyd's Underwriter: A member of Lloyd's of London who underwrites insurance at Lloyd's.

Loan Value: The amount of money which a policyholder may borrow on the sole security of a life insurance policy.

Loss: The decrease or disappearance of value, usually in an unexpected or at least relatively unpredictable manner. An economic loss is the undesirable end result of risk.

Loss Accumulation: The potential of retained risks becoming burdensome lid sufficient number of losses occur during a one year period.

Losses and Loss Adjustment Expenses: This item represents the total reserves for unpaid losses and loss adjustment expenses, including reserves for incurred but not reported losses, in any, and supplemental reserves established by the company. It is the total for all lines of business and all accident years.

Losses Incurred: The amount of loss for which an insurer is liable during a certain allocated period of time. Incurred losses include losses paid, losses incurred but not yet reported, and losses reported but not yet paid. Paid losses include all losses disbursed during that same period.

Losses Outstanding: Unpaid amounts for which the insurance company is liable.

Losses Paid: Amounts which have been paid to the insured or others.

Loss Exposure: The possibility that a particular property or person may suffer loss from a specific peril.

Loss of Consortium: Loss of companionship of a mate.

Loss of License Insurance: An income protection plan which provides coverage for occupational disability to professional pilots in the event they lose their medical certificates, or authority to exercise the privileges of their airman certificates.

Loss of Use: Compensation made to an insured against loss resulting from the inability to use property, such as an aircraft in furtherance of his business.

Loss Other Than Collision: Applies to all automobile physical damage losses except those specifically excluded. For example, losses by falling objects, fire, theft, hail and so forth.

Loss Payable Provision: A clause sometimes contained within a policy that provides payment of a loss for which the insurer is liable to the insured, to someone other than the insured; a third party who has an insurable interest in the property covered under the terms of an insurance contract.

Loss Prevention: An attempt by companies to prevent losses from occurring by reducing hazards.

Loss Ratio: The ratio of incurred losses and loss adjustment expenses to net premiums earned, expressed as a percent. This ratio measures the company's underlying profitability, or loss experience, on its total book of business.

Loss Reduction: A risk management program which seeks to reduce the potential severity of a loss. An example is the installation of a sprinkler system.

Major Air Carriers: A class of certificated air carriers that provide scheduled passenger and cargo service primarily between high-density cities. Included are: Alaska, America West, American, Continental, Delta, DHL Airway, Federal Express, Northwest, Southwest, TWA, United, United Paracel Post and US Airway. Gross revenue must exceed $1 billion.

Major Medical Insurance: Health insurance to finance the expense of major illness and injury, characterized by large benefit maximums ranging up to $250,000 (or with no limit); the insurance, above an initial deductible, reimburses the major part of all charges for hospital, doctor, private nurses, medical appliance, prescribed out-of-hospital treatment, drugs and medicines. The insured person as coinsurer pays the remainder.

Malfeasance: The perpetration of an unlawful act.

Malicious Mischief: Purposeful destruction of another person's property.

Management Company: A aviation company responsible for the crew, maintenance, ground support, insurance, record-keeping and overall operation of the aircraft on behalf of an aircraft owner or several owners.

Master Policy: A policy issued to an employer or trustee, establishing a group insurance plan for designated members of an eligible group.

Master-Servant Rule: In law, it is called *respondeat superior* (Latin), which means that the Master (i.e., employer) is answerable for the actions of his Servant (employee). *See also* Negligence, Imputed; and Vicarious Liability.

Material Fact: (1) A fact that is essential to a case, either to the plaintiff or defendant. (2) The fundamental reason for a contract.

Medicaid: State programs of public assistance to persons regardless of age whose income and resources are insufficient to pay for health care. Title XIX of the Federal Social Security Act provides matching federal funds for financing state Medicaid programs, effective January I, 1966.

Medical Payments Insurance: An insuring clause under which the insurer agrees to pay medical, surgical, hospital, and funeral expenses up to the limit shown in the policy, regardless of the liability of the insured who can be included under this option. Medical payments coverage protects the pilot and crew members as well as passengers.

Medical Payments Insuring Agreement: *See* Medical Payments Insurance.

Medicare: The hospital insurance system and the supplementary medical insurance for the aged created by the 1965 amendments to the Social Security Act and operated under the provisions of the Act.

Mental Distress: Threatening or harassing a person that results in a serious mental affliction such as a nervous breakdown.

Minimum Group: The least number of employees permitted under a state law to effect a group for life insurance coverage. The purpose is to maintain some sort of proper division between individual policy insurance and the group forms.

Minimum Pilot Requirements: The minimum or lowest hourly requirement for pilots operating the insured aircraft.

Misrepresentation: A representation which is untrue. It may be used by the insurance company to void the contract only if the misrepresentation is material.

Montreal Convention: A special amendment to the Warsaw Convention increasing the limit of liability on international flights to $75,000.

Moored Deductible: A deductible which applies while the aircraft is tied in the water.

Moral Hazards: *See* Hazard, Moral.

Morale Hazards: *See* Hazard, Morale.

Morality: The incidence of deaths in a well- defined class of persons. The death rate.

Mortality Table: A statistical table showing the death rate at each age, usually expressed as so many per thousand.

Mortgage Clause: *See* Loss Payable Provision.

Mortgagee: The lender of funds, secured by a mortgage on property.

Mortgagor: The person who borrows money and gives a mortgage on his property as security.

Multiple-line Carrier: An insurance company that writes several kinds of insurance.

Mutual Company: A cooperative corporation in which the customers (insureds) are also the owners. The policy holders also participate in the operations of the company, at least through voting rights, and in the sharing of the company's financial gains or losses. It is organized for the purpose of providing insurance at low cost. There are no stockholders. *See also* Stock Insurance Company.

Named Insured: The actual policyholder who is specifically named in the policy.

Named Perils: A term under which specific causes giving rise to a loss may be classified as hazards.

Named Perils Policy: A policy that specifies the perils covered. The commercial property form offers the Basic Form that lists eleven perils and the Broad Form that lists sixteen perils.

National Association of Insurance Commissioners (NAIC): The association of insurance commissioners of various states formed to promote national uniformity in the regulation of insurance.

Negligence: Failure to do what a reasonable, careful, conscientious person is expected to do; doing something that a reasonable, careful, conscientious person would not do.

Negligence, Comparative: A principle in a suit to recover damages that compares the negligence of the defendant to that of the plaintiff.

Negligence, Concurrent: A situation in which both the plaintiff and the defendant contributed toward the injury for which damages are sought.

Negligence, Contributory: A failure on the part of the plaintiff to exercise ordinary, proper care, thus contributing toward an accident.

Negligence, Degree of: The determination as to whether negligence was slight, moderate, or willful. The more willful and severe the negligence, the greater the penalty potentially imposed.

Negligence, Gross: (1) Failure to act where duty demands that one act. (2) Acting in such a manner that one ignores the safety of others. (3) Willful neglect.

Negligence, Imputed: That negligence for which a person is responsible because the negligent act was committed by someone acting in his behalf and under his direction. See Vicarious Liability.

Negligence Per Se: Violation of a statute or regulation resulting in harm to a plaintiff who is within the class of persons intended to be protected by the statute or regulation.

Net Premium: Is the portion of the premium for which the insurance company is responsible. It does not include the part of the premium that covers expenses, contingencies (commissions paid to agents) or profits. Why not profit? Because net premium is only potential profit at this point. The insurance company does not yet know whether it will be paid with this money or if the insurance company will get to keep it once it becomes earned premium.

Net Premiums Earned: This item represents the adjustment of the net premiums written for the increase or decrease during the year of the liability of the company for unearned premiums. When an insurance company's business is increasing in amount from year to year, the earned premiums will usually be less than the written premiums. With the increased volume, the premiums are considered fully paid at the inception of the policy so that at the end of a calendar period, the company must set up premiums, representing the unexpired terms of the policies. On a decreasing volume, the reverse is true.

Net Premiums Written: This item represents gross premium written, direct and reinsurance assumed, less reinsurance ceded.

Net Underwriting Income: Net premiums earned less incurred losses, loss adjustment expenses, underwriting expenses incurred, and dividends to policyholders.

Nonadmitted Carrier: An insurance company which is not licensed to write in a given state or locality.

Noncancellable Guaranteed Renewable Policy: An individual health/disability insurance policy that the insured person has the right to continue in force until a specified age, such as to age 65, by the timely payment of premiums. During this period, the insurer has no right to unilaterally make any changes in any provision of the policy while it is in force.

Noncontributory Plans: A group insurance plan in which the employer pays the total cost of the benefits.

Nondisabling Injury: An injury that may require medical care, but does not result in loss of working time or income.

Nonforfeiture Option: One of the choices available to the life insurance policyholder if he discontinues premium payments on a policy with a cash value. This may be taken in cash, as extended term insurance or as reduced paid-up insurance.

Non-Owned Hull (Aircraft Damage Liability): Insurance designed for pilots flying rented, borrowed, or club aircraft, or for students flying flight-school aircraft, covering the value of the aircraft.

Non-Ownership Liability: *See* Aircraft Non-ownership Liability.

Nonparticipating Life Insurance: Life insurance on which the premium is calculated to cover as closely as possible the anticipated costs of insurance protection with no dividends payable.

Nuisance: A dangerous or defective condition.

Obligation: Something a person is bound to do or bound not to do; a moral or legal duty.

Occurrence: An accident, including continuous or repeated exposure to conditions, which results in bodily injury or property damage neither expected nor intended from the standpoint of the insured.

Old-Age, Survivors, and Disability Insurance: *See* Social Security

Omnibus Clause: A provision extending coverage to persons other than the named insured(s).

Ordinary Life Insurance: Life insurance usually issued in amounts of $1,000 or more with premiums payable on an annual, semiannual, quarterly or monthly basis. The term also is used to describe the type of permanent whole life insurance where the insured pays the premium for his whole life. Such a policy also is called straight life.

Organized Flying Adjusters: An organization of independent aviation adjusters.

Overinsurance: The aggregate benefits available in a contract of insurance exceed the possible amount of loss to which it is applicable. Overinsurance may give rise to a moral hazard.

Owner: A person who has the legal title to property; a proprietor.

Package Policy: Including multiple coverages into a single policy. For example, the Comprehensive General Liability policy which includes airport liability, hangarkeepers and products liability is a package policy.

Parol (Oral) Evidence Rule: This rule states that in the absence of mistake or fraud, the document that is prepared is presumed to represent the intent of the parties, and no oral evidence will be admissible to contradict its written terms.

Particular Risks: Are personal in origin an effect and tend to arise out of individual occurrences. Examples would include: the loss of income due to death or disability, and the loss of property by such perils as fire, windstorm, theft and vandalism.

Passengers: Persons in, on, or boarding an aircraft for the purpose of riding in it, or alighting from it after a ride, flight or attempted flight.

Passive Risk Retention: When risks are inadvertently retained due to an improperly done risk analysis and/or failure to keep it updated.

Pension Plans, Qualified: There are two major types of qualified pension plans that receive favorable tax treatment under the Internal Revenue Code. They are the defined benefit plan and the defined contribution plan.

Peril: Is the actual cause of a loss such as a fire, windstorm, theft, collision, negligence, crime, premature death and so forth.

Permanent and Total Disability: *See* Disability, Permanent and Total.

Permanent Life Insurance: A phrase used to cover any form of life insurance except term; generally insurance that accrues cash value, such as whole life or universal life.

Permission: Legal consent to perform an act, without such consent the act would be illegal; the license to do something; sufferance.

Personal Contract: The insurance contract is a personal one because it depends on the personal characteristics of the applicant. For this reason the policy cannot be transferred to another without the consent of the company.

Personal Effects Floater: All risk protection for the insured on personal property while traveling or otherwise located away from his residence. Personal property includes securities, jewelry, clothing, money, cameras, etc.

Personal Injury Liability: Liability because of false arrest, libel, slander, or invasion of privacy.

Personal Injury Protection (PIP): A no-fault type of coverage that pays the insured, relatives living in the insured's home, passengers other than family members, and licensed persons who drive the car with the insured's permission for certain accident-related medical expenses regardless of who caused the accident.

Personal Liability: An obligation of a person, as distinguished from an obligation enforceable against property. Also, the personal responsibility of an agent while acting on someone else's behalf.

Personal Property: Movable objects owned by individuals, such as securities, jewelry, furniture, clothing, money, etc. Personal property is also called chattel.

Phoenix Aviation Mangers, Inc.: Founded in 1983, the company is a wholly owned subsidiary of Old Republic International Corporation. Primarily concentrates on general aviation risks. The company acquired the book of business from Southern Marine & Aviation (SMAU) in 1995.

Physical Damage: Direct and accidental physical loss of, or damage to property (an aircraft). The term does not infer loss of use or any residual depreciation in value, if any, after repairs have been made.

Physical Damage Insuring Agreement: Covers the insured automobile for losses caused by collision and loss other than collision such as fire, theft and falling objects.

Physical Hazard: *See* Hazard, Physical

Physical Injury: (1) Damage to one's own body. (2) In reference to property, physical injury exists when something interferes with one's ability to use one's own property.

Pilferage: Stealing, especially taking a portion rather than all that one could take, in order that the theft not be discovered; filching.

Pilot Accident Policy: Covers crew members while flying any aircraft. Benefits provide for loss of life, limb, or sight, as well as total disability. Medical expense can also be included under this coverage.

Policy: *See* Insurance.

Policy Dividend: A refund of part of the premium on a participating life insurance policy reflecting the difference between the premium charged and actual experience. Policy dividends may be paid to the policyholder in cash, used to reduce future premiums, left with the company to accumulate at interest, used to purchase participating paid-up additions, or used to purchase one-year term insurance.

Policyholder: *See* Insured.

Policy Loan: A loan made by a life insurance company from its general funds to a policyholder on the security of the cash value of his or her policy.

Policy Period: The length of time during which an insurance contract is in effect.

Pollution Liability Coverage: Protects the insured for losses from fuel tank leaks or spills.

Portfolio Program: Introduced by the Insurance Services Offices (ISO), this program is designed to eliminate the redundancy in coverage provisions and to incorporate updated, simplified language.

Possession: Exclusive control and occupancy of property; the right to live on and enjoy, without interference, land or other property.

Post Selection: Deciding whether or not to get rid of undesirable insureds.

Power of Attorney: (1) A written document stating that one appoints another to act on his behalf as an agent, giving him the authority to carry out certain specified acts. (2) A written document giving an attorney the authority to appear in court on someone's behalf.

Pre-Launch and Manufacturers' Coverage: Indemnifies the insured for loss or damage to the sset during manufacture, testing, shipping and integration with the launch vehicle.

Premium: The amount of money (consideration) that is decided upon by the insurer to be adequate to provide insurance for a particular risk, or category of risks.

Premium, Deposit: An initial payment made by the insured at the time insurance is issued under a temporary binder.

Premium, Earned: A portion or ratio of premium that has been paid to an insurance company, that covered the expired segment of the policy period.

Premium, Return: A refund of paid-up premium to a policyholder. It is computed either on a short-rate basis if the insured request cancellation, or pro rata if the company terminates coverage.

Premium, Unearned: Premium that in a sense is on-deposit with the insurer, to cover the unexpired portion of the policy period.

Preselection: Deciding whether or not to accept or reject a new insured.

Principal Sum: The amount payable in one sum in the event of accidental death and in some cases accidental dismemberment.

Private-use Airports: Airports not open to the general public, but are restricted to the use of their owners and invited guests of the owners on an exclusive basis.

Producer: *See* Agent; and Broker.

Products Liability: Insurance which protects the manufacturer or distributor of a product against claims arising from the use of that product.

Professional Liability Insurance: Insurance that protects a professional, like a flight instructor, from malpractice suits.

Promissory Warranty: An absolute guarantee on the part of the insured that he or she will perform some duty in the future.

Proof of Loss: A statement that provides insurers with the facts necessary to determine the existence and extent of their liability.

Property Damage: See Liability Insurance, Property Damage

Proportional Reinsurance: Reinsurance agreements under which premiums and losses are shared in some common proportion.

Proximate Cause: Refers to the major cause of injury or damage.

Public Law 15: Subjects regulation of insurance to the federal government but Congress has allowed the states to continue with this responsibility so long as it is done effectively.

Public-use Privately Owned Airports: Airports that are located on the outskirts of a metropolitan area and serve as the general aviation airport for the community.

Public-use Publicly Owned Airports: Airports that range in size from the major airports serving a metropolitan area to a small single grass strip owned by a local community.

Punitive Damages: *See* Damages, Punitive.

Pure Risk: Exists when there is a chance of loss, but not a chance of a gain.

Purpose of Use Categories: Use of an aircraft is generally classified as: (1) airline, (2) business and pleasure, (3) industrial aid, (4) commercial, and (5) special use.

Pyramiding: The problem of having multiple deductibles apply to one occurrence when various coverages (policies) apply, each with separate deductibles.

Qualified Pension Plans: *See* Pension Plans, Qualified.

Quota Share Reinsurance: Reinsurance arrangements in which each insurer accepts a certain percentage of premiums and losses in a given line of insurance.

Ratemaking: The pricing of insurance.

Rating Bureaus: Develop rates for various lines of insurance.

Real Property: Real estate or land with any type of permanent structures.

Reasonable expectation doctrine: When insurance policy language is ambiguous the courts will interpret the policy to mean what a reasonable buyer would expect it to mean.

Reciprocal Exchange: An interinsurance association that is a form of cooperative insurance in the sense that each policyholder is insured by all of the others; and he, on the other hand, insures them. Neither a Mutual Insurer, nor an Exchange like Lloyd's, the major characteristics of reciprocals are: the dual nature of each insured as an insurer; a system of individual accounts for each subscriber; and the use of an attorney -in -fact who is an appointed advisory committee to manage the business. The committee has final authority in matters affecting the reciprocal. Underwriting earnings, if any, are paid in cash as dividends to subscribers.

Reinstatement: The re-establishment of insurance coverage under the terms of a policy which had lapsed because of nonpayment of premium.

Reinsurance: An agreement between an insurance company and another insurer, insuring the original insurer from possible loss or liability. In other words, reinsurance shares the risk taken by the original insurer.

Reinsurer: An insurance company that accepts a portion of a risk from the ceding company.

Release: (1) To give up a right or claim; to relinquish. (2) A discharge from duty or obligation. (3) The freeing of a prisoner, such as a release from custody.

Renewable Term Insurance: Term insurance which can be renewed at the end of the term, at the option of the policyholder and without evidence of insurability, for a limited number of successive terms. The rates increase at each renewal as the age of the insured increases.

Renewal: The extension of an insurance contract after its expiration date by the issuance of a new policy which supersedes the old one.

Rental Value Insurance: Designed to cover the loss of income due to a covered peril making the rental property untenantable.

Replacement Cost: The cost to replace the property today with new materials of like kind and quality.

Replacement Value: When a hangar is insured for replacement value, it eliminates the factor of depreciation in a settlement of a loss. The intent is to permit the insured to replace the damaged property without adding funds from sources other than the proceeds of the insurance policy.

Reporting Forms: Enable companies to report fluctuating levels of insured inventories such as parts or aircraft at periodic intervals.

Representation: An act by which a person through silence or admission, leads another to believe that certain conditions are true, when in actuality they are not true.

Reserve: The amount that must be carried as a liability in the financial statement of an insurer, to provide for future commitments under policies outstanding.

Res Ipsa Loquitur: "The thing speaks for itself" (Latin). A legal phrase meaning that the facts, testimony, and circumstances are so clear that one can conclude, without a doubt, that a certain act or omission of an act caused a particular damage or injury.

Restricted (or limited) Chemical Drift (RC): RC coverage applies to insecticides, fungicides, fertilizers or seeds only. No herbicides are covered under RC coverage including defoliants and desiccants.

Retrocessional Reinsurance: When the reinsurer obtains reinsurance from another reinsurer.

Rider: *See* Endorsement.

Riot: An unlawful, violent, public disturbance caused by three or more persons, resulting in a breach of the peace and endangerment of non-participants.

Risk: The subject of insurance whether an individual person, or an inanimate object. The uncertainty concerning financial loss. In insurance law, the danger and its extent of a loss of the property that is insured (the chance of loss).

Risk Analysis Questionnaire: A survey form used by risk managers in identifying potential loss exposures.

Risk and Insurance Management Society (RIMS): An association of risk managers whose primary function is the improvement of the management of risk through the dissemination of management and legislative information to its members.

Risk Avoidance: The risk is avoided or the activity is discontinued once the hazards are known.

Risk Control: Various techniques that are used to alter the exposure to loss and in so doing, reduce the firm's expected property, liability, and personal losses or to make the annual loss experience more predictable.

Risk Finance: The methods of financing the losses that do occur. The two methods used are risk transfer and active risk retention.

Risk Management: The systematic identification of a company's exposures to the risk of loss, and with decisions on the best methods for handling these exposures in relation to corporate profitability.

Risk Management Audit: A method of identifying, controlling, and protecting all pure risks faced by a firm. It is an objective analysis of the entire risk management program and is usually conducted by someone outside the organization.

Risk Transfer: The decision by a risk manager to transfer the burden of a loss to an insurance company by purchasing insurance or to some other person or group of persons.

Robbery: Taking of property by a person causing or threatening to cause bodily harm.

Roth IRA: An additional type of IRA created by Congress in 1997 that allows earnings that accumulate in the IRA to be withdrawn after age 59½ on a tax free basis.

Salvage: Damaged property which in the event of a total loss, can be sold by the insurance company on behalf of the named insured.

Satellite: Any object orbiting another in space such as a planet or in the case of commercial use, orbiting a man-made object.

Second-injury Funds: Established in all states except Georgia, to facilitate employment of physically handicapped workers. When a worker suffers an injury which qualifies only as a partial disability, but due to a previous injury, the worker is permanently disabled, the second-injury fund pays the difference.

Segregation: A risk handling technique that focuses on reducing an organizations dependence on a single asset by making individual losses smaller and perhaps more predictable.

Selection: The process of determining the kinds of risks that are acceptable which an insurer continually revises based upon updated risk management information.

Self-Employed Retirement Plan: A qualified retirement plan available to the proprietors of unincorporated businesses and their employees. In many respects, these plans are similar to pension plans.

Self-Insurance: The setting aside of funds by companies or individuals to meet future losses out of this reserve.

Service Benefit Contracts: Blue Cross and Blue Shield are called service benefit contracts because they provide a level of service without regard to the actual dollar cost. Hospitals provide services to policyholders and are reim bursed under contract by these organizations.

Settlement: (1) The ending of a dispute through an agreement. (2) The payment to an insured or other third parties by an insurance company once liability has been established, and a value placed on the claim.

Severity: The amount of loss that is apt to be sustained.

Short Rate: The rate charged for a period which is less than that for which the policy was originally written. It is higher than the pro rata rate.

Simple-IRA: A tax deferred retirement plan provided by employers with fewer than 100 employees who do not maintain or contribute to any other retirement plan.

Single Limit Legal Liability: Liability coverage that provides one limit for bodily injury and property damage (including or excluding passengers) which represents the insurer's maximum liability for one claim or for any combination of claims which might arise from one occurrence.

Single Transaction Entry Bond (SEB): This bond is used by companies that import infrequently and have no need for continuous coverage.

Social Security: The Federal benefit program covering the majority of workers in the United States and funded by contributions from employers and employees. Survivor, disability and retirement benefits are paid to eligible beneficiaries.

Space Insurance: Provides coverage for the ownership, operation or use of spacecraft providing first party hull coverage and third party liability coverage.

Space Treaty: Convention on International Liability (1972) provides for damages caused by space objects.

Spares Endorsement: Provides all risk coverage for physical damage or loss to spare parts which are owned, leased, consigned, or are in the care, custody, or control of the insured under a written agreement.

Special Damages: Damages that reflect the financial contributions in terms of support and services the beneficiary could reasonably have expected had the decedent lived.

Special Purposes Use: Use of an aircraft for special purposes such as aerial applications, aerial advertising, aerial photography, fire fighting, fish spotting, mosquito control, police traffic control, pipeline/powerline surveillance, weather modifications, and wildlife conservation.

Specification Defense: A defense for private contractors in negligent actions where the designer provides the speci fications and the private contracting manufacturer has no reason to know that the design specifications pose a hazard.

Specific Insurance: Refers to a definite dollar amount of coverage to each stated property.

Speculative Risks: Risks that involve the possibility of a loss or a gain. Gambling is a good example of a speculative risk.

Split-dollar Life Insurance: Is used to recruit and retain top performing employees. This plan increases an employee's financial security by increasing death benefits to surviving dependents and provides savings for future use.

Standard Deviation: Is a statistical calculation that measures the concentration of the losses about their mean or average, and aids in improving the accuracy for predicting future losses.

State of the Art Defense: Refers to the limits of technological expertise and scientific knowledge relevant to the industry at a particular time.

Static Risks: Risks caused by the normal perils of nature and the dishonesty of their individuals, and involve either the damage or destruction of an asset or a change in its possession as a result of dishonesty or human failure.

Statute: A law passed by the legislative branch of a government.

Statutes of Limitation: Provide a time limit within which a plaintiff can file suit. The period of time permitted varies with the jurisdiction and the nature of the cause of action.

Statute of Repose: Prescribes a time limit within which a plaintiff can file suit. Generally applies to manufacturers of long-lasting products, such as aircraft which are subject to the possibility of liability claims years after the manufacture and sale of the product.

Statutory Law: Created by the enactment of a law, relating to a statute or law; existing as the result of a statute.

Stock Insurance Companies: Incorporated business organizations which are structured as profit-making ventures, and are owned by stockholders who provide surplus capital. Stockholders are entitled to any of the residual profits after losses and expenses have been paid, and proper reserves have been established. Stock companies usually operate through agents, who are customarily paid on a commission basis.

Straight Deductible: A common deductible found in single -engine business and pleasure policies. Normally $50 ground-no motion and $250 in flight and taxiing.

Straight Life Insurance: Whole life insurance on which premiums are payable for life. Also referred to as ordinary life.

Strict Liability: Manufacturers and merchandisers of products are held liable for injuries caused by defective products sold by them, regardless of the manufacturers' fault or negligence. Strict liability is distinguished from absolute liability in that the plaintiff must prove the product unreasonably dangerous.

Subrogation: The doctrine of subrogation gives the insurer whatever rights the insured possessed against third parties who are responsible for a loss. The right of subrogation by the insurer is limited in amount to the loss payment which has been made to the named insured. In order to actually recoup its loss payment, the insurer must prove the liability of the wrongdoer, and that the negligent party has the financial ability to pay for the loss he caused.

Supplementary Payments: A policy provision whereby the insuring company agrees to pay any and all costs levied against an insured in preparation of a legal defense should a loss occur.

Surety: A person who binds himself to pay a certain sum or to perform a certain act for another person who is also bound to pay the said sum or to perform the said act.

Surplus Lines: Insurance that is available from an acceptable nonadmitted carrier, through a broker who is specially licensed to place such coverage. The insurance must be unavailable in the admitted market, and the nonadmitted insurer must meet specific requirements of the state or country of the domiciled insurance company.

Surplus Share Reinsurance: A reinsurance arrangement whereby the ceding company assumes 100 percent of all losses up to an agreed amount.

Survival Statutes: Provide that a cause of action for personal or other injury shall not abate because of the death of a party. Some states have held that survival actions are available only if death was not instantaneous and the decedent experienced suffering prior to death.

Syndicates: Underwriting members of Lloyd's of London join a syndicate which is like a company. Each syndicate specializes in some class of insurance marine, non-marine, or aviation. Members participate in the profits or losses of the syndicate relative to the proportion of their financial interest.

Systems Protection or Boiler and Machinery Insurance: coverage for property usually excluded in the standard property policy.

Temporary Use of Substitute Aircraft: A policy clause that enables an insured to use another non-owned aircraft of similar type, horsepower, and seating capacity for such a time that the insured's aircraft is being repaired or serviced.

Tenants' Improvement and Betterments Insurance: Covers the insured's interest in a building that is occupied, but not owned by the insured.

Territorial Limits: Stipulations in an aviation insurance policy that define the geographical boundaries in which coverage is provided to an insured.

Third Party: (1) Someone who is not directly connected with a contract, a deal, a lawsuit, an occurrence, etc., but who may be affected by its outcome. (2) Persons other than the plaintiff or defendant who are brought into a case.

Time Sharing Agreement: The lease of an aircraft with flight crew to another party, and no charge is made other than specified direct operating expenses.

Title: The right of ownership of property; the just possession of one's own property.

Title Insurance: Insurance that a purchaser of property takes out, in order to protect himself against loss should the title in some way prove defective.

Tort: A wrong committed by one person against another; a civil, not a criminal wrong; a wrong arising out of a contract; a violation of a legal duty that one person has toward another. (Negligence and Libel are Torts.)

Tort-feasor: A wrongdoer; a term formerly applied to a defendant who has injured a plaintiff.

Total Loss: The result of an occurrence (unforeseen event) in which the insuring company makes a judgment that the repair of property (the insured aircraft) would be equal to or greater in cost than replacement.

Transponder Coverage: Provides protection against the loss of the transponder.

Transportation Costs: A provision in the hull and liability policy indicating that, in the event a partial loss, the aircraft must be transported by the least expensive method to a repair station. Some policies stipulate a percentage of the insured value as a limitation.

Travel Accident Policy: A limited contract covering only accidents while an insured person is traveling, usually on a commercial carrier.

Treaty Reinsurance: A reinsurance agreement where the reinsurer automatically assumes a portion of the ceding company's liability on every risk written.

Trespass: An unlawful and/or violent interference with the person or property of another; an unauthorized entry upon and/or damage to the land of another.

Trespasser: One who ventures upon the property of others without the latter's knowledge or consent.

Tricycle Landing Gear: The two main wheels are aft of the center of gravity and a third wheel is under the nose.

Trip Insurance: Insurance that is issued on a special basis to cover a particular trip, usually one that will go beyond the territorial limits contained in the insured's policy.

Umbrella Liability Insurance: Excess insurance, usually with a substantial deductible, and also providing coverage for many risks not included in the basic coverage.

Underinsurance: The aggregate benefits available in a contract of insurance are inadequate to meet amount of loss to which they are applicable.

Underwriter, Direct: An insurance company that deals directly with the insured, without agents or brokers, utilizing employees as underwriters.

Underwriting: The selection and rating of risks which are offered to an insurer. The entire process is based upon the proper selection, and rating of risks that the insurer feels will have the greatest likelihood of being profitable for the firm.

Unearned Physical Damage Premium: A pro rata return of the unearned portion of the hull premium in the event of total loss.

Unilateral Contract: A contract in which there is an act in exchange for a promise. The act is on the part of the insured by paying the premium and the promise is made by the insurance company to cover certain risks.

Uninsured/Underinsured Motorist Insuring Agreement: Promises to pay the insured an amount he or she could have collected from the insurer of a negligent uninsured/underinsured driver if the driver had carried adequate automobile liability insurance.

United States Aircraft Insurance Group (USAIG): Formed in 1928, USAIG is the oldest and largest of the domestic aviation insurers. The group represents over 30 of the world's major insurance companies and under writes all classes of aviation insurance including the major air carriers, manufacturers and airports.

Universal Life Insurance: A flexible premium life insurance policy under which the policyholder may change the death benefit from time to time (with satisfactory evidence of insurability for increases) and vary the amount or timing of premium payments. Premiums (less expense charges) are credited to a policy account from which mortality charges are deducted and to which interest is credited at rates which may change from time to time.

Utmost Care and Skill: Phrase used denoting the greatest diligence and aptitude (skill) that can be exercised in the performance of a particular act.

Utmost Good Faith: The insurance contract must contain a greater degree of good faith than an ordinary commercial contract because the insurance buyer is not in a good position to inspect and interpret the policy.

Valid: Legally binding; sufficient, justifiable; complying with necessary regulations and formalities.

Valued Basis: A stated value policy sets an agreed amount on the value of the property to be insured. Under such a valued policy, an owner of an aircraft would receive compensation for the actual amount of insurance carried on the hull, less any deductible.

Vandalism: The senseless, willful destruction of or injury to property.

Variable Annuity: An annuity contract in which the amount of each periodic income payment fluctuates. The fluctuation may be related to security market values, a cost of living index, or some other variable factor.

Variable Life Insurance: Life insurance under which the benefits relate to the value of assets behind the contract at the time the benefit is paid. The amount of death benefits payable would, under variable life policies that have been proposed, never be less than the initial death benefit payable under the policy.

Vesting: Guarantee that an employee gains ownership to all or some portion of employer contributions even if employment terminates before retirement.

Vesting, Cliff: One hundred percent vesting after ten years of service.

Vesting, Graded: Twenty-five percent vesting after five years of service, plus 5 percent for each additional year of service up to ten years, plus an additional 10 percent each year thereafter.

Vicarious Liability: The responsibility of one person for the acts of another.

Void: Having no legal or binding effect; null; ineffectual.

Waiver: The voluntary giving up or renouncing of a right, benefit, or privilege.

Waiver of Premium: A provision that under certain conditions a life insurance policy will be kept in full force by the company without further payment of premiums. It is used most often in the event of total and permanent disability.

Warranty: (1) A statement that certain facts are true, made by one party to a contract and accepted by the other party as true. (2) An agreement to make up for any damages that result from a false representation of facts.

Warranty, Breach of: *See* Breach of Warranty

Warranty, Expressed: A statement by an insured person that certain facts exist and are true, with such a statement (warranty) appearing on the face of the insurance contract. An affirmation of fact or promise made by the seller to a buyer which relates to goods.

Warranty, Implied: A warranty which is assumed to be part of a contract even though it is not specifically spelled out. Also the assumption that a manufacturer's product is fit and safe for the purpose for which it is sold.

Warsaw Convention: A multilateral treaty intended to regulate international airline transportation uniformly and establish a limitation on liability. *See also* Montreal Agreement.

Wear and Tear: The normal deterioration of a component due to extensive use.

Weekly Indemnity: A coverage which can be included as part of the guest voluntary settlement coverage. In the event the insured becomes totally disabled, weekly indemnity coverage provides a weekly payment (normally limited to 80 percent of the insured's average weekly wage) for up to 52 weeks.

Whole Life Insurance: Life insurance payable to a beneficiary at the death of the insured, whenever that occurs. Premiums may be payable for a specified number of years (limited payment life) or for life (straight life).

Willful Misconduct: A standard in which the defendant intentionally performed an act with the knowledge that it was likely to result in injury or reckless disregard of the consequences.

Workers' Compensation Insuring Agreement: Insurance against liability imposed on certain employers to pay benefits and furnish care to employees injured, and to pay benefits to dependents of employees killed in the course of or arising out of their employment.

World Aviation Directory: A quarterly publication listing all aviation organizations within various industries such as airlines, airports, and so forth. The insurance section lists all major companies, agencies, and brokers handling aviation insurance.

Writ: A formal order of a court, in writing, ordering someone who is out of court to do something.

Wrong: A breach of legal duty, based upon a standard of conduct that is determined by what a prudent person would have done or not done in similar circumstances.

Wrongful Death Statutes: Designed to compensate the decedent's beneficiaries for the pecuniary loss incurred by the wrongful death.

Zone of Danger: A rule under which a plaintiff may recover for emotional distress if the plaintiff was in personal danger of impact due to the defendant's negligence.

Appendix

Self-Tests

CHAPTER 1 **SELF-TEST**

MULTIPLE CHOICE: Circle the letter that corresponds to the best answer.

1. The first aviation insurance policy was written by:
   a. Associated Aviation Underwriters.
   b. Insurance Company of North America.
   c. Lloyd's of London.
   d. Travelers Insurance Company

2. The Travelers Insurance Company eventually became a member of the following aviation insurance group:
   a. Aero Insurance Underwriters.
   b. Royal-Globe Insurance Companies.
   c. Aero Associates.
   d. United States Aircraft Insurance Group.

3. One of the earliest aviation insurance agencies was:
   a. Caroon and Black.
   b. Barber and Baldwin.
   c. Johnson and Higgins.
   d. Marsh and McLennan.

4. The Air Commerce Act of 1926:
   a. required minimum limits of liability for the air carriers.
   b. established the first airway rules and regulations.
   c. created the Federal Aviation Agency.
   d. provided subsidies for several of the early aviation insurers.

5. The first aviation insurance pool in the United States was:
   a. AAU.
   b. Aero Insurance Underwriters
   c. ABC Plan.
   d. USAIG.

6. The individual who originated the idea of group aviation underwriting was:
   a. David C. Beebe.
   b. Horatio Barber.
   c. Eddie Rickenbacker.
   d. Owen C. Torrey.

7. The group approach to underwriting aviation risks was initially proposed for all of the following reasons, EXCEPT:
   a. it appealed to American patriotism.
   b. it would create a monopoly.
   c. it was the most economical way to write aviation insurance.
   d. it would be staffed by specialists in aviation.

8. This company entered the aviation insurance market in 1949 as a direct writer and solicited business primarily from members of AOPA:
   a. Aviation Insurance Managers.
   b. American Mercury Insurance Company.
   c. Aviation Office of America.
   d. AVEMCO.

9. The investigation of the aviation industry by the Senate Subcommittee on Antitrust and Monopoly in 1960 resulted in:
   a. the breakup of USAIG.
   b. a number of penalties being imposed on the three leading markets.
   c. indictments of key officers of the two major pools.
   d. none of the above.

10. This company has become a leading source in assembling insurers of space policies:
    a. AON Risk Services.
    b. J&H Marsh & McLennan.
    c. International Space Brokers.
    d. All of the above.

11. The group approach to underwriting benefits member companies for all of the following reasons, EXCEPT:
    a. economies of operation.
    b. spreads the risk.
    c. increases premium share.
    d. facilitates reinsurance arrangements.

12. The number of aviation insurers during the 1960's.
    a. increased
    b. decreased
    c. remained about the same
    d. at first increased and then decreased sharply

13. All of the following factors have had a significant effect on smaller general aviation aircraft sales, EXCEPT:
    a. fuel and maintenance costs.
    b. products liability.
    c. federal regulations.
    d. foreign competition.

14. During the late 1980's:
    a. Cessna Aircraft Company dropped its piston aircraft production.
    b. Beech Aircraft Corporation operated without the benefit of product liability coverage.
    c. Piper Aircraft Corporation was acquired by Raytheon Corporation.
    d. Mooney Aircraft filed for bankruptcy.

15. Between 1980 and 1985:
    a. income from insurance company investments increased significantly offsetting depressed premium rates.
    b. general aviation aircraft shipments decreased slightly.
    c. the number of private civil suits and the size of the awards increased.
    d. the number of FBOs increased resulting in more competition for their insurance business by the carriers.

16. All of the following took place during the late 1980's, EXCEPT:
    a. intense competition causing premium rates to reach record lows.
    b. increased airline mergers.
    c. a weakening of the U.S. dollar vis-a-vis European currencies.
    d. a deteriorating safety record for the major air carriers.

17. The real test of strength of the American Aviation insurance market came during the early 1950's when:
    a. the first jets were tested.
    b. commercial jets were tested.
    c. helicopters were first used for commercial purposes
    d. corporate aviation grew at a rapid pace.

18. Which of the following statements is NOT correct?
    a. Cessna was acquired by Textron in 1992.
    b. The Beech name was replaced by Raytheon in 1997.
    c. The New Piper Aircraft Corporation was formed in 1995 by M. Stuart Millar.
    d. Beech acquired the rights to Mitsubishi's Diamond business jet in 1986.

19. Learjet was acquired by:
    a. Bombardier
    b. The New Piper Aircraft Corporation
    c. Raytheon
    d. Euralair

20. During the 1980's, the number of FBO's.
    a. increased slightly.
    b. declined by two-thirds.
    c. declined slightly.
    d. stayed about the same.

21. Following passage of the General Aviation Revitalization Act in 1994:
    a. Cessna resumed production of single-engine aircraft.
    b. The New Piper Aircraft Corporation was formed.
    c. The number of new general aviation aircraft shipments increased.
    d. All of the above.

22. Southeastern Aviation Underwriters (SEAU) was acquired by ______________ in 1983.
    a. AAU
    b. AIG
    c. AON Risk Services
    d. Avemco

23. All of the following factors contributed to the fierce competition in aviation insurance during the late 1980's and early 1990's, EXCEPT:
    a. Consolidation in the airline industry.
    b. Growth in the size of awards as courts became more liberal.
    c. Growth in the number of insurance carriers.
    d. Decline in the number of new general aviation aircraft shipments.

24. The General Aviation Revitalization Act of 1994:
    a. limited the amount of punitive damages that could be awarded.
    b. limited the amount of compensatory damages that could be awarded.
    c. imposed an 18-year statute of repose.
    d. provided a subsidy to the light-aircraft manufacturers.

25. Which of the following acquisitions that took place in the late 1990's is NOT correct?
    a. Phoenix Aviation Managers acquired Southern Marine and Aviation in 1995.
    b. Avemco was acquired by HCC Insurance Holdings in 1997.
    c. The Great American Insurance Companies acquired the book of aviation business from Aviation Office of America in 1997.
    d. American International Group (AIG) acquired U.S. Specialty Insurance Company in 1996.

26. Overall Aviation insurance premiums in late 2001 and throughout 2002:
    a. drifted upward.
    b. softened.
    c. increased significantly.
    d. were relatively stable.

TRUE/FALSE: Circle *T* if the statement is true, *F* if it is false.

T F 1. The Travelers Insurance Company was the first aviation insurer in the United States.

T F 2. Most of the early aviation insurance policies did not include hull coverage.

T F 3. J. Brooks B. Parker assisted in placing insurance for Pan American World Airways during that airline's formative years.

T F 4. The Air Mail Act of 1925 required the first licensing of aircraft and airmen.

T F 5. The USAIG and AAU were formed immediately following World War I.

T F 6. The two predominant aviation insurance markets up to the end of World War II were Aero Insurance Underwriters and USAIG.

T F 7. Established in 1932, the Board of Aviation Underwriters ceased operations in 1965 during the extremely competitive period in aviation underwriting.

T F 8. The Royal-Globe Insurance Companies entered the aviation field in 1948 following their withdrawal from Aero Insurance Underwriters.

T F 9. The Aircraft Builders Counsel, Inc ., (ABC) was formed in 1952 to provide aircraft liability coverage.

T F 10. The growth in all segments of the aviation industry during the 1960's and 1970's resulted in the establishment of a number of aviation insurers.

T F 11. The group approach to underwriting aviation risks is generally more advantageous to insurers than agents and brokers.

T F 12. The Senate Subcommittee investigating aviation insurance industry practices in the late 1950's concluded that too much competition was hurting individual insurers.

T F 13. In 1963 AVEMCO replaced American Mercury Insurance Company as the designated insurer for the AOPA.

T F 14. Growth in the number of new general aviation aircraft during the 1960's reduced competition because there was enough business for everyone.

T F 15. By 1985 the products liability cost per new aircraft produced exceeded the average selling price of many two and four place aircraft.

T F 16. General Aviation accidents per 100,000 aircraft hours increased during the 1980's, which was the primary reason for the rise in products liability premiums.

T F 17. Historically, up to the 1980's, the general aviation industry had paralleled the economic cycle of the national economy.

T F 18. The world's airlines suffered a record number of passenger fatalities in 1985.

T F 19. While the air carriers experienced sharp premium reductions during the late 1980's, FBO's and general aviation aircraft owners saw their rates rise slightly.

T F 20. Aero Insurance Underwriters became a major underwriting market by the late 1940's.

T F 21. Beech Aircraft was acquired by Textron in 1992.

T F 22. By 1986 Cessna Aircraft Company decided to drop its jet aircraft production and self-insure up to $100 million because of its concentration on light single-engine aircraft.

T F 23. During the 1980's, the number of FBO's in the United States declined by more than two-thirds.

T F 24. The number of new general aviation aircraft shipments increased during the late 1990's.

T F 25. The General Aviation Revitalization Act of 1994 limited products liability suits and provided subsidies to light aircraft manufacturers.

T F 26. The size of the active general aviation aircraft fleet declined during the period of 1980 to 1995.

T F 27. Price competition in the aviation insurance market was fierce during the late 1980's and early 1990's.

T F 28. Phoenix Aviation Managers acquired Southern Marine and Aviation Underwriters in 1995.

T F 29. Avemco is now a subsidiary of the American International Group (AIG).

T F 30. The first five years of the new millenium were a period of relative calm in the U.S. aviation industry.

Answers to Chapter 1 Self-Test

Multiple Choice

1. c	6. a	11. c	16. d	21. d	26. c
2. d	7. b	12. a	17. b	22. b	
3. b	8. b	13. d	18. c	23. c	
4. b	9. d	14. a	19. a	24. c	
5. d	10. d	15. c	20. b	25. d	

True/False

1. T	6. F	11. F	16. F	21. F	26. T
2. T	7. F	12. F	17. T	22. F	27. T
3. T	8. T	13. T	18. T	23. T	28. T
4. F	9. F	14. F	19. F	24. T	29. F
5. F	10. T	15. T	20. F	25. F	30. F

CHAPTER 2 SELF-TEST

MULTIPLE CHOICE: Circle the letter that corresponds to the best answer.

1. Companies like The Boeing Company, Honeywell and United Technologies are members of:
   a. ATA.
   b. AIA.
   c. NBAA.
   d. GAMA.

2. Companies like Cessna, Mooney, and The New Piper Aircraft are members of:
   a. ADMA.
   b. AOPA.
   c. AIA.
   d. GAMA.

3. The principal aviation insurance coverage purchased by the aircraft and component parts manufacturers is:
   a. aircraft liability.
   b. aircraft hull.
   c. products liability.
   d. construction and alterations.

4. Certificated air carriers such as Delta and American are commonly referred to as:
   a. low farecarriers.
   b. legacy carriers.
   c. leading carriers.
   d. large trunk carriers.

5. Corporate operated aircraft flown by professional pilots are referred to as which of the following classes of business?
   a. business and pleasure.
   b. commercial.
   c. industrial aid.
   d. special use.

6. The nation's approximately 2,400 fixed base operators operate about ___aircraft for air taxi, instructional, and rental purposes.
   a. 20,000
   b. 25,000
   c. 30,000
   d. 35,000

7. The purpose of aircraft for "special use" would include all of the following EXCEPT:
   a. police traffic control.
   b. flying club.
   c. powerline patrol.
   d. mosquito control.

8. Which of the following coverages is unique to airport owners and operators?
   a. non-ownership liability.
   b. airport premises liability.
   c. medical payments.
   d. air meet liability.

9. Special aircraft hull and liability policies have been designed for owners and operators of this fast-growing segment of the aviation industry:
   a. helicopters.
   b. ultralights.
   c. seaplanes.
   d. amphibians.

10. The personal non-owned aircraft policy is primarily designed for:
    a. corporate pilots.
    b. student pilots.
    c. private pilots.
    d. ultralight pilots.

11. If the FAA decides that an unsafe condition exists which warrants immediate corrective action, it may issue a(an):
    a. airworthiness directive.
    b. defective component alert.
    c. service bulletin.
    d. service letter.

12. Air carriers carry a wide range of insurance coverages, including:
    a. hull and liability.
    b. premises liability.
    c. automobile liability.
    d. all of the above.

13. Air Taxi operators must exercise which degree of care towards their passengers?
    a. the highest
    b. normal
    c. reasonable
    d. ordinary

14. Air carriers owe a duty of ______care to other aircraft which may be damaged as a result of the carrier's negligence.
    a. the highest
    b. normal
    c. reasonable
    d. ordinary

15. Guest Voluntary Settlement (Admitted Liability) coverage is only provided for which of the following classes of business?
    a. Air Carriers
    b. Fixed Base Operators
    c. Industrial Aid Operators
    d. Flying Clubs

16. Which of the following statements regarding the liability of FBOs is not correct?
    a. An FBO may be held vicariously liable for the negligence of a student or renter pilot.
    b. The oil companies normally cover an FBO's liability for pumping contaminated fuel.
    c. An FBO is generally under no duty to determine whether a product manufactured by another is defective.
    d. An FBO's liability for aircraft storage depends on the principles of bailment.

17. Notice to Airmen (NOTAMs):
    a. advise pilots of defective aircraft components.
    b. are issued by airports advising pilots of unsafe conditions.
    c. are FAA weather advisories.
    d. are none of the above.

18. Which of the following statements is not correct?
    a. The majority of aircraft accidents are attributable to pilot error.
    b. The pilot-in-command (PIC) of an aircraft is directly responsible for and is the final authority in the operation of an aircraft.
    c. The duty of reasonable care that a pilot owes his or her passengers depends upon his or her experience.
    d. Pilot negligence can arise as a result of improperly operating the controls in the cockpit.

19. Which of the following situations would be considered a negligent act by a pilot?
    a. flying with an elapsed medical certificate
    b. flying into a known hazard such as adverse weather
    c. a student pilot carrying passengers
    d. a private pilot flying for hire

20. When the FAA approves an aircraft design, the manufacturer receives a(an):
    a. airworthiness certificate.
    b. design certificate.
    c. production certificate.
    d. type certificate.

21. The primary source of weather information for aviation use is the:
    a. air traffic controllers.
    b. FAA Flight Service Station.
    c. FAA Flight Standards District Office.
    d. airport weather advisories.

22. Negligence on the part of the FAA can arise when an air traffic controller gives the pilot-in- command inaccurate or misleading information in all of the following areas, EXCEPT:
    a. aeronautical charts.
    b. aircraft performance characteristics.
    c. weather information.
    d. aircraft separation standards.

23. Most general aviation aircraft are operated by:
    a. Corporations.
    b. FBO's.
    c. business and pleasure operators.
    d. special use operators.

24. An aircraft manufacturer may be held liable for:
    a. design-induced errors.
    b. inadequate instructions.
    c. defective parts.
    d. all of the above.

25. Which of the following statements regarding airport liability is correct?
    a. Commercial airports owe the public the highest degree of care.
    b. Liability incurred in the terminal area is primarily the responsibility of tenants.
    c. Notification of off airport hazards such as nearby powerlines and bird nesting areas are the responsibility of the FAA.
    d. Where the airport takes full possession and control of an aircraft, a bailment is created which imposes a duty to use ordinary care in safeguarding the plane.

26. The General Aviation Revitalization Act of 1994:
    a. provided tax benefits to light aircraft manufacturers.
    b. limited a manufacturer's liability.
    c. restricted suits against FBOs.
    d. did all of the above.

27. Non-owned aircraft physical damage coverage is frequently purchased by:
    a. FBOs
    b. Airport operators.
    c. individual aircraft owners.
    d. flight instructors.

28. A coverage frequently purchased by airport owners and operators is:
    a. non-owned aircraft physical damage.
    b. non-owned aircraft liability.
    c. contractual liability and independent contractors liability.
    d. war risks.

29. The Federal Tort Claim Act (FTCA):
    a. provides a limited waiver of the Federal government's sovereign immunity.
    b. allows U.S. citizens to bring suit against foreign companies in U.S. courts.
    c. limits a manufacturer's liability by placing an 18 year statute of repose.
    d. does none of the above.

TRUE/FALSE: Circle *T* if the statement is true, *F* if it is false.

T F 1. Major corporations are planning for the eventual industrialization of outer space, which is expected to increase the demand for new aviation insurance coverages.

T F 2. Virtually all of the major aerospace manufacturers are members of the Aircraft Distributors and Manufacturers Association (ADMA).

T F 3. Grounding coverage is frequently purchased by the major air carriers.

T F 4. Most general liability policies exclude aviation liability, and consequently many subcontractors who manufacture aircraft parts and components purchase aircraft products liability.

T F 5. The small non-certificated regional air carriers are one of the fastest growing segments of the airline industry.

T F 6. The airlines, as a class of business, represent a tremendous premium volume for relatively few insurance markets.

T F 7. Guest voluntary settlement (admitted liability) coverage is generally limited to industrial aid risks.

T F 8. The majority of civil aircraft in the United States are used for commercial purposes.

T F 9. Fixed base operators, as a class of aviation insurance, are considered excellent by underwriters because FBOs are all subject to strict FAA regulations.

T F 10. There are over 18,000 airports in the United States.

T F 11. A manufacturer may be held liable for not providing adequate warnings and instructions.

T F 12. Failure to respond to an AD notice may subject an aircraft owner to criminal and civil prosecution including revocation of the airworthiness certificate.

T F 13. Northwest Airlines is classified as a regional carrier.

T F 14. As common carriers, charter operators have a duty to exercise reasonable care for the safety of their passengers.

T F 15. Air carriers only owe a duty of ordinary care to persons injured on the ground.

T F 16. Liability arising out of fixed base operations is basically limited to their owned aircraft and line services.

T F 17. Aircraft sales organizations can be held liable for breach of any express warranties or breach of the implied warranty of merchantability.

T F 18. An aircraft dealer may have a duty of inspection and a subsequent duty to warn others in selling a used aircraft.

T F 19. When an FBO assumes the position of bailee, it owes the aircraft owner a duty of ordinary care.

T F 20. Liability incurred for injuries to persons in the terminal area generally is the responsibility of the air carriers and concessionaires, not the airport authority.

T F 21. When a pilot is operating an aircraft on behalf of his or her employer on company business, the pilot's liability can be imputed to the pilot's employer.

T F 22. The duty of an airport to maintain its premises in a safe condition extends beyond the runways to include the airspace used for takeoffs and landing approaches.

T F 23. Pilots flying under Visual Flight Rules (VFR) are required under the FARs to "see and avoid" and to separate themselves from other air traffic.

T F 24. Pilot liability can sometimes be established on a theory other than negligence.

T F 25. The payment of punitive damages does not apply in the case of a pilot flying under the influence of alcohol or drugs.

T F 26. Aerial application has been considered an ultrahazardous activity by some jurisdictions.

T F 27. Air traffic controllers have a duty of due care to pilots and as such, the government is not immune from liability for ATC negligence.

T F 28. Accidents involving ATC separation requirements may result in FAA liability.

T F 29. The General Aviation Manufacturers Association (GAMA) represents companies that produce missiles and space systems as well as light aircraft.

T F 30. Corporate operated aircraft flown by professional pilots have a safety record that compares favorably with that of the scheduled air carriers.

T F 31. Most oil companies assume all liability incurred by FBO's in pumping contaminated fuel.

T F 32. The personal non-owned aircraft policy is primarily designed for individuals who rent, borrow or lease aircraft.

T F 33. The majority of aircraft accidents are attributable to mechanical failure.

T F 34. Violation of an FAR may constitute negligence per se depending on state law.

T F 35. An aircraft flown by a flying club would be considered special use aircraft.

T F 36. The General Aviation Revitalization Act of 1994 restricted the issuance of AD notices by the FAA.

T F 37. The number of FBOs in the U.S. declined during the 1980s and '90s

T F 38. The 1996 FAA Reauthorization Bill charged the FAA with promotion and regulation of civil aviation.

T F 39. Failure to issue a NOTAM advising pilots of a dangerous condition existing at an airport might result in a liability claim under the FAA's responsibility in publishing aeronautical charts.

LISTING:

1. List five areas of exposure in which an FBO can incur liability.

   a.______________________________

   b.______________________________

   c.______________________________

   d.______________________________

   e.______________________________

2. The FAA can incur liability in any of the following six areas:

   a.______________________________

   b.______________________________

   c.______________________________

   d.______________________________

   e.______________________________

   f.______________________________

Answers to Chapter 2 Self-Test

Multiple Choice

1. b	6. a	11. a	16. b	21. b	26. b
2. d	7. b	12. d	17. d	22. b	27. a
3. c	8. d	13. a	18. c	23. c	28. c
4. b	9. b	14. a	19. b	24. d	29. a
5. c	10. c	15. c	20. d	25. d	

True/False

1. T	6. T	11. T	16. F	21. T	26. T	31. F	36. F
2. F	7. T	12. T	17. T	22. T	27. T	32. T	37. T
3. F	8. F	13. F	18. T	23. T	28. T	33. F	38. F
4. T	9. F	14. F	19. T	24. T	29. F	34. T	39. F
5. T	10. T	15. T	20. F	25. F	30. T	35. F	

LISTING

1. a. line service
   b. maintenance and repair service
   c. aircraft sales and service
   d. charter and rental service
   e. premises liability also, fuel sales, products sales, corporate flight services, pilot training and other specialized services.

2. a. certification of aircraft
   b. certification of airmen
   c. air weather information
   e. aeronautical charts
   f. airport hazards

CHAPTER 3 SELF-TEST

MULTIPLE CHOICE: Circle the letter that corresponds to the best answer.

1. Combined aircraft hull and liability policies first appeared during the:
   a. 1950's.
   b. 1960's.
   c. 1970's.
   d. 1980's.

2. Avemco is an example of a:
   a. directing-writing company.
   b. underwriting group.
   c. multiple-line company.
   d. company who sells its policies through agents and brokers.

3. Formerly based in St. Louis, this aviation insurer specializing in underwriting FBOs, became a wholly owned subsidiary of Avemco in 1985.
   a. Crump Aviation Underwriters.
   b. Aviation Office of America.
   c. National Aviation Underwriters.
   d. Associated Aviation Underwriters.

4. One of the two largest aviation insurance pools, this underwriter was formed by the merger of Associated Aviation Underwriters and the British Aviation Insurance Group:
   a. American Aviation Underwriters.
   b. Global Aerospace.
   c. AIG Aviation
   d. Phoenix Aviation Managers

5. Approximately how many major domestic aviation insurers are there today?
   a. 6
   b. 8
   c. 10
   d. 12

6. Which of the following reasons caused the number of aviation insurance markets to decrease in the last two decades compared to the number In the 1960's and 1970's?
   a. The need for adequate reinsurance.
   b. Lower rates were offered by Lloyd's of London.
   c. The variety of aircraft being produced was too much to develop an adequate spread of risks.
   d. Competition increased and there was a leveling-off of the number of active general aviation aircraft.

7. Which of the following statements concerning a Lloyd's underwriting member is not correct?
   a. All members of Lloyd's are required to provide capital equivalent to their risk assessed capital requirement.
   b. All members must be British subjects.
   c. All members must make annual contributions to Lloyd's Central Fund.
   d. All members must join a syndicate.

8. Which of the following qualities must a good agent possess?
   a. knowledge of the insurance business.
   b. good contacts with the aviation insurance markets.
   c. an effective claim follow-up service.
   d. all of the above.

9. In choosing among insurers, the nature of their services should be considered. In doing so, which of the following factors is/are important: (1) fairness of an insurer's claim service; (2) speed of claim service; (3) provision of additional services, such as loss prevention and safety where needed; (4) unquestioned claim payments to the insured.
   a. (1) only.
   b. (1), (2) and (4).
   c. (1),(2) and (3).
   d. (1), (2), (3) and (4).

10. The only persons who may present business to underwriters at Lloyd's are:
    a. large domestic brokers.
    b. domestic agents appointed by Lloyd's.
    c. Lloyd's brokers.
    d. Any agent or broker. There are no restrictions.

11. Aviation has remained a specialty line of insurance primarily because of the:
    a. unique underwriting requirements.
    b. relatively low total premium generated worldwide compared to other lines.
    c. catastrophe nature of the risks.
    d. relatively large number of homogeneous exposure units.

12. Large multiple-line companies such as Liberty Mutual and Hartford Fire Insurance Company are members of:
    a. Ace USA International & Specialty Aerospace
    b. AIG Aviation, Inc.
    c. HCC Aviation Insurance.
    d. USAIG.

13. In addition to business and pleasure risks, this insurer specializes in agricultural aircraft.
    a. Phoenix Aviation Managers
    b. AIG Aviation, Inc.
    c. Avemco Insurance Company
    d. HCC Aviation Insurance Group

14. The actual underwriting market at Lloyd's is called a(an):
    a. Lloyd's broker.
    b. Name.
    c. syndicate.
    d. underwriting member.

15. Best's Insurance Reports: Property Liability includes all of the following information on insurers, EXCEPT:
    a. underwriting results.
    b. claims handling philosophy.
    c. adequacy of reserves.
    d. soundness of investments.

16. Oldest and largest of the aviation insurance groups is:
    a. AIG, Aviation, Inc.
    b. USAIG.
    c. Global Aerospace.
    d. HCC Aviation Insurance Group

17. In 1983 ______________________ acquired the book of aviation insurance from the former Southeastern Aviation Underwriters (SEAU).
    a. HCC Aviation Insurance Group.
    b. Ace USA International & Specialty Aerospace.
    c. Phoenix Aviation Managers.
    d. AIG Aviation.

18. AIG Aviation, Inc., acquired the following company in 1997:
    a. Aviation Office of America (AOA).
    b. Aviation & Marine Insurance Group (AMIG).
    c. Southern Aviation Underwriters (SAU).
    d. Commercial Aviation Underwriters (COMAV).

19. Avemco was acquired in 1997 by:
    a. HCC Insurance Holdings.
    b. Great American Insurance Companies.
    c. American International Group.
    d. Phoenix Aviation Managers.

20. In 1995 Phoenix Aviation Managers started an Airport and Special Risks Division after acquiring the book of business from the former:
    a. Aviation Office of America (AOA).
    b. National Aviation Underwriters (NAU).
    c. Southern Marine & Aviation Underwriters (SMAU).
    d. Southern Aviation Underwriters (SAU).

21. Which of the following insurers is currently writing aviation insurance?
    a. Signal Aviation Underwriters.
    b. Commercial Aviation Insurance (COMAV).
    c. Crump Aviation Underwriters.
    d. U.S. Specialty Insurance Company.

22. Which of the following statements concerning Lloyd's is NOT correct?
    a. More than half of the aviation market's premiums are from North American risks.
    b. Lloyd's is not a company as such, but an association of individual and corporate underwriting members.
    c. All syndicates write aviation insurance.
    d. Corporate and individual members must also make annual contributions to Lloyd's Central Fund.

23. The only persons who may present business to underwriters at Lloyd's are:
    a. selected agents and brokers only.
    b. Lloyd's brokers only.
    c. selected agents and brokers including Lloyd's brokers.
    d. surplus lines brokers.

24. In 1998 the Aviation Insurance Association (AIA) established their ____________________ program.
    a. Certified Aviation Insurance Professional (CAIP).
    b. Chartered Aviation Underwriter (CAU).
    c. Certificated Aviation Underwriting Professional (CAUP).
    d. Accredited Aviation Insurance Executive (AAIE).

25. A market for antique and homebuilt aircraft would be:
    a. AIG, Aviation, Inc.
    b. ACE USA Aerospace.
    c. Phoenix Aviation Managers.
    d. U.S. Specialty Insurance Company.

TRUE/FALSE: Circle *T* if the statement is true, *F* if it is false.

T F 1. There are approximately 300 insurance companies in the United States which write aviation coverages, and the majority are members of some pool or association.

T F 2. HCC Aviation Insurance is one of the two major direct- writing aviation insurance companies.

T F 3. AIG Aviation, Inc. is the designated insurer of the Aircraft Owners and Pilots Association (AOPA).

T F 4. Formed in 1928, USAIG is one of the largest of the domestic aviation underwriters, representing some of the world's major insurance companies.

T F 5. Underwriting members at Lloyd's of London are formed into syndicates.

T F 6. All american agents and brokers doing business with Lloyd's must work through an approved Lloyd's broker.

T F 7. Each Lloyd's syndicate generally accepts less than 100 percent of a particular line of business.

T F 8. Direct-writing companies always offer lower rates than companies selling their insurance through independent agents and brokers.

T F 9. Companies that pass off all or virtually all of a risk through various reinsurance arrangements are called captive agents.

T F 10. A broker is generally looked upon as the agent of the insured and not of the insurer.

T F 11. The two largest aviation insurers, USAIG and Global Aerospace only accept business through brokers and independent agencies that represent their member companies.

T F 12. Munich Re and Mitsui Nichido are member companies of AIG Aviation, Inc.

T F 13 AIG Aviation, Inc. underwrites all classes of business except commuter/regional carriers.

T F 14. The former Crump Aviation Underwriters which specialized in helicopters and agricultural operators is now part of Phoenix Aviation Managers.

T F 15. ACE USA International & Specialty specializes in airport and satellite risks.

T F 16. Aviation Syndicates within Lloyd's can only accept business through brokers approved by the Committee of Lloyd's.

T F 17. The CPCU professional insurance designation stands for Certified Professional Company Underwriter.

T F 18. USAIG's aerospace coverages include launch and initial operations insurance for satellites and in-orbit satellite insurance.

T F 19. AIG Aviation, Inc. was created from the former Southeastern Aviation Underwriters (SEAU) in 1983.

T F 20. ACE USA International & Specialty Aerospace was the result of a merger in 1982 between Royal-Globe Insurance Companies and INA Corporation.

T F 21. The former Aviation Office of America (AOA) is now a part of the HCC Aviation Insurance Group.

T F 22. The Special Risk Department of HCC Aviation specializes in warbirds, antique, float and homebuilt aircraft.

T F 23. U.S. Specialty Insurance Company is now part of the HCC Insurance Holdings, Inc.

T F 24. In 1995 Phoenix Aviation Managers, Inc. started an airport and special risks division after acquiring the book of business from Southern Marine & Aviation Underwriters (SMAU).

T F 25. In 1998 Phoenix Aviation Managers established an agricultural division.

T F 26. Corporate members of Lloyd's now represent more than half of the underwriting capacity.

T F 27. Only aviation syndicates of Lloyd's are permitted to write aviation business because of the catastrophe nature of the business.

T F 28. All Lloyd's policies are backed by the market's unique four levels of security: The premiums trust funds, individual and corporate members' funds at Lloyd's, the personal resources of individual members and the Central Fund.

T F 29. The Aviation Insurance Association (AIA) is located in Kansas City, Missouri.

T F 30. The Certified Aviation Insurance Professional (CAIP) designation is fast becoming the standard of professionalism in the aviation insurance industry.

MATCHING: Match the descriptor on the right with the aviation insurance company on the left.

________1. USAU.

________2. Phoenix Aviation Managers

a. The only direct writing company.

b. Headquartered in Atlanta, this company was created from the former SEAU.

_______3.	Avemco Insurance Company	c.	This company is a major aviation insurer of airline risks.
_______4.	ACE USA International & Specialty Aerospace	d.	A market for antique and homebuilt aircraft.
_______5.	AIG Aviation, Inc.	e.	Established an agricultural division in 1998.
_______6.	HCC Aviation	f.	This company specializes in airport and satellite risks.

LISTING: List five factors which an insured should consider in selecting an agent or broker to handle aviation insurance.

1. ______________________________

2. ______________________________

3. ______________________________

4. ______________________________

5. ______________________________

Answers to Chapter 3 Self-Test

Multiple Choice

1. a	6. d	11. c	16. b	21. d
2. a	7. b	12. d	17. d	22. c
3. c	8. d	13. a	18. d	23. b
4. b	9. c	14. c	19. a	24. a
5. a	10. c	15. b	20. c	25. d

True/False

1. T	6. T	11. T	16. T	21. F	26. T
2. F	7. T	12. F	17. F	22. T	27. F
3. F	8. F	13. F	18. T	23. T	28. T
4. T	9. F	14. T	19. T	24. T	29. T
5. T	10. T	15. T	20. F	25. T	30. T

Matching

1. c	2. e	3. a	4. f	5. b	6. d

LISTING

a. knowledge of the insurance business.
b. type of aviation insurance written.
c. number of insurers represented.
d. knowledge of the aviation industry.
e. experience in handling aviation claims

(Other answers might include: continuing education; and respect of clients, competitors, insurers, and claim adjusters.)

CHAPTER 4 SELF-TEST

MULTIPLE CHOICE: Circle the letter that corresponds to the best answer.

1. From a risk management perspective, risk is best described as:
   a. uncertainty.
   b. loss itself.
   c. cause of loss.
   d. chance of loss.

2. The major function of insurance is to:
   a. remove the risk of misfortune.
   b. substitute certainty for uncertainty.
   c. shift the burden of all financial losses to the insurance company.
   d. none of the above are major functions of insurance.

3. The long-run relative frequency of a loss defines:
   a. degree of risk.
   b. law of large numbers.
   c. chance of loss.
   d. pure risk.

4. Which of the following identifies a classification of risk which is NOT the responsibility of the risk manager?
   a. pure risks.
   b. dynamic risks.
   c. static risks.
   d. both b and c.

5. A speculative risk differs from a pure risk because:
   a. a speculative risk might result in a financial gain.
   b. pure risks result in a financial loss.
   c. speculative risks are more predictable.
   d. speculative risks have a greater catastrophic exposure.

6. If an airplane is damaged by a windstorm, the direct loss is the actual cost of repairs. The indirect loss is:
   a. expense of renting a replacement airplane.
   b. loss of revenue due to the inability to fly charter.
   c. time and effort required to arrange for repairs.
   d. all of the above are examples of indirect losses.

7. All of the following are perils except:
   a. collision.
   b. theft.
   c. negligence.
   d. physical hazards.

8. Hazards are usually classified into the following three categories:
   a. physical, mental and moral.
   b. physical, moral, and morale.
   c. personal, property, and moral.
   d. perils, loss exposures, and chance of loss.

9. Adverse selection is a term used to describe:
   a. the choice of the wrong insurance contract to fit a specific need.
   b. an underwriting error on the part of an insurance company.
   c. the tendency of poor risks to seek insurance.
   d. a loss situation in which the chance of loss cannot be determined.

10. To be successful in shifting the burden of a financial loss to a negligent third party:
    a. you must be able to prove negligence in a court of law.
    b. the negligent party must have sufficient resources.
    c. the airplane must not have been financed.
    d. both a and b are required.

11. According to the law of large numbers, as the number of exposure units is increased:
    a. the chance of loss declines.
    b. the chance of loss increases.
    c. the accuracy of predictions increases.
    d. the accuracy of predictions should remain the same.

12. All of the following are required for an insurable risk except
    a. a large number of homogeneous units.
    b. the loss must be accidental.
    c. the article insured may be easily replaced from current income.
    d. loss must be definite.

13. Reinsurance:
    a. is insurance for the insurance companies.
    b. is an agreement between the insurance company and the insured.
    c. selects the risks to be insured and then negotiates the premium with the insured.
    d. has very little involvement in aircraft liability insurance.

14. Reinsurance agreements where the reinsurer automatically assumes a portion of the risk is called:
    a. proportional reinsurance.
    b. quota share reinsurance.
    c. treaty arrangement..
    d. facultative arrangement.

15. The insurance company which issues a policy under a reinsurance agreement is called:
    a. reinsurer.
    b. ceding company.
    c. primary company.
    d. both b and c.

16. The type of reinsurance is surplus share. Ceding company's retention limit (line) is $400,000. The insured hull value is $900,000. What proportion will the reinsurer pay when there is a $600,000 loss?
    a. $ 200,000
    b. 266,667
    c. 400,000
    d. 633,333

17. The mean or average of past accident losses for a sample population is 6. The standard deviation for this data is 3. How many aircraft would the underwriter need to be prepared to pay for to be 95.45 percent certain of the actual outcome?
    a. 6
    b. 9
    c. 12
    d. 15

TRUE/FALSE Circle *T* if the statement is true, *F* if it is false.

T F 1. A statistician, economist, decision theorist, and an insurance theorist would all define risk differently.

T F 2. From an insurance standpoint, risk is only involved with financial losses.

T F 3. Risks can be divided into fundamental and particular risks.

T F 4. Dynamic risks are group risks, like floods.

T F 5. Moral hazards involve an attitude of carelessness.

T F 6. A peril is the actual cause of the loss.

T F 7. A physical hazard is anything that is likely to cause a loss, such as a fire, a windstorm, or a crash.

T F 8. An accident is defined as an event which is unexpected, unforeseen, and outside the control of the insured.

T F 9. Since a loss must be definite to be an insurable risk, the aircraft which is lost in flight would not be covered.

T F 10. Transferring risks to an insurance company is only feasible when the loss will cause some hardship.

T F 11. For the insurance mechanism to work, a large number of homogeneous units must be present.

T F 12. The basic purpose of reinsurance is to concentrate the risk with one large insurance company.

T F 13. The basic purpose of reinsurance is to spread the losses to protect an insurance company against catastrophic loss.

T F 14. Proportional reinsurance or pro rata includes quota share and surplus share reinsurance.

T F 15. Under surplus share reinsurance, the reinsurer agrees to accept insurance in excess of the ceding company's retention limit or line.

Answers to Chapter 4 Self-Test

Multiple Choice

1. a	6. d	11. c	16. d
2. b	7. d	12. c	17. c
3. c	8. b	13. a	
4. b	9. c	14. c	
5. a	10. d	15. d	

True/False

1. T	6. T	11. T
2. T	7. F	12. F
3. T	8. T	13. T
4. F	9. F	14. T
5. F	10. T	15. T

CHAPTER 5 SELF- TEST

MULTIPLE CHOICE: Circle the letter that corresponds to the best answer.

1. Risk managers:
   a. are responsible for identifying all exposures that create pure risks.
   b. establish programs to handle the identified pure risks.
   c. are responsible for all risks which effect corporate profitability.
   d. both a and b.

2. The differences between risk management and insurance management include all of the following except
   a. risk management views the purchase of insurance as only one method of dealing with pure risks.
   b. risk management deals with both insurable and uninsurable pure risks.
   c. insurance management evolved from the field of risk management.
   d. insurance management focuses only on one method of dealing with pure risks.

3. The goal of risk management is to:
   a. purchase insurance most efficiently.
   b. see that the firm does not incur any financial losses.
   c. make sure that the business does not incur catastrophic financial losses.
   d. oversee toss prevention programs.

4. The major advantage of using a risk analysis questionnaire during the risk identification step is to:
   a. assure that all hidden exposures are uncovered.
   b. reduce the time required to conduct the survey.
   c. allow the delegation of conducting the survey to others.
   d. receive a premium credit from the insurance company.

5. Which of the following risk analysis areas has the greatest potential financial loss?
   a. loss of real property.
   b. theft by employees.
   c. loss of revenue due to property damage.
   d. liability.

6. All of the following types of pure risks are a concern to the risk manager EXCEPT:
   a. real and personal property losses.
   b. inventory losses due to product obsolescence.
   c. death of a key employee.
   d. theft by an employee.

7. Risk managers consider which one of the four dimensions of risk measurement the most important?
   a. frequency.
   b. severity.
   c. predictability.
   d. probability.

8. Risk control can be achieved by
   a. loss reduction
   b. risk avoidance
   c. loss prevention
   d. all of the above

9. All of the following are examples of loss reduction methods except:
   a. safety programs.
   b. frequent inspections of the premises.
   c. installing sprinkler systems.
   d. venting paint room fumes.

10. Risks most appropriate for transfer would have the following characteristics:
    a. low probability and high severity.
    b. high probability and low severity.
    c. low probability and low severity.
    d. high probability and high severity.

11. When evaluating pure risks, the risk manager should focus on:
    a. the availability of alternative methods of dealing with the risk.
    b. techniques available to reduce the risk.
    c. the potential severity of the loss and the firms ability to pay for the losses.
    d. the probability that a loss wilt occur.

12. Passive risk retention occurs when:
    a. the risk manager cannot calculate the dollar amount of the loss.
    b. risks are inadvertently retained due to an improperly conducted risk analysis.
    c. identified risks are determined to be catastrophic.
    d. both a and b.

13. The term self-insurance:
    a. means the same thing as risk retention.
    b. identifies those risks which meet certain criteria for risk retention.
    c. is useful for risks which have been passively retained.
    d. both b and c are correct.

14. The type of risk which has the highest probability of being successfully self-insured is:
    a. a fleet of 15 airplanes.
    b. an FBO who owns six hangars on the airport property.
    c. workers' compensation for an employer with 1,500 employees.
    d. none of the above are candidates for self -insurance.

15. Risk transfer can be accomplished by:
    a. purchasing insurance.
    b. entering into hold-harmless agreements.
    c. negotiating terms of a contract.
    d. all of the above.

16. A corporation in the 34 % income tax bracket will actually only pay $ ______ when a $5,000 deductible is subtracted from their settlement check.
    a. $0
    b. 1,700
    c. 3,300
    d. 5,000

17. The principles and concepts of risk management:
    a. are inappropriate for small FBOs.
    b. are too expensive for small airports to use.
    c. can be implemented by all firms to better manage pure risk exposures.
    d. are only useful when a risk manager is employed by the firm.

18. Which of the following risks should never be retained by a business firm?
    a. loss of a key person.
    b. hull coverage for a new corporate aircraft.
    c. liability for operating an airplane.
    d. both b and c.

19. The risk management task can be viewed as a:
    a. decision-making process.
    b. cause and effect process.
    c. management process.
    d. ongoing auditing process.

20. The characteristics of a self-insurance program include all of the following except
    a. probability of loss should be high severity and low frequency.
    b. ability of the firm to build necessary reserves.
    c. exposure units must be geographically dispersed.
    d. sufficient exposure units to allow the law of large numbers to work.

21. Which of the following valuating standards is most appropriate for determining the insured value of property subject to rapid changes in technology, like computers?
    a. replacement cost.
    b. market value.
    c. historical cost.
    d. functional replacement cost.

TRUE/FALSE: Circle *T* if the statement is true, *F* if it is false.

T F 1. Risk managers are responsible for identifying all exposures that create both pure and speculative risks and establish programs to handle them.

T F 2. In small firms, the risk management function is often the responsibility of the treasurer or controller.

T F 3. An insurance manager and a risk manager have the same job description.

T F 4. Risk and Insurance Management Society (RIMS) is a trade association made up of professional risk managers.

T F 5. Growth in size, complexity, and diversification of business firms is one of the major factors influencing the evolution of the risk management process.

T F 6. Once the risks of loss have been identified the next step is to select the appropriate techniques for handling them.

T F 7. The two methods of handling risk under the risk control category are risk retention and loss prevention.

T F 8. Installing burglar alarms in a hangar is an example of risk control.

T F 9. Passive risk retention occurs when risks are inadvertently retained due to an improperly done risk analysis.

T F 10. Self-insurance is not really insurance at all because there is no transfer of risk to others.

T F 11. A risk retention program and a self-insurance program are the same.

T F 12. One of the major advantages of a self-insurance program is the improved loss experience due to closer involvement by key company personnel.

T F 13. Risk transfer can be accomplished without the purchase of an insurance policy.

T F 14. Losses which have been evaluated and judged to have high severity and high frequency characteristics should be transferred to an insurance company.

T F 15. Those risks characterized as high frequency and low severity should be retained.

T F 16. A business firm in the 34% income tax bracket pays losses from retained risks with .34 cent dollars.

T F 17. A risk management audit is usually conducted by someone outside the organization.

T F 18. One of the most efficient and economical products offered by the insurance industry is the packaged policy.

T F 19. Safety groups are usually formed by industry trade organizations and provide a small business an opportunity to handle risk exposures efficiently.

T F 20. Studies show that a reduction in the severity of loss is a better indicator of savings in a loss control program than a reduction in the total number of accidents.

Answers to Chapter 5 Self-Test

Multiple Choice

1. d	6. b	11. c	16. c	21. d
2. c	7. b	12. b	17. c	
3. c	8. d	13. b	18. c	
4. a	9. d	14. c	19. d	
5. d	10. a	15. d	20. a	

True/False

1. F	6. F	11. F	16. F
2. T	7. F	12. T	17. T
3. F	8. T	13. T	18. T
4. T	9. T	14. F	19. T
5. T	10. T	15. T	20. F

CHAPTER 6 SELF-TEST

MULTIPLE CHOICE: Circle the letter that corresponds to the best answer.

1. The principle of indemnity provides that:
   a. the agent must be paid a fair commission for his work.
   b. aircraft insurance cannot be written for minor children.
   c. those responsible for injury to others must pay them indemnity.
   d. one cannot make a profit from his insurance policy.

2. Which of the following may not have an insurable interest in an aircraft:
   a. the owner.
   b. the airport operator.
   c. the lessee.
   d. the mortgagee.

3. Which of the following statements concerning subrogation is not correct?
   a. It only applies after the insured has been indemnified.
   b. It prevents the insured from collecting twice.
   c. It only applies to property insurance.
   d. It is of great importance in the case of hull insurance.

4. All of the following are true statements EXCEPT:
   a. Punitive damages do not apply in liability cases.
   b. Punitive damages are in excess of compensation for injuries.
   c. Punitive damages are made to punish the defendant.
   d. Punitive damages are made to discourage others form wrong.

5. Claims arising from torts are based on:
   a. negligence.
   b. intentional interference.
   c. strict liability.
   d. all of the above.

6. Which of the following is not generally considered to be one of the essential requirements of a negligent act?
   a. existence of a legal duty to protect the injured party.
   b. existence of a liability contract on trespassers.
   c. failure to exercise requisite care.
   d. reasonably close causal relationship between the breach of duty toward the claimant and the claimant's injury.

7. In most jurisdictions, a property owner owes the highest degree of care to:
   a. a trespasser.
   b. a licensee.
   c. an invitee.
   d. the degree of care owed is the same to all.

8. Vicarious liability refers to:
   a. res ipsa loquitur.
   b. imputed negligence.
   c. guest laws.
   d. sovereign immunity.

9. Which of the following is not generally considered a defense against allegations of negligence?
   a. assumption of risk.
   b. last- clear- chance.
   c. comparative negligence.
   d. tort-feasor.

10. In a liability case, the job of the jury is to:
    a. settle disputes over questions of fact.
    b. settle disputes over the law.
    c. interpret contracts.
    d. do all of the above.

11. Examples of intentional interference are: (l) assault and battery; (2) libel and slander; (3) bailment and conversion; (4) trespass and false arrest.
    a. (l)only.
    b. (1)and(4)only.
    c. (l), (2) and (3) only.
    d. (l), (2) and (4) only.

12. The doctrine of contributory negligence:
    a. has been replaced in many jurisdictions by the doctrine of comparative negligence.
    b. is a defense that benefits the injured party.
    c. is currently applied only in the field of employer's liability.
    d. applies only in the case of aircraft accidents.

13. This body of law, often referred to as "judge-made law," consists of past court decisions.
    a. public law.
    b. statutory law.
    c. common law.
    d. administrative law.

14. Torts arise out of all of the following, except:
    a. criminal acts.
    b. intentional acts.
    c. strict liability.
    d. negligence.

15. Violation of an FAA regulation resulting in harm to a plaintiff would be an example of:
    a. strict liability.
    b. res ipsa loquitur.
    c. negligence per se.
    d. vicarious liability.

16. Strict liability most often involves:
    a. airlines.
    b. manufacturers.
    c. corporate aircraft owners.
    d. air taxi operators.

17. Manufacturing defects fall into all of the following categories, EXCEPT:
    a. design defects.
    b. safety defects.
    c. manufacturing flaws.
    d. marketing defects.

18. The offensive or harmful contact of another without his or her express or implied consent is called:
    a. assault.
    b. battery.
    c. defamation.
    d. physical distress.

19. Which of the following statements is NOT correct?
    a. The government contractor's defense will only protect the manufacturer if the design defect was in compliance with specifications required under a government contract.
    b. Specification defense applies to private contracts as well as government contracts.
    c. Specification defense applies to marketing defects as well as design defects.
    d. State of the art defense refers to the limits of technological expertise at a particular time.

20. Express warranties:
    a. must be written.
    b. arise through operation of law rather than by the agreement of the parties.
    c. are an affirmation of fact or promise made by the seller to the buyer.
    d. are none of the above.

21. The implied warranty of merchantability requires:
    a. an agreement by or knowledge on the seller.
    b. that the product sold be reasonably fit.
    c. that the buyer rely on the seller's judgment.
    d. none of the above.

22. Which of the following is NOT a bailee?
    a. An FBO that ties down an individual's aircraft.
    b. An individual who loans his aircraft to a friend.
    c. An airline that does maintenance work on another carrier's aircraft.
    d. All of the above are bailees.

23. Variables included in determining the amount recoverable for special damages include all of the following, EXCEPT:
    a. financial support.
    b. loss of inheritance.
    c. grief and mental anguish.
    d. family services.

24. In determining financial support for survivors, the courts have included all of the following in determining the decedent's normal work-life expectancy, EXCEPT:
    a. hereditary factors.
    b. economic status.
    c. marital status.
    d. occupation.

25. The loss of society and companionship would be considered:
    a. special damage.
    b. punitive damage.
    c. general damage.
    d. none of the above.

26. Punitive damages:
    a. in civil cases have increased significantly in recent years.
    b. are awarded to punish or make an example of a defendant.
    c. often exceed the compensatory damage award by a much greater amount.
    d. All of the above.

27. Wrongful death statutes:
    a. place an absolute ceiling on the amount recoverable.
    b. specify those persons qualified to bring an action.
    c. do not recognize recovery for loss of consortium.
    d. All of the above.

28. An award for damages would generally be higher in the case where the victim is a(an):
    a. business person.
    b. child.
    c. elderly person.
    d. homemaker.

29. Statutes of repose:
    a. usually provide a shorter period of time than statutes of limitation.
    b. are designed to permit insurers to determine an actuarial limit to the risk exposure.
    c. commence with the cause of action.
    d. b and c are correct.

30. Proponents of statutes of repose argue that:
    a. evidence concerning manufacture of the product may no longer be available.
    b. intervening misuse or alteration of the product over the years makes it difficult to prove a product was defective at manufacture.
    c. the safe use of a product for many years is evidence that the product was not defective at manufacture.
    d. All of the above.

31. All of the following are objectives of the Foreign Sovereign Immunities Act, except:
    a. to codify the restrictive principle of sovereign immunity.
    b. to regulate international airline transportation uniformly.
    c. to assist in executing a judgment against a foreign state.
    d. to provide a statutory procedure for suing a foreign state.

32. The Montreal Agreement ratified by the United States in 2003 required air carriers to make payments up to approximately $ __________ to families of the deceased passengers.:
    a. $25,000.
    b. $50,000.
    c. $75,000.
    d. $144,000.

33. The limitation of liability on international flights does not apply in all of the following cases, EXCEPT:
    a. willful misconduct of the air carrier.
    b. persons traveling on government business.
    c. persons who did not receive adequate notice of the liability rules.
    d. a and b

34. In general, GARA established a (an) _________ year window in which general aviation aircraft and component parts manufacturers can be sued for defective products.
    a. 5
    b. 10
    c. 18
    d. 20

35. The Aviation Disaster Family Assistance Act of 1996 established a _______ waiting period before any attorney, insurance company or airline litigation representative can contact victims or their families.
    a. one week
    b. 10 days
    c. two weeks
    d. 30 days

TRUE/FALSE: Circle *T* if the statement is true, *F* if it is false.

T F 1. Administrative law consists of the great body of past court decisions.

T F 2. Under Public Law 15, insurance has been held to be subject to regulation by the federal government.

T F 3. When there is no insurable interest in an insurance policy, it becomes a gambling contract.

T F 4. In the property or liability field, insurable interest is generally only required at the time of loss.

T F 5. Proximate cause is a legal term which refers to the many factors which contribute to injury or damage.

T F 6. Loss of consortium means pain and suffering following an injury.

T F 7. A guest is usually defined as one who has not paid for his transportation.

T F 8. "The thing speaks for itself" refers to the doctrine of res ipso loquitur.

T F 9. A breach of contract arises when one party to a contract refuses to fulfill his part of the bargain.

T F 10. When property is given over to the care of another party, a legal relation of implied warranty arises.

T F 11. Comparative negligence, when claimed, is a defense used by the plaintiff.

T F 12. Negligence may be defined as the failure of a person to exercise the proper degree of care required by the circumstances.

T F 13. Possession may give the holder of property an insurable interest.

T F 14. Civil wrongs are divided into three types: criminal acts, torts, and breaches of contracts.

T F 15. The term which the law applies to the companionship of a mate is called vicarious liability.

T F 16. Absolute liability may result from persons or organizations engaging in certain ultrahazardous activities.

T F 17. Gross negligence involves the willful or wanton disregard of the life or property of another person.

T F 18. A situation in which the thing that caused the accident is so obvious and clearly would not have occurred if proper care was exercised is known as the doctrine of res ipsa loquitur.

T F 19. Strict liability is the same as absolute liability.

T F 20. When a warning or instruction is absent or inadequate, a marketing defect is said to exist.

T F 21. Government contractor defense and specification defense only apply to design defects.

T F 22. Noise created by a low-flying aircraft may give rise to an action under trespass.

T F 23. An implied warranty requires that the product sold be reasonably fit for the general purpose for which it is manufactured and sold.

T F 24. The party to whom property is entrusted is referred to as the bailor.

T F 25. States are fairly similar in determining the extent of financial loss recoverable and the method used in calculating an award.

T F 26. Promotions and merit pay increases can be included in determining estimated gross income over a decedent's life expectancy.

T F 27. Minor children have received financial support for the loss of their parents' guidance.

T F 28. Some jurisdictions deny recovery for funeral expenses, reasoning that death is inevitable and so the expense would be incurred eventually even had death occurred naturally.

T F 29. Grief and mental anguish are now recognized as compensable in virtually all jurisdictions.

T F 30. The preimpact rule permits a cause of action for the negligent cause of emotional distress only where it is accompanied by some physical injury.

T F 31. The majority of states now recognize recovery for loss of consortium for the death of a spouse.

T F 32. Extraneous circumstances regarding the private lives of the beneficiaries are not admitted in calculating damages.

T F 33. In those states with guest statutes, a guest passenger cannot recover for damage unless the host operator is found to have been guilty of "gross" or "willful and wanton" negligence.

T F 34. A statute of repose commences to run with the manufacture or sale of the product.

T F 35. The only difference between a statute of limitation and statute of repose is the degree of negligence that must be proved.

T F 36. Most major international air carriers flying into the United States have waived their right to assert the defense of sovereign immunity.

Answers to Chapter 6 Self-Test

Multiple Choice

1. d
2. d
3. c
4. a
5. d
6. b
7. c
8. b
9. d
10. a
11. d
12. a
13. c
14. a
15. c
16. b
17. b
18. b
19. c
20. c
21. b
22. b
23. c
24. c
25. c
26. d
27. b
28. a
29. b
30. d
31. b
32. c
33. b
34. c
35. d

True/False

1. F
2. F
3. T
4. T
5. F
6. F
7. T
8. T
9. T
10. T
11. F
12. T
13. T
14. F
15. F
16. T
17. T
18. T
19. F
20. T
21. T
22. T
23. T
24. F
25. F
26. T
27. T
28. T
29. F
30. F
31. T
32. F
33. T
34. T
35. F
36. T

CHAPTER 7 SELF-TEST

MULTIPLE CHOICE: Circle the letter that corresponds to the best answer.

1. For a valid contract there must be an exchange of values by the parties. This prerequisite is called:
   a. legal purpose.
   b. consideration.
   c. bilateral.
   d. competent parties.

2. Which of the following statements is true?
   a. applicant for insurance makes an offer to the insurance company.
   b. coverage starts immediately after the offer has been made.
   c. applications for insurance must be written.
   d. both a and c are true.

3. The prerequisite for a valid contract, legal purpose, is primarily concerned with:
   a. the presence of an insurable interest.
   b. not insuring aircraft hauling contraband.
   c. making sure that the insurance is socially acceptable.
   d. competent parties.

4. All of the following areas would be covered in an application for aircraft hull and liability insurance EXCEPT:
   a. identification of the applicant.
   b. description of the aircraft.
   c. coverages and limits desired.
   d. premium costs for each coverage area.

5. A binder:
   a. represents a portion of the premium given to the agent at the time of submitting the application.
   b. is a temporary contract.
   c. is as detailed as the policy which it represents.
   d. is a standard form used by all insurance companies.

6. All of the following will appear on the declarations page EXCEPT:
   a. date of the policy.
   b. coverage limits.
   c. insuring agreements.
   d. insured value of the aircraft.

7. The purpose of exclusions is to eliminate:
   a. duplicate coverages in other policies.
   b. coverage not needed by a typical insured.
   c. unique or specialized coverages.
   d. all of the above.

8. Endorsements:
   a. generally require additional premiums.
   b. modify coverages or terms of a policy.
   c. are used by insurance companies mainly to exclude coverages.
   d. both a and b.

9. An aleatory contract is:
   a. a contract of unequal exchange of value.
   b. a contract principally drawn up by one party.
   c. is the result of long negotiations.
   d. is the same as a commutative contract.

10. A contract of adhesion:
    a. eliminates the element of bargaining over terms.
    b. is a contract when an act is exchanged for a promise.
    c. is a contract prepared entirely by one party.
    d. both a and c.

11. Unique characteristics of insurance policies include all of the following except :
    a. personal.
    b. bilateral.
    c. conditional.
    d. unilateral.

12. An applicant for aviation insurance must make a full and fair disclosure to the agent because the policy is a (an):
    a. unilateral contract.
    b. contract of good faith.
    c. aleatory contract.
    d. personal contract.

13. Which of the following statements are true?
    a. material information known by the agent pertaining to the risk is deemed to be known by his company.
    b. the agent has primary responsibility to the insurer.
    c. the powers of insurance agents are generally the same for most lines of insurance.
    d. both a and b are true statements.

14. A is a statement by the applicant made prior to, or at the time of, making the contract.
    a. waiver
    b. warranty
    c. representation
    d. all of the above

15. Representations:
    a. are part of the application for insurance.
    b. are about the same as warranties.
    c. do not exist in airport insurance.
    d. usually are continuing.

16. Warranties:
    a. have the effect, in general, of waivers.
    b. are collateral inducements to a contract being formed.
    c. are part of the contract.
    d. may be oral.

17. Remaining silent when there is a duty to speak is:
    a. a misrepresentation.
    b. concealment.
    c. the parol evidence rule.
    d. fraud.

18. A pilot warranty in an aircraft hull and liability policy is an example of a (an):
    a. promissory warranty.
    b. waiver.
    c. affirmative warranty.
    d. endorsement.

19. Which of the following would permit the insurance company to void your aircraft hull and liability policy?
    a. concealing the fact that it took you 80 hours to earn your private pilot's license.
    b. misstating the place where you first learned to fly.
    c. failure to indicate that you are flying subject to a waiver from the FAA.
    d. both a and c.

20. Agents are primarily responsible to:
    a. insurance companies they represent.
    b. insureds.
    c. neither the insured nor the insurance company because they are independent agents.
    d. both on an equal basis.

21. Which of the following is not generally considered among the agents' authorities?
    a. contractual.
    b. implied.
    c. assumed.
    d. apparent.

22. Authority which is necessarily granted by the courts in order for the agent to carry out contractual duties is called:
    a. contractual.
    b. implied.
    c. expressed.
    d. apparent.

23. Waiver:
    a. is the same thing as estoppel.
    b. involves the relinquishment of a known right.
    c. is an obsolete doctrine, seldom used in insurance today.
    d. is an exception to the principle of indemnify.

24. A broker:
    a. is particularly important in aviation insurance due to the technical nature of the risks.
    b. attempts to obtain the best coverage for the client.
    c. is the agent of the insurance company.
    d. both a and b.

TRUE/FALSE: Circle *T* if the statement is true, *F* if it is false.

T F 1. For a contract to be valid, the premium must have been paid.

T F 2. The consideration of the insurance company is the promise to pay for losses caused by covered perils.

T F 3. In most states, the applicant must be either married or age 21 to be judged a competent party.

T F 4. Since the courts have ruled that insurance does not qualify as a necessity of life, it is unwise to contract with a minor.

T F 5. An insurance policy is not for a legal purpose when no insurable interest exists.

T F 6. A standard form application must be submitted to make a legal offer for insurance.

T F 7. A binder provides evidence of coverage until the actual policy is issued.

T F 8. The source for the date on the declaration page of an aviation hull and liability comes from the submitted application blank.

T F 9. Insuring agreements state the dollar limits of coverage.

T F 10. Exclusions reduce the broad coverage provided in the insuring agreements.

T F 11. Conditions in the policy outline the duties of the parties to the contract.

T F 12. Endorsements can only be used to increase coverage or change the premium.

T F 13. Named pilot coverage is preferable to the open pilot warranty.

T F 14. Insurance is a bilateral contract because it involves two parties.

T F 15. Insurance is a personal contract but can be transferred to another.

T F 16. A misrepresentation of any fact by the applicant will void the coverage.

T F 17. A warranty must be included in the policy to be enforceable.

T F 18. Requiring the installation of a burglar alarm in the airport hangar is an example of a promissory warranty.

T F 19. A breach of a warranty may void coverage even though there was no causal connection between the accident and the breach.

T F 20. Unlike representations, warranties are conclusively presumed to be material.

T F 21. The parol evidence rule refers to the rights of a defendant not testify on his or her own behalf.

T F 22. Concealment involves the deliberate misstatement of a material fact.

T F 23. Fraud is the deliberate attempt to mislead a third party.

T F 24. The relationship between agents and insurance companies is based upon the law of agency.

T F 25. Implied authority is that which the public believes the agent to possess.

T F 26. In the majority of states where contribute-to-the-loss standard for the breach of a warranty is used the burden is placed upon the insurer to prove that the breach related to the loss.

Answers to Chapter 7 Self-Test

Multiple Choice

1. b	6. c	11. b	16. c	21. c
2. d	7. d	12. b	17. b	22. b
3. a	8. d	13. d	18. c	23. b
4. d	9. a	14. c	19. c	24. d
5. b	10. d	15. a	20. a	

True/False

1. F	6. F	11. T	16. F	21. F	26. F
2. T	7. T	12. F	17. T	22. F	
3. F	8. T	13. F	18. T	23. T	
4. T	9. F	14. F	19. T	24. T	
5. T	10. T	15. F	20. T	25. F	

CHAPTER 8 SELF-TEST

MULTIPLE CHOICE: Circle the letter that corresponds to the best answer.

1. The two most common aircraft hull coverages purchased are:
   a all risks-ground and flight and all risks-not in flight.
   b. all risks-ground and flight and all risks-not in motion.
   c. all risks-not in flight and all risks-not in motion.
   d. all risks-not in motion and specified perils.

2. The definition of aircraft includes all of the following EXCEPT:
   a. navigating or radio equipment while temporarily removed.
   b. an engine removed for overhaul.
   c. a spare engine.
   d. tools and equipment normally carried aboard the aircraft.

3. Deductibles are used for all of the following reasons EXCEPT:
   a. to keep the rates in line.
   b. to eliminate small claims.
   c. to decrease the physical hazard.
   d. to decrease the moral hazard.

4. Which of the following types of deductible only applies to losses up to a stated amount? Once that amount is exceeded, the entire loss is paid in full.
   a. straight.
   b. disappearing.
   c. aggregate.
   d. franchise.

5. Which of the following hull losses would be covered?
   a. blown tire as a result of a rough landing.
   b. cracked windshield caused by freezing.
   c. damaged landing gear as a result of a hijacking attempt.
   d. electrical breakdown as a result of deteriorating wires.

6. Which of the following costs would not be covered in the event of a partial loss in which repairs were made by an FBO?
   a. new parts.
   b. transportation costs.
   c. labor expenses, including overtime.
   d. labor expenses, excluding overtime.

7. Which of the following is NOT a duty of the insured in the event of loss?
   a. have the damage appraised within 30 days.
   b. protect the aircraft from further loss or damage.
   c. file a sworn proof of loss within 60 days.
   d. assist and cooperate with the company.

8. If the insured and the insurer fail to agree on the amount of loss:
   a. the company can deny coverage.
   b. the insured can bring the company to court.
   c. each shall select a disinterested appraiser.
   d. the company shall select a disinterested appraiser.

9. Which of the following endorsements is of particular interest to lien holders?
   a. loss of use.
   b. component parts schedule.
   c. subrogation clause.
   d. breach of warranty.

10. Loss of use coverage:
    a. is generally provided under the basic hull coverage.
    b. is a separate coverage primarily designed for business and pleasure risks.
    c. includes all expenses associated with renting or leasing a substitute aircraft.
    d. does not apply if the insured has available another aircraft of similar type without charge.

11. The bodily injury excluding passengers coverage would cover all except one of the following accidents. Which accident would NOT be covered?
    a. An aircraft crashes into a farmhouse causing injury to several members of the household.
    b. An aircraft, while taxiing, blows debris causing eye injuries to several persons standing in the vicinity of the runway.
    c. A guest is injured when he trips and falls from the boarding platform of the aircraft on static display in an air show.
    d. An occupant (other than the pilot) of the aircraft suffers multiple fractures of both legs when the aircraft crashes.

12. Which of the following statements concerning medical payments coverage is NOT correct?
    a. Funeral expenses are included.
    b. It only applies to passengers.
    c. Payment is made regardless of legal liability.
    d. It discourages liability suits.

13. Admitted liability:
    a. must be at the written request of the injured party.
    b. requires a full release for all bodily injury after the payment is made.
    c. does not apply to the crew members.
    d. is designed primarily for employees.

14. The "omnibus clause," under definition of insured, covers liability incurred by all of the following EXCEPT:
    a. another pilot flying the aircraft with the named insured's permission.
    b. guest passengers.
    c. employees of the named insured for suits other than fellow employees.
    d. any FBO who flies the named insured's aircraft.

15. Which of the following situations would NOT be excluded under the liability coverage?
    a. bodily injury to a fellow employee.
    b. defending suits even if the suits are groundless.
    c. liability assumed under an agreement with an FBO.
    d. personal property of the named insured.

16. Temporary use of substitute aircraft applies:
    a. only when the named insured's aircraft is withdrawn from normal use because of its breakdown, repair, servicing, loss, or destruction.
    b. to any aircraft for any reason as long as it is not used for a period exceeding seven days.
    c. to any non-owned aircraft which is used as a temporary substitute.
    d. none of these.

17. A fairly standard territorial limit under an aircraft hull and liability policy would include the United States and:
    a. Central America.
    b. Canada and Mexico.
    c. Canada and the Caribbean islands.
    d. Mexico and the Bahamas.

18. Which of the following is not a reason for a company to purchase aircraft non-ownership liability coverage?
    a. Employees may rent, charter, or borrow non-owned aircraft.
    b. Employees may fly their own aircraft on company business.
    c. Limits of liability under other contracts may not be adequate.
    d. The company may lease a non-owned aircraft on an annual basis.

19. The named insured is required to waive subrogation rights and assume all liability when using:
    a. major hub airports.
    b. military installations.
    c. seaplane bases.
    d. general aviation airports.

20. No changes to the policy are allowed without approval by the:
    a. agent or broker.
    b. insurance company.
    c. FAA.
    d. local airport authority.

21. All of the following are unique characteristics of aviation insurance, EXCEPT:
    a. limited number of exposure units.
    b. catastrophe exposure.
    c. binding authority by agents and brokers.
    d. relatively few insurers.

22. The declarations page of the hull and liability policy includes:
    a. information from which underwriters make their judgment on risk selection and premium.
    b. statements that are made a part of the contract.
    c. insuring agreements.
    d. a and b.

23. Limited commercial use does not include:
    a. student instruction.
    b. rental to others.
    c. industrial aid.
    d. passenger carrying for hire.

24. Special purposes use include all of the following, EXCEPT:
    a. crop dusting.
    b. industrial aid.
    c. fire fighting.
    d. banner towing.

25. Deductibles generally do not apply to losses caused by:
    a. fire.
    b. theft.
    c. robbery and vandalism.
    d. all of the above.

26. In flight commences:
    a. with the actual takeoff run.
    b. after the wheels have lifted off the runway.
    c. once the aircraft leaves the flight pattern.
    d. upon reaching cruise altitude.

27. Which of the following causes of the loss or damage to tires would NOT be covered?
    a. theft.
    b. vandalism.
    c. malicious mischief.
    d. blowout as a result of a hard landing.

28. A common hull endorsement found on policies covering older aircraft is the:
    a. Breach of Warranty.
    b. Unearned Hull Premium.
    c. Automatic Hull Value Increase.
    d. Component Parts Schedule.

29. All of the following are factors that must be considered in determining the limit of liability to be carried, EXCEPT:
    a. firm's assets.
    b. type of passengers carried (e.g., employees vs. guests).
    c. extent of flying into high-density areas and catastrophe exposure.
    d. the amount other firms carry.

30. Liability coverage protects the insured for:
    a. liability assumed under most contracts.
    b. damage to cargo carried aboard the insured aircraft.
    c. intentional injury to an intoxicated passenger interfering with the safe operation of the aircraft.
    d. injury to employees.

31. Which of the following statements regarding guest voluntary settlement coverage is correct?
    a. It applies to industrial aid and limited commercial risks only.
    b. It does not apply to crew members because their only recourse is workers' compensation.
    c. It is designed to make it unnecessary for an insured's guest to resort to legal action to secure compensation for injury.
    d. A legal release signed by the insured is necessary.

32. Which of the following statements regarding the assumed liability exclusion is NOT correct?
    a. Some policies have been broadened to include assumed liability under incidental contracts.
    b. Insurers generally want to review all contracts in which the insured assumes liability.
    c. Most insurers will approve hold-harmless agreements for flights into military installations.
    d. Most insurers will remove this exclusion, upon request of the insured.

33. A standard territorial limit under an aircraft hull and liability policy includes the:
    a. United States and Canada.
    b. United States, Canada, and Mexico.
    c. United States, Canada, Mexico, and the Bahama Islands.
    d. North America.

34. A shared-use agreement between companies operating a large turbojet multiengine aircraft in which one company leases their aircraft to another company in exchange for equal time is called a(an):
    a. lease exchange.
    b. time sharing agreement.
    c. joint ownership.
    d. interchange agreement.

35. Under a time sharing agreement, all of the following charges are allowed, EXCEPT:
    a. travel expenses of the passengers, including food, lodging, and ground transportation.
    b. hangar and tie-down costs away from the aircraft's base of operations.
    c. insurance obtained for the specific flight.
    d. in flight food and beverages.

36. Because any remuneration received by an aircraft owner may void the "use" provision of the policy:
    a. it should be avoided except for reimbursement of operating expenses.
    b. full details of the arrangement should be submitted to the insurer.
    c. an extension for commercial use must be included.
    d. all of the above.

37. Which of the following situations is least attractive in the case of an insured operating his aircraft for occasional commercial purposes?
    a. Extending his policy to provide for commercial use.
    b. Providing his business and pleasure and commercial use under an air taxi operator's policy.
    c. Covering the commercial use under the air taxi operator's policy and keeping his own policy for business and pleasure purposes.
    d. All of the above are equally unattractive.

38. Which of the following statements concerning holding companies is NOT correct?
    a. Remuneration to the holding company by the users may constitute commercial use.
    b. The actual users, if considered to be renters would be subject to subrogation in the event of a hull loss.
    c. Naming the actual users as named insureds would provide non-ownership liability coverage for them and their employees.
    d. Each case involving a holding company should be reviewed with their underwriter.

39. In the event of loss the insured must do all of the following, EXCEPT:
    a. Arrange for the aircraft to be protected.
    b. If sued, the insured must forward all documents to the insurer.
    c. The insured may be required to obtain medical and other records.
    d. The insured must accept at his own expense any payment required by governmental authorities.

40. In the event that transportation of the aircraft is required following an accident:
    a. the most expedient method must be used.
    b. the least expensive method must be used.
    c. the aircraft must be transported to the insured's home airport.
    d. the aircraft must be disassembled by an authorized mechanic.

41. This coverage is designed to reimburse the insured for extra expense of obtaining another plane when his own business-used aircraft is out of service due to damage covered by the policy.
    a. Temporary use of substitute aircraft.
    b. Loss Payable clause.
    c. Loss of use.
    d. Automatic physical damage coverage.

42. This coverage provides legal liability protection for property damage to non-owned aircraft at the named insured's premises and in the care, custody or control of the named insured. It usually applies only while the aircraft is on the ground.
    a. Non-owned aircraft physical damage.
    b. Loss of use.
    c. Hangarkeepers legal liability.
    d. Aircraft non-ownership liability.

43. Personal Injury liability.
    a. provides legal liability protection for false arrest, assault or battery, defamation, libel and slander.
    b. provides personal protection for lost or damaged baggage or personal effects.
    c. includes host liquor liability.
    d. provides legal liability protection for goods, merchandise and property belonging to others.

44. This coverage provides reimbursement of expenses incurred for food, lodging and travel of passengers to complete a given flight.
    a. Rental Expense of Temporary Replacement Parts.
    b. Extra Expense for Substitute Aircraft.
    c. Personal Injury Liability.
    d. Trip Interruption.

45. Which of the following statements is NOT correct regarding an Interchange Agreement?
    a. Both companies will carry hull and liability coverage on their respective aircraft.
    b. Both companies need to be named as a loss payee with a Breach of Warranty endorsement with respect to hull coverage on each others policy.
    c. With respect to hull coverage, each company must waive their subrogation rights against the other company while each is using the other's aircraft.
    d. Each company will need a clause in their respective policies stating that the other company's policy is primary while using the other company's aircraft.

46. Naming each party as an insured is needed under a(an):
    a. Interchange Agreement.
    b. Time-sharing Agreement.
    c. Joint Ownership Agreement.
    d. All of the above.

47. Under a Fractional ownership arrangement:
    a. each owner normally carries their own hull coverage.
    b. the manufacturer normally provides hull coverage and names the owners as loss payees.
    c. the individual owners normally waive subrogation rights against one another.
    d. a management company will normally carry the hull coverage.

48. A management company providing the crew, maintenance, ground support, insurance record-keeping and overall operation of the aircraft is usually used in which of the following arrangement?
    a. Interchange agreement.
    b. Fractional ownership.
    c. Exclusive dry lease
    d. Time-sharing agreement.

49. Holding companies are established for ownership of a company aircraft for all of the following reasons, EXCEPT:
    a. tax purposes.
    b. to limit liability exposure.
    c. to establish commercial operations.
    d. a and b.

50. Which of the following statements regarding aircraft hull and liability insurance is correct?
    a. Policy terms and wording are similar.
    b. Comparing coverage offered by different insurers on the same risk is relatively easy.
    c. Policy forms can vary within the same company.
    d. Reinsurance treaties are similar because of the limited number of companies.

TRUE/FALSE: Circle *T* if the statement is true, *F* if it is false.

T F 1. An aircraft might be "in flight" according to the aircraft hull and liability policy even though it is, in fact, on the ground.

T F 2. All risks-ground and flight coverage also provides for disappearance of aircraft if unreported 60 days after takeoff.

T F 3. The most common type of deductible is the aggregate deductible.

T F 4. A deductible, if applicable, is always subtracted in case of a total loss.

T F 5. Fire, lightning, explosion, and theft losses are not subject to a deductible.

T F 6. The hull coverage excludes any loss or damage to the aircraft caused by war.

T F 7. Hull coverage would not apply to an engine destroyed by fire while it was removed from the aircraft for an overhaul.

T F 8. If a policy were written on a valued basis, the company would pay the actual cash value of the aircraft in the event of total loss.

T F 9. Some policies provide for a return of any unearned hull premium in the event of a partial loss.

T F 10. Component parts schedules are normally attached to policies covering older aircraft.

T F 11. The value of all salvage following the payment of a total loss shall inure to the benefit of the company.

T F 12. Coverage for newly acquired aircraft is normally provided under hull insurance.

T F 13. Aircraft liability arising out of the ownership, maintenance, or use of an aircraft is, in general, based on the law of negligence.

T F 14. The term "occurrence" is broader than the term "accident."

T F 15. A single-limit of liability can be written either excluding or including passengers.

T F 16. Only reasonable expenses incurred for hospital and surgical procedures are payable under the medical coverage.

T F 17. Non-ownership liability provides the owner of aircraft with protection should he rent or lease his aircraft.

T F 18. Weekly indemnity can be included as part of the medical payments coverage.

T F 19. If medical payments coverage is provided, it can be used to satisfy a workers' compensation claim in the event of injury to an employee.

T F 20. "Use of other aircraft" only applies to the named insured (if an individual) and his spouse with respect to the operation of any non-owned aircraft.

T F 21. When two or more aircraft are insured under a policy, the terms of the policy apply separately to each.

T F 22. Because the insurance policy is a personal contract, an insured may assign it to another party in the event the aircraft is sold.

T F 23. If the named insured cancels his policy, a short rate penalty applies.

T F 24. Guest voluntary settlement limits of liability are not in addition to the legal limits of liability.

T F 25. Authority to bind risks or amend coverages is rarely given to agents and brokers in the aviation insurance field.

T F 26. Most aviation policies begin and end at 12:01 a.m.

T F 27. Any financial institution holding a mortgage on the aircraft must be listed under the declarations.

T F 28. An open pilot warranty means that there is no minimum hourly requirement.

T F 29. Hull coverage is designed to protect owners, lessors, lessees, borrowers, and renters.

T F 30. All risk-not in flight is a popular coverage.

T F 31. Standard deductibles for commercial risks are generally lower than business and pleasure risks because the aircraft are flown by professional pilots.

T F 32. A franchise deductible applies to a loaner engine that is damaged as a result of ingesting rocks, hail stones, birds, and other foreign objects.

T F 33. Loss or damage arising out of a hijacking would normally be covered unless it was carried out by some governmental authority.

T F 34. If a policy is written on a valued basis, a total loss would be settled on the basis of actual cash value.

T F 35. Hull coverage normally applies to temporary substitute aircraft if reported to the company within one week after its use.

T F 36. War-risks coverage only applies in the case of a declared war.

T F 37. Flights requiring a waiver or permit from the FAA are usually excluded unless the insured notifies the company.

T F 38. If the named insured is an individual, the liability coverages apply while operating non- owned aircraft.

T F 39. Non-ownership liability coverage normally limits the consecutive number of days coverage will apply.

T F 40. Airport Premises liability coverage can be included under the Aircraft Hull and Liability policy.

T F 41. When products liability for sale of the insured aircraft is covered the policy must be in force at the time of the accident.

T F 42. Baggage liability coverage is provided under virtually all aviation policies but the limits offered vary considerably among carriers.

T F 43. Territorial limits can normally be extended for one trip or on a blanket basis for little or no additional premium.

T F 44. Insureds that are reimbursed for use of their aircraft are covered so long as no profit is made.

T F 45. Actual funds must be exchanged for an insurer to deny coverage in the case of a reimbursement arrangement between an insured and another party.

T F 46. A time sharing agreement involves the lease of an airplane with flight crew to another party.

T F 47. Most major aviation insurers will endorse a noncommercial policy without charge to avoid any conflict resulting from reimbursement arrangements provided they are notified in advance.

T F 48. An attractive way to cover occasional commercial usage is to have an air taxi operator pick up this exposure under his policy.

T F 49. The remuneration to a holding company, established for the ownership of an aircraft, may constitute commercial use and void a policy written for industrial aid purposes.

T F 50. Buying aircraft hull and liability insurance is very similar to buying automobile insurance.

T F 51. Flying Clubs would be considered special uses under the purpose of use on the Declarations page.

T F 52. The least expensive method of transportation must be used in the event the aircraft must be moved following an accident.

T F 53. In the event that the insured and insurer fail to agree on the amount of loss the only recourse is for the insured to sue the insurer.

T F 54. Payments under guest voluntary settlement coverage are subject to a full release for all bodily injury is obtained from the insured.

T F 55. Permanent and total disability coverage can be provided in conjunction with guest voluntary settlement whether weekly indemnity coverage is written or not.

T F 56. Non-Owned aircraft physical damage coverage is basically in-flight hangarkeepers legal liability coverage.

T F 57. Extra expense for substitute aircraft provides reimbursement of expenses incurred for food, lodging and travel of passengers to complete a given flight.

T F 58. Under an exclusive dry lease arrangement the lessor normally only provides the aircraft and maintenance.

T F 59. Under a management company arrangement the management company will normally carry the hull and liability coverage for the owner under its own fleet insurance policy.

T F 60. Each fractional owner normally carries their own hull insurance.

T F 61. Reduced taxes and limitation of liability are the primary reasons why businesses establish holding companies.

T F 62. The insurance considerations for an interchange agreement are basically the same for each owner/user.

COVERAGE: Answer the following questions on the basis of the named insured having an aircraft hull and liability policy in force providing coverage under all liability insuring agreements. Indicate whether or not the policy would respond for the person seeking coverage by circling the yes or no preceding the question. Each numbered question gives a situation which stands by itself.

yes no 1. X, the named insured, is sued by the widow of passenger Y, who was killed in a crash.

yes no 2. X, the named insured, lends his plane to friends Y and Z. After the crash Y sues Z, the pilot, for injuries that Y sustained.

(3-5). X, the named insured, lends his plane to Y with instructions to let no one else fly it. Y, nevertheless, lends it to Z without the knowledge or implied consent of X. Z crashes the aircraft into a house and:

yes no 3. the occupants sue X.

yes no 4. the occupants sue Y.

yes no 5. the occupants sue Z.

yes no 6. X, an aircraft dealer, has sold an aircraft to Y, the named insured. Several days later after servicing, X flew the aircraft toward Y's home field and crashed into Z's home. Will X be covered under Y's policy?

yes no 7. The named insured instructs employee A to use the aircraft for business purposes. In the course of such use, A injures another employee, B. B sues A.

(8-9). X, the named insured, signs an agreement with the local FBO assuming all liability for any losses arising out of the use of the FBO's tie -down area. A windstorm occurs and X's aircraft is blown into Y's aircraft. Y sues X for tying down his aircraft in an insecure manner and enjoins the FBO for having poorly secured tie-down stakes.

yes no 8. Is X covered?

yes no 9. Is the FBO covered?

yes no 10. X, the named insured, while taxiing his aircraft on the ramp area injures an airport employee who sues X?

Answers to Chapter 8 Self-Test

Multiple Choice

1. b	11. d	21. c	31. c	41. c
2. c	12. b	22. d	32. d	42. c
3. c	13. b	23. d	33. b	43. a
4. d	14. d	24. b	34. d	44. d
5. c	15. b	25. d	35. a	45. b
6. c	16. a	26. a	36. b	46. d
7. a	17. b	27. d	37. c	47. d
8. c	18. d	28. d	38. c	48. b
9. d	19. b	29. d	39. d	49. d
10. d	20. b	30. c	40. b	50. c

True/False

1. T	10. T	19. F	28. F	37. T	46. T	55. T
2. T	11. T	20. T	29. F	38. T	47. T	56. T
3. F	12. T	21. T	30. F	39. T	48. F	57. F
4. F	13. T	22. F	31. F	40. T	49. T	58. F
5. T	14. T	23. T	32. F	41. T	50. F	59. T
6. T	15. T	24. T	33. T	42. F	51. F	60. F
7. F	16. F	25. T	34. F	43. T	52. T	61. T
8. F	17. F	26. T	35. F	44. F	53. F	62. T
9. F	18. F	27. T	36. F	45. F	54. F	

Coverage

1. Yes	3. Yes	5. No	7. No	9. No
2. Yes	4. Yes	6. No	8. No	10. Yes

CHAPTER 9 **SELF- TEST**

MULTIPLE CHOICE: Circle the letter that corresponds to the best answer.

1. The declarations page of the airport premises liability policy includes all of the following EXCEPT:
   a. the policy period.
   b. coverages and limits of liability.
   c. insuring agreements.
   d. description of premises.

2. Which of the following situations would NOT be excluded under the airport liability policy?
   a. liability arising out of an air show sponsored by the insured, for which a charge is made
   b. liability assumed under an agreement with a fuel supplier
   c. liability arising out of the operation of vehicles operated on the airport property
   d. liability arising out of work performed by independent contractors

3. Medical payments coverage is not designed to cover:
   a. the insured's employees.
   b. independent contractors employed by the insured.
   c. municipal workers
   d. answers a and b are not covered.

4. "Completed operations" under products liability includes:
   a. the sale of new and used aircraft.
   b. aircraft repairs, "servicing and installation of parts and accessories.
   c. fuel and oil sales.
   d. sale of aircraft parts and accessories.

5. The following coverage is basically a form of bailee insurance:
   a. Products liability.
   b. Air meet liability.
   c. Contractual liability.
   d. Hangarkeepers liability.

6. Hangar keepers' liability:
   a. excludes coverage for aircraft in the insured's care, custody, or control.
   b. provides coverage for aircraft rented or loaned to the insured while the aircraft is on the ground.
   c. is written with a limit per aircraft and a limit per occurrence.
   d. only covers the insured's liability for maintenance and repair work done on aircraft.

7. A renter pilot may purchase individual non -ownership liability coverage for all of the following reasons EXCEPT:
   a. the basic bodily injury and property damage liability includes physical damage to the non-owned aircraft.
   b. the limits of liability under the owner's policy may be inadequate for the renter.
   c. he may be excluded under the owner's policy.
   d. answers a and c are exceptions.

8. Consequential loss can best be described as:
   a. indirect loss.
   b. chemical liability.
   c. a large direct loss.
   d. non-ownership loss.

9. Many suppliers of aircraft components purchase aircraft products liability coverage because:
   a. their loss experience is very poor.
   b. most other products liability insurance policies exclude all aviation exposures.
   c. they need grounding coverage which is provided under the basic policy.
   d. most aircraft accidents involve minor aircraft components.

10. The basic ultralight aircraft policy provides:
    a. physical damage coverage.
    b. premises liability coverage.
    c. medical payments coverage.
    d. admitted liability coverage.

11. The Comprehensive General Liability policy includes coverage for:
    a. aircraft owned by the insured.
    b. aircraft non -ownership liability.
    c. independent contractors liability.
    d. air meet liability.

12. Which of the following exclusions is found under all liability contracts and generally cannot be amended?
    a. assumed liability
    b. contractual liability.
    c. war-risks liability.
    d. products liability.

13. The premium for various coverages under the airport premises liability policy is determined by all of the following methods, EXCEPT:
    a. area of the premises.
    b. number of admissions.
    c. number of aircraft operations.
    d. sales.

14. The products liability coverage contains three limits of liability—a per person, a per accident, and a(an):
    a. aggregate limit.
    b. occurrence limit.
    c. completed operations limit.
    d. hangar keepers' liability limit.

15. A common method of determining hangarkeepers' limits is to cover the value of the in the operator's care, custody, or control at any one time.
    a. minimum aircraft and maximum total aircraft
    b. maximum aircraft and average total aircraft
    c. average aircraft and maximum total aircraft
    d. average aircraft and average total aircraft

16. Personal injury liability covers claims arising out of:
    a. bodily injury.
    b. intentional torts.
    c. property damage.
    d. medical payments to the insured.

17. Air meet liability coverage provided under an airport liability policy is designed to protect the:
    a. sponsor.
    b. participants.
    c. local municipality.
    d. public.

18. All of the following situations are examples of why a company should purchase non-ownership liability coverage, EXCEPT:
    a. employees flying their own aircraft on company business.
    b. company officials rent, borrow, or charter aircraft.
    c. employees fly on company business as guests in another company's aircraft.
    d. company officials lease a non-owned aircraft for six months.

19. Umbrella liability insurance is designed to:
    a. reimburse the insured for the cost of renting a substitute aircraft while the insured's aircraft is undergoing repairs.
    b. add additional coverage above a specific amount up to a specified limit.
    c. provide an aggregate amount for all losses over a stated amount for the policy year.
    d. fill the gaps in liability protection associated with basic coverages or self-insured retentions.

20. Loss of Use coverage:
    a. is particularly beneficial to business and pleasure aircraft operators.
    b. takes effect immediately following an aircraft's removal from service.
    c. only applies while the insured's aircraft is undergoing repairs following an accident.
    d. only applies for one year following an accident.

21. Loss of license insurance:
    a. pays the pilot a predetermined amount per month immediately following the loss of his or her medical certificate.
    b. covers a period from one to five years following the loss of his or her medical certificate.
    c. will pay a preselected lump sum of money, less the amount paid out in monthly payments, after predetermined number of months.
    d. only applies if the pilot is permanently and totally disabled.

22. The inspection and surveys clause gives the company the right to:
    a. make inspections and surveys at any time.
    b. audit the insureds books.
    c. make recommendations.
    d. all of the above.

23. Assumed liability under which of the following contracts would NOT be covered?
    a. a lease of premises.
    b. architectural drawings.
    c. an elevator maintenance agreement.
    d. a municipal ordinance.

24. Which of the following statements regarding products liability coverage is correct?
    a. Completed operations refers to the sale of fuel and oil.
    b. The coverage applies to accidents off and on the airport premises.
    c. Three limits of liability apply: a per person, a per accident, and an aggregate policy limit.
    d. a and c are correct.

25. Aircraft non-ownership liability may be purchased by a corporation for all of the following reasons, EXCEPT:
    a. An employee, unknown to the company, may fly an aircraft on business.
    b. the limits under the owners policy be inadequate.
    c. They may be held liable for physical damage to the non-owned aircraft.
    d. The corporation may have an infrequent need for a non-owned aircraft to supplement their own aircraft.

26. Advertising injury liability provides coverage for:
    a. oral or written publication of material that slanders or libels a person or organization.
    b. breach of contract.
    c. the failure of products or services to conform with advertised quality or performance.
    d. the wrong description of the price of products or services.

27. Which of the following insurers specializes in aircraft operators engaged in aerial application?
    a. Phoenix Aviation Managers
    b. Reliance National Aviation
    c. Avemco Insurance Company
    d. CIGNA Aerospace

28. Liability coverage for aerial applications can be written in the following ways, EXCEPT:
    a. excluding chemical drift (XC).
    b. restricted (or limited) chemical drift (RC).
    c. including chemical drift (IC).
    d. comprehensive chemical drift (CC).

29. Most states require a commercial aerial applicator to carry minimum liability limits of:
    a. BI $100/300,000
PD $100,000
    b. BI $10/20,000
PD $10,000
    c. BI $250/500,000;
PD $250,000
    d. BI and PD $1,000,000

30. Restricted (or limited) chemical drift (RC) coverage:
    a. is basically designed to only cover liability incurred by the agricultural aircraft.
    b. only applies to insecticides, fungicides, fertilizers and seeds.
    c. includes substantial consequential losses.
    d. excludes adjacent field coverage

31. Light-sport aircraft are generally defined by their limitations. All of the following are limitations, EXCEPT:
    a. Take-off weight of 1,232 pounds.
    b. A stalling speed in the landing configuration of 39 knots.
    c. A speed in straight and level flight of 115 knots.
    d. Four occupants.

32. All of the following categories of aircraft would need an experimental airworthiness certificate, EXCEPT:
    a. Vintage aircraft.
    b. Flying club aircraft.
    c. Warbird.
    d. air racing aircraft.

TRUE/FALSE: Circle *T* if the statement is true, *F* if it is false.

T F 1. The two prerequisites for determining the dividing point between premises operations and products completed operations are: (l) possession must be relinquished and (2) the occurrence must take place off the premises.

T F 2. Airport premises liability coverage is primarily designed for airport owners, not tenants.

T F 3. Many exclusions are included in the airport premises liability policy because there are other policies designed to cover such risks.

T F 4. The inspection and surveys clause gives the company the right to inspect the insured's premises and to audit his books.

T F 5. Most airport liability policies provide automatic coverage for new premises and operations for 30 days.

T F 6. Contractual liability is normally provided on a blanket basis because of the numerous contracts between airport operators and tenants.

T F 7. Liability arising out of the work performed by independent contractors is automatically covered under the airport premises liability contract.

T F 8. An aggregate limit only applies in the case of products liability.

T F 9. Air meet liability is normally designed to protect the sponsor and the participants in an air show.

T F 10. Non-owned aircraft physical damage coverage is basically subrogation coverage.

T F 11. Airport premises liability coverage does not extend to include the automobile parking facilities.

T F 12. Fixed Base Operators normally do not need airport premises liability coverage because this exposure is picked up under their aircraft hull and liability policy.

T F 13. Elevators and escalators are covered automatically under the basic airport liability policy.

T F 14. Medical payments coverage under the airport premises liability policy is designed to cover employees and independent contractors employed by the insured as well as members of the public.

T F 15. Approval of contractual liability by underwriters is generally done on a very selective basis.

T F 16. Independent contractors employed by the insured carry their own liability coverage, therefore, it is generally not necessary for an airport operator to cover this exposure.

T F 17. Deductibles do not apply to fire, lightning, or explosion losses under the hangar keepers' liability coverage.

T F 18. Advertising injury liability protects an insured against misappropriation of advertising ideas or infringement upon another's copyright or title.

T F 19. Aerial application is often written with a deductible applicable to the liability coverage.

T F 20. There is generally no need for non-ownership liability protection if a company is covered as an insured under the owner's policy.

T F 21. Grounding coverage is provided as an extension under air meet liability.

T F 22. Excess aggregate insurance is popular among aircraft and component manufacturers.

T F 23. Loss of use coverage is particularly attractive to commercial aircraft operators.

T F 24. Loss of license insurance will pay the pilot a predetermined amount per month immediately following the loss of his or her medical certificate.

T F 25. Employees of an airport are covered as insureds but only while working at the airport described in the declarations.

T F 26. Medical payments coverage excludes tenants injured on their property.

T F 27. Airport liability policies basically follow the OLT and CGL forms.

T F 28. Any liability arising from the ownership or operation of automobiles or other vehicles is excluded under airport premises liability.

T F 29. Most airport liability policies do not provide automatic coverage for new premises and operations because underwriters must review the particular risk.

T F 30. Theft of an aircraft would be included under hangarkeepers liability.

T F 31. Individual non-ownership liability is largely negated because renter pilots and flight training students are covered under most FBO policies.

T F 32. Corporations buy non-ownership liability coverage because they are frequently unaware that some of its personnel are flying on company business.

T F 33. Umbrella liability insurance is designed to fill the gaps in liability protection associated with basic coverages or self-insured retentions.

T F 34. The pilot accident policy, is a limited exposure, covering only those accidents resulting from exposure to aircraft.

T F 35. Liability insurance needs of aerial applicators differ somewhat from those of the regular aircraft owner or operator.

T F 36. Adjacent field coverage provides protection for drift onto crops owned by the same farmer the applicator is contracted to spray for.

T F 37. Comprehensive chemical drift (CC) coverage only applies to insecticides, fungicides, fertilizers or seeds.

T F 38. Aerial applicators are subject to a special short-rate table in the event of cancellation.

T F 39. Vintage aircraft and warbirds must have a standard airworthiness certificate issued by the FAA.

T F 40. One of the markets writing experimental aircraft is U.S. Specialty Insurance Company.

MATCHING: Match the coverage applicable to each of the following accidents. (indicate a, b, c, or d)

COVERAGE

a. Airport premises B1.
b. Airport premises PD.
c. Hanger keepers' flight or ground.
d. Products BI or PD.

_______1. X's aircraft was tied down by FBO's employee on FBO's tie -down area. X's aircraft was destroyed by a windstorm.

_______2. A gasoline truck, operated by fueling service company T located at the airport, damaged A's automobile in the airport parking lot.

_______3. D slipped on some oil spilled on the apron area, which R's mechanic failed to clean up after working on an aircraft.

_______4. R's line employee lit up a cigarette after fueling E's aircraft. A fire ensued, causing considerable damage to E's aircraft.

_______5. R's counter employee failed to inform an incoming pilot, via unicorn, that the county maintenance crew was cutting the grass landing strip. F's aircraft was damaged when he tried to avoid hitting the mower.

_______6. R's line employee pumped contaminated gasoline into Z's aircraft causing him to crash after takeoff.

Answers to Chapter 9 Self-Test

Multiple Choice

1. c	5. d	9. b	13. c	17. a	21. c	25. c	29. a
2. c	6. c	10. a	14. a	18. d	22. d	26. a	30. b
3. d	7. a	11. c	15. d	19. d	23. b	27. a	31. d
4. b	8. a	12. c	16. b	20. c	24. c	28. c	32. b

True/False

1. T	6. F	11. F	16. F	21. F	26. T	31. F	36. T
2. F	7. F	12. F	17. T	22. T	27. T	32. T	37. F
3. T	8. T	13. F	18. T	23. T	28. F	33. T	38. T
4. T	9. F	14. F	19. T	24. T	29. F	34. T	39. F
5. T	10. T	15. T	20. F	25. F	30. F	35. T	40. T

Matching

1. c	2. b	3. a	4. b	5. b	6. d

CHAPTER 10 SELF-TEST

MULTIPLE CHOICE: Circle the letter that corresponds to the best answer.

1. The basic function of underwriting is to:
   a. avoid insuring people who are likely to have losses.
   b. make certain that only very good risks are insured.
   c. generate as high a premium volume as possible.
   d. avoid adverse selection.

2. The aircraft hull and liability application requires all of the following information EXCEPT:
   a. insured value of aircraft.
   b. the purpose for which the aircraft will be used.
   c. name of the home airport.
   d. hangar or tie -down charge per month.

3. The minimum pilot requirements for a single-engine retractable gear aircraft would normally include:
   a. any student pilot or better.
   b. any private pilot or better.
   c. any private pilot with a minimum of 200 total logged hours.
   d. any private pilot with a minimum of 50 total logged hours in the model.

4. Corporate aircraft flown by professional pilots would be classified as:
   a. business and pleasure use.
   b. industrial aid use.
   c. airline use.
   d. special use.

5. An aircraft used for rental and instruction would be classified as:
   a. special use.
   b. industrial aid use.
   c. full commercial use.
   d. limited commercial use.

6. Products liability premiums are based on:
   a. the number of products sold.
   b. the gross receipts.
   c. the type and size of the FBO.
   d. the use to which the products are put.

7. Rate making in aviation insurance:
   a. is usually done on a cooperative basis.
   b. must be accomplished through rating bureaus and cannot be done by individual companies because of the limited spread of risk.
   c. differs from price setting in other businesses since prices must be set before costs are known.
   d. none of these.

8. The base rate for hull insurance is expressed as a rate per:
   a. $100 of insured value.
   b. $1,000 of insured value.
   c. number of estimated hours flown.
   d. days at risk.

9. Guest voluntary settlement coverage is primarily available for:
   a. business and pleasure risks.
   b. industrial aid risks.
   c. commercial risks.
   d. airline risks.

10. All of the following are unique problems faced by aviation underwriters, EXCEPT:
    a. limited spread of risks.
    b. selection of risks.
    c. catastrophe loss.
    d. diversification of risks.

11. Diversification of risks refers to the differing:
    a. make and model of aircraft.
    b. values of similar aircraft.
    c. use of aircraft.
    d. all of the above.

12. Which of the following statements concerning basic underwriting information is NOT correct?
    a. Coverage normally attaches and expires at 12:01 a.m.
    b. Avionics equipment can often represent up to one -third of the aircraft value.
    c. The law of large numbers works better the greater the number of aircraft at a particular airport.
    d. Higher deductibles are often required for tied-down aircraft.

13. Underwriters would probably require additional information on which of the following statements in the application?
    a. Aircraft is tied-down at a large general aviation airport in the Midwest.
    b. Aircraft is used by a flying club.
    c. Aircraft is flown from the Midwest to Florida quite often.
    d. There is an outstanding encumbrance on the aircraft in the amount of $10,000 to the First National Bank.

14. A second class medical certificate expires every:
    a. six months.
    b. twelve months.
    c. eighteen months.
    d. twenty-four months.

15. Total hours logged as pilot-in-command (PIC) means:
    a. total flying hours.
    b. total flying hours required by the FAA to qualify for certain licenses and ratings.
    c. total logged flying hours.
    d. none of the above.

16. All of the following factors are important to an underwriter in evaluating a pilot's flight history, EXCEPT:
    a. Have there been any citations for a violation of FARs?
    b. Where and when did the pilot first learn to fly?
    c. Has the pilot been involved in an aircraft accident?
    d. Is the pilot flying subject to a medical waiver from the FAA?

17. Which of the following statements concerning a pilot's flight experience is correct?
    a. The Federal Aviation Administration requires that all PIC hours be logged.
    b. Underwriters are particularly concerned in knowing the pilot's hours flown during the last 90 days.
    c. Pilot warranties generally do not hold up in a court of law because they overstate logged hours.
    d. Unlike a student pilot, a private pilot can log time as PIC while receiving instruction with a flight instructor aboard the aircraft.

18. Underwriters are concerned with four principal areas when insuring aircraft. They include all of the following, EXCEPT:
    a. operational characteristics of the aircraft.
    b. the abilities of the pilot.
    c. geographical considerations.
    d. the purpose for which the aircraft is to be used.

19. An aircraft's susceptibility to loss is a function of any of the following factors, EXCEPT:
    a. age.
    b. manufacturer.
    c. construction.
    d. configuration.

20. An underwriter may impose certain minimum hourly requirements or restrictions in the pilot warranty for a pilot:
    a. who is transitioning from a fixed-gear aircraft to a retractible-gear aircraft and has little or no experience in the latter type.
    b. who is planning a flight into a high-density traffic area.
    c. who carries a single-limit of liability coverage.
    d. all of the above.

21. As a general guideline underwriters will require single-engine retractible-gear aircraft to be operated by a private pilot having at least total logged hours.
    a. 100
    b. 200
    c. the FAA minimum
    d. 500

22. Limited commercial use:
    a. includes charter flights.
    b. excludes business and pleasure usage.
    c. includes rental and instruction.
    d. excludes rental but includes instruction.

23. Underwriters are particularly concerned with two factors when evaluating helicopter risks. They are the:
    a. manufacturer and purpose of use.
    b. purpose of use and pilot qualifications.
    c. pilot qualifications and geographical area of operations.
    d. geographical area of operations and operating characteristics.

24. Under a hull and liability reporting form policy:
    a. hull rates are the same for all insured aircraft.
    b. the deposit premium is generally equal to 75 percent of the estimated annual premium.
    c. coverages can be written on a rate per diem or per flying hour but not a combination of both.
    d. if the actual hours flown during the year exceed the estimate upon which the flying hour rate was determined, the additional premium is considered fully earned.

25. Which of the following statements regarding underwriting is NOT correct:
    a. GARA has prompted more lawsuits against FBOs.
    b. One of the key factors in underwriting airports is the extent to which the airport engages in service operations such as fueling and hangaring aircraft.
    c. Underwriting experience for helicopters has improved considerably since the 1970s.
    d. Commercial aircraft risks are subject to fewer partial hull losses than other purpose of use categories because of pilot experience.

26. The products liability classification that would normally take the highest rate per $1,000 of gross receipts is:
    a. sale of used aircraft.
    b. aircraft servicing and repair.
    c. sale of aircraft parts.
    d. sale of gas and oil.

27. Limited spread of risks leads to:
    a. more credible statistics.
    b. less credible statistics.
    c. less diversification in risks.
    d. less rapidity of change in models.

28. Which of the following statements regarding tied-down aircraft is NOT correct?
    a. Higher deductibles may be required.
    b. There is a higher incidence of theft.
    c. A surcharge on the hull rate is typical.
    d. Some companies refuse to write tied-down aircraft.

29. An aircraft's configuration means:
    a. year of manufacture.
    b. wood frame, tubular steel or aluminum.
    c. conventional or tricycle landing gear.
    d. seating capacity.

30. Which of the following statements regarding pilots is correct?
    a. Less than 50 percent of the non-airline accidents involve some degree of pilot error.
    b. Most companies agree on minimum pilot requirements.
    c. Underwriters will often impose pilot restrictions beyond those required by federal licensing regulations.
    d. Most underwriters agree that total time is more important than recency of experience in the model.

31. Which purpose of use would flying clubs fall under?
    a. Special use.
    b. Commercial use.
    c. Limited commercial.
    d. Business and Pleasure.

32. All of the following factors would be considered in underwriting hangarkeepers liability, EXCEPT:
    a. type of aircraft hangared and tied-down.
    b. general housekeeping practices.
    c. average value of any one aircraft hangared or tied-down.
    d. aggregate value of all aircraft.

33. Which of the following statements is NOT correct?
    a. FBO's generally prefer reporting form policies.
    b. Legal liability coverage for commercial risks is generally higher than industrial aid.
    c. Hangarkeeper liability rates are fairly standard throughout the industry.
    d. Products liability rates vary according to the product classification.

34. The primary purpose of underwriting is to:
    a. offer a broad selection of classifications for rating purposes.
    b. obtain a profitable distribution of risks.
    c. accept the best risks at competitive prices.
    d. all of the above.

35. All of the following are part of the preselection process of underwriting, EXCEPT:
    a. offering insureds restricted coverage.
    b. requiring an antitheft device.
    c. instructions to agents advising general underwriting requirements.
    d. no exceptions - all of the above are part of the preselection process.

TRUE/FALSE: Circle *T* if the statement is true, *F* if it is false.

T F 1. The underwriting process includes preselection and post-selection of risks.

T F 2. Underwriting sources include applications, agent's comments, and inspection reports.

T F 3. An aircraft's susceptibility to loss can be a function of any number of factors relative to its age, construction, and general configuration.

T F 4. Underwriters often impose pilot standards in the form of minimum hours beyond those required by federal regulations.

T F 5. An aircraft used exclusively for charter purposes would be classified as limited commercial.

T F 6. Liability premiums for commercial risks are generally much higher than business and pleasure risks.

T F 7. The one item of the declarations which has the most significance for aircraft liability coverage is the certificated passenger capacity.

T F 8. The airport liability policy provides automatic coverage for all hazards connected with the operation of an airport.

T F 9. A corporation with no known aircraft exposure other than their employees' use of commercial airlines would have no need for non-owned aircraft liability coverage.

T F 10. The pricing problem in insurance is simpler than that in most other businesses.

T F 11. Underwriting involves the profitable distribution of risks.

T F 12. Aviation underwriting is greatly assisted by the National Bureau of Casualty Underwriter which has developed rating manuals for all classes of aviation business.

T F 13. Eliminating undesirable insureds is called preselection.

T F 14. "Select or be selected against" means choosing only the best risks and canceling all marginal accounts.

T F 15. Production(marketing) and underwriting are more likely to conflict in a small branch office.

T F 16. If a multiengine aircraft has two crew seats plus five passenger seats but is often operated with one pilot and six passengers the rating should be based on the five passenger seats.

T F 17. A surcharge on the hull rate is common for tied-down aircraft based at certain airports because of weather conditions or a higher incidence of theft.

T F 18. Some underwriters will not insure aircraft used for certain purposes regardless of the premium.

T F 19. A pilot who holds a first or second class medical certificate which has expired, may continue to fly under certain circumstances.

T F 20. A private or commercial pilot can only log time as PIC while he or she is the sole manipulator of an aircraft that he or she is properly rated for.

T F 21. An FAA flight (biennial) review can be waived if the pilot has logged at least 50 hours during the past year.

T F 22. Underwriters will often impose minimum pilot warranties that are in excess of FAA requirements for operating a particular aircraft.

T F 23. If an insured meets FAA minimum requirements for operating a particular aircraft underwriters will generally not impose any restrictions.

T F 24. Generally underwriters require a copilot to be aboard all turboprop aircraft.

T F 25. Most underwriters agree that recency of experience and experience in the model are more important than total time in evaluating a pilot.

T F 26. An aircraft used for charter and rental purposes but not instruction would be classified as limited commercial use.

T F 27. Improvements in rotor blades and other materials in recent years have not significantly affected helicopter safety.

T F 28. Considerably less information is needed in underwriting airports than aircraft.

T F 29. Medical payments coverage can be written to include or exclude crew members.

T F 30. A hull and liability reporting form policy can be written on a per diem or per flying hour basis but not a combination of both.

T F 31. FBOs generally prefer reporting form policies because premiums, even though subject to a deposit and minimums, are less expensive than an annual payment.

T F 32. Most airports outsource service operations functions such as fueling and hangaring aircraft to FBOs.

T F 33. Hangarkeepers' liability rates largely depend upon whether or not the insured stores aircraft or does repair and servicing work.

T F 34. It is important from an underwriting standpoint to have as many rating classifications as possible.

T F 35. Limited spread of risks combined with diversification makes aviation underwriting more difficult than many other lines of insurance.

T F 36. The business of an applicant can be helpful in determining how the aircraft is going to be used.

T F 37. A surcharge on the hull rate is typical for tied-down aircraft.

T F 38. A third class medical certificate expires every 12 months.

T F 39. Age of the aircraft is no longer a problem since single-engine aircraft production resumed after the General Aviation Revitalization Act.

T F 40. Over 70 percent of the non-airline accidents involve some degree of mechanical failure.

T F 41. The accident record for industrial aid aircraft operators compares very favorably with that of the major airlines.

T F 42. In underwriting helicopter risks purpose of use and pilot qualifications are the two most important factors.

T F 43. Housekeeping practices by the insured is an important factor in underwriting hangarkeepers' liability coverage.

T F 44. Based on an annual exposure of 1,200 hours, a hull rate of $7.20/$100 and an insured value of $40,000 this FBO's monthly premium would be $260.00.

T F 45. Aircraft servicing and repair normally takes the highest rate per $1,000 of gross receipts.

LISTING:

1. An underwriter is interested in four principal areas when insuring aircraft hull and liability risks. They are:

   a.______________________________

   b.______________________________

   c.______________________________

   d.______________________________

2. List the correct purpose of use next to the following descriptions:

   a. An FBO provides aircraft and pilot to fly several executives on a business trip.________________

   b. A sales representative uses his own aircraft to cover his territory.________________

   c. A utility company uses a Cessna 150 for powerline patrol.________________

   d. A corporation rents its aircraft to another company for business and pleasure usage.________________

e. A corporate-owned aircraft is flown by corporate-employed professional pilots on flights in which no charge is made.__________

3. The basic information needed to offer a hull and liability quotation include:

a.__________

b.__________

c.__________

d.__________

e.__________

f.__________

g.__________

h.__________

i.__________

j.__________

k.__________

l.__________

Answers to Chapter 10 Self-Test

Multiple Choice

1. d	6. b	11. d	16. b	21. b	26. b	31. d
2. d	7. c	12. c	17. b	22. c	27. b	32. a
3. c	8. a	13. b	18. a	23. b	28. d	33. c
4. b	9. b	14. b	19. b	24. d	29. c	34. b
5. d	10. b	15. d	20. a	25. d	30. c	35. d

True/False

1. T	7. T	13. F	19. T	25. T	31. F	37. T	43. T
2. T	8. F	14. F	20. T	26. F	32. T	38. F	44. F
3. T	9. F	15. T	21. F	27. F	33. T	39. F	45. T
4. T	10. F	16. F	22. T	28. F	34. F	40. F	
5. F	11. T	17. T	23. F	29. T	35. T	41. T	
6. T	12. F	18. T	24. T	30. F	36. T	42. T	

LISTING

1. a. the type of aircraft to be insured.
   b. the abilities of the pilot.
   c. geographical considerations.
   d. the purpose for which the aircraft is to be used.

2. a. full commercial.
   b. business and pleasure.
   c. special use.
   d. limited commercial.
   e. industrial aid.

3. a. Name and address of the applicant.
   b. Business of the applicant.
   c. Effective time and data of coverage.
   d. The type(s) and limit(s) of liability coverage desired.
   e. The type of aircraft physical damage (hull) coverage desired and deductibles.
   f. Description of the aircraft.
   g. Whether the aircraft is normally hangared or tied down and the name of the airport.
   h. Purpose of use.
   i. Territorial limits.
   j. Pilots who will operate the aircraft.
   k. Pilot's physical and flight history.
   l. Loss payee in addition to the named insured

CHAPTER 11 SELF-TEST

MULTIPLE CHOICE: Circle the letter that corresponds to the best answer.

1. Approximately _______ of the world's passenger traffic is concentrated in the U.S. air transportation system.
   a. one-third
   b. one-half
   c. two-thirds
   d. three quarters

2. All of the following are major or legacy airlines, EXCEPT:
   a. Delta Air Lines
   b. Northwest Airlines
   c. Southwest Airlines
   d. Continental Airlines

3. All of the following criteria are considered to be major factors to be considered by underwriters in the airline risk selection process, EXCEPT:
   a. Management strength and stability
   b. Routes flown and hub airports served.
   c. Capital Structure.
   d. Business plan.

4. Airline passenger liability coverage is generally quoted on a basis of a rate per 1000:
   a. Available seat miles (ASMs)
   b. Revenue Passenger Miles (RPMs)
   c. Available Ton Miles (ATMs)
   d. Passengers enplaned

5. Airlines rates in general are based on:
   a. claims experience.
   b. capacity available.
   c. competition and market environment
   d. all of the above.

6. _____________ is an arrangement where a number of co-insurers participate in an airline placement on a percentage basis.
   a. Shared limit.
   b. Facultative participation.
   c. Quota share
   d. Surplus line

7. Which of the following statements regarding hull deductibles is NOT true?
   a. Deductibles can be as high as One Million Dollars for wide-body aircraft.
   b. Deductibles generally do not apply to smaller turbo-prop airline equipment.
   c. Deductibles generally apply on an occurrence basis.
   d. There are varying aggregate deductible schemes that can be used depending on the willingness and financial ability of the insured to share the risk.

8. The most prominent satellites in use today are:
   a. Geostationary satellites.
   b. Low earth orbit (LEO) satellites.
   c. Military satellites.
   d. None of the above.

9. The most popular launch vehicle for geostationary satellites used for commercial purposes is:
   a. Delta II
   b. Titan
   c. Pegasus
   d. Ariane

10. Pre-Launch and Manufacturers' coverage indemnifies the insured for physical loss or damage to the satellite during:
    a. manufacture only.
    b. manufacture and testing only.
    c. manufacture, testing, and shipping only.
    d. manufacture, testing, shipping and integration with the launch vehicle.

11. Pre-Launch and Manufacturers' coverage ceases:
    a. after manufacture and testing.
    b. at intentional ignition of the launch vehicle.
    c. upon receipt of the satellite by the launch provider.
    d. Upon shipment of the satellite to the launch provider.

12. Launch providers:
    a. can purchase coverage for a replacement launch in the event the satellite is not placed in the proper orbit.
    b. cannot purchase coverage for a replacement launch.
    c. can only purchase coverage under the satellite owner's policy.
    d. face the least risk during the launch phase and consequently the cost of insurance is nominal.

13. The 1972 Convention on International Liability for Damages caused by Space Objects is commonly referred to as the:
    a. Warsaw Convention (amended).
    b. International Air Law Agreement.
    c. Space Treaty.
    d. Sovereignty of Airspace Conference.

14. Which of the following statements concerning launch liability exposures is **NOT** true?
    a. All launches must be licensed by the FAA and the application for license must include a possible loss analysis.
    b. The FAA will require a specified limit of liability to be carried by the launch provider.
    c. The major launch providers purchase third party liability coverage under their comprehensive aviation products liability program.
    d. Currently, the government will share the risk on a quota share basis.

15. Coverage for damage that a satellite might cause to another satellite:
    a. is available in the London market but seldom purchased because of the limited exposure and relatively high cost.
    b. is provided under In-Orbit third party liability coverage.
    c. has become less popular today because of the decline in the number of operators with low earth orbit launches.
    d. is provided under Launch Risk Guarantee insurance.

16. Which of the following statements regarding underwriting space insurance is **NOT** correct?
    a. There are relatively few launches per year and they are not homogeneous because of the different launch providers and satellite manufacturers.
    b. Space underwriters and brokers rely on industry consultants for advice.
    c. The space underwriting process is a relatively short one.
    d. Insurance is written on a quota share basis with each insurer only taking a percentage of the risk.

17. An insured value for a satellite:
    a. is similar to determining an insured value for an aircraft.
    b. includes replacement costs, including the cost to manufacture, launch, finance and insure.
    c. is basically what it cost to manufacture.
    d. is determined by the insurer in consultation with the broker.

18. Which of the following statements regarding the policy period of a space policy is true?
    a. The launch (attachment of risk) may take place several years after the policy has been bound.
    b. Underwriters must manage a long tail of exposures several years after policy inception.
    c. Generally, a deposit premium of ten percent of the full premium is due at policy inception.
    d. All of the above statements are true.

19. Termination of risk under a space policy can be:
    a. As early as at the end of launch.
    b. 180 days following launch.
    c. 60 months following launch.
    d. All of the above.

20. Deductibles for space programs can take any one of the following forms, EXCEPT:
    a. one launch failure out of a series of launches.
    b. within the definition of a partial loss where it may specify that a total loss does not occur under 75 percent of a satellite's operational life has been lost.
    c. a straight deductible of a certain dollar amount.
    d. can take the form of a straight exclusion of a component on a satellite that has failed on other satellites of the same module.

True/False: Circle *T* if the statement is true, *F* if it is false

T F 1. The dawn of the modern jet transport era began in 1968.

T F 2. Traffic carried by regional air carriers has increased significantly during the past thirty years.

T F 3. Cargo carriers operate airline equipment but do not publish a schedule.

T F 4. Normally deductibles do not apply to airline equipment.

T F 5. Pricing airline physical damage coverage depends on the individual and combined fleet value of hulls at risk.

T F 6. An individual air carrier may experience an increase in premiums on renewal even though they may not have had any claims.

T F 7. The lead co-insurer on an airline placement generally receives the same rates as other co-insureds or following market.

T F 8. Financial security of the underwriter refers to the ability to service accounts and offer fair prices.

T F 9. In the case of hull coverage, underwriters will generally set a rate on the average fleet value for a particular type of aircraft.

T F 10. Underwriters are generally adverse to providing profit sharing and no-claims bonus schemes for airlines because loss experience can vary considerably from year to year.

T F 11. The first space insurance policy was written in the mid-1960s.

T F 12. Space insurance is typically purchased by commercial entities and not by governmental agencies.

T F 13. Some LEO satellites are small enough that many can be launched at the same time on the same launch vehicle.

T F 14. Delay or termination coverage protects the insured from financial losses caused by covered perils which delay or terminate a satellite program.

T F 15. Prior to the mid-1980s satellite owners, not launch providers provided Launch Risk Guarantee Insurance.

T F 16. It is generally more advantageous for the launch provider to purchase coverage through the satellite owner.

T F 17. All parties to a launch (satellite owner, manufacturer, subcontractors and the government) agree to cross-waiver of liability against all other parties.

T F 18. Third party liability coverage is typically purchased by the satellite owner and includes the launch provider as an additional insured.

T F 19. In-orbit third party liability coverage is designed to protect the launch provider for property damage to the satellite.

T F 20. Each insurer may quote a different premium for their quota share (percentage) of the risk.

T F 21. The insured value of a satellite is very broad and includes more than that of the satellite itself.

T F 22. The attachment of risk under a space policy may not take place for up to three years after the policy has been bound.

T F 23. A partial loss involving a satellite is virtually non-existent.

T F 24. Attachment of risk can take place at intentional ignition or at lift-off depending on contractual conditions.

T F 25. Reinsurance has become a major factor in recent years in the space market.

Answers to Chapter 11 Self-Test

Multiple Choice

1. a	5. d	9. d	13. c	17. b
2. c	6. c	10. d	14. d	18. d
3. b	7. b	11. b	15. b	19. d
4. b	8. a	12. a	16. c	20. c

True/False

1. F	6. T	11. T	16. F	21. T
2. T	7. F	12. T	17. T	22. T
3. F	8. F	13. T	18. F	23. F
4. F	9. T	14. T	19. F	24. T
5. T	10. F	15. T	20. F	25. F

CHAPTER 12 SELF-TEST

MULTIPLE CHOICE: Circle the letter that corresponds to the best answer.

1. One of the purposes of the commercial property declarations page is to:
   a. explain the various insuring agreements.
   b. describe the premises to which coverage applies.
   c. list the appropriate exclusions.
   d. identify common policy conditions.

2. All of the following are common policy conditions found in the Commercial Property Policy EXCEPT:
   a. a non-renewal by the insurer requires 30 day notice to the insured.
   b. insurer has the right to audit books and records of the insured.
   c. changes in policy terms can be made by written endorsement.
   d. insured's rights and duties under the policy can be transferred to another with written consent from the insurer.

3. To the extent of loss payment made by the insurer, the insured's rights of recovery against others for that loss are transferred to the insurer described in the following policy provision:
   a. other insurance.
   b. subrogation.
   c. pro rata clause.
   d. legal action against the insurer.

4. Property insurance rates:
   a. are regulated by the states and are developed and managed by rating bureaus.
   b. are influenced by the loss experience in a given area.
   c. are the same throughout a specific area, regardless of type of building construction.
   d. both a and b.

5. FBOs which have widely fluctuating levels of business personal property could benefit from a:
   a. reporting form.
   b. named peril policy.
   c. larger deductible.
   d. agreed value coverage.

6. The commercial property policy is an all risk policy which:
   a. has specified peril coverage.
   b. is cheaper than the named peril policy.
   c. covers all perils not otherwise excluded.
   d. requires the insurer to show that the loss was caused by a peril specifically listed.

7. Replacement cost:
   a. is the same as book value.
   b. is the same as market value.
   c. is based on the original cost of the property.
   d. is the cost to replace the property today with new materials of like kind and quality.

8. Actual cash value basis is:
   a. preferred over replacement basis due to depreciation.
   b. defined as replacement minus depreciation.
   c. the same as book value.
   d. both b and c.

9. In determining replacement value for a building:
   a. it is wise to engage the services of an appraiser.
   b. the use of purchase price is acceptable.
   c. the insurer will inspect and determine the correct dollar amount for you.
   d. the cost of foundations and other underground property should be included in the value.

10. Statistics gathered by fire-rating bureaus indicate that:
    a. about 85% of all building losses are for less then 20% of the value of the building.
    b. only five % of building losses result in damages which exceed 50% of property value.
    c. the necessity to insure for full value is lessened.
    d. all of the above.

11. A commercial building policy with an 80% coinsurance clause will pay $ minus the deductible for a $40,000 covered fire toss. (Insured value = $200,000; replacement value at the time of the loss = $275,000)
    a. $36,114
    b. 36,364
    c. 39,750
    d. 40,000

12. Under the provision of the coinsurance clause:
    a. the insured agrees to maintain insurance equal to some selected percentage of replacement value.
    b. the insured agrees to pay a stated percentage of each dollar of loss.
    c. the replacement value of the property is determined at the inception of the policy.
    d. the stated percentage is only imposed for total losses.

13. Blanket insurance:
    a. is designed to cover all buildings at the same location.
    b. is an alternative approach for stating dollar coverage for multiple locations.
    c. is beneficial for multiple locations, but does require a 90% coinsurance clause.
    d. both b and c.

14. Business income insurance
    a. indemnifies a business for all loss of income during the time the building in untenantable due to a covered peril.
    b. is written subject to a coinsurance clause.
    c. will not reimburse for lost profits.
    e. both a and c.

15. Premises burglary:
    a. requires evidence of forcible entry.
    b. means taking property by a person causing or threatening to cause bodily harm.
    c. covers tosses from vandalism.
    d. covers losses of automobiles which were parked on the premise.

16. Pollution Liability insurance:
    a. provides coverage for all pollution exposures for an FBO or airports.
    b. is used by risk managers to show financial responsibility for underground fuel leaks.
    c. is available with very low deductible for small firms.
    d. requires that all underground fuel tanks more than 20 years old be replaced.

17. Inland Transit insurance would be appropriate when the owner of property ships by:
    a. common carrier.
    b. firm's airplane.
    c. contract carrier.
    d. both a and c.

18. The legal liability of a common carrier:
    a. is really absolute liability.
    b. greatly exceeds that of ordinary care.
    c. is reduced when the damage was caused by an act of God.
    d. both b and c.

19. An Inland Transit Policy is purchased:
    a. to protect personal property owned by the insured while in transit.
    b. with a single limit of liability per occurrence.
    c. to protect personal property shipped to customers on an F.0.B. point of destination basis.
    d. all of the above.

20. Cargo Liability Coverage Endorsement:
    a. covers the insured's cargo in transit by air.
    b. only covers property of others.
    c. covers property even though no charge is being made.
    d. includes coverage for live animals, fish, and reptiles.

TRUE/FALSE: Circle *T* if the statement is true, *F* if it is false.

T F 1. The adoption of ISO's Portfolio Program was required of all property and casualty insurance companies as of January 1, 1986.

T F 2. The definition of "building" in the Commercial Property Form includes permanently installed fixtures.

T F 3. Individual insurance companies inspect business properties and determine the rate which they wish to charge the insured.

T F 4. Fire resistant construction, existence of sprinkler systems, and located within a protected fire district will have a positive effect on the cost of Commercial Property insurance.

T F 5. Reporting Form allows the insured to pay premiums in installments.

T F 6. Named peril policies list the perils covered thus eliminate the necessity of any exclusions.

T F 7. An important advantage of the all risk approach is that it is more difficult for insurers to deny coverage.

T F 8. Book value of an asset reflects its current market value and should serve as the basis for insurance.

T F 9. Replacement value and market value are often not the same.

T F 10. Loss settlement statistics show that there is a high degree of probability that losses suffered to real property will be partial losses.

T F 11. Insurance companies will allow the risk manager to select coverage limits less than the replacement value of the building.

T F 12. If the insured agrees to a coinsurance clause and fails to maintain the required percentage of replacement value, a penalty will be assessed on all partial losses.

T F 13. It is the responsibility of the insurance company to make sure that the amount of insurance purchased meets the selected coinsurance percentage.

T F 14. An insurance company will suspend the coinsurance clause requirement if Agreed Value coverage provision is activated.

T F 15. Under the blanket insurance form, one amount of insurance covers all property located at multiple locations.

T F 16. Most insurers require an 80% coinsurance clause when coverage is written on a blanket basis.

T F 17. Blanket insurance is also appropriate for contents coverage.

T F 18. An example of an indirect loss is the loss of revenue due to the inability to service maintenance customers under contract when the building was damaged by fire.

T F 19. Extra Expense insurance and Business Interruption insurance should not be purchased together since they address two different indirect loss situations.

T F 20. Rental Value insurance reimburses the landlord for the amount which the property could have been rented if the rental property is untenantable due to a covered peril.

T F 21. An example of Extra Expense insurance is the cost of moving into temporary quarters.

T F 22. Theft, disappearance, and destruction coverage is in effect all risk coverage for money and securities.

T F 23. A special condition of burglary coverage is that if a covered loss occurs, the coverage is suspended for the balance of the policy period.

T F 24. Earthquake insurance only covers damage caused by earthquakes.

T F 25. Federal laws require owners of underground fuel storage tanks to demonstrate financial responsibility of at least $500,000.

T F 26. An air waybill of lading (AWB) is a written contract setting forth the terms and conditions of the bailment.

T F 27. A common carrier becomes an insurer of goods thus relieving the owner of any responsibility.

T F 28. An Inland Transit policy excludes shipments made by air unless via regularly scheduled airlines.

T F 29. A Spares Endorsement provides all risk coverage for spare parts which are owned, leased, or consigned to the insured.

T F 30. Cargo Liability Coverage Endorsement covers baggage, luggage, wearing apparel, and personal effects of passengers.

Answers to Chapter 12 Self-Test

Multiple Choice

1. b	6. c	11. b	16. b
2. a	7. d	12. a	17. d
3. b	8. b	13. d	18. d
4. d	9. a	14. b	19. d
5. a	10. d	15. a	20. b

True/False

1. F	6. F	11. T	16. F	21. T	26. T
2. T	7. T	12. T	17. T	22. T	27. F
3. F	8. F	13. F	18. T	23. F	28. T
4. T	9. T	14. T	19. T	24. F	29. T
5. F	10. T	15. T	20. T	25. F	30. F

CHAPTER 13 SELF-TEST

MULTIPLE CHOICE: Circle the letter that corresponds to the best answer.

1. Under English common law, a worker:
   a. had no more right against the employer than a member of the public.
   b. injured on the job could bring suit against the employer.
   c. was compensated by the employer for medical bills and lost wages without the necessity of proving negligence.
   d. both a and b.

2. All of the following are considered minimum work requirements under common law EXCEPT:
   a. providing a safe working environment.
   b. providing proper tools and machinery for the job.
   c. providing suitable safety rules.
   d. compensating for injuries caused by fellow workers.

3. Which of the following is NOT one of the common law defenses used by employers in the early 19OOs to reduce their employee liability?
   a. fellow -servant rule.
   b. contributory negligence.
   c. last clear chance.
   d. assumption of risk.

4. An injured worker must be unable to work because of a work related injury for before weekly indemnity (replacement income) can start:
   a. 24 hours
   b. 3 days
   c. 1 days
   d. no waiting period, income starts immediately

5. Which of the following is a false statement?
   a. employers will be liable only for injuries where negligence is proven.
   b. workers' compensation laws were passed by state governments starting in 1903.
   c. the first state to pass workers' compensation laws was Maryland.
   d. injuries primarily caused by intoxication of the worker are not subject to compensation benefits.

6. Employees covered by workers' compensation:
   a. give up their right to sue the employer except for gross negligence in some states.
   b. are entitled to the stated schedule of benefits as a matter of right.
   c. receive replacement income benefits over time, rather than in a lump sum.
   d. all of the above.

7. Workers' Compensation laws:
   a. require all employers to show financial responsibility.
   b. were passed to assure adequate compensation to workers injured on and off the job.
   c. require all payments to go through the employer first.
   d. both b and c are incorrect statements.

8. The workers' compensation insuring agreement:
   a. requires all payments to go directly to the worker or dependents of the worker.
   b. does not have any exclusions.
   c. does not state any maximum limit of insurer's liability.
   d. all of the above.

9. The employer's liability portion of the Workers' Compensation policy is designed to cover the employer's liability in all of the following EXCEPT:
   a. standard limit of $100,000 for each accident.
   b. $500,000 occupational disease aggregate.
   c. suits arising out of illegal employment of minors.
   d. lost wages due to a lockout of striking employees.

10. Select the false statement. Most workers' compensation laws:
    a. are compulsory.
    b. provide coverage for executives.
    c. require all employees to be covered except those belonging to unions and those employed by small firms (less than 25 employees).
    d. require an employee-employer relationship.

11. All of the following are used as criteria to classify a worker as an independent contractor rather than an employee EXCEPT:
    a. employee pays all social security taxes.
    b. worker uses their own equipment.
    c. work is performed away from employer's premises.
    d. employer has no control over employee's work hours.

12. The benefits provided by workers' compensation include:
    a. child care for injured worker's children.
    b. 100 % income replacement up to 6 months.
    c. rehabilitation.
    d. guaranteed job placement to a less hazardous one.

13. Which of the following statements is false?
    a. due to inflation, all states increase the replacement income annually.
    b. after a waiting period, injured workers are provided a weekly income until they are able to return to work.
    c. the size of the weekly income is generally a percentage of the worker's average weekly wage.
    d. total temporary disability is the most common type.

14. Medical expense benefits from workers' compensation:
    a. are generally reimbursed on an 80/20 basis.
    b. include doctor and hospital costs, and any expense incurred at home if medically necessary, even child care.
    c. pay 100% of all medical expenses.
    d. none of the above are correct.

15. Rehabilitation under workers' compensation involves all of the following activities EXCEPT:
    a. guaranteed job placement.
    b. physical therapy.
    c. psychological evaluations.
    d. vocational training.

16. Second injury funds have been established to:
    a. provide additional funds to workers who are injured twice at the same job.
    b. facilitate employment of physically handicapped workers.
    c. assist dependents of workers who are killed on the job from second injuries.
    d. reimburse workers for lost wages which result from a second injury within a one year period.

17. The premium for Workers' Compensation insurance:
    a. is typically based upon a percentage of employer's payroll.
    b. is typically the same for all employers in the same industrial classification.
    c. can run between 10 and 30%.
    d. all of the above.

18. A workers' compensation cost control program would include all of the following EXCEPT:
    a. installation of a sprinkler system.
    b. installing loss control incentive programs.
    c. encouraging key executives to become involved.
    d. conducting a safety program audit.
19. An aggressive workers' compensation cost control program will have its greatest impact on:
    a. workers' compensation premiums.
    b. employee turnover.
    c. reduction in pension costs.
    d. employee morale.
20. All of the following vehicles are typically insured under a Business Auto Policy EXCEPT:
    a. private passenger cars owned by a corporation.
    b. trucks leased to a partnership.
    c. private passenger cars leased by individuals and used in business.
    d. specialty vehicles, like fire trucks, owned by corporations.

21. In addition to the stated limits of liability in a Business Auto Policy, the liability insuring agreement will also pay:
    a. cost of defending suits.
    b. premiums on appeal bonds.
    c. loss of earnings up to $500 per day.
    d. only a and b are correct.

22. Major exclusions in the liability insuring agreement of the Business Auto Policy include:
    a. bailee.
    b. assumed liability through a contract.
    c. pollution.
    d. all of the above are excluded.

23. The following split limits were purchased: $250,000/500,000/100,000 in a Business Auto Policy. The total amount this policy will pay to the following three persons who were negligently injured is: Party A-$1 00,000; Party B-$250,000; and Party C-$300,000.
    a. $250,000.
    b. 500,000.
    c. 600,000.
    d. 650,000.

24. Which of the following automobile coverages is written on a no-fault basis?
    a. medical payments.
    b. property damage liability.
    c. comprehensive coverage.
    d. both a and c.

25. Which insuring agreement of the Business Auto Policy will pay to repair the corporation's automobile which ran off the road and overturned?
    a. comprehensive.
    b. collision.
    c. property liability.
    d. not a covered peril.

26. Uninsured/underinsured motorist coverage:
    a. applies to bodily injury only in the majority of states.
    b. includes injury by a hit and run automobile.
    c. is required coverage in the majority of states.
    d. both a and b.

27. All of the following are excluded perils from collision coverage EXCEPT:
    a. breakage of glass.
    b. contact with a bird or animal.
    c. upset.
    d. falling objects.

28. All of the following play a major role in determining automobile insurance rates EXCEPT:
    a. annual mileage.
    b. type of vehicle.
    c. age of drivers.
    d. income of drivers.

29. All of the following coverages included in a Business Auto Policy are candidates for risk retention EXCEPT:
    a. collision.
    b. comprehensive.
    c. liability.
    d. medical payments.

30. Which of the following protects employers from losses caused by dishonest acts of employees:
    a. Fidelity bonds
    b. Surety bonds
    c. Blanket bonds
    d. Both a and c

31. Surety bonds are often referred to as:
    a. fidelity bonds.
    b. performance bonds.
    c. blanket bonds.
    d. discovery bonds.

32. Examples of surety bonds include all of the following EXCEPT:
    a. supply contract bonds.
    b. liability bonds.
    c. bail bonds.
    d. bid bonds.

33. All of the following are normal coverages under state mandated Personal Injury Protection (PIP) statutes up to a specified dollar limit EXCEPT:
    a. 80% of reasonable medical expenses.
    b. 60% of wage replacement.
    c. $ 5,000 damage to the automobile
    d. $ 5,000 burial expenses

TRUE/FALSE: Circle *T* if the statement is true, *F* if it is false.

T F 1. Workers' compensation laws modify the law that requires the injured person toprove negligence to receive compensation from the defendant.

T F 2. Assumption of risk is a defense used by a defendant to relieve themselves of liability in negligence suits.

T F 3. Workers' compensation laws are federal laws, but are administered by the states.

T F 4. By 1948, all states had operational workers' compensation laws.

T F 5. Workers' compensation laws are no-fault laws.

T F 6. Contributory negligence is not a defense which can be used in workers' compensation cases.

T F 7. Most states will allow employers to self-insure their workers' compensation risk.

T F 8. The Workers' Compensation Policy will protect employers from the liability of illegally employing minors.

T F 9. The Workers' Compensation Policy introduced in 1984 includes two standard coverages: workers' compensation and employers' liability.

T F 10. A standard coverage under a Workers' Compensation Policy is protection for employees injured out of state.

T F 11. Some states like Florida, require compensation coverage only when total employees exceed six.

T F 12. In all states, workers' compensation coverage is compulsory.

T F 13. Corporate officers can elect to be excluded from workers' compensation coverage.

T F 14. Owners who operate their businesses as sole proprietorships or partnerships are not usually covered by workers' compensation.

T F 15. Pilots who moonlight by flying single trips for a fee, would be covered if injured while flying.

T F 16. Wage replacement is a major benefit under workers' compensation.

T F 17. After six months, workers' compensation income stops, and is replaced by social security disability benefits.

T F 18. An industrial accident which results in the loss of sight is classified as a partial permanent disability.

T F 19. Workers' compensation benefits even include funeral expenses.

T F 20. The largest percentage of workers who are disabled make a complete recovery and return to work promptly.

T F 21. Funds to assist in rehabilitation expenses come from the Federal Vocational Rehabilitation Act.

T F 22. Since all states pay the same level of workers' compensation benefits, payroll costs for premiums will not vary from state to state.

T F 23. Workers' compensation premiums are quite sensitive to the frequency and severity of injuries suffered on the job.

T F 24. Small firms belonging to a group plan can benefit from an experience rating system.

T F 25. The use of pre-employment physicals has proven to be ineffective in reducing workers' compensation premiums.

T F 26. Autos acquired by a business during a Business Auto Policy year will be automatically covered for 30 days without notification to the insurer..

T F 27. Limits of liability for business autos are written on a single limit basis rather than a split liability basis.

T F 28. Medical payments coverage under a Business Auto Policy is no-fault charge.

T F 29. Medical payments coverage covers paying and non-paying guests.

T F 30. Limits of liability for uninsured motorists coverage usually match the limits selected for liability to third parties.

T F 31. Collision is defined as the upset or collision with another object with a covered automobile.

T F 32. Damage to covered autos caused by floods will be covered under other than collision coverage in a Business Auto Policy.

T F 33. Actual cash value and market value of an automobile are essentially the same.

T F 34. As in aviation hull coverage, valued policies are available for insuring business autos.

T F 35. Physical damage coverage for older automobiles is a candidate for risk retention.

T F 36. Each year, thefts by employees probably amount to several times the loss from individuals outside the firm.

T F 37. There are three types of fidelity bonds available to risk managers: individual, scheduled, and blanket.

T F 38. Blanket fidelity bonds are usually written with aggregate limit of liability per policy year.

T F 39. Under fidelity bonds, losses which are only provable by inventory shortages are not covered.

T F 40. Surety bonds are useful when engaging the services of independent contractors.

T F 41. Federal Employment Compensation Act provides workers' compensation for military personnel.

Answers to Chapter 13 Self-Test

Multiple Choice

1. d	6. d	11. c	16. b	21. d	26. d	31. b
2. d	7. d	12. c	17. d	22. d	27. c	32. b
3. c	8. d	13. a	18. a	23. b	28. d	33. c
4. c	9. d	14. c	19. a	24. d	29. c	
5. a	10. c	15. a	20. c	25. b	30. d	

True/False

1. T	6. T	11. F	16. T	21. T	26. T	31. T	36. T
2. T	7. T	12. F	17. F	22. F	27. F	32. T	37. T
3. F	8. T	13. T	18. T	23. T	28. T	33. T	38. F
4. T	9. T	14. T	19. T	24. T	29. T	34. F	39. T
5. T	10. F	15. F	20. T	25. F	30. T	35. T	40. T
							41. F

CHAPTER 14 **SELF-TESTS**

MULTIPLE CHOICE: Circle the letter that corresponds to the best answer.

1. The major advantage of a Roth IRA over a traditional IRA is that:
   a. the owner has total control over the investments
   b. there are no penalties for early withdrawals
   c. all proceeds received after age 59 ½ are income tax free
   d. contributions are considered an income reduction

2. Employee benefits accomplish all of the following EXCEPT:
   a. reduce the overall payroll costs.
   b. help recruit and retain employees.
   c. favorably affect employee moral.
   d. provide benefits which some employees would not voluntarily have.

3. Employee benefits which are insurance based:
   a. are required by state statutes.
   b. include life, disability, medical care, and retirement plans.
   c. are inexpensive since employees pay the majority of the costs through payroll deductions.
   d. are only available to employers with 25 or more employees.

4. Which of the following is (are) generally not required for enrolling in a group life insurance plan?
   a. physical exam.
   b. individual application.
   c. binder equal to one -twelfth of the annual premium.
   d. both a and b.

5. Group life insurance is:
   a. usually term insurance.
   b. usually whole life or ordinary life insurance.
   c. usually written on a contributory basis.
   d. only payable to the employee's spouse.

6. When an employee terminates, the group term insurance policy:
   a. coverage continues for 60 days.
   b. allows the employee to continue the insurance on a term basis.
   c. permits the employee to convert the group life coverage to an individual permanent life insurance policy within 31 days after termination.
   d. allows the employee within 90 days of termination to convert the group policy to an individual one.

7. The amount of group life insurance death benefit an employee receives will depend:
   a. upon the employee's desires.
   b. upon how generous the employer wants to be.
   c. upon some criterion like annual salary or job classification.
   d. both b and c.

8. Universal life insurance:
   a. is an alternative to term insurance since the premiums are about the same.
   b. is not a wise choice because of the low guaranteed values.
   c. is quite flexible and can be continuously tailored to fit the employee's needs.
   d. can only be purchased as an individual policy.

9. At age 35, the chance of experiencing total disability of three months or more prior to age 65 is:
   a. 25%.
   b. 33 %.
   c. 45%.
   d. 50%.

10. The most common level of income replacement chosen by employers in group disability plans is:
    a. 50%.
    b. 65%.
    c. 90%.
    d. 100%.

11. Which of the following definitions of disability is the most favorable to the insurance company?
    a. inability of the employee to engage in his/her own occupation.
    b. inability of the employee to engage in any reasonable occupation for which he/she is or might easily become qualified.
    c. inability of the employee to engage in any occupation.
    d. all three definitions have the same liability to the insurance company.

12. The premium cost to the employer for a Long Term Disability Program depends on all the following EXCEPT:
    a. definition of disability.
    b. the date the firm started in business.
    c. the nature of the firm.
    d. age and sex composition of the firm.

13. The annual cost of group term insurance:
    a. is usually split on an 80/20 basis with employees.
    b. is usually paid 100% by the employer.
    c. is a 100% deductible expense for both the employer and employee.
    d. both b and c.

14. Techniques used in medical care insurance programs to shift some of the cost to the employee include:
    a. an annual deductible of $250 to $500.
    b. a coinsurance clause like 80% insurance company / 20% the insured.
    c. a waiting period of three days to two weeks.
    d. both a and b.

15. A 1985 federal law, Consolidated Omnibus Budget Reconciliation Act (COBRA):
    a. requires the employer to pay 100% of all premiums for group life insurance.
    b. was passed due to discrimination in employee sick leave benefits.
    c. requites employers with 20 or more employees to allow terminated employees to continue health expense insurance for up to 18 months.
    d. permits handicapped employees to receive life and medical expense group insurance.

16. Advantages of Health Maintenance Organizations (HMOs) include:
    a. employee receives all medical care under one roof.
    b. reduces administrative costs when compared with insured plans.
    c. employee has freedom of choice among physicians.
    d. both a and b.

17. Blue Cross and Blue Shield organizations:
    a. were formed as profit making organizations.
    b. are decreasing in number and importance.
    c. write policies which are called expense reimbursement contracts.
    d. none of the above is correct.

18. Currently, _____ % of all employees must rely on Social Security and personal savings for income after retirement.
    a. 30
    b. 40
    c. 50
    d. 60

19. The primary focus of the Employee Retirement Income Security Act of 1974 (ERISA) was to:
    a. establish standards for pension plans to provide better guarantees and equality.
    b. require employers to provide their employees with income after retirement.
    c. stop employers from requiring employees from contributing to their own retirement plans.
    d. provide survivor benefits for retired workers.

20. Vesting provisions in pension plans:
    a. are concerned with ownership of employer contributions upon termination of employment prior to retirement.
    b. are elective by the employee.
    c. determine the percentage of contributions by employer and employee.
    d. determine the age and length of service required for eligibility to start the retirement program.

21. Defined benefit plans:
    a. are favored by firms which are aggressive and willing to take risks.
    b. are favored by paternalistic firms.
    c. continue to be the plan of choice for new plans.
    d. both a and c.

22. Defined contribution plans:
    a. specify the dollar amount of retirement income the employee will receive.
    b. continue to be the most popular type of pension plan
    c. require the employer to make a fixed and regular contribution.
    d. are usually noncontributory.

23. Contributions made to a qualified pension plan:
    a. by the employee are treated as an income reduction.
    b. by the employer as a business expense.
    c. by the employer are tax deferred to the employee.
    d. all of the above.

24. Retirement planning for the employee is the easiest with a:
    a. pay-as-you-go plan.
    b. defined contribution plan.
    c. defined benefit plan.
    d. offset integration plan.

25. All of the following are characteristics of a SIMPLE (IRA) EXCEPT:
    a. employer has no obligation to make annual contributions.
    b. must make the plan available to all eligible employees.
    c. employees have the right to withdraw the funds after age 59 ½ without penalty.
    d. participants are 100% vested from the beginning of the plan.

26. Keogh plans:
    a. can only be a defined contribution plan.
    b. are primarily used by large corporations for their key persons.
    c. have a maximum employee contribution in any one year of 25% of compensation or $30,000, which ever is smaller.
    d. are the same as individual retirement accounts.

27. Most employees can make contributions up to $ ______ per year to their IRA.
    a. $1,000
    b. 1,500
    c. 2,000
    d. 4,000

28. Once an IRA has been started, an employee must make minimum contributions of:
    a. $ 0.
    b. 100.
    c. 1,000.
    d. 2,000.

29. Employees who establish an IRA:
    a. have complete control over the management of their contributions.
    b. pay current income taxes on the contributions, but income taxes on the earnings are deferred.
    c. are not eligible for a company sponsored pension plan.
    d. can withdraw the funds after 10 years without penalty.

30. Key limitations imposed by the Internal Revenue Code on Section 401 (k) plans include:
    a. age 21.
    b. employer matching of employee's contributions.
    c. a maximum annual salary reduction.
    d. tax exemption of employee's contributions.

31. Business use of life insurance includes all of the following excepts
    a. key-person life insurance.
    b. funding cross-purchase agreements.
    c. split-dollar plans.
    d. funding IRAs.

32. Which of the following business uses of life insurance would require some form of permanent life insurance?
    a. cross-purchase agreement
    b. deferred compensation plan
    c. key- person insurance
    d. none of these uses require permanent life insurance

TRUE/FALSE: Circle *T* if the statement is true, *F* if it is false.

T F 1. Employee benefit plans include plans like unemployment compensation which are underwritten by the federal government.

T F 2. A March 2004 study showed that fifty-one percent of workers had access to group life insurance.

T F 3. Most employers have accepted the cost of funding employee benefit plans as an integral part of the cost of doing business.

T F 4. Because of their minor costs, small FBOs can provide all of the typical voluntary benefit programs to their employees.

T F 5. The two most popular employee benefit plans are group life insurance and pension plans.

T F 6. Due to the nature of group life insurance plans, individual employees are not required to show evidence of insurability.

T F 7. Each employee will receive a policy to show evidence of group insurance.

T F 8. Noncontributory plans are ones where the employer pays the total cost of the benefits.

T F 9. Group term insurance does provide some savings that the employee receives upon termination or retirement.

T F 10. Most group term plans limit the death benefit per employee to $50,000.

T F 11. In most firms, the age composition tends to remain level.

T F 12. If whole life insurance is used in the group plan, the beneficiary will receive the face amount of the insurance plus the cash value.

T F 13. The cash value in a whole life policy is available on a loan basis at an interest rate stated in the policy.

T F 14. Universal life insurance is actually a more modern version of the traditional ordinary life policy.

T F 15. Group temporary disability income insurance is a candidate for risk retention.

T F 16. Generally, disabilities due to on the job accidents are excluded from coverage under group disability plans.

T F 17. Dependents of the employee are often eligible for coverage under both group life and medical care plans.

T F 18. To manage the rising cost of medical care plans, larger firms are turning to self-insurance.

T F 19. Tax treatment of medical care premiums is a major reason why employers are willing to pay up to 100% of their cost.

T F 20. HMOs have become an important alternative in the delivery of health care for employees.

T F 21. A major criticism of HMOs is that employees do not have freedom in selecting health care providers.

T F 22. Vesting is concerned with employee contributions to a retirement plan.

T F 23. Roth IRAs provide tax free income at retirement.

T F 24. The number of companies offering defined benefit plans to employees today is decreasing.

T F 25. Defined benefit plans do not allow early retirement.

T F 26. Some defined benefit plans use social security benefits in their determination of retirement benefits.

T F 27. Treating employee contributions to a retirement plan as an income reduction, is the same as exempting them from any income taxes.

T F 28. Keogh plans can be either a defined benefit plan or a defined contribution plan.

T F 29. Self-employed persons can put an unlimited amount into their Keogh plans each year.

T F 30. All earnings from traditional IRAs are tax deferred.

T F 31. Any invasion of IRA funds prior to age 59 and one- half will result in a 15% tax penalty.

T F 32. An employee can have an unlimited number of IRAs, but is limited to the current annual per person contribution level.

T F 33. The beneficiary of a key-person insurance policy is the employee's spouse.

T F 34. Split-dollar life insurance is useful in recruiting and retaining key persons.

Answers to Chapter 14 Self-Test

Multiple Choice

1. c	6. c	11. c	16. d	21. b	26. c	31. d
2. a	7. d	12. b	17. d	22. c	27. d	32. b
3. b	8. c	13. b	18. b	23. d	28. a	
4. d	9. b	14. d	19. a	24. c	29. a	
5. a	10. b	15. c	20. a	25. a	30. c	

True/False

1. F	6. T	11. T	16. T	21. T	26. T	31. F
2. T	7. F	12. F	17. F	22. F	27. F	32. T
3. T	8. T	13. T	18. T	23. T	28. T	33. F
4. F	9. F	14. T	19. T	24. T	29. F	34. T
5. F	10. T	15. T	20. T	25. F	30. T	

Index